Cognitive Communication Disorders

Third Edition

Cognitive Communication Disorders

Third Edition

Michael L. Kimbarow,
PhD, CCC-SLP, FASHA

PLURAL
PUBLISHING
INC.

5521 Ruffin Road
San Diego, CA 92123

e-mail: information@pluralpublishing.com
Website: http://www.pluralpublishing.com

Typeset in 10.5/13 Palatino by Flanagan's Publishing Services, Inc.
Printed in the United States of America by McNaughton & Gunn, Inc.

Library of Congress Cataloging-in-Publication Data

Names: Kimbarow, Michael L., 1953– editor.
Title: Cognitive communication disorders / [edited by] Michael L. Kimbarow.
Description: Third edition. | San Diego, CA : Plural, [2021] | Includes
   bibliographical references and index.
Identifiers: LCCN 2019011615 | ISBN 9781635501568 (alk. paper) | ISBN
   1635501563 (alk. paper)
Subjects: | MESH: Cognition Disorders—complications | Communication
   Disorders—etiology
Classification: LCC RD594 | NLM WM 204 | DDC 617.4/81044—dc23
LC record available at https://lccn.loc.gov/2019011615

Contents

Preface

Welcome to the third edition of *Cognitive Communication Disorders*. As I write this, it's hard to fathom that five years have gone by since the second edition was published and almost 10 years have elapsed since the inaugural release of the book in 2011. I'm grateful and appreciative that the text remains a valuable resource for instructors, students, and clinicians dealing with the diverse population of individuals with cognitive communication disorders.

There's a challenge in developing a third edition of a book. The goal is to find the right balance between maintaining the foundation that made it a resource in the first place and refreshing the content in a manner that ensures its ongoing relevancy to the reader. I believe the third edition has met the challenge in a number of ways.

First, I'm grateful to the authors who remain with the text (Margaret Blake, Fofi Constantinidou, Nidhi Mahendra, Carole Roth, and Sarah Wallace) and were again excited to revise and update their contributions from the second edition. I'm grateful to the new authors who have come on board for the third edition, some as coauthors, Jessica Brown (traumatic brain injury [TBI]) and Kathryn Hardin (mild TBI); Sarah Villard, who took on a complete revision of the chapter on attention; and Maya Henry and Heather Dial, who

contributed a new chapter on primary progressive aphasia.

Second, readers familiar with the first and second editions will note some significant changes to this text as a direct result of user feedback solicited by the Plural Publishing team. These include the addition of a chapter on primary progressive aphasia and a major revision to the chapter on mild TBI to include sports-related concussive disorders. Also new to the third edition is the inclusion of a case study in each chapter to demonstrate the clinical applications of the information presented by their respective author(s).

Finally, all the contributors have refreshed and updated their material with the latest evidence-based research. The rapid pace of advances in our understanding of the cognitive foundations of communication and advances in clinical management of individuals who have cognitive communication disorders are reflected in the updated content in each chapter.

The book remains organized in the same fashion as the previous two editions. The first three chapters (attention by Dr. Sarah Villard, memory by Dr. Fofi Constantinodou, and executive function by Dr. Mary Purdy) provide the foundational understanding of the cognitive systems that support communication. Each of these distinguished authors provides information on the current state of knowledge regarding their respective cognitive domain and go on to address issues related to clinical management of disorders specific to each.

The book then pivots to the juncture where cognition and communication meet in the clinical populations of associated with right hemisphere disorders (Chapter 4, Dr. Margaret Blake), primary progressive aphasia (Chapter 5, Drs. Maya Henry and Heather Dial), dementia (Chapter 6, Dr. Nidhi Mahendra), mild TBI/concussion (Chapter 7, Drs. Carole Roth and Kathryn Hardin), and traumatic brain injury (Drs. Brown, Wallace, and Kimbarow).

With gratitude to all the contributors to the third edition, I trust you will find this latest edition worthy to take its place next to the first two.

—Michael L. Kimbarow,
PhD, CCC-SLP, FASHA
San Mateo, CA

Acknowledgments

To my wife, Joyce, for the love and joy of every day together. You make my world a better place.

My continued thanks and gratitude to all the contributing authors for sharing your outstanding work and expertise for this edition. It's my privilege to know you and to work with you and I look forward to many more years of the same.

Finally, my thanks to the Plural Publishing team for your continued support of the book and your invitation to produce a third edition to ensure it remains current and relevant to the reader.

Contributors

Margaret Lehman Blake, PhD, CCC-SLP
Professor and Chair
Communication Sciences & Disorders
University of Houston
Houston, Texas
Chapter 4

Jessica Brown, PhD, CCC-SLP
Assistant Professor
Speech, Language, and Hearing Sciences
University of Arizona
Tucson, Arizona
Chapter 8

Fofi Constantinidou, PhD, CCC-SLP, CBIS, FASHA, FACRM
Professor of Language Disorders and Clinical Neuropsychology
Director, Center for Applied Neuroscience
University of Cyprus
Nicosia, Cyprus
Chapter 2

Heather R. Dial, PhD
Postdoctoral Fellow
Department of Communication Sciences and Disorders
Moody College of Communication
University of Texas at Austin
Austin, Texas
Chapter 5

Kathryn Y. Hardin, PhD, CCC-SLP
Assistant Professor
Marcus Institute for Brain Health, University of Colorado Anschutz Medical Campus
Department of Physical Medicine & Rehabilitation
University of Colorado School of Medicine
Aurora, Colorado
Chapter 7

Maya L. Henry, PhD, CCC-SLP
Assistant Professor
Department of Communication Sciences and Disorders
Moody College of Communication
University of Texas at Austin
Austin, Texas
Chapter 5

Michael L. Kimbarow, PhD, CCC-SLP, FASHA
Professor
Department of Communicative Disorders and Sciences
San Jose State University
San Jose, California
Chapter 8

Nidhi Mahendra, PhD, CCC-SLP
Associate Professor
Department of Communicative Disorders and Sciences
San Jose State University
San Jose, California
Chapter 6

Mary H. Purdy, PhD, CCC-SLP
Professor
Department of Communication
    Disorders
Southern Connecticut State University
New Haven, Connecticut
Chapter 3

**Carole R. Roth, PhD, CCC-SLP,
FASHA**
Head, Division of Speech Pathology
Department of Otolaryngology
Naval Medical Center San Diego
Assistant Professor
Uniformed Services University of
    Health Sciences
San Diego, California
Chapter 7

Sarah Villard, PhD, CCC-SLP
Postdoctoral Fellow
Department of Speech, Language &
    Hearing Sciences
Boston University
Boston, Massachusetts
Chapter 1

Sarah E. Wallace, PhD, CCC-SLP
Associate Professor
Department of Speech-Language
    Pathology
Duquesne University
Pittsburgh, Pennsylvania
Chapter 8

1

Attention

Sarah Villard

Introduction

Interest in the cognitive skill of attention within the field of speech-language pathology has increased considerably over the past two to three decades. Although attention is not specifically a language skill, it is an essential cognitive process that may interact with language and communication in several different ways. Impairments in attention have been observed in individuals with a number of different neurologically acquired and degenerative conditions, including stroke, traumatic brain injury, and various types of dementia. Even in aphasia, traditionally conceptualized as a language-specific impairment, attention deficits have frequently been noted and are becoming increasingly of interest. Researchers in communication sciences and disorders are continuing to refine the ways in which principles of attention can be applied to better understand neurogenic impairments, and clinicians who assess and treat cognitive communication disor-

ders now routinely consider attention alongside other cognitive-linguistic abilities.

The aim of this chapter is to discuss the construct of attention as it relates to clinical practice in speech-language pathology. In order to properly contextualize this discussion within the historical literature on attention, we will start with an overview of some basic principles of attention, as well as several major historical models and theories of attention from the neuropsychological literature on healthy populations. The discussion will then shift to the ways in which attention manifests in specific acquired and degenerative cognitive communication disorders, as well as the ways in which existing models of attention may be able to enhance our understanding of these disorders. Next, principles of assessment and treatment of attention within the field of speech-language pathology will be outlined, and some specific assessment tools will be described. Finally, a case study will be presented as an example of how these principles and tools might be applied to better understand the role of attention in the assessment and treatment of an individual patient.

Central Principles of Attention

A major challenge in studying the cognitive skill of attention is defining precisely what attention is. Most of us have a general sense of what it entails —after all, "attention" is a familiar term that occurs frequently and flexibly in everyday conversation. We may casually comment that an individual has a short or long "attention span"; we may remind someone that important information is forthcoming ("Pay attention!"); we may talk about "attention to detail" or about "drawing someone's attention" to something. We may associate the idea of attention with concepts such as distraction or multitasking or meditation, or with the feeling of suddenly realizing we have just read the same paragraph over several times without absorbing any of its content. And particularly in recent years, with the ever-increasing ubiquity of scrolling, texting, news feeds, and social media, many of us report an increasing sense of concern about whether our habit of scanning and flitting from image to image and from page to page could be negatively impacting our ability to focus on a single topic for longer periods of time.

These everyday references to attention, however, are sprawling and imprecise, and it is difficult to extract from them a definitive definition of this construct. Is attention one thing or many things? Is it about how *long* we can pay attention? Is it about how *well* we can pay attention? Or is it more

about how many things we (think we) can pay attention to at the same time? How can we measure an individual's attention, and what does that mean? And—most importantly for our discussion here—how does attention fit into the assessment and treatment of cognitive communication disorders?

The first step in considering how attention may manifest in clinical populations will be to consider the ways in which the neuropsychological literature has defined attention in healthy people. This is no small undertaking, as a variety of models and theories of attention have been proposed over the past seven or so decades, and each one characterizes attention somewhat differently. We will consider a number of major historical models of attention in this chapter. However, before delving into specifics, it may be useful to first outline several broad, fairly universal principles of attention that are inherent in multiple models.

The first central principle of attention is that it is always defined in relation to a stimulus: You always pay attention *to* something. A stimulus can be either external (originating from the environment) or internal (originating from within the individual). Examples of external stimuli could include a funny story your sister tells you about her dog, the rapidly falling shapes in a game of Tetris, the lyrics of "Bohemian Rhapsody," or this chapter you're currently reading. Some examples of internal stimuli are a mental grocery list, a major decision you're trying to think through, or a childhood memory. In some cases, you might also be attending (or attempting to attend) to multiple stimuli at once. For example, you might be writing an email while also watching a talk show and dividing or switching your attention between the two. The important takeaway here, however, is that in order for attention to take place, at least one stimulus must be involved.

A second, related principle of attention that relates primarily to external stimuli is that the modality of the stimulus should always be identified and noted. We can attend, for example, to an auditory stimulus such as a radio news program or an intercom announcement; likewise, we can also attend to a visual stimulus such as a silent film or a chess game. Many of the objects we attend to on a daily basis consist of a combination of auditory and visual stimuli; an action film, a live dance performance, a thunderstorm, and a family member speaking to us from across the dinner table all fall into this category. Additionally, although it is common to think of attention in terms of the visual, auditory, or combined visual-auditory modalities, it is certainly also possible to attend through other modalities—reading Braille, for example, requires attention through the tactile modality. We may also attend to simple everyday stimuli such as the wind on our face (another tactile stimulus), to the smell of something baking in the next room (an olfactory stimulus), or to the taste of an apple (a gustatory stimulus).

Another notable feature of attention is that it is thought to be closely connected to other processes such as memory and executive function, as well as to the effective use of language to communicate. From a certain perspective, you might even say that attention functions as a prerequisite that must be fulfilled before certain other cognitive-linguistic operations can be successfully carried out. For example, how could you possibly recall a set of verbal directions if you were not able to pay attention to the directions when they were originally given? How could you harness executive function to create and execute a plan without directing some attention toward that plan? How could effective communication occur without attention to the topic or attention to a communication partner's message? Attention is necessary for all of these cognitive-linguistic activities. This interconnectedness of attention with other cognitive-linguistic skills can present a challenge in studying attention in an experimental or evaluation context, as it can be difficult to cleanly separate from other processes. This issue will be further explored later on when discussing the assessment of attention.

This brings us to perhaps the two most important features of attention as it is understood in the neuropsychological literature: *capacity limitation* and *selection*, concepts that are closely related to one another and should be considered in tandem. The first, capacity limitation, refers to the fact that the human attention system can only process a limited number or amount of stimuli at once. The second, selection, represents the ability of this system to focus on stimuli that are most relevant to its behavior, goals, or interests, while ignoring or filtering out stimuli that are less relevant. We could consider capacity limitation to be a weak point of the human attention system and selection to be a complementary strong point: We may not be able to attend to everything at once, but at least we can be somewhat selective about which stimuli we *do* want to attend to.

The psychologist William James, who wrote about attention in the late

19th century, summed up the ideas of capacity limitation and selection nicely in the following passage:

> [Attention] is taking possession by the mind, in clear and vivid form, of one out of what seem several simultaneously possible objects or trains of thought. Focalization, concentration, of consciousness are of its essence. It implies withdrawal from some things in order to deal effectively with others and is a condition which has a real opposite in the confused, dazed, scatterbrained state which in French is called distraction. (James, 1890/1950, pp. 403–404)

While James's characterization is somewhat more philosophical than evidence based, it nicely expresses the idea that in many everyday situations, a multiplicity of different stimuli competes for our attention, and if we are to "deal effectively" with any of them, we must (consciously or subconsciously) select specific stimuli on which to focus our attention and find a way to ignore the others. As an illustration, think of all the many stimuli that might bombard you as you enter a busy restaurant: the sights of tables, chairs, lights, menus, the décor, the hostess, servers, and other patrons, as well as the sounds of clinking glasses and silverware, the music, and the numerous conversations unfolding simultaneously around you. Due to capacity limitations, it would be difficult if not impossible to attend fully to all of these stimuli at once. Even in a calmer, less complicated situation (e.g., if you were sitting alone on the couch reading a book), capacity limitations would likely still be at play. In this case, the multiple stimuli competing for your attention might consist of the words on

the page, the feel of the book in your hand, the light in the room, the ticking clock, your occasionally vibrating phone, and the distant hum of a lawnmower or of cars going by outside, as well as perhaps internal stimuli such as thoughts about dinner or about a conversation you had earlier in the day.

Typically, selection is based on which stimulus or stimuli are most relevant to the task or behavior we are currently engaged in. In the above example in which your chosen task is reading, presumably with the goal to finish the chapter, the book is the relevant stimulus and most other stimuli in your environment are irrelevant by comparison. In the restaurant example, the most relevant stimulus might be the hostess as she asks how many are in your party. Ideally, you would want to select and attend to these relevant stimuli, while ignoring or filtering out stimuli that are less relevant.

Theories and Models of Attention

Having outlined some fundamental principles of attention, we will now discuss several of the most influential theories and models of attention that have emerged in the neuropsychological literature since this cognitive skill began to be studied systematically and in depth, in the mid-20th century. In general, models of attention tend to fall into one of three categories: models that attempt to explain selection, models that focus on capacity limitations, and models that delineate different subtypes of attention. Major examples of each of these three types of models will be discussed in turn. Where relevant, important experimental findings will also be described.

Theories and Models of Selection

Much of the literature on attentional selection has been influenced by early investigations of the "cocktail party problem" in the 1940s and 1950s. The "cocktail party problem," a term originally coined by Colin Cherry (1953), refers to the challenge of selectively attending to a target speech stream when other, less relevant, auditory information is also present. As the term suggests, this phenomenon is exemplified by the experience of engaging in conversation with a friend at a noisy cocktail party, surrounded by a bevy of other conversations, and trying to selectively attend to what that friend is saying while filtering out all the other audible talkers (for a recent review of the cocktail party problem, see Bronkhorst, 2015). Early work on the cocktail party problem sought to identify factors that make this type of selective listening more—or less—successful. An early experiment by Cherry (1953) included a dichotic listening task, in which two different speech streams were presented to a listener simultaneously, one in each ear via headphones. The listener was asked to attend to the ongoing message in one ear, repeating it aloud as it was heard (a task known as "shadowing"). It was found that when listeners were asked to shadow the message in one ear but were later asked about the voice and message played into the other, unattended ear, they were typically unable to report

anything about that unattended message other than global acoustic information about the speaker (e.g., whether they had perceived a male or female voice). This is a clear example of selection, in which the listener selected one message to process, at the expense of the other.

A subsequent experiment by Broadbent (1952) added to this work, expanding the understanding of the role of attention in selective listening. In this experiment, subjects listened to two messages spoken by two different voices, but instead of the two messages being played simultaneously and funneled to different ears (as in the dichotic listening experiment above), the messages were serially interleaved, word-by-word. The subject heard the first word of the first message, followed by the first word of the second message, followed by the second word of the first message, followed by the second word of the second message, and so on. The subject was instructed at the start to listen and respond to only *one* of these two messages. Results suggested that presenting sentences in this way caused confusion for the subject or, as Broadbent termed it, "failures of attention in selective listening."

The finding that interleaved, non-overlapping speech could negatively impact processing of a target message was critical because previous work on selective listening had mostly asked listeners to attend to target speech in the presence of sustained, overlapping background noise (e.g., Egan & Wiener, 1946). In these experiments, difficulty understanding the target was usually attributed to time-frequency overlap between the target and the masker (i.e., the irrelevant or distractor stimulus).

Because the auditory system processes sounds in time-frequency units, any time-frequency unit containing strong energy originating from the masker could result in a reduced ability of the listener to detect energy in that same unit originating from the target. This would not be considered a failure of the listener's attention abilities but rather a physiologically based inability of the listener's peripheral auditory system to detect target energy. Broadbent's (1952) experiment, however, demonstrated that even in a paradigm with zero time-frequency overlap between target and masker, confusion could still occur. The existence of masking effects that cannot be explained by time-frequency overlap between target and masker has been confirmed by a number of more recent studies using more technologically advanced methods (e.g., Arbogast, Mason, & Kidd, 2002; Brungart, Chang, Simpson, & Wang, 2006). This additional level of masking, now known as "informational masking," is thought to be due to higher order, central processing factors including attention (for a review, see Kidd & Colburn, 2017). Researchers have also identified a number of factors that influence the extent to which listeners are able to selectively attend to target speech, including degree of spatial separation between target and masker (e.g., Freyman, Balakrishnan, & Helfer, 2001), degree of linguistic similarity of the target and masker (Brouwer, Van Engen, Calandruccio, & Bradlow, 2012), and familiarity of the target and masker languages (e.g., Van Engen & Bradlow, 2007). Such findings are highly relevant to attentional selection in everyday situations, particularly in relation to auditory stimuli.

Early work on auditory selective attention also produced three notable theories about the process whereby the human attention system may select relevant stimuli and filter out irrelevant stimuli. These theories are known as the *early filter theory*, the *filter attenuation model*, and the *late filter model*. These models were all designed to explain the steps involved in attentional selection; however, they differ from one another in the specifics of those steps. The *early filter theory* (Broadbent, 1958) suggests that all stimuli receive preliminary analysis of general features such as location or intensity but that irrelevant or unattended stimuli are filtered out at a relatively early stage of processing, while the attended stimulus is selected and goes on to receive additional processing. The *filter attenuation model* (Treisman, 1960) was developed later, based in part on results that called the early filter theory into question. Specifically, it was found that even though subjects in dichotic listening tasks were usually unable to report any content from the unattended ear, they were sometimes able to report part of this content if it was highly salient (Moray, 1959; Treisman, 1960). Like the early filter model, the filter attenuation model posits that relevant stimuli are selected early on for further processing; however, in the filter attenuation model, unselected stimuli are not completely filtered out but rather are attenuated, making them potentially available for further analysis later on. Finally, the *late filter* (or *late selection*) model (Deutsch & Deutsch, 1963) theorized that all stimuli are analyzed in the early stages of processing and that selection of the target stimulus occurs later and is based on "importance weighting." Although all three models have influenced the study of attention, a number of more recent studies have lent support to Treisman's filter attenuation model (e.g., Cowan, 1997; Driver, 2001). A fourth, more recent model has suggested that the extent to which irrelevant stimuli are ignored may depend on the perceptual load and cognitive control load of the relevant information (Lavie, 1995; Lavie, Hirst, de Fockert, & Viding, 2004). This model offers a possible compromise between the earlier models of selection.

In addition to the theories described above, which are all based on work in auditory attention, several influential theories of selection have developed from work on visual attention. One of these is the spotlight theory of attention (Posner, Snyder, & Davidson, 1980), which suggests that visual cues can trigger the formation of a "spotlight" in a specific location of the visual field, and as a result, an object in that location receives enhanced processing. It has been argued that the idea of attention as a spotlight may have limitations in dynamic visual scenes (i.e., those involving object movement) (Driver & Baylis, 1989); however, the basic analogy of attention as a mechanism that highlights a specific visual object in a potentially complex scene is still highly intuitive and useful. Although the idea of a "spotlight" lends itself most easily to visual attention, it can also be applied to auditory attention (Fritz, Elhilali, David, & Shamma, 2007).

A related theoretical principle of visual attention is that of object formation. Object formation is the concept that humans, when presented with a complex mixture of sensory information (sometimes known as a visual or auditory "scene"), tend to perceptually group the sensory information in this scene into specific "objects" (Desimone & Duncan, 1995). This grouping is typically based on perceived spatial location, as well as on other qualities (e.g., color and contour in the visual modality). To give a simple visual example, if you see a blue circle on your left, a green square on your right, and a yellow circle straight ahead, you will almost certainly, and without thinking much about it, perceive these areas of color as 3 separate objects (rather than as 2 objects or 11 objects or as simply a cluttered mess) and will attend to them as such. Shinn-Cunningham (2008) extended the theory of object formation to apply to auditory attention as well, defining an auditory object as "a perceptual entity that, correctly or not, is perceived as coming from one physical source" (p. 2). If you hear a bark that you perceive to be coming from your left, a meow that sounds like it's coming from your right, and a chirp straight ahead, then your brain will use this information to form three auditory objects originating from three different animals. Object formation, whether visual or auditory, is relevant to attentional selection: The attention system may be considered to be selecting between competing perceptual objects.

Theories and Models of Capacity Limitation

Another group of theories of attention has focused not on selection per se but rather on the limits of attentional capacity. Attentional capacity has frequently been considered and studied in the context of dual-task experiments, in which a subject is asked to pay attention to two sets of stimuli at the same time and to split their attention between the two. Dual-task experiments are often thought to recruit divided attention processes and can be thought of as a form of multitasking. Because successful multitasking can (depending on the tasks) place high demands on the attention system, dual-task paradigms can be an effective way of determining at what point an individual's capacity limit has been reached. Researchers often manipulate the difficulty or salience of one or both tasks in order to determine how these changes will impact subjects' performance. Dual-task experiments in the neuropsychological literature have also frequently been used to examine age-related differences in attentional capacity (e.g., Künstler et al., 2018; McDowd & Craik, 1988; Naveh-Benjamin, Craik, Guez, & Kreuger, 2005).

One of the most well-known theories of attention, the *resource allocation theory* (Kahneman, 1973), offers an account of capacity limitations in the attention system, as well as an explanation of how attention functions during dual-task experiments. According to the resource allocation theory, humans are able to flexibly allocate resources from a single cognitive pool to various cognitive tasks. This cognitive pool of resources is considered to be limited in capacity, such that when more resources are taken up by one task, fewer resources remain to be allocated to other tasks. This may result in decreased task performance when multiple tasks are engaged in simultaneously, as in dual-task paradigms. Kahneman also observed that when two tasks required detection of stimuli through the same modality

(e.g., visual), performance declined more than it did when the two tasks involved stimuli from different modalities. Kahneman termed this phenomenon "structural interference" and theorized that it occurs when both tasks use the same input channels. Other researchers, however, have proposed alternative explanations for structural interference, specifically that there may exist a number of different resource pools, each specialized for a cognitive processing domain (e.g., Gopher, Brickner, & Navon, 1982; Navon & Gopher, 1979; Wickens, 1980). For example, different resource pools might exist for verbal versus spatial processing or for visual versus auditory processing (Wickens, 1980).

A competing theory of attentional capacity limitations is the *central bottleneck model* (Pashler, 1994). This model argues that cognitive resources, particularly those related to response selection, must be sequentially allocated to specific tasks, rather than being simultaneously allocated to multiple tasks. The implication of the central bottleneck model is that attention capacity limitations are ultimately due to the "bottleneck" created when attention must be switched back and forth between one task and another.

Models Delineating Attentional Subtypes

A third group of models of attention has focused on dividing the vast and multifaceted construct of attention into different subtypes. Note that some of these models overlap to some extent in terms of the subtypes they identify.

An early theory put forth by Schneider and Shiffrin (1977) and Shiffrin and Schneider (1977) proposed a dichotomy between *automatic* versus controlled processing. Automatic processing is described as processing that is the result of learned sequences, is not impacted by capacity limitations, and requires no control from the individual. Controlled processing, conversely, is described as being controlled by the individual and subject to capacity limitations. Later studies have suggested that a simple dichotomy between automatic and controlled processes may be too oversimplified (e.g., Kahneman & Treisman, 1984); however, this binary distinction continues to be frequently referenced. While Shiffrin and Schneider's model is not technically an attention model—in fact, automatic processing is considered to be able to occur without attention—it has been influential in thinking about the ways attention may or may not be under voluntary control. It is also related to concepts of top-down versus bottom-up attention, which will be further discussed below.

One of the most influential attention models of the past three decades was proposed by Posner and Petersen (1990). This model, groundbreaking in part because it was based on findings from neuroimaging and lesion studies, included three components: *orienting*, *target detection*, and *alerting*. The first of these, *orienting*, involves the direction of attention toward a specific location. If a person is instructed or cued to direct their attention or gaze toward a particular location, subsequent stimuli that occur in that location will be processed and responded to sooner than stimuli in other locations. Cueing toward a target location can be either overt (in which the gaze is directed toward the location) or covert (in which attention but not gaze is directed toward the location). Subsequent work has described orienting as a process that can be either top-down (goal directed) or bottom-up (stimulus directed) (Corbetta & Shulman, 2002; Shulman & Corbetta, 2012). Posner and Petersen (1990) also discuss three specific mechanisms believed to be involved in the orienting subsystem: disengaging (detaching attention from a currently focused location), moving (shifting attention to a new location), and engaging (fixing attention on a new target). Evidence for orienting and for these three mechanisms has been provided by studies of covert visual attention (e.g., Posner, Inhoff, Friedrich, & Cohen, 1987; Posner, Walker, Friedrich, & Rafal, 1984). See the Assessment of Attention section in this chapter for a description of one such task, the Covert Orienting of Visual Attention (COVAT) (Posner & Cohen, 1980). The second component of Posner and Petersen's model, *target detection*, which was later renamed the *executive control* system in an update to the model (Petersen & Posner, 2012), is involved in the effortful control of attention, which includes processes such as conflict resolution and error detection. The third and final component of the model, *alertness*, is the ability to prepare for, and sustain alertness to, relevant stimuli. Alertness is thought to primarily impact response rate: states of higher alertness can facilitate faster response times but also higher error rates in response selection. Posner and Petersen's (1990) model was updated in 2012 to reflect more recent findings from neuroimaging, developmental, pharmacological, and genetic studies (Petersen & Posner, 2012); however, the basic principles of the model remain the same.

Another notable framework of attentional types was proposed by Mirsky and colleagues (Mirsky, Anthony, Duncan, Ahearn, & Kellam, 1991). This model comprises four subtypes: *focus, sustain, shift*, and *attention for outcomes*. In this model, *focus* refers to the ability to select target stimuli from an array; *sustain* refers to the ability to maintain focus on selected stimuli, as well as to alertness; *shift* refers to the ability to flexibly adapt attentive focus; and *attention for action* is the process by which we connect stimuli (input) with a response to that stimuli (output). This model shares some basic concepts with Posner and Petersen's model discussed above. Rather than being rooted in neuroimaging studies, however, it was based on results of neuropsychological testing of a large sample of healthy adult control subjects, neuropsychiatric patients, and elementary school-age children.

One final model that has been particularly influential in the evolution of assessment and treatment of attention in individuals with cognitive communication disorders is the clinically based model developed by Sohlberg and Mateer (1987, 2001b). McKay Sohlberg, a speech-language pathologist, and Catherine A. Mateer, a clinical neuropsychologist, developed and proposed an attentional framework specifically for understanding and evaluating attention deficits in clinical populations. This model comprised a hierarchical taxonomy of types of attention based on the authors' clinical observations and experience and was intended to be useful for clinicians in classifying and treating patients' attentional impairments.

Sohlberg and Mateer's (1987, 2001b) original framework included five specific types of attention, which they arrange in a hierarchy based on task demands. The first and most basic type of attention in the model, *focused attention*, was defined as a fundamental, low-level ability to orient and respond to specific stimuli in any modality. The next, *sustained attention*, referred to the ability to maintain attention to an ongoing, repetitive task for a period of time. Sohlberg and Mateer noted that sustained attention might involve the recruitment of working memory to hold the task instructions in mind and might require a response set. The next type of attention in the model was *selective attention*, defined as the ability to sustain attention to a target stimulus in the presence of irrelevant or distractor stimuli; here, too, working memory and a response set might be involved. Next in the hierarchy came *alternating attention*, or the ability to flexibly switch back and forth between different tasks and task instructions. Finally, Sohlberg and Mateer included *divided attention*, or the ability to engage in multiple tasks simultaneously, as the most demanding type of attention in their model.

The original five-element version of Sohlberg and Mateer's model continues to be widely used in clinical settings; however, the authors updated their framework in 2010 to "reflect the functional importance of executive control and working memory, and the lack of clarity around the concept of divided attention" (Sohlberg & Mateer, 2010, p. 7). This updated framework is simpler, comprising two major components: *sustained attention* and *executive control of attention*, where executive control of attention is a category that includes working memory, selective attention, suppression, and alternating attention (Table 1–1). The revised framework no longer includes divided attention; instead, the skill of attending to two tasks simultaneously is represented by alternating attention (a subcomponent of executive control of attention). Note that Sohlberg and Mateer's updated model reflects a change in the way that attention and working memory are conceptualized relative to one another. In the earlier model, working memory was considered to be a feature of sustained attention, whereas in the updated model, working memory is a subcomponent of executive control of attention.

Characterizing Attention: Other Considerations

Before moving on to examine the literature on attention in cognitive communication disorders, we will briefly discuss three additional concepts related to the

Table 1–1. Sohlberg and Mateer's (2010) Clinical Taxonomy of Attention

Attention Component	Description	Representative Task
Sustained	Ability to maintain attention during continuous and repetitive activities	Monitoring a spoken list for target words
Executive control		
Selective	Selectively process information while inhibiting responses to nontarget information	Listening to a spoken passage in the presence of background noise and/or distracting visual stimuli
Alternating	Ability to shift focus between tasks, stimuli, or response sets; mental flexibility	Switching back and forth between listening to a spoken passage and reading text
Suppression	Ability to control impulsive responding	Inhibiting automatic responses during a task; "thinking before acting"
Working memory	Ability to hold and manipulate information in mind	Doing math in one's head

Source: From Biel and Hula (2016).

characterization of attention that do not fit neatly into any of the above models but will be useful to keep in mind when considering the assessment and treatment of attention. They are the differences (and similarities) between visual attention and auditory attention, the consideration of variability, and the role of effort in attention.

Auditory Versus Visual Attention

Since many of studies on attention have been focused specifically on either visual attention or auditory attention, it is worth thinking about the ways in which visual and auditory attention can differ. Auditory attention is almost always time dependent, driven by the source of the stimulus. As an example, the experience of reading a book with your eyes is somewhat different from the experience of listening to an audiobook. With visual reading, you can read at any pace you like, but there may be only one speed at which you can listen to an audiobook (or possibly several, depending on the device you're using). Similarly, during visual reading, your eyes can jump around the page, whereas when listening to an audiobook, it may be harder to skip around or locate a particular sentence. Similar principles hold true for the ways in which visual and auditory attention can be studied in experimental settings or assessed by standardized tests. Some tasks in one modality may have no close equivalent in the other modality. A notable example is a visual search task, in which an individual might be given a sheet of paper with many letters of the alphabet scattered on it and asked to circle all of the Ks. The individual could use a vari-

ety of different strategies to find all the Ks: searching quickly or slowly, from left to right or from top to bottom, etc. It would be difficult to create an auditory version of this task; the closest equivalent might be a task in which an individual is asked to listen to a series of letters spoken aloud and raise their hand whenever they hear a K. In this task, the individual must listen to the letters in the order they are spoken—they cannot formulate a strategy that involves listening to the letters at a certain speed or in a certain order. Likewise, some types of auditory attention tasks, such as the experiments described earlier in which an individual is asked to attend to target speech in the presence of an auditory masker, may have no clear visual equivalent.

Time-Based Variability in Attention

Another concept to keep in mind when considering how to measure attention is the extent to which attention in a given situation is expected to be sustained over time. In some situations, successful attention might involve orienting and responding to a single stimulus, but in many situations, successful attention requires sustained focus to an ongoing stimulus over a longer period of time: a minute, 2 minutes, 5 minutes. Attention could also vary from day to day: If an individual is given the same task to complete on several different days, performance may fluctuate to some degree from day to day. This concept of *intra-individual variability* has been shown to be related to age, with older individuals showing higher degrees of variability than younger individuals (Dykiert, Der,

Starry, & Deary, 2012; MacDonald, Li, & Bäckman, 2009). It has also been shown to be elevated in individuals with neurocognitive disorders, including traumatic brain injury (TBI) (e.g., Bleiberg, Garmoe, Halpern, Reeves, & Nadler, 1997; Stuss, Pogue, Buckle, & Bondar, 1994), dementia (Hultsch, MacDonald, Hunter, Levy-Bencheton, & Strauss, 2000; Murtha, Cismaru, Waechter, & Chertkow, 2002), and aphasia (Villard & Kiran, 2015, 2018). On a related note, attention can also decrease over time, particularly during a longer task; this declining performance is known as a decrement in performance over time (Sarter, Givens, & Bruno, 2001).

Attention and Effort

One final issue that may be useful to consider when assessing attention is the relationship between attention and effort. Effort—like attention—can be very difficult to define, making the relationship between the two challenging to measure. Kahneman's (1973) influential theory posits a very close relationship between attention and effort, even suggesting that the two terms are synonymous. As a result, attention and effort have often been equated in the psychological and neuropsychological literature, though this conceptualization has also been questioned (Bruya & Tang, 2018). While effort may be difficult to define in relation to attention, it is relevant to how taxing or fatiguing an individual perceives a task to be and may therefore be useful to consider in clinical contexts. Researchers have utilized a variety of different tools to study effort during tasks requiring attention. One example is pupillometry, which involves measuring involuntary changes in pupil diameter during a task and is considered to reflect the amount of cognitive effort put forth by an individual (Kahneman & Beatty, 1966). Pupillometry is thought to be particularly sensitive to changes in the allocation of attention (see Laeng, Sirois, & Gredebäck, 2012, for a review). Functional magnetic resonance imaging (fMRI) has also been used to examine brain regions recruited during tasks requiring effortful attention (e.g., Hervais-Adelman, Carlyon, Johnsrude, & Davis, 2012), as has functional near-infrared spectroscopy (fNIRS) (Wijayasiri, Hartley, & Wiggins, 2017). Effort during a variety of types of tasks can also been assessed through self-report, for example, by asking the individuals to subjectively rate their effort during a specific task or item (e.g., Schepker, Haeder, Rennies, & Holube, 2016).

Attention in Neurogenic Cognitive Communication Disorders

This section summarizes the research on attention deficits that may occur in several acquired/degenerative neurological disorders. While attention may not necessarily be the most salient deficit in many patient profiles, it can interact closely with other cognitive-linguistic abilities and therefore can be important to consider when choosing assessment approaches and designing treatment programs. The diagnoses discussed in this section are traumatic brain injury, aphasia, and dementia. From this point forward, when possible, we will refer to subtypes of attention using Sohlberg and Mateer's (1987, 2001b) original taxonomy, as well as Posner and Petersen's (1990) model.

Traumatic Brain Injury

Traumatic brain injury (TBI) is a general term that refers to any damage to the brain caused by sudden trauma (see Chapter 8 of this book for more on TBI). As such, it encompasses a number of different types of injuries, as well as a wide range of resulting patterns of impairment and recovery. Depending on the specific case, TBI could involve a closed or open head injury, diffuse axonal injury (widespread shearing of white matter in the brain), contusion (bruising of the brain), increased intracranial pressure, hypoxia, and/or several other types of initial injuries or sequelae. In the most recent update to the *Diagnostic and Statistical Manual of Mental Disorders* (5th ed.; *DSM-V*; American Psychiatric Association, 2013), TBI has been reclassified as *neurocognitive disorder due to traumatic brain injury*, under the heading *major or minor neurocognitive disorders*, and may be marked by decreased cognitive skills in areas including complex attention, executive function, learning, and memory, among others.

While cognitive impairments in TBI can vary substantially from patient to patient, attention has very frequently been observed to be impacted. However, the manifestation and extent of cognitive impairments in TBI can vary based on a multitude of factors, including severity and type of initial injury, extent and type of complications, age of the patient, and premorbid functioning, making it difficult to draw general conclusions. For this reason and others, the available literature has yielded mixed results on the presence and extent of different types of attentional impairment in TBI patients.

Despite the variability within the TBI population, however, a number of studies have provided evidence that patients with TBI do exhibit impairments in sustained attention (Bonnelle et al., 2011; Chan, 2002; Manly et al., 2003; Whyte, Polansky, Fleming, Coslett, & Cavallucci, 1995). Sleep disorders and disturbances are also widely studied in TBI, and some of the research on sustained attention in TBI has overlapped with research on arousal, fatigue, or sleepiness in this population. A number of studies examining sleep disturbances in TBI have suggested that these disturbances are associated with deficits in sustained attention (Bloomfield, Espie, & Evans, 2010; Castriotta, Wilde, Lai, Atanasov, Masel, & Kuna, 2007).

There is also some evidence that selective attention, or the ability to resist distraction, is impaired in TBI. One study found that individuals with TBI exhibited slower reaction times than controls when visual distractions were presented immediately following a target stimulus, suggesting distractibility during response preparation (Whyte, Fleming, Polansky, Cavallucci, & Coslett, 1998). A subsequent study by the same group observed TBI patients and healthy controls completing tasks both with and without distractions and concluded that TBI patients were significantly less attentive than controls in both conditions (Whyte, Schuster, Polansky, & Adams, & Coslett, 2000); however, evidence that distractions posed additional difficulties for patients (beyond the difficulties present when no distractions were involved) was weak. Other studies on selective attention in TBI have found evidence of visual selective attention deficits in patients relative to controls (Bate, Mathias, & Crawford, 2001), associations between selective attention and fatigue (Ziino & Ponsford, 2006), and evidence of deterioration of performance over time on a selective attention task (Schnabel & Kydd, 2012). Divided attention has often been found to be impaired in TBI as well, although findings regarding the specifics of this impairment have varied from study to study. It has been suggested that this is due to marked differences in the tasks used in different studies to examine divided attention and that tasks with fewer memory or controlled processing components may not be sensitive to differences between TBI patients and controls (Park, Moscovitch, & Robertson, 1999). Impairments in executive attention or executive control of attention have also been noted in TBI (e.g., Niogi et al., 2008; Ríos, Periáñez, & Muñoz-Céspedes, 2004).

A key complication in assessing and understanding attention deficits in TBI stems from difficulty separating impaired (which sometimes means *slowed*) attention from slowed cognitive processing in general. Research suggests that patients with TBI do typically exhibit overall slowed cognitive processing relative to healthy controls (Ben-David, Nguyen, & van Lieshout, 2011; Ríos et al., 2004). Some studies have argued that slowed processing and attention are two separate impairments in TBI patients (Dymowski, Owens, Ponsford, & Willmott, 2015; Mathias & Wheaton, 2007). Other studies, however, have concluded that slowed process-

ing speed may significantly contribute to the observed attention impairments in TBI (Ponsford & Kinsella, 1992) or may even fully explain them (Willmott, Ponsford, Hocking, & Schönberger, 2009). In short, results on this point are mixed, and the relationship between attention and slowed processing is still under discussion in the TBI literature.

Much of the research on attention in TBI has been motivated by understanding the ways in which individuals engage in everyday tasks such as activities of daily living (ADLs) and their level of competence or safety while doing so. Some studies have specifically examined the link between attention deficits and cognitive failures during everyday tasks in TBI patients, with somewhat mixed results. A widely cited study by Robertson and colleagues (Robertson, Manly, Andrade, Baddeley, & Yiend, 1997) found significant associations between performance on a sustained attention task, severity of brain damage (assessed by a coma scale and posttraumatic amnesia duration), and everyday slips in attention (as reported by caregivers of the study participants). The particular sustained attention task used in this study was the Sustained Attention to Response Test (SART) (Robertson, Manly, Andrade, et al., 1997), which is described at greater length in the Assessment portion of this chapter. However, a later study was unable to replicate Robertson and colleagues' key findings (Whyte, Grieb-Neff, Gantz, & Polansky, 2006). Finally, a study by Dockree and colleagues (2006) found evidence that errors during a divided attention task were correlated with everyday cognitive failures.

There has also been a substantial amount of work on TBI and driving, a task considered to require higher-level forms of attention (e.g., drivers might recruit divided attention when checking to see if it is safe to change lanes while also maintaining safety in their current lane). There is some evidence that impaired divided attention following TBI may be associated with reduced safety in driving (Brouwer, Ponds, Van Wolffelaar, & Van Zomeren, 1989; Brouwer, Withaar, Tant, & Van Zomeren, 2002; Cyr et al., 2009). However, a systematic review on studies examining prediction of driving capacity after TBI concluded that due to methodological limitations in many studies, there is still no reliable way to predict driving abilities in TBI (Ortoleva, Brugger, Van der Linden, & Walder, 2012).

Finally, a note on neglect. Brain injury—as well as other etiologies, notably right hemisphere stroke—can result in unilateral neglect, also known as hemispatial neglect. Patients with neglect have decreased abilities to detect, orient to, or respond to stimuli on the side of space contralateral to the lesion (in the majority of neglect cases, right hemisphere damage results in left neglect). Although neglect can be considered a form of impaired attention, it will not be discussed at length here. For a thorough discussion of right hemisphere disorder and neglect, the reader is referred to Chapter 4 of this book.

Aphasia

Aphasia in most cases results from a stroke or injury to the language-dominant hemisphere of the brain (the left hemisphere in most but not all individuals) and is characterized by a decrease in receptive and/or expressive language abilities. As a result, the bulk of the research on aphasia has centered on language impairments and on damage to language centers in the brain. However, while language deficits are typically considered the most salient feature of aphasia, many individuals with aphasia have been found to have attention deficits as well (for reviews, see Kurland, 2011; Murray, 1999). A growing body of research is examining the extent and role of decreased attention in this population, and there is an increasing sense that gaining a better understanding of attention deficits in aphasia is not only theoretically important but also clinically relevant, in terms of both the assessment and treatment of aphasia.

Notably, a number of studies have provided evidence that the attention deficits in aphasia are domain-general in nature—in other words, attention deficits in aphasia are evident not just on linguistic tasks but also on nonlinguistic tasks (e.g., Erickson, Goldinger, & LaPointe, 1996; Hunting-Pompon, Kendall, & Bacon Moore, 2011; Kreindler & Fradis, 1968; Laures, Odell, & Coe, 2003; Peach, Newhoff, & Rubin, 1992; Robin & Rizzo, 1989; Villard & Kiran, 2015). An important point in studying attention in aphasia is that if an attention task that involves linguistic stimuli is administered to a patient with known language deficits, it will be difficult to conclude that impaired performance is necessarily due to deficits in attention. The above-referenced studies all removed this confound through the use of nonlinguistic tasks. Their findings demonstrate that persons with aphasia exhibit attentional impairments in situations where no language is required, suggesting that the attention impairment in aphasia is, at least to some extent, domain-general.

An interesting feature of aphasia—possibly connected to attention impairments in this population—is that substantial within-person, or *intraindividual,* variability has been observed on a variety of different types of language tasks (Cameron, Wambaugh, & Mauszycki, 2010; Caplan, Waters, DeDe, Michaud, & Reddy, 2007; Freed, Marshall, & Chuhlantseff, 1996; Howard, Patterson, Orchard-Lisle, & Morton, 1985; Kreindler & Fradis, 1968). It is not unusual to observe an individual with aphasia correctly name a picture or answer a question one moment but then be unable to repeat this behavior a few moments later—even if shown the exact same picture or asked the exact same question. This variability has been observed not only from moment to moment but also from day to day. Work by McNeil and colleagues (Hula & McNeil, 2008; McNeil, 1982, 1983; McNeil, Odell, & Tseng, 1991) has suggested that this variability in performance, along with several other features of aphasia such as stimulability and preserved metalinguistic knowledge, indicates that individuals with aphasia have not lost their representations of language in the brain, as is often assumed. Rather, McNeil and colleagues argue, these individuals experience a fluctuating ability to access these representations due to a failure to effectively and efficiently *allocate* attentional resources (see McNeil, Hula, & Sung, 2011, for a review). On a related note, recent work has shown that individuals with aphasia not only demonstrate variability on language tasks but

also demonstrate elevated variability on attention tasks relative to controls and that this variability is evident not only when measured from moment to moment (Villard & Kiran, 2018) but also when measured from day to day (Villard & Kiran, 2015).

Evidence supporting the existence of divided attention deficits and/or attention allocation deficits in aphasia has been presented in a number of studies. One study implemented a nonlinguistic dual-task experiment using an auditory tone discrimination task and the Wisconsin Card Sorting Task (WISC) (Grant & Berg, 1981), a test of set-shifting involving visual categorization of colored symbols (Erickson et al., 1996). Results showed that while patients and controls performed similarly while focusing on only one task, patient performance was significantly worse than that of controls during the dual-task condition, suggesting that these patients exhibited deficits in attention allocation and/or differences in capacity limitations. Another study by Murray, Holland, and Beeson (1997) also found evidence of divided attention deficits in aphasia using a primary linguistic listening task combined in one condition with a secondary linguistic task and in another condition with a secondary nonlinguistic task. When a secondary task was added, patient performance decreased more than control performance, suggesting that patients had more difficulty allocating attention between the two tasks. Additionally, patient performance was worse when the secondary task was linguistic. More recently, Heuer and Hallowell (2015) used eye-tracking during a dual-task paradigm in which participants were asked to complete two tasks: One was an auditory sentence comprehension task and one was a visual search task. Murray (2018) also found evidence of reduced resource allocation in patients with aphasia during a divided attention task involving sentence comprehension as well as tone discrimination. Results suggested that while all participants experienced more difficulty in a dual-task relative to a single-task condition, participants with aphasia experienced additional difficulty allocating attention between the two tasks.

The question of whether language deficits in aphasia could be driven or exacerbated by underlying attention deficits, or if these two impairments simply co-occur, is still under discussion in the literature. The view put forth by McNeil and colleagues (described above) implies a relatively strong influence of attention on language performance in aphasia, such that impaired attention is at the root of language deficits in aphasia. Others, such as Murray (1999) and Villard and Kiran (2017), have suggested a somewhat weaker view, in which attention deficits influence language performance in aphasia to some extent but can only partially explain the linguistic deficit. Some studies have examined this question by looking at the relationship between attention severity and language severity in aphasia. If attention deficits do in fact drive language deficits in aphasia, we would expect poorer attention skills to be associated with poorer language skills. One study by Murray (2012) reported significant associations between scores on standardized attention tests and standardized language tests in patients with aphasia. Another, however, though it found connections

between lesion location and performance on an experimental attention task, did not see associations between performance on that same attention task and overall severity of aphasia (Murray et al., 1997).

Additionally, a number of studies have investigated visuospatial attention in aphasia; findings from these studies have suggested that individuals with aphasia may orient or respond to objects in their visual field differently than healthy controls. Generally, severe visuospatial deficits in the form of visual neglect are associated with damage to the right hemisphere (refer to Chapter 4 for more on this topic); however, there is also evidence that left hemisphere stroke can cause visual neglect. In a recent study on 117 patients with acute left hemisphere stroke, 17.4% were found to have symptoms of visual neglect (Beume et al., 2017). An earlier study by Petry and colleagues found that patients with aphasia following left hemisphere stroke demonstrated slowed reaction times responding to stimuli in their right visual field when they were given a misleading, or invalid, cue prior to the stimulus, whereas controls did not show this difficulty (Petry, Crosson, Rothi, Bauer, & Schauer, 1994).

Other recent research on visuospatial attention in patients with aphasia has used eye-tracking to examine eye gaze patterns of individuals with aphasia while attending to visual stimuli. Thiessen and colleagues used eye-tracking to examine visual attention patterns in individuals with aphasia and healthy individuals while looking at visual scenes (Thiessen, Beukelman, Hux, & Longenecker, 2016). Results suggested that the visual attention exhibited by patients with aphasia differed from that exhibited by healthy controls in several ways, including a higher tendency to look at background images in a scene, as well as a lower degree of responsiveness to engagement cues. Additionally, a study by Heuer, Ivanova, and Hallowell (2017) found evidence that when looking at multiple-choice image displays, physical stimulus characteristics had a notable influence on visual attention in patients with aphasia. Such findings may prove relevant to the development and optimization of visual displays in augmentative-alternative communication (AAC) devices for persons with aphasia.

Dementia

With the most recent update to the *DSM*, the terminology referring to the various types of dementia has been reconfigured. Specifically, the diagnostic category that had previously been labeled *delirium, dementia, amnestic, and other cognitive disorders* has been renamed *major/minor neurocognitive disorders*. This category includes a number of more specific etiologies, including neurocognitive disorder due to Alzheimer's disease, dementia with Lewy bodies, vascular neurocognitive disorder, and frontotemporal neurocognitive disorder. Despite these official changes to the diagnostic nomenclature, the more familiar terms Alzheimer's disease, dementia with Lewy bodies, vascular dementia, and frontotemporal dementia continue to be widely used in clinical and research settings and will therefore be employed here as well.

Research suggests that attention impairments are common in dementia and that deficits in different domains of attention may be helpful in differentiating certain types of dementia (Foldi, Lobosco, & Schaefer, 2002; Harciarek & Jodzio, 2005). However, dementia with Lewy bodies (DLB) is the only subtype of progressive neurocognitive disorders for which attention deficits are a key diagnostic feature. In the fourth consensus report of the Dementia with Lewy Bodies Consortium (McKeith et al., 2017), one of the core features of DLB is listed as "fluctuating cognition with pronounced variations in attention and alertness" (p. 90). Importantly, these fluctuations manifest early on in patients with DLB, which may aid in differentiating this cognitive disorder from others in which marked deficits in attention appear only later, after the disease has progressed further. Variability in processes such as attention may cause patients with DLB to appear to lose focus during ordinary activities or to "zone out." This variability during everyday situations is typically brief and is not related to specific task demands (Metzler-Baddeley, 2007).

In other types of dementia, such as Alzheimer's disease, vascular dementia, and frontotemporal dementia, attention is not considered to be a diagnostic criterion and is therefore not typically the main focus of assessment or management of the disease. However, even in these types of dementia, information about patients' attention skills may prove valuable during the diagnostic process and may also be relevant when designing plans of treatment or care. In Alzheimer's disease (AD), attentional abilities certainly decline as the disease progresses and are notably impaired during the later stages (Foldi et al., 2002; McGuinness, Barrett, Craig, Lawson,

& Passmore, 2010; Perry & Hodges, 1999). Different subtypes of attention, however, may begin to decline at different stages. Patients with AD have been found to have relatively preserved sustained attention abilities until the later stages of the disease (Calderon et al., 2001), whereas higher-level forms of attention, such as executive control and divided attention, have been shown to be impaired even in early AD (Baddeley, Baddeley, Bucks, & Wilcock, 2001; Foldi et al., 2002; Perry & Hodges, 1999). There is also some evidence that AD patients and DLB patients demonstrate similar deficits in selective attention (Calderon et al., 2001).

Additionally, several recent studies suggest that small changes in attention may be associated with preclinical AD biomarkers such as increased levels of amyloid in the brain (Gordon et al., 2015; Lim et al., 2016). Gaining a better understanding of preclinical AD and mild cognitive impairment (MCI) is a major of focus in AD research today, as improving early detection of AD could lead to the development of treatments for individuals whose abilities have not yet been substantially impaired by the disease. There is also evidence that visual selective attention abilities may be helpful in predicting the progression of AD in individual patients (Chau et al., 2017).

Regarding frontotemporal dementia, researchers have suggested that selective attention, as measured by subtests of the Test of Everyday Attention (TEA) (Robertson, Ward, Ridgeway, & Nimmo-Smith, 1994), described in the Assessment section of this chapter, is more impaired in the frontal variant of FTD than in the temporal variant or in AD (Perry & Hodges, 2000). Patients

with vascular dementia have been found to have attention deficits as well (Akanuma et al., 2016).

Assessment of Attention

This section will describe some widely available tests of attention that may be used in clinical and/or research settings to evaluate attention in individuals with cognitive communication disorders. Before jumping into the details of these tests, however, it may be helpful to begin by outlining some important considerations in approaching an assessment of attention and choosing appropriate tools.

As discussed in the previous section, attention comprises a variety of subtypes. While these subtypes may overlap in some respects (e.g., basic sustained attention is necessary in order for successful selective attention to occur) they are often assessed separately. It is essential, therefore, to choose attention measures that assess the subtype (or subtypes) of attention that are most relevant to the patient being assessed. To begin with, this should involve considering the patient's current abilities. For example, it would probably not be appropriate to administer a challenging dual-task assessment to a patient known to have inconsistent alertness or difficulty focusing on a simple task for more than a few seconds. Similarly, a basic sustained attention measure might not be sensitive enough to detect subtler attention deficits in a higher-level patient hoping to return to work.

Next, when selecting a test of attention—or a test of any cognitive-linguistic skill, for that matter—test validity should be carefully examined. Test validity can be defined as the extent to which a test measures what it claims to measure (Thorndike, 1997). It includes several subcomponents, two of which—construct validity and ecological validity—will be discussed here. The first, construct validity, is whether the results of a test are really a reflection of the construct it purports to assess. Theoretically, anyone could create a new test and name it "My New Test of Selective Attention"; however, this would not necessarily mean that the test-takers' scores on this measure were at all indicative of their selective attention abilities. A published test should provide specific information about construct validity, including a research-based description of the theoretical construct that the test aims to measure, as well as an explanation of how the developed test relates to this construct. A comprehensive analysis of construct validity will involve statistical testing (e.g., a factor analysis conducted on test data from a normative sample), comparison of scores on the test in question with scores on other established tests believed to measure the same construct, and/or other quantitative procedures.

The second type of validity that is important to consider is ecological validity, which is how well individuals' performance on a test of a given skill reflects the way they are able to apply that skill in a functional, real-world context (Sbordone, 2001). Ecological validity is particularly important to think about when selecting tests of attention, as many available tests of attention involve repetitive listening or computer-based tasks that may differ considerably from most real-world situations. It is important to consider to what extent such tests are—or are not—reflective of patients' attention abilities in everyday contexts (Bate, Mathias, & Crawford, 2001a; Kim et al., 2005). The concept of ecological validity, along with related principles of treatment (e.g., generalizability of trained skills), is one we will return to again later in this chapter. Note that there can often be somewhat of a trade-off between construct validity and ecological validity. A highly structured, repetitive, computer-based attention test may have high construct validity but low ecological validity. A patient or caregiver questionnaire about attentional lapses in everyday situations, on the other hand, could have high ecological validity but limited construct validity.

Another complication in selecting tests of attention is the fact that attention can be difficult to tease apart from other cognitive-communicative abilities such as executive function, language processing, and visual/auditory processing. After all, most real-world activities requiring attention require other skills as well. For example, a child listening to a bedtime story is attending to the story, but he is also processing the language he hears. Similarly, a teenager playing a video game is attending to the game, but she is also visually processing what she sees on the screen. The same principle holds true for the clinical assessment of attention, and for many patients, this point can introduce complications. An attention task requiring the patient to attend to written words or letters, for example, could be problematic if administered to a patient with aphasia, alexia, or visual impairment, as these other impairments would cloud interpretation of the resulting scores. On a somewhat different note, the patient's native language or bilingual/multilingual status should also be considered, as administering a test in English to a patient who is nonnative speaker or English could impact results. Literacy level based on educational background should also be taken into account if written words are presented. Additionally, many tests of attention may require additional cognitive abilities of the patient: Short-term and/or working memory may be required to retain and apply the task instructions, or executive function may be required to plan and execute a response. The full range of processes required for a particular task should therefore be identified when choosing a test of attention, with potentially confounding issues considered.

Other factors that should be considered when selecting test materials include the purpose and goals of assessment. In some cases, the purpose of assessing attention may be to demonstrate that the individual has an attention deficit that warrants rehabilitative treatment. In these cases, a norm-referenced test with high validity and sufficient guidance for thorough interpretation of results would be appropriate. In other cases, the purpose might be to track improvement in attention over time, perhaps in relation to the implementation of an attention treatment program. (For situations in which the test is expected to be administered again following treatment, issues such as test-retest reliability and practice effects should be taken into account.) Test selection should also be related to the goals and concerns of the patient or family. Depending on the setting, these goals may be centered on safety, inde-

pendence, discharge to a lower level of care, improvement of maintenance of functional abilities, or personal factors. Finally, as is true when evaluating any cognitive-linguistic skills, the presence or absence of impairment should never be based on the results of a single measure. Instead, several complementary methods of assessment should be used to paint a full picture of the patient's ability in a given domain.

With these considerations in mind, let us now look at some of the available tests of attention that may be used by speech-language pathologists in clinical or research settings. This list is intended to be representative, but it is by no means exhaustive. Many of the tests described below are used in clinical settings (see Table 1–2 for a summary of these); however, some descriptions of well-known tests typically used in research settings are also included. As noted earlier, the evaluation of attention overlaps with the evaluation of other cognitive processes; therefore, some tests that may often be considered to measure attention are described in other chapters of this book. The reader is referred to Chapter 3 for descriptions of the Trail Making Test, Stroop test, and other executive function tests, and to Chapter 4 for descriptions of visual neglect tests such as the Behavioral Inattention Test (Wilson, Cockburn, & Halligan, 1987a, 1987b) and the Catherine Bergego Scale (Azouvi et al., 2003).

Test of Everyday Attention

One widely used and fairly comprehensive tool designed to assess a number of different subtypes of attention is the Test of Everyday Attention (TEA) (Rob-

Table 1–2. Selected Assessment Tasks and Instruments for Evaluating Attention in Clinical Settings

Test	Component(s) of Attention and Related Processes Assessed
Test of Everyday Attention	
Map Search	Selective attention
Telephone Search	Sustained and selective attention
Telephone Search With Counting	Divided attention
Elevator Counting	Sustained attention
Elevator Counting With Distraction	Working memory, alternating attention
Visual Elevator	Alternating and sustained attention
Auditory Elevator With Reversal	Alternating attention, working memory
Lottery	Sustained attention
Attention Process Training—Test	Sustained, selective, alternating, and divided attention
WAIS-IV	
Digit Span Forward	Sustained attention
Digit Span Backward	Sustained attention, working memory
Digit Sequencing	Sustained attention, working memory
Brief Test of Attention	Divided attention, working memory
Symbol Digit Modalities Test	Divided attention, visual scanning and tracking, perceptual motor speed
Paced Auditory Serial Addition Task	Sustained and divided attention, speed of processing
Conners' Continuous Performance Test	Sustained, selective, and divided attention
Moss Attention Rating Scale	Restlessness/distractibility, initiation, sustained attention
Rating Scale of Attentional Behavior	General attention, ability to focus

Source: Adapted from Biel and Hula (2016).

ertson et al., 1994). This measure was designed for adults aged 18 to 80 and is intended to take approximately 60 minutes to administer. Initial validation performed by the developers involved analysis of scores from 154 unimpaired individuals, as well as 80 unilateral stroke patients, as well as comparison of these scores with performance on previously existing tests of attention. Brief descriptions of the eight TEA subtests are provided below. All subtests were designed around the theme of an imagined trip to Philadelphia.

- *Map Search:* The test-taker is given a map of Philadelphia and asked to find and circle as many restaurant symbols (a knife and fork) as they can in 2 minutes. Two scores are taken from this task: the number of symbols circled in 1 minute and the number of symbols circled in 2 minutes.
- *Telephone Search:* The test-taker is given a telephone directory and asked to cross out specific symbols.
- *Telephone Search Dual Task:* As in the Telephone Search, the test-tasker is asked to cross out specific symbols in a telephone directory; however, he or she is also asked to simultaneously count auditory tones. Scores on Telephone Search and Telephone Search Dual Task can be compared to determine the decrement in performance when a second task is added.
- *Elevator Counting:* In this auditory task, the test-taker is instructed to pretend he or she is in an elevator in which the visual floor number indicator is not working. The test-taker is presented with a series of tones and asked to count these tones to determine what floor he or she is "on."
- *Elevator Counting With Distraction:* This task is identical to Elevator Counting, except that two types of tones (medium-pitched and high-pitched) are presented. The

test-taker is asked to count the medium tones and ignore the high ones.

- *Visual Elevator:* In a visual version of the elevator task, the test-taker is presented with a series of pictured stimuli including elevator doors and arrows pointing up or down and is asked to keep track of what floor he or she is on (with the arrows indicating a switch in the up/down direction).
- *Auditory Elevator With Reversal:* The final elevator task is an auditory version of the visual elevator task, in which the test-taker is asked to keep track of what floor he or she is on by counting medium auditory tones. In this task, high and low tones indicate a change in direction.
- *Lottery:* The test-taker is presented with series of spoken letters and numbers. He or she is instructed to listen for a target number and, each time he or she hears it, to write down the preceding two letters.

Analysis of the TEA subtests provides a good illustration of how the constructs of specific attentional subtypes can be difficult to identify, separate, and measure. Available analyses of TEA results have yielded differing results about which TEA subtests measure which attentional subtypes. For example, the authors' principal components analysis of their normative sample data during development and validation of the test suggested that the TEA subtests load on four factors: visual selective attention/speed, attentional switching, sustained attention, and auditory-verbal working memory. However, more recent studies of a

Cantonese version of the TEA in individuals with and without TBI (Chan & Lai, 2006; Chan, Lai, & Robertson, 2006) found evidence for a three-factor structure consistent with Posner and Petersen's (1990) model, including sustained attention, visual selection, and attentional switching. These differing structures have included conflicting interpretations of specific tasks. For example, the authors' original analysis found that the Visual Elevator task loaded onto the attentional switching factor. However, a different study found that while accuracy on this task loaded onto an attentional switching factor, the timing score loaded onto a sustained attention factor (Chan & Lai, 2006), and another study found the task overall to load onto a sustained attention factor (Bate et al., 2001a).

The TEA has several key advantages. To begin with, it is theory based and is considered to have high construct validity. It also includes instructions for three different administrations (where each includes slight variations in stimuli), which increases the validity of multiple administrations. It may also be useful, in situations where time for testing may be limited, to selectively administer one or several subtests of the TEA (although this approach may not provide a full picture of the patient's attention skills).

However, there are also limitations to administering the TEA. As a structured test, it is considered to have only moderate ecological validity. Additionally, the evidence on the sensitivity of the TEA to differences between healthy individuals and individuals with neurological impairment is somewhat mixed. The authors of the test found

differences in performance between healthy individuals and those with brain injury (Robertson, Ward, Ridgeway, & Nimmo-Smith, 1996). However, a later study examined performance on the TEA in 35 patients recovering from severe TBI and 35 age- and education-matched controls and found significant group differences in scores on only two of the eight subtests (Map Search and Telephone Search) (Bate et al., 2001a). Finally, the authors note that the TEA should be used with caution in individuals who have known sensory deficits such as reduced visual or auditory acuity and that ceiling or floor effects may be an issue for some subtests.

Attention Process Training Test

The Attention Process Training Test (APT-Test; Sohlberg & Mateer, 2001a) was designed based on the authors' original theoretical framework of attentional subtypes, with the goal of providing clinicians with a tool to systematically assess attention deficits in sustained attention, selective attention, alternating attention, and divided attention. The APT-Test tasks are highly structured and involve both visual and audio-recorded stimuli. This test was originally designed for use with the APT-I and APT-II attention treatment programs; the more recently released APT-III program (see the Treatment portion of this chapter for additional information on this) was not designed to be used with the APT-Test. Nevertheless, the APT-Test is still available and may be useful in contexts where highly structured assessment of specific attentional types is desirable.

Digit Span

A simple and common attention task is the digit span task, versions of which are included in many comprehensive cognitive and neuropsychological batteries, such as the Wechsler Adult Intelligence Scale (WAIS-IV) (Wechsler, 2008). In the digit span task, the test administrator reads aloud a sequence of digits at the rate of one digit per second while the test-taker listens. When the sequence is finished, the test-taker repeats the digits in either forward or backward order (as instructed prior to the task). In other forms of the digit span task, the test-taker may be instructed to manipulate the digits in some way, such as sequencing them into ascending order. Typically, the test begins with a span of two digits, with subsequent items increasing the span, up to eight or nine digits. Two sequences of each length are presented, progressing to longer sequences until the patient misses both sequences at a given level. The length of the longest repeated sequence is the digit span score.

Although digit span is a relatively straightforward task, it also provides another example of overlapping constructs. While forward digit span certainly requires attention to the presented sequences, it can also be considered a test of short-term verbal memory (Lezak, Howieson, Bigler, & Tranel, 2012). Similarly, the backward and sequencing digit span tasks likely recruit working memory, as well as, possibly, visuospatial processing (Black, 1986; Larrabee & Kane, 1986; Rapport, Webster, & Dutra, 1994). It should also be recognized that while a digit span task may be appropriate for an individual who has no known difficulty with speech or numbers, it may not be the best choice for patients with aphasia, apraxia, acalculia, or other deficits that could complicate the interpretation of performance. Additionally, there is somewhat conflicting information about how the digit span scores should be understood and about the sensitivity and specificity of digit span scores in differentiating performance in healthy individuals versus a variety of patient populations (see Schroeder, Twumasi-Ankrah, Baade, & Marshall, 2012, for a review). Notably, some studies have found no reliable difference between backward digit span scores in healthy individuals and individuals with TBI in the chronic stage of recovery (Bate et al., 2001a; Vallat-Azouvi, Weber, Legrand, & Azouvi, 2007).

Brief Test of Attention

The Brief Test of Attention (BTA) (Schretlen, Bobholz, & Brandt, 1996) was developed to be a quick test of auditory divided attention. This measure includes two parts. In the first part, the test-takers listen to sequences of letters and numbers read aloud at the rate of one per second (e.g., "M-6-3-R-2"); after each sequence, they are expected to report how many numbers they heard. In the second part, the test-takers listen to the same sequences of letters and numbers; this time, after each sequence, they are expected to report how many letters they heard. In each of the two parts, the sequences start with four items and increase to 18 items. Psychometric testing and validation conducted by the developers of the BTA, involving 926 patients and healthy individuals, suggest that the BTA has good construct validity (Schretlen et al., 1996). However, like many tests of attention, it may also recruit other processes such as auditory working memory and language comprehension.

Symbol Digit Modalities Test

In the Symbol Digit Modalities Test (SDMT) (Smith, 1991), the test-taker is presented with a sheet of paper containing a sequence of symbols, as well as a symbol-digit coding key, in which each digit from 1 to 9 is paired with a symbol. The test-taker is asked to provide the digit corresponding to each symbol in the sequence and is given 90 seconds to do so. The SDMT has been considered by some studies to be a measure of visual selective attention (Bate et al., 2001a; Chan, 2000) and by others to be a measure of divided attention (Ponsford & Kinsella, 1992). In addition to requiring attention, the successful completion of this task requires complex visual scanning abilities, processing speed, and memory (Bate et al., 2001a). It has been shown to be sensitive in differentiating individuals with TBI from healthy individuals (Ponsford & Kinsella, 1992). Although the SDMT is traditionally a pencil-and-paper test, computerized versions have also been developed and used in research settings (e.g., Forn et al., 2009; Tung et al., 2016).

Paced Auditory Serial Addition Test

The Paced Auditory Serial Addition Test (PASAT), originally developed by Gronwall and Sampson (1974) for the purpose of detecting minor cognitive impairments in concussion patients, measures sustained attention, divided attention, and processing speed and likely recruits working memory as well. The PASAT is a challenging task in which a series of random digits (usually 50 or 60) are presented auditorily to the test-taker. Each time a digit is presented (with the exception of the first digit), the test-taker is expected to add that digit to the previous digit and provide the response (a number between 2 and 18). Divided attention is required to add the new number with the previous one while also holding the new number in mind so it can be added to the following number. Research on this test in patients with TBI suggests that it is sensitive to mild deficits. However, it may also be sensitive to factors not related to neurological impairment, such as age, IQ, and mathematical ability; notable practice effects have also been observed (Tombaugh, 2006).

Conners' Continuous Performance Test

Conners's Continuous Performance Test Second Edition (CPT II) (Conners, 2000) was originally designed for use in children and adolescents with attention-deficit hyperactivity disorder (ADHD); however, it may be useful for assessing attention deficits in other populations and ages as well. Studies examining clinical utility of the CPT-II in TBI have found group differences between moderate-to-severe TBI patients and age-matched controls (Zane, Gfeller, Roskos, & Bucholz, 2016). Like the SART, the CPT-II asks test-takers to respond to all presented items *except* a specific target; in this case, a series of letters are presented on the screen and test-takers are instructed to respond to all letters *except* "X." The CPT II provides several indices of performance, including attentiveness, impulsivity, sustained attention, and consistency of response time.

Covert Orienting of Visual Attention

The Covert Orienting of Visual Attention (COVAT) task (Posner & Cohen, 1980) was designed to assess an individual's ability to disengage, move, and engage attention. In this computerized task, the test-takers are seated in front of a computer and instructed to keep their eyes focused on a fixation located at the center of the screen during the entire task. For each item, a spatial cue (right or left) appears, followed by a target (also on the right or left). The subject is expected to then press a button indicating the location of the target. In some of the trials, the target appears on the cued side (congruent trials); in other trials, the target appears on the noncued side (incongruent trials). The ratio of congruent to incongruent trials can be varied in the COVAT, but typically 50% or more of the targets appear in the location designated by the cue. In order to respond to incongruent trials, the test-takers need to disengage their attention from the cue, move their attention to the side of the screen opposite the visual cue, and then reengage their focus on the target. One study comparing performance on the COVAT in severe TBI patients and age-matched controls found no differences in the two groups' ability to disengage, move, and engage during incongru-

ent trials, though they did find that the patients were significantly slower than the controls in responding (Bate, Mathias, & Crawford, 2001b). Another TBI study on the COVAT revealed that participants with TBI demonstrated an impaired ability to use correct cues (Cremona-Meteyard, Clark, Wright, & Geffen, 1992). One study also found the COVAT to be sensitive to attention deficits in Alzheimer's disease (Wright, Cremona-Meteyard, Geffen, & Geffen, 1994). The COVAT has primarily been used for research purposes and is seldom seen in clinical settings.

Sustained Attention to Response Test

The Sustained Attention to Response Test (SART) (Robertson, Manly, Andrade, et al., 1997) is a computerized task designed to assess sustained attention. The test-takers are presented with a series of 225 random digits on a screen at unpredictable intervals. They are instructed to press a button as quickly as possible each time they see a digit, unless the digit is a 3, in which case they are told they should *not* press the button. This type of task is categorized as a go/no-go task and relies on the ability of the subject to remain vigilant toward an infrequently occurring target stimulus and to inhibit an accustomed response when that target appears; such inhibition is thought to require attentional control. SART scores have been shown to differ between healthy individuals and TBI patients, especially those with damage to the frontal lobes (Manly, Davison, Heutink, Galloway, & Robertson, 2000; Manly, Robertson, Galloway, & Hawkins, 1999; Manly et al.,

2003; Robertson, Manly, Andrade, et al., 1997). The SART was originally designed for use in research settings and is not frequently used in clinical evaluations.

Attention Network Test

The Attention Network Test (ANT) (Fan et al, 2002) was designed to assess the 3 attention networks—alerting, orienting, and executive control—identified by Posner and Petersen (1990). In this computerized task, the test-takers see a fixation on the screen in front of them, followed by a visual cue that may provide spatial information, followed by an arrow stimulus pointing to the left or right, which may be presented with or without distractor arrows pointing in the opposite direction. The ANT collects data about error rate as well as reaction time, and information about the three attention networks can be obtained through analysis of the results. This test has been used in a number of different research settings and has often been modified to fit the goals of specific studies; auditory versions have also been developed (e.g., Roberts, Summerfield, & Hall, 2006).

Clinician-Completed Rating Scales of Attention

In addition to the measures listed above, all of which require the patient to sit and complete specific tasks in a controlled testing environment, there are also a number of attention rating scales available. An attention rating scale takes a markedly different approach to the assessment of a patient's attention. The patient is not asked to sit and take a test; instead, a clinician rates the patient on a variety of behaviors related to attention. In order for such scales to be used effectively, the clinician must be familiar with the patient's behavior and must have had substantial opportunity to interact with the patient in everyday situations, usually over the course of 2 or more days. Rating scales tend to have high ecological validity due to their focus on patient behavior and capabilities in everyday environments; however, they can also have disadvantages, such as subjectivity of clinician judgments or application to limited settings.

One such scale is the Moss Attention Rating Scale (MARS) (Hart et al., 2006; Whyte, Hart, Bode, & Malec, 2003; Whyte, Hart, Ellis, & Chervoneva, 2008). This measure includes 22 scales, including "initiates communication with others," "performs better on tasks when directions are given slowly," and "sustains conversation without interjecting irrelevant or off-topic comments." Analysis of the MARS provided by the authors suggests that it measures three factors (restlessness/distraction, initiation, and sustained/consistent attention) (Hart et al., 2006). The authors of the MARS have provided evidence that it has good construct validity and interrater reliability and that it is sensitive to change over time (Hart, Whyte, Ellis, & Chervoneva, 2009; Whyte et al., 2008). It has also been shown to be predictive of 1-year outcomes of disability in TBI patients (Hart et al., 2009). Disadvantages of the MARS include a somewhat limited scope of validation—it was designed for use mainly with moderate-to-severe TBI patients and has been evaluated only in inpatient (acute and subacute rehab) settings.

Another example of an attention rating scale is the Rating Scale of Attentional Behavior (Ponsford & Kinsella, 1991), a tool that includes 14 specific scales, such as "performed slowly on mental tasks" and "unable to pay attention to more than one task at a time." Initial validation of the Rating Scale of Attentional Behavior noted that it demonstrated good interrater reliability between professionals from the same discipline but weaker interrater reliability between professionals from different disciplines. It was also found to correlate moderately with scores on other, more impairment-based tests of attention. Like the MARS, the Rating Scale of Attentional Behavior may be most useful in a limited population and setting (in this case, patients with severe TBI in a rehabilitation setting).

Quick Attention Screenings and Informal Observation

We turn our focus now to yet another approach to the assessment of attention. While the neuropsychological tests and behavior scales detailed above can provide valuable and, in some cases, relatively comprehensive information about patients' attention abilities, it should be recognized that an in-depth assessment of attention skills is ambitious and may not be feasible in all clinical settings, especially when a clinician is tasked with assessing and treating a variety of cognitive-linguistic skills in a limited period of time. Additionally, some inpatient facilities may have guidelines designed to standardize or streamline screening procedures, and depending on the setting, the available testing materials may be limited. For these reasons, comprehensive attention testing may not always be realistic.

In such cases, attention can still be examined to some extent through the use of standard cognitive screening/evaluation tools that assess a variety of domains of cognitive functioning. A few examples of cognitive tests that are not specific to attention but may be encountered in rehabilitation or skilled nursing settings include the Montreal Cognitive Assessment (MoCA; Nasreddine et al., 2005), the Brief Cognitive Assessment Tool (BCAT; Mansbach, MacDougall, & Rosenzweig, 2012), the Cognitive Log (Cog-Log; Alderson & Novack, 2003), the Cognitive-Linguistic Quick Test (CLQT; Helm-Estabrooks, 2001), and the Mini-Mental State Examination (MMSE; Folstein, Folstein, & McHugh, 1975). While none of these tests are specific to attention, they may provide an opportunity to learn something about the patient's attention skills, either through the administration of specific items or through informal observation of the patient and their overall performance. Note, however, that many of the tasks included in these shorter cognitive screening tools may recruit multiple processes, such as working memory, attention, and problem solving, and are no substitute for a fine-grained assessment of attention. If attention impairments are suspected, a more in-depth assessment would ideally follow.

To give an example, the MoCA includes a short "Attention" section including one forward digit span item, one backward digit span item, a short vigilance task, and a serial subtraction task. Additionally, the MoCA includes a clock drawing task, which is not considered to be a task that specifically evaluates attention; however, informal observation of the patients during the clock drawing may provide some basic information about their ability to attend to a task for several minutes. While these tasks would not provide specific, in-depth, or definitive information about the patients' attention abilities, they may allow the clinician to gain some basic insight, which may then guide further assessment. Observing the patients' language and behavior during informal conversation can also be valuable, as it may reveal more about their ability to attend to a task or conversation for a sustained period of time.

Treatment of Attention

A sizable amount of the available literature on cognitive-behavioral attention treatment in patients with acquired neurological deficits has focused on patients with TBI, with another moderately sized group of studies examining attention treatment in stroke. Interestingly, a somewhat separate line of research investigating possible attention treatments in patients with aphasia has also evolved. Attention is typically not a primary focus of treatment for most types of dementia. For a review of how attention may be taken into consideration when designing treatment plans for patients with dementia, see Choi and Twamley (2013).

Approaches used to treat attention in neurogenically impaired populations can be divided into several groups, including direct training of

attention, training of specific everyday skills requiring attention, training in self-management of attention deficits, environmental modifications, self-management strategies, and the implementation of external aids. The first two approaches listed, direct training and training of specific skills, can be considered restorative approaches, meaning that they are intended to improve function. The other approaches listed are considered to be more compensatory in nature, meaning that they are strategies to help compensate for, or accommodate, the deficit. This section includes a discussion of each of these approaches, followed by an overview of the literature specifically on treatment of attention in aphasia.

Direct Training

The goal of direct training is to treat the underlying attention impairment, usually through the use of repetitive, decontextualized tasks. There is substantial evidence in the literature suggesting that direct training in attention does result in improved performance on trained tasks, on tasks similar to the trained tasks, and on neuropsychological measures (e.g., Sohlberg & Mateer, 1987; Sohlberg, McLaughlin, Pavese, Heidrich, & Posner, 2000; Sturm, Willmes, Orgass, & Hartje, 1997). However, it is essential to recognize that improvements on repetitive attention tasks may not necessarily generalize to improved attention function in everyday, real-world situations. Several reviews have concluded that there is insufficient evidence that direct training of attention is effective for improving functional outcomes, at least as a stand-alone method (e.g., Cicerone et al., 2011, 2019; Michel & Mateer, 2006; Park & Ingles, 2001; Ponsford et al., 2014). One systematic review examining the efficacy of computerized cognitive rehabilitation of attention and executive function in acquired brain injury did find evidence that these types of direct training methods may be effective; however, the authors acknowledge that many of the studies reviewed had notable methodological limitations such as small sample size or inadequate control groups (Bogdanova, Yee, Ho, & Cicerone, 2016). More research on this topic is therefore needed.

Attention Process Training (APT-III) (Sohlberg & Mateer, 2010) is an example of a widely utilized program that uses the direct training approach. APT-III is the most updated version of the program; the second edition (APT-II) (Sohlberg, Johnson, Paule, Raskin, & Mateer, 2001) continues to be widely used in clinical settings as well. APT-II is based on Sohlberg and Mateer's original attention framework and involves a series of tasks that build upon one another, starting with sustained attention, then moving to selective, alternating, and divided attention. Auditory tasks include listening for target words in presented strings, either in quiet or in the presence of competing background noise; visual tasks include search tasks or reading, with or without visual distractions. Tasks are adapted as difficulty levels increase from sustained attention up through divided attention. There is evidence that APT-II may be effective in treating attention deficits following stroke (Barker-Collo et al., 2009). The updated APT-III is aligned with Sohlberg and Mateer's (2010) revised attention model. It also includes additional training in metacognitive strategies and self-monitoring, is computer-based, and supports home practice.

Over the past decade or so, there has been a notable increase in the appearance and popularity of computer-based and tablet-based training programs targeting attention and other cognitive skills. These programs, which in many cases are marketed to the general public, can be considered a form of direct training of attention and are worth discussing here for several reasons. For one thing, there is literature suggesting that some of these programs could be able to help facilitate improvements in attention. For example, one study on the use of the program CogMed (Pearson Company) in TBI patients suggested that it may be able to help patients improve attention and working memory (Westerberg et al., 2007), and another study suggested that training in CogMed may result in fewer cognitive failures in everyday life (Lundqvist et al., 2010). Another widely available cognitive training program, Lumosity (Lumos Labs, San Francisco, CA), has been shown in at least one study to facilitate improvements on an untrained measure of visual attention (Finn & McDonald, 2011). Another study found that a combination of Lumosity and APT-III resulted in a small amount of generalization to standardized measures (Zickefoose, Hux, Brown, & Wulf, 2013). The reader is referred to Sigmundsdottir, Longley, and Tate (2016) for a more in-depth review of a wider variety of computer- and tablet-based programs.

However, while it is true that there is some preliminary evidence suggesting the potential utility of computer-

and tablet-based cognitive training programs, there is still insufficient evidence to definitively support the effectiveness of these methods in facilitating real improvements in everyday functioning for patients with TBI (Sigmundsdottir et al., 2016). It is important to keep in mind that cognitive training programs should be subjected to the same scrutiny and held to the same scientific, evidence-based standards as any other potential treatment method. Additionally, since many cognitive training programs are available on the Internet for potential independent use by patients, the role of clinician-guided training versus independent home practice should be considered before implementing or recommending this type of treatment approach (Cicerone et al., 2011; Connor & Shaw, 2016). For further discussion of the issues and questions surrounding cognitive training programs in a variety of populations, see also Rabipour and Raz (2012).

Training of Specific Functional Skills Requiring Attention

A second approach to attention treatment attempts to narrow the gap between impairment-based training and generalization to everyday situations by treating attention in the context of real-world activities of daily living. A notable review by Park and Ingles (2001) found that specific skills treatments showed greater effects than direct, impairment-based treatments, particularly when control conditions were taken into account. This finding led them to suggest that rehabilitation efforts will be most effective when they focus on skills of functional importance

to patients. Park and Ingles also emphasize the role of "neuropsychological scaffolding" in training specific skills. Neuropsychological scaffolding refers to the ways in which a clinician may identify the simpler component parts involved in a more complex task and break these parts down so the patient can practice each one individually—a step that may be necessary for successful practice of the task but that some patients may not be able to take on their own. Specific skills trained may include ADLs such as preparing food, bathing, or dressing. In these cases, collaboration with other disciplines such as occupational therapy or physical therapy can be valuable.

Self-Management Strategies, External Aids, and Environmental Modifications

Finally, attention may be treated through the use of compensatory techniques such as self-management strategies, external aids, and/or environmental modifications. These approaches can be implemented in somewhat overlapping ways and therefore will be discussed here as a group.

The self-management approach to treating attention consists of instructing and training the patient in strategies for self-management of attentional difficulties in everyday functional settings. A self-management strategy could be specific to a particular routine. For example, individuals who have difficulty maintaining consistent attention throughout their entire morning routine might be instructed to post a list next to the bathroom mirror that includes each of the tasks they need to complete (e.g., wash face, brush teeth, floss, brush hair). Note that this strategy could be considered to be a self-management tool that addresses not only attention but also memory and executive function. Self-management strategies can also be more general, making them potentially applicable to many situations—for instance, a patient could be taught to verbally mediate her or his actions (i.e., describe each step of a task while completing it) or to verbally rehearse important information. There also exist self-management strategies designed specifically to improve attention, comprehension, and memory while reading, such as the PQRST (preview, question, read, summarize, test) method and the SQ3R (survey, question, read, recite, review) method.

Some self-management strategies may also involve the use of external aids, including timed electronic reminders. One example is Goal Management Training (GMT) (Levine et al., 2011), a metacognitive approach that trains patients to pause periodically during a task to monitor performance and define goal hierarchies, sometimes using audible tones as cues. Another strategy suggested by Sohlberg and Mateer (2001b), which targets self-management of orientation, memory, and attention, is to set a watch to beep at the top of each hour and to ask oneself the following questions whenever it beeps: "What am I currently doing? What was I doing before this? What am I supposed to do next?" as a way to help manage orienting, attention, and memory. Other examples of self-management/strategy training combined with external aids that have been piloted include content-free cueing (Fish et al., 2007) and NeuroPage (Wilson, Emslie, Quirk,

& Evans, 2001; Wilson, Emslie, Quirk, Evans, & Watson, 2005). In a recent systematic review, Gillespie, Best, and O'Neill (2012) found strong evidence supporting the use of devices that provide alerts to individuals with cognitive impairments, drawing their attention to stimuli that are either external (e.g., bringing one's attention back to a current task) or internal (e.g., shifting one's attention to a goal in memory).

Environmental modifications, while typically designed to help with memory or executive function (Gillespie et al., 2012), can also help compensate for the effects of attention impairments. Environmental modifications are often designed and implemented by the clinician and then carried over by the patient, possibly with some degree of assistance from family members or other caregivers. Examples could include a computer system or app designed to help with organization or time-based reminders, the implementation of filing systems, or the modification of the home environment to reduce visual or auditory distractions (Sohlberg & Mateer, 2001b).

As with any treatment method, self-management strategies, external aids, and environmental modifications should be carefully selected or designed, tailored for the individual patient, and customized to evolve with patients' needs over time (Lopresti, Mihailidis, & Kirsch, 2004). Ideally, patients themselves should be actively involved in choosing and developing these kinds of strategies, and implementation should involve adequate training and practice time, social and/or environmental supports, and a maintenance program to assess outcomes (Sohlberg & Mateer, 2001b).

Notes on Selecting, Combining, and Implementing Treatment Approaches

A number of reviews and meta-analyses have compared the different types of approaches discussed above, and while recommendation are somewhat mixed, several commonalities emerge. In general, findings from these reviews have recommended a combination of two or more approaches in treating attention, such as direct attention training combined with instruction in metacognitive strategies, or strategy training combined with environmental modifications (Cicerone et al., 2011, 2019; Michel & Mateer, 2006; Ponsford et al., 2014).

The *Cognitive Rehabilitation Manual* (Haskins, 2012), developed by the American Congress of Rehabilitation Medicine, recommends several principles that are applicable for both self-management strategies and direct attention training. These principles are to select theory-based treatment approaches; to organize treatment in a hierarchical way, beginning with simpler forms of attention and building upon them; to base treatment decisions on ongoing patient performance data; to help patients work toward generalization of treatment tasks to real-world situations; and to flexibly adapt treatment according to patients' changing needs.

Attention Treatments Designed for Patients With Aphasia

Treating attention in aphasia is often conceptualized differently than treating attention in other neurologically impaired populations. Although attention deficits are common in aphasia,

they are usually not as salient as language deficits. As a result, improving attention is typically not the primary goal of treatment for either the patient or the clinician. Research on attention and treatment in aphasia has therefore been motivated by slightly different questions than research on attention treatment in TBI. Some of the work on attention in aphasia has examined whether attention and other cognitive abilities may be able to predict language treatment outcomes in aphasia (Lambon Ralph, Snell, Fillingham, Conroy, & Sage, 2010). Other studies have investigated the possible utility of using treatment that incorporates—or consists of—attention training to try to address language deficits.

Several studies have examined the effects of direct, impairment level treatment of attention in patients with aphasia. The APT-II program (Sohlberg et al., 2001) has been used to target attention in patients with aphasia in a number of studies. For example, two case studies examined whether APT-II training would be effective in facilitating mild reading impairments secondary to aphasia (Coelho, 2005; Sinotte & Coelho, 2007). Differences observed from pre- to posttreatment included improved reading comprehension and decreased reading effort (Coelho, 2005), as well as decreased variability in the comprehension of longer reading passages, which the authors theorized could be due to improved attention allocation (Sinotte & Coelho, 2007). Another case study found that APT-II training facilitated some degree of improvement on standardized testing of cognitive abilities, but no changes in everyday attention or communication abilities were noted (Murray, Keeton, &

Karcher, 2006). Several other small studies piloting the use of other direct attention training programs have been conducted (e.g., Helm-Estabrooks, 2011; Helm-Estabrooks, Connor, & Albert, 2000), with one utilizing a combined direct training and metacognitive facilitation method (Lee & Sohlberg, 2013). In general, findings from these studies have provided only modest support for the potential of direct attention training in remediating linguistic or cognitive deficits in aphasia. Additional evidence, including studies with larger sample sizes, would be necessary before direct attention training could be clinically recommended for patients with aphasia.

More recently, Peach and colleagues have developed a different type of approach for patients with aphasia, called language-specific attention treatment (L-SAT) (Peach, Nathan, & Beck, 2017; Peach, Schenk, Nathan, & Beck, 2018), in which sustained attention, attentional switching, and auditory-verbal working memory are implicitly incorporated into a systematic, skill-based language treatment program targeting lexical and sentence processing. L-SAT is based upon the idea that treating attention within the language domain may be of greater use than direct training of attention in patients with aphasia and that language treatment can be structured in such a way that attentional processes are heavily recruited. This approach could perhaps be considered a specific skills training approach tailored to the specific skill of communication. Preliminary results from a small study by the test developers suggest that L-SAT may be successful in facilitating language recovery and auditory-verbal working memory in patients with aphasia whose attention deficits are not severe (Peach et al., 2017).

Finally, there are also a growing number of tablet-based apps designed specifically for use by persons with aphasia (for reviews, see Des Roches & Kiran, 2017; Kurland, 2014; Swales, Hill, & Finch, 2016). Some of these apps target attention and other cognitive skills in addition to language. One example is Constant Therapy (The Learning Corp, Newton, Massachusetts), a tablet-based program created to remediate a variety of cognitive-linguistic skills in patients with aphasia. The creators of Constant Therapy have provided evidence suggesting that consistent use of the app (involving individualized programs targeting a variety of cognitive-linguistic skills) may facilitate improved performance on standardized tests of various language and cognitive abilities, including improvements in attention (Des Roches, Balachandran, Ascenso, Tripodis, & Kiran, 2015).

Finally, it is worth briefly mentioning that in recent years, several studies have investigated mindfulness meditation as a possible tool for remediation of attention and/or language in individuals with aphasia (e.g., Laures-Gore & Marshall, 2016; Marshall, Laures-Gore, & Love, 2018; Orenstein, Basilakos, & Marshall, 2012), as well as TBI (McMillan, Robertson, Brock, & Chorlton, 2002). Though small positive effects have been reported in some cases, there is currently insufficient evidence that mindfulness meditation is effective in remediating attention skills in neurologically impaired populations.

Case Study

The following case study is intended to provide an example of how the principles of assessment and treatment of attention discussed in this chapter might be applied in a specific clinical case. This case study is based on a composite of several patients encountered by the author in clinical settings.

A 69-year-old patient, KW, has just been admitted to the rehabilitation unit of a skilled nursing facility following a head injury sustained during a fall at home. KW spent 2 weeks in acute care following the injury, prior to being transferred to this facility for continued recovery and possible discharge to home, depending on progress. KW also has a history of right-hemisphere stroke (2 years prior to this admission). Following her stroke 2 years ago, she was diagnosed with a mild cognitive communication disorder; however, due to steady progress, she was subsequently determined to be safe to return to an independent living situation with regular help from family members living nearby.

Notes from the acute facility from the current admission suggest that KW demonstrates reduced insight, reduced short-term memory, reduced attention, and perseveration on specific topics. KW lives alone in a first-floor apartment; her niece visits her once a day after work to bring over groceries and to do a little cooking and cleaning. The patient also cooks light meals for herself, manages her medications with supervision from her niece, and spends much of the day watching TV or chatting on the phone with friends or relatives. She does not drive. The patient's niece is concerned that the patient may fall again.

An initial brief cognitive screening in this facility indicates that the patient can name the month (but not the date) and can state that she is here because of a fall. However, she is unconvinced that use of her walker is necessary (though she has been instructed consistently by nursing staff to

use it), and she has difficulty maintaining a conversational topic, often jumping from topic to topic and continually perseverating on several specific topics, such as stories about her next-door neighbor in the apartment complex where she lives at home.

As the facility's speech-language pathologist, you are tasked with evaluating KW's cognitive communication skills and, if appropriate, designing a treatment plan. Your facility recommends administration of the MoCA as an initial evaluation procedure for all patients with a suspected or diagnosed cognitive communication disorder. With this information in mind, some clinical questions going forward may include:

1. Is additional attention-related testing appropriate for KW?
2. How does attention relate to the goals of KW and her family?
3. Should attention be incorporated into treatment for KW and, if so, how?

One of the primary issues at stake is whether or not KW can safely return to her previous living environment. Questions involved in this issue include whether she can continue to manage her medications and cook, whether she can complete ADLs independently, and how likely she is to sustain another fall.

Attention Testing

Since your facility recommends use of the MoCA, you begin with this test. KW has notable difficulty with the items under the Attention subheading. She also requires occasional redirection to the task throughout the 15-minute assessment. Her clock drawing is missing both hands, as well as the numbers "4" and "11." Based on this testing, as well as other observations of the patient such as her difficulty in maintaining a conversational topic, you decide to complete additional attention testing.

Since KW is new to you and to the facility, you conclude that an attention rating scale is not appropriate at this time, as you would need to have in-depth knowledge of her daily functioning in order to complete one. Because you have limited evaluation time and also want to assess some other domains of cognitive functioning, you decide to administer the Map Search, Telephone Search, Elevator Counting, and Elevator Counting With Distraction subtests of the TEA in order to assess KW's sustained and selective attention abilities. Impairments are noted on all subtests. You also speak with the occupational therapist and physical therapist to find out more about KW's functioning during ADLs and learn that she needs frequent cueing to stay on task and to sequence steps of ADLs.

Goals and Treatment

Because KW appears to exhibit a variety of cognitive deficits, including not only impaired attention but also reduced insight, impaired orientation, and impaired short-term memory, you as the clinician will likely need to make decisions about how to target multiple skills in treatment. With this in mind, however, initial short-term objectives for this patient specifically targeting attention could include one or more of the following:

- The patient will successfully use a written external aid for medication management, given a once-per-day check-in, in 80% of measured opportunities.
- The patient will sustain a single conversational topic for 3 minutes in a structured conversational setting, given a visual cue and no more than two verbal reminders to stay on topic, in 80% of measured opportunities.
- The patient will complete three steps of an activity of daily living, given a written external aid and training in a verbal mediation strategy, in 80% of measured opportunities.
- The patient will state two personally relevant strategies learned via metacognitive training, such as verbal mediation of the steps involved in an ADL and use of a written external aid, in 80% of measured opportunities.

Treatment will be guided by the final objectives chosen and will combine specific skills training with training in metacognitive strategies and use of compensatory external aids, which may include posted reminders and lists with check-off boxes. The treatment program will also include strategies and practice in topic maintenance during structured conversation. Additionally, co-treatment sessions with occupational therapy are planned in order to determine implementation of strategies and aids during ADLs. Finally, KW's niece will be educated on how to assist with these strategies. Treatment will include ongoing monitoring of progress toward objectives, and treatment data and observations will be presented at interdisciplinary meetings to help track KW's progress and determine a safe and appropriate discharge setting.

Summary

Attention is both a fundamental cognitive skill essential for many simple tasks and a complex neuropsychological construct. Key dimensions of the human attention system include capacity limitations, selection of relevant stimuli to attend to, and allocation of attentional resources during dual-task situations. Attention comprises a number of different subtypes, including sustained attention, selective attention, and divided attention; the specifics of these subtypes are under debate and can differ from model to model. Attention processing overlaps substantially with other skills such as executive function, working memory, and communication. Patients with acquired and degenerative neurological conditions—including brain injury, aphasia, and dementia—often exhibit attention deficits along with deficits in other, related skill areas. Key responsibilities of clinicians treating patients with suspected attention impairments include identifying whether an attention impairment is indeed present, determining if attention treatment is warranted, and designing appropriate treatment programs. Tools for assessing attention should be carefully and specifically selected, and results of assessments should be considered within the context of the patient's overall profile, as well as within relevant theoretical frameworks. Treatment for attention should be based on patient characteristics, abilities, and goals.

References

Akanuma, K., Meguro, K., Kato, Y., Takahashi, Y., Nakamura, K., & Yamaguchi, S. (2016). Impaired attention function based on the Montreal Cognitive Assessment in vascular dementia patients with frontal hypoperfusion: The Osaki-Tajiri project. *Journal of Clinical Neuroscience, 28,* 128–132.

Alderson, A. L., & Novack, T. A. (2003). Reliable serial measurement of cognitive processes in rehabilitation: The Cognitive Log. *Archives of Physical Medicine and Rehabilitation, 84*(5), 668–672.

American Psychiatric Association. (2013). *Diagnostic and statistical manual of mental disorders* (5th ed.). Arlington, VA: Author.

Arbogast, T. L., Mason, C. R., & Kidd, G., Jr. (2002). The effect of spatial separation on informational and energetic masking of speech. *Journal of the Acoustical Society of America, 112*(5), 2086–2098.

Azouvi, P., Olivier, S., De Montety, G., Samuel, C., Louis-Dreyfus, A., & Tesio, L. (2003). Behavioral assessment of unilateral neglect: Study of the psychometric properties of the Catherine Bergego Scale. *Archives of Physical Medicine and Rehabilitation, 84*(1), 51–57.

Baddeley, A. D., Baddeley, H. A., Bucks, R. S., & Wilcock, G. K. (2001). Attentional control in Alzheimer's disease. *Brain, 124,* 1492–1508.

Barker-Collo, S. L., Feigin, V. L., Lawes, C. M., Parag, V., Senior, H., & Rodgers, A. (2009). Reducing attention deficits after stroke using attention process training: A randomized controlled trial. *Stroke, 40*(10), 3293–3298.

Bate, A. J., Mathias, J. L., & Crawford, J. R. (2001a). Performance on the Test of Everyday Attention and standard tests of attention following severe traumatic brain injury. *Clinical Neuropsychologist, 15*, 405–422.

Bate, A. J., Mathias, J. L., & Crawford, J. R. (2001b). The covert orienting of visual attention following severe traumatic brain injury. *Journal of Clinical and Experimental Neuropsychology, 23*, 386–398.

Ben-David, B. M., Nguyen, L. L., & van Lieshout, P. H. (2011). Stroop effects in persons with traumatic brain injury: Selective attention, speed of processing, or color-naming? A meta-analysis. *Journal of the International Neuropsychological Society, 17*(2), 354–363.

Beume, L., Martin, M., Kaller, C. P., Klöppel, S., Schmidt, C. S. M., Urbach, H., Egger, K., . . . Umarova, R. M. (2017). Visual neglect after left-hemispheric lesions: A voxel-based lesion–symptom mapping study in 121 acute stroke patients. *Experimental Brain Research, 235*(1), 83–95.

Biel, M., & Hula, W. (2016). Attention. In M. Kimbarow (Ed.), *Cognitive communication disorders* (2nd ed., pp. 1–48). San Diego, CA: Plural Publishing.

Black, F. W. (1986). Digit repetition in brain-damaged adults: Clinical and theoretical implications. *Journal of Clinical Psychology, 42*, 770–782.

Bleiberg, J., Garmoe, W. S., Halpern, E. L., Reeves, D. L., & Nadler, J. D. (1997). Consistency of within-day and across-day performance after mild brain injury. *Neuropsychiatry, Neuropsychology, & Behavioral Neurology, 10*(4), 247–253.

Bloomfield, I. L., Espie, C. A., & Evans, J. J. (2010). Do sleep difficulties exacerbate deficits in sustained attention following traumatic brain injury? *Journal of the International Neuropsychological Society, 16*(1), 17–25.

Bogdanova, Y., Yee, M. K., Ho, V. T., & Cicerone, K. D. (2016). Computerized cognitive rehabilitation of attention and executive function in acquired brain injury: A systematic review. *Journal of Head Trauma Rehabilitation, 31*(6), 419–433.

Bonnelle, V., Leech, R., Kinnunen, K. M., Ham, T. E., Beckmann, C. F., De Boissezon, X., . . . Sharp, D. J. (2011). Default mode network connectivity predicts sustained attention deficits after traumatic brain injury. *Journal of Neuroscience, 31*(38), 13442–13451.

Broadbent, D. E. (1952). Failures of attention in selective listening. *Journal of Experimental Psychology, 44*(6), 428.

Broadbent, D. E. (1958). *Perception and communication*. London, UK: Pergamon Press.

Bronkhorst, A. W. (2015). The cocktail-party problem revisited: Early processing and selection of multi-talker speech. *Attention, Perception, & Psychophysics, 77*(5), 1465–1487.

Brouwer, S., Van Engen, K. J., Calandruccio, L., & Bradlow, A. R. (2012). Linguistic contributions to speech-on-speech masking for native and non-native listeners: Language familiarity and semantic content. *Journal of the Acoustical Society of America, 131*(2), 1449–1464.

Brouwer, W. H., Ponds, R. W., Van Wolffelaar, P. C., & Van Zomeren, A. H. (1989). Divided attention 5 to 10 years after severe closed head injury. *Cortex, 25*(2), 219–230.

Brouwer, W. H., Withaar, F. K., Tant, M. L., & Van Zomeren, A. H. (2002). Attention and driving in traumatic brain injury: A question of coping with time-pressure. *Journal of Head Trauma Rehabilitation, 17*(1), 1–15.

Brungart, D. S., Chang, P. S., Simpson, B. D., & Wang, D. (2006). Isolating the energetic component of speech-on-speech masking with ideal time-frequency segregation. *Journal of the Acoustical Society of America, 120*(6), 4007–4018.

Bruya, B., & Tang, Y. Y. (2018). Is attention really effort? Revisiting Daniel Kahneman's influential 1973 book Attention and Effort. *Frontiers in Psychology, 9*(1133), 1–10.

Calderon, J., Perry, R. J., Erzinclioglu, S. W., Berrios, G. E., Dening, T. R., & Hodges, J. R. (2001). Perception, attention, and working memory are disproportionately impaired in dementia with Lewy bodies compared with Alzheimer's disease. *Journal of Neurology, Neurosurgery, and Psychiatry, 70*, 157–164.

Cameron, R. M., Wambaugh, J. L., & Mauszycki, S. C. (2010). Individual variability on discourse measures over repeated sampling times in persons with aphasia. *Aphasiology, 24*(6–8), 671–684.

Caplan, D., Waters, G., DeDe, G., Michaud, J., & Reddy, A. (2007). A study of syntactic processing in aphasia I: Behavioral (psycholinguistic) aspects. *Brain and Language, 101*(2), 103–150.

Castriotta, R. J., Wilde, M. C., Lai, J. M., Atanasov, S., Masel, B. E., & Kuna, S. T. (2007). Prevalence and consequences of sleep disorders in traumatic brain injury. *Journal of Clinical Sleep Medicine, 3*(4), 349–356.

Chan, R. C. (2000). Attentional deficits in patients with closed head injury: A further study to the discriminative validity of the Test of Everyday Attention. *Brain Injury, 14*, 227–236.

Chan, R. C. K. (2002). Attention deficits in patients with persisting postconcussive complaints: A general deficit or specific component deficit? *Journal of Clinical and Experimental Neuropsychology, 24*, 1081–1093.

Chan, R. C., & Lai, M. K. (2006). Latent structure of the Test of Everyday Attention: Convergent evidence from patients with traumatic brain injury. *Brain Injury, 20*, 653–659.

Chan, R. C., Lai, M. K., & Robertson, I. H. (2006). Latent structure of the Test of Everyday Attention in a non-clinical Chinese sample. *Archives of Clinical Neuropsychology, 21*, 477–485.

Chau, S. A., Herrmann, N., Sherman, C., Chung, J., Eizenman, M., Kiss, A., & Lanctot, K. L. (2017). Visual selective attention toward novel stimuli predicts cognitive decline in Alzheimer's disease patients. *Journal of Alzheimer's Disease, 55*(4), 1339–1349.

Cherry, E. C. (1953). Some experiments on the recognition of speech, with one and two ears. *Journal of the Acoustical Society of America, 25*, 975–979.

Choi, J., & Twamley, E. W. (2013). Cognitive rehabilitation therapies for Alzheimer's disease: A review of methods to improve treatment engagement and self-efficacy. *Neuropsychology Review, 23*(1), 48–62.

Cicerone, K. D., Goldin, Y., Ganci, K., Rosenbaum, A., Wethe, J. V., Langenbahn, D. M., . . . Trexler, L. (2019). Evidence-based cognitive rehabilitation: Systematic review of the literature from 2009 through 2014. *Archives of Physical Medicine and Rehabilitation*. Advance online publication.

Cicerone, K. D., Langenbahn, D. M., Braden, C., Malec, J. F., Kalmar, K., Fraas, M., . . . Azulay, J. (2011). Evidence-based cognitive rehabilitation: Updated review of the literature from 2003 through 2008. *Archives of Physical Medicine and Rehabilitation, 92*(4), 519–530.

Coelho, C. (2005). Direct attention training as a treatment for reading impairment in mild aphasia. *Aphasiology, 19*(3–5), 275–283.

Conners, C. K. (2000). *Conners' Continuous Performance Test II.* Toronto, Canada: Multi-Health Systems.

Connor, B. B., & Shaw, C. (2016). Case study series using brain-training games to treat attention and memory following brain injury. *Journal of Pain Management, 9*(3), 217–226.

Corbetta, M., & Shulman, G. L. (2002). Control of goal-directed and stimulus-driven attention in the brain. *Nature Reviews Neuroscience, 3*, 201–215.

Cowan, N. (1997). *Attention and memory.* New York, NY: Oxford University Press.

Cremona-Meteyard, S. L., Clark, C. R., Wright, M. J., & Geffen, G. M. (1992). Covert orientation of visual attention after closed head injury. *Neuropsychologia*, *30*(2), 123–132.

Cyr, A. A., Stinchcombe, A., Gagnon, S., Marshall, S., Hing, M. M. S., & Finestone, H. (2009). Driving difficulties of brain-injured drivers in reaction to high-crash-risk simulated road events: A question of impaired divided attention? *Journal of Clinical and Experimental Neuropsychology, 31*(4), 472–482.

Des Roches, C. A., Balachandran, I., Ascenso, E. M., Tripodis, Y., & Kiran, S. (2015). Effectiveness of an impairment-based individualized rehabilitation program using an iPad-based software platform. *Frontiers in Human Neuroscience, 8,* 1015.

Des Roches, C. A., & Kiran, S. (2017). Technology-based rehabilitation to improve communication after acquired brain injury. *Frontiers in Neuroscience, 11,* 382.

Desimone, R., & Duncan, J. (1995). Neural mechanisms of selective visual attention. *Annual Review of Neuroscience, 18*(1), 193–222.

Deutsch, J. A., & Deutsch, D. (1963). Attention: Some theoretical considerations. *Psychological Review, 70*(1), 80.

Dockree, P. M., Bellgrove, M. A., O'Keeffe, F. M., Moloney, P., Aimola, L., Carton, S., & Robertson, I. H. (2006). Sustained attention in traumatic brain injury (TBI) and healthy controls: Enhanced sensitivity with dual-task load. *Experimental Brain Research, 168*(1–2), 218–229.

Driver, J. (2001). A selective review of selective attention research from the past century. *British Journal of Psychology, 92*(1), 53–78.

Driver, J., & Baylis, G. C. (1989). Movement and visual attention: The spotlight metaphor breaks down. *Journal of Experimental Psychology: Human Perception and Performance, 15*(3), 448.

Dykiert, D., Der, G., Starr, J. M., & Deary, I. J. (2012). Age differences in intra-individual variability in simple and choice reaction time: Systematic review and meta-analysis. *PLoS One, 7*(10), e45759.

Dymowski, A. R., Owens, J. A., Ponsford, J. L., & Willmott, C. (2015). Speed of processing and strategic control of attention after traumatic brain injury. *Journal of Clinical and Experimental Neuropsychology, 37*(10), 1024–1035.

Egan, J. P., & Wiener, F. M. (1946). On the intelligibility of bands of speech in noise. *Journal of the Acoustical Society of America, 18*(2), 435–441.

Erickson, R. J., Goldinger, S. D., & LaPointe, L. L. (1996). Auditory vigilance in aphasic individuals: Detecting nonlinguistic stimuli with full or divided attention. *Brain and Cognition, 30*(2), 244–253.

Fan, J., McCandliss, B. D., Sommer, T., Raz, A., & Posner, M. I. (2002). Testing the efficiency and independence of attentional networks. *Journal of Cognitive Neuroscience, 14*(3), 340-347.

Finn, M., & McDonald, S. (2011). Computerised cognitive training for older persons with mild cognitive impairment: A pilot study using a randomised controlled trial design. *Brain Impairment, 12*(3), 187–199.

Fish, J., Evans, J. J., Nimmo, M., Martin, E., Kersel, D., Bateman, A., . . . Manly, T. (2007). Rehabilitation of executive dysfunction following brain injury: "Content-free" cueing improves everyday prospective memory performance. *Neuropsychologia, 45,* 1318–1330.

Foldi, N. S., Lobosco, J. J., & Schaefer, L. A. (2002). The effect of attentional dysfunction in Alzheimer's disease: Theoretical and practical implications. *Seminars in Speech and Language, 23,* 139–150.

Folstein, M. F., Folstein, S. E., & McHugh, P. R. (1975). "Mini-mental state": A practical method for grading the cognitive state of patients for the clinician. *Journal of Psychiatric Research, 12*(3), 189–198.

Forn, C., Belloch, V., Bustamante, J. C., Garbin, G., Parcet-Ibars, M. À., Sanjuan, A., . . . Ávila, C. (2009). A symbol digit modalities test version suitable for functional MRI studies. *Neuroscience Letters, 456*(1), 11–14.

Freed, D. B., Marshall, R. C., & Chuhlantseff, E. A. (1996). Picture naming variability: A methodological consideration of inconsistent naming responses in fluent and nonfluent aphasia. *Clinical Aphasiology*, *24*, 193–205.

Freyman, R. L., Balakrishnan, U., & Helfer, K. S. (2001). Spatial release from informational masking in speech recognition. *Journal of the Acoustical Society of America*, *109*(5), 2112–2122.

Fritz, J. B., Elhilali, M., David, S. V., & Shamma, S. A. (2007). Auditory attention—focusing the searchlight on sound. *Current Opinion in Neurobiology*, *17*(4), 437–455.

Gillespie, A., Best, C., & O'Neill, B. (2012). Cognitive function and assistive technology for cognition: A systematic review. *Journal of the International Neuropsychological Society*, *18*(1), 1–19.

Gopher, D., Brickner, M., & Navon, D. (1982). Different difficulty manipulations interact differently with task emphasis: Evidence for multiple resources. *Journal of Experimental Psychology: Human Perception and Performance*, *8*, 146–157.

Gordon, B. A., Zacks, J. M., Blazey, T., Benzinger, T. L., Morris, J. C., Fagan, A. M., . . . Balota, D. A. (2015). Task-evoked fMRI changes in attention networks are associated with preclinical Alzheimer's disease biomarkers. *Neurobiology of Aging*, *36*(5), 1771–1779.

Grant, D. A., & Berg, E. A. (1981). *Wisconsin Card Sorting Test*. Odessa, FL: Psychological Assessment Resources.

Gronwall, D., & Sampson, H. (1974). *The psychological effects of concussion*. Auckland, New Zealand: Auckland University Press.

Harciarek, M., & Jodzio, K. (2005). Neuropsychological differences between frontotemporal dementia and Alzheimer's disease: A review. *Neuropsychology Review*, *15*(3), 131–145.

Hart, T., Whyte, J., Ellis, C., & Chervoneva, I. (2009). Construct validity of an attention rating scale for traumatic brain injury. *Neuropsychology*, *23*, 729–735.

Hart, T., Whyte, J., Millis, S., Bode, R., Malec, J., Richardson, R. N., & Hammond, F. (2006). Dimensions of disordered attention in traumatic brain injury: Further validation of the Moss Attention Rating Scale. *Archives of Physical Medicine and Rehabilitation*, *87*, 647–655.

Haskins, E. C. (2012). *Cognitive rehabilitation manual: Translating evidence-based recommendations into practice*. Reston, VA: American Congress of Rehabilitation Medicine.

Helm-Estabrooks, N. (2001). *Cognitive Linguistic Quick Test*. San Antonio, TX: The Psychological Corporation.

Helm-Estabrooks, N. (2011). Treating attention to improve auditory comprehension deficits associated with aphasia. *Perspectives on Neurophysiology and Neurogenic Speech and Language Disorders*, *21*(2), 64–71.

Helm-Estabrooks, N., Connor, L. T., & Albert, M. L. (2000). Treating attention to improve auditory comprehension in aphasia. *Brain and Language*, *74*(3), 469–472.

Hervais-Adelman, A. G., Carlyon, R. P., Johnsrude, I. S., & Davis, M. H. (2012). Brain regions recruited for the effortful comprehension of noise-vocoded words. *Language and Cognitive Processes*, *27*(7–8), 1145–1166.

Heuer, S., & Hallowell, B. (2015). A novel eye-tracking method to assess attention allocation in individuals with and without aphasia using a dual-task paradigm. *Journal of Communication Disorders*, *55*, 15–30.

Heuer, S., Ivanova, M. V., & Hallowell, B. (2017). More than the verbal stimulus matters: Visual attention in language assessment for people with aphasia using multiple-choice image displays. *Journal of Speech, Language, and Hearing Research*, *60*(5), 1348–1361.

Howard, D., Patterson, K., Franklin, S., Orchard-Lisle, V., & Morton, J. (1985). Treatment of word retrieval deficits in aphasia. *Brain*, *108*(8), 17–29.

Hula, W. D., & McNeil, M. R. (2008, August). Models of attention and dual-task performance as explanatory constructs in aphasia. *Seminars in Speech and Language, 29*(3), 169–187.

Hultsch, D. F., MacDonald, S. W., Hunter, M. A., Levy-Bencheton, J., & Strauss, E. (2000). Intraindividual variability in cognitive performance in older adults: Comparison of adults with mild dementia, adults with arthritis, and healthy adults. *Neuropsychology, 14*(4), 588.

Hunting-Pompon, R., Kendall, D., & Bacon Moore, A. (2011). Examining attention and cognitive processing in participants with self-reported mild anomia. *Aphasiology, 25*(6–7), 800–812.

James, W. (1950). *The principles of psychology.* New York, NY: Dover. (Original work published 1890)

Kahneman, D. (1973). *Attention and effort.* Englewood Cliffs, NJ: Prentice-Hall.

Kahneman, D., & Beatty, J. (1966). Pupil diameter and load on memory. *Science, 154*(3756), 1583–1585.

Kahneman, D., & Tresiman, A. (1984). Changing views of attention and automaticity. In R. Parasuraman & D. A. Davies (Eds.), *Varieties of attention* (pp. 29–61). New York, NY: Academic Press.

Kidd, G., & Colburn, H. S. (2017). Informational masking in speech recognition. In J. C. Middlebrooks, J. Z. Simon, A. N. Popper, & R. R. Fay (Eds.), *The auditory system at the cocktail party* (pp. 75–109). New York, NY: Springer.

Kim, J., Whyte, J., Hart, T., Vaccaro, M., Polansky, M., & Coslett, H. B. (2005). Executive function as a predictor of inattentive behavior after traumatic brain injury. *Journal of the International Neuropsychological Society, 11*, 434–445.

Kreindler, A., & Fradis, A. (1968). *Performances in aphasia: A neurodynamical diagnostic and psychological study.* Paris, France: Gauthier-Villars.

Künstler, E. C., Penning, M. D., Napiór-kowski, N., Klingner, C. M., Witte, O. W., Müller, H. J., . . . Finke, K. (2018). Dual task effects on visual attention capacity in normal aging. *Frontiers in Psychology, 9*(1564), 1–12.

Kurland, J. (2011). The role that attention plays in language processing. *Perspectives on Neurophysiology and Neurogenic Speech and Language Disorders, 21*(2), 47–54.

Kurland, J. (2014, February). iRehab in aphasia treatment. *Seminars in Speech and Language, 35*(1), 3–4.

Laeng, B., Sirois, S., & Gredebäck, G. (2012). Pupillometry: A window to the preconscious? *Perspectives on Psychological Science, 7*(1), 18–27.

Lambon Ralph, M. A., Snell, C., Fillingham, J. K., Conroy, P., & Sage, K. (2010). Predicting the outcome of anomia therapy for people with aphasia post CVA: Both language and cognitive status are key predictors. *Neuropsychological Rehabilitation, 20*(2), 289–305.

Larrabee, G. J., & Kane, R. L. (1986). Reversed digit repetition involves visual and verbal processes. *International Journal of Neuroscience, 30*, 11–15.

Laures, J., Odell, K., & Coe, C. (2003). Arousal and auditory vigilance in individuals with aphasia during a linguistic and nonlinguistic task. *Aphasiology, 17*(12), 1133–1152.

Laures-Gore, J., & Marshall, R. S. (2016). Mindfulness meditation in aphasia: A case report. *NeuroRehabilitation, 38*(4), 321–329.

Lavie, N. (1995). Perceptual load as a necessary condition for selective attention. *Journal of Experimental Psychology: Human Perception and Performance, 21*(3), 451.

Lavie, N., Hirst, A., De Fockert, J. W., & Viding, E. (2004). Load theory of selective attention and cognitive control. *Journal of Experimental Psychology: General, 133*(3), 339.

Lee, J. B., & Sohlberg, M. M. (2013). Evaluation of attention training and metacognitive facilitation to improve reading comprehension in aphasia.

American Journal of Speech-Language Pathology, 22(2), S318–S333.

Levine, B., Schweizer, T. A., O'Connor, C., Turner, G., Gillingham, S., Stuss, D. T., . . . Robertson, I. H. (2011). Rehabilitation of executive functioning in patients with frontal lobe brain damage with goal management training. *Frontiers in Human Neuroscience, 5,* 9.

Lezak, M. D., Howieson, D. B., Bigler, E. D., & Tranel, D. (2012). *Neuropsychological assessment* (5th ed.). New York, NY: Oxford University Press.

Lim, Y. Y., Snyder, P. J., Pietrzak, R. H., Ukiqi, A., Villemagne, V. L., Ames, D., . . . Rowe, C. C. (2016). Sensitivity of composite scores to amyloid burden in preclinical Alzheimer's disease: Introducing the z-scores of attention, verbal fluency, and episodic memory for nondemented older adults composite score. *Alzheimer's & Dementia: Diagnosis, Assessment & Disease Monitoring, 2,* 19–26.

Lopresti, F, E., Mihailidis, A., & Kirsch, N. (2004). Assistive technology for cognitive rehabilitation: State of the art. *Neuropsychological Rehabilitation, 14*(1–2), 5–39.

Lundqvist, A., Grundström, K., Samuelsson, K., & Rönnberg, J. (2010). Computerized training of working memory in a group of patients suffering from acquired brain injury. *Brain Injury, 24*(10), 1173–1183.

MacDonald, S. W., Li, S. C., & Bäckman, L. (2009). Neural underpinnings of within-person variability in cognitive functioning. *Psychology and Aging, 24*(4), 792.

Manly, T., Davison, B., Heutink, J., Galloway, M., & Robertson, I. H. (2000). Not enough time or not enough attention? Speed, error and self-maintained control in the Sustained Attention to Response Test (SART). *Clinical Neuropsychological Assessment, 3*(10), 167–177.

Manly, T., Owen, A. M., McAvinue, L., Datta, A., Lewis, G. H., Scott, S. K., . . . Robertson, I. H. (2003). Enhancing the sensitivity of a sustained attention task to frontal damage: Convergent clinical and functional imaging evidence. *Neurocase, 9,* 340–349.

Manly, T., Robertson, I. H., Galloway, M., & Hawkins, K. (1999). The absent mind: Further investigations of sustained attention to response. *Neuropsychologia, 37*(6), 661–670.

Mansbach, W. E., MacDougall, E. E., & Rosenzweig, A. S. (2012). The Brief Cognitive Assessment Tool (BCAT): A new test emphasizing contextual memory, executive functions, attentional capacity, and the prediction of instrumental activities of daily living. *Journal of Clinical and Experimental Neuropsychology, 34*(2), 183–194.

Marshall, R. S., Laures-Gore, J., & Love, K. (2018). Brief mindfulness meditation group training in aphasia: Exploring attention, language and psychophysiological outcomes. *International Journal of Language & Communication Disorders, 53*(1), 40–54.

Mathias, J. L., & Wheaton, P. (2007). Changes in attention and information-processing speed following severe traumatic brain injury: A meta-analytic review. *Neuropsychology, 21,* 212–223.

McDowd, J. M., & Craik, F. I. (1988). Effects of aging and task difficulty on divided attention performance. *Journal of Experimental Psychology: Human Perception and Performance, 14*(2), 267.

McGuinness, B., Barrett, S. L., Craig, D., Lawson, J., & Passmore, A. P. (2010). Attention deficits in Alzheimer's disease and vascular dementia. *Journal of Neurology, Neurosurgery, and Psychiatry, 81,* 157–159.

McKeith, I. G., Boeve, B. F., Dickson, D. W., Halliday, G., Taylor, J. P., Weintraub, D., . . . Bayston, A. (2017). Diagnosis and management of dementia with Lewy bodies: Fourth consensus report of the DLB Consortium. *Neurology, 89*(1), 88–100.

McMillan, T., Robertson, I. H., Brock, D., & Chorlton, L. (2002). Brief mindfulness training for attentional problems after traumatic brain injury: A randomised control treatment trial. *Neuropsychological Rehabilitation, 12*(2), 117–125.

McNeil, M. R. (1982). The nature of aphasia in adults. In N. J. Lass, L. V. McReynolds, J. L. Northern, & D. E. Yoder (Eds.), *Speech, language, and hearing: Vol. II. Pathologies of speech and language* (pp. 692–740). Philadelphia, PA: Saunders.

McNeil, M. R. (1983). Aphasia: Neurological considerations. *Topics in Language Disorders, 3*, 1–19.

McNeil, M., Hula, W., & Sung, J. E. (2011). The role of memory and attention in aphasic language performance. In J. Guendouzi, F. Loncke, & M. J. Williams (Eds.), *The handbook of psycholinguistic and cognitive processes: Perspectives in communication disorders* (pp. 551–578). New York, NY: Psychology Press.

McNeil, M. R., Odell, K., & Tseng, C. H. (1991). Toward the integration of resource allocation into a general theory of aphasia. *Clinical Aphasiology, 20*, 21–40.

Metzler-Baddeley, C. (2007). A review of cognitive impairments in dementia with Lewy bodies relative to Alzheimer's disease and Parkinson's disease with dementia. *Cortex, 43*, 583–600.

Michel, J. A., & Mateer, C. A. (2006). Attention rehabilitation following stroke and traumatic brain injury: A review. *Europa Medicophysica, 42*, 59–67.

Mirsky, A. F., Anthony, B. J., Duncan, C. C., Ahearn, M. B., & Kellam, S. G. (1991). Analysis of the elements of attention: A neuropsychological approach. *Neuropsychology Review, 2*(2), 109–145.

Moray, N. (1959). Attention in dichotic listening: Affective cues and the influence of instructions. *Quarterly Journal of Experimental Psychology, 11*, 56–60.

Murray, L. L. (1999). Review attention and aphasia: Theory, research and clinical implications. *Aphasiology, 13*(2), 91–111.

Murray, L. L. (2012). Attention and other cognitive deficits in aphasia: Presence and relation to language and communication measures. *American Journal of Speech-Language Pathology, 21*, S51–S64.

Murray, L. L. (2018). Sentence processing in aphasia: An examination of material-specific and general cognitive factors. *Journal of Neurolinguistics, 48*, 26–46.

Murray, L. L., Holland, A. L., & Beeson, P. M. (1997). Auditory processing in individuals with mild aphasia: A study of resource allocation. *Journal of Speech, Language, and Hearing Research, 40*, 792–808.

Murray, L. L., Keeton, R. J., & Karcher, L. (2006). Treating attention in mild aphasia: Evaluation of Attention Process Training–II. *Journal of Communication Disorders, 39*(1), 37–61.

Murtha, S., Cismaru, R., Waechter, R., & Chertkow, H. (2002). Increased variability accompanies frontal lobe damage in dementia. *Journal of the International Neuropsychological Society, 8*(3), 360–372.

Nasreddine, Z. S., Phillips, N. A., Bédirian, V., Charbonneau, S., Whitehead, V., Collin, I., . . . Chertkow, H. (2005). The Montreal Cognitive Assessment, MoCA: A brief screening tool for mild cognitive impairment. *Journal of the American Geriatrics Society, 53*(4), 695–699.

Naveh-Benjamin, M., Craik, F. I., Guez, J., & Kreuger, S. (2005). Divided attention in younger and older adults: Effects of strategy and relatedness on memory performance and secondary task costs. *Journal of Experimental Psychology: Learning, Memory, and Cognition, 31*(3), 520.

Navon, D., & Gopher, D. (1979). On the economy of the human-processing system. *Psychological Review, 86*, 214–255.

Niogi, S. N., Mukherjee, P., Ghajar, J., Johnson, C. E., Kolster, R., Lee, H., . . . McCandliss, B. D. (2008). Structural dissociation of attentional control and memory in adults with and without mild traumatic brain injury. *Brain, 131*(12), 3209–3221.

Orenstein, E., Basilakos, A., & Marshall, R. S. (2012). Effects of mindfulness meditation on three individuals with aphasia. *International Journal of Language & Communication Disorders, 47*(6), 673–684.

Ortoleva, C., Brugger, C., Van der Linden, M., & Walder, B. (2012). Prediction of driving capacity after traumatic brain injury: A systematic review. *Journal of Head Trauma Rehabilitation, 27*(4), 302–313.

Park, N. W., & Ingles, J. L. (2001). Effectiveness of attention rehabilitation after an acquired brain injury: A meta-analysis. *Neuropsychology, 15*, 199–210.

Park, N. W., Moscovitch, M., & Robertson, I. H. (1999). Divided attention impairments after traumatic brain injury. *Neuropsychologia, 37*, 1119–1133.

Pashler, H. (1994). Dual-task interference in simple tasks: Data and theory. *Psychological Bulletin, 116*, 220–244.

Peach, R. K., Nathan, M. R., & Beck, K. M. (2017, February). Language-specific attention treatment for aphasia: Description and preliminary findings. *Seminars in Speech and Language, 38*(1), 5–16.

Peach, R. K., Newhoff, M., & Rubin, S. S. (1993). Attention in aphasia as revealed by event-related potentials: A preliminary investigation. *Clinical Aphasiology, 21*, 323–333.

Peach, R. K., Schenk, K. A., Nathan, M. R., & Beck, K. M. (2018). Construct validity, external validity, and reliability for a battery of language-specific attention tasks. *Aphasiology, 32*(6), 618–645.

Perry, R. J., & Hodges, J. R. (1999). Attention and executive deficits in Alzheimer's disease: A critical review. *Brain, 122*(3), 383–404.

Perry, R. J., & Hodges, J. R. (2000). Differentiating frontal and temporal variant frontotemporal dementia from Alzheimer's disease. *Neurology, 54*, 2277–2284.

Petersen, S. E., & Posner, M. I. (2012). The attention system of the human brain: 20 years after. *Annual Review of Neuroscience, 35*, 73–89.

Petry, M. C., Crosson, B., Rothi, L. J. G., Bauer, R. M., & Schauer, C. A. (1994). Selective attention and aphasia in adults: Preliminary findings. *Neuropsychologia, 32*(11), 1397–1408.

Ponsford, J., & Kinsella, G. (1991). The use of a rating scale of attentional behavior. *Neuropsychological Rehabilitation, 1*(4), 241–257.

Ponsford, J., & Kinsella, G. (1992). Attentional deficits following closed-head injury. *Journal of Clinical and Experimental Neuropsychology, 14*(5), 822–838.

Ponsford, J. L., Downing, M. G., Olver, J., Ponsford, M., Acher, R., Carty, M., & Spitz, G. (2014). Longitudinal follow-up of patients with traumatic brain injury: Outcome at two, five, and ten years post-injury. *Journal of Neurotrauma, 31*(1), 64–77.

Posner, M. I., & Cohen, Y. (1980). Covert orienting of visuospatial attention task. In G. G. Stelmach & J. Requin (Eds.), *Tutorials in motor behaviour* (pp. 243–258). Amsterdam, The Netherlands: North-Holland Publishing.

Posner, M. I., Inhoff, A. W., Friedrich, F. J., & Cohen, A. (1987). Isolating attentional systems: A cognitive-anatomical analysis. *Psychobiology, 15*, 107–121.

Posner, M. I., & Petersen, S. E. (1990). The attention system of the human brain. *Annual Review of Neuroscience, 13*(1), 25–42.

Posner, M. I., Snyder, C. R., & Davidson, B. J. (1980). Attention and the detection of signals. *Journal of Experimental Psychology: General, 109*(2), 160.

Posner, M. I., Walker, J. A., Friedrich, F. J., & Rafal, R. D. (1984). Effects of parietal injury on covert orienting of attention. *Journal of Neuroscience, 4*(7), 1863–1874.

Rabipour, S., & Raz, A. (2012). Training the brain: Fact and fad in cognitive and behavioral remediation. *Brain and Cognition, 79*(2), 159–179.

Rapport, L. J., Webster, J. S., & Dutra, R. L. (1994). Digit span performance and unilateral neglect. *Neuropsychologia, 32*, 517–525.

Ríos, M., Periáñez, J. A., & Muñoz-Céspedes, J. M. (2004). Attentional control and slowness of information processing after severe traumatic brain injury. *Brain injury, 18*(3), 257–272.

Roberts, K. L., Summerfield, A. Q., & Hall, D. A. (2006). Presentation modality influences behavioral measures of alerting, orienting, and executive control. *Journal of the International Neuropsychological Society, 12*(4), 485-492.

Robertson, I. H., Manly, T., Andrade, J., Baddeley, B. T., & Yiend, J. (1997). "Oops!": Performance correlates of everyday attentional failures in traumatic brain injured and normal subjects. *Neuropsychologia, 35*, 747–758.

Robertson, I. H., Ward, T., Ridgeway, V., & Nimmo-Smith, I. (1994). *The Test of Everyday Attention (TEA)*. Bury St. Edmunds, UK: Thames Valley Test Company.

Robertson, I. H., Ward, T., Ridgeway, V., & Nimmo-Smith, I. (1996). The structure of normal human attention: The Test of Everyday Attention. *Journal of the International Neuropsychological Society, 2*(6), 525–534.

Robin, D. A., & Rizzo, M. (1989). The effect of focal cerebral lesions on intramodal and cross-modal orienting of attention. *Clinical Aphasiology, 18*(1), 61–74.

Sarter, M., Givens, B., & Bruno, J. P. (2001). The cognitive neuroscience of sustained attention: Where top-down meets bottom-up. *Brain Research Reviews, 35*(2), 146–160.

Sbordone, R. J. (2001). Limitations of neuropsychological testing to predict the cognitive and behavioral functioning of persons with brain injury in real-world settings. *NeuroRehabilitation, 16*, 199–201.

Schepker, H., Haeder, K., Rennies, J., & Holube, I. (2016). Perceived listening effort and speech intelligibility in reverberation and noise for hearing-impaired listeners. *International Journal of Audiology, 55*(12), 738–747.

Schnabel, R., & Kydd, R. (2012). Neuropsychological assessment of distractibility in mild traumatic brain injury and depression. *The Clinical Neuropsychologist, 26*, 769–789.

Schneider, W., & Shiffrin, R. A. (1977). Controlled and automatic human information processing: I. Detection, search, and attention. *Psychological Review, 84*, 1–66.

Schretlen, D., Bobholz, J. H., & Brandt, J. (1996). Development and psychometric properties of the Brief Test of Attention. *The Clinical Neuropsychologist, 10*(1), 80–89.

Schroeder, R. W., Twumasi-Ankrah, P., Baade, L. E., & Marshall, P. S. (2012). Reliable Digit Span: A systematic review and cross-validation study. *Assessment, 19*(1), 21–30.

Shiffrin, R. A., & Schneider, W. (1977). Controlled and automatic human information processing: II. Perceptual learning, automatic attending, and a general theory. *Psychological Review, 84*, 127–190.

Shinn-Cunningham, B. G. (2008). Object-based auditory and visual attention. *Trends in Cognitive Sciences, 12*(5), 182–186.

Shulman, G. L., & Corbetta, M. (2012). Two attentional networks. In M. I. Posner (Ed.), *Cognitive neuroscience of attention* (2nd ed., pp. 113–128). New York, NY: Guilford.

Sigmundsdottir, L., Longley, W. A., & Tate, R. L. (2016). Computerised cognitive training in acquired brain injury: A systematic review of outcomes using the International Classification of Functioning (ICF). *Neuropsychological Rehabilitation, 26*(5–6), 673–741.

Sinotte, M. P., & Coelho, C. A. (2007). Attention training for reading impairment in mild aphasia: A follow-up study. *NeuroRehabilitation, 22*(4), 303–310.

Smith, A. (1991). *Symbol Digit Modalities Test*. Los Angeles, CA: Western Psychological Services.

Sohlberg, M. M., Johnson, L., Paule, L., Raskin, S. A., & Mateer, C. A. (2001). *Attention Process Training–II: A program to address attentional deficits for persons with mild cognitive dysfunction* (2nd ed.). Wake Forest, NC: Lash & Associates.

Sohlberg, M. M., & Mateer, C. A. (1987). Effectiveness of an attention-training program. *Journal of Clinical and Experimental Neuropsychology, 9*, 117–130.

Sohlberg, M. M., & Mateer, C. A. (2001a). *Attention Process Training* (2nd ed.). Wake Forest, NC: Lash & Associates.

Sohlberg, M. M., & Mateer, C. A. (2001b). *Cognitive rehabilitation: An integrative neu-*

ropsychological approach. New York, NY: Guilford Press.

Sohlberg, M. M., & Mateer, C. A. (2010). *APT-III: Attention Process Training: A direct attention training program for persons with acquired brain injury*. Youngsville, NC: Lash & Associates.

Sohlberg, M. M., McLaughlin, K. A., Pavese, A., Heidrich, A., & Posner, M. I. (2000). Evaluation of Attention Process Training and brain injury education in persons with acquired brain injury. *Journal of Clinical and Experimental Neuropsychology, 22,* 656–676.

Sturm, W., Willmes, K., Orgass, B., & Hartje, W. (1997). Do specific attention deficits need specific training? *Neuropsychological Rehabilitation, 7,* 81–103.

Stuss, D. T., Pogue, J., Buckle, L., & Bondar, J. (1994). Characterization of stability of performance in patients with traumatic brain injury: Variability and consistency on reaction time tests. *Neuropsychology, 8*(3), 316.

Swales, M. A., Hill, A. J., & Finch, E. (2016). Feature rich, but user-friendly: Speech pathologists' preferences for computer-based aphasia therapy. *International Journal of Speech-Language Pathology, 18*(4), 315–328.

Thiessen, A., Beukelman, D., Hux, K., & Longenecker, M. (2016). A comparison of the visual attention patterns of people with aphasia and adults without neurological conditions for camera-engaged and task-engaged visual scenes. *Journal of Speech, Language, and Hearing Research, 59*(2), 290–301.

Thorndike, R. M. (1997). *Measurement and evaluation in psychology and education.* Upper Saddle River, NJ: Prentice-Hall.

Tombaugh, T. N. (2006). A comprehensive review of the Paced Auditory Serial Addition Test (PASAT). *Archives of Clinical Neuropsychology, 21,* 53–76.

Treisman, A. (1960). Contextual cues in selective listening. *Quarterly Journal of Experimental Psychology, 12,* 242–248.

Tung, L. C., Yu, W. H., Lin, G. H., Yu, T. Y., Wu, C. T., Tsai, C. Y., . . . Hsieh, C. L.

(2016). Development of a Tablet-based symbol digit modalities test for reliably assessing information processing speed in patients with stroke. *Disability and Rehabilitation, 38*(19), 1952–1960.

Vallat-Azouvi, C., Weber, T., Legrand, L., & Azouvi, P. (2007). Working memory after severe traumatic brain injury. *Journal of the International Neuropsychological Society, 13*(5), 770–780.

Van Engen, K. J., & Bradlow, A. R. (2007). Sentence recognition in native-and-foreign-language multi-talker background noise. *Journal of the Acoustical Society of America, 121*(1), 519–526.

Villard, S., & Kiran, S. (2015). Between-session intra-individual variability in sustained, selective, and integrational non-linguistic attention in aphasia. *Neuropsychologia, 66,* 204–212.

Villard, S., & Kiran, S. (2017). To what extent does attention underlie language in aphasia? *Aphasiology, 31*(10), 1226–1245.

Villard, S., & Kiran, S. (2018). Between-session and within-session intra-individual variability in attention in aphasia. *Neuropsychologia, 109,* 95–106.

Wechsler, D. (2008). *Wechsler Adult Intelligence Scale–IV*. San Antonio, TX: Pearson.

Westerberg, H., Jacobaeus, H., Hirvikoski, T., Clevberger, P., Östensson, M.-L., Bartfai, A., & Klingberg, T. (2007). Computerized working memory training after stroke—a pilot study. *Brain Injury, 21*(1), 21–29.

Whyte, J., Fleming, M., Polansky, M., Cavallucci, C., & Coslett, H. B. (1998). The effects of visual distraction following traumatic brain injury. *Journal of the International Neuropsychological Society, 4,* 127–136.

Whyte, J., Grieb-Neff, P., Gantz, C., & Polansky, M. (2006). Measuring sustained attention after traumatic brain injury: Differences in key findings from the sustained attention to response task (SART). *Neuropsychologia, 44,* 2007–2014.

Whyte, J., Hart, T., Bode, R. K., & Malec, J. F. (2003). The Moss Attention Rating Scale for traumatic brain injury: Initial psychometric assessment. *Archives of Physical Medicine and Rehabilitation, 84,* 268–276.

Whyte, J., Hart, T., Ellis, C. A., & Chervoneva, I. (2008). The Moss Attention Rating Scale for traumatic brain injury: Further explorations of reliability and sensitivity to change. *Archives of Physical Medicine and Rehabilitation, 89,* 966–973.

Whyte, J., Polansky, M., Fleming, M., Coslett, H. B., & Cavallucci, C. (1995). Sustained arousal and attention after traumatic brain injury. *Neuropsychologia, 33*(7), 797–813.

Whyte, J., Schuster, K., Polansky, M., Adams, J., & Coslett, H. B. (2000). Frequency and duration of inattentive behavior after traumatic brain injury: Effects of distraction, task, and practice. *Journal of the International Neuropsychological Society, 6,* 1–11.

Wickens, C. D. (1980). The structure of attentional resources. In R. S. Nickerson (Ed.), *Attention and performance VIII* (pp. 239–258). Hillsdale, NJ: Erlbaum.

Wijayasiri, P., Hartley, D. E., & Wiggins, I. M. (2017). Brain activity underlying the recovery of meaning from degraded speech: A functional near-infrared spectroscopy (fNIRS) study. *Hearing Research, 351,* 55–67.

Willmott, C., Ponsford, J., Hocking, C., & Schönberger, M. (2009). Factors contributing to attentional impairments after traumatic brain injury. *Neuropsychology, 23*(4), 424.

Wilson, B., Cockburn, J., & Halligan, P. (1987a). *Behavioural Inattention Test manual.* Suffolk, UK: Thames Valley Test Company.

Wilson, B., Cockburn, J., & Halligan, P. (1987b). Development of a behavioral test of visuospatial neglect. *Archives of Physical Medicine and Rehabilitation, 68,* 98–102.

Wilson, B. A., Emslie, H. C., Quirk, K., & Evans, J. J. (2001). Reducing everyday memory and planning problems by means of a paging system: A randomised control crossover study. *Journal of Neurology, Neurosurgery, and Psychiatry, 70,* 477–482.

Wilson, B. A., Emslie, H., Quirk, K., Evans, J., & Watson, P. (2005). A randomized control trial to evaluate a paging system for people with traumatic brain injury. *Brain Injury, 19,* 891–894.

Wright, M. J., Cremona-Meteyard, S. L., Geffen, L. B., & Geffen, G. M. (1994). The effects of closed head injury, senile dementia of the Alzheimer's type, and Parkinson's disease on covert orientation of visual attention. *Australian Journal of Psychology, 46*(2), 63–72.

Zane, K. L., Gfeller, J. D., Roskos, P. T., & Bucholz, R. D. (2016). The clinical utility of the Conners' Continuous Performance Test–II in traumatic brain injury. *Archives of Clinical Neuropsychology, 31*(8), 996–1005.

Zickefoose, S., Hux, K., Brown, J., & Wulf, K. (2013). Let the games begin: A preliminary study using Attention Process Training-3 and Lumosity™ brain games to remediate attention deficits following traumatic brain injury. *Brain Injury, 27*(6), 707–716.

Ziino, C., & Ponsford, J. (2006). Selective attention deficits and subjective fatigue following traumatic brain injury. *Neuropsychology, 20*(3), 383.

2

Principles of Human Memory: An Integrative Clinical Neuroscience Perspective

Fofi Constantinidou

Introduction

Memory is probably the most studied cognitive system in both human and animal behavioral literature. Researchers from various theoretical and philosophical backgrounds, including cognitive psychology, neuropsychology, education, neurolinguistics, neurobiology, cognitive science, nuclear medicine, neurology, neuroscience, psychiatry, and computer science, have contributed to different aspects of the memory literature and to our conceptualization of animal and human memory mechanisms. Perhaps the fascination with memory systems is a result of our understanding that learning and memory are essential for species' survival. Furthermore, for humans, in addition to survival, memory is critical to conceptual knowledge development and

language acquisition, higher reasoning abilities, and effective decision making. Specifically, learning and memory allow for progression through various levels of problem solving and are essential for generating responses and modifying responses following feedback. Given that memory is an integral part of most daily activities, children learn how to develop strategies to reduce the demands on memory. Working memory capacity and the ability to incorporate encoding, organization, and retrieval strategies improve during elementary school years, as there is significant improvement in verbal learning performance between older and younger children (Constantinidou, Danos, Nelson, & Baker, 2011). Working memory and episodic memory performance can be frequently affected in patients with neurologic and psychiatric conditions as a result of focal and diffuse brain lesions or due to a functional disruption of working memory and executive functioning networks hampering the deployment of memory strategies (Behnken et al., 2010; Constantinidou, 1999; Voss, Galvan, & Gonsalves, 2011).

Memory impairment is probably the most common observable clinical symptom in a variety of organic brain conditions leading to neuropsychological impairment. In fact, memory decline is considered to be the hallmark of neurodegenerative disorders, such as pathologic aging (i.e., mild cognitive impairment and dementia), and is a common disorder in acquired brain injury, epilepsy disorders, and psychiatric conditions such as major depression and psychosis. However, memory disorders are not uniform and their presentation and severity are dependent on the disrupted brain networks. In addition, memory networks are facilitated by other cognitive systems such as attention and executive networks; hence, damage to these systems can compound the memory impairment.

Cognitive theory organizes human cognition into a hierarchy of basic and complex processes-systems. Basic processes such as sensory perception, attention, and memory underlie more complex systems, including categorization, problem solving, reasoning, language, and abstract thought processes.

Neurobiological research in humans and animals provides support for the cognitive systems generated by cognitive theory. When these systems are disrupted, the observable outcomes include predictable cognitive deficits. Neurologic disorders may produce focal brain damage (e.g., resulting from a stroke or a contained neoplastic lesion) or complex diffuse lesions as in the case of traumatic brain injury, aggres-

sive neoplasms, and degenerative disorders such as multiple sclerosis and Alzheimer's disease. Neuropsychiatric conditions, such as major depression, bipolar disorder, and psychosis interfere with normal functioning of cognitive networks, leading to cognitive and thought dysfunction. The aforementioned complex conditions can result in both focal and diffuse cortical and subcortical disruptions and a cascade of neurobiological changes that can be bilateral and extensive. The challenge of rehabilitation is first to assess the patient's abilities and then implement effective and efficient treatment modalities that will enable the survivor to maximize his or her level of functioning in the face of focal or diffuse systemic disruption.

The purpose of this chapter is to apply cognitive theory, as well as current findings in cognitive neuroscience and brain research, and to present contemporary theoretical models of memory processes with a focus on adult-acquired memory disorders. Consistent with the previous editions, the chapter uses an integrative life-span approach to present information on the organization of memory systems and discusses assessment methodologies, types of memory disorders, and treatment planning principles for the management of memory disorders.

Cognitive Theory and Memory

The concept of modularity is perhaps the most influential guiding principle of modern cognitive neuroscience. This view of local representation was prominent in the early history of cognitive psychology and referred to the strong claim that specific faculties could be completely delineated into separate neural areas (Fodor, 1983). Contemporary cognitive neuroscience proposes a "weak" modularity framework, suggesting that the simple computations and their underlying neural substrates are relatively localized and loosely autonomous (Kosslyn & Koenig, 1992). Neurons within these systems are tuned to specific characteristics in the environment (i.e., to the fundamental frequency of an auditory stimulus; to the light intensity of a visual stimulus), but that tuning is broad and, therefore, the response of the neuron gradually declines when the stimulus departs from the cell's preferred stimulus (Farah, 1990). Complex cognitive activities are accomplished by the coordination and communication among these more specialized modules. Basic processing principles governing how processing takes place appear to hold across systems, and these principles may be formulated in terms of computational styles or strategies. That is, cognitive activities spanning a variety of tasks may be rule governed (i.e., based on a set of explicit rules), similarity governed (according to a prototype), or through extensive experience or preexisting propensities be accomplished automatically (through the development of procedures, implicit learning, and expertise). Individual differences/preferences, task demands, and characteristics of the environment will determine which processing strategies and systems will be utilized (Constantinidou & Thomas, 2017).

The "weak modularity framework" has led the way to a new generation of research focusing on identifying and characterizing functional systems and their basic components. As part of this effort, researchers search for basic processing principles that hold across different functional systems that may dictate how different situations lead the brain to recruit different processing strategies. This line of research integrates various methodologies spanning from both traditional cognitive psychology (involving behavioral measures of accuracy and response times) to modern cognitive neuroscience (utilizing brain imaging and lesion/damage dissociation logic) in order to identify major systems and their processing characteristics. The reader is referred to Constantinidou and Thomas (2017) for more detailed information on cognitive theory and a more in-depth discussion of basic and complex cognitive processes. This chapter follows the multiple systems model, although considerations of memory processes or stages (e.g., encoding, storage and retrieval) are also discussed as they operate across the various subsystems. According to the systems model, memory can be broken down into smaller subsystems or functional units, and in line with the weak modularity theory, the coordinated, interactive, and integrated efforts of these subsystems result into effective human memory functioning.

Theoretical Framework for Human Memory: Multiple Stage Models

In the last 50 years, several models of memory functioning have been proposed. The model of memory implemented in this chapter combines Baddeley's theory of working memory (Baddeley, 1986, 2000, 2001, 2003; Baddeley, Allen, & Hitch, 2011; Baddeley & Hitch, 1974) and subsequent updates (Baddeley et al., 2011; Doherty & Logie, 2016) with Tulving's and Squire's models of long-term memory and subsequent updates (Schacter & Tulving, 1994; Squire, 1992). This framework has considerable utility in populations with memory disorders.

Memory is organized with respect to both time and contents (Markowitsch, 1995). On the basis of behavioral evidence (Brown, 1958; Peterson & Peterson, 1959) and neuropsychological data (Milner, 1966), the distinction between a short-term and a long-term retention system was the first to be made (e.g., Atkinson & Shiffrin, 1968). Atkinson and Shiffrin (1968) distinguished between short- and long-term memory stores. The short-term store was considered to be temporary and of limited capacity, whereas the long-term store was considered to be permanent. Initially, the nature of the information handled within these time-delineated systems was thought to be unitary and earlier models influenced by cognitive science and computer science conceptualized memory as a single system consisting of several stages or processes (Atkinson & Shiffrin, 1968; Sohlberg & Mateer, 2001). Concepts such as encoding, consolidation, storage, and retrieval were coined to explain the various stages of information processing. While the stage model has been replaced by a content-based subdivision incorporating multiple memory systems and subsystems, certain terminology from the stage models of memory has been retained and can be useful for understanding memory performance when working with patients with memory impairments (Constan-

tinidou & Thomas, 2017; Sanders, Nakase-Thomson, Constantinidou, Wertheimer, & Paul, 2007). *Encoding* refers to the early processing of the material (to be learned). How well information is encoded can contribute to how well it is stored for later use and eventually recalled. Encoding encompasses a variety of operations that can be performed on material to be learned, including simple repetition through rehearsal and organizing material in a way that is meaningful (e.g., creating an acronym to assist with recall of word lists) (Sanders et al., 2007). Encoding is highly dependent on frontal lobe mechanisms.

Consolidation refers to the process via which recently encoded information is transferred into permanent storage. Consolidation is more efficient after successful encoding. Recent events in comparison to past events are more vulnerable to forgetting as a result of trauma or disease because their consolidation process was not complete. During the consolidation stage, information is susceptible to proactive and retroactive interference. That is, recently learned information can hamper the storage and recall of newly learned material (proactive interference), whereas retroactive interference implies that competing information can hamper the successful storage and recall of recently learned material. Once the consolidation process is complete, then information has entered permanent storage. The medial temporal lobe area networks and structures are important for effective consolidation.

Storage refers to the way that information is held in memory for future use. Encoding and storage are interactive processes in that the quality of the encoding process can affect the way that information is stored. Once a memory is placed in the long-term store, it is considered to be permanent unless disrupted by a pathologic process. In addition, stored information is vulnerable to time and not all information entered into the permanent storage system is available for spontaneous retrieval (Constantinidou, 1998). Hence, opportunities for rehearsal increase the opportunity for future recall of stored information (Tulving, 1966).

Retrieval refers to the act of pulling information from storage, typically from the long-term store. On most memory tests, this is measured via *delayed recall* paradigms consisting of free recall and recognition tasks. Immediate recall presumably does not necessitate retrieval of information from long-term memory, because the material is still being held in the short-term/working memory system and may be undergoing encoding processes, such as rehearsal. For example, on a story recall task, recall of the information immediately after presentation relies on the short-term store. Recall of the information 30 minutes after presentation relies on the long-term store. Persons with retrieval deficits often benefit from presentation of information in a recognition format, such as a multiple-choice or yes/no format. Improved recognition over free recall performance points to the fact that information was not lost due to storage or rapid forgetting difficulties; decline in free recall could be due to inability to access the information successfully, resulting from retrieval deficits or impaired or unsuccessful encoding. During information retrieval, the individual is able to monitor the success of the process and

individuals with strong memories, and meta-memories are able to delineate whether the retrieved information is correct. The frontal lobes are activated during the retrieval process in order to implement strategies and search in the correct schemas; the hippocampi are activated as they may need to hold multiple pieces of information for brief periods of time during the retrieval process (Constantinidou, 1998).

Encoding, storage, and retrieval are considered to be interactive processes and require mediation by the executive network. Disruptions in frontal-subcortical networks can interfere with these memory processes. Specifically, the way information is encoded can affect the form in which it is stored, which can later affect its retrieval. The ability of the individual to implement active memory strategies and organize information meaningfully into already existing schemas increases the likelihood for successful retrieval at a later time. For example, word lists are more likely to be recalled when they can be organized by semantic category such as foods, animals, colors, and so on. Similarly, a new mathematical formula is more likely to be remembered if students can build on existing knowledge (e.g., the formula for calculating a standard deviation is built on the formula used to calculate averages). Persons with frontal lobe damage and executive functioning deficits may perform better on story recall tasks when compared to list learning paradigms because their impaired ability to impose structure on material is more obvious with the unstructured word list.

There also is evidence that the act of retrieving information can strengthen its representation in long-term storage.

For example, it has been shown that repeated retrieval of information from long-term store strengthens memories, increasing the probability that information will be accurately retrieved at a later time (Tulving, 1966). Furthermore, the strength of representations is influenced by how the information is initially learned, including the frequency and spacing of stimulus presentation at encoding (Sohlberg, Ehlhardt, & Kennedy, 2005), the depth of semantic encoding (Craik & Lockhart, 1972), and the type of stimulus presentation (Christoforou, Constantinidou, Shoshilou, & Simos, 2013; Constantinidou et al., 2011).

Our discussion of the human memory systems integrates the aforementioned terms as they assist in our understanding of memory performance in adults with neurologic disorders. Table 2–1 depicts information on human memory divisions, functions, and anatomic structures.

Short-Term/Working Memory

The term "short-term memory," which was coined in the 1950s, gave way to the more contemporary concept of "working memory" in recent decades. Contemporary views of working memory incorporate the initial concepts of short-term memory, which is limited in both capacity and function but consists of multiple components that require the coordination of multiple cognitive resources.

When information arrives via the sense organs, that is, perceptually encoded, it is deposited into an immediate working memory system that is divided into three subsystems specialized for different functions (Baddeley et al., 2011): a control system—the *executive network* of attention (please refer to Chapter 1 on Attention) and two slave systems each handling different types of information: (a) the *visuospatial sketchpad* and (b) the *phonological, or articulatory, loop*. Visual (e.g., color and shape), spatial (i.e., location and orientation), and haptic (e.g., kinesthetic, tactile) information is held and manipulated in the *visuospatial sketchpad*. Recent evidence suggests that visual working memory is not unitary, and during maintenance, the brain segregates visual information depending on the physical attributes of each piece of information (e.g., shape, orientation, color, motion, spatial location; Baddeley et al., 2011; Doherty & Logie, 2016; Konstantinou, Constantinidou, & Kanai, 2017). Cortical areas that are involved in visual perception (the occipital lobe) and spatial orienting (the parietal areas, especially the right parietal lobe) subserve the operations of the visuospatial sketchpad (Baddeley et al., 2011; Doherty & Logie, 2016; Farah, 1988; Jonides et al., 1993; Konstantinou et al., 2017).

Sounds (e.g., phonological and music) as well as linguistically encoded information (e.g., sign and lip reading) are stored and processed by the *phonological* or *articulatory loop*, a term that emphasizes its prototypical activity of recycling acoustic and linguistic information to keep it in conscious awareness. Baddeley et al. (2011) proposed a *memory buffer* mechanism responsible for integrating information between the phonological and visuospatial systems and storing information that exceeds the span capacities of the two subsystems. The neuroanatomic correlates of this additional system have not been confirmed, but it seems that its functions

Table 2–1. Human Memory Systems

System	Subsystems	Divisions	Function	Brain Structure
Working memory	Central executive		Attention control	Bilateral fronto-parietal regions Prefrontal lobes/cortical-subcortical networks
	Visuospatial sketchpad	Nonverbal visuospatial store	Hold visual information	Occipital/parietal Insular Cortex
	Phonological loop	Phonological store	Hold acoustic information	Left temporal-parietal Left supramarginal gyrus
		Subvocal rehearsal	Refreshes store content	Broca's area Cerebellum
	Buffer	Integration of information from visuo-spatial and phonological systems	Use of strategy	Frontal lobe
Long-term memory	Explicit	Semantic	General facts	Medial temporal lobe (MTL) Left cerebellum
		Episodic	Autobiographical experiences	Left MTL Diencephalon Amygdala
		Prospective	Delayed Intentions	Rostral Prefrontal
	Implicit	Procedural	Motor and cognitive skill	Basal ganglia Motor cortex
		Perceptual representation Encoding	Priming/perceptual	Occipital lobes Stimulus-dependent primary sensory areas MTL
		Simple associative/classical conditioning		Throughout central nervous system Cerebellum

might be dependent on the frontal lobe. This working memory buffer deploys effective organization strategies (such as chunking) and pulls information from long-term memory stores that will assist with semantic processing and information manipulation and organization into already known schemata or create new schemata. Demanding working memory tasks that exceed the typical span of 7 (±2) items and tasks that require delayed recall after presentation will require active engagement of the buffer for successful task completion.

Studies of the capacity of auditory working memory often use a task in which a sequence of items (e.g., letters or digits) is presented to a subject who must reproduce them immediately from memory in the correct order. The length of the longest sequence (in terms of number of digits/letters) correctly produced, termed the *letter* or *digit span*, is an index of the size of short-term memory, which some believe is correlated with IQ measures of intelligence (Kyllonen & Christal, 1990). However, others suggest that this span reflects the capacity of the phonological loop rather than the entire working memory system, and the role of the phonological loop in general cognitive function has been called into question (Baddeley, 1995; Conway et al., 2005; Unsworth & Engle, 2007). The phonological loop appears to be necessary, however, for language acquisition, either the early childhood learning of a native language or multiple languages (Gathercole & Baddeley, 1990), or in adult learning of foreign languages (Baddeley, Papagno, & Vallar, 1988; Papagno, Valentine, & Baddeley, 1991).

True working memory capacity of the executive network that has been shown to relate to higher cognitive functioning (Salthouse, 2005) is better measured by tasks that require either dual processing or inhibiting prepotent responses, both activities that are the hallmark of flexible control of attention (Colfesh & Conway, 2007; Conway et al., 2005; Kane & Engle, 2002, 2003). Tests that measure static spans (e.g., forward span of the Wechsler Adult Intelligence Scale–IV [WAIS-IV] or the Wechsler Memory Scale–IV [WMS-IV]) are dissociable from those that measure the more active processes involved in attentional control such as digit span backward and verbal learning paradigms like the Rey Auditory Verbal Learning Test or the California Verbal Learning Test (Conway et al., 2005; Kane et al., 2004; Sanders et al., 2007).

Doherty and Logie (2016) demonstrated that processing accuracy is affected during dual-task processing when task demands exceed the measured memory span. Furthermore, in the case of visual memory, capacity limits in visual short-term memory (VSTM) are correlated with sustained activity in the dorsal and ventral visual streams responsible for perception of spatial and object information, respectively. Voxel-based morphometry (VBM) analyses revealed dissociable neuroanatomical correlates of spatial versus object VSTM reflected in interindividual variability in the gray matter density of the inferior parietal lobule and the left insula, respectively (Konstantinou et al., 2017).

Patients with significant disruptions in the executive and attentional control systems, such as patients who sustained moderate to severe brain injury, or patients with amnestic mild cognitive impairment, typically demonstrate difficulty in allocating resources and actively organizing (and encoding) incoming information (Kennedy et al., 2009; Konstantinou et al., 2017; Metzler-Baddeley et al., 2012). However, research indicates that these patients are able to learn how to implement strategies or to follow external organizational schemes (Constantinidou, Thomas, & Robinson, 2008; Crosson, Cooper, Lincoln, Bauer, & Velozo, 1993; Goldstein, Levin, Boake, & Lohrey, 1990; Kennedy & Krause, 2011).

Long-Term Memory

Some incoming information undergoes the process known as consolidation, which results in it being stored in various long-term retention systems. The different routes to storage, together with the distinctions among the kinds of information permanently stored, define the various hierarchical subsystems of long-term memory. At the top level of the taxonomy adopted by many cognitive neuroscientists (e.g., Schacter & Tulving, 1994; Squire & Zola-Morgan, 1991) is the divide between information that can be consciously declared to have been learned or experienced (*explicit, or declarative, memory*) and information whose learning is reflected only by changes in future behavior as a result of the prior experience without conscious remembrance (*implicit, or nondeclarative, memory*). The kinds of items deemed declarative include general knowledge or facts about the world termed *semantic memory* and personal,

autobiographical recollection of experiences, termed *episodic memory*. The exact locus of stored memories is not known (Thompson & Krupa, 1994), but it has been suggested that various cortical sites involved in perception may hold perceptual memories regarding events, whereas general factual knowledge is likely to be represented at least in the temporal cortex (Gazzaniga, Ivry, & Mangun, 1998).

Both semantic and episodic memories are thought to require a functioning medial temporal lobe system (hippocampus, amygdala, and adjacent cortex but especially the hippocampus) for their learning (Smith, Urgolites, Hopkins, & Squire, 2014; Squire & Knowlton, 1995; Squire & Zola-Morgan, 1991). Lesions in the medial temporal lobe structures result in pronounced *anterograde* amnesia in comparison to *retrograde* amnesia. That is, patients will experience difficulty recalling new events that occur after the injury (anterograde amnesia). They perform poorly on the standard measures of declarative memory such as free recall and recognition of newly studied material such as word lists, paragraphs, and figures. The patients can recall a new experience for a few seconds, before it fades, reflecting an intact immediate recall or span performance. In contrast, their ability to recall events prior to the injury (retrograde amnesia) is largely intact, with the exception of events immediately preceding insult, perhaps because the injury process interrupted the consolidation process. The role of the medial temporal system appears to be one of storage or consolidation of short-term memories rather than one of retrieval given that individuals with amnesia can retrieve remote memories with little difficulty.

There has been some debate in the literature regarding the role of the hippocampus in semantic memories (Tulving, Hayman, & MacDonald, 1991; Vargha-Khadem et al., 1997). A prevailing position states that hippocampal damage will affect the episodic memory system to a greater extent than the semantic system. However, a study by Manns, Hopkins, and Squire (2003) demonstrated that hippocampal damage interferes with the acquisition of new semantic/factual knowledge. In addition, patients experienced retrograde amnesia for semantic information, but that span was limited to a few years. Hence, the authors concluded, the hippocampus supports both episodic and semantic knowledge, but it has a time-limited role in the acquisition and storage of semantic knowledge (Manns et al., 2003).

Explicit memories not only are vulnerable to disruption following medial temporal brain lesions and traumatic brain injury (TBI) but also are relatively vulnerable in healthy individuals, and episodic memories typically are more vulnerable than semantic memories. Most people could not remember the event or moment during which they learned that 1 meter equals 100 centimeters, unless this information was associated with an event of emotional significance. Although semantic or factual memory appears to be strengthened by repeated exposure (especially in the presence of interfering or distracting information), episodic memory by its nature cannot undergo repeated exposure. It appears that most episodic memories fade unless they include or are accompanied by some emotion-ally significant experience or there is a systematic and accurate recount of the events, that is, rehearsal of information (McGaugh, 2000).

Similar to episodic memory, prospective memory is also vulnerable to brain pathology and to interference. Prospective memory refers to delayed intentions. Test paradigms typically design tasks that require an intention (e.g., an act) to be carried out at a later time. The time between the assigned intention and the time to act (retention interval) is filled with an ongoing activity that typically prevents rehearsal (Gonen-Yaacovi & Burgess, 2012). Imaging studies indicate that during prospective memory paradigms, the rostral prefrontal cortex (Brodmann's 10) is a key area of activation during the creation, maintenance, and execution of intentions.

Implicit memory consists of a heterogeneous collection of different types of memories that are generally preserved in the loss of declarative memory ability. These implicit memory systems are quite distinct from one another and rely on entirely different brain structures. They include procedural memory, priming, and classical conditioning. The development of *procedural memory* is independent of the hippocampal formation and mesial temporal lobe structures but appears to depend on the basal ganglia, especially the caudate nucleus (Ashby & Waldron, 2000; Ewert, Levin, Watson, & Kalisky, 1989). Procedural memory typically is divided into two major subtypes, which, on their surface, appear to be quite different but appear to depend on the integrity of similar brain systems. One of the major categories is *motor skill* memory; the other is *cognitive skill* or *reference memory*. If an individual learned how to ride a skip rope today, and her episodic memory is intact, tomorrow she will report having remembered the experience. However, even if she has no explicit memory of the experience (due to hippocampal damage), she will demonstrate intact motor skill memory as manifested by her improved ability to skip rope. Subjects with lesions invading the motor and premotor areas of the frontal cortex frequently display difficulty in motor skill learning. Yet, if their hippocampus is intact, they will recall the experience of attempting to skip rope.

Reference or cognitive skill memory (i.e., the memory of the procedures that are necessary to win a game or solve a problem) constitutes the second kind of procedural memory. This form of memory does not refer to explicit declarative memory for the rules of the game but refers to the acquisition of successful strategies. An individual with a medial temporal lobe lesion could improve his or her skill at board games, such as checkers, without recalling ever playing the game before. Thus, the solution of some complex cognitive tasks does not require explicit memory but rather repeated exposure to a specific situation and rules for solutions. Quite possibly, the learned strategies are a collection of observations of cause and effects that are reinforced according to the principles of operant or instrumental conditioning. Consequently, patients with medial temporal lobe lesions may benefit from the repetitive nature of certain activities in cognitive rehabilitation and become more adapted and independent without necessarily demonstrating improvement in explicit memory tasks. Domain-specific memory training capitalizes on procedural memory. The patient receives training for specific tasks relating to his or her work demands or daily activities. Although functional performance on these tasks typically does not translate to generalization to new tasks, the patient's level of functioning and independence (on the specific activities) may improve. Both forms of procedural learning (motor skill and cognitive skill) involve the basal ganglia; however, motor skill learning appears to be dependent on the integrity of the motor areas of the neocortex, including the premotor strip, and cognitive skill learning appears to be more dependent on sensory cortices in the parietal and occipital lobes (Ewert et al., 1989).

Another type of implicit memory relates to *priming* phenomena. Priming refers to the facilitation in the processing, detection, or identification of an item as a consequence of its prior exposure in tasks not requiring conscious recollection (Schacter, 1992). Classic research paradigms of priming involve an initial study of items, such as a list of words, under the disguise of some ruse instructions, followed with a nonmemory task such as lexical decision ("is this letter string a word or nonword?"), word identification ("what is this word?"), or word-stem completion ("wo_ _"). The typical finding is that lexical decisions and word identifications occur more quickly or require less stimulus energy to achieve a given level of performance for words previously seen. In the word-stem completion task, subjects tend to supply words seen from the earlier list to complete the partial words (Schacter, 1987). Other, nonverbal paradigms implemented include dot patterns and geometric paradigms.

Several studies have demonstrated that priming is dependent on a different anatomical system than explicit memory. Individuals with amnesia who fail traditional tests of explicit memory exhibit normal priming (Graf & Mandler, 1984; Jacoby & Witherspoon, 1982; Schacter, 1985; Shimamura & Squire, 1984). Individuals with damage to perceptual areas such as the occipital lobe show normal performance on explicit measures of memory but do not evidence priming (Gabrieli, Fleischman, Keane, Reminger, & Morel, 1995), and performance on standard recognition and recall tasks can be dissociated from priming tasks in normal subjects (Graf & Mandler, 1984; Graf, Mandler, & Haden, 1982; Jacoby & Dallas, 1981; Tulving, Schacter, & Stark, 1982). Priming appears to be perceptual in nature as any surface change of the stimulus (e.g., font changes for word stimuli or changes in picture orientation for visual stimuli), from prior exposure to test, can reduce its effect (Biederman & Cooper, 1991; Cave & Squire, 1992; Graf & Ryan, 1990; Jacoby & Hayman, 1987; Roediger & Blaxton, 1987). Priming is mediated by the corresponding sensory cortices (visual priming in visual cortex, auditory priming in auditory cortex, etc.). This system responsible for priming is referred to as the perceptual representation system in Schacter's framework (e.g., Schacter, 1990) and is the system involved in the initial perception and encoding of a stimulus (Constantinidou & Thomas, 2017).

Although research studies provide evidence that priming is supported by nontemporal lobe structures, brain imaging studies suggest that the medial temporal lobe may also have a role in implicit learning as well as for information relating to meaningful implicit tasks (Beauregard, Gold, Evans, & Chertkow, 1998; Smith et al., 2014). Koenig et al. (2008) implemented a prototype extraction task during an fMRI task to assess implicit learning of a meaningful novel visual category in young adults, in healthy older adults, and in adults with Alzheimer's disease (AD). As expected, occipital deactivation was observed consistent with perceptually based implicit learning and lateral temporal cortex deactivation reflecting implicit acquisition of the category's semantic nature. In addition, young adults showed medial temporal lobe (MTL) activation during the exposure and test period, suggesting involvement of explicit memory as well. In contrast, adults with AD who had significant MTL atrophy did not show MTL activation, and their performance on the implicit memory task was not as strong as their healthy counterparts. The other patterns of cortical activation/deactivation associated with implicit learning were similar to the healthy controls. The authors concluded that patients with AD appear to engage a cortically based implicit memory mechanism, whereas their relative deficit on this task may reflect their MTL disease. These findings suggest that implicit and explicit memory systems collaborate in neurologically intact individuals performing a seemingly implicit memory task.

A final category of implicit memory includes simple *classical conditioning* and associative learning of the sort often studied in animal learning research. These simple forms of learning, evidenced even in invertebrates, may reflect principles of neuronal plasticity in general such as Hebbian learning or long-term potentiation. That is, repeated stimulation of a postsynaptic neuron by a presynaptic neuron results in synaptic efficiency. There is some evidence for the special role of the cerebellum in classical conditioning of discrete motor responses, such as eye-blinks in the presence of air-puffs (Thompson & Krupa, 1994). Most neurologic disorders do not disrupt this form of learning provided that the patient is conscious and not in a coma or vegetative state and has preserved basic cognitive functioning. This type of memory is mentioned here to provide a complete picture of what is known regarding memory systems (Constantinidou, Thomas, & Best, 2004).

Assessment of Memory Functions

The above sections describe different categories of memories emphasizing the nature of the memory content as revealed by dissociations of the effects of variables on performance using different types of tasks and materials. Most forms of memory assessment, especially in clinical neuropsychological contexts, rely heavily on explicit measures (Lezak, 1995; Lezak, Howieson, & Loring, 2004) as this type of memory is most characteristic of human cognitive performance and seems to be most influenced by brain pathology. Table 2–2 depicts common tests that assess memory in relationship to the systems model of memory. Table 2–3 depicts testing paradigms relating to the systems model.

Assessment of memory abilities needs to follow an integrative multidisciplinary approach. In most rehabilitation settings, memory assessment is part of the cognitive assessment process and conducted by speech-language pathologists and neuropsychologists. Professionals have an array of formal and informal tools designed to test different aspects of memory. To select the appropriate tools, the goals of assessment need to be taken into consideration (Vakil, 2012). Answers to the following questions could provide guidance for appropriate test selection:

■ *What is the goal of the assessment?* Is the goal to obtain a global indication of cognitive function or to provide a thorough memory assessment in order to develop treatment goals? For instance, most global tests of cognition will assess certain aspects of memory; however, they are not designed to provide a thorough assessment of memory. Hence, the clinician needs to be aware of this limitation when administering a general cognitive test. If the test results suggest a memory decline, or if the purpose of assessment is to evaluate memory functions, testing should be followed up with a comprehensive memory assessment.

■ *Is the patient able to participate in standardized testing procedures?* For instance, patients in the acute recovery process post TBI, who are experiencing posttraumatic amnesia and are disoriented, agitated, and unable to engage in sustained attention tasks, as a general rule, cannot participate in thorough formal working memory testing. Results from such testing are not considered clinically reliable. Assessments should focus on testing orientation skills (such as the Galveston Orientation and Amnesia Test) and obtaining informal measures of memory and cognitive function.

Table 2–2. Commonly Administered Tests and Their Relationship to the Systems Memory Model

Batteries/Screens

Testing Task	Test	Immediate Recall	Delayed Recall	Recognition	Forced Choice
List learning memory	RBANS	+	+	+	
Supraspan lists (>9 items per list)	NAB	+	+	+	
	WJ-IV	+			
Subspan lists (<7 items per list; typically single presentation)	ABCD	+		+	
	COGNISTAT	+	+	+	
	RIPA-II	+	+		
	SCATBI	+	+		
Paragraph memory	ABCD	+	+		
	ADP	+			
	NAB	+		+	
	SCATBI	+	+		
	RBANS	+		+	

Memory Assessments

Testing Task	Test	Immediate Recall	Delayed Recall	Recognition	Forced Choice
List learning memory	CVLT-II	+	+	+	+
Supraspan lists (>9 items per list)	HVLT-R	+	+	+	
	RAVLT	+	+	+	
	WMS-IV	+	+	+	
	TOMAL-2	+	+		
Subspan lists (<7 items per list; typically single presentation)	DTLA-A	+			
Paragraph memory	RBMT-3	+	+		
	TOMAL-2	+			
	WMS-IV	+	+	+	

Testing Task	Batteries/Screens					Memory Assessments				
	Test	Immediate Recall	Delayed Recall	Recog-nition	Forced Choice	Test	Immediate Recall	Delayed Recall	Recog-nition	Forced Choice
Paired associates learning						TOMAL-2	+			
						WMS-IV	+	+		
Digit span task or serial recall task—backward (verbal)	WAIS-IV	+				DTLA-A	+			
	WJ-IV	+				TOMAL-2	+			
						WMS-IV	+			
Picture recall	WJ-IV			+		BVRT	+			
	NAB	+	+	+	+	CVMT	+	+	+	
						RMT	+			
						TOMAL-2			+	
						WMS-IV	+	+		
Figure recall	RBANS	+	+			DTLA-A	+			
						WMS-IV	+	+		
						RCFT	+	+	+	
						TOMAL-2		+	+	

continues

Table 2–2. *continued*

Testing Task	Batteries/Screens					Memory Assessments				
	Test	Immediate Recall	Delayed Recall	Recog- nition	Forced Choice	Test	Immediate Recall	Delayed Recall	Recog- nition	Forced Choice
Visual span task or serial recall task— backward						WMS-IV	+			
						TOMAL-2	+			
Visual-auditory learning	WJ-IV	+	+			TOMAL-2	+			

Note. The above list is not intended as an exhaustive list of tests, and inclusion of a test on the table does not imply endorsement by the author. Furthermore, some categorization of the aforementioned "testing tasks" stimulates debate. It is important to keep in mind that the individual's approach to a task may lead to the use of a variety of cognitive functions. As an example, if a patient approaches the task passively, there may not be a demand on executive functioning. However, if a participant chooses to semantically organize the words on a list-learning task, the use of executive functions will ensue. Moreover, one needs to keep in mind the potential of a test to tap into multiple cognitive functions. BVRT = Benton Visual Retention Test; COGNISTAT = Cognitive Status Examination; CVLT-III = California Verbal Learning Test–III; CVMT = Continuous Visual Memory Test; HVLT-R = Hopkins Verbal Learning Test–Revised; NAB = Neuropsychological Assessment Battery; RAVLT = Rey Auditory Verbal Learning Test; RBANS = Repeatable Battery for the Assessment of Neuropsychological Status; RCFT = Rey Complex Figure Test; RMT = Warrington's Recognition Memory Test; WAIS-IV = Wechsler Adult Intelligence Scale–IV; WMS-IV = Wechsler Memory Scale–IV; ADP = Aphasia Diagnostic Profiles; ABCD = Arizona Battery for Communication Disorders of Dementia; RIPA-II = Ross Information Processing Ability–II; SCATBI = Scales of Cognitive Ability for Traumatic Brain Injury; RBMT-3 = Rivermead Behavioural Memory Test–3; TOMAL-2 = Test of Memory and Learning–2; DTLA-A= Detroit Test of Learning Aptitude–Adult; WJ-IV= Woodcock Johnson-IV PsychoEducational Battery-Tests of Cognitive Abilities.

Table 2–3. Testing Paradigms and their Relationship to the Systems Memory Model

Testing Task	Short-Term Store (Working Memory)			Long-Term Store	
	Visual	Phono-logical	Central Executive	Declarative Memory	Non-declarative Memory
List Learning Memory					
Supraspan Lists (>9 items per list)					
Immediate Recall (IR)		+	+		
Delayed Recall (DR)			+	+	
Recognition (Rec)			+	+	
Forced Choice (FC)			+	+	
Subspan Lists (<7 items per list; typically single presentation)					
Immediate Recall		+	+		
Delayed Recall			+	+	
Recognition			+	+	
Paragraph Memory					
Immediate Recall		+	+		
Delayed Recall			+	+	
Recognition			+	+	
Paired Associates Learning					
Immediate Recall		+	+		
Delayed Recall			+	+	
Recognition			+	+	

continues

Table 2–3. *continued*

Testing Task	Short-Term Store (Working Memory)			Long-Term Store	
	Visual	Phono-logical	Central Executive	Declarative Memory	Non-declarative Memory
Digit Span Task or Serial Recall Task—Backward (verbal)					
Immediate Recall		+	+		
Prospective Task		+	+	+	
Visual-Auditory Learning					
Immediate Recall	+	+	+		
Delayed Recall			+	+	
Picture Recall					
Immediate Recall	+		+		
Delayed Recall			+	+	
Recognition			+	+	
Figure Recall					
Immediate Recall	+		+		
Delayed Recall			+	+	
Recognition			+	+	
Visual Span Task or Serial Recall Task—Backward					
Immediate Recall	+		+		
Procedural Memory Tasks (e.g., pursuit rotor)			+		+

Once posttraumatic amnesia (PTA) is resolved, and the patient is able to sustain attention to complete test tasks, then formal memory testing can be implemented.

- *What is the theoretical framework of memory adopted by the test and how does it relate to contemporary theoretical models of memory?*
- *What aspects of memory does the test assess? How do these aspects relate to the patient's neurological disease/ condition?*
- *What are the psychometric properties of the test? Content validity, interitem reliability, test-retest reliability, and standardization process (including population demographics)?* Are the patient's cultural, linguistic, educational, and socioeconomic strata represented in the normative sample?
- *How does the assessment relate to the model of International Classification of Functioning Disability and Health (ICF) (WHO, 2001)?*

Screening Tools

Screening tests are designed to detect a disease state. For that reason, screenings have several advantages:

a. Brief and time efficient
b. Often tap on a wide array of cognitive processes
c. Easy to administer
d. Typically have good face validity
e. Often known to many disciplines such as the Folstein Mini Mental State Examination (MMSE; Folstein, Folstein, & Hugh, 1975), the Montreal Cognitive Assessment

(Nasreddine et al., 2005), the Ross Information Processing Assessment II (RIPA-II; Ross-Swain, 1996), or the Repeatable Battery of Assessment of Neuropsychological Status (RBANS; Randolph, Tierney, Mohn, & Chase, 1998).

Clinicians should be cautioned that often patients with mild memory decline (as in the case of patients with amnestic mild cognitive impairment or mild TBI) may perform well on screening tests because these tools assess memory only crudely. Patients who fail the screening or who are suspected of having memory decline should be administered comprehensive memory tests designed to assess and diagnose memory deficits.

Relating Memory Models to Memory Assessment

Memory assessment can be organized according to the systems of memory processes such as working memory versus long-term memory and types of memory, such as verbal versus nonverbal, declarative versus nondeclarative. Testing tasks may incorporate the following types of activities:

- *Immediate Recall:* The examinee is asked to spontaneously (i.e., without hints/cues) recall stimulus material immediately following presentation.
- *Delayed Recall:* The examinee is asked to spontaneously recall stimulus materials presented at an earlier time interval (i.e., 20 to 30 minutes).

■ *Recognition:* Performance of examinee when asked to recognize target stimuli among distracter materials.

■ *Forced-Choice Recall:* The examinee is read pairs of words and asked to choose the word from each pair that was from a specific list read previously. This task is helpful in identifying those who simulate memory deficits.

Immediate recall should incorporate manipulation of information versus mere repetition of information to be considered a working memory task. Manipulation of information requires the involvement of the central executive system, which is an integral component of working memory. The type of stimulus (i.e., verbal or nonverbal) will determine as to whether the phonological or visual-spatial sketchpad is activated in the immediate recall task. Each of the above testing tasks assesses a different aspect of memory. Hence, memory assessment should incorporate all of them.

Assessment of Verbal Memory

The following types of stimuli typically are implemented in the assessment of verbal memory (auditory or visual) memory:

■ Letters
■ Words
■ Names
■ Numbers
■ Paragraphs
■ Pictures of familiar objects and faces

Photos of familiar objects and people are considered verbal (even though they are visual stimuli) because most people will assign verbal labels to pictorial stimuli. Pictorial stimuli need to be abstract to escape verbal labeling (Lezak, 1983). The most common verbal working memory paradigms include one of the following activities:

■ *Verbal Learning Tasks* (e.g., serial presentation of words that may or may not be related). Stimulus words may be presented in three to five learning trials. Multiple scores may be generated from this type of task representing the examinee's ability to benefit from repetition and other cognitive constructs such as attention. Formal verbal list learning tasks often have recall of stimulus materials at various delay intervals. During subspan learning tasks, typically, the words are only presented once and then the patient is asked to recall the items from the list.

■ *Paragraph/Story Recall* (e.g., a story that incorporates meaningful material along with episodic information). Most paragraph recall paradigms incorporate immediate and delayed recall conditions.

■ *Paired Associates Learning* (e.g., presenting pairs of words together and later on presenting one of the pair items and requesting the patient to recall the other item)

■ *Digit Span or Serial Recall Task* (e.g., presenting a series of digits or letters to be remembered and gradually increasing the number of items)

■ *Prospective Memory Tasks* (e.g., requesting to carry out an intention at a later time)

Comprehensive memory assessment typically incorporates all of the above tasks because patient performance may vary across them. For example, patients who have difficulty implementing organization and encoding strategies may perform poorly on multitrial verbal learning paradigms consisting of word lists that exceed the normal span of seven to nine items. Their recognition performance may be better than their free recall abilities (Constantinidou, 1998). During paragraph/story recall, the patients may perform comparatively better (than their free recall performance on list learning tasks) because stories provide contextual support and inherent organization since they follow a logical sequence. Hence, story recall facilitates encoding for patients who have a more passive learning style.

Patients with normal auditory attention span may perform well on digit span tasks by remembering five to nine items. In order for digit or serial recall tasks to engage working memory mechanisms, they need to involve manipulation of information (which involves the central executive system) or exceed the capacity of the human span (e.g., nine items or chunks of information). Therefore, the backward recall of digits or serial recall is considered a working memory task versus the forward recall task.

Prospective memory tasks also have gained popularity in the recent years because they resemble real-life situations. The patient is asked to remember and carry on a task or intention at a later time (e.g., to turn off the radio in 15 minutes). Therefore, the integrative work of attention, episodic buffer, and executive abilities are needed to complete the task successfully.

Assessment of Nonverbal Memory

The following types of stimuli typically are implemented in the assessment of nonverbal memory:

- Abstract designs
- Complex figures
- Unfamiliar melodies
- Spatial positions
- Unfamiliar faces

The most common nonverbal working memory paradigms include one of the following activities:

- *Complex Figure Test* (copy, immediate, delayed, and recognition conditions)
- *Picture Recall* of unfamiliar faces (immediate and delayed condition)
- *Spatial Span Tasks* (forward and backward)
- *Spatial Navigation* paradigms

Similar to its verbal memory counterpart, visual-spatial memory assessment needs to incorporate a variety of paradigms that test visual organization abilities, learning, recall, and recognition of information. Complex (abstract) figure recall tasks have considerable clinical utility for the assessment of visual-spatial skills. Most tasks require an initial copy of the figure followed by immediate, delayed, and recognition conditions. During the copy administration, the clinician can observe the patient's ability to organize visual information and his or her visual construction skills. Patients who, during the copy administration, demonstrate difficulty grasping the general organizational theme of the figure predictably will have difficulty recalling information during the immediate and recall conditions. Patients with TBI often copy figures using a piecemeal approach because of difficulty processing complex multiple pieces of information at once (Lezak, 1995).

Most patients will demonstrate similar immediate and delayed recall performance of abstract figures unless they suffer from pronounced forgetting (Lezak et al., 2004).

Furthermore, subgroups of patients with perceptual problems may perform better during the recall conditions than the copy administration because of delayed perceptual organization skills.

As mentioned previously, pictorial stimuli of familiar objects are considered verbal tasks because humans assign verbal labels to photos. However, presentation and subsequent recall of unfamiliar faces has a higher probability of escaping verbal encoding and are typically used in visual-spatial memory testing. It has been demonstrated that some individuals will use verbal encoding strategies to organize perceptual features of objects (Constantinidou & Kreimer, 2004) and unfamiliar faces. However, damage in the posterior right hemispheres can result in difficulty in remembering faces, and this difficulty is characteristic of patients with right hemisphere focal lesions.

Spatial span tasks typically incorporate memory for location in a two- or three-dimensional space. The number of items to recall gradually increases until the spatial span capacity is reached (typically five to nine items). Like its verbal counterpart (i.e., the digit span), spatial paradigms should incorporate backward recall because it requires manipulation of information and engages the executive mechanisms of working memory.

Spatial navigation paradigms involve route finding or mental rotation paradigms in a three-dimensional space.

Memory assessment typically includes immediate recall to determine span capacity and learning performance. A 20- to 30-minute delayed recall will provide information about the patient's ability to transfer newly acquired information into long-term memory, thus making predictions regarding learning and storage capacity. Delayed recall paradigms typically involve free recall and recognition performance. Patients with difficulty in actively retrieving information have poorer free recall scores than recognition scores. However, if information has not been transferred into long-term storage, then recognition performance will also be affected.

Contextual Assessment of Memory

In addition to test performance on the aforementioned formal tasks, clinicians should consider the WHO-ICF framework and obtain information on how the patient performs in different contexts. Central to the WHO-ICF model is the interaction between the health condition that results in impairment in certain body functions and structures and how that condition and impairment can affect the execution of activity required for participation in meaningful tasks and roles. The model stresses the contribution of contextual factors, such as the environment (i.e., support services, environmental adaptations) and personal factors (i.e., patient motivation, coping mechanisms, and psychosocial functioning) that can contribute to the individual's ability to engage in social, educational, and vocational activities. The intimate interplay between contextual and health factors contributes to differences among patients in levels of activity and participation and resulting disability (Constantinidou & Kennedy, 2017; WHO, 2001).

Structured questionnaires such as the Everyday Memory Questionnaire–Revised (EMQ-R; Royle & Lincoln, 2008) with good psychometric properties provide a liable tool of subjective memory deficits and can complement formal clinical tests. Furthermore, considering the interplay between memory and executive functions, questionnaires such as the Dysexecutive Questionnaire–Revised (DEX-R;Simblett, Ring, & Bateman, 2017)) and the Behavior Rating Inventory of Executive Function (BRIEF; Gioia, Isquith, & Kenworthy, 2000) can provide information about the patient's functioning and goal-directed behavior during everyday activities. The latter provide the opportunity for an informant to provide information regarding the patient's performance. Discrepancies between the informant rating and the patient ratings offer information on self-awareness deficits. Using the DEX, self-awareness deficits were evident in young adults with chronic TBI at 5.5 years postinjury in the Social and Self-Regulation and Motivation and Attention domains (Pettemeridou & Constantinidou, 2018).

Specific Types of Memory Disorders

There are several types of memory disorders associated with different neuropathologies. Therefore, it is important for the clinician and the rehabilitation team in general to have a thorough understanding of how the brain pathology can affect cognition and memory abilities. Papanicolaou (2006) in the book, *The Amnesias*, discusses extensively the most common types of memory disorders associated with normal aging, dementia, limbic system damage, brain injury, acute confusional state, epilepsy, and psychiatric disorders. Most of these conditions involve anterograde and/or retrograde memory loss.

Anterograde amnesia (AA) refers to the difficulty learning and remembering new information/events after the onset of the memory loss. Most memory assessment procedures discussed in this chapter addresses anterograde memory. In contrast, *retrograde amnesia* (RA) refers to loss of information that occurred prior to the onset of the memory impairment. The length of RA typically decreases in patients with nondegenerative acquired brain conditions and prior memories fill the gaps. However, the most recent events (such as what happened minutes prior to the incident that caused brain injury) are vulnerable to RA effects in comparison to older events. The vulnerability of the events might be because their consolidation process was disrupted and information was not transferred into long-term memory. In contrast, patients with degenerative conditions such as Alzheimer's disease initially don't demonstrate RA during the early phases of the disease. However, as the disease progresses, their RA worsens and patients have significant difficulty with autobiographical memory, remembering previous events, and recalling previously acquired knowledge.

Acquired brain injury often results in *posttraumatic amnesia* (PTA). PTA includes the period of RA plus AA. The onset of RA is the last memory remembered prior to the injury; the end of AA is the point of complete return to continuous memory after the injury. The Galveston Orientation and Amnesia Test (GOAT; Levin, O'Donnell, & Grossman, 1979) can be used to assess a patient's orientation during the acute and subacute stage. This can be administered several times during the day until recovery of orientation and PTA resolution is demonstrated (Levin et al., 1979). The duration of PTA is used as an indicator of brain injury severity along with other critical variables such as length of impaired consciousness, initial Glasgow Coma Scale score, presence of focal neurologic signs, and neuroimaging results.

The Role of Processes and Strategies in Memory Performance

The current view of the organization of memory and its processes has been developed in part from studies investigating focal lesions in humans and animals. However, certain neuropathologies such as TBI and Alzheimer's disease cause diffuse neuronal disruption. Subsequently, multiple memory systems may be affected (Barak, Vakil, & Levy, 2013; Constantinidou, 1998; Millis & Ricker, 1994; Sanders et al., 2007).

Standardized memory testing provides quantitative information regarding the patient's memory performance. In order to interpret this information in a meaningful manner, the clinicians should examine and consider memory strategies implemented by the patient during the various memory tasks. For example, early cognitive studies of memory formation focusing on the stage model argued that certain ways of organizing the to-be-remembered material lead to more durable memory traces (Craik & Lockhart, 1972). Consequently, if the individual elaborated on the deeper meaning of items, emphasizing connections to already learned material or involving visual imagery (Paivio, 1971, 1976), those items would be less subject to forgetting than items merely rehearsed by being recycled in the phonological loop. This idea of (elaboration) has been exploited in various prescriptions of strategies to improve memory performance in cognitive rehabilitation (Barak et al., 2012; Crosson & Buenning, 1984; Goldstein et al., 1990; Levin, 1989; Wilson, 1987; Yubero, Gil, Paul, & Maestú, 2011).

Active elaboration clearly places demands on working memory, especially on executive control mechanisms (of the frontal lobes) responsible for the planning and sequencing of currently active mental operations. Patients with TBI may present normal immediate recall (suggesting an intact auditory span), but a passive learning style can interfere with their ability to implement effective strategies and acquire new words during supraspan tasks like the Auditory Verbal Learning Test (AVLT) (Constantinidou, 1998).

Studies incorporating demanding multitrial tasks such as the AVLT and the California Verbal Learning Test (CVLT) also demonstrated a decline in active memory processes secondary to brain injury (Constantinidou & Neils, 1995; Konstantinou, Pettemeridou, Stamatakis, Seimenis, & Constantinidou, 2019; Lezak, 1995; Millis & Ricker, 1994). Furthermore, research with the CVLT

2. PRINCIPLES OF HUMAN MEMORY   75

and AVLT indicates that decreased memory performance could be due to inefficiency in guiding the retrieval process (Constantinidou, 1999), especially in the presence of right frontal lobe damage (Konstantinou et al., 2019; Nyberg, Cabeza, & Tulving, 1996) or due to aging (Blachstein, Greenstein, & Vakil, 2012). Difficulty in transferring of information from working memory to long-term memory (i.e., consolidation) can be disrupted by the appearance of distracting or interfering material (Waugh & Norman, 1965) as well as by failure to appropriately organize information. Patients suffering from TBI seem to be most vulnerable to the debilitating effects of interference possibly due to insult to the frontal lobes, especially the left frontal (Konstantinou et al., 2016; Nyberg et al., 1996) or the medial temporal lobe areas (Konstantinou et al., 2016, 2019). Studies following TBI suggest that immediate recall (measured by span tasks) appears to be intact (Brooks, 1975; O'Donnell, Radtke, Leicht, & Caesar, 1988). However, when interference is imposed, memory performance is significantly affected, indicating difficulties in consolidating declarative information into long-term memory (Brooks, 1975; Constantinidou, 1999). Interference can be introduced in the form of a delay or in the form of a competing stimulus (O'Donnell et al., 1988). Even a 10-second delay between stimulus presentation and response has been reported to affect recall performance (Constantinidou & Prechel, 1996).

Research demonstrates that patients who don't apply active memory strategies tend to have a decreased rate of learning compared to normal subjects, and their ability to recognize information is superior to their free recall performance. In contrast, subgroups of patients who apply active memory typically show improvements in their working memory capacity (Constantinidou, 1999; Constantinidou & Neils, 1995; Spikman, Berg, & Deelman, 1995). Consequently, teaching patients how to implement active memory strategies may be a useful therapy approach to memory rehabilitation.

The ability to apply strategies that guide learning and recall of information has also been associated with the "cognitive reserve" (CR) hypothesis. According to the CR hypothesis, individuals with higher reserve are able to cope with brain pathology through some form of active compensatory strategy better than those with lower reserve. Thus, greater CR could allow individuals to cope better with the cognitive changes associated with aging or brain injury, by promoting more flexible usage of cognitive processes and implementation of new strategies (Brickman et al., 2011; Singh-Manoux et al., 2011). CR is not a unitary theoretical construct and variables such as education, social and cognitive engagement, vocabulary knowledge, and reading abilities have been incorporated in latent model analyses in order to define it and determine its prognostic utility in rehabilitation (Giogkaraki, Michaelides, & Constantinidou, 2013; Levi, Rassovsky, Agranov, Sela-Kaufman, & Vakil, 2013). Giogkaraki et al. (2013) reported that higher levels of CR have a moderating role in reducing the direct negative effect of age on verbal episodic memory and on executive function in healthy aging. Consequently, in addition to injury or disease-specific characteristics, CR could be another parameter for consideration during patient rehabilitation.

Implications for Rehabilitation

In order to decide how to plan therapy goals and organize memory rehabilitation, the clinician needs to have a thorough understanding of the underlying brain pathology and its impact on overall cognition and health status. Most patients with neurologic conditions, who experience memory deficits, also demonstrate difficulties in other cognitive domains such as executive, attention, categorization, language, and psychosocial functioning. Hence, it is imperative to obtain complete information regarding the patient's history and neuropsychological status for effective management and treatment planning.

Memory rehabilitation and, more extensively, cognitive rehabilitation fall under two primary categories: *restorative* and *compensatory*. *Restorative* rehabilitation is based on neuroanatomic and neurophysiologic models of learning, suggesting that neuronal growth and synaptogenesis result directly from repeated exposure and repetition of stimulation through experience (Squire, 1987). Consequently, cognitive training potentially could lead to the development of new neuronal networks, which could facilitate reorganization of partially damaged systems, reduce cognitive impairment, and improve function (Constantinidou et al., 2004).

An increasing body of evidence supports the use of memory retraining (see reviews by Cicerone et al., 2005; Cicerone et al., 2011; Cicerone et al., 2019). Memory therapy focusing on restorative principles incorporates a variety of methodologies such as attention training, semantic organization and asso-

ciation, rehearsal techniques, chunking and rhyming strategies, and organization strategies such as *wh*-questions. Studies with patients who sustained moderate severe brain injuries and had difficulty organizing incoming information demonstrated that participants were able to learn how to implement strategies or to follow external organizational schemes. Training activities that incorporate self-regulation, organize incoming information, and require allocation of attentional resources to a task train the central executive system of working memory (Crosson et al., 1993; Goldstein et al., 1990; Kennedy & Krause, 2011).

On the other side of the spectrum, the *compensatory* rehabilitation approach operates under the assumption that some functions cannot be recovered or restored completely. Therefore, the patient needs to use specific strategies to improve functional performance without relying on the restoration of the damaged neurocognitive systems (Coelho, DeRuyter, & Stein, 1996; Kennedy & Coelho, 2005). The restorative and compensatory approaches, where appropriate, could be used together in memory rehabilitation to maximize performance (Constantinidou & Thomas, 2017). Compensatory strategies, including environmental modifications, are also implemented in the acute management of sports concussion, where formal cognitive treatment is typically not warranted for the majority of the cases. During the acute phases of the injury, concentration, learning, and retention deficits are prominent for several days and the patient's improvement is closely monitored by an interdisciplinary team (Knollman-Porter, Constantinidou, Beardslee, & Dailey,

2019). Environmental modifications and use of external memory aids are especially useful during the first weeks of the recovery process.

Patients with severe memory impairment benefit more from external memory aids and alerting devices for activities of daily living, provided that they receive extensive training for the use of the strategy/device (Cicerone et al., 2005, 2011). Specific external memory strategies such as the implementation of a memory notebook or a smartphone may be beneficial for everyday (or prospective) memory functions such as remembering important dates and appointments (McDonald et al., 2011; Sohlberg & Mateer, 1989; Wilson, Emslie, Quirk, & Evans, 2013). Furthermore, patients with moderate severe TBI, as well as normal older adults with memory decline due to normal aging, benefit from pictorial presentation of verbal material rather than auditory presentation of information alone (Constantinidou & Baker, 2002; Constantinidou, Neils, Bouman, Lee, & Shuren, 1996). Hence, the type of stimulus presentation modality may affect learning and recall, with the pictorial modality resulting in better recall and recognition performance. Regardless of the method used, a key component to establishing consistent and effective use of compensatory strategies includes self-awareness training and the use of strategies to solve functional problems. In other words, the patient needs to "buy in" to the functional utility of the strategy (Armstrong, McPherson, & Nayar, 2012). Patients with extensive neurologic involvement and executive functioning deficits demonstrate difficulty transferring new knowledge acquired in therapy to novel situations.

In these patients, domain-specific treatment of memory may be a successful therapy method. Domain-specific therapy is designed to meet the needs of a given task or activity (hence the term "domain"). Its success may be attributed to the fact that it incorporates procedural memory, repetition, and routine building (Glisky, 1992; Parente & Anderson-Parente, 1989), which is less affected by cortical disease or injury. The case study below illustrates this approach to managing difficulties associated with memory decline.

Nondeclarative memory tends to be more resistive to several types of cortical brain pathology as compared to declarative memory. However, the application of newly learned skills to novel situations and problems likely will be unsuccessful as it requires declarative knowledge of strategies, as well as intact executive abilities (Malec, 1996), frequently impaired in the dementias, TBI, and frontal lobe pathology (Stuss, 2011).

There has been a great deal of emphasis in the recent years for the early and timely diagnosis of pathologic aging (i.e., mild cognitive impairment) and dementia. Interestingly, in a large cohort study, older adults were aware of their memory deficits before their informants, as evidenced by significant differences in the memory factor of the DEX (Demetriadou, Michaelides, Bateman, & Constantinidou, 2018). The benefit of early detection relates to the notion that, during the early stages of the disease, therapy can benefit from the relatively intact nondeclarative system and help the patient implement strategies to maximize independence. Furthermore, in a small unpublished study, patients with

MCI were able to learn new strategies to support categorization abilities (Constantinidou & Nikou, 2014). Through the Categorization Program, which was originally designed to remediate cognitive deficits in patients with TBI (Constantinidou et al., 2008), patients were able to demonstrate learning as measured by improvement on a variety of hierarchical categorization tasks. Strategies such as repetition, errorless learning, and cued recall were instrumental to the learning process, and outcomes indicate that declarative learning is possible even during amnestic MCI.

Concepts such as *metacognition* and *metamemory* are used in the rehabilitation literature referring to the individual's ability for self-awareness regarding his or her cognitive and memory abilities. These functions are developed through experience and rely heavily on executive abilities and frontal lobe networks. Patients who have difficulty in this area may not be aware of their deficits and subsequently may see no need for rehabilitation or implementation of strategies discussed during therapy. Patients who are able to benefit from increased self-awareness training can learn about the nature of their memory problem and how specific strategies implemented in therapy can improve memory functioning. Furthermore, therapy may incorporate metamemory training to help patients predict their performance on certain tasks (Sohlberg & Mateer, 2001). Improvement of self-awareness has been linked to rehabilitation success (Armstrong et al., 2012; Kennedy & Coehlo, 2005; Kennedy & Krause, 2011). It is based on the expectation that the patient assumes greater responsibility for his deficits and imple-

ments strategies to facilitate effective performance (Constantinidou & Kennedy, 2017).

Case Study: Patient With Mild Cognitive Impairment

Mr. SS is a retired 78-year-old engineer with 18 years of education (BA and MSc degrees). He is a native of Cyprus and attended university in Greece. He worked for 40 years in a private company as a survey engineer and retired at age 65. About 3 years ago, he began noticing "memory lapses." He described them as episodes of forgetting various events during the day (including conversations) and misplacing things or forgetting to do important tasks to the extent that he was feeling worried. Forgetting names of familiar people and word-finding problems during conversation were also frequent phenomena. He was a veteran of the Cypriot independence struggle (1955–1959) and enjoyed reading history books and attending various lectures on the same matter. He reported having trouble retaining information he read and found himself rereading information in order to retain it. These difficulties affected his quality of life, but he attributed them to getting older. Mr. SS belongs to a retirement club whose members participate in the Neurocognitive Study for Aging (NEUROAGE). NEUROAGE is a longitudinal study on aging in Cyprus, established in 2009 to examine health, demographic, and biological factors contribute to cognitive aging in Greek Cypriot participants (Constantinidou, Christodoulou, & Prokopiou, 2012). The study has a rolling admission process (e.g., participants can enter the study at any time) and NEUROAGE participants are assessed at baseline and are subsequently being followed every 2 years. Participants whose performance deviates from the expected ranges for age and education are followed up further and are referred for medical and rehabilitation services.

Assessment Battery and Procedures

Mr. SS volunteered to participate in the NEUROAGE project. Testing was conducted at the Center for Applied Neuroscience, University of Cyprus, which is the host organization for the project. The project incorporates the following battery of tests in order to assess key areas of impairment and function following the WHO-ICF model. All tests have been adapted in Greek and have been used in prior research by our team. Following are the measures organized in domains.

1. Cognitive Screening: MMSE (Fountoulakis, Tsolaki, Chantzi, & Kasis, 2000)
2. Attention/concentration: The Greek version of Trail Making Test A (also processing speed), Digit Span Forward and Backwards (Wechsler Memory Scale III [WMS-III]), and Visual Span Forward and Backwards (WMS-III) (Wechsler, 1997)
3. Working Memory: Rey Complex Figure Test—recall and recognition (Myers & Myers, 1995), Greek version of the Hopkins

Verbal Learning Test (HVLT; Benedict, Schretlen, Groninger, & Brandt, 1998; adapted in Greek, see Giogkaraki et al., 2013), and Greek Story Recall (Immediate and Delayed) (Constantinidou & Ioannou, 2008)
4. Executive Function: Copy administration of the Rey Complex Figure, Symbol Digits Modalities Test (Smith, 1982), Control Oral Word Association (COWAT; Kosmidis et al., 2004), Greek version Trail Making Test B (Zalonis et al., 2008), and Greek version of the Dysexecutive Questionnaire from the BADS (Demetriadou et al., 2018)
5. Language: Greek version of the Boston Naming Test (Simos, Kasselimis, & Mouzaki, 2011), short version of the Peabody Picture Vocabulary Test (Simos et al., 2011), and word reading and pseudowords (Simos, Sideridis, Kasselimis, & Mouzaki, 2013)
6. Greek version of Quality of Life & Outcome Measures: WHOQOL-BREF (Ginieri-Coccossis et al., 2011)
7. Psychosocial Measures: Geriatric Depression Scale (Fountoulakis et. al., 1999)

Test Results

Raw scores were converted to z scores according to age and years of education. As indicated in Figure 2–1, Mr. SS performed at the mean or above the mean on all measures, with the exception of the learning trials and delayed recall on the HVLT and the immediate and

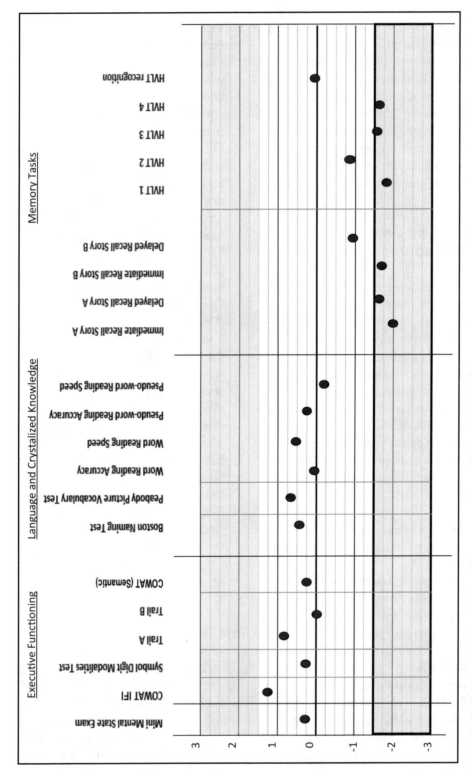

Figure 2–1. The plot of the test scores converted as z scores. Performance on the MMSE and on Executive, Language, and Memory domains. Fluctuations between + or – 1 z score is considered within the average range for age and educational level.

delayed recall of the story recall tasks. Notably, his performance on the general screening test (MMSE was well within the normal range, score of 28). From a psychosocial perspective, he did not report elevated depression symptomatology that could explain the presenting cognitive symptoms. Performance on the DEX did not indicate discrepancies with the scores assigned by his informant and no meaningful changes were noted in executive functioning. Notably, the patient noticed more cognitive changes than his son, who provided the informant rating. The objective measures of the test battery in conjunction with his subjective measures of memory difficulties indicate that Mr. SS's performance is consistent with amnestic MCI. Figure 2–1 is the plot of the test scores converted as z scores.

Recommendations

The patient was referred to the collaborating neurologist for a medical evaluation, which included a clinical examination, an imaging study, and laboratory workup. Medical etiologies for cognitive decline were excluded. MRI findings were negative other than mild hyperintensities in the deep white matter (classification: FAZEKAS grade 1, punctuate foci of ischemic nature), associated with vascular changes, a finding that is not uncommon in older adults. Fazekas grade of 2 or 3 is associated with pathological aging or vascular dementia. Furthermore, the patient had no history of cardiovascular risk factors, including hyperlipidemia or diabetes. Family history was negative for dementia. The confirmed diagnosis was amnestic MCI.

Neurocognitive Treatment

The short-term goals of treatment were (1) to implement the systematic use of compensatory strategies to facilitate memory performance and (2) to improve neurocognitive functioning through systematic remedial neurocognitive training with the Categorization Program. The long-term objective was to help the patient remain at a high functioning level and delay further neurocognitive decline through the use of strategies that would maintain instrumental activities of daily living and participation.

The patient was enrolled in neurocognitive treatment two times per week, which included psychoeducational training on cognitive decline and the implementation of memory strategies in order to help Mr. SS compensate for his deficits. Memory strategies included the use of a planner and smartphone for prospective memory tasks with reminders and establishment of procedures that could ensure successful implementation of the strategies. For example, the patient would generate a daily "to-do" list before dinnertime and would review the information every morning at breakfast. In addition, he was trained on the use of wh-questions during reading as well as implementing note-taking of important names, characters for longer text. Domain-specific strategies were also implemented to manage memory difficulties and improve recall for content relevant to his hobby, reading and attending lectures about history.

Hierarchical neurocognitive training was implemented with the Categorization Program (CP; Constantinidou et al., 2008). The CP is a rigorous systematic, hierarchical, eight-level program initially designed as a restorative cognitive rehabilitation program in adults with acquired brain injury. Initial research findings (Constantinidou et al., 2005) and a subsequent randomized controlled trial (Constantinidou et al., 2008) indicate that the CP is an effective therapy tool for adults with brain injury who exhibit categorization deficits. In a small unpublished study with older adults with MCI, the CP was also found effective in improving cognitive performance. Constantinidou et al. (2008) offered the following explanations regarding the active ingredients of the CP:

■ The CP addresses both aspects of categorization, novel category learning, and categorization of established concepts or categories. It incorporates concrete visual stimuli and gradually progresses into abstract concepts through the use of repetition, cueing, and strategy building that facilitate learning.

■ The CP was built using a very systematic hierarchical structure that corresponds to the neurodevelopmental categorization and cognitive processes hierarchy.

■ Tasks gradually increase in difficulty and cognitive abstraction. CP tasks begin with basic feature identification and feature extraction (such as color, shape, and size) and progress to higher levels of concept formation and abstraction (such as rule-based decision making).

■ The program integrates cognitive processes such as executive skills, attention, organization, conceptual reasoning, linguistic flexibility, and explicit memory for the completion of the categorization tasks.

■ The redundancy and the repetition integrated in each level, along with the extensive cueing systems and errorless learning principles, provide support and organization for participants with more passive learning styles. The program provides a standardized approach to categorization training, yet it incorporates mastery criteria for each level in order to account for individual differences.

Treatment Duration

Twelve weeks per 3 times per week at 60 minutes. One time was devoted to memory strategies and other two times to the CP training.

Treatment Outcome Measures

Memory log of memory difficulties prior to treatment and during treatment. Log of use of strategies during targeted activities (e.g., reading, attending lectures). In addition, the CP training included three tests measuring change in skills learning during the training administered at baseline and at the end of the 12-week training and four probe tasks designed to test generalizability of performance. For a more in-depth discussion of the training and dependent measures, the reader is referred to Constantinidou et al. (2008).

Treatment Results

The patient demonstrated systematic usage of memory strategies on 80% of targeted tasks. In addition, he reported reduction in memory difficulties on a daily basis to 30%. He completed the CP training and demonstrated gains in the three CP tests by 30%. In addition, his performance on the CP probe tasks consistently improved from baseline (score 18/30) to 20/30, 24/30, and 26/30 for the subsequent administrations.

Conclusions

Neurocognitive treatment for Mr. SS incorporated compensatory memory strategies and hierarchical cognitive retraining. Treatment captured intact procedural memory in order to establish routines that incorporated the memory strategies. The patient was highly motivated and aware of his deficits as demonstrated by performance on the tests and during treatment. Consequently, his engagement and eagerness to improve was a significant key ingredient to treatment success. This case also illustrates the value of including domain-specific tests in our assessment strategy. In relationship with the memory model incorporated in this chapter, had we relied on the cognitive screening of the MMSE, we would miss the memory impairment demonstrated by performance on verbal learning (HVLT) and story recall tasks.

will disrupt the efficiency of memory networks. The extent of disruption and its impact on social and professional activities will depend on the severity of the memory impairment and how this impairment can interfere with participation in social, educational, and vocational activities (see ICF model; WHO, 2001).

Memory abilities are interdependent with other cognitive skills such as attention and executive functioning. In fact, the multiple systems model of memory incorporates a central executive control system that coordinates the function of two subslave systems (phonological loop and visuospatial sketchpad). Hence, disruption in the efficiency of this multiple-system network can result in difficulty acquiring new information as in anterograde amnesia.

Comprehensive memory assessment is an integral component of cognitive and neuropsychological assessment. Test results along with information regarding the patient's overall cognitive and psychosocial status, personal/professional goals, and overall health should be taken into consideration in order to make an accurate diagnosis, determine prognosis, and develop an effective management plan to maximize the patient's level of functioning and participation into the community.

Conclusions

The ability to acquire new information and recall it at a later time is an important cognitive ability necessary for survival and for the acquisition of important cognitive functions such as language, reasoning, and problem solving. Research and clinical experience indicate that most brain pathologies

References

Armstrong, J., McPherson, K., & Nayar, S. (2012). External memory aid training after traumatic brain injury: 'making it real.' *British Journal of Occupational Therapy, 75*(12), 541–548.

Ashby, F. G., & Waldron, F. G. (2000). The neuropsychological basis of category learning. *Current Directions in Psychological Science, 9,* 10–14.

Atkinson, R. C., & Shiffrin, R. M. (1968). Human memory: A proposed system and its control processes. In K. W. Spence & J. T. Spence (Eds.), *The psychology of learning and motivation* (Vol. 2, pp. 89–195). New York, NY: Academic Press.

Baddeley, A. D. (1986). *Working memory.* Oxford, UK: Oxford University Press.

Baddeley, A. D. (1995). *Working memory.* In M. S. Gazzaniga (Ed.), *The cognitive neurosciences* (pp. 755–764). Cambridge, MA: MIT Press.

Baddeley, A. D. (2000). The episodic buffer: A new component of working memory? *Trends in Cognitive Sciences, 4,* 417–423.

Baddeley, A. D. (2001). Is working memory still working? *American Psychologist, 56*(11), 851–864.

Baddeley, A. D. (2003). Working memory and language: An overview. *Journal of Communication Disorders, 36,* 189–208.

Baddeley, A. D., Allen, R. J., & Hitch, G. J. (2011). Binding in visual working memory: The role of the episodic buffer. *Neuropsychologia, 49*(6), 1393–1400.

Baddeley, A. D., & Hitch, G. (1974). Working memory. In G. A. Bower (Ed.), *The psychology of learning and motivation* (Vol. 18, pp. 47–89). New York, NY: Academic Press.

Baddeley, A. D., Papagno, C., & Vallar, C. (1988). When long-term learning depends on short-term storage. *Journal of Memory and Language, 27,* 586–595.

Barak, O., Vakil, E., & Levy, D. A. (2013). Environmental context effects on episodic memory are dependent on retrieval mode and modulated by neuropsychological status. *Quarterly Journal of Experimental Psychology, 66*(10), 2008–2022.

Beauregard, M., Gold, D., Evans, A. C., & Chertkow, H. (1998). A role for the hippocampal formation in implicit memory: A 3-D PET study. *NeuroReport, 9,* 1867–1873.

Behnken, A., Schöning, S., Gerß, J., Konrad, C., de Jong-Meyer, R., Zwanzger, P., & Arolt, V. (2010). Persistent non-verbal memory impairment in remitted major depression—Caused by encoding deficits? *Journal of Affective Disorders, 122*(1), 144–148.

Benedict, R. H. B., Schretlen, D., Groninger, L., & Brandt, J. (1998). Hopkins Verbal Learning Test–Revised: Normative data and analysis of inter-form and test-retest reliability. *Clinical Neuropsychologist, 12,* 43–55.

Biederman, I., & Cooper, E. E. (1991). Priming contour-deleted images: Evidence for intermediate representations in visual object recognition. *Cognitive Psychology, 23,* 393–419.

Blachstein, H., Greenstein, Y., & Vakil, E. (2012). Aging and temporal order memory: A comparison of direct and indirect measures. *Journal of Clinical and Experimental Neuropsychology, 34*(1), 107–112.

Brickman, A. M., Siedlecki, K. L., Muraskin, J., Manly, J. J., Luchsinger, J. A., Yeung, L. K., . . . Stern, Y. (2011). White matter hyperintensities and cognition: Testing the reserve hypothesis. *Neurobiology of Aging, 32*(9), 1588–1598.

Brooks, D. N. (1975). Long-term and short-term memory in head injured patients. *Cortex, 11,* 329–340.

Brown, J. A. (1958). Some tests of the decay theory of immediate memory. *Quarterly Journal of Experimental Psychology, 10,* 12–21.

Cave, C. B., & Squire, L. S. (1992). Intact and long-lasting repetition priming in amnesia. *Journal of Experimental Psychology: Learning, Memory, and Cognition, 18,* 509–520.

Christoforou, C., Constantinidou, F., Shoshilou, P., & Simos, P. G. (2013). Single-trial linear correlation analysis: Application to characterization of stimulus modality effects. *Frontiers in Computational Neuroscience, 7,* 15.

Cicerone, K. D., Dahlberg, C., Malec, J. F., Langenbahn, D. M., Felicetti, T., Kneipp, S., . . . Catanese, J. (2005). Evidence-based cognitive rehabilitation: Updated review of the literature from 1998 through 2002.

Archives of Physical Medicine and Rehabilitation, 86, 1681–1692.

Cicerone, K. D., Goldin, Y., Ganci, K., Rosenbaum, A., Wethe, J. V., Langenbahn, D. M., . . . Trexler, L. (2019). Evidence-based cognitive rehabilitation: Systematic review of the literature from 2009 through 2014. *Archives of Physical Medicine and Rehabilitation.*

Cicerone, K. D., Langenbahn, D. M., Braden, C., Malec, J. F., Kalmar, K., Fraas, M., . . . Ashman, T. (2011). Evidence-based cognitive rehabilitation: Updated review of the literature from 2003 through 2008. *Archives of Physical Medicine and Rehabilitation, 92*(4), 519–530.

Coelho, C. A., DeRuyter, F., & Stein, M. (1996). Treatment efficacy: Cognitive communicative disorders resulting from traumatic brain injury in adults. *Journal of Speech and Hearing Research, 39,* 5–17.

Colfesh, G. J. H., & Conway, A. R. A. (2007). Individual differences in working memory capacity and divided attention in dichotic listening. *Psychonomic Bulletin and Review, 14,* 699–703.

Constantinidou, F. (1998). Active memory strategies following moderate-to-severe head injury: In search of important components. *Hearsay, 12*(1), 20–26.

Constantinidou, F. (1999). The effects of stimulus modality on interference and recognition performance following brain injury. *Journal of Medical Speech-Language Pathology, 7*(4), 283–295.

Constantinidou, F., & Baker, S. (2002). Stimulus modality and verbal learning performance in normal aging. *Brain and Language, 82*(3), 296–311.

Constantinidou, F., Christodoulou, M., & Prokopiou, J. (2012). The effects of age and education on executive functioning and oral naming performance in Greek Cypriot adults: The neurocognitive study for the aging. *Folia Phoniatrica et Logopaedica, 64*(4), 187–198.

Constantinidou, F., Danos, M. A., Nelson, D., & Baker, S. (2011). Effects of modality presentation on working memory in school-age children: Evidence for the pictorial superiority hypothesis. *Child Neuropsychology, 17*(2), 173–196.

Constantinidou, F., & Ioannou, M. (2008). The effects of age and language on paragraph recall performance: Findings from a preliminary cross-sectional study. *Psychologia, 15,* 342–361.

Constantinidou, F., & Kennedy, M. (2017). Traumatic brain injury in adults. In P. Coppens & I. Papathanasiou (Eds.), *Aphasia and related neurogenic communication disorders* (2nd ed., pp. 421–450), Burlington, MA: Jones & Bartlett Learning.

Constantinidou, F., & Kreimer, L. T. (2004). Feature description and categorization of common objects after traumatic brain injury: The effects of a multi-trial paradigm. *Brain and Language, 89*(1), 216–225.

Constantinidou, F., & Neils, J. (1995). Stimulus modality and verbal learning in moderate to severe closed head injury. *Journal of Head Trauma Rehabilitation, 10,* 90–100.

Constantinidou, F., Neils, J., Bouman, D., Lee, L., & Shuren, J. (1996). Pictorial superiority during verbal learning tasks in moderate to severe closed head injury: Additional evidence. *Journal of General Psychology, 123*(3), 173–184.

Constantinidou, F., & Nikou, M (2014, July). *Categorization training for persons with mild cognitive impairment: A feasibility study.* Oral presentation at the 11th Neuropsychological Rehabilitation Satellite Meeting, Limassol, Cyprus.

Constantinidou, F., & Prechel, D. (1996). *Is the initial memory span recovered following moderate to severe brain injury?* Unpublished manuscript, Miami University, Oxford, OH.

Constantinidou, F., & Thomas, R. D. (2017). Principles of cognitive rehabilitation in TBI: An integrative neuroscience approach. In M. Ashley & D. Hovda (Eds.), *Traumatic brain injury: Rehabilitation, treatment, and case management* (4th ed., pp. 513–540). Boca Raton, FL: Taylor & Francis: CRC Press.

Constantinidou, F., Thomas, R. D., & Best, P. (2004). Principles of cognitive rehabilitation: An integrative approach. In M. J. Ashley (Ed.), *Traumatic brain injury rehabilitation: Rehabilitative treatment and case management* (2nd ed., pp. 337–366). Boca Raton, FL: CRC Press.

Constantinidou, F., Thomas, R. D., & Robinson, L. (2008). Benefits of categorization training in patients with traumatic brain injury during post–acute rehabilitation: Additional evidence from a randomized controlled trial. *Journal of Head Trauma Rehabilitation, 23*(5), 312–328.

Constantinidou, F., Thomas, R. D., Scharp, V. L., Laske, K. M., Hammerly, M. D., & Guitonde, S. (2005). Effects of categorization training in patients with TBI during post acute rehabilitation: Preliminary findings. *Journal of Head Trauma Rehabilitation, 20*(2), 143–157.

Conway, A. R. A., Kane, M. J., Bunting, M. F., Hambrick, D. Z., Wilhelm, O., & Engle, R. W. (2005). Working memory span tasks: A methodological review and user's guide. *Psychonomic Bulletin and Review, 12*, 769–786.

Craik, F. I. M., & Lockhart, R. S. (1972). Levels of processing: A framework for memory research. *Journal of Verbal Learning and Verbal Behavior, 11*, 671–684.

Crosson, B., & Buenning, W. (1984). An individualized memory retraining program after closed-head injury: A single-case study. *Journal of Clinical Neuropsychology, 6*(3), 287–301.

Crosson, B., Cooper, P. V., Lincoln, R. K., Bauer, R. M., & Velozo, C. A. (1993). Relationship between verbal memory and language performance after blunt head injury. *Clinical Neuropsychologist, 7*(3), 250–267.

Demetriadou, M., Michaelides, M., Bateman, A., & Constantinidou, F. (2018). Measurement of everyday dysexecutive symptoms in normal aging with the Greek version of the Dysexecutive Questionnaire–Revised. *Neuropsychological Rehabilitation.* Advance online publication.

Doherty, J. M., & Logie, R. H. (2016). Resource-sharing in multiple-component working memory. *Memory & Cognition, 44*(8), 1157–1167.

Ewert, J., Levin, H. S., Watson, M. G., & Kalisky, Z. (1989). Procedural memory during posttraumatic amnesia in survivors of severe closed head injury. *Archives of Neurology, 46*, 911–916.

Farah, M. J. (1988). Is visual imagery really visual? Overlooked evidence from neuropsychology. *Psychological Review, 95*, 307–317.

Farah, M. J. (1990). *Visual agnosia: Disorders of object recognition and what they tell us.* Cambridge, MA: MIT Press.

Fodor, J. A. (1983). *The modularity of mind.* Cambridge, MA: MIT Press.

Folstein, M. F., Folstein, S. E., & McHugh, P. R. (1975). "Mini-mental status": A practical method for grading the cognitive state of patients for the clinician. *Journal of Psychiatric Research, 12*(3), 189–198.

Fountoulakis, K. N., Tsolaki, M., Chantzi, H., & Kazis, A. (2000). Mini Mental State Examination (MMSE): A validation study in Greece. *American Journal of Alzheimer's Disease and Other Dementias, 15*, 342–345.

Fountoulakis, K. N., Tsolaki, M., Iacovides, A., Yesavage, J., O'Hara, R., Kazis, A., & Ierodiakonou, C. (1999). The validation of the short form of Geriatric Depression Scale (GDS) in Greece. *Aging Clinical and Experimental Research, 11*, 367–372.

Gabrieli, J. D. E., Fleischman, D. A., Keane, M. M., Reminger, S. L., & Morel, F. (1995). Double dissociation between memory systems underlying explicit and implicit memory in the human brain. *Psychological Science, 6*, 76–82.

Gathercole, S., & Baddeley, A. D. (1990). Phonological memory deficits in language-disordered children: Is there a causal connection? *Journal of Memory and Language, 29*, 336–360.

Gazzaniga, M. S., Ivry, R. B., & Mangun, G. R. (1998). *Cognitive neuroscience: The biology of the mind*. New York, NY: W. W. Norton.

Ginieri-Coccossis, M., Triantafillou, E., Tomaras, V., Soldatos, C., Mavreas, V., & Christodoulou, G. (2011). Psychometric properties of WHOQOL-BREF in clinical and health Greek populations: Incorporating new culture-relevant items. *Psychiatrike*, 23(2), 130–142.

Giogkaraki, E., Michaelides, M., & Constantinidou, F. (2013). The role of cognitive reserve in cognitive aging: Results from the Neurocognitive Study on Aging. *Journal of Clinical and Experimental Neuropsychology, 35*(10), 1024–1035.

Gioia, G. A., Isquith, P. K., Guy, S. C., & Kenworthy, L. (2000). Test review behavior rating inventory of executive function. *Child Neuropsychology, 6*(3), 235–238.

Glisky, E. L. (1992). Computer-assisted instruction for patients with traumatic brain injury: Teaching of domain-specific knowledge. *Journal of Head Trauma Rehabilitation, 7*(3), 1–12.

Goldstein, F. C., Levin, H. S., Boake, C., & Lohrey, J. H. (1990). Facilitation of memory performance through induced semantic processing in survivors of severe closed-head injury. *Journal of Clinical and Experimental Neuropsychology, 12*(2), 286–300.

Gonen-Yaacovi, G., & Burgess, P. (2012). Prospective memory: The future for future intentions. *Psychologica Belgica, 52*, 2–3.

Graf, P., & Mandler, G. (1984). Activation makes words more accessible, but not necessarily more retrievable. *Journal of Verbal Learning and Verbal Behavior, 23*, 553–568.

Graf, P., Mandler, G., & Haden, P. (1982). Simulating amnesic symptoms in normal subjects. *Science, 218*, 1243–1244.

Graf, P., & Ryan, L. (1990). Transfer-appropriate processing for implicit and explicit memory. *Journal of Experimental Psychology: Learning, Memory, and Cognition, 16*, 978–992.

Jacoby, L. L., & Dallas, M. (1981). On the relationship between autobiographical memory and perceptual learning. *Journal of Experimental Psychology: General, 110*, 306–340.

Jacoby, L. L., & Hayman, C. A. G. (1987). Specific visual transfer in word identification. *Journal of Experimental Psychology: Learning, Memory and Cognition, 13*, 456–463.

Jacoby, L. L., & Witherspoon, D. (1982). Remembering without awareness. *Canadian Journal of Psychology, 32*, 300–324.

Jonides, J., Smith, E. E., Koeppe, R. A., Awh, E., Minoshima, S., & Mintun, M. A. (1993). Spatial working memory in humans as revealed by PET. *Nature, 363*, 623–625.

Kane, M. J., & Engle, R. W. (2002). The role of prefrontal cortex in working-memory capacity, executive attention, and general fluid intelligence: An individual-differences perspective. *Psychonomic Bulletin and Review, 9*, 637–671.

Kane, M. J., & Engle, R. W. (2003). Working-memory capacity and the control of attention: The contributions of goal neglect, response competition, and task set to Stroop interference. *Journal of Experimental Psychology: General, 132*, 47–70.

Kane, M. J., Hambrick, D. Z., Tuholski, S. W., Wilhelm, O., Payne, T. W., & Engle, R. W. (2004). The generality of working memory capacity: A latent variable approach to verbal and visuospatial memory span and reasoning. *Journal of Experimental Psychology: General, 133*, 189–217.

Kennedy, M. R., & Coelho, C. (2005). Self-regulation after traumatic brain injury: A framework for intervention of memory and problem solving. *Strategies, Seminars in Speech and Language, 26*(4) 242–255.

Kennedy, M. R., & Krause, M. O. (2011). Self-regulated learning in a dynamic coaching model for supporting college students with traumatic brain injury: Two case reports. *Journal of Head Trauma Rehabilitation, 26*(3), 212–223.

Kennedy, M. R., Wozniak, J. R., Muetzel, R. L., Mueller, B. A., Chiou, H. H., Pantekoek, K., & Lim, K. O. (2009). White matter and neurocognitive changes in adults with chronic traumatic brain injury. *Journal of the International Neuropsychological Society, 15*(1), 130–136.

Knollman-Porter, K., Constantinidou, F., Beardslee, J., & Dailey, S. (2019). Multidisciplinary management of collegiate sports-related concussions. *Seminars in Speech & Language, 40*(1), 3–12.

Koenig, P., Smith, E. E., Troiani, V., Anderson, C., Moore, M., & Grossman, M. (2008). Medial temporal lobe involvement in an implicit memory task: Evidence of collaborating implicit and explicit memory systems from fMRI and Alzheimer's disease. *Cerebral Cortex, 18*(12), 2831–2843.

Konstantinou, N., Constantinidou, F., & Kanai, R. (2017). Discrete capacity limits and neuroanatomical correlates of visual short-term memory for objects and spatial locations. *Human Brain Mapping, 38*(2), 767–778.

Konstantinou, N., Pettemeridou, E., Seimenis, I., Eracleous, E., Papacostas, S. S., Papanicolaou, A. C., & Constantinidou, F. (2016). Assessing the relationship between neurocognitive performance and brain volume in chronic moderate-severe traumatic brain injury. *Frontiers in Neurology, 7*, 29.

Konstantinou, N., Pettemeridou, E., Stamatakis, E. A., Seimenis, I., & Constantinidou, F. (2019). Altered resting functional connectivity is related to cognitive outcome in males with moderate-severe TBI. *Frontiers in Neurology, 9*, 1163.

Kosmidis, M. C., Vlahou, C. H., Panagiotaki, P., & Kiosseoglou, G. (2004). The verbal fluency task in the Greek population: Normative data and clustering and switching strategies. *Journal of the International Neuropsychology Society, 10*, 164–172.

Kosslyn, S. M., & Koenig, O. (1992). *Wet mind: The new cognitive neuroscience.* New York, NY: Free Press.

Kyllonen, P. C., & Christal, R. E. (1990). Reasoning ability is (little more than) working-memory capacity. *Intelligence, 14*, 389–433.

Levi, Y., Rassovsky, Y., Agranov, E., Sela-Kaufman, M., & Vakil, E. (2013). Cognitive reserve components as expressed in traumatic brain injury. *Journal of the International Neuropsychological Society, 19*(6), 664–671.

Levin, H. S. (1989). Memory deficit after closed-head injury. *Journal of Experimental Psychology, 12*(1), 95–103.

Levin, H. S., O'Donnell, V. M., & Grossman, R. G. (1979). The Galveston Orientation and Amnesia Test: A practical scale to assess cognition after head injury. *Journal of Nervous and Mental Disease, 167*, 675–684.

Lezak, M. D. (1983). *Neuropsychological assessment* (2nd ed.). New York, NY: Oxford University Press.

Lezak, M. D. (1995). *Neuropsychological assessment* (3rd ed.). New York, NY: Oxford University Press.

Lezak, M. D., Howieson, D. B., & Loring, D. W. (2004). *Neuropsychological assessment* (4th ed.). Oxford, UK: Oxford University Press.

Malec, J. F. (1996). Cognitive rehabilitation. In R. W. Evans (Ed.), *Neurology and trauma* (pp. 231–248). Philadelphia, PA: W. B. Saunders.

Manns, J. R., Hopkins, R. O., & Squire, L. (2003). Semantic memory and the human hippocampus. *Neuron, 38*, 127–133.

Markowitsch, H. J. (1995). Anatomical basis of memory disorders. In M. S. Gazzaniga (Ed.), *The cognitive neurosciences* (pp. 765–779). Cambridge, MA: MIT Press.

McDonald, A., Haslam, C., Yates, P., Gurr, B., Leeder, G., & Sayers, A. (2011). Google calendar: A new memory aid to compensate for prospective memory deficits following acquired brain injury. *Neuropsychological Rehabilitation, 21*(6), 784–807.

McGaugh, J. L. (2000). Memory: A century of consolidation. *Science, 287*, 248–251.

Metzler-Baddeley, C., Hunt, S., Jones, D. K., Leemans, A., Aggleton, J. P., & O'Sullivan, M. J. (2012). Temporal association tracts and the breakdown of episodic memory in mild cognitive impairment. *Neurology, 79*(23), 2233–2240.

Milner, B. (1966). Amnesia following operation on the temporal lobes. In C. W. M. Whitty & O. L. Zangwill (Eds.), *Amnesia* (pp. 109–133). London, UK: Butterworth.

Millis, S. R., & Ricker, J. H. (1994). Verbal learning patterns in moderate and severe traumatic brain injury. *Journal of Clinical and Experimental Neuropsychology, 16*, 498–507.

Myers, J. E., & Meyers, K. R. (1995). *Rey Complex Figure Test and Recognition Trial.* Odessa, FL: Psychological Assessment Resources.

Nasreddine, Z. S., Phillips, N. A., Bédirian, V., Charbonneau, S., Whitehead, V., Collin, I., & Chertkow, H. (2005). The Montreal Cognitive Assessment, MoCA: A brief screening tool for mild cognitive impairment. *Journal of the American Geriatrics Society, 53*(4), 695–699.

Nyberg, L., Cabeza, R., & Tulving, E. (1996). PET studies of encoding and retrieval: The HERA model. *Psychonomic Bulletin and Review, 3*, 135–148.

O'Donnell, J. P., Radtke, R. C., Leicht, D. J., & Caesar, R. (1988). Encoding and retrieval processes in learning-disabled, head-injured, and nondisabled young adults. *Journal of General Psychology, 115*, 335–368.

Paivio, A. (1971). *Imagery and verbal processes.* New York, NY: Holt, Rinehart, & Winston.

Paivio, A. (1976). Imagery in recall and recognition. In J. Brown (Ed.), *Recall and recognition.* New York, NY: John Wiley & Sons.

Papagno, C., Valentine, T., & Baddeley, A. D. (1991). Phonological short-term memory and foreign language vocabulary learning. *Journal of Memory and Language, 30*, 331–347.

Papanicolaou, A. (2006). *The amnesias: A clinical textbook of memory disorders.* New York, NY: Oxford University Press.

Parente, R., & Anderson-Parente, J. K. (1989). Retraining memory: Theory and application. *Journal of Head Trauma Rehabilitation, 4*(3), 55–65.

Peterson, L. R., & Peterson, M. J. (1959). Short-term retention of individual verbal items. *Journal of Experimental Psychology, 58*, 193–198.

Pettemeridou, E., & Constantinidou, F. (2018). Brain volume predicts self-awareness and quality of life in chronic moderate-severe TBI. *Archives of Physical Medicine and Rehabilitation, 99*(11), e156–e157.

Randolph, C., Tierney, M. C., Mohr, E., & Chase, T. N. (1998). The Repeatable Battery for the Assessment of Neuropsychological Status (RBANS): Preliminary clinical validity. *Journal of Clinical and Experimental Neuropsychology, 20*(3), 310–319.

Roediger, H. L., & Blaxton, T. A. (1987). Retrieval modes produce dissociations in memory for surface information. In D. S. Gorfein & R. R. Hoffman (Eds.), *The Ebbinghous Centennial Conference* (pp. 349–379). Hillsdale, NJ: Erlbaum.

Ross-Swain, D. (1996). *Ross Information Processing Assessment, 2nd ed. (RIPA-2).* Austin, TX: Pro-Ed.

Royle, J., & Lincoln, N. B. (2008). The Everyday Memory Questionnaire–Revised: Development of a 13-item scale. *Disability and Rehabilitation, 30*(2), 114–121.

Salthouse, T. A. (2005). Relations between cognitive abilities and measures of executive functioning. *Neuropsychology, 19*, 532–545.

Sanders, A., Nakase-Thomson, R., Constantinidou, F., Wertheimer, J., & Paul, D. (2007). Memory assessment on an interdisciplinary rehabilitation team: A theoretically based framework. *American Journal of Speech-Language Pathology, 16*, 316–330.

Schacter, D. L. (1985). Priming of old and new knowledge in amnesic patients and normal subjects. *Annals of the New York Academy of Sciences, 444*, 44–53.

Schacter, D. L. (1987). Implicit memory: History and current status. *Journal of Experi-*

mental Psychology: Learning, Memory and Cognition, 13, 501–518.

Schacter, D. L. (1990). Perceptual representation systems and implicit memory: Toward a resolution of the multiple memory systems debate. In A. Diamond (Ed.), *Development and neural bases of higher cognitive functions* (pp. 543–571). New York, NY: New York Academy of Sciences.

Schacter, D. L. (1992). Understanding implicit memory: A cognitive neuroscience approach. *American Psychologist, 47,* 559–569.

Schacter, D. L., & Tulving, E. (1994). *Memory systems.* Cambridge, MA: MIT Press.

Shimamura, A. P., & Squire, L. R. (1984). Paired-associate learning and priming effects in Amnesia—A neuropsychological study. *Journal of Experimental Psychology–General, 113,* 556–570.

Simblett, S. K., Ring, H., & Bateman, A. (2017). The Dysexecutive Questionnaire Revised (DEX-R): An extended measure of everyday dysexecutive problems after acquired brain injury. *Neuropsychological Rehabilitation, 27*(8), 1124–1141.

Simos, P. G., Kasselimis, D., & Mouzaki, A. (2011). Age, gender, and education effects on vocabulary measures in Greek. *Aphasiology, 25,* 475–491.

Simos, P., Sideridis, G. D., Kasselimis, D., & Mouzaki, A. (2013). Reading fluency estimates of current intellectual function: Demographic factors and effects of type of stimuli. *Journal of the International Neuropsychological Society, 19,* 1–7.

Singh-Manoux, A., Marmot, M. G., Glymour, M., Sabia, S., Kivimäki, M., & Dugravot, A. (2011). Does cognitive reserve shape cognitive decline? *Annals of Neurology, 70*(2), 296–304.

Smith, A. (1982). *Symbol Digit Modalities Test (SDMT). Manual (Revised).* Los Angeles, CA: Western Psychological Services.

Smith, N. C., Urgolites, J. Z., Hopkins, O. R., & Squire, R. L. (2014). Comparison of explicit and incidental learning strategies in memory-impaired patients. *PNAS, 111,* 475–479.

Sohlberg, M. M., Ehlhardt, L., & Kennedy, M. (2005). Instructional techniques in cognitive rehabilitation: A preliminary report. *Seminars in Speech and Language, 26*(4), 268–279.

Sohlberg, M. M., & Mateer, C. A. (1989). *Introduction to cognitive rehabilitation.* New York, NY: Guilford Press.

Sohlberg, M. M., & Mateer, C. A. (2001). *Cognitive rehabilitation: An integrative neuropsychological approach.* New York, NY: Guilford Press.

Spikman, J. M., Berg, I. J., & Deelman, B. G. (1995). Spared recognition capacity in elderly and closed-head injury subjects with clinical memory deficits. *Journal of Clinical and Experimental Neuropsychology, 17,* 29–34.

Squire, L. R. (1987). *Memory and brain.* New York, NY: Oxford University Press.

Squire, L. R. (1992). Memory and the hippocampus: A synthesis from findings with rats, monkeys, and humans. *Psychological Review, 99,* 195–231.

Squire, L. R., & Knowlton, B. J. (1995). Learning about categories in the absence of memory. *Proceedings of the National Academy of Sciences of the United States of America, 92,* 12470–12474.

Squire, L. R., & Zola-Morgan, S. (1991). The medial temporal lobe memory system. *Science, 253,* 1380–1386.

Stuss, D. T. (2011). Functions of the frontal lobes: Relation to executive functions. *Journal of the International Neuropsychological Society, 17*(5), 759–765.

Thompson, R. F., & Krupa, D. J. (1994). Organization of memory traces in the mammalian brain. *Annual Review of Neuroscience, 17,* 519–550.

Tulving, E. (1966). Subjective organization and effects of repetition in multi-trial free-recall learning. *Journal of Verbal Learning and Verbal Behavior, 5,* 193–197.

Tulving, E., Hayman, C. A. G., & MacDonald, C. A. (1991). Long-lasting perceptual priming and semantic learning in amnesia: A case experiment. *Journal of Experi-*

mental Psychology: Learning, Memory, and Cognition, 17, 595–617.

Tulving, E., Schacter, D. L., & Stark, H. A. (1982). Priming effects in word-fragment completion are independent of recognition memory. *Journal of Experimental Psychology: Learning, Memory, and Cognition, 8,* 352–373.

Unsworth, N., & Engle, R. W. (2007). On the division of short-term and working memory: An examination of simple and complex span and their relations to higher order abilities. *Psychological Bulletin, 133,* 1038–1066.

Vakil, E. (2012). Neuropsychological assessment: Principles, rationale, and challenges. *Journal of Clinical and Experimental Neuropsychology, 34*(2), 135–150.

Vargha-Khadem, F., Gadian, D. G., Watkins, K. E., Connelly, A., Van Paesschen, W., & Mishkin, M. (1997). Differential effects of early hippocampal pathology on episodic and semantic memory. *Science, 277,* 376–380.

Voss, J. L., Galvan, A., & Gonsalves, B. D. (2011). Cortical regions recruited for complex active-learning strategies and action planning exhibit rapid reactivation during memory retrieval. *Neuropsychologia, 49*(14), 3956–3966.

Waugh, N. C., & Norman, D. A. (1965). Primary memory. *Psychological Review, 72,* 89–104.

Wechsler, D. (1997). *Wechsler Memory Scale®– Third edition (WMS-III)* (3rd ed.). San Antonio, TX: Harcourt Assessment.

Wilson, B. A. (1987). *Rehabilitation of memory.* London, UK: Guilford.

Wilson, B. A., Emslie, H. C., Quirk, K., & Evans, J. J. (2013). Reducing everyday memory and planning problems by means of a paging system. In B. A. Wilson (Ed.), *The assessment, evaluation and rehabilitation of everyday memory problems: Selected papers of Barbara A. Wilson* (pp. 96–107). Hove, UK: Psychology Press.

World Health Organization. (2001). *International classification of functioning, disability and health.* Geneva, Switzerland: Author.

Yubero, R., Gil, P., Paul, N., & Maestú, F. (2011). Influence of memory strategies on memory test performance: A study in healthy and pathological aging. *Aging, Neuropsychology, and Cognition, 18,* 497–515.

Zalonis, I., Kararizou, E., Triantafyllou, N. I., Kapaki, E., Papageorgiou, S., Sgouropoulos, P., & Vassilopoulos, D. (2008). A normative study of the Trail Making Test A and B in Greek adults. *Clinical Neuropsychologist, 22*(5), 842–850.

3

Executive Functions: Theory, Assessment, and Treatment

Mary H. Purdy

Introduction

Executive function is a complex neuropsychological construct that overlaps with, yet is distinct from, attention and memory as described in the previous chapters. Though specific definitions vary among researchers, it is generally agreed that executive functions play a critical role in goal-directed and purposeful behavior and assist in planning, organizing, initiating, and adapting effectively and flexibly as the situation demands (Lezak, Howieson, Bigler, & Tranel, 2012). Consider the following example. As the speech-language pathologist on the brain injury unit of the rehabilitation hospital, you are about to begin a 45-minute talk on communication disorders following traumatic brain injury for the Family Education Series. The program director pulls you aside right before you begin and says you have 30 minutes. You immediately determine the change in expectations (15 minutes less time), plan your strategy (cut down on several

sections, or eliminate an entire section), then select and execute your strategy. As you move through your talk, you simultaneously monitor the time and adjust the content as needed.

When executive functioning is disrupted, everyday activities become challenging. This is demonstrated through the following cases (all names have been changed): Lucinda, a 40-year-old artist and graphic designer, cannot complete projects and meet deadlines since she sustained a traumatic brain injury in a car accident; Brian, a 56-year-old self-employed salesman who also suffered a traumatic brain injury, cannot schedule appointments or plan travel routes efficiently, or adequately describe his products to his customers; Jennie, a 43-year-old mother of three children reports problems keeping track of her children's schedules and getting dinner ready on time after sustaining a right hemisphere hemorrhage. All three individuals demonstrated preservation of basic cognitive skills yet could not regulate these skills to carry out more complex tasks. Because executive functions are required in virtually all daily life activities, it is critical for speech-language pathologists to understand the nature of executive functions and their relation to cognitive-communicative behavior.

This chapter reviews the theoretical basis of executive functioning, its neuroanatomic correlates, its impact on communication, and issues related to assessment and management. The case of Brian mentioned earlier will be embedded throughout the chapter to illustrate specific concepts.

Defining Executive Functions

Many definitions of executive function exist and the components and nomenclature vary, often depending on the specific field of study (e.g., cognitive psychology, educational psychology, neuropsychology). Miyake, Emerson, and Friedman (2000) identified some of the issues to be considered when reviewing the executive function literature. First, concepts among the different models may overlap. Second, researchers may use the same terms to refer to conceptually different functions or use different terms to refer to the same function. Finally, there is a lack of agreement among researchers on the issue of whether executive functions should be considered unitary (a single, general construct with multiple interrelated subprocesses) or nonunitary (a collection of dissociable or independent processes).

Luria (1966) introduced the concept of executive functions after systematically observing problem-solving behavior in individuals who sustained frontal lobe damage. He documented that these individuals typically lacked a specific plan, did not acknowledge constraints of a problem, and were impulsive, a phenomenon he described as an impairment in self-regulation. Luria concluded that problem-solving behavior was dependent on a number of overarching skills, or executive functions, including anticipation (setting realistic expectations, understanding consequences), planning (organization), execution (flexibility, maintaining set), and self-monitoring (emotional control, error recognition). Many models of executive functions have been developed over the years. Stuss and Benson (1986) and Lezak (1995) developed models of executive function that are closely related to Luria's, although the nomenclature is different. Stuss and Benson identified initiation of behavior, planning, sequencing, and organization as primary components of executive functioning. Stuss and Alexander (2000) later placed executive functions in the middle of a hierarchical framework. According to this model, executive functions receive input from lower-level, or basic processes (e.g., attention, memory, language, perception), as well as higher-level metacognitive processes. Lezak proposed a four-component executive function model: volition (including self-awareness and self-monitoring), planning, purposive action, and effective performance.

Sohlberg and Mateer (2001) conceptualized a clinical model of executive functions involving six components including: (1) initiation and drive (activation or starting of a cognitive system), (2) response inhibition (stopping automatic or prepotent response tendencies), (3) task persistence (maintaining a behavior until task completion), (4) organization (organizing and sequencing of information), (5) generative thinking (creating multiple solutions to a problem and thinking in a flexible manner), and (6) awareness (monitoring and modifying one's own behavior). Keil and Kaszniak (2002) categorized the cognitive processes of executive functions into four domains: (1) planning, scheduling, strategy use, and rule adherence; (2) generation, fluency, and initiation; (3) shifting and suppression; and (4) concept formation and abstract reasoning. Table 3–1 provides a comparison of these models.

Other fields (e.g., developmental, educational, and cognitive psychology) view executive functions as part of the metacognitive system. Metacognition, or thinking about thinking, includes self-awareness (or metacognitive beliefs), self-monitoring, and self-control of cognition while performing an activity (Kennedy & Coelho, 2005). Metacognitive beliefs are created and updated by new experiences and situations; thus, there is a dynamic relationship between metacognitive beliefs and ongoing, daily routines and new experiences. Because everyday routines are automatic, they do not require explicit self-monitoring. However, in order to successfully perform a task that is novel, one must be able to detect what is different, monitor performance, make a strategy decision, and execute the strategy (Kennedy & Coelho, 2005).

Although definitions and specific components of executive functioning vary, there is agreement that the primary cognitive processes comprising executive functions include initiation, prob-

Table 3–1. A Comparison of Executive Function Theories

Luria (1966)	Stuss and Benson (1986)	Lezak (1995)	Sohlberg and Mateer (2001)	Keil and Kaszniak (2002)
Anticipation	Initiation	Volition	Initiation and drive	Planning, scheduling, strategy use, rule adherence
Planning	Planning	Planning	Response inhibition	Generation, fluency, initiation
Execution	Sequencing	Purposive action	Task persistence	Shifting and suppression
Self-monitoring	Organization	Effective performance	Organization	Concept formation and abstract reasoning
			Generative thinking	
			Awareness	

lem solving, mental flexibility, planning, judgment, inhibition, abstract reasoning, and self-regulation and metacognition (Kennedy et al. 2008; Lezak et al., 2012; Sohlberg & Mateer, 2001; Stuss, 1991). It is important to realize that these components are not mutually exclusive; rather, they interact and overlap. Table 3–2 provides definitions and examples of these components.

Cognitive Processing and Regulation: Integration of Attention, Memory, and Working Memory

Embedded within executive function models are the concepts of cognitive processing and regulation of cognitive resources (Goldstein, Naglieri, Princiotta, & Otero, 2014). Every task we perform requires activating a number of specific cognitive processes, and each cognitive process takes up some of the resources (e.g., attention) we have available to perform the task. These cognitive processes may be carried out automatically or with conscious control. Automatic processing is effortless and rapid and conducted unconsciously due to permanent connections that are developed over repeated practice. On the other hand, controlled processing is slow, effortful, and completely conscious. Actions are performed by temporarily activating and attending to a sequence of steps under conscious control of the individual (Goldstein et al., 2014). Controlled processing may become automatic with repeated practice (Schneider & Chein, 2003). The more automatic a task is, the fewer resources it requires, thereby leaving more resources available for other tasks. For example, when you are driving to school, you can most likely simultaneously listen to the radio and have a conversation without really thinking of where you are going since you have driven the route numerous times. However, if you are driving in a new city and trying to follow directions to a place you have never been before, the radio may need to be turned off and the conversation ceased so you can devote your attention to where you are going.

Brain injury results in diminished recruitment of anterior brain structures required for attention (Shah et al., 2017), essentially reducing the pool of resources available for cognitive processing. In addition, the amount of resources required to do a previously automatic activity increases, leaving even fewer resources available for processing other information, and performance suffers. Therefore, driving to a familiar place may now take up all the person's resources and there are none left to devote to the radio or conversation. Figure 3–1 illustrates this concept of resource allocation.

Switching your attention from the conversation to your driving is an example of how automatic responses may be overwritten or inhibited via cognitive control. Our ability to consciously control our actions allows us to adapt from situation to situation depending upon the specific goal. Posner and Snyder (1975) first introduced the concept of cognitive control. They proposed there is a separate executive branch of the attentional system that directs attention to selected aspects of the environment. Shallice (2002) also suggested that attention can be regulated and proposed a supervisory attentional

Table 3–2. Executive Function Components and Related Problems

Component	Example of Component Deficit
Initiation is the action of beginning a goal-directed task (Lezak et al., 2012).	Susan has an appointment at 3:00. It's now 2:30 and she knows she should leave but she can't seem to get going.
Problem solving involves identifying the problem, generating potential solutions, choosing a solution, and evaluating the outcome (Cantor et al., 2014).	Jon was invited away for the weekend. He had an appointment scheduled for the Saturday he'd be away. He did not attempt to reschedule the appointment and had to pay a "no show" fee.
Mental flexibility (cognitive flexibility, set-shifting) is the ability to change a course of action or thought based on the shifting demands of a situation (Lezak et al., 2012).	Max tried to turn on the TV with the remote but the TV did not turn on. He kept pointing the remote at the screen and pressing buttons, becoming increasingly agitated when the TV failed to turn on. He attempted the same solution over and over again despite its ineffectiveness.
Planning involves setting objectives and determining a course of action for achieving those actions (Lezak et al., 2012).	Jennie wanted to have chicken, broccoli, and potatoes for dinner. She started cooking them all at same time. She did not plan for different cooking times, and thus the broccoli burned and the chicken was dry.
Judgment involves being able to discern the potentially good and harmful aspects of a situation, and act in a way that makes sense (Hinrichs et al., 2016).	Lucinda has insulin-dependent diabetes and is on a restricted carbohydrate diet. She went out to dinner with friends and ordered pasta, garlic bread, and ice cream.
Inhibition is the ability to select appropriate responses and suppress unwanted actions (Bender et al., 2016).	Mary met her friend for lunch and told her that her new haircut makes her look like a poodle.
Reasoning is the process of forming conclusions, judgments, or inferences from facts or premises (Higginson, Thompson, Benjamin, & Rosales, 2017).	Jerome wants to ask Tasha to the movies. Tasha works on Fridays until 7:30 p.m. Jerome asked Tasha to go with him to a 7:15 movie on Friday.
Self-regulation involves the regulation of one's thoughts, emotional responses, actions, and motivations in order to behave in an expected way for a given situation (Kennedy & Coelho, 2005).	Just as he was being picked up to go to the movie, Juan received a phone call informing him he did not get a job he wanted. Juan hung up the phone and began to curse. He continued with his rantings at the theater and was asked to leave.

continues

Table 3–2. *continued*

Component	Example of Component Deficit
Metacognition is awareness and understanding of one's own thoughts and skills and how you learn information (Kennedy & Coelho, 2005).	George regularly attended class but didn't study for his exam, and he failed. His next exam was coming up. He figured that because he went to every class since the last exam, he would do well, but he failed.

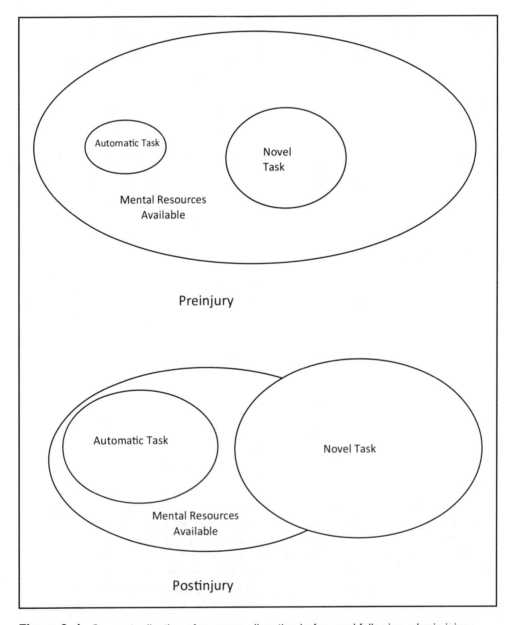

Figure 3–1. Conceptualization of resource allocation before and following a brain injury.

system that acts as a mediator to inhibit competing actions and select an action that would result in achievement of the goal.

Similarly, Baddeley and Hitch (1974) embedded the concept of a central executive, or control system, within their model of working memory. In addition to the central executor, their working memory model contains two subsidiary storage systems, the phonological loop and the visuospatial sketchpad, which are responsible for temporarily storing verbal and nonverbal information, respectively. The central executor performs operations on the information held within these storage systems. For example, during goal-directed behavior, relevant strategies to accomplish a task are held within the appropriate storage system and the central executor selects the most appropriate strategy for completing the task, reviews it, and modifies it as necessary (Serino et al., 2006). To illustrate this concept, consider Brian, the salesman who wants to persuade a customer to buy his product. In order to explain the similarities and differences between his product and a customer's current product, he needs to call up the specific features of the two items and hold those in the phonological loop storage system while the central executor sorts through, organizes, and pulls out the features relevant to the customer's needs. Figure 3–2 provides an illustration of this concept.

Anatomic Correlates of Executive Functions

Executive functions have been associated with the frontal lobes as far back as 1840 when the case of Phineas Gage was presented (see Ratiulon, Talos, Haker, Lieberman, & Everett, 2004). While working on the railroad, Phineas Gage was pierced through his frontal lobe with a large iron rod. Although the majority of his left frontal lobe was destroyed, Phineas survived. However, significant changes in his behavior and personality became apparent. He was described as disinhibited and hyperactive, behaviors currently associated with executive functioning.

The frontal lobes are the largest of the four human lobes and are dramatically larger than those in animals lower on the phylogenetic scale. This implies that the frontal lobes drive higher-level human behavior (Filley, 2000). The prefrontal area is divided into subsections (dorsolateral, ventrolateral, orbitofrontal, dorsomedial, and ventromedial), each subserving different neurobehavioral functions. The link between executive functions and the frontal lobes has been based on both studies of individuals with localized lesions (Alvarez & Emory, 2006) and on task-based functional magnetic resonance imaging studies (D'Esposito, Postle, & Rypma, 2000). The dorsolateral prefrontal cortex is associated with the manipulation of information held "on line." The ventrolateral prefrontal cortex assists with control of attention, vigilance, and inhibition. Orbitofrontal cortex is associated with personality and the maintenance of appropriate social behavior (Alvarez & Emory, 2006; D'Esposito et al., 2000; Filley, 2000; O'Reilly, 2010).

However, there is clear evidence that the symptoms attributed to executive dysfunction are not restricted to damage to frontal areas. Numerous neural connections have been identified

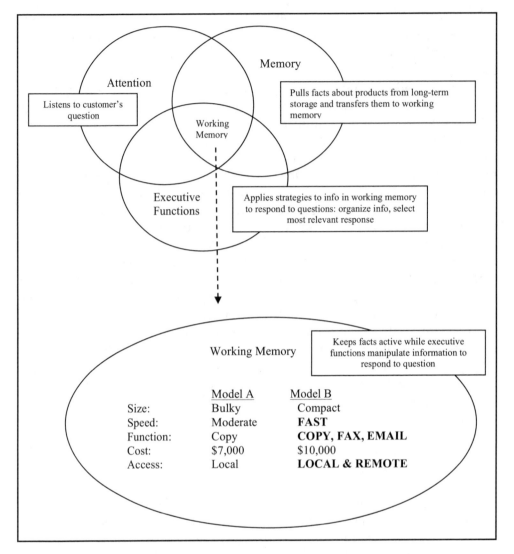

Figure 3–2. Conceptualization of the relationships among attention, memory, executive functions, and working memory in responding to customer's question, "Why should I buy Model B?"

among the frontal lobes, temporal lobes, parietal lobes, cerebellum, and subcortical structures (Cummings, 1993; Schmahmann, 2010; Vataja et al., 2003), and the persistent deficits in mental flexibility, set shifting, planning, and other executive function processes result from damage to the integrity of these white matter tracts that connect brain regions (Caeyenberghs et al., 2014). Greater white matter pathology, or diffuse axonal injury (DAI), predicts greater cognitive deficits (Caeyenberghs et al., 2014; Kinnunen, et al., 2011). Diffusion tensor imaging (DTI) has been used to examine neural networks and structural connectivity to more specifically identify the impact of

DAI on cognitive functioning. Results have revealed disruption and weaker integration of networks related to executive functioning following brain injury, resulting in a limited capacity to integrate information across brain regions (Caeyenberghs et al., 2014; Table 3–3).

Executive Dysfunction in Clinical Populations

Acquired Brain Injury

Impairments of executive functions are among the most enduring cognitive deficits seen following traumatic brain injury (Marsh, Ludbrook, & Gaffaney, 2016). A wide range of deficits has been documented in this population, including difficulties with problem solving, reasoning, planning, and emotional self-regulation, and these problems have a significant impact on functional outcome following injury (Spitz, Pons-ford, Dion, & Maller, 2012). Individuals who suffer a stroke may also present with executive dysfunction. Following right hemisphere stroke, individuals may exhibit problems with planning, problem solving, cognitive flexibility, inhibition, and/or less cohesive and coherent connected speech (Annoni et al., 2003; Barker, Young, & Robinson, 2017; Lehman-Blake, Duffy, Myers, & Tompkins, 2002). In addition, many individuals with right hemisphere brain damage may display an unawareness of their problems, referred to as anosognosia (Hartman-Maeir, Soroker, Ring, & Katz, 2002). Left hemisphere stroke can also lead to executive dysfunction.

Individuals with aphasia may have problems with planning and cognitive flexibility that exacerbate language diffi-culties and may interfere with the reha-bilitation process (Nicholas & Connor, 2017; Purdy, 2002; Purdy & Koch, 2006; Ramsburger, 2000).

There is a substantial amount of lit-erature emerging regarding the effect of single and multiple concussions on neuropsychological functioning. Sev-eral studies have reported persistent deficits in executive functioning in ath-letes and veterans impacting academic and vocational performance following sports-related concussions (Belanger, Spiegel, & Vanderploeg, 2010) and blast injuries (Lippa, Pastorek, Benge, & Thornton, 2010). When an indi-vidual sustains multiple concussions, cognitive decline may continue for years after the last injury (Guskiewicz et al., 2005).

Dementia

Executive dysfunction may be a promi-nent clinical feature of many dementing diseases (Ramanan et al., 2017). It has been well documented in Alzheimer's disease (AD) and has been correlated with impaired instrumental activities of daily living (Marshall et al., 2011). Executive dysfunction, manifested primarily through behavioral deficits, may occur throughout the course of AD and frequently is associated with other neuropsychiatric features (Swan-berg, Tractenberg, Mohs, Thal, & Cum-mings, 2004). Vascular dementia is the second most common form of dementia after AD. It is characterized by loss of executive function with milder memory

Table 3–3. Neurobehavioral Correlates of the Prefrontal Cortex

	Connections (Superior to Inferior)	Functions	Consequences of Lesions
Dorsolateral	Parietal cortex Caudate nucleus Global pallidus Substantia nigra Thalamus	Monitors and adjusts behavior using working memory and executive functions	Executive function deficit Disinterest/ emotional reactivity Decreased attention to relevant stimuli
Ventrolateral	Temporal cortex Amygdala Posterior cingulate Parahippocampal gyrus Inferior parietal lobe	Response inhibition Goal-appropriate response selection Attentional control Vigilance	Emotional dysregulation Poor attention and vigilance
Orbitofrontal	Temporal, parietal Insula Globus pallidus Caudate nucleus Substantia nigra Amygdala Thalamus Cerebrocerebellar circuit	Personality Emotional input Social behavior Suppression of distracting signals	Emotional lability Disinhibition Distractibility Social inappropriateness
Dorsomedial	Temporal, parietal Caudate nucleus Global pallidus Substantia nigra Cingulate Thalamus	Arousal Motivation Initiation of activity	Apathy Decreased drive/ awareness Akinetic-abulic syndrome Mutism
Ventromedial	Amygdala Temporal lobe Prelimbic cortex	Emotional control, empathy	Impaired judgment Inappropriate social behavior

loss as compared with AD and is associated with cerebral brain infarction or hemorrhage (Schneck, 2008). Individuals with frontotemporal dementia also show greater executive function impairment than memory impairment following administration of a formal neuropsychological battery (Huey et al., 2009). These individuals also present with prominent behavioral changes, including disinhibition, apathy, perseveration, and cognitive inflexibility (Elderkin-Thompson, Boone, Hwang, & Kumar, 2004; Slachevsky et al., 2004).

Neurologic Disease

A systematic review of executive functioning in early stage Parkinson's disease revealed consistent evidence of cognitive deficits across a variety of executive function tests (Kudlicka, Clare, & Hindle, 2011). Insufficient dopamine to the dorsal frontal striatal pathways is the likely cause of executive dysfunction, primarily characterized by impairments in task-switching and feedback usage (Ravizza, Goudreau, Delgado, & Ruiz, 2012). Reports have indicated that patients with a new diagnosis of amyotrophic lateral sclerosis (ALS) have a comorbid diagnosis of cognitive impairment, particularly executive dysfunction (Burke et al., 2017; Phukan et al., 2012). Cognitive impairment, including executive dysfunction, frequently occurs in individuals with multiple sclerosis, making it difficult to maintain employment and participate in everyday activities (Flavia, Stampatori, Zanotti, Parrinello, & Capra, 2010).

Cognitive-Communicative Consequences of Executive Dysfunction

Social or cognitive communication deficits following brain injury occur primarily from a breakdown in the interactional use of language and cognitive functions and are primarily evident at the level of discourse rather at the linguistic word or sentence level (Steel & Togher, 2018). Successful communication requires individuals to plan and use language flexibly across contexts, inhibit inappropriate responses, and continuously update information in working memory as context and social cues change over time (Byom & Turkstra, 2017). Thus, social communication is cognitively challenging and places high demands on executive functions. There is some evidence that executive function impairments are associated with social communication deficits; however, whether this relationship is correlational or causal remains an area of debate (Byom & Turkstra, 2017).

Zimmerman, Gindri, deOliveira, and Fonseca (2011) examined the relationship between pragmatic behavior and executive function skills and found that individuals with traumatic brain injury exhibited difficulty on conversational and narrative discourse tasks, which was associated with a general profile of executive dysfunction affecting mainly working memory, initiation, inhibition, planning, and switching. The conversational and narrative discourse problems of individuals with right brain damage were predominantly related to working memory and verbal initiation impairments. McDonald et al.

(2014) reported speakers with traumatic brain injury failed to address the perspective of others on a variety of high- and low-cognitive flexibility tasks, which was due to problems with executive control. Impaired executive function has also been associated with poor comprehension of social implications (Channon & Watts, 2003) and inaccurate or poorly structured discourse (Coelho, 1995; Coelho, Grela, Corso, Gamble, & Feinn, 2005; Le, Coelho, Mozieko, Krueger, & Grafman, 2014; Marini, Zettin, & Galetto, 2014). Pearce, Cartwright, Cocks, and Whitworth (2016) reported that reduced inhibition speed contributed to disinhibited communication behaviors. Poor control of inhibition has been linked to significant social implications and poor vocational outcomes for individuals with brain injury (McDonald, Togher, & Code, 2013).

Though not explicitly documented as the result of executive dysfunction, additional observations of individuals with traumatic brain injury showed that their conversational skills may be characterized by difficulty responding to open-ended questions, presenting new information, organizing discourse, and adapting to interlocutor knowledge (Rousseaux, Verigneaux, & Kozlowski, 2010). Discourse production been described as lacking in macrostructure (e.g., omission or sequencing errors of essential steps or story episodes), cohesion (e.g., inaccurate or nonspecific use of pronouns and other referents), and informativeness (e.g., omission of important units of information, or inclusion of inaccurate information) (Coelho, 2002; Davis & Coelho, 2004). Pragmatic and social communication deficits following right brain damage may include difficulty comprehending abstract language and humor, making inferences, differentiating between relevant and irrelevant information, and interpreting extralinguistic or contextual information (Bryan & Hale; 2001; Lehman-Blake et al., 2002; Purdy, Belanger, & Liles, 1993; Tompkins, Bloise, Timko, & Baumgaertner, 1994).

World Health Organization's International Classification of Functioning Framework (WHO-ICF)

The American Speech-Language-Hearing Association (ASHA) promotes the use of the WHO-ICF (2001) to guide assessment and treatment decisions (ASHA, 2004). This classification system was developed to supplement the International Classification of Diseases (ICD), in recognition of the fact that a person's disease process (e.g., stroke) does not predict function (e.g., functional communication). There are two primary components to the ICF: Functioning and Disability and Contextual Factors. Functioning and Disability includes Body Function and Structure (Impairment), which describe the specific anatomy and physiology of the body and resulting impairment (e.g., brain damage resulting in a cognitive communication impairment). Activity and participation describe the impact of the impairment on a person's functional status, including changes in interpersonal interactions, self-care and independence, and roles in life, among other things. Contextual Factors include Environmental Factors and Personal Factors. Environmental Factors are things that are not within the person's control such as family, work, public policy, and cultural beliefs. Personal Factors include things such as age, motivation, and coping styles. Figure 3–3 provides an example of how this framework may be applied to Brian.

Assessment

General Assessment Issues

Decision making regarding assessment will depend on a range of factors relating to the clinical setting, the patient's stage of recovery, the purpose of the assessment, and resources available (Steel & Togher, 2018).

It is very difficult to assess executive functioning in the acute care hospital very soon after neurologic injury. The patient is often overwhelmed with medical testing and visits from doctors, nurses, and occupational and physical therapists. Fatigue and pain medication may decrease the patient's level of alertness. As the patient moves through the continuum of care and becomes less dependent on caregivers, there is more potential for executive function deficits to present themselves and the therapist is more likely to obtain reliable results from executive function tests.

For individuals with traumatic brain injury, the Ranchos Los Amigos (RLA) Scale of Cognitive Functioning level (Hagen, Malkamus, & Durham, 1972) may help guide assessment decisions for evaluation of executive functioning. In general, patients at RLA Levels I through IV are not appropriate for executive function testing due to their overall low level of functioning and/or agitation. Patients at RLA Levels V and

VI may demonstrate generalized confusion and global cognitive deficits, and administration of a brief assessment of general cognitive functioning may be appropriate. As the patient progresses through these stages of confusion, the clinician may observe behaviors associated with executive dysfunction such as reduced error awareness, self-monitoring, initiation, and planning, but at this stage, it is difficult to differentiate between specific executive function deficits versus underlying global cognitive dysfunction. By the time patients reach RLA VII and VIII, the general confusion has subsided and executive dysfunction can be more reliably diagnosed. At these stages, individuals are more aware of their deficits and can often describe specific activities that are challenging. The clinician can do a task analysis of the specific troublesome activities, hypothesize about the executive function processes needed to successfully perform the activities, and select a test battery that addresses those specific executive function processes.

There are some unique challenges related to assessment of executive functions. The broad definition and multiple components constituting the construct of executive functions may compromise the validity of assessment. Inadequate concurrent and predictive validity have been cited as a weakness of most executive function tests (Mueller & Dollaghan, 2013). There is a need to come to consensus on the definition of the construct of executive function so valid assessment may be achieved (Keil & Kaszniak, 2002; Mueller & Dollaghan, 2013).

Another challenge of executive function assessment is the paradox between testing in a structured environment and

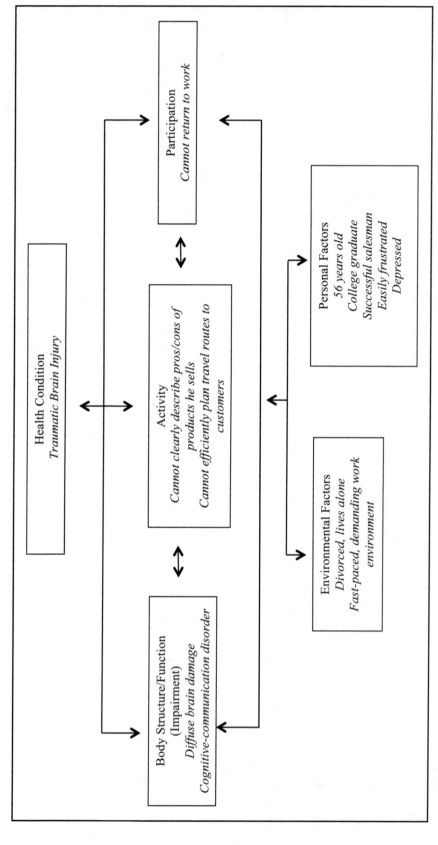

Figure 3–3. Example of the World Health Organization International Classification of Functioning as applied to Brian.

the need to observe self-directed goal setting, planning and organization of behavior, monitoring and evaluation of performance, and flexible shifting in strategy use. Testing protocols typically provide structure and cues for initiation, maintenance of on-task behavior, and explicit goals, reducing the likelihood of exposing executive dysfunction (Lezak et al., 2012).

To increase the reliability of results and making an accurate diagnosis of executive dysfunction, it is important to use a variety of tests and measures. Tests of executive functions often tap a variety of fundamental as well as higher-level cognitive skills and clients may do poorly for a number of reasons (Delis, Kaplan, & Kramer, 2001). Results from a single test may over- or under-estimate a client's executive abilities. A client with executive dysfunction may do well if his problematic components were not tapped by the measure used, causing the clinician to overestimate the client's skills. Conversely, a client may do poorly, not because of impaired executive skills, but due to a problem with a more fundamental process such as visual perception, language, or attention. For example, patients who have suffered a right hemisphere stroke may have significant visual perceptual problems, and clinicians should select tests that do not rely heavily on visual perception. Likewise, for patients with left brain damage and aphasia, selected tests should not have a heavy linguistic load. For this reason, it is important for the clinician to be aware of more basic cognitive deficits before administering executive function batteries so tests may be interpreted appropriately.

In an ideal world, the clinician would select both impairment-based and activity/participation assessment measures that assist with identifying strengths and challenges related to executive functioning. Impairment-based measures may provide information on the specific components affected as well as the severity of the disorder. Activity/participation-based tools are helpful in determining the impact of the executive function impairment on the patient's ability to carry out daily tasks at home and the prognosis for returning to work or school. However, the current health-care environment does not permit clinicians to perform extensive evaluations, so they must design their assessment protocols to gather as much information as possible in as little time as possible. Consultation with other team members (psychology, occupational therapy, physical therapy) will help provide a more complete picture of the patient's executive function profile and prevent redundancy in testing. In fact, the need for increased efficiency and accountability in service delivery necessitates the integration of findings and the reduction of overlap among disciplines (Joint Commission on Interprofessional Relations, 2007).

Case History

Assessment of executive functions should begin with a detailed case history. Information can be obtained through a medical record review and interviews with the patient and a reliable contact person.

Medical Record Review

Information related to the patient's acute medical history such as the type, locus, and extent of brain damage; presence/ length of coma; and medical complications (WHO Body Structure/Function) provides information relevant to recovery and prognosis. Information on the client's level of education and occupation (e.g., WHO Personal Factors) is important for the clinician to know in order to estimate the type and extent of demands previously placed on the executive function system. This information also helps with interpretation of test results. Knowledge of the client's residential setting, marital status, and support system (WHO Environmental Factors) will help the clinician plan for discharge.

Information regarding the patient's current cognitive status should be obtained. Behaviors associated with executive dysfunction (e.g., impulsivity, disinhibition, lack of awareness of cognitive problems, off-target or disorganized responses to questions) may be documented by other health professionals. If the patient has been evaluated previously, reports should be reviewed prior to additional testing of executive functioning. Having a general idea of the potential severity of a problem will assist the clinician in developing an assessment protocol. For example, if it is known that a patient has a significant attentional problem, testing will need to be brief. Likewise, if a client has a concurrent aphasia, executive functioning tests with a high linguistic load should be avoided.

Interview

Interviewing patients regarding their medical history, perception of the cognitive and situational changes since the injury, and the personal goals they wish to achieve through rehabilitation provides the clinician with information on the patient's awareness and insight, attitude regarding the injury, and ability to cope with the changes (WHO Personal Factors). Interviewing a reliable informant regarding any changes in behavior, communication, or cognitive function can aid in establishing hypotheses regarding potential executive function problems and help with identifying potential assessment tools.

Refer to Table 3–4 for Brian's medical history.

Impairment-Based Assessment of Executive Functioning (WHO-ICF Body Structure and Function)

As mentioned previously, formal test batteries of executive function have many limitations; however, using the best available evidence on assessment, combined with clinician experience and expertise, allows clinicians to make informed decisions regarding choosing an appropriate assessment battery. Given the broad definition of executive functioning and the overlapping nomenclature, it is difficult to organize tests according to specific criteria or processes. However, Keil and Kazniak (2002) provide a useful framework (p. 306). They divided tests of executive functioning into four broad categories:

1. Tests of planning, scheduling, strategy use, and rule adherence: Includes tests that require creation of subgoals, temporal sequencing, strategy generation and application, using environmental feedback to guide behavior, and self-monitoring.

Table 3–4. Brian's Case History

Category	Information	Relevance to Assessment
Medical history	• 56-year-old male • MVA 3 months ago • Upon admission to ER was confused and agitated (RLA IV) • Initial CT scan = negative • Follow-up MRI = evidence of DAI • Improved to RLA VI by discharge 2 weeks postadmission	Still relatively early in recovery Good progress in 2 weeks DAI = likelihood of executive function problems
Rehabilitation history	• Inpatient rehabilitation for 4 weeks • Transitional living program for 6 weeks • Safe for discharge home independently • Given medical clearance to drive • Rec. outpatient rehab for persistent moderate executive function deficits and mild memory problems	Made good progress during rehab Safe at home, but how does he do logistically (manage son's schedule, meals, grocery shopping, bills)? Does he plan to go back to work?
Sensory and motor status	• No difficulty hearing • Wears glasses for distance only (driving) • No upper or lower extremity deficits	No restrictions/ limitations for participating in assessment
Educational and vocational history	• College graduate • Successful self-employed salesman of office equipment	Likely had good executive function skills prior to injury since he was skillful in planning and managing his time and persuading customers to purchase expensive equipment.
Psychosocial background	• Divorced • 19-year-old son living at home, going to community college • Speaks English	Limited support system

continues

Table 3–4. *continued*

Category	Information	Relevance to Assessment
Interview: Patient	• Attempted to go back to work (against medical advice) • Was late for his appointment with customer • Couldn't answer customer's questions re: differences/pros/cons of newer copier and fax machines • Became flustered and "mind went blank" • Complained that everything takes longer to do than it used to	Questionable judgment, but does acknowledge when he has problems Potential deficits in working memory, verbal reasoning, organization, time management
Interview: Son	• Mostly still acts like Dad, but "flakey" at times • Forgets items at grocery store • Dinner is usually later than planned • Takes him longer to do the usual things around the house, gets frustrated when he can't get everything done • I can't always follow what he's trying to tell me	Problems identified are consistent with patient report

2. Tests of generation, fluency, initiation: Includes tests that require generation of concepts and compliance with environmental constraints, and measure lack of monitoring (i.e., through perseverative errors).

3. Tests of shifting and suppression: Includes tests that require shifting between tasks (i.e., set) and inhibition of external or internal/overlearned responses.

4. Tests of concept formation and abstract reasoning: Includes tests that require formation of concepts and conceptualization of abstract relationships.

It should be noted that these categories are not mutually exclusive and some tests may address executive functions in more than one category. Table 3–5 contains a list of commonly used impairment-based tests of executive functioning and the specific executive process(es) addressed according to the test's author or as reported in the literature.

Table 3–5. Executive Function Processes Addressed in Impairment-Based Executive Function Assessments

		Planning, Strategy Use, Rule Adherence	Generation, Fluency, Initiation	Shifting, Suppression	Concept Formation, Abstract Reasoning
D-KEFS	Trail Making			X	
	Verbal Fluency		X	X	
	Design Fluency		X	X	
	Color-Word Interference			X	
	Sorting			X	X
	20 Questions	X			X
	Word Context				X
	Towers	X			
	Proverbs				X
WCST				X	X
CLQT	Generative Naming		X		
	Design Generation		X		
	Symbol Trails			X	
	Mazes	X		X	
COWAT			X		
Porteus Mazes		X		X	

Note. D-KEFS = Delis-Kaplan Executive Function System (Delis, Kaplan, & Kramer, 2001); WCST = Wisconsin Card Sorting Test (Grant & Berg, 1948); CLQT = Cognitive-Linguistic Quick Test (Helm-Estabrooks, 2001); COWAT = Controlled Oral Word Association Test (Benton, Hamsher, Rey, & Sivan, 1994); Porteus Mazes = Porteus, 1965.

Delis-Kaplan Executive Function System

The Delis-Kaplan Executive Function System (D-KEFS; Delis et al., 2001) measures a wide spectrum of verbal and nonverbal executive functions. The national standardization study of the test included over 1,700 neurologically normal subjects, ages 8 to 89 years, carefully selected to match the demographic characteristics of the population in the United States. Each subtest is designed to differentiate between fundamental cognitive problems (e.g., word level reading, numerical or alphabetic sequencing, task comprehension) and executive dysfunction (e.g., cognitive flexibility). Each subtest is designed to be a stand-alone instrument that can be administered individually or along with other subtests. Several of the subtests have been published previously or occurred in the research literature. The D-KEFS is composed of the following nine subtests:

1. *Trail Making Test* (previously published by Reitan & Wolfson, 1985). This test addresses flexibility of thought or switching behavior. There are three conditions that must be completed successfully in order to draw conclusions about flexibility: visual cancellation task, connect numbers in order, and connect letters of the alphabet in order. The primary task involves alternating between numbers and letters, in ascending order (e.g., 1-A, 2-B, 3-C).

2. *Verbal Fluency Test* (e.g., Benton, Hamsher, Rey, & Sivan, 1994; Borkowski, Benton, & Spreen, 1967). Individuals must generate as many words as they can in a specified category within 1 minute. This test comprises three testing conditions: generation of words by letter (phonemic knowledge), by category (semantic knowledge), then alternating between two semantic categories (flexibility/ shifting). It addresses initiation, shifting, and self-monitoring of responses to prevent repetition of a previously stated item.

3. *Design Fluency Test.* This test requires the patient to create unique designs by using exactly four straight lines to make connections among 10 dots. Condition 1 provides a basic test of design fluency (connect filled dots). Condition 2 measures design fluency and response inhibition (connect only the empty dots and inhibit connecting the filled dots). Condition 3 measures design fluency and cognitive flexibility (create designs by alternately connecting filled and empty dots).

4. *Color-Word Interference Test* (previously published as the Stroop Test; Trenerry, Crosson, DeBoe, & Leber, 1989). This test examines the subject's ability to inhibit an overlearned or automatic verbal response in order to generate a conflicting response. The test contains two basic tasks: naming patches of color and reading color names printed in black ink. The higher-level task involves stating the color of the ink while inhibiting reading the word (e.g., for the word GREEN printed

in BLUE ink, the patient must respond "blue" and inhibit the natural tendency to read the word "green").

5. *Sorting Test* (previously known as the California Sorting Test; Delis, Squire, Bihrle, & Massman, 1992). This test measures concept formation, abstract reasoning, and flexibility. There are two conditions: Free Sorting and Sort Recognition. In Free Sorting, the subject is presented with six cards that display words and various perceptual features (e.g., diagonal lines or printed shapes) and is asked to sort the cards into two groups, three cards per group. After each sort, the participant is asked to provide the rule used for sorting, then is instructed to sort the cards in a different manner (eight possible sorts). In Sort Recognition, the examiner sorts the cards and the subject identifies the sorting rule.

6. *Twenty Questions Test.* This subtest measures concept formation and planning. The subject is presented with a stimulus page depicting pictures of 30 common objects and must determine a target item using the fewest number of yes/no questions possible.

7. *Word Context Test.* This subtest addresses deductive reasoning and concept formation. The individual attempts to discover the meaning of a made-up word on the basis of its use in five clue sentences. The clues begin very vague ("A ____ is a food"), then subsequently become more specific ("A ____ a day keeps the doctor away").

8. *Tower Test* (previously published as the Tower of London; Shallice, 1982). This subtest addresses planning, rule adherence, and flexibility. The object of this test is to move three to five varying in size (from small to large) from a starting position to a goal position in the fewest number of moves possible while adhering to specific rules (e.g., cannot put a large disk on top of a smaller disk).

9. *Proverb Test* (previously published as The California Proverb Test; Delis, Fridlund, Kramer, & Kaplan, 1984). This test addresses concept formation and abstract reasoning. It consists of eight sayings that are presented in two formats: Free Inquiry and Multiple Choice. For the Free Inquiry condition, the proverbs are read individually to the examinee, who attempts to interpret them orally without assistance or cues. For the Multiple-Choice condition, the same eight proverbs are presented in written form along with four alternative written choices.

Wisconsin Card Sorting Test

The Wisconsin Card Sorting Test (Grant & Berg, 1948) examines the client's ability to identify abstract categories and shift cognitive set. It contains 128 cards depicting one to four colored shapes. Patients must determine a sorting strategy according to a criterion that an examiner has in mind (e.g., color, shape, or number) and that is deduced from the examiner's feedback (i.e., "right" or "wrong"). Once a client successfully completes 10 consecutive sorts, the examiner changes the criterion without alerting the individual and the individual must determine the new rule for sorting.

Cognitive-Linguistic Quick Test

The Cognitive-Linguistic Quick Test (CLQT) (Helm-Estabrooks, 2001) may be used as a screening test for quick identification of strengths and weaknesses in five cognitive domains (attention, memory, executive functions, language, and visuospatial skills). Although population norms are not provided, cutoff scores were determined for two age groups (18–69 and 70–89) based on two research studies involving 235 neurologically normal adults (Helm-Estabrooks, 2002). Four of the 10 tasks address executive functioning: Generative Naming, Design Generation, Symbol Trails, and Mazes. The generative naming and design tests are similar to the verbal and design fluency tasks described previously but do not include a set-shifting condition.

> *Symbol Trails.* This task is similar to the Trail Making Test described previously; however, to reduce the linguistic load of the task, participants connect shapes in order from smallest to largest. First, participants connect triangles, then circles, then alternate between triangles and circles progressing from small to large (e.g., small triangle–small circle; medium triangle–medium circle). The task addresses shifting and suppression.

> *Mazes.* Participants must create a path through two mazes (easy and difficult) without going into any dead ends or crossing lines. The task addresses planning and suppression.

Controlled Oral Word Association Test

The Controlled Oral Word Association Test (COWAT; Benton et al., 1994) is a measure of verbal fluency and is a subtest of the Multilingual Aphasia Examination. It uses the three-letter set of C, F, and L to assess phonemic fluency. Individuals are given 1 minute to name as many words as possible beginning with the target letter.

Porteus Mazes

Porteus Mazes (Porteus, 1965) consist of a series of 10 mazes, each increasing in complexity. Individuals must plan the sequence of their responses, then execute the response while self-monitoring and inhibiting error responses as they progress through the mazes.

Activity/Participation Assessments

Assessments that address activity/participation include both standardized tests and observational/performance-based tasks (Tables 3–6 and 3–7).

Standardized Tests

Functional Assessment of Verbal Reasoning and Executive Strategies. The Functional Assessment of Verbal Reasoning and Executive Strategies (FAVRES; MacDonald, 2005) is an assessment tool particularly attractive to professionals interested in assessing the

Table 3–6. Executive Function Processes Addressed in Activity/Participation Assessments

		Planning, Strategy Use, Rule Adherence	Generation, Fluency, Initiation	Shifting, Suppression	Concept Formation, Abstract Reasoning
FAVRES	Planning an Event	X		X	
	Scheduling a Workday	X		X	
	Making a Decision			X	X
	Building a Case			X	X
FAVRES Reasoning Subskills	Getting the Facts				X
	Eliminating Irrelevant Facts				X
	Weighing Relevant Choices				X
	Flexibility			X	
	Generating Alternatives		X		
	Predicting Outcome				X
BADS	Rule Shift Card			X	
	Action Program	X			
	Key Search	X			
	Temporal Judgment				X
	Zoo Map	X		X	
	Modified Six Elements	X			

Note. FAVRES = Functional Assessment of Verbal Reasoning and Executive Strategies (MacDonald, 2005); BADS = Behavioral Assessment of Dysexecutive Syndrome (Wilson, Alderman, Burgess, Emslie, & Evans, 1996).

Table 3–7. Observation/Performance-Based Measures

Behavior Rating Inventory of Executive Functions–Adult (BRIEF-A)
The Dysexecutive Questionnaire (DEX) (Burgess, Alderman, Wilson, Evans, & Emslie, 1996)
Frontal Systems Behavior Scale (FrsBe)
Profile of Executive Control System (PRO-EX)
Executive Function Route Finding Task
Cognitive Estimation Task
American Multiple Errands Test

impact of executive dysfunction on a variety of real-life tasks dependent on communication skills. Performance on this test was positively associated with sustaining employment in skilled jobs after traumatic brain injury (Meulenbroek & Turkstra, 2016). Each task presents a novel problem that contains large amounts of information that must be comprehended and integrated prior to making a decision. Two tasks examine planning (sequencing, organizing, and prioritizing tasks with time constraints), and two tasks examine inhibition (examinee's ability to inhibit inappropriate remarks in response to conditions presented in the task). The tasks are scored in terms of efficiency of the performance, accuracy of the solution, and the quality of the rationale provided. Following administration of each primary task, a variety of reasoning skills are assessed, including the client's ability to identify facts, eliminate irrelevant information, predict potential outcomes or consequences, generate alternative solutions, and provide a rationale for choices made. This information is helpful for treatment planning.

The normative sample for the FAVRES included 52 adults with acquired brain damage and 101 neurologically normal adults aged 18 to 79. The test was found to accurately differentiate individuals with acquired brain injury from neurologically normal peers (MacDonald & Johnson, 2005). Overall performance on the FAVRES is significantly related to cognitive measures of attention, speed of processing, memory, and executive functioning, establishing its concurrent validity (Avramović et al., 2017). The four tasks are:

1. *Planning an Event.* This task addresses planning, sequencing, organizing, and flexibility. The client is provided with "newspaper" listings of upcoming events and is asked to choose an activity to do with a child given specific constraints (e.g., day of week, cost).
2. *Scheduling a Workday.* This task addresses planning, sequencing, organizing, and prioritizing tasks by degree of importance and time requirements. The client is given a list of tasks that must be

completed during the workday. The time required to complete the task and specific constraints are provided (e.g., project must be picked up by mail service by a certain time).

3. *Making a Decision.* This task addresses inhibition and reasoning. The client must determine an appropriate gift for a couple based on information provided in a script from a telephone conversation.

4. *Building a Case.* This task addresses reasoning, organization, sequencing, and suppression. The client assumes the role of a dissatisfied customer who must write a letter to a "contractor" regarding the damage sustained from a leaky roof.

The Behavioral Assessment of Dysexecutive Syndrome. The Behavioral Assessment of Dysexecutive Syndrome (BADS; Wilson, Alderman, Burgess, Emslie, & Evans, 1996) was designed to assess a wide spectrum of executive function abilities and to predict everyday problems arising from dysexecutive syndrome. Normative data were obtained from 216 neurologically healthy control subjects aged between 16 and 87 years and 78 individuals who presented with a variety of neurological disorders (closed head injury, encephalitis, dementia, and stroke). The BADS demonstrates high discriminant validity and predictive validity (e.g., caregivers' ratings of executive problems were predicted by their brain-injured relatives' performance on the BADS). It also has high interrater reliability, but only moderate test-retest reliability. This could be because repeated testing results in decreased novelty (Wilson et al., 1996).

The test contains six tasks and the Dysexecutive Questionnaire. Performance on the six tasks yields a profile score ranging from 0 to 4 and incorporates both accuracy and time. Each task is designed to assess a specific component of executive functioning.

1. *Rule Shift Card Test.* The client is asked to respond to a given rule (say "yes" if the card is red and "no" if the card is black), then respond to a new rule (say "yes" if the previous card was red and "no" if the previous card was black). This subtest addresses cognitive flexibility and inhibition.

2. *Action Program Test.* The client must figure out how to get a cork out of a glass using a variety of objects while following specific rules. This subtest addresses planning and problem solving.

3. *Key Search Test.* The client is provided with a paper containing a square representing a football field and is instructed to draw a route to search the field for a set of lost keys. This subtest assesses planning and self-monitoring.

4. *Temporal Judgment Test.* The client responds to questions about the length of time required for common occurrences (e.g., time required for a routine dental examination). This subtest examines problem solving and reasoning.

5. *Zoo Map Test.* The client is provided with a map and must draw a route around the "zoo" while following specific rules. There are two conditions, one

with structure and one without structure. This subtest assesses planning and cognitive flexibility.

6. *Modified Six Elements Test* (originally described by Shallice & Burgess, 1991). The client must complete three tasks, each containing two parts, in a specified amount of time, while adhering to specific rules. Skills assessed by this subtest include planning, organization, and self-monitoring.

Performance-Based Measures of Executive Functioning

The true test of executive functioning is successful completion of daily life goals. Observation of the client in a variety of contexts and under various conditions provides invaluable information on how the client performs independently without the structure that is often provided during formal testing. It may appear that a client knows what to do for a given task and may complete the task under structured conditions; however, when required to spontaneously carry out the task, performance may break down. Reliance on structured tests of executive functions may lead to underestimation of the difficulty individuals will have in real-world contexts (Ylvisaker & Feeney, 1998). Direct observation of functional behaviors also allows the clinician to assess the effect of corrective feedback with clients. Response to feedback often highlights the likelihood of a client's participation and success in rehabilitation (Manchester, Priestley, & Jackson, 2004). For these reasons, observation of individuals in real settings, performing

real activities, is encouraged. Observational/performance assessments are listed in Table 3–7.

Behavior Rating Inventory of Executive Function–Adult Version. The Behavior Rating Inventory of Executive Function–Adult Version (BRIEF-A; Roth, Isquith, & Gioia, 2005) is a standardized measure that assesses executive functioning of individuals in their everyday environment. There are two formats: Self-Report and Informant. The assessment is composed of 75 items within nine scales that measure various aspects of executive functioning on the basis of frequency of occurrence (never, sometimes, often): Inhibit, Self-Monitor, Plan/Organize, Shift, Initiate, Task Monitor, Emotional Control, Working Memory, and Organization of Materials. The scales form two broad indexes: Behavior Regulation and Metacognition. It can be administered in approximately 10 to 15 minutes and has strong internal consistency, interrater reliability, construct validity, and concurrent validity.

The Dysexecutive Questionnaire (DEX). The DEX (Burgess et al., 1996) is part of the BADS. It is a 20-item questionnaire designed to sample emotional, motivational, behavioral, and cognitive changes in a person with suspected executive dysfunction. One version is designed for the subject to complete and another version is designed for someone who is close to the individual, such as a relative or caregiver. Instructions are given to the participant to read 20 statements describing common problems of everyday life and to rate them according to their personal experience. Each item is scored on a

5-point scale according to its frequency from "never" (0 point) to "very often" (4 points).-The total score may range from 0 to 80, with the higher score representing more significant deficits in executive functioning.

Frontal Systems Behavior Scale. The Frontal Systems Behavior Scale (FrsBe; Grace & Malloy, 2001) was developed to identify and quantify behavioral problems associated with frontal lobe dysfunction. It consists of three scales (Apathy, Disinhibition, and Executive Function) and a total of 46 items. It can be completed by the patient and/or caregiver. It can be administered in approximately 10 to 15 minutes and has good reliability, construct validity, convergent validity, and discriminant validity.

Profile of Executive Control System. The Profile of Executive Control System (PRO-EX; Braswell et al., 1992) is a tool that helps the clinician organize and interpret observational data. The PRO-EX is divided into seven scales delineating specific executive abilities, including Goal Selection, Planning/Sequencing, Initiation, Execution, Time Sense, Awareness of Deficits, and Self-Monitoring. Ideally, the clinician observes the client performing several multistep activities (e.g., cooking and money management) in a variety of settings (e.g., clinic, home). At the completion of the task, the clinician rates performance on each scale from "able, only with physical prompting" to "independent."

Executive Function Route-Finding Task. In the Executive Function Route-Finding Task (EFRT; Boyd, Sautter, Bailey, Echols, & Douglas, 1987; Lezak, 1995), the client is faced with a novel problem to solve: finding a specific, but unfamiliar location within the building where the testing takes place. No specific instructions are provided to the client regarding how the task may be completed. The task requires integration of a number of processes, including initiation, planning, and self-monitoring. Performance is rated on a 4-point scale in the areas of (1) Task Understanding, (2) Incorporation of Information Seeking, (3) Retaining Directions, (4) Error Detection, (5) Error Correction, and (6) On-Task Behavior. Additional problems that may contribute to performance are noted in emotional, communicative, interpersonal, and perceptual abilities.

Cognitive Estimation Test. The Cognitive Estimation Test (CET; MacPherson et al., 2014) was originally published by Shallice and Evans (1978) and was recently updated by MacPherson and colleagues (2014). The CET requires patients to mentally manipulate known facts to formulate reasonable answers to questions for which some relevant information may be known, but the exact answer is unknown (e.g., How many segments are there in an orange?). Participants are informed that there is no exact answer for most questions and they should make a reasonable estimation. All questions require numerical responses. This test provides information about a patient's semantic memory, planning, working memory, and self-monitoring.

American Multiple Errands Test. The American Multiple Errands Test (AMET;

Aitken, Chase, McClue, & Ratcliff, 1993) was modified from the original Multiple Errands Test (Shallice & Burgess, 1991). It allows the clinician to observe the client in a real shopping environment. Prior to arrival at the shopping center, the client is provided with instructions, a nominal amount of money, and a watch. Activities to be completed include purchasing six items as quickly and cheaply as possible, sending a postcard with specific information to the clinician, and meeting the clinician at a certain time and place. The client's performance is rated in terms of successful task completion, rule breaks, and use of efficient strategies. McCue, Pramuka, Chase, and Fabry (1995) compared client's performance on this test to standardized tests of executive functioning and found that performance on the AMET was poorer than on standard executive function tests, and no strong associations were found among these measures. This suggests that the AMET is more sensitive in identification of executive dysfunction since it detected deficits that were not identified on formal measures. More recently, a virtual reality version of the Multiple Errands Test (Raspelli et al., 2011) was developed for the assessment of executive functions. Raspelli and colleagues established ecological and construct validity when the measure was used with stroke patients.

Morrison et al. (2013) revised the scoring system of the original MET (MET-R) in order to quantify the observed behaviors. New variables to be counted included total time, number of locations visited, number of tasks completed, number of passes, and number of rule breaks. It was found that the MET-R reliably differentiated individu-

als with mild strokes from neurologically normal individuals.

Cognitive-Communication Assessment

Current guidelines for cognitive-communication assessment after traumatic brain injury (TBI) recommend considering the communication needs of individuals, the communicative context, and the communication partner through use of both standardized and nonstandardized assessments (Togher et al., 2014). Numerous assessments and methods of analyses have been described in the literature; however, clinical use of these methods is infrequent (Frith, Togher, Ferguson, Levick, & Docking, 2014; Riedemann & Turkstra, 2018). Select measures and methods of assessment of cognitive communication are described below and listed in Table 3–8.

La Trobe Communication Questionnaire. The La Trobe Communication Questionnaire (LCQ; Douglas, Flaherty, & Snow, 2000) is a measure of perceived communicative ability based on information gathered from the patient and close others. It consists of two 30-question forms that assess how the individual with brain injury and his or her communication partner perceive communication quality. A sample item is "When talking to others do you [does your family member] say or do things others might consider rude or embarrassing?" Perceptions are recorded on a 4-point Likert scale ranging from rarely/never to frequent/always. However, since the LCQ is reliant on self and other awareness of communication changes, it may be less useful during

Table 3–8. Cognitive-Communication Measures

LaTrobe Communication Questionnaire (LCQ)
Pragmatic Profile of Impairments in Communication (PPIC)
The Adapted Kagan Scales
Discourse Analysis Measures
Narrative
Macrolinguistic
Microstructural
Macrostructural
Story Grammar
Conversation
Obliges, comments, clarification
Exchange Structure Analysis

the early stages of recovery, particularly in the hospital environment (Steel, Ferguson, Spencer, & Togher, 2017).

The Pragmatic Profile in of Impairment in Communication. The Pragmatic Profile in of Impairment in Communication (PPIC) (originally the PFIC) (Linscott, Knight, & Godfrey, 1996) is a clinician-rated assessment of videotaped interactions. It has 10 feature summary scales (Literal Content, General Participation, Quantity, Quality, Internal Relation, External Relation, Clarity of Expression, Social Style, Subject Matter, and Aesthetics), which assess the severity of the impairment, and 84 behavioral items rated by frequency of occurrence. The inclusion of both frequency of behaviors and severity ratings makes this instrument useful for measuring changes (Steel & Togher, 2018). Although the PPIC is commonly used in TBI research, this assessment is not yet available for commercial use but may be obtained by contacting the authors.

The Adapted Kagan Scales. Kagan et al. (2004) developed two scales to assess the outcome of partner training for persons with aphasia: the Measure of Participation in Conversation (MPC) scale, which assesses how well the person with aphasia is able to engage in interactions, and the Measure of Support in Conversation (MSC), which evaluates the ability of the communication partner to acknowledge and reveal his or her partner's competence. Togher, Power, Tate, McDonald, and Rietdijk (2010) modified the scales to incorporate supports identified as appropriate for individuals with cognitive communication deficits such as developing collaborative intent, cognitive support, emotional support, positive questioning style, and collaborative turn taking. This tool enables examination of the conversation as a mutual activity.

Discourse Tasks and Measures. Discourse samples can be elicited using a variety of tasks, including picture descriptions, story retell, story generation, procedural descriptions, or conversation. Analysis may be conducted across different levels, including microlinguistic, microstructural, macrostructural, or superstructural (e.g., story grammar) (Coelho, 2007). For example, Cannizzaro and Coelho (2013) used a story retell task and segmented the narrative into T-units (a main clause and its subordinate clauses), then coded them into story grammar components (essential episodes consisting of initiating events, attempts, and direct consequences). Stubbs et al. (2018) used a simple procedural discourse task ("tell me how you would make a cheese and Vegemite sandwich") and examined productivity (number of meaningful words, total number of utterances, speaking time, speech rate, and words per minute) and macrostructure (number of essential steps, optional steps, and low content elements according to a checklist). Although these analyses are time-consuming, they can provide valuable information regarding communication strengths and weakness, which can inform the direction of treatment and document change over time (Stubbs, et al., 2018).

Conversational discourse has been analyzed using an appropriateness paradigm that analyzed speaker initiations (obliges, comments, understanding, and clarification) and speaker responses (adequate: minimum response, adequate, adequate plus; inadequate: no response, partially unintelligible, completely unintelligible, delayed) (Youse et al., 2011). Bogart, Togher, Power, and Docking (2012) used exchange structure analysis (Halliday, 1994) to analyze conversations between individuals with traumatic brain injury and their friends. In exchange structure analysis, exchanges, or moves, are coded as synoptic (giving or requesting information) or dynamic (perform the function of negotiating meaning and assist with communication breakdown and repair).

Brian's Assessment Results

Brian's goal was to return to work, so the assessment was designed to obtain information related to facilitating successful employment. The FAVRES was selected because of its predictive validity and because it captures behaviors consistent with areas in which Brian reported difficulty. In addition, the Zoo Map subtest of the BADS was used to assess the benefit of structure on planning ability. Testing took place over two sessions. The interview was conducted and FAVRES Subtests 1, 3, and 4 were administered in the first session (60 minutes). FAVRES Subtest 2 and the BADS Zoo Map subtest were administered in the second session, and preliminary results were reviewed (45 minutes).

As can be seen in Table 3–9, Brian accurately completed Subtests 1 (Planning Event) and 3 (Making a Decision) on the FAVRES. He provided a logical rationale for Subtest 3 but was a bit vague on Subtest 1. However, his performance on both subtests was inefficient as he took longer than average to provide his responses. He had more difficulty with Subtests 2 (Scheduling) and 4 (Building a Case). He was overwhelmed with the scheduling task. He successfully scheduled 5 of the 12 tasks

Table 3–9. Brian's Assessment Results

Brian was assessed over two sessions		
Session 1 (1 hour): Interview, FAVRES Subtests 1, 3, 4		Session 2 (45 minutes): FAVRES Subtest 2, BADS–Zoo Maps

Tool	Rationale	
FAVRES	Patient wants to return to work; high predictive validity; captures behaviors consistent with areas in which patient reported difficulty	

	Planning an Event			Scheduling			Making a Decision			Building a Case		
	Raw	Percentile	SS	Raw	Percentile	SS	Raw	Percentile	SS	Raw	Percentile	SS
Accuracy	5	100	108	3	3	51	5	100	107	3	2	41
Rationale	4	15	69	0	6	58	5	100	103	4	29	59
Time (minutes)	10	11	79	27	3	72	11	9	86	18	11	77

	Planning an Event	Scheduling	Making a Decision	Building a Case	Total
Getting the facts	3/5	3/5	5/5	3/5	14/20
Eliminating irrelevant	1/1	1/1	1/1	1/1	4/4
Weighing facts	0/1	0/1	1/1	1/2	2/5
Flexibility	1/1	0/1	0/1	0/1	1/4
Generating	9	9	8	7	33
Predicting consequences	4/4	3/4	4/4	2/2	13/14
TOTAL	18	16	19	14	69

<3 percentile, <70 SS

continues

Table 3–9. *continued*

Tool	Rationale		
BADS	**Has difficulty planning routes for work—determine benefit of structure**		
	Zoo Map Subtest Version 1 (no structure)	Sequence Score = 1/8	
	Zoo Map Subtest Version 2 (with structure)	Sequence Score = 8/8	
Strengths		**Weaknesses**	
Initiation		Efficiency	
Attention		Organization	
Comprehension		Strategy Use	
Persistence		Flexibility	
Insight			
Benefits from structure			

Note. FAVRES = Functional Assessment of Verbal Reasoning and Executive Strategies; D-KEFS = Delis-Kaplan Executive Function System.

and omitted the others, despite taking a long time to work it out. He did not provide a rationale for his responses. His written response on the Building a Case subtest identified three of seven problems and he offered two potential solutions, though vague. Overall, his letter was disorganized and did not clearly define the problem.

On the reasoning questions following the primary FAVRES test, Brian performed relatively well with predicting outcomes, eliminating irrelevant information, getting the facts, and generating alternative solutions. Weighing the facts and flexibility of thinking were challenging.

On Version 1 of the BADS Zoo Map subtest, he achieved a sequence score of 1 out of a possible 8. He had difficulty determining alternate options when confronted with a problem and broke several rules in his attempts to create a route. In contrast, when provided with structure on Version 2, he achieved a sequence score of 8/8 and successfully completed the task.

Brian demonstrated several strengths during the assessment, including initiation, attention comprehension, persistence, and insight. His challenges were in the areas of flexibility, organization, efficiency, and strategy use. Overall, his test results are consistent with his subjective complaints and provide information needed to develop an effective treatment plan.

Treatment

In general, treatment approaches for executive function deficits attempt to either restore cognitive functions or train use of strategies to compensate for impaired functions. The strongest research evidence favors compensatory treatments that train individuals with traumatic brain injury to use strategies to circumvent executive function impairments in daily activities (Raymer, Roitsch, Redman, Michalek, & Johnson, 2018). The treatments described below are compensatory in nature.

Selection of a therapy approach depends on many factors, not the least of which is the clinician's theoretical belief of the nature of executive functioning. Additional factors to consider include the time since injury; severity of dysexecutive symptoms; co-occurrence of other cognitive deficits; client's level of awareness; rehabilitation priorities of client, family, and staff; and support available in the environment (Sohlberg & Mateer, 2001).

Treatment approaches vary in the amount of structure provided for task completion and in the amount of effort expended by the client. Individuals whose injuries were relatively recent or who display significant dysexecutive symptoms may benefit from a very structured approach. The amount of structure should decrease and the effort expended by the client should gradually increase as the client's symptoms begin to abate.

Rehabilitation priorities of the client and family also must be considered. There may be specific tasks that are important for the client to perform in order to increase independence and decrease the burden placed on the family. In this instance, training of a specific activity may be warranted. For example, if an individual is unable to groom and dress himself due to poor initiation, planning, or sequencing skills, adaptive procedures may be developed and aimed specifically at those activities. Likewise, if a client cannot get to scheduled appointments on time due to poor time management, a program directed toward accurately gauging the passage of time may be implemented.

Guiding Principles

Treatment approaches for executive function deficits emphasize the manner of instruction rather than specific tasks. They incorporate a number of principles that have been found to facilitate learning and generalization as well as self-regulation. Guiding principles embedded in many executive function treatments include provision of structure, systematic instruction, collaboration, meaningful contexts, and metacognitive strategy instruction. Although these principles are briefly reviewed below individually, there is overlap in the manner in which they are integrated into the treatment. Refer to Table 3–10.

Structure

A recurring theme in rehabilitation is the role of structure in management of executive functions. It is well understood that individuals with executive function problems perform better when structure is provided, that is, when there is a built-in organizational plan. What is less understood is what type of structure can be provided to improve performance on real-life activities and how to fade the structure to promote independence.

Jackson et al. (2014) defined three types of structure that may be used in rehabilitation: anchors, scaffolding,

Table 3–10. Executive Function Treatments

Guiding Principles
  Structure
  Systematic Instruction
  Collaboration
  Context
  Metacognitive Strategy Instruction

Treatment Protocols
  Instructional Techniques
    Plan, Implement, Evaluate (PIE)
    TEACH-M
    Training Assistive Technology in the Environment (TATE)

Organization Strategies
  Problem-Solving Therapy
  Interactive Strategy Modeling Training
  Goal Management Training
  Strategic Memory Advanced Reasoning Training (SMART)
  Goal-Oriented Attentional Self-Regulation (GOALS)
  Time Management
  Awareness Training

Cognitive-Communication Interventions

Environmental Supports

and strategies. *Anchors* relate to routines that are well established in an individual's life. They are bound by time and environmental cues and may include routines (e.g., steps for getting ready in the morning) or ways to organize our environment (e.g., keeping things in set places). In rehabilitation, it is beneficial to use previously established anchors whenever possible and to establish new anchors as necessary. *Scaffolding* involves developing systems to maintain or reestablish anchors and may include use of organizational and memory aids to help engage the patient in the process of establishing structure. Initially, the clinician provides reminders, prompts, encouragement, and reinforcement to use these aids. However, the goal is to reduce dependence on these external cues and foster independence. *Strategies* are what help transition the patient to independent use of aids in the natural environment. Training patients to use strategies must be done systematically, which is another guiding principle, discussed below.

Systematic Instruction

While it is a common practice to introduce strategies to compensate for executive function deficits, use of these strategies may be unsuccessful due to lack of effective instruction and/or lack of instruction that targets maintenance and generalization of the strategies (Powell et al., 2012). However, it has been demonstrated that strategies can be successfully acquired and used in real-life situations when they are trained systematically (Ehlhardt et al., 2008; Powell et al., 2015; Sohlberg & Turkstra, 2011).

Systematic instruction is a method that focuses on *how* the instruction is designed and delivered. It emphasizes error control (e.g., errorless learning), particularly during the acquisition phase of an instructional target (Sohlberg & Turkstra, 2011). Several studies have found error control techniques to be helpful in teaching specific information to traumatically brain-injured individuals (Cohen, Ylvisaker, Hamilton, Kemp, & Claiman, 2010; Hunkin, Squires, Aldrich, & Parkin, 1998; Manly, Hawkins, Evans, Woldt, & Robertson,

2002), as well as to persons with dementia (Jang, Lee, & Yoo, 2015; Kessels & Hensken, 2009). Systematic instruction also builds in factors influencing maintenance and generalization such as high amounts of correct practice, distributed practice spaced retrieval, effortful processing and self-generation, and use of metacognitive strategies (to be discussed later) (Sohlberg, Ehlardt, & Kennedy, 2005). Error control is not emphasized during generalization and maintenance stages since there is evidence that error-based learning (trial and error) may be more beneficial than errorless learning in transferring skills to new tasks or environments (Ownsworth, 2017).

Powell et al. (2012) clearly summarized the components to include when designing instructional methods. First, conduct a detailed assessment of the learner's needs and abilities, including determining the environments in which the instructional targets will be used. Second, complete a task analysis by breaking the instructional targets into component parts. Third, carefully select and sequence examples. Delivery or implementation of instructional components includes (1) ongoing assessment of the learner's performance to gauge mastery; (2) preinstruction of component skills; (3) modeling of the skill by the instructor prior to learner practice; (4) carefully faded support; (5) frequent, correct, distributed practice and review; (6) immediate corrective feedback; (7) individualized instructional pacing to facilitate engagement; and (8) strategy instruction (p. 87).

Collaboration

A strong partnership between the clinician and the person with brain injury provides the foundation for the therapeutic process (Medley & Powell, 2010). Patients' experience of a bond with their therapist is related to increasing patients' awareness, which in turn is predictive of patients' compliance with a therapeutic plan (Trahan, Pepin, & Hopps, 2006). The bond, or therapeutic alliance, between the therapist and the patient can be strengthened by agreement on therapy goals and methods to achieve these goals (Schonberger, Humle, & Teasdale, 2006). Thus, collaboration and client-centeredness are necessary components of effective goal-setting practice (Prescott, Fleming, & Doig, 2015).

Goal attainment scaling (GAS) is a collaborative technique that has been used in many studies for developing individualized and meaningful goals and evaluating progress toward goal attainment (Grant & Ponsford, 2014). It involves the following steps: (1) specify an overall goal and break it down into a set of component goals, (2) assign a weight for each goal according to priority, (3) specify a continuum of possible outcomes, (4) determine initial or current performance, (5) intervene for a specified period, (6) determine performance attained on each objective, and (7) evaluate extent of attainment (Cardillo & Choat, 1994). GAS can be a useful tool for assessing outcomes in terms of improvement in performance of important daily activities (Grant & Ponsford, 2014).

Context

Ylvisaker and Feeney (1998) reported that successful management of executive function problems is related to the personal relevance of the treatment and the extent to which the treatment uses supports from the person's everyday life. They emphasized that "positive behavioral momentum," that is, providing a context in which the individual can succeed, is critical to success. Over the years, many treatment approaches have emphasized training in contextually rich, relevant environments using meaningful materials. Training that occurs within naturalistic contexts are more socially valid and thus more likely to generalize into real-life situations (Togher et al., 2014; Ylvisaker et al., 2007). For example, training assistive technology for cognition in the environments in which the technology will be used has resulted in positive outcomes (Powell, Glang, & Ettel, 2013). Similarly, treatment to improve conversational skills was more effective when individuals with traumatic brain injury practiced these skills at home and during social events compared to when they did not practice in those contexts (Togher, MacDonald, Tate, Power, & Rietdijk, 2013).

Metacognitive Strategy Instruction

Metacognition, or thinking about your thinking, includes self-awareness, self-monitoring, and self-control of cognition while performing an activity (Kennedy & Coelho, 2005). Metacognitive strategy instruction (MSI) teaches individuals to regulate their own behavior by breaking complex tasks into steps while thinking strategically. It is a practice standard for adults with traumatic brain injury who have difficulty with problem solving, organization, and planning (Kennedy et al., 2008) and is a primary component of numerous treatment studies. MSI does not emphasize training of a specific skill or task but rather guides the integration and internalization of self-regulation processes through direct instruction. This includes helping individuals identify an appropriate goal, predict their performance in advance of the activity, identify possible solutions based on their predictions, self-monitor or assess their performance during an activity, and change their behavior if the goal is not met (Kennedy et al., 2008). Interventions aimed to improve problem solving, planning, organization, and reasoning were found to be beneficial when treatments included individualized goal setting, use of metacognitive approaches that encouraged self-regulation or self-monitoring, internalization or self-instruction, structure and practice in a variety of real-life environments, and explicit feedback or training in self-evaluation systems (i.e., videotaping), whether offered in group or individual formats (Kennedy et al., 2008).

Treatment Protocols

Examples of specific treatments that have incorporated the above principles are described below.

Instructional Techniques

Plan, Implement, Evaluate. Sohlberg and Turkstra (2011) described a framework for systematic instruction that can be used when training specific facts and concepts, multistep routines, or use of external aids: Plan, Implement, Evaluate (PIE). In the planning stage, the clinician needs to ask *who* the learner is, *what* type of information is to be trained, *where* will the skill be used, *why* is the skill being trained, and *how* will the outcome be evaluated. The Implementation stage has three phases: Initial Acquisition, Mastery and Generalization, and Maintenance. During each of these phases, the clinician needs to consider the specific stimuli to be used, the practice regimen (e.g., error-control methods, massed practice, and intensive practice), and the level of cognitive engagement (e.g., prediction and reflection). When evaluating the effectiveness of the instructional technique, the specific outcome needs to be identified (e.g., the client will independently use an electronic calendar to recall and attend meetings). Data to be collected within the session (e.g., how many steps were recalled; how many trials were needed to reach criteria), as well as generalization and maintenance probes, should also be considered in advance (e.g., if recording speech appointments in calendar was trained in treatment, probe whether patient spontaneously recorded PT appointments).

TEACH-M. Elhardt, Sohlberg, Glang, and Albin (2005) designed a direct instructional package (TEACH-M) to facilitate learning and retention of steps for using an e-mail program. The specific components of the TEACH-M program include: *T*ask analysis (broke task into seven steps), *E*rrorless learning (modeled each step; patient practice step one, then one and two, then one, two, three, etc.), *A*ssess performance (baseline then probe before introducing a new step), *C*umulative review (regularly review previously learned skills), *H*igh rates of correct practice trials (e.g., spaced retrieval practice), and *M*etacognitive strategy training (e.g., patient predict performance). Using this technique, the five participants learned the seven-step e-mail program (seven of seven steps correct over three consecutive sessions) in 7 to 15 treatment sessions. Participants reported the most helpful parts of learning the program were watching the instructor model the steps and the high frequency of practice.

Training Assistive Technology in the Environment. Training Assistive Technology in the Environment (TATE; Powell, Harwick, et al., 2013) is an instructional package that was developed to assist clinicians train the use of assistive technology for cognition (ATC) to compensate for cognitive impairments. The package includes training videos, needs assessment forms, sample scripts, and data tracking tools (available at https://cbirt.org/research/completed-proj ects/tate-training-assistive-technology-environment-toolkit).

Powell and colleagues (2015) used the information in the TATE Toolkit to guide selection and training of an assistive technology device to facilitate workplace success for a 50-year-old woman with chronic cognitive deficits (over 20 years) following a cerebral hemorrhage from an arteriovenous malformation. Treatment began with a needs assessment to determine past and current use of technology and facilitate selection of the most appropriate device and apps to manage her current needs. Then three job requirements identified as challenging were chosen as treatment targets and appropriate apps to facilitate performance were selected. Task analyses for using each app were completed, and a variety of practice examples were selected

to facilitate generalization of each app across relevant work situations. Systematic instruction was delivered across three phases: initial acquisition, generalization, and maintenance. Initial acquisition involved three steps to minimize errors: (1) modeling with faded cues and support until the participant consistently performed each step with 100% accuracy; (2) frequent, correct, distributed practice with review; and (3) immediate, corrective feedback in response to errors. Generalization was promoted by conducting training in a variety of locations within the work setting. Regular review sessions were conducted to facilitate maintenance of learned skills. Results demonstrated regular usage of the apps with better recall of work-related tasks and information, and skills were maintained up to 1 year following treatment.

Organization Strategies

Turkstra and Flora (2002) provided treatment to a 49-year-old man with executive function problems following a traumatic brain injury. Specific deficits related to organization of information prevented him from successfully returning to work as a social worker. He reported difficulty with note-taking during interviews and writing reports; therefore, treatment addressed development of a report structure (e.g., , S.O.A.P. format: Subjective, Objective, Assessment, Plan) that included carrier phrases to elicit and organize information (e.g., "The client talked about . . . " "I said to the client . . . "). He was provided with numerous opportunities to practice using the forms in a variety of role play scenarios. Following 21 one-hour sessions over 10 weeks, he generated more accurate, detailed, and organized reports and became successfully employed.

Problem-Solving Therapy

Treatment of problem-solving skills has been addressed in both individual and group therapy sessions. In their meta-analysis of executive function interventions, Kennedy et al. (2008) found that many of the interventions for problem solving used steps that included self-monitoring, self-recording of performance, making strategy decisions based on goals, and adjusting or modifying the plan based on self-assessment and/or external feedback. Cantor et al. (2014) designed a problem-solving program incorporating these principles and generated an acronym to guide the patient through the problem-solving process: SWAPS.

1. <u>S</u>top! Is there a problem?
2. <u>W</u>hat is the problem?
3. <u>A</u>lternatives and options to solve the problem
4. <u>P</u>ick and plan the chosen option
5. <u>S</u>atisfied with the outcome of the plan

Cantor et al. (2014) used this problem-solving approach, along with training in attention, emotional self-regulation, and use of external aids, with 98 individuals with traumatic brain injury. During the 12-week program (3 hours per week), the participants were trained to use the SWAPS strategy to address any problematic situations that they encountered in life, including making decisions, handling interpersonal difficulties, and dealing with crises. Following training, significant gains were made in problem-solving skills. No significant gains were made in attention or emotional self-regulation following treatment targeting these areas.

Rath, Simon, Langenbahn, Sherr, and Diller (2003) conducted a randomized control study examining the effect of group treatment on problem-solving ability in outpatients with traumatic brain injury. Participants were assigned to either a "innovative problem-solving group" or a "conventional cognitive rehabilitation group." The problem-solving group treatment was divided into two parts: a problem-orientation component, which emphasized emotional self-regulation, and a problem-solving skills component, which emphasized "clear-thinking" and trained a systematic, step-by-step model of cognitive-behavioral problem-solving skills. Each of the 24 sessions followed a specific agenda, which included review of the previous session, didactic instruction, discussion, role-play, and assignment of homework exercises. During discussion of real-life problems, worksheets were used to help participants identify problematic contexts, warning signs of a problem, their reactions to the problems, possible strategies to manage the problem, and a plan to implement the strategy. In the problem-solving skills component, participants were taught to compensate for deficits caused by their injuries by asking "clear-thinking questions" in order to think their way through each step of the problem-solving skills model. Individuals who received the problem-solving treatment demonstrated greater gains on several standardized measures of problem-solving as well as improvement in everyday problem situations and their self-assessment of their problem-solving skills when compared to individuals who received conventional cognitive rehabilitation.

Interactive Strategy Modeling Training

The purpose of Interactive Strategy Modeling Training (ISMT) is to teach participants to use metacognitive strategies to solve verbal problems. In a study by Marshall et al. (2004), the participants and the examiner worked together to solve verbal problems through systematic question asking. The task was based on the Twenty Questions Task of Mosher and Hornsby (1966), and the training incorporated principles from educational psychology, including reciprocity (equal partnership/interactive) and exemplary modeling. Participants were presented with a grid containing 32 familiar words and had to determine a target word. The words could be grouped according to various semantic or perceptual categories. The examiner and participant exchanged roles of "problem solver" and "instructor." The examiner modeled strategies (i.e., constraint seeking questions) and provided the rationale for using the strategy (i.e., eliminated many of the options). Reinforcement was provided to the participant when appropriate questions were asked and guessing was avoided. Results demonstrated improved problem solving, characterized by requiring fewer questions to solve the problem and use of more constraint-seeking questions.

Goal Management Training

Goal Management Training (GMT) is intended to promote a mindful approach to problem solving by raising awareness of attentional lapses and reinstating cognitive control (Levine et al., 2011). It combines education of key concepts such as the distinction between absentmindedness and present-mindedness, slipups that occur in daily life, habitual responding (e.g., "auto-pilot"), stopping and thinking, task performance and feedback, and discussion of participants' own personal task failures and successes (Levine et al., 2011). Levine et al. (2000) conducted two experiments to determine the effect of GMT on the completion of multistep tasks. Clients were trained to actively consider six stages designed to facilitate self-regulation of their behavior during completion of common paper-and-pencil tasks designed to mimic tasks that are problematic for clients with goal neglect. The specific stages were:

1. STOP (ask themselves what they are doing)
2. DEFINE (define the main task)
3. LIST (list all steps required)
4. LEARN (ask themselves whether they know all the steps)
5. DO IT (execute the task)
6. CHECK (asking if they are doing what they planned to do)

Levine and colleagues found that GMT was associated with significant gains on completion of the tasks. In a later study, Levine and colleagues (2011) compared GMT to a general education approach. Both groups received seven 2-hour sessions. Results showed significant gains on a variety of executive function tasks following GMT. Tornas et al. (2016) conducted a randomized control study examining the effect of GMT with the addition of external cueing via text messages compared to a general brain health education program and found that GMT was an effective metacognitive strategy training method for enhancing successful completion of tasks in daily life situations. Effects were maintained and improved after 6 months, suggesting that skills learned in GMT were consolidated in real-life contexts after the end of training. When GMT was used with veterans with blast injuries, gains were made on tests of executive function; however, there was a lack of generalization from the clinic to everyday activities (Waid-Ebbs et al., 2014).

GMT has also found to be effective for managing executive dysfunction following stroke. Schweizer et al. (2008) used GMT with a patient who sustained a cerebellar hemorrhage due to rupture of an arteriovenous malformation. Following seven weekly 2-hour sessions, the patient made gains in sustained attention, planning, and organization on standardized tests as well as in real-life activities, including return to work.

Strategic Memory and Reasoning Training

The Strategic Memory and Reasoning Training (SMART) protocol (Vas, Chapman, Cook, Elliott, & Keebler, 2011) was developed to enhance the ability to abstract the gist of information presented in various formats. The program uses a top-down hierarchical strategy-based approach to train individuals to construct generalized meanings with no direct emphasis on recall of explicit facts. The program begins with strategies to strategically attend to incoming information and filter out less relevant details. The next stage focuses on integration of explicit content with preexisting knowledge to form gist-based representations. The final stage addresses generalization by evaluating information from different perspectives. Vas et al. (2011) examined the effects of SMART versus a general education program on 24 participants with traumatic brain injury who engaged in 18 hours of training during 12 group sessions conducted over 8 weeks. Results showed that the SMART program resulted in improved gist-reasoning, with generalization to untrained tasks of working memory, and improvements were sustained over a 6-month period. These findings were replicated in a second study (Vas et al., 2016). Additionally, gains were evident in executive function and psychological health. Physiologic changes were also evident, demonstrated by an increase in cerebral blood flow to bilateral precuneus and anterior cingulate cortex, and left inferior frontal region and left insula.

Goal-Oriented Attentional Self-Regulation

The Goal-Oriented Attentional Self-Regulation (GOALS) program emphasizes two key components: regulation of distractibility and application of goal-oriented attentional self-regulation to the identification, selection, and execution of self-generated goals (Novakovic-Agopian et al., 2018). Mindfulness-based attention regulation is applied to redirect cognitive processes toward task-relevant activities and filter nonrelevant noise using the metacognitive strategy of "Stop-Relax-Refocus" (p. 2787). Goal Management

Training and Problem-Solving Therapy (previously described above) were used to objectively describe their goals and extensively practice and apply the strategies. After ten 2-hour group sessions, three individual 1-hour sessions, and 20 hours of home practice over 5 weeks, 33 veterans with brain injury significantly improved on tests of attention and executive function, complex task performance, and emotional regulation (Novakovic-Agopian et al., 2018). These results were consistent with a previous study using GOALS with a civilian group of individuals with brain injury (Novakovic-Agopian et al., 2011).

Time Management

Many individuals with brain injuries can no longer accomplish tasks as efficiently as they had previously or regulate their behavior according to time constraints. These difficulties may be due to specific deficits in planning and organization or generalized slowed information processing. Tasks and behaviors that are carried out daily vary regarding the amount of time needed to initiate and complete the task and the speed with which action needs to be taken. For any task, decision making can be hierarchically organized into three levels, depending on the amount of time pressure present (Winkens, Van Heugten, Wade, & Fasotti, 2009). At the first level, no time pressure is experienced in relation to task completion because there is enough time to make a decision. Consider the act of driving. You need to determine where you are going, how you will get there, and the amount of time needed. This requires planning and organization, but typically there is no time pressure associ-

ated with the task since the plan can be determined well in advance. The next level relates to anticipating events and adapting behavior before time pressure builds up. For example, while driving you need to make decisions about you speed and how closely you follow the car in front of you. Some degree of time pressure is present, but it is manageable. Tasks at the third level require immediate decisions and actions in order to prevent failure, such as suddenly hitting the breaks and turning the wheel to avoid a collision.

Time Pressure Management (TPM) is an approach that teaches individuals strategies to either "prevent" or "manage" time pressure (Fasotti, Livacs, Eling, & Brouwer, 2000). TPM is carried out in three stages. The first stage addresses increasing awareness that mental slowness is a problem and can significantly impact daily life. During the second stage, the patients are informed that their speed of processing is not likely to return to normal, but the strategy "Let me give myself enough time" (Winkens et al., 2009, p. 52) can help them deal with their slowness. The last stage of TPM emphasizes strategy application and generalization by training under more distracting and difficult conditions.

Fasotti et al. (2000) used a TPM program to target speed of processing deficits in 12 brain-injured patients. A control group of 10 brain-injured individuals received "Concentration Therapy," during which they were instructed to pay careful attention to information presented. Both groups viewed a series of nine brief videotapes and were instructed to retell as much of what they heard on tapes as possible. The results showed that information intake improved significantly for both groups; however, TPM produced greater gains than concentration training and appeared to generalize to other measures of speed and memory function. Winkens et al. (2009) used a TPM program with 20 patients who had suffered a stroke. A control group of 17 stroke patients received usual care. The primary outcome measures were performance on an Information Intake Task and the number of strategies used during four tasks on the Mental Slowness Observation Test. Immediately posttreatment, both groups showed improvement in strategy usage. However, at 3 months posttreatment, only the TPM group showed a statistically significant decrease in the time required to complete everyday tasks while maintaining their level of accuracy.

Manly et al. (2002) took a different approach to teaching time management. They used a modification of Shallice and Burgess's six-element test to determine the effect of using auditory alerts to facilitate time management and completion of goals. Participants were told to imagine they worked in a hotel and had five tasks they needed to work on for a total of 15 minutes (sorting conference labels into alphabetical order, proofreading the hotel leaflet, sorting the charity collection, looking up telephone numbers, and compiling customer bills). They were told they would not have sufficient time to complete each task but had to do at least some of each task. In the first condition, participants independently worked on the tasks. In a second condition, participants were informed an auditory "beep" would be heard periodically, and they might find it helpful to use the tone as a reminder to think about what

they were doing and the overall aim of the task. Manly and colleagues found that participants with head injuries performed significantly worse on the task than control participants without brain injury during the independent condition. However, when the experimental group was provided with intermittent auditory tones, their performance improved to the level of the control group on several of the measures. Manly et al. suggested selective facilitation of a specific process may have considerable value in managing executive dysfunction. They concluded that, if one aspect of the executive system can be environmentally supported (i.e., use of an auditory tone), other aspects of problem solving and organization may be adequately demonstrated.

Awareness Training

Sohlberg et al. (2005) suggested several methods to help clients experience and integrate knowledge about changes in their functioning to improve awareness of their deficits. These methods incorporate metacognitive principles such as attending to and reflecting on specific behaviors or actions. Clients may be encouraged to predict performance on a variety of tasks that are both within and outside of their skill level. Clinicians can help their clients reflect on their predictions and performance to help the clients recognize their abilities and limitations. Another method involves asking clients to track their performance on tasks they select to monitor while using or not using different compensatory strategies. This helps the clients learn which strategies work or don't work. Finally, specific goal setting can also be used to increase awareness and track performance. Establishing meaningful goals can also help motivate clients to participate in treatment.

Comparison of predicted performance and actual behavior has been used both as a measure of unawareness and as a management approach for unawareness (Goverover, Johnston, Toglia, & Deluca, 2007; Schlund, 1999). Goverover et al. (2007) used a randomized control design to examine the effect of awareness training conducted during completion of instrumental activities of daily living. The experimental group was asked to predict their performance before completing the activity and estimate their performance after completion, while the control group simply completed the task. The experimental group showed significant gains completing daily living tasks and self-regulation. No change was evident in the control group. Similarly, Schlund (1999) evaluated three individuals' awareness by comparing predicted memory test scores with actual memory test scores. Following testing, an awareness training program was implemented, which involved estimating performance on various tasks, followed by specific feedback on actual performance. Over time, the differences between the predicted and actual performance decreased, suggesting increased awareness.

Cognitive-Communication Interventions

Behavioral treatments to enhance cognitive communication can be classified as impairment based or context sensitive (Finch, Copley, Cornwell, & Kelly, 2016). Impairment-based approaches focus solely on restoring a specific damaged cognitive function such as emotion perception or verbal interaction skills. Context-sensitive treatments use a combination of impairment-based interventions, functional activities, and context-supported participation to help individuals engage in their desired everyday activities. A systematic review of behavioral interventions found both impairment-based and context-sensitive treatments resulted in improved cognitive communication skills. However, maintenance of the skills up to 6 months posttreatment was found only for the context-sensitive approach (Finch et al., 2016). Treatments typically were conducted in a group format, though some programs also included individual sessions. Intervention procedures were variable among studies and included discussion, modeling, role-playing, verbal or visual (videotaped) feedback, self-monitoring, behavioral rehearsal, and social reinforcement.

Gabbatore et al. (2015) designed a cognitive pragmatic treatment that addressed comprehension and production aspects of communicative competence for individuals with traumatic brain injury. The activities were designed to increase inferential abilities that would allow participants to fill in the gap that may occur between what a person says and what the person intends to communicate. Comprehension tasks focused on matching linguistic utterances with paralinguistic information such as tone of voice, facial expressions, and body movements. Production training was aimed at helping participants modulate their communication according to a particular context. Treatment was provided twice a week for 12 weeks. Following treatment, participants demonstrated higher levels of social appropriateness, sensitivity to the context, and social judgment.

Environmental Supports

The goal of environmental adaptations is to set up a client's home or work setting to circumvent or prevent problems that may arise due to impairments in executive functioning (Sohlberg & Mateer, 2001). Environmental adaptations also may be used concurrently with direct instruction techniques.

Environmental adaptations can be organized into four broad categories: modification of task demands, organization of physical space, cuing/prompting, and manipulation of physiologic factors.

Mateer (1999) suggests a number of ways in which task demands may be reduced, including breaking the task down into smaller steps, removing or minimizing stimuli that may elicit inappropriate behavior, providing breaks to minimize fatigue or frustration, allowing clients extra time to complete tasks, and reducing or eliminating environmental distractions.

Organization of physical space also can reduce the demands on a client's executive function system. In order for this approach to be successful, the clinician must systematically examine the client's environment and obtain input from the client and family so as to understand where difficulties may arise. Specific organizational techniques may include identifying designated areas for items and activities; providing a centralized space for a calendar, schedules, and other things related to planning; and creating a filing system for management of bills, letters, and other important items.

The provision of cues or prompts may be helpful in management of dysexecutive symptoms of clients, particularly for clients who may demonstrate adequate knowledge of the steps required in various executive tasks but fail to apply this knowledge when the need arises. A variety of verbal and written reminders or other external cues may be helpful. For example, a list of tasks to be completed or items to take to school may be generated; steps in specific routines ("wake-up" and "bed-time") can be established and written down, and schedules to facilitate time management may be created. Sohlberg, Sprunk, and Metzelaar (1988) reported improvements in initiation following training with an external cueing system.

Finally, Sohlberg and Mateer (2001) suggest it is important to monitor different physiological factors that regulate internal states since disruptions in nutrition, sleep, activity level, and medications may negatively affect performance. Implementation of specific routines such as always taking medications with meals or going to bed at the same time each night can be useful in preventing fatigue. In addition, patients can be encouraged to monitor their level of fatigue by "checking in" during completion of challenging activities.

Brian's Treatment Plan

Brian's overall goal was to return to work. Treatment began with collaborating to establish meaningful, achievable goals. This was accomplished through discussion of his experiences to date ("What happened when you tried to return to work?") and the introduction of metacognitive strategies to problem-solve through the situation ("What do you think the problem was? What could you do differently to be more successful? Given these issues, what do you think you could reasonably accomplish by the end of therapy?"). Following these discussions, it was determined that scheduling appointments would be the focus of treatment. Specific long-term goals were developed using Goal Attainment Scaling (Table 3–11).

A task analysis of the procedure for scheduling appointments was completed collaboratively. Brian brainstormed to write out all steps related to the overall task of scheduling (sequential order was not necessary at this point), which helped him become aware of the complexity of the task. The items were then reorganized into subtasks (preparation, contacting the customer, and traveling to the appointment), and

prompting was provided as needed to add details. Templates, checklists, and a script were created over the next several sessions (Table 3–12). The guiding principles discussed earlier in the chapter were incorporated in training use of the templates and script (Table 3–13). Homework included reviewing his customers' records and entering information from technical manuals for equipment into templates. Because there were multiple models for each type of product and the volume of information was overwhelming, only information for copy machines was entered into templates. Initially, assignments were very explicit. As treatment progressed, Brian identified what he needed to do to prepare for the next session. Each session began with a review of the homework and discussion of the process ("How did it go? What was easy? Challenging? Anything unexpected?"). Then the script was practiced with "customers" during various role-play situations. Immediate, corrective feedback was

Table 3–11. Sample Goal Attainment Scaling

Value Number	Meaning	Example
+2	Much more than expected level of outcome	I will schedule four appointments per week, using strategies
+1	Somewhat more than expected level of outcome	I will schedule three appointments per week, using strategies
0	Expected level of outcome	I will schedule two appointments per week, using strategies
−1	Somewhat less than expected level of outcome	I will schedule one appointment per week, using strategies
−2	Much less than expected level of outcome	I will schedule two appointments per month, using strategies

Note. Brian reported meeting with two to three customers per day prior to his accident.

Table 3–12. Sample Template and Checklist

PREPARATION		Notes	
Before calling the customer, review the customer's records	1. When did we last meet?	1.	
	2. What did he buy?	2.	
	3. Is there a newer model?	3.	
	a. How is it different?*		3a
	b. Other models?*		3b
	4. What else was he interested in?	4.	
	5. Is there any other product that would be helpful for the customer?	5.	
	*Complete equipment template with information for customer's current product and one recommended product		

GETTING THERE	Check off when completed
Two days before appointment	
1. Find address on Google Maps	1.
2. Note time it takes to get there	2.
3. Add 30 minutes	3.
4. Calculate total time you need to get there	4.
5. Calculate the time you need to leave	5.
6. Write time you need to leave and time of appointment in calendar	6.
7. Gather relevant cheat sheets and brochures	7.
Day before appointment	
1. Find address on Google Maps	1.
2. Print out route—read through three times	2.
3. Check appointment time and time you need to leave	3.
4. Review relevant cheat sheets and brochures	4.
Morning of appointment	
1. Check Google Maps—any change in time to get there? (accident, rush hour)	1.
2. Adjust time for travel, if necessary, remembering to add 30 minutes	2.
3. Review cheat sheets	3.
4. Put cheat sheets and print out of route in car	4.

continues

Table 3–12. *continued*

SAMPLE SCRIPT	

Before calling, gather props
     1. Calendar
     2. Relevant cheat sheets
	Notes

1. Hi Mr. _____	
2. It's been awhile. We haven't had a chance to talk since _____	
3. How is the _____ working?	
4. Is it meeting your needs?	
5. Are there other jobs or tasks you need some help with?	
6. I'd like to come see you again and show you some new products.	

7. What day works for you?
     Check calendar.
     If there is nothing on your calendar, ask	

8. "What time?" *If you already have something scheduled, state:*	
9. I'm sorry, I already have an appointment that day. What other day are you available? *Write down customer's name and time of appointment in your calendar.*	
10. Great! I look forward to meeting with you on _____.	

provided if a step was missed (e.g., did not write the appointment in his calendar), and the script was started again from the beginning. As Brian became accustomed to using the script successfully, constraints or problems were spontaneously introduced to encourage problem solving and flexibility.

Brian was seen for treatment twice a week (45-minute sessions) for 10 weeks to develop and practice the script and cheat sheets, then once a week for 8 more weeks, during which time he attempted to schedule appointments with customers. Treatment sessions were used to review the week (Was he

Table 3–13. Guiding Principles Incorporated Into Brian's Treatment Program

Collaboration	Identified Goals Using Goal Attainment Scaling
Context	All stimuli and activities were related to Brian's job
Structure	Generated templates, checklists, and a script to aid in organization of information
Systematic instruction	Conducted task analysis; practiced scripts with a variety of "customers" in a variety of situations; provided immediate, corrective feedback; gradually faded structure and increased patient effort following successful completion of activities
Metacognitive strategy instruction	Regularly reflected on performance, factors influencing performance, and ways to modify tasks to increase success

successful in meeting his goal? Why or why not?) and tweak the script as necessary. By the eighth week, he had scheduled two appointments per week for 3 consecutive weeks and he was discharged from therapy.

Summary

Executive dysfunction is a common consequence of brain injury. Comprehensive assessment and careful attention to the design and implementation of treatment can result in positive outcomes and improved participation in meaningful activities.

References

Aitken, S., Chase, S., McClue, M., & Ratcliff, G. (1993). An American adaptation of the Multiple Errands Test: Assessment of executive abilities in everyday life. *Archives of Neurology, 8*, 212.

Alvarez, J. A., & Emory, E. (2006). Executive function and the frontal lobes: A meta-analytic review. *Neuropsychological Review, 16*, 17–42. doi:10.1007/s11065-006-9002-x

American Speech-Language-Hearing Association. (2004). *Preferred practice patterns for the profession of speech-language pathology* [Preferred practice patterns]. *Retrieved* from http://www.asha.org/policy

Annoni, J. M., Khateb, A., Gramigna, S., Staub, F., Carota, A., Maaeder, P., & Bogousslavsky, J. (2003). Chronic cognitive impairment following laterothalamic infarcts: A study of 9 cases. *Archives of Neurology, 60*, 1439–1443.

Avramović, P., Kenny, B., Power, E., McDonald, S., Tate, R., Hunt, L., . . . Togher, L. (2017). Exploring the relationship between cognition and functional verbal reasoning in adults with severe traumatic brain injury at six months post injury. *Brain Injury, 31*(4), 502–516. doi: 10.1080/02699052.2017.1280854

Baddeley, A., & Hitch, G. (1974). Working memory. In G. Bower (Ed.), *The psychology of learning and motivation* (pp. 47–89). New York, NY: Academic Press.

Barker, M., Young, B., & Robinson, G. (2017). Cohesive and coherent connected speech deficits in mild stroke. *Brain and Language, 168,* 23–36. doi:10.1016/j.bandl .2017.01.004

Belanger, H., Spiegel, E., & Vanderploeg, R. (2010). Neuropsychological performance following a history of multiple self-reported concussions: A meta-analysis. *Journal of the International Neuropsychological Society, 16*(2), 262–267.

Benton, A. L., Hamsher, K., Rey, G. J., & Sivan, A. B. (1994). *Multilingual Aphasia Examination* (3rd ed.). San Antonio, TX: Psychological Corporation.

Bogart, E., Togher, L., Power, E., & Docking, K. (2012). Casual conversations between individuals with traumatic brain injury and their friends. *Brain Injury, 26*(3), 221–233. doi:10.3109/02699052.2011.648711

Borkowski, J., Benton, A., & Spreen, O. (1967). Word fluency and brain damage. *Neuropsychologia, 5,* 135–140.

Boyd, T. M., Sautter, S., Bailey, M. B., Echols, L. D., & Douglas, J. W. (1987, February). *Reliability and validity of a measure of everyday problem solving.* Paper presented at the annual meeting of the International Neuropsychological Society, Washington, DC.

Braswell, D., Hartey, A., Hoornbeek, S., Johansen, A., Johnson, L., Schultz, J., & Sohlberg, M. (1992). *The profile of executive control system.* Gaylord, MI: Northern Rehabilitation Services.

Bryan, K. L., & Hale, J. B. (2001). Differential effects of left and right cerebral vascular accidents on language competency. *Journal of the International Neuropsychological Society, 7,* 655–664.

Burgess, P. W., Alderman, N., Wilson, B. A., Evans, J. J., & Emslie, H. (1996). The Dysexecutive Questionnaire. In B. A. Wilson, N. Alderman, P. W. Burgess, H. Emslie, & J. J. Evans (Eds.), *Behavioural assessment of the dysexecutive syndrome.* Bury St Edmunds, UK: Thames Valley Test Company.

Burke T., Lonergan, K., Pinto-Grau, M., Elamin, M., Bede, P., Madden, C., . . .

Pender, N. (2017). Visual encoding, consolidation, and retrieval in amyotrophic lateral sclerosis: Executive function as a mediator, and predictor of performance. *Amyotrophic Lateral Sclerosis Frontotemporal Degeneration, 18*(3–4), 193–201. doi:10 .1080/21678421.2016.1272615

Byom, L., & Turkstra, L. (2017). Cognitive task demands and discourse performance after traumatic brain injury. *International Journal of Language and Communication Disorders, 52*(4), 501–513.

Caeyenberghs, K., Leemans, A., Leunissen, I., Gooijers, J., Michiels, K., Sunnaert, S., & Swinnen, S. (2014). Altered structural networks and executive deficits in traumatic brain injury patients. *Brain Structure and Function, 219,* 193–209.

Cannizzaro, M., & Coelho, C. (2013). Analysis of narrative discourse structure as an ecologically relevant measure of executive function in adults. *Journal of Psycholinguistic Research, 42,* 527–549. doi:10. 1007/s10936-012-9231-5

Cantor, J., Ashman, T., Dams-O'Connor, K., Dijkers, M., Gordon, W., Spielman, L., . . . Oswald, J. (2014). Evaluation of the Short-Term Executive Plus intervention for executive dysfunction after traumatic brain injury: A randomized controlled trial with minimization. *Archives of Physical Medicine and Rehabilitation, 95*(1), 1–9.

Cardillo, J. E., & Choate, R. O. (1994). Illustrations of goal setting. In T. Kiresuk, A. Smith, & J. Cardillo (Eds.), *Goal attainment scaling: Applications, theory and measurement* (pp. 15–60). London, UK: Erlbaum.

Channon, S., & Watts, M. (2003). Pragmatic language interpretation after closed head injury: Relationship to executive functioning. *Cognitive Neuropsychiatry, 8,* 243–260.

Coelho, C. (1995). Impairments of discourse abilities and executive functions in traumatically brain-injured adults. *Brain Injury, 9*(5), 471–477.

Coelho, C. (2002). Story narratives of adults with closed head injury and non-brain injured adults: Influence of socioeconomic status, elicitation task, and executive functioning. *Journal of Speech, Language, and Hearing Research, 45*, 1232–1248.

Coelho, C. (2007). Management of discourse deficits following traumatic brain injury: Progress, caveats, and needs. *Seminars in Speech Language, 28*(2), 122–128. doi:10.1055/s-2007-970570.

Coelho, C., Grela, B., Corso, M., Gamble, A., & Feinn, R. (2005). Microlinguistic deficits in the narrative discourse of adults with traumatic brain injury. *Brain Injury, 19*(13), 1139–1145. doi:10.1080/02699050500110678

Cohen, M., Ylvisaker, M., Hamilton, J., Kemp, L., & Claiman, B. (2010). Errorless learning of functional life skills in an individual with three aetiologies of severe memory and executive function impairment. *Neuropsychological Rehabilitation, 20*(3), 355–376.

Cummings, J. L. (1993). Frontal-subcortical circuits and human behavior. *Archives of Neurology, 50*, 873–880.

Davis, G. A., & Coelho, C. (2004). Referential cohesion and logical coherence of narration after closed head injury. *Brain and Language, 89*, 508–523.

Delis, D. C., Fridlund, A. J., Kramer, J., & Kaplan, E. (1984). California Proverb Test. In P. McReynolds, J. C. Rosen, & G. J. Chelune (Eds.), *Advances in psychological assignment* (pp. 101–132). New York, NY: Plenum Press.

Delis, D. C., Kaplan, E., & Kramer, J. H. (2001). *Delis-Kaplan executive function system examiner's manual.* San Antonio, TX: Psychological Corporation.

Delis, D. C., Squire, L. R., Bihrle, A. M., & Massman, P. J. (1992). Componential analysis of problem-solving ability: Performance of patients with frontal lobe damage and amnesic patients on a new sorting test. *Neuropsychologia, 30*, 683–697.

D'Esposito, M., Postle, B. R., & Rypma, B. (2000). Prefrontal cortical contributions to working memory: Evidence from event related fMRI studies. *Experimental Brain Research, 133*, 3–11.

Douglas, J., O'Flaherty, C., & Snow, P. (2000). Measuring perception of communicative ability: The development and evaluation of the La Trobe Communication Questionnaire. *Aphasiology, 14*(3), 251–268.

Ehlhardt, L., Sohlberg, M., Kennedy, M., Coelho, C., Ylvisaker, M., Turkstra, L., & Yorkston, K. (2008). Evidence-based practice guidelines for instructing individuals with neurogenic memory impairments: what have we learned in the past 20 years? *Neuropsychological Rehabilitation, 18*(3), 300–342. doi:10.1080/09602010701733190

Ehlhardt, L. A., Sohlberg, M. M., Glang, A., & Albin, R. (2005). TEACH-M: A pilot study evaluating an instructional sequence for persons with impaired memory and executive functions. *Brain Injury, 19*(8), 569–583.

Elderkin-Thompson, V., Boone, K. B., Hwang, S., & Kumar, A. (2004). Neurocognitive profiles in elderly patients with frontotemporal degeneration or major depressive disorder. *Journal of the International Neuropsychological Society, 10*, 753–771.

Fasotti, L., Kovacs, F., Eling, P., & Brouwer, W. H. (2000). Time pressure management as a compensatory strategy training after closed head injury. *Neuropsychological Rehabilitation, 10*, 47–65.

Filley, C. M. (2000). Clinical neurology and executive dysfunction. *Seminars in Speech and Language, 21*, 95–108.

Finch, E., Copley, A., Cornwell, P., & Kelly, C. (2016). Systematic review of behavioral interventions targeting social communication difficulties after traumatic brain injury. *Archives of Physical Medicine and Rehabilitation, 97*, 1352–1365. doi:10.1016/j.apmr.2015.11.005

Flavia, M., Stampatori, C., Zanotti, D., Parrinello, G., & Capra, R. (2010). Efficacy and specificity of intensive cognitive rehabilitation of attention and executive functions in multiple sclerosis. *Journal of the Neurological Sciences, 288*(1), 101–105.

Frith, M., Togher, L., Ferguson, A., Levick, W., & Docking, K. (2014). Assessment practices of speech-language pathologists for cognitive communication disorders following traumatic brain injury in adults: An international survey. *Brain Injury, 28*(13/14), 1657–1666. doi:10.3109/02699052.2014.947619

Gabbatore, I., Sacco, K., Angeleri, R., Zettin, M., Bara, G., & Bosco, F. (2015). Cognitive pragmatic treatment: A rehabilitative program for traumatic brain injury individuals. *Journal of Head Trauma Rehabilitation, 30*(5), E14–E28. doi:10.1097/HTR.0000000000000087

Goldstein, S., Naglieri, J., Princiotta, D., & Otero, T. (2014). Introduction: A history of executive functioning as a theoretical and clinical construct. In S. Goldstein & J. Naglieri (Eds.), *Handbook of executive functioning* (pp. 3–12). New York, NY: Springer.

Goverover, Y., Johnson, M., Toglia, J., & Deluca, J. (2007). Treatment to improve self-awareness in persons with acquired brain injury. *Brain Injury, 21*(9), 913–923. doi:10.1080/02699050701553205

Grace, J., & Malloy, P. (2001). *Frontal systems behavior scale professional manual.* Lutz, FL: Psychological Assessment Resources.

Grant, D. A., & Berg, E. A. (1948). A behavioral analysis of reinforcement and ease of shifting to new responses in a Weigel-type card-sorting problem. *Journal of Experimental Psychology, 38*, 404–411.

Grant, M., & Ponsford, J. (2014). Goal Attainment Scaling in brain injury rehabilitation: Strengths, limitations, and recommendations for future applications. *Neuropsychological Rehabilitation, 24*(5), 661–677. doi:10.1080/09602011.2014.901228

Guskiewicz, K. M., Marshall, S. W., Bailes, J., McCrea, M., Cantu, R. C., Randolph, C., & Jordan B. D. (2005). Association between recurrent concussion and late-life cognitive impairment in retired professional football players. *Neurosurgery; 57*, 719–726.

Hagen, C., Malkamus, D., & Durham, P. (1972). *Levels of cognitive functioning.* Downey, AZ: Ranchos Los Amigos Hospital.

Halliday, M. (1994). *An introduction to functional grammar* (2nd ed.). London, UK: Edward Arnold.

Hartman-Maeir, A., Soroker, N., Ring, H., & Katz, N. (2002). Awareness of deficits in stroke rehabilitation. *Journal of Rehabilitative Medicine, 34*(4), 158–164.

Helm-Estabrooks, N. (2001). *Cognitive-Linguistic Quick Test.* San Antonio, TX: Psychological Corporation.

Helm-Estabrooks, N. (2002). Cognition and aphasia: A discussion and a study. *Journal of Communication Disorders, 35*, 171–186.

Huey, E., Govelia, E., Paviol, S., Pardini, M., Krueger, F., Zamboni, G., . . . Grafman, J. (2009). Executive dysfunction in frontotemporal dementia and corticobasal syndrome. *Neurology, 72*(5), 453–459.

Higginson, C., Thompson, T., Benjamin, A., & Rosales, A. (2017). Construct validity of the Functional Assessment of Verbal Reasoning and Executive Strategies (FAVRES). *Brain Injury, 31*(13–14), 1087–1812.

Hunkin, N. M., Squires, E. J., Aldrich, F. K., & Parkin, A. J. (1998). Errorless learning and the acquisition of word processing skills. *Neuropsychological Rehabilitation, 8*, 433–449.

Jackson, H., Hague, G., Daniels, L., Aguilar, R., Carr, D., & Kenyon, W. (2014). Structure to self-structuring: Infrastructure and processes in neurobehavioral rehabilitation. *NeuroRehabilitation, 34*, 681–694. doi:10.3233/NRE-141082

Jang, J., Lee, J., & Yoo, D. (2015). Effects of spaced retrieval training with errorless learning in the rehabilitation of patients with dementia. *Journal of Physical Therapy Science, 27*(9), 2735–2738.

Joint Committee on Interprofessional Relations Between the American Speech-Language-Hearing Association and

Division 40 (Clinical Neuropsychology) of the American Psychological Association. (2007). *Structure and function of an interdisciplinary team for persons with acquired brain injury.* Retrieved from http://www.asha.org/policy

Kagan, A., Winckel, J., Black, S., Duchan, J. F., Simmons-Mackie, N., & Square, P. (2004). A set of observational measures for rating support and participation in conversation between adults with aphasia and their conversation partners. *Topics in Stroke Rehabilitation, 11*(1), 67–83.

Keil, K., & Kaszniak, A. W. (2002). Examining executive function in individuals with brain injury: A review. *Aphasiology, 16*(3), 305–335.

Kennedy, M. R., & Coelho, C. (2005). Self-regulation after traumatic brain injury: A framework for intervention of memory and problem solving. *Seminars in Speech and Language, 26*(4), 242–255.

Kennedy, M. R., Coelho, C., Turkstra, L., Ylvisaker, M., Sohlberg, M. M., Yorkston, K., . . . Kan, P.F. (2008). Intervention for executive functions after traumatic brain injury: A systematic review, meta-analysis and clinical recommendations. *Neuropsychological Rehabilitation, 18,* 257–299.

Kessels, R., & Hensken, L. (2009). Effects of errorless skill learning in people with mild-to-moderate or severe dementia: A randomized controlled pilot study. *NeuroRehabilitation, 25*(4), 307–312. doi:10 .3233/NRE-2009-0529

Kinnunen, K. M., Greenwood, R., Powell, J. H., Leech, R., Hawkins, P. C., Bonnelle, V., . . . Sharp, D. J. (2011). White matter damage and cognitive impairment after traumatic brain injury. *Brain, 134*(2), 449–463. doi:10.1093/brain/awq347

Kudlicka, A., Clare, L., & Hindle, J. V. (2011). Executive functions in Parkinson's disease: Systematic review and meta-analysis. *Movement Disorders, 26,* 2305–2315.

Le, K., Coelho, C., Mozieko, J., Krueger, F., & Grafman, J. (2014), Does brain volume loss predict cognitive and narrative discourse performance following traumatic brain injury? *American Journal of Speech–Language Pathology, 23,* S271–S284.

Lehman-Blake, M., Duffy, J. R., Myers, P. S., & Tompkins, C. A. (2002). Prevalence and patterns of right hemisphere cognitive/communicative deficits: Retrospective data from an inpatient rehabilitation unit. *Aphasiology, 16,* 537–547.

Levine, B., Robertson, I. H., Clare, L., Carter, G., Hong, J., Wilson, B. A., . . . Stuss, D. T. (2000). Rehabilitation of executive functioning: An experimental-clinical validation of Goal Management Training. *Journal of the International Neuropsychological Society, 6,* 299–312.

Levine, B., Schweizer, T., O'Connor, C., Turner, G., Gillingham, S., Stuss, D., . . . Robertson, I. (2011). Rehabilitation of executive functioning in patients with frontal lobe brain damage with Goal Management Training. *Frontiers in Human Neuroscience, 5*(9), 1–9.

Lezak, M. D. (1995). *Neuropsychological assessment* (3rd ed.). Oxford, UK: Oxford University Press.

Lezak, M., Howieson, D., Bigler, E., & Tranel, D. (2012). *Neuropsychological assessment* (5th ed.). New York, NY: Oxford University Press.

Linscott, R., Knight, R., & Godfrey, H. (1996). The Profile of Functional Impairment in Communication (PFIC): A measure of communication impairment for clinical use. *Brain Injury, 10*(6), 397–412.

Lippa, S., Pastorek, N., Benge, J., & Thornton, G. (2010). Post-concussive symptoms after blast and non-blast-related mild traumatic brain injuries in Afghanistan and Iraq war veterans. *Journal of the International Neuropsychological Society, 16*(5), 856–866.

Luria, A. R. (1966). *Higher cortical functions in man.* New York, NY: Basic Books.

MacDonald, S. (2005). *Functional assessment of verbal reasoning and executive strategies.* Ontario, Canada: CCD Publishing.

MacDonald, S., & Johnson, C. (2005). Assessment of subtle cognitive-communication deficits following acquired brain injury:

A normative study of the Functional Assessment of Verbal Reasoning and Executive Strategies (FAVRES). *Brain Injury, 19*(2), 895–902. doi:10.1080/0269 9050400004294

MacPherson, S. E., Wagner, G. P., Murphy, P., Bozzali, M., Cipolotti, L.& Shallice, T. (2014). Bringing the Cognitive Estimation Task into the 21st century: Normative data on two new parallel forms. *PLoS ONE, 9*(3), e92554. doi:10.1371/journal.pone.0092554

Manchester, D., Priestley, N., & Jackson, H. (2004). The assessment of executive functions: coming out of the office. *Brain Injury, 18*(11), 1067–1081.

Manly, T., Hawkins, K., Evans, J., Woldt, K., & Robertson, I. (2002). Rehabilitation of executive function: Facilitation of effective goal management on complex tasks using periodic auditory tests. *Neuropsychologia, 40,* 271–281.

Marini, A., Zettin, M., & Galetto, V. (2014). Cognitive correlates of narrative impairment in moderate traumatic brain injury. *Neuropsychologia, 64,* 282–288.

Marsh, N., Ludbrook, M., & Gaffaney, L. (2016). Cognitive functioning following traumatic brain injury: A five-year follow-up. *NeuroRehabilitation, 38*(1), 71–78. doi:10.3233/NRE-151297

Marshall, G., Rentz, D., Frey, M., Locascio, J., Johnson, K., & Sperling, R. (2011). Executive function and instrumental activities of daily living in mild cognitive impairment and Alzheimer's disease. *Alzheimers Dementia, 7*(3), 300–308.

Marshall, R. C., Karow, C. M., Morelli, C. A., Iden, K. K., Dixon, J., & Cranfill, T. B. (2004). Effects of interactive strategy modeling training on problem-solving by persons with traumatic brain injury. *Aphasiology, 18*(8), 659–673.

Mateer, C. (1999). The rehabilitation of executive disorders. In D. Stuss, G. Winocur, & I. Robertson (Eds.), *Cognitive neurorehabilitation* (pp. 314–332). Cambridge, UK: Cambridge University Press.

McCue, M., Pramuka, M., Chase, S., & Fabry, P. (1995). Functional assessment procedures for individuals with severe cognitive disabilities. *American Rehabilitation, 20*(3), 17–27.

McDonald, S., Gowland, A., Randall, R., Fisher, A., Osborn Crowley, K., & Honan, C. (2014). Cognitive factors underpinning poor expressive communication skills after traumatic brain injury: Theory of mind or executive function? *Neuropsychology, 28,* 801–811.

McDonald, S., Togher, L., & Code, C. (Eds.). (2013). *Social and communication disorders following traumatic brain injury* (2nd ed.). Hove, UK: Psychology Press.

Medley, A., & Powell, T. (2010). Motivational interviewing to promote self-awareness and engagement in rehabilitation following acquired brain injury: A conceptual review. *Neuropsychological Rehabilitation, 20*(4), 481–508. doi:10.1080/09602010903 529610

Meulenbroek, P., & Turkstra, L. (2016). Job stability in skilled work and communication ability after moderate-severe traumatic brain injury. *Disability and Rehabilitation, 38*(5), 452–461. doi:10.3109/096382 88.2015.1044621

Miyake, A., Emerson, M. J., & Friedman, N. P. (2000). Assessment of executive functions in clinical settings: Problems and recommendations. *Seminars in Speech and Language, 21*(2), 169–183.

Morrison, M., Giles, G., Ryan, J., Baum, C., Dromerick, A., Polatajko, H., & Edwards, D. (2013). Multiple Errands Test–Revised (MET-R): A performance-based measure of executive function in people with mild cerebrovascular accident. *American Journal of Occupational Therapy, 13*(4), 460–468.

Mosher, F. A., & Hornsby, J. R. (1966). On asking questions. In J. S. Bruner, R. Oliver, J. R. Greenfield, J. R. Hornsby, M. Kenner, N. Maccoby, et al. (Eds.), *Studies in cognitive growth* (pp. 86–102). New York, NY: Wiley.

Mueller, J., & Dollaghan, C. (2013). A systematic review of assessments for identifying executive function impairment in adults with acquired brain injury. *Journal of Speech, Language, and Hearing Research*, *56*, 1051–1064.

Nicholas, M., & Connor, L. (2017). People with aphasia using AAC: Are executive functions important? *Aphasiology, 31*(7), 819–836. doi:10.1080/02687038.2016.1258539

Novakovic-Agopian, T., Chen, A., Rome, S., Abrams, G., Castelli, H., Rossi, A., . . . D'Esposito, M. (2011). Rehabilitation of executive functioning with training in attention regulation applied to individually defined goals: A pilot study bridging theory, assessment, and treatment. *Journal of Head Trauma Rehabilitation, 26*, 325–338.

Novakovic-Agopian, T., Kornblith, E., Abrams, G., Burciaga-Rosales, J., Loya, F., D'Esposito, M., & Chen, A. (2018). Training in goal-oriented attention self-regulation improves executive functioning in veterans with chronic traumatic brain injury. *Journal of Neurotrauma, 35*, 2784–2795. doi:10.1089/neu.2017.5529

O'Reilly, R. A. (2010). The what and how of prefrontal cortical organization. *Trends in Neuroscience, 33*, 355–361. doi:10.1016/j.tins.2010.05.002

Ownsworth, T., Fleming, J., Tate, R., Beadle, E., Griffin, J., Kendall, M., . . . Shum, D. (2017). Do people with severe traumatic brain injury benefit from making errors? A randomized controlled trial of error-based and errorless learning. *Neurorehabilitation and Neural Repair, 31*(12), 1072–1082. doi:10.1177/1545968317740635

Pearce, B., Cartwright, J., Cocks, N., & Whitworth, A. (2016). Inhibitory control and traumatic brain injury: The association between executive control processes and social communication deficits. *Brain Injury, 30*(13–14), 1708–1717. doi:10.1080/02699052.2016.1202450

Phukan, J., Elamin, M., Bede, P., Jordan, N., Gallagher, L., Byrne, S., . . . Hardiman, O. (2012). The syndrome of cognitive impairment in amyotrophic lateral sclerosis: A population-based study. *Journal of Neurology, Neurosurgery and Psychiatry, 83*(1), 102–108.

Porteus, S. D. (1965). *Porteus Maze Test. Fifty years application.* Palo Alto, CA: Pacific.

Posner, M., & Snyder, C. (1975). Attentional and cognitive control. In R. L. Solso (Ed.), *Information processing and cognition* (pp. 55–85). Abingdon, UK: Erlbaum.

Powell, L. E., Glang, A., & Ettel, D. (2013). Systematic assessment and instruction of assistive technology for cognition (ATC) following brain injury: An introduction. *Perspectives on Neurophysiology and Neurogenic Speech and Language Disorders, 23*(2), 59–68. doi:10.1044/nnsld23.2.59

Powell, L., Glang, A., Ettel, D., Todis, B., Sohlberg, M., & Albin, R. (2012). Systematic instruction for individuals with acquired brain injury: Results of a randomized controlled trial. *Neuropsychological Rehabilitation, 22*(1), 85–112. doi:10.1080/09602011.2011.640466

Powell, L., Glang, A., Pinkelman, S., Albin, R., Harwick, R., Ettel, D., & Wild, M. (2015). Systematic instruction of assistive technology for cognition (ATC) in an employment setting following acquired brain injury: A single case, experimental study. *NeuroRehabilitation, 37*, 437–447. doi:10:3233/NRE-151272

Powell, L. E., Harwick, R., Glang, A., Todis, B., Ettel, D., Saraceno, C., . . . Albin, R. (2013). TATE: Training Assistive Technology in the Environment Toolkit. Retrieved from https://cbirt.org/research/completed-projects/tate-training-assistive-technology-environment-toolkit

Prescott, S., Fleming, J., & Doig, E. (2015). Goal setting approaches and principles used in rehabilitation for people with acquired brain injury: A systematic scoping review. *Brain Injury, 29*(13–14), 1515–1529. doi:10.3109/02699052.2015.1075152

Purdy, M. (2002). Executive functioning in aphasia. *Aphasiology, 16* (4/5/6), 549–557. doi:10.1080/02687030244000176

Purdy, M., Belanger, S., & Liles, B. (1993). Right brain damaged subjects' ability to use context in inferencing. In P. Lemme (Ed.), *Clinical aphasiology* (p. 21). Austin, TX: Pro-Ed.

Purdy, M., & Koch, A. (2006). Prediction of strategy usage by adults with aphasia. *Aphasiology, 20*(2/3/4), 337–348. doi:10.1080/02687030500475085

Ramanan, S., Bertoux, M., Flanagan, E., Irish, M., Piguet, O., Hodges, J., & Hornberger, M. (2017). Longitudinal executive function and episodic memory profiles in behavioral-variant frontotemporal dementia and Alzheimer's disease. *Journal of the International Neuropsychological Society, 23*(1), 34–43. doi:10.1017/S1355617716000837

Ramsberger, G. (2000). Executive functions: What are they and why do they matter? *Seminars in Speech and Language, 21*(2), 93.

Raspelli, S., Pallavicini, F., Carelli, L., Morganti, F., Poletti, B., Corra, B., & Silani, V. (2011). Validation of a neuro virtual reality-based based version of the Multiple Errands Test for the assessment of executive functions. *Studies in Health Technology and Informatics, 167*(1), 92–97. doi:10.3233/978-1-60750-766-6-92

Rath, J. F., Simon, D., Langenbahn, D. M., Sherr, R. L., & Diller, L. (2003). Group treatment of problem-solving deficits in outpatients with traumatic brain injury: A randomized outcome study. *Neuropsychological Rehabilitation, 13*, 461–488. doi:10.1080/09602010343000039

Ratiulon, P., Talos, F., Haker, S., Lieberman, D., & Everett, P. (2004). The tale of Phineas Gage, digitally remastered. *Journal of Neurotrauma, 21*(5), 637–643. doi:10.1089/089771504774129964

Ravizza, S. M., Goudreau, J., Delgado, M. R., & Ruiz, S. (2012). Executive function abilities in Parkinson's disease: Contributions of the fronto-striatal pathways to action and feedback processing. *Cognitive, Affective, & Behavioral Neuroscience, 12*(1), 193–206.

Raymer, A. Roitsch, J., Redman, R., Michalek, A., & Johnson, R. (2018). Critical appraisal of systematic reviews of executive function treatments in TBI. *Brain Injury, 32*(12–14), 1601–1611. doi:10.1080/02699052.2018.1522671

Reitan, R. M., & Wolfson, D. (1985). *The Halstead-Reitan Neuropsychology Test Battery.* Tucson, AZ: Neuropsychology Press.

Riedeman, S., & Turkstra, L. (2018). Knowledge, confidence, and practice patterns of speech-language pathologists working with adults with traumatic brain injury. *American Journal of Speech-Language Pathology, 27*(1), 181–191. doi:10.1044/2017_AJSLP-17-0011

Roth, R., Isquith, P., & Gioia, G. (2005). *Behavior Rating Inventory of Executive Function–Adult Version* (BRIEF-A). Lutz, FL: Psychological Assessment Resources.

Rousseaux, M., Verigneaux, C., & Kozlowski, O. (2010). An analysis of communication in conversation after severe traumatic brain injury. *European Journal of Neurology, 17*, 922–929.

Schlund, M. W. (1999). Self-awareness: Effects of feedback and review on verbal self-reports and remembering following brain injury. *Brain Injury, 13*(5), 375–380.

Schmahmann, J. D. (2010). The role of the cerebellum in cognition and emotion: Personal reflections since 1982 on the dysmetria of thought hypothesis, and its historical evolution from theory to therapy. *Neuropsychological Review, 20*, 236–260.

Schneck, M. (2008). Vascular dementia. *Top Stroke Rehabilitation, 15*(1), 22–26.

Schneider, W., & Chein, J. (2003). Controlled and automatic processing: Behavior, theory, and biological mechanisms. *Cognitive Science 27*(3), 525–559. doi:10.1207/s15516709cog2703_8

Schonberger, M., Humle, F., & Teasdale, T. (2006). Subjective outcome of brain injury rehabilitation in relation to the therapeutic working alliance, client compliance and awareness. *Brain Injury, 20*(12), 1271–1282. doi:10.1080/02699050601049395

Schweizer, T., Levine, B., Rewilak, D., O'Connor, C., Turner, G., Alexander, M., . . . Stuss, D. (2008). Rehabilitation of executive functioning after focal damage to the cerebellum. *Neurorehabil Neural Repair, 22*(1), 72–77.

Serino, A., Ciaramelli, E., DiSantantonio, A., Malagù, S., Servadei, F., & Làdavas, E. (2006). Central executive system impairment in traumatic brain injury. *Brain Injury, 20*(1), 23–32.

Shah, S., Goldin, Y., Conte, M., Goldfine, A., Mohamadpour, M., Fidali, B., & Schiff, N. (2017). Executive attention deficits after traumatic brain injury reflect impaired recruitment of resources. *NeuroImage: Clinical, 14*, 233–241.

Shallice, T. (1982). Specific impairments of planning. *Philosophical Transactions of the Royal Society of London, 298*, 198–209.

Shallice T. (2002). Fractionation of the supervisory system. In D. T. Stuss & R. T. Knight (Eds.), *Principles of frontal lobe function* (pp. 261–277). New York, NY: Oxford University Press.

Shallice, T., & Burgess, P. (1991). Deficits in strategy application following frontal lobe damage in man. *Brain, 114*, 727–741.

Shallice, T., & Evans, M. (1978). The involvement of the frontal lobes in cognitive estimation. *Cortex, 14*, 294–303.

Slachevsky, A., Villalpando, J. M., Sarazin, M., Hahn-Barma, V., Pillon, B., & Dubois, B. (2004). Frontal assessment battery and differential diagnosis of frontotemporal dementia and Alzheimer disease. *Archives of Neurology, 61*, 1104–1107.

Sohlberg, M. M., Ehlhardt, L., & Kennedy, M. (2005). Instructional techniques in cognitive rehabilitation: A preliminary report. *Seminars in Speech and Language, 26*, 268–279.

Sohlberg, M. M., & Mateer, C. A. (2001). *Cognitive rehabilitation: An integrative neuropsychological approach.* New York, NY: Guilford Press.

Sohlberg, M. M., Sprunk, H., & Metzelaar, K. (1988). Efficacy of an external cuing system in an individual with severe frontal lobe damage. *Journal of Cognitive Rehabilitation, 6*(4), 36–41.

Sohlberg, M. M., & Turkstra, L. (2011). *Optimizing cognitive rehabilitation: Effective instructional methods.* New York, NY: Guilford Press.

Spitz, G., Ponsford, J. L., Rudzki, D., & Maller, J. J. (2012). Association between cognitive performance and functional outcome following traumatic brain injury: A longitudinal multilevel examination. *Neuropsychology, 26*(5), 604–612. doi:10.1037/a0029239

Steel, J., Ferguson, A., Spencer, E., & Togher, L. (2017). Social communication assessment during post-traumatic amnesia and the post-acute period after traumatic brain injury. *Brain Injury, 31*(10), 1320–1330. doi:10.1080/02699052.2017.1332385

Steel, J., & Togher, L. (2018). Social communication assessment after TBI: A narrative review of innovations in pragmatic and discourse assessment methods. *Brain Injury.* doi:10.1080/02699052.2018.1531304

Stubbs, E., Togher, L., Kenny, B., Fromm, D., Forbes, M., MacWhinney, B., . . . Power, E. (2018). Procedural discourse performance in adults with severe traumatic brain injury at 3 and 6 months post injury. *Brain Injury, 32*(2), 167–181. doi:10.1080/02699052.2017.1291989

Stuss, D. T. (1991). Self, awareness, and the frontal lobes: A neuropsychological perspective. In J. Strauss & G. R. Goethals (Eds.), *The self: Interdisciplinary approaches* (pp. 255–278). New York, NY: Springer-Verlag.

Stuss, D., & Alexander, M. (2000). Executive functions and the frontal lobes: A conceptual view. *Psychological Research, 63*, 289-298.

Stuss, D. T., & Benson, D. F. (1986). *The frontal lobes.* New York, NY: Raven Press.

Swanberg, M., Tractenberg, R., Mohs, L., Thal, J., & Cummings, J. (2004). Executive dysfunction in Alzheimer disease. *Archives of Neurology, 61*(4), 556–560. doi:10.1001/archneur.61.4.556

Togher, L., McDonald, S., Tate, R., Power, E., & Rietdijk, R. (2013). Training communication partners of people with severe traumatic brain injury improves everyday conversations: A multicenter single blind clinical trial. *Journal of Rehabilitation Medicine, 45,* 637–645. doi:10.2340/16501977

Togher, L., McDonald, S., Tate, R., Rietdijk, R., & Power, E. (2016). The effectiveness of social communication partner training for adults with severe chronic TBI and their families using a measure of perceived communication ability. *Neuro-Rehabilitation, 38*(3), 243–255.

Togher, L., Power, E., Tate, R., McDonald, S., & Rietdijk, R. (2010). Measuring the social interactions of people with traumatic brain injury and their communication partners: The adapted Kagan scales. *Aphasiology, 24*(6–8), 914–927. doi:10.1080/02687030903422478

Togher, L., Wiseman-Hakes, C., Douglas, J., Stergiou-Kita, M., Ponsford, J., Teasell, R., . . . Turkstra, L. (2014). INCOG recommendations for management of cognition following traumatic brain injury, Part IV: Cognitive communication. *Journal of Head Trauma Rehabilitation, 29*(4), 353–368. doi:10.1097/HTR.0000000000000071

Tompkins, C. A., Bloise, C. G. R., Timko, M. L., & Baumgaertner, A. (1994). Working memory and inference revision in brain-damaged and normally aging adults. *Journal of Speech and Hearing Research, 37,* 96–912.

Tornas, S., Lovstad, M., Solbakk, A., Evans, J., Endestad, T., Hol, P., . . . Stubberud, J. (2016). Rehabilitation of executive functions in patients with chronic acquired brain injury with goal management training, external cueing, and emotional regulation: A randomized controlled trial. *Journal of the International Neuro-psychological Society, 22,* 436–452. doi:10.1017/S1355617715001344

Trahan, E., Pepin, M., & Hopps, S. (2006). Impaired awareness of deficits and treatment adherence among people with traumatic brain injury or spinal cord injury. *Journal of Head Trauma Rehabilitation, 21,* 226–235.

Trenerry, M. R., Crosson, B., DeBoe, J., & Leber, W. R. (1989). *Stroop neuropsychological screening test manual.* Lutz, FL: Psychological Assessment Resources.

Turkstra, L., & Flora, T. L. (2002). Compensating for executive function impairments after TBI: A single case study of functional intervention. *Journal of Communication Disorders, 35,* 467–482.

Vas, A., Chapman, S., Aslan, S., Spence, J., Keebler, M., Rodriguez-Larrain, G., . . . Krawczyk, D. (2016). Reasoning training in veteran and civilian traumatic brain injury with persistent mild impairment. *Neuropsychological Rehabilitation, 26*(4), 502–531. doi:10.1080/09602011.2015.1044013

Vas, A., Chapman, S., Cook, L., Elliott, A., & Keebler, M. (2011). Higher-order reasoning training years after traumatic brain injury in adults. *Journal of Head Trauma Rehabilitation, 26*(3), 224–239. doi:10.1097/HTR.0b013e318218dd3d

Vataja, R., Pohjasvaara, T., Mantyla, R., Ylikoski, R., Leppavuori, A., Leskela, M., . . . Erkinjuntti, T. (2003). MRI correlates of executive dysfunction in patients with ischaemic stroke. *European Journal of Neurology, 10*(6), 625–631.

Waid-Ebbs, J. K., Daly, J., Wu, S., Berg, W. K., Bauer, R., Perlstein, W., & Crosson, B. (2014). Response to goal management training in veterans with blast-related mild traumatic brain injury. *Journal of Rehabilitation Research and Development, 51*(10), 1555–1566. doi:10.1682/JRRD.2013.12.0266

Wilson, B. A., Alderman, N., Burgess, P. W., Emslie, H., & Evans, J. J. (1996). *Behavioural assessment of the dysexecutive syndrome.* St Edmunds, UK: Thames Valley Test Company.

Winkens, I., Van Heugten, C., Wade, D., & Fasotti, L. (2009). Training patients in time pressure management, a cognitive strategy for mental slowness. *Clinical Rehabilitation, 23,* 79–90.

World Health Organization. (2001). *International classification of functioning, disability, and health (ICF).* Geneva, Switzerland: Author.

Ylvisaker, M., & Feeney, T. J. (1998). *Collaborative brain injury intervention.* San Diego, CA: Singular.

Ylvisaker, M., Turkstra, L., Coelho, C., Yorkston, K., Kennedy, M., Sohlberg, M., & Avery, J. (2007). Behavioral interventions for children and adults with behavior disorders after TBI: A systematic review of the evidence. *Brain Injury, 21*(8), 769–805.

Youse, K., Gathof, M., Fields, R., Lobianco, T., Bush, H., & Noffsinger, J. (2011). Conversational discourse analysis procedures: a comparison of two paradigms. *Aphasiology, 25*(1), 106–118. doi:10.1080/02687031003714467

Zimmermann, N., Gindri, G., deOliveira, C., & Fonseca, R. (2011). Pragmatic and executive functions in traumatic brain injury and right brain damage: An exploratory comparative study. *Dementia & Neuropsychologia, 5*(4), 337–345.

4

Cognitive Communication Deficits Associated With Right Hemisphere Brain Damage

Margaret Lehman Blake

History

Throughout the mid- to late 20th century, deficits associated with damage to the right hemisphere (RHD) were observed and reported. Visuoperceptual deficits and symptoms of visuospatial neglect were reported in the 1940s (see Heilman, Watson, & Valenstein, 1985); difficulties with comprehending or expressing emotion were described in the 1950s. In the 1960s and 1970s, reports of communication problems associated with RHD were published. Critchley (1962, as cited in Critchley, 1991) and Eisenson (1962) both reported deficits in processing abstract, emotional, and metaphorical information following damage to the right hemisphere. In the 1970s, Gardner and his colleagues at the aphasia research cen-

ter at the Boston Veterans Administration hospital published reports of communication deficits in individuals with RHD. Their awareness of these problems grew out of aphasia research, in which they included adults with RHD as a brain-damaged control group, to evaluate whether aphasic deficits were due to brain damage in general or to the left hemisphere specifically. When they examined the results for the RHD "control" group, they found that although these individuals did not exhibit typical aphasic language impairments, they also did not perform like a control group of individuals without brain damage. Deficits were observed in a variety of areas, including appreciating humor, understanding connotative versus denotative meanings, and appreciating metaphorical and other nonliteral meanings (Wapner, Hamby, & Gardner,

1981). Around the same time, Myers (1979) was reporting similar deficits and discussing the role of the speech-language pathologist in assessment and treatment of these clients.

A seminal article by Wapner and colleagues (Wapner et al., 1981) and a book about cognitive-communication processes associated with the right hemisphere (Perecman, 1983) stimulated work in the 1980s. Many studies were conducted to explore the types of deficits exhibited by adults with RHD and to describe RHD profiles. Characteristics noted included a lack of specific, relevant information in narratives (Cimino, Verfaellie, Bowers, & Heilman, 1991; Joanette, Goulet, Ska, & Nespoulous, 1986); difficulties understanding or relating emotional concepts in stories (Bloom, Borod, Obler, & Koff, 1990; Borod, Koff, Lorch, & Nicholas, 1985); overpersonalization of responses (Wapner et al., 1981); poor organization of story retellings (Myers, 1979; Wapner et al., 1981); inclusion of tangential or off-topic comments in their responses (Wapner et al., 1981); difficulties interpreting humor and responding appropriately to humor (Brownell, Michel, Powelson, & Gardner, 1983; Gardner, Silverman, Wapner, & Zurif, 1978); reduced abilities in determining morals or themes of stories (Benowitz, Moya, & Levine, 1990; Delis, Wapner, Gardner, & Moses, 1983; Mackisack, Myers, & Duffy, 1987; Moya, Benowitz, Levine, & Finklestein, 1986; Rehak et al., 1992); and impairments in understanding connotative or nonliteral meanings (Brownell, Potter, Mishelow, & Gardner, 1984; Gardner & Denes, 1973; Myers & Linebaugh, 1981; Van Lancker & Kempler, 1987). One conclusion drawn from the patterns observed was that RHD communication deficits affected the comprehension and use of complex linguistic material (Wapner et al., 1981).

In the 1990s, theories were proposed to explain the underlying deficits. Myers (1990) suggested an *inference failure* was the basis for many deficits associated with RHD. This label was not meant to indicate a complete failure of inferencing processes but rather inefficient or incomplete inferencing (just as aphasia literally means "without language" but in practice means difficulties with language). The inference failure account was based on observations and reports of difficulties with inferring meanings in both verbal and visual modalities. It suggested that inferencing processes impacted both early and late stages of cognitive processing and that inferencing was a central deficit in adults with RHD. The hypothesis was never directly tested and has not been revisited in its original form.

Other accounts followed, several of which were designed to explain inferencing difficulties. One suggests the problems are caused by an inability to generate inferences (Beeman, 1998). Another account proposes that initial inference generation is intact but that the problem lies in the inhibition, or suppression, of meanings that are less likely or that become inappropriate for a given context (Tompkins, Baumgaertner, Lehman, & Fassbinder, 2000; Tompkins, Fassbinder, Blake, Baumgaertner, & Jayaram, 2004; Tompkins, Lehman-Blake, Baumgaertner, & Fassbinder, 2001a, 2001b). Other accounts implicate Theory of Mind, or one's ability to understand that other people have ideas, beliefs, and views that differ from one's own (Balaban, Friedmann, & Ziv, 2016; Griffin et al., 2006; Happe, Brownell, & Winner, 1999; Martin & McDonald, 2003); the complexity of processing required for interpreting discourse and pragmatics (Monetta & Joanette, 2003; Monetta, Ouellet-Plamondon, & Joanette, 2006); and the interruption of executive function networks based in the frontal lobes (Martin & McDonald, 2003). These theories are discussed in more detail later as they relate to discourse and pragmatic deficits in adults with RHD. They also are used as suggested foundations for developing theoretically based treatments in the absence of evidence for efficacy of treatment in these areas.

There is no commonly used label for communication deficits associated with RHD. Some labels that routinely appear in both research and clinical diagnoses include cognitive-communication deficits, cognitive-linguistic deficits, or nonaphasic language deficits. The label "right hemisphere syndrome" also has been used. A syndrome generally has specific signs and symptoms associated with it, and given that with RHD there is a wide variety of deficits and no readily apparent pattern of those deficits (Blake, Duffy, Myers, & Tompkins, 2002; Ferré, Fonseca, Ska, & Joanette, 2012), "RH syndrome" is perhaps a misnomer. Two other labels that have been suggested include *pragmatic aphasia* (Joanette & Ansaldo, 1999) and *apragmatism* (Myers, 2001). These were selected to highlight the centrality of pragmatic deficits to the communication problems associated with RHD. To date, neither of these labels has been accepted for general clinical use. In this chapter, the label cognitive communi-cation disorder (CCD) will be used to refer to impairments in cognition and/or communication that commonly occur after RHD.

Characteristics

Cognitive deficits associated with RHD include attention, executive function, and awareness. Deficits in memory commonly are addressed clinically, but there are few studies that specifically address such deficits following RHD, and thus they will not be discussed here. There is no reason to believe that descriptions of memory deficits and evidence-based treatments discussed in other chapters would not be applicable to adults with RHD.

Attentional deficits include general deficits in the ability to focus attention, sustain attention over time, and alternate or divide attention between different tasks or stimuli. One particular type of attentional disorder is unilateral neglect (UN), in which an individual has difficulty attending to stimuli presented contralateral to the side of lesion.

Deficits in executive function impact organization, sequencing, problem solving, reasoning, judgment, and insight. Another cognitive deficit common to adults with RHD is anosognosia, or reduced awareness/recognition of deficits.

Communication deficits associated with RHD affect speech, language, and pragmatics. Disruptions of interpretation and production of prosodic contours to express meaning and emotion can be affected in aprosodia. Language-processing deficits can affect interpretation of nonliteral language, ambiguities, and other language that can have multiple meanings as well as the use of linguistic context to interpret meaning. Efficiency and effectiveness of spoken language can also be affected. Pragmatic deficits include use and interpretation of facial expression, eye contact, turn taking, and communicating within social norms (e.g., selecting appropriate topics of conversation based on the listener and the environment).

Prevalence and Patterns of Deficits

The population of adults with RHD is extremely heterogeneous both in the range of severity (which is seen in all neurologic communication disorders) and in terms of presentation. Results from several studies using different methodologies have suggested that over 80% of adults with RHD in inpatient rehabilitation settings have CCD. For the general population of adults with RHD, the proportion with CCD is closer to 50% (Blake et al., 2002; Côté, Payer, Giroux, & Joanette, 2007).

In terms of frequency of occurrence of deficit areas, Blake and colleagues (Blake et al., 2002) reported that cognitive deficits, including attention, unilateral neglect, memory, and executive function, were diagnosed more often than were communication deficits (e.g., aprosodia, pragmatics). This pattern was replicated in a survey of speech-language pathologists in 2018 (Blake & Ramsey, 2018). It is unclear whether the findings truly reflect the incidence of these various deficits or are a by-product of the available assessment tools. This will be discussed later in the assessment section.

There are few studies that evaluate patterns of co-occurrence, so conclusions are tentative at best, but deficits in learning/memory and attention may co-occur, as do some executive functions (organization, sequencing) and characteristics of slowed processing. Aprosodia and deficits affecting pragmatics or aspects of interpersonal interactions also may tend to occur together (Blake et al., 2002). Within aspects of communication, Ferré and colleagues (Ferré et al., 2012) report subgroups characterized by (a) severe deficits across multiple areas including conversation, semantic judgments, prosody, and nonliteral language interpretation; (b) emotional prosody and conversation; and (c) semantic judgments and linguistic prosody.

Impact of Deficits

Knowledge obtained from research with people with aphasia and traumatic brain injury (TBI) indicates that impairments in communication and cognition can have substantial effects on social, emotional, and vocational outcomes. Research on stroke survivors (both left and right hemisphere strokes) has linked the presence of cognitive deficits, unilateral neglect, and anosognosia to the length of stay in acute and subacute settings as well as functional status upon discharge and the likelihood of being discharged to an independent living setting (e.g., Appelros, 2007; Gillen, Tennen, & McKee, 2005; Vossel, Weiss, Eschenbeck, & Fink, 2013; Wee & Hopman, 2005).

Deficits associated with RHD can also impact caregivers and social participation. Hillis and Tippett (2014) found that changes in an RHD stroke survivor's level of empathy was the most important change reported by caregivers and was more important than hemiparesis or cognitive deficits. Hewetson and colleagues (Hewetson, Cornwell, & Shum, 2017) interviewed a group of adults with RH stroke and found that those who were diagnosed acutely with a CCD were more likely than those without CCD to experience changes in social participation that affected several specific areas: occupational activities, interpersonal relationships, and independent living skills.

Cognition

Attention

General Attention

General forms of attention, including focused, sustained, alternating, and divided attention (as discussed in Chapter 1), all may be affected by

RHD. For example, individuals with RHD may have difficulty focusing on assessment or treatment tasks, especially when there are distractors present. They also may have difficulty sustaining attention for several minutes at a time. Deficits in either focused or sustained attention may negatively affect communication. The client will have difficulty focusing on a conversation or not be able to maintain his focus on conversations or reading material. Imagine being in a conversation in which your attention starts to drift away from the speaker. Your comprehension of the conversation topic will be decreased because you miss some information. If the information was not critical, then you can refocus on the conversation and still get the gist of it. On the other hand, if you miss critical information, then your understanding will be incomplete at best or possibly incorrect (Table 4–1). Alternating and divided attention, in part because they are more complex forms of attention, frequently are affected by RHD.

Table 4–1. Example of Comprehension Affected by Attentional Deficits

You are talking with your friend Marisol about a wedding she attended. Marisol says: *"The bridesmaid dresses were hideous! They were an awful color of pink, and the style was really unflattering on some of the bridesmaids. But you should have seen Katie's cousin Lucas! He just turned 5 last month. He is so cute! I could hardly take my eyes off of him during the ceremony."*
The highlighted areas indicate areas in which your attention was drawn away from the conversation. The first part missed, about the color of the dresses, may not create difficulties with interpreting or understanding the conversation, because you know that Marisol didn't like the dresses. However, if you didn't know Lucas before and your attention was drawn away from the conversation when your friend mentioned that he was only 5 years old, you might infer that Lucas is a young adult and that your friend is interested in getting to know him better. This small lapse of attention could cause an error in comprehension and a miscommunication.

Unilateral Neglect

Unilateral Neglect (UN; also called hemineglect, visuoperceptual neglect, or hemispatial neglect) is a specific attentional disorder in which the brain does not process stimuli that appear in, or originate from, the side contralateral to the cerebral lesion (e.g., individuals do not process information from the left side of space after a lesion to the right hemisphere). Sometimes UN is described as the person "ignoring" information from one hemispace. This term should be used cautiously, as the word ignore suggests that the person is aware of the stimulus and chooses not to attend to it. In contrast, UN is not a conscious ignoring of information but a decreased ability to process that information.

UN may occur after damage to either cerebral hemisphere. Left UN resulting from damage to the right hemisphere is more severe and lasts longer than right UN resulting from left hemisphere damage (Bowen, McKenna, & Tallis, 1999; Mesulam, 1981). Thus, although right UN occurs at approximately the same frequency as left UN, clinicians are less likely to see it because it resolves relatively quickly, or it is masked by other disorders such as aphasia (Cocchini, Beschin, & Della Sala, 2012). The remaining discussion focuses on left UN caused by RHD.

UN can affect motor and somatosensory systems as well as auditory and visual modalities. In left motor neglect, patients do not use their left limbs to the extent possible. For example, an individual may not use his left arm to propel his wheelchair, or for tasks that require both hands (e.g., unscrewing a tube of toothpaste), even if there is only mild weakness present (Laplane & Degos, 1983). Tactile neglect occurs when a person does not process sensory stimulation on the contralateral side of the body above and beyond any sensory deficit that may be present. A person with auditory neglect may exhibit impairments in processing sounds that originate from the left side (Eramudugolla, Irvine, & Mattingley, 2007; Pavani, Husain, Ladavas, & Driver, 2004; Zimmer, Lewald, & Karnath, 2003). Auditory neglect can be difficult to identify because of the bilateral (although unequal) representation of sounds in the auditory cortex and from the transmission of sound through space such that sounds that originate on the left side are detected and processed by both ears (just softer and slightly later in time for the contralateral ear). Auditory neglect may manifest as a difficulty in localizing sounds, particularly those that originate from the left side of space (Brozzoli, Demattè, Pavani, Frassinetti, & Farnè, 2006). Errors attributed to auditory neglect tend to correlate with the severity of visual neglect, suggesting a deficit of multimodal spatial processing (Pavani, Làdavas, & Driver, 2002).

Unilateral visuospatial neglect (UVN) is the most common type of UN. Estimates of prevalence are quite broad, ranging anywhere from 13% to 81% of patients with RHD (Barrett et al., 2006). The range may be due to spontaneous recovery in some patients, or to the variable sensitivity of tests for UVN. The latter is discussed in the section on assessment. UVN affects one's ability to attend to visual information from the left visual field or the left side of an object. UVN is not an all-or-none phenomenon: Some individuals can shift their attention to stimuli in the left visual space when cued to do so; some demonstrate excessive variation in response times to left-sided stimuli (Anderson, Mennemeier, & Chatterjee, 2000); others can attend to items in the left hemispace when there are no competing stimuli on the right side. The latter behavior has been attributed to a "magnetic" attraction to items on the right, which grab one's attention (Bartolomeo & Chokron, 2002; Mark, Kooistra, & Heilman, 1988). The client then has difficulty disengaging attention from that stimulus in order to shift attention to another one (Siéroff, Decaix, Chokron, & Bartolomeo, 2007).

UVN can result from damage to a variety of regions of the right hemisphere, including parietal or frontal cortices or the white matter tracts connecting them. Lesions to subcortical structures, including the thalamus and the basal ganglia, also may result in UVN (Arene & Hillis, 2007; Bartolomeo, Thiebaut De Schotten, & Doricchi, 2007; Karnath, Fruhmann Berger, Küker, & Rorden, 2004; Mesulam, 2000; Shinoura et al., 2009; Yue, Song, Huo, & Wang, 2012).

A phenomenon often observed along with UVN is extinction (Chechlacz, Rotshtein, Demeyere, Bickerton, & Humphreys, 2014; de Haan, Karnath, & Driver, 2012). For a patient with RHD, extinction presents as a response to a left-sided stimulus only when that stimulus is presented in isolation. When bilateral simultaneous stimulation is presented (e.g., touch both arms or present two objects, one to the left and one to the right of midline), the person reports only sensing the stimulus on the right.

There are subtypes of UVN defined by frames of reference: *what* aspect of a stimulus is neglected, and *where* neglected items are in relation to the person. The two most well-described types are *viewer-centered* (or egocentric) and *stimulus* or *object-centered* (also called allocentric) UVN (e.g., Chatterjee, 1994). In viewer-centered UVN, individuals fail to attend to the left side of space from their perspective. When asked to copy a scene (e.g., Figure 4–1A), they copy only items that are on the right side of the scene. In contrast, with object-centered UVN, individuals may copy only the right side of each object, regardless of where the items appear in the visual scene. Figure 4–1B demonstrates a combination of viewer- and object-centered neglect. Viewer-centered UVN is the more common type, and very few patients have both types. In 150 participants with new onset of a right hemisphere stroke, Hillis (2006) reported 28% exhibited viewer-centered neglect, 5% had object-centered, and 2% demonstrated a combination of both.

There are three types of UVN related to the region of personal space affected (Appelros, Nydevik, Karlsson, Thorwalls, & Seiger, 2004; Buxbaum et al., 2004). Individuals with *personal* neglect fail to attend to the left side of their body. They may not comb the left side of their hair, shave the left side of their face, or dress the left side of their body. Personal neglect has been linked to damage to the supramarginal gyrus in the right parietal lobe (Bartolomeo et al., 2007). Individuals with *peripersonal* neglect do not attend to information within the left space within an arm's reach. These individuals demonstrate neglect on paper/pencil tasks, reading tasks, and when eating or locating objects on a table in front of them.

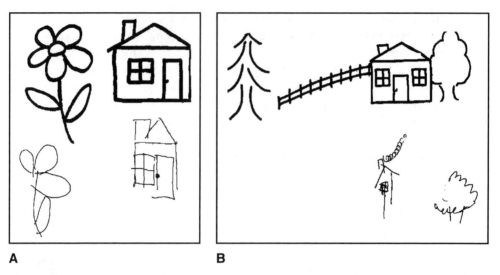

A   **B**

Figure 4–1. A. Viewer-centered neglect: the patient omitted the leftmost features of the drawing on the left side of the page. **B.** Object and viewer-centered neglect: the patient omitted the left-sided detail of the two items he drew, as well as all items to the left of midline on the page.

Peripersonal neglect is more common, reported in 23% of a sample, versus 8% with personal neglect (Appelros et al., 2004). The third type is extrapersonal neglect, which is reduced attention to the left side of space beyond an arm's reach. Individuals with extra-personal neglect may not notice people or objects that are on the left side of the room. Thus, they may not be able to "find" the TV or window that is on the left side. Hillis (2006) reported dissociations between these types of neglect. For example, individuals can have personal, but not peripersonal neglect, and vice versa. Peri- and extra-personal neglect have been linked to lesions of the superior temporal gyrus, inferior frontal gyrus, and/or frontoparietal attentional networks (Bartolomeo et al., 2007).

Unconscious processing of information within the neglected hemispace has been repeatedly documented (e.g., Marshall & Halligan, 1988; Vuilleumier,

Schwartz, Clarke, Husain, & Driver, 2002; Vuilleumier, Schwartz, Husain, Clarke, & Driver, 2001). Individuals with UVN demonstrate processing of color and shape, and even identity and meaning without conscious awareness of seeing the stimuli. This phenomenon can be used in treatment, as will be discussed later in this chapter.

UVN can affect reading and writing. The terms "neglect dyslexia" and "neglect dysgraphia" have been used to describe the resulting deficits. An individual with neglect dyslexia may have difficulty reading the beginnings (leftmost characters) of words or sentences (Reinhart, Schaadt, Adams, Leonhardt, & Kerkhoff, 2013; Ronchi et al., 2016; Vallar, Burani, & Arduino, 2010). Thus, the word *baseball* may be read as *ball*, or *hiking* as *king*. Sometimes there can be replacement of letters on the left side, resulting in *snake* being read as *lake*. This is thought to be due to the brain adding in letters to create a meaningful word given the nonword created by letters on the right side (-*ake*).

Neglect dysgraphia can have one or more of the following characteristics: writing that begins near the midline of a page as opposed to the left margin (for individuals who read languages written left-to-right), letter perseverations, perseverations of lines (e.g., crossing at multiple times), and inappropriate gaps between letters in words (Cubelli, Giducci, & Consolmagno, 2000; Ellis, 1998).

Executive Function

Executive function deficits caused by stroke are well documented (Adamit et al., 2015; Levine et al., 2015; Middleton et al., 2014; Park et al., 2015). Unfortunately, few studies independently examine right versus left hemisphere stroke, so there are little data specifically about RHD. As described in a previous chapter, the frontal lobes are critical for executive function processes. It is unclear whether the cognitive deficits present in adults with RHD are due to damage specifically to the right frontal lobe or if the right hemisphere in general plays a special role in such cognitive processes (Martin & McDonald, 2003; McDonald, 2000). Carefully controlled research is needed to further assess this question.

Many of the conclusions drawn about executive function deficits in adults with RHD are extrapolated from these individuals' deficits in visuoperception and complex communication, including discourse and pragmatics. For example, deficits in inferencing, integration, and problem-solving com-

munication breakdowns may be due to more general executive function deficits in integration, reasoning, and problem solving. Although this makes sense logically, it needs to be explored further.

Awareness

Reduced awareness of deficits and their consequences, also referred to as anosognosia, often is considered a hallmark of RHD. Estimates of prevalence range from 7% to 77% in individuals with unilateral strokes (Orfei et al., 2007). The variability may be due to spontaneous recovery and the time point of evaluation or different sensitivities of assessment measures. Additionally, awareness can be influenced by a variety of factors, including motivation, fatigue, salience, complexity of a task, or competing demands on a patient (Toglia & Kirk, 2000).

A variety of theories have been proposed to explain the reduced awareness of deficits, including a relatively general deficit in cognition, an impairment in encoding new sensorimotor memories into long-term memory, and an interruption in a feed-forward process that sends sensory information forward to frontal motor systems for comparisons between anticipated actions and actual performance (see Blake, 2018, or Orfei et al., 2007, for reviews). Anosognosia frequently co-occurs with neglect, in which individuals are not aware that they are not processing items in the left side of space. Adults with RHD may have reduced awareness of hemiplegia as well as CCDs, including problems with prosody, affect, general communication, or executive function. They also may not have a good awareness of the consequences of their deficits (e.g., they cannot drive because they have UN).

The terms "denial" or "denial of deficits" frequently are used in relation to reduced awareness following RHD, but these terms should be used with caution. Denial is considered a psychological issue, in which a patient is aware of a deficit on some level and fails to accept its existence (either consciously or unconsciously). Differences in responses to feedback have been documented for individuals with psychological denial versus anosognosia or lack of awareness of deficits (Giacino & Cicerone, 1998; Prigatano, 2014). Individuals with denial may show resistance or anger to feedback about their deficits, while those with anosognosia are surprised or perplexed when shown their performance deficiencies.

Anosodiaphoria is a term meaning a reduced concern about deficits. Some individuals with RHD can report that they have deficits, but they do not seem to be bothered by them (Barrett et al., 2006; Orfei et al., 2007). This may be related to a reduced appreciation of the limitations caused by the deficits.

Anosognosia has important consequences for treatment. Individuals who are not aware of their deficits or the consequences of those deficits are not as likely to actively participate in therapy and often have poorer outcomes (Jehkonen et al., 2001; Katz, Hartman-Maeir, Ring, & Soroker, 2000; Vossel et al., 2013).

Communication

Communication deficits associated with RHD affect speech production as well as the production and comprehension of discourse. Discourse can broadly be defined as two or more connected sentences, and relies on appropriate links (explicit or implicit) between sentences or ideas, and integration of information across sentences. Adults with RHD may exhibit deficits in interpretation of intent, providing or generating links, and using context to aid comprehension. Context, broadly, includes not only verbal information within the text or discourse but also things such as intonation, facial expression, knowledge of another's beliefs or intentions, prosody, and relevant world knowledge.

Prosody and Affect

Deficits in the use and comprehension of prosodic contours to express meaning and emotion have been attributed to RHD. The term "aprosodia" is used to describe such deficits in the production or comprehension of variations in pitch, duration, loudness, and pause time (Ross, 1981). A variety of classification schemes have been developed based on the communicative function of prosody. According to Peppé (2009), pragmatic prosody is used to draw attention to specific information primarily through emphatic stress. Grammatical prosody aids in segmenting clauses and differentiating word and sentence types, such as questions and statements. Affective prosody is used to convey mood and emotion. Finally, indexical prosody includes idiosyncratic speech patterns, such as Barack Obama's characteristic cadence or the "upspeak" used by so many young females in which all statements are produced with rising intonation.

In the RHD research, grammatical and pragmatic subtypes are commonly grouped together under the label *linguistic prosody*. Some reports suggest that linguistic prosody is controlled primarily by the left hemisphere, although other work suggests it is controlled bilaterally or primarily by the right hemisphere (Baum & Pell, 1999; Walker, Daigle, & Buzzard, 2002; Walker, Pelletier, & Reif, 2004). Linguistic prosody may be affected after RHD, but the focus of the majority of research and assessment tools is emotional or affective prosody.

Affective or emotional prosody involves intonation patterns used to convey emotion (e.g., "I hate it when I do that," spoken in an off-handed or joking manner versus the same statement proclaimed with anger). Emotional prosody repeatedly has been linked to the right hemisphere (Baum & Pell, 1999; Ethofer et al., 2006; Kotz, Kalberlah, Bahlmann, Friederici, & Haynes, 2013; Walker et al., 2002; Wildgruber, Ethofer, Grandjean, & Kreifelts, 2009; Witteman, van Ijzendoorn, van de Velde, van Heuven, & Schiller, 2011).

Expressive affective aprosodia is characterized by difficulty producing prosodic contours to convey mood or emotion. Speech produced by an individual with expressive aprosodia sounds monotone and flat. The listener may perceive the rate of speech as fast if grammatical and pragmatic aspects of prosody are affected and there are few prosodic contours to segment words, phrases, and sentences. Receptive affective aprosodia involves difficulty interpreting mood or emotion expressed through tone of voice. This can affect identification of emotion (e.g., anger versus disgust versus surprise) but also

the differentiation of strength of emotion (Pell, 2006). The impact is broader than just emotion. Some adults with aprosodia have difficulty interpreting attitude or intent, such as determining whether someone is conveying confidence or politeness through prosody (Pell, 2007).

Extending beyond prosody, the linguistic and visual expression or comprehension of affect also can be impaired after RHD. In terms of production, adults with RHD use fewer emotionally charged words to describe pictures or events (Bloom, Borod, Obler, & Gerstman, 1992; Bloom et al., 1990; Borod et al., 2000). They are less likely to convey emotion through facial expression (Blonder et al., 2005; Heath & Blonder, 2003) and have difficulty interpreting nonverbal cues of speaking partners. Recognition of affective information may be poorer than expected given the clients' visuospatial skills, indicating a deficit specific to affect. One estimate suggests that up to 70% of adults with RHD have difficulty with recognition of facial expression or affective prosody (Bowers, Blonder, & Heilman, 1991).

The prevalence of aprosodia following right hemisphere stroke is virtually unknown, with estimates of 20% to 80% (Blake et al., 2002; Dara, Bang, Gottesman, & Hillis, 2014). The impact of aprosodia and affective processing deficits is unclear. The ability to recognize emotion after traumatic brain injury is not strongly correlated with functional outcomes (Milders, Fuchs, & Crawford, 2003; Osborne-Crowley & McDonald, 2016; Saxton, Younan, & Lah, 2013), but spouses and caregivers rate prosodic deficits as being as important as left-sided hemiparesis (Hillis & Tippett, 2014).

Comprehension: Nonliteral Language and Inferences

Difficulties interpreting nonliteral language have long been associated with RHD. Deficits have been reported in comprehension of metaphors, similes, idioms, and indirect questions (e.g., Can you tell me the time?). Nonliteral phrases have both a literal meaning and the intended nonliteral meaning. In the example of the indirect question above, a literal interpretation of the question would require a yes/no answer (e.g., "Yes, I am able to tell you the time"). However, the intended meaning typically is "*Would* you tell me what time it is." Comprehenders must determine the most likely intended meaning to make an appropriate response.

Another form of going beyond literal interpretations is the ability to make inferences. An inference is information that is not explicitly stated but must be inferred from the context. There are different types of inferences, categorized by the type of information to be inferred and the amount of time and/or mental resources needed to make the inference. One continuum commonly used has "bridging" or "local coherence" inferences on one end and "elaborative" inferences on the other (McKoon & Ratcliff, 1992). Bridging inferences are those that are needed to link adjacent sentences to make a coherent story. These include processes such as linking pronouns to their proper antecedents. For example, in the text, "Sandy held Francis' hand as they crossed the street. She and her son were going to the playground." bridging inferences are needed to link "she" to "Sandy" and "son" to "Francis." These are considered bridging inferences because they

are necessary to link (or bridge) the two sentences together. Bridging inferences are generated quickly and with very little drain on mental resources by healthy young adults, older adults, and adults with RHD (Graesser, Singer, & Trabasso, 1994; Kiefer, 1993; Mckoon & Ratcliff, 1992).

On the other end of the continuum are "elaborative inferences." These are inferences that are not necessary for comprehension but can enhance one's interpretation and may speed up processing of future information (Garrod, Brien, Morris, & Rayner, 1990; Matsuki et al., 2011). In the example above, one would not need to infer that Francis is a child. However, this elaboration may be made based on other clues in the story (e.g., he was holding his mother's hand and they were going to a playground), and integration of this information with one's world knowledge: It would be unusual for a grown man to hold his mother's hand or go to a playground with his mother. Another type of elaborative inference is a predictive inference, in which a reader/comprehender predicts what will happen next. One might predict that Francis will swing or slide at the playground. Again, these inferences are not necessary to comprehend the short discourse. But if the story continues, "Francis first ran to the slide. He climbed up the ladder and slid down, landing with a bump," comprehenders will process this information more quickly if it matched their prediction.

Generation of inferences requires use of contextual cues. There has been controversy in the literature regarding whether adults with RHD can use context. Some work indicates that they are unable to use context to generate some types of inferences (Beeman, 1998; Hough, 1990; Rehak et al., 1992). Other work indicates that the use of context is relatively preserved (Blake & Lesniewicz, 2005; Blake, Tompkins, Scharp, Meigh, & Wambaugh, 2015; Brownell, Potter, & Bihrle, 1986; Lehman-Blake & Tompkins, 2001; Leonard, Waters, & Caplan, 1997; Tompkins & Scott, 2013). The truth likely lies somewhere in between: There is not an all-or-none deficit, and research is needed to determine the conditions under which difficulties are minimized.

The long-standing description of difficulties with inferencing and nonliteral language has depicted adults with RHD as overly literal and incapable of appreciating nonliteral meanings or information that is not explicitly stated. Recent research, along with careful examination of older reports, indicates that this conclusion is not tenable. In fact, adults with RHD can make inferences. Myers (Myers, 1999b) provides examples of generation of inferences. One task was to describe Norman Rockwell's "Waiting Room" picture. The picture shows three men and a boy all looking in the same direction, consternation on some faces, and a bandage on one man's head. Responses included comments such as, "they're sitting in a pew at church," "they've returned home from war," and "they're watching a movie." All of these responses involve inferences about what is portrayed in the picture. However, none of them integrate *all* of the available cues to arrive at the *most appropriate* interpretation: that they are in a doctor's waiting room.

Difficulty integrating multiple cues was demonstrated in a study by Blake and Lesniewicz, (2005). Individuals with and without RHD read stories that either strongly suggested one specific outcome (high-predictability condition: a widow would sell her anniversary ring because she needed money) or that suggested that inference as one of several possible outcomes (low-predictability condition: she might sell the ring, but had other options). Contextual cues supporting the target outcome were interspersed throughout the story. The results indicated that for the high-predictability condition, adults without brain damage generated the target outcome (sell) and were quite sure that was the correct interpretation (e.g., "She *will* sell the ring"). They did not mention many other alternative outcomes. The participants with RHD also generated the target outcome and said that it was likely to occur. However, they also produced many other alternatives (e.g., she'll get it cleaned instead, she'll ask her family for money, she'll just get it appraised). The responses suggested that although the individuals with RHD were able to use contextual cues to generate an elaborative (predictive) inference, they were unable to integrate multiple cues to help narrow down their ideas to one most likely outcome.

The ability to integrate multiple cues and to be able to revise an initial interpretation appears to be one source of the difficulties underlying nonliteral language and inferencing. A second component is the ability to revise initial interpretations based on new information. Brownell and Tompkins and their colleagues (Brownell et al., 1986; Tompkins, Bloise, Timko, & Baumgaertner, 1994) demonstrated that adults with RHD can have difficulties when they must change an initial interpretation. A classic example is, "Barbara grew tired of the history book. She had already spent five years writing it." After reading only the first sentence, most comprehenders believe that Barbara was reading the book. The second sentence changes that interpretation, from reading to writing the book. Adults with RHD are able to revise an initial interpretation, but it takes longer for them to do so than adults without brain damage (Tompkins et al., 1994). The cost of taking time to revise the interpretation may lead to more general comprehension problems. If this story occurred within a conversation, comprehenders may lose track of what is said next if they are slow to revise their initial interpretation. Alternatively, if they continue to process new incoming information and do not take the time to make the revision, they may continue to think that Barbara was reading the book, which again would cause general comprehension problems.

Adults with RHD have been reported to have difficulty appreciating humor (Cheang & Pell, 2006; Shammi & Stuss, 1999; Winner, Brownell, Happe, Blum, & Pincus, 1998). Humor often relies on revising interpretations. Consider the joke, "When she was 65, my grandmother started walking two miles a day. Now she's 71 and we have no idea where she is." To appreciate the humor, comprehenders must revise their interpretation of "walking two miles a day" from someone returning home each day after a walk to someone walking away, two miles at a time, resulting in being thousands of miles away. Individuals with RHD again may have difficulty with this reinterpretation process, resulting in confusion and lack of appreciation of the humorous intent.

A brief review of models of comprehension is needed to help explain the difficulties described above. Several models propose a two-stage comprehension process (Gernsbacher, 1990; Mckoon & Ratcliff, 1992). The first is an activation or construction phase, which is context free. Multiple meanings and ideas are generated. When one hears the word "spring," for example, a variety of meanings and features are generated. These might include a season, flowers blooming, a wire coil, a mattress, a small creek. The second phase is an integration phase, in which meanings are integrated into a context. Irrelevant or less important meanings are pruned away, or suppressed, to focus the interpretation of the material. If the word appeared in the sentence, "He went fishing in the spring," one would quickly suppress the "coil" meaning of the word but may keep the "season" and the "water" meanings activated, waiting for more information to help resolve the ambiguity. If the sentence is followed by, "There were more fish there than in the polluted pond," then one would suppress the "season" meaning based on the contextual bias toward the "water" meaning.

Within a two-stage comprehension framework, most evidence suggests that RHD comprehension deficits occur primarily at the integration stage. These individuals generally are able to generate meanings and inferences (even multiple meanings) but have difficulty with integrating information to select the most appropriate interpretation. Some research indicates that some deficits may occur in the construction phase, particularly in activating and sustaining activation of distantly related meanings (Beeman, Bowden, & Gernbacher, 2000; Bouaffre & Faita-Ainseba, 2007; Tompkins, Scharp, Meigh, & Fassbinder, 2008).

Discourse Production and Pragmatics

Discourse production refers to the content and organization of verbal output, whereas pragmatics refers to the use of language in communicative interactions. There is overlap between discourse production and pragmatics, although some concepts belong more clearly to one category or the other. Organization of a story, for instance, is a component of discourse production, whereas use of appropriate eye contact is a component of pragmatics. However, many other characteristics can fit into either category. These include content and word choice, such as whether the topic is appropriate given the setting or conversation partner. Due to the difficulty in clearly separating out these two concepts, they are discussed together.

A variety of aspects of discourse production have been evaluated in adults with RHD, including organization, coherence, topic selection and maintenance, quantity, and turn-taking. Across 24 studies, over 34 different aspects of production have been examined through a variety of tasks including story retelling, picture description, procedural discourse, personal storytelling, and conversation. Examination of the findings yields few consistent results or patterns of performance. As seen in Table 4–2, the most consistent result is the use of fewer emotional words.

Conclusions that can be drawn are quite vague. Some adults with RHD may have disorganized, tangential, and/or egocentric discourse production (Brady, Armstrong, & Mackenzie, 2006; Chantraine, Joanette, & Ska, 1998; Cherney, Drimmer, & Halper, 1997; Marini, Carlomagno, Caltagirone, & Nocentini, 2005). Discourse may not be cohesive, such that individual sentences are not clearly tied together. Good cohesion

Table 4–2. Summary of Results From Studies of RHD Discourse Production

Variable Measured	Task		
	Storytelling	Picture Description	Conversation
Coherence/cohesion	No deficits		No deficits
Structure	No deficits	No deficits	Conflicting results
Content	Conflicting results	Conflicting results	No deficits
Productivity	Conflicting results	Conflicting results	
Appropriateness: number of emotional words	Deficit present	Deficit present	
Nonverbals (eye contact, turn taking)			Deficit present

includes appropriate use of pronouns and transition words. Adults with RHD may use ambiguous pronouns (e.g., John and Alex went to the store because *he* needed some milk), leaving the communication partner confused about who did what. Coherence may also be a problem. Coherence refers to how a story fits together as a whole: whether or not all the pieces are relevant and if they are appropriately tied together. Discourse after RHD can be disjointed, wandering, and not really have a point. Brady, Mackenzie, and Armstrong (2003) reported that adults with RHD produced stories in which there was no clear demarcation of main topics and subtopics, but rather each piece of information was given equal importance. This causes confusion to listeners, who have difficulty discerning the main points from the asides. Adults with RHD may have difficulty staying on topic, being whisked away by tangential thoughts and details that are elaborated upon. Poor coherence may contribute to confusion over the intent of the discourse. Listeners may walk away from a conversation with someone with RHD wondering what the point was.

The content of discourse by adults with RHD may not always be appropriate, as suggested above. They may be egocentric in their conversation (Chantraine et al., 1998; Mackenzie, Begg, Lees, & Brady, 1999; Wapner et al., 1981). They also may talk about personally sensitive topics in inappropriate situations.

In terms of quantity, some adults may exhibit verbosity in which they talk more than is socially acceptable (Mackisack et al., 1987; Trupe & Hillis, 1985). Those with verbosity may talk a lot but not convey much information. Their productions can lack informativeness. For example, they may assume that the listener knows what they do and not provide adequate background information. Alternatively, they may give too much information, including information that is not appropriate for the situation. Others may have paucity of speech, in which they say very little (Mackenzie, Begg, Brady, & Lees, 1997). Verbosity and paucity of speech appear to occur with similar frequency after RHD (Blake et al., 2002).

Specifically in relation to pragmatics, one study suggests that some adults with RHD may take more turns and talk more per turn than adults without brain damage and may have reduced eye contact (Kennedy, 2000). Additionally, they may not be sensitive to the listener, in terms of how much the listener knows. They also may have difficulty reading nonverbal cues indicating the listener's reaction to the conversation (e.g., a puzzled look if he is not following the conversation, a bored look, or a look of surprise or shock in response to an inappropriate topic). The difficulties with reading or interpreting nonverbal cues may be related to visuoperceptual deficits and/or difficulties interpreting affective information.

Theory of Mind

Another account of RHD deficits is that these individuals have difficulty with Theory of Mind (ToM). ToM refers to one's ability to understand that another person has ideas, beliefs, feelings, and emotions that differ from one's own (Aboulafia-Brakha, Christe, Martory, & Annoni, 2011; Balaban, Friedmann, & Ziv, 2016; Happe et al., 1999; Winner et al., 1998). This theory is most commonly used to describe deficits associated with autism spectrum disorders. ToM is thought to be controlled by a "mentalizing network" of regions in both right and left hemispheres that control understanding others' ideas and beliefs (cognitive ToM) as well as understanding others' feelings and emotions (affective ToM) (Hillis, 2014; Shamay-Tsoory, Tomer, Goldsher, Berger, & Aharon-Peretz, 2004). Deficits affecting ToM can cause problems with interpretation of sarcasm or irony, recognizing social faux pas, and some aspects of language production, including the use of pronouns and explicit references (e.g., the tall man vs. the man in referring to a picture of two men) (Balaban, Friedmann, & Ariel, 2016; Balaban, Friedmann, & Ziv, 2016) that depend on consideration of what a listener knows in order to avoid ambiguity.

Assessment

Assessment of adults with RHD and diagnosis of cognitive and communication deficits is challenging for several reasons. First, there are few measures with strong psychometric properties (validity and reliability) available for this population. Earlier it was noted that cognitive deficits appear to be more prevalent than communication disorders after RHD. Clinicians have a variety of cognitive assessments available that were developed primarily for adults with TBI. There are fewer readily available assessments for pragmatics, aprosodia, or the kinds of language deficits associated with RHD. Thus, these areas may not be assessed as often. Sec-

ond, there are no obvious patterns or co-occurrences of deficits that can aid in guiding the diagnostic process. Thus, unlike with aphasia, there are no clear subtypes of RHD for which you know that if the client has difficulty with X, she will also have difficulty with Y, but Z will be preserved. Third, in the general population, there is a broad range of what is considered "normal" within the areas of cognition and communication affected by RHD so it is difficult to set a solid cutoff to diagnose deficits. Finally, cultural background influences aspects of pragmatics and communication and must be taken into consideration during the assessment process. For example, use of eye contact, the amount of personal sharing that is considered appropriate, and the use of direct versus indirect statements all can vary across cultures.

Assessment of adults with RHD should include observation as well as objective measures. Observation of an individual in conversations with familiar and unfamiliar people can give the clinician a sense of how well the person communicates, his or her use of pragmatic rules such as turn-taking and eye contact, and appropriate choice of content. Clinicians also can observe the client in other settings, such as in a waiting room or physical therapy gym, to see how well she or he attends in noisy environments.

Talking with family or close friends is essential for accurate diagnosis of pragmatic and other communication deficits. Given the wide range of communicative behaviors seen in the general population, it is important to find out what behaviors are different from the client's premorbid state. Speech-language pathologists (SLPs), due to our in-depth knowledge of communication, may overdiagnose deficits when we see behaviors that appear inappropriate when family members report that the behaviors have not changed following the stroke (Baron, Goldsmith, & Beatty, 1999).

Additionally, many of the communication deficits ascribed to RHD, including egocentric, inefficient, and disorganized discourse production, have also been attributed to normal aging processes (Ellis, Henderson, Wright, & Rogalski, 2016; Wright, 2016). More research is needed to determine what level of performance can be expected in a normally aging population, and what characteristics exhibited by stroke survivors should be considered deficits that deserve to be addressed in treatment. One study found that SLPs who were experienced in assessment and treatment of neurogenic communication disorders had distinct biases in judging discourse of healthy older adults versus discourse of individuals with RHD (Blake, 2006). One-third of the clinicians accurately judged which samples belonged to healthy older adults versus those with RHD. Another third had a very loose criterion for "normal," in that they frequently judged discourse produced by individuals with RHD to be normal. The final third had a very strict criterion and classified many of the healthy older adults' discourse samples as being produced by individuals with RHD. With no clear explanation for why these biases occur, one must be cautious in interpreting diagnoses or test scores that are based on subjective ratings of performance without input from families to help determine what is "normal" for any given client.

General Assessment Tools

Several batteries have been designed specifically for RHD. These include the Right Hemisphere Language Battery (RHLB; Bryan, 1994), the Mini Inventory of Right Brain Injury (MIRBI-R; Pimental & Kingsbury, 2000), the Burns Brief Inventory of Communication and Cognition (Burns, 1997), the Rehabilitation Institute of Chicago Evaluation Clinical Management of Right Hemisphere Dysfunction-Revised (RICE-3; Halper, Cherney, & Burns, 2010), and the Montreal Protocol for the Evaluation of Communication (Protocole MEC; Joanette et al., 2015). The MEC is available in French, Portuguese, Brazilian Portuguese, and English. Most of these batteries have subtests to measure attention (at least unilateral neglect); language production; discourse comprehension; comprehension and/or use of abstract, metaphorical, or inferential language; pragmatics; and prosody or affect.

All of these assessment tools have weaknesses in terms of their validity, reliability, and/or scope (see Blake, 2018, for a detailed review of these and other assessment tools). The majority of the older tools were designed to measure symptoms reported in the literature and observed clinically but do not have a strong theoretical basis. Additionally, they may not be sensitive to mild deficits, and many of the subtests for pragmatics and other areas (e.g., prosody, discourse production) rely on subjective judgments.

Some assessment tools designed for clients with traumatic brain injury, described in other chapters in this book, may be appropriate for adults with RHD. Reviews of formal (Turkstra et al.,

2005) and nonstandardized (Coelho, Ylvisaker, & Turkstra, 2005) assessment tools either designed for or appropriate for individuals with traumatic brain injury may be one source for clinicians to find tools that may be appropriate for assessing specific deficits for specific clients.

Assessing Cognition

Attention

General Attention. Observation of a client can provide information about how well he or she is able to attend in quiet situations and when noise is present (e.g., a radio or TV on in the background; conversations in the hallway). Tests of attention (discussed in Chapter 1) may be appropriate for use with adults with RHD. Additionally, tests for UVN (described below) also can be used to gauge general attention, by counting the number of missed targets in a scanning task on both sides of the page; individuals with general attentional deficits may make errors on both left and right sides of the page.

Unilateral Visuospatial Neglect.. Assessment of UVN generally involves one or more paper/pencil tasks, including line, letter, or shape cancellation tasks; line bisection; copying; and drawing. The Behavioral Inattention Test (Wilson, Cockburn, & Halligan, 1987) is a standardized measure commonly used for assessing the presence and severity of neglect. In addition to the six "conventional" (paper/pencil) tasks, there are subtests involving reading a map, a menu, and a clock; dialing a phone;

sorting coins and cards; and identifying items in a picture scene. It has become apparent that this and other standardized assessments are inadequate for several reasons. First, the tasks assess only peripersonal neglect in structured tasks. Arene and Hillis (2007) describe an individual who scored within normal limits on such standard paper/pencil tasks but demonstrated difficulty with personal care tasks and was unable to maneuver through a doorway without hitting the left side of the entrance. Second, the sensitivity of tasks varies considerably. Reports of sensitivity range from 19% to 100% for commonly used tasks and tests (Barrett et al., 2006). Lindell and colleagues (Lindell et al., 2007) administered 19 different neglect tests to a group of individuals with RHD. Most of the tasks assessed peripersonal neglect, with a few that measured neglect of far space or personal space. None of the tests, in isolation, identified more than 50% of people with neglect. The most sensitive tests were random shape cancellation, complex line bisection, and star cancellation, which together identified 88% of those with neglect. An additional three tasks (two-part picture, article reading, and finding objects in a pictured scene) had to be added to achieve 100% identification of peripersonal neglect. Representational drawing, such as drawing a clock or a person, was the least sensitive when used alone, identifying only 6% of cases.

Executive Function and Awareness

There are no standardized tests of cognition or executive function specifically created for, or standardized on, adults with RHD. Clinicians can use general tests of cognition or executive function as deemed appropriate. A variety of measures exist for the assessment of anosognosia related to cognition, UN, or pragmatics, including the Awareness Questionnaire (Sherer, Hart, & Nick, 2003), the Patient Competency Rating Scale (Borgaro & Prigatano, 2003; Prigatano & Klonoff, 1998), and the Self Awareness of Deficit Interview (Fleming, Strong, & Ashton, 1996). Most were designed for adults with TBI but may be relevant and appropriate for individuals with RHD. Several include comparisons between responses from patients versus family or professionals (see also Blake, 2018; Orfei et al., 2007).

Assessment of Communication

Prosody and Affect

There are four batteries for assessing prosody and affect, including the Aprosodia Battery (Ross, Thompson, & Yenkosky, 1997), the Comprehensive Affect Testing System (Froming, Levy, Schaffer, & Ekman, 2006), the Florida Affect Battery (Bowers et al., 1991), and the New York Emotion Battery (Borod, Welkowitz, & Obler, 1992). The Aprosodia Battery assesses only affective prosody—the ability to produce or identify emotion conveyed through prosody. All of the others are broader and include affective facial expression as well as prosody. The reliability and validity of most of these assessments are weak or have not been reported. The exception is the Florida Affect Battery, which has reasonable reliability and validity. Audio files containing both semantically neutral and affective sentences produced with or without emotional prosody were created and validated by Ben-David and colleagues (Ben-David, van Lieshout, & Leszcz, 2011).

The files are available in both Hebrew and English (https://goo.gl/oNcfrI).

Discourse and Pragmatics

There are a few standardized tools for assessment of comprehension and production of discourse/pragmatics. The Discourse Comprehension Test (DCT; Brookshire & Nicholas, 1983) is a measure of reading and auditory comprehension. Stories are 10 to 15 sentences long, and questions target details and main ideas that are either explicitly stated or must be inferred. The Awareness of Social Inferences Test (TASIT; McDonald, Flanagan, & Rollins, 2002) consists of video vignettes. Two or three actors interact in each scene, and the client answers questions about the intent of statements made and emotions conveyed. Subtests include identification of emotion and interpretation of social exchanges, including sincere exchanges, white lies, and sarcasm. The test was designed for adults with TBI, and there are few data specific to RHD. It was constructed in Australia, so some individuals may have difficulty with the slight accents and some phrases that are not common in American English. Both the DCT and TASIT involve answering questions after the stimulus stories, thus creating memory demands that may affect performance.

Assessment of discourse production and pragmatics can focus on communication components or the functional outcomes of communicative interactions. Assessment of pragmatic components or skills typically involves a broad range of skills, including use of verbal and nonverbal communication, and conversational "rules" (e.g., eye contact, turn-taking). Functional communication measures focus on the outcome of an interaction rather than components that go into conveying a message. Penn (1999) suggests that pragmatic assessments should include four components. First, the clinician should conduct the assessment in a social, communicative environment that allows and facilitates open communication. Second, the clinician should evaluate language and communicative effectiveness as well as cognitive skills that could affect communication, such as impaired attention or memory. Third, the clinician should assess how well a client adapts to an environment, whether he is able to change communicative style to match the context (e.g., talking with a friend versus a doctor). Fourth, the clinician must assess how the pragmatic deficits affect the person's interactions, those around him, and, more broadly, his life.

Treatment

The evidence-based triangle provides a framework for making clinical decisions regarding intervention. The corners of the triangle represent (1) current best evidence, (2) clinical expertise, and (3) client/patient values. The latter two are discussed first, and then the current best evidence is discussed in detail for specific deficits associated with RHD.

Clinical expertise in RHD, as with any neurogenic cognitive or communication disorder, begins with a solid knowledge of normal processes and the effects of brain injury on such processes. Knowledge about assessment and treatment procedures is also needed. The knowledge then must be coupled with clinical experiences to aid in the recognition and accurate diagnosis of the deficits and development of treatments. Opportunities for obtaining such knowledge is more challenging than for other neurogenic communication disorders. A survey of presentations offered over a 3-year period at the annual convention of the American Speech-Language-Hearing Association (ASHA) indicated that, on average, there were over 200 presentations on aphasia, approximately 50 related to TBI and over 30 on dementia, but fewer than 10 specific to RHD.

Awareness and consideration of a client's own wants, needs, and values is an important component of any treatment plan. These help a clinician determine treatment goals and select tasks and stimuli that are of interest to the client. The client should be actively involved in choosing treatment goals. This helps create ownership of the goals and treatment plans, which increases motivation and participation. This is especially important for individuals with anosognosia, who may not see the need for treatment.

In terms of current best evidence, there is a paucity of treatment efficacy research for disorders associated with RHD. The exception is UVN, for which there are many treatments, some with solid evidence of efficacy. On the positive side, there is a large body of research on cognitive deficits caused by TBI that can inform practice with RHD. Clinicians still must critically evaluate the use of such treatments and carefully measure outcomes to ensure that the treatments are creating meaningful change due to differences in the neurophysiology and neuropathology of TBI and stroke and demographic differences in the populations (e.g., individuals with TBI are predominantly young males while strokes tend to affect older adults) that could impact the effectiveness of the treatments.

Treatment for Disorders of Attention

General Attention Deficits

Most treatments for general attention deficits have been designed for adults with attentional deficits caused by TBI (see Chapter 8). As discussed in that chapter, combinations of direct training and strategy training may be the most efficacious. As noted above, careful measurement of treatment outcomes is important because attentional deficits related to RHD may not respond to treatment in the same way as those caused by TBI. For example, results from a systematic review of randomized control trials indicated that participants with RHD had better outcomes following divided attention treatment than those with TBI (Virk, Williams, Brunsdon, Suh, & Morrow, 2015). In another study, Sturm (Sturm & Willmes, 1991) reported that generalization from attention training to other cognitive and communication abilities was better for TBI than RHD participants.

Unilateral Visuospatial Neglect

Treatment for neglect has been studied more than any other deficit associated with RHD and many reviews of neglect treatment have been published

(Bowen, Hazelton, Pollock, & Lincoln, 2013; Cappa et al., 2005; Cicerone et al., 2011; Luauté, Halligan, Rode, Rossetti, & Boisson, 2006; Pernet, Jughters, & Kerckhofs, 2013; Yang, Zhou, Chung, Li-Tsang, & Fong, 2013). Conclusions from the research indicate that there is substantial evidence to support the use of visual scanning and prism adaptation treatments in adults with USN, and there are several other treatments that have some empirical support. One of the major weaknesses of the USN treatment literature is that assessment and treatment focus primarily on viewer-centered, peripersonal neglect. Few studies evaluate other forms of USN to determine how the presence of one or more forms of neglect might impact response to treatment or if there is generalization from one form to another. There are only a few studies of treatments for other forms of neglect (Barrett et al., 2006; Hillis, 2006).

Treatments for UN can be categorized as either top-down or bottom-up. Top-down attentional treatments improve individuals' performance via cognitive strategies. Visual scanning falls into this category. Bottom-up treatments, in contrast, are designed to increase attention to left-sided stimuli through manipulation of attentional systems or the stimuli themselves. Bottom-up treatments include general attention treatments, prism adaptation, external sensory stimulation (such as caloric stimulation, neck vibration), and treatments designed to expand the attentional window. Some treatments include both bottom-up and top-down features, such as visuomotor treatments (Barrett et al., 2006; Hillis, 2006; Saevarsson, Halsband, & Kristjansson, 2011).

Visual scanning training is recommended as a practice standard (Cicerone et al., 2011). Specific methods vary but the essential component is repeated scanning from left to right and back again. Targets can be letters, words, objects, shapes, images, and so on. Scanning treatments often involve a hierarchy. Manipulation of the number, size, and visual complexity of the targets and the use of distractors can be used to alter difficulty. Remembering that USN is an attentional deficit will aid in developing a hierarchy of difficulty. Things that are likely to grab attention (large, bright stimuli; blinking lights; photos or names of family members) can be used to make the task easier. Examples of how to manipulate targets are provided in Table 4–3. Evidence from visual scanning treatment studies suggests that while improvements

Table 4–3. Sample Stimulus Manipulations for Treatment of Unilateral Visuospatial Neglect

Feature	Manipulation	Rationale
Size of target	Large → small	Greater visual demands in identifying smaller targets
Number of targets	Few → many	Greater attentional demands with more stimuli
Visual saliency of targets	Bright colors → subdued colors Blinking targets → solid targets	Greater visual demands in distinguishing targets that do not "pop out" from background
Emotional or personal saliency of targets	Emotionally stimulating targets (spiders, snakes, beautiful sunrise, pictures of patient or family members) → neutral targets (cow, tree, pictures of unknown people)	Meaningful or emotionally laded pictures/words may stimulate unconscious processing that grabs attention; neutral items will not
Presence of distractors	None → many	Greater attentional, visual, and cognitive demands in differentiating targets from distractors and inhibiting responses to distractors
Similarity of distractors	Visually distinct from targets → visually similar to targets	Greater attentional and visual demands in differentiating targets from distractors
Location of targets	Few on right side → many on right side	More items on right side will stimulate the "magnetic attraction" to the right side and hinder attentional shifts to left visual space

routinely occur on the tasks practiced in therapy, generalization to other tasks or situations does not always occur. Thus, it is important to match the therapy tasks to the goals. For example, if the patient's goal is to be able to read magazines, then scanning treatment needs to involve words, sentences, and paragraphs.

Limb Activation Training (Bailey, Riddoch, & Crome, 2002; Robertson, McMillan, MacLeod, Edgeworth, & Brock, 2002) is a form of visuomotor treatment based on the idea that activation of right hemisphere motor regions associated with movement of the left arm or leg might "spill over" to enhance activation of right hemisphere attentional circuits. In this therapy, the patient is prompted to move his or her left arm or leg during scanning tasks. Movement of the left limbs requires right hemisphere activation; the pairing of such movement with visual scanning is thought to be more effective than the scanning alone. The Lighthouse Strategy takes the visuomotor training one step further by adding visualization of the beam of a lighthouse paired with the movement of the head from left to right and back again (Niemeier, Cifu, & Kishore, 2001). Outcomes from visuomotor treatments differ across studies, but improvement has been reported on neglect measures, reading, motor function, and navigation in the environment. Gains reported from visuomotor treatments are similar to those for visual scanning treatments (Luukkainen-Markkula, Tarkka, Pitkänen, Sivenius, & Hämäläinen, 2009; Priftis, Passarini, Pilosio, Meneghello, & Pitteri, 2013).

General attention or alertness treatments are designed to reduce the severity of UN by targeting the general attentional system. Several treatments and programs have been developed, but the benefits generally are short lived (DeGutis & Van Vleet, 2010; Robertson, Tegnér, Tham, Lo, & Nimmo-Smith, 1995; Sturm, Thimm, Kust, Karbe, & Fink, 2006; Thimm, Fink, Küst, Karbe, & Sturm, 2006).

Externally driven bottom-up treatments include prism glasses and sensory stimulation. These must be conducted in collaboration with the appropriate colleagues (e.g., neurologists, neurophthalmologists) because they involve multiple sensory and neural systems. Prism glasses distort the visual images to one side. Initially, if the visual field is distorted to the right, the viewer will reach too far to the right to reach an object. Over time, the brain adapts to the distortion so that the reach is on target. When the glasses are removed, viewers experience a reversal of the perceptual distortion to the left side. For individuals with neglect, prism glasses with a rightward distortion have been used to create a "hyperneglect." After adaptation and then removal of the glasses, a leftward distortion is noted, with greater processing of items in the left side of space (Barrett & Muzaffar, 2014; Fortis et al., 2010; Newport & Schenk, 2012; Rossetti et al., 1998; Rusconi & Carelli, 2012). Positive effects from prism glasses have been reported to last hours to days.

Sensory stimulation techniques increase eye movement and attentional focus to the left side through neck vibration, optokinetic stimulation (watching vertical lines move leftward across a screen), or caloric vestibular stimulation (putting cold water into the ear to create leftward beating nystagmus).

All have resulted in at least transient reduction in severity of UN (Kerkhoff & Schenk, 2012; Reinhart, Schindler, & Kerkhoff, 2011; Ronchi et al., 2013), and added benefits have been reported for combinations of visual scanning and sensory stimulation techniques (Pitteri, Arcara, Passarini, Meneghello, & Priftis, 2013; Priftis et al., 2013).

The only published treatments for stimulus- or object-centered neglect are bottom-up treatments designed to draw attention leftward or expand the window of visual attention. The rationale for the latter is to expand the space, or window, of attentional focus so that for a small object, details on the left side of an object will fall within the window (Hillis, Mordkoff, & Caramazza, 1999). This was accomplished by interspersing dime-sized circles with quarter-sized circles. In order to perceive the quarter-sized circles, the patient's attentional window had to expand. This resulted in the patient being able to identify features on the left side of a dime-sized stimulus, because that was well within the attentional window.

The impact of object-centered neglect on word reading can be reduced by adding meaningless characters to the beginning of a word (Hillis, 2006). These characters become the leftmost region of a word and exist in the space that previously had been neglected. For example, attempts to read the word *brother* will be more accurate when presented as xxxbrother.

Other suggested treatments that have not been studied empirically include manipulating stimuli to encourage leftward movement of attention, either explicitly or unconsciously (Myers, 1999b; Tompkins, 1995). This can be done by having a client outline a paper with his finger before beginning a task, to establish the boundaries to be attended to. The use of stimuli that cross the midline also may shift attention leftward, particularly if the stimulus cannot be identified without processing details that appear on the left. Examples include (a) line drawings of objects for which critical, differentiating information is only on the left side (e.g., a hammer with the head on the left and the handle on the right) and (b) words presented at midline, for which no shorter word can be created by the letters on the left side of midline (e.g., "mountain" or "pencil"). Items that are connected also may draw attention to the left, as opposed to those that are separate (e.g., interlocking circles versus a line of circles that do not touch each other).

Perceptual grouping and feature detection may impact the extent of USN on specific tasks (Brooks, Wong, & Robertson, 2005). Taking advantage of how human visual processing works can enable individuals with UVN to respond faster to stimuli on the left side of space: the presence of a connector joining left and right stimuli, stimuli with collinear edges (e.g., squares versus circles, in which an imaginary line can be drawn extending from the top surface of one square to the next), or when items were grouped by a peripheral border, such as a circle drawn around target stimuli. Treatments involving manipulation of stimuli need to be carefully evaluated to determine their efficacy and whether changing stimuli can create lasting changes in leftward attention.

External cues such as red lines along the left margin or the examiner exhorting, "look to the left" are commonly used in clinical practice to serve as anchors or reminders, or perhaps to capitalize on unconscious processing. For the latter, the presence of a bright or otherwise salient stimulus in the left margin may aid in an unconscious shift of attention toward the left. There is no evidence to support the use of external cues; often they are embedded into treatment programs but have not been independently assessed to determine what benefits they add. There is extensive evidence from the TBI literature that external cues are not as effective as internal cues in the long term for a variety of reasons. First, performance gains usually are lost when the external cues are removed, and unless a patient/client has someone to set the cues for them, they will obviously have no benefit. Second, in the cognitive disorders literature, there is a well-established disconnect between knowing and doing. While a patient may know that she needs to look to the left and start at the left edge of a page, she may not be able to use those strategies in all situations.

Treatment for Deficits of Executive Function and Awareness

Currently, there are no efficacy data for treatment of cognitive deficits or anosognosia specifically resulting from RHD. Some studies include adults with cognitive deficits caused by either TBI or focal lesions, but most do not separate out results based on etiology or location of lesion, making it difficult to determine whether or not adults with RHD respond the same way as adults with TBI. In the absence of evidence specific to RHD, clinicians may use the questions provided below to evaluate cognitive treatments designed for adults with TBI described in previous chapters, to see if they might be appropriate for individual clients with RHD.

Evidence for treatment of awareness deficits from the TBI literature suggests that feedback, experiential learning, and metacognitive strategies may be useful (Cheng & Man, 2006; Cicerone et al., 2011; Goverover, Johnston, Toglia, & Deluca, 2007; Youngjohn & Altman, 1989). In group settings, verbal feedback can come not only from the clinician but also from other group members. For some clients, feedback from peers may be more powerful in creating awareness than feedback from a clinician. Video feedback reduces the metacognitive demands of monitoring performance online. It may be difficult for some clients to catch errors when they are focused on completing a task. Giving them the opportunity to view a video after the fact allows them to focus on evaluating the performance. Another benefit is that clients can see for themselves when errors are made, which again may be more powerful in increasing awareness than hearing feedback from a clinician.

Treatment for Communication Disorders

Aprosodia

Leon, Rosenbek, and colleagues (Leon et al., 2004; Rosenbek et al., 2004) have reported results of two types of treatments for expressive aprosodia. The treatments were constructed based on theories of the underlying deficits causing aprosodia. The cognitive-linguistic treatment is based on the theory that expressive aprosodia results from an inability to access emotional linguistic structures and the prosodic patterns related to different emotions. The clinician provides the patient with information about prosodic characteristics that convey different emotions. A variety of cues, including the appropriate facial expression and a written description of the prosodic features are provided, and the cues are gradually faded over a six-step hierarchy (Table 4–4).

A second treatment, the motoric-imitative treatment, is based on the theory that aprosodia is a type of motor speech deficit, in which individuals are unable to program the speech mechanism to produce emotional prosodic patterns. The treatment focuses on imi-

Table 4–4. Aprosodia Treatment Hierarchies

Cognitive-Affective Treatment for Aprosodia
Sample sentence: "You are insulting me" 1. Clinician provides a written description of tone of voice; client explains it back to the clinician. 2. Client matches name of emotion to description and matches picture of facial expression to description. 3. Client reads target sentence with appropriate prosody. Description, name, and face are available. 4. Client reads sentence with appropriate prosody. Name and face are available. 5. Client reads sentence with appropriate prosody. Only the face is available. 6. Client reads sentence with appropriate prosody. No cues are available.
Motoric-Imitative Treatment for Aprosodia
Sample sentence: "We just had a new baby" 1. Clinician reads sentence with appropriate prosody and facial expression. Client and clinician produce the sentence in unison. 2. Clinician reads sentence with appropriate prosody and facial expression. Client repeats the sentence. 3. Clinician reads sentence with appropriate prosody (covers face to remove visual cues). Client repeats the sentence. 4. Clinician reads sentence with neutral intonation. Client repeats the sentence with appropriate intonation. 5. Clinician asks a question to elicit the production of the target sentence. Client produces the sentence with appropriate prosody. 6. Client is asked to produce the sentence with appropriate prosody, while imagining he or she is speaking to family member.

Source. Rosenbek et al. (2006).

tation of appropriate prosodic patterns, with cues faded over a six-step process (see Table 4–4).

As there was no clear support in the literature for one treatment (theory) over the other, all participants received both types of therapy, in random order. Results indicated that both treatments were efficacious. The one administered first was the most effective (regardless of type of treatment), and further gains were observed for most participants after the second therapy. Gains generalized within types of prosody trained. For example, after treatment, participants were able to produce a variety of "happy" sentences using appropriate "happy" prosody. Gains did not generalize to emotions not trained. Thus, participants were unable to produce appropriate fearful prosody after treatment, as fear was not trained during therapy. Four of the six participants available for follow-up demonstrated maintenance of gains 3 months after treatment ended.

Discourse and Pragmatics

A small number of treatments have been developed to target specific areas of language comprehension affected by RHD. Contextual Constraint Treatment (Blake et al., 2015; Tompkins, Scharp, Meigh, Blake, & Wambaugh, 2012) was designed to implicitly stimulate and increase the efficiency of coarse coding and suppression mechanisms to improve narrative comprehension. Stimuli were developed with a hierarchy of contextual bias to capitalize on the preserved use of strong contextual cues to aid in comprehension. Results from a multiple-baseline design indicated gains not only in speed of responses to

the individual items but, more importantly, to general comprehension. The treatment is not available for clinical use at this time due to the complexity of individually programming the computerized administration. However, the takeaway is that broad language processes can be improved by increasing the efficiency of component processes (coarse coding and suppression). Offline, interactive treatments using the principles of contextual bias are described below.

A metaphor interpretation treatment was designed to improve comprehension of nonliteral meanings of novel phrases (Lundgren, Brownell, Cayer-Meade, Milione, & Kearns, 2011). The treatment involves generating meanings and features of words, and linking overlapping meanings to create a nonliteral interpretation of a metaphor. For example, for the metaphor, "a family is a cradle," features of the words "family" and "cradle" would be identified, and those that overlap would be connected to create a nonliteral meaning. Four of the five participants showed gains on the treatment task, but only one exhibited improvement on a standardized test of figurative language comprehension. No measures of generalization were reported, so it is unclear whether or not the gains affect general communication.

Several programs to address social communication and pragmatics have been developed for adults with TBI. These may be a good starting place for developing treatments for adults with TBI (Braden et al., 2010; Dahlberg et al., 2007; Huckans et al., 2010).

Given the absence of treatment efficacy data specifically for communication disorders associated with RHD, two avenues for selecting treatments are suggested (Blake, 2007). The first is to develop treatments based on existing theories of underlying disorders. The second is to select treatments originally designed for other populations (e.g., adults with traumatic brain injury) whose deficits appear to overlap with those associated with RHD.

Theoretically Based Treatments. There are theories of how the intact, healthy right hemisphere functions and how it contributes to language and communication (Beeman, 1998; Tompkins, Klepousniotou, & Scott, 2013; Tompkins & Scott, 2013). These accounts suggest that the intact RH is important for discourse comprehension processes, including activating broad meanings of words (including abstract meanings, infrequent or less familiar meanings, and distantly related features), integrating ideas and information across sentences, generating inferences to determine main ideas, and integrating world knowledge with information being comprehended. Extrapolating to the RHD population, these accounts predict that damage to the RH will result in difficulties generating inferences and main ideas, and problems integrating across sentences. Although the predictions fit with general descriptions of adults with RHD, the theories tend to overestimate the problems encountered in this population, for example, suggesting that all inferencing processes will be abolished. This is akin to predicting that because the left hemisphere is important for comprehending language, all left hemisphere strokes will severely impair comprehension. There is much evidence in the RHD literature suggesting that individuals with

RHD do have some intact inferencing processes and that they can generate strongly suggested inferences. Thus, it is difficult to justify treatments based solely on the theories of normal RH functioning.

The suppression deficit hypothesis, described above, purports that adults with RHD have difficulty *suppressing* unwanted meanings to allow rapid selection of the most appropriate meaning for a given context. Treatments that emphasize identification of contextual cues that guide interpretation of meaning may be useful. Stories, cartoons, and statements in which a change or revision of an initial interpretation is needed can be used as stimuli. Puns and jokes can be a good source of material, such as the one presented earlier about Grandma walking two miles a day. Headlines are another source of stimuli, as they can sometimes have different meanings, such as, "Police chase snakes through downtown," in which the reader must determine if the police were chasing snakes, or if their chase went through many downtown streets. Clients may be asked what their initial interpretation is, then given a new sentence that supports the alternate meaning (e.g., "Three boa constrictors escaped from an open cage in a downtown pet store"). The clients should be encouraged to identify clues in the context that indicate which meaning is correct.

Treatments that emphasize the use of context and contextual cues may facilitate processing in the integration phase of comprehension (see examples in Table 4–5). The clinician can discuss words or sentences that have alternative meanings and how those meanings can be informed by context. The

Table 4–5. Examples of Stimuli for Contextually-Based Treatment

Homophones: Word Pairs
second–line vs. second–minute
fan–sports vs. fan–breeze
pitcher–water vs. pitcher–baseball
yard–grass vs. yard–distance
jam–toast vs. jam–cars

Homophones: Sentences
He was *second* in line.
It took her a *second* to recognize him.
He took a *survey* of the land.
He took a *survey* online.
The baseball *fan* cheered for his team.
She wanted to buy a new ceiling *fan*.
He spilled the *pitcher* of water.
The *pitcher* threw a curveball.
I sat in the *row* behind her.
He did not know how to *row* the boat.
The dog ran through the neighbor's *yard*.
He was tackled on the ten-*yard* line.

Ambiguous Sentences
The man stopped the robber with a bat.
The man stopped the robber using his bat. OR
The man stopped the robber who had a bat.
The woman was walking through the store with pillows.
She walked with pillows in her hand through the store. OR
She walked through the store which sells pillows.
The pitcher was full.
The pitcher was full of water. OR
The baseball pitcher just finished eating a whole pizza.

Common Idioms
You are dead meat.
That puts the icing on the cake.
He is working around the clock.
It's like finding a needle in a haystack.
She is about to open a can of worms.
My mother put her foot down about staying out late.
Have your cake and eat it too.

English language is full of homographs and homophones that can be used (e.g., yard, pitcher). Context can be provided by presenting word pairs (e.g., yard–grass versus yard–inch) or putting ambiguous words into sentences. Ambiguous sentences also can be used and then additional sentences added to provide a context with which to interpret the meaning.

If a client appears to have difficulty with nonliteral language (e.g., idioms or metaphors), it is important to determine if he or she has problems only when the idiom is presented in isolation or if the problem persists when it appears in context, also. Many idioms can be interpreted by surrounding context. For example, the expression, "he's a tall drink of water" may not be familiar to some people. If I use that as an example of an idiom in front of a classroom, some of the students will have no idea what it means. However, if we were standing in a bar, and I pointed out a tall handsome man standing on the other side of the room, the student would probably quickly determine the intended meaning. In the increasingly multicultural American society, there are many individuals who may not be familiar with some American idioms. If a client is unfamiliar with an idiom, a clinician can add a context and guide the client in determining the meaning based on the context.

As noted earlier, contextual information is not restricted to language. Contextual cues are present in picture description stimuli, particularly those that are inferentially complex, such as Norman Rockwell paintings. Myers (1999a, 1999b) suggests guiding clients through picture descriptions, asking questions to draw attention to various facets. These may include determining relationships between characters in the picture (e.g., parents vs. children) or the roles of individuals (doctors, teachers, etc.). Various other features, such as facial expressions, signs, and postures, also can provide clues as to the full interpretation of a picture.

These techniques for identifying relevant contextual cues can also be used to address deficits of ToM or deficits based on the Social Inferencing account. Scenarios can be developed in which a client has to use information about relationships or what knowledge each person has to determine the intent of a conversation or comment (Blake, 2007; Lehman Blake, 2018; Myers, 1999a). For example, consider the following scenario: "Peter had a big surprise planned for Sarah. The previous day he had confirmed plans for a big screen TV to be delivered to their house while she was at work. When Sarah walked into the living room that evening, she exclaimed, 'I can't believe you did this without my knowing!'" Sarah's statement would be interpreted as expressing surprise at the gift. However, if the sentence, "Peter was upset when he realized that Sarah had been behind him as he confirmed the delivery time," was inserted into the scenario, then Sarah's exclamation would take on a new meaning, being teasing or sarcastic. Clients can read through such scenarios and discuss how new information (context) may change interpretations. Clients can be guided through determining what contextual cues are important and which are not.

Another account of RHD deficits is the executive function deficits model (Martin & McDonald, 2003), which proposes that many pragmatic deficits associated with RHD are a result of impairments in executive functioning. Martin and McDonald suggest that RHD causes damage to frontal lobes or the extensive executive function networks that are controlled primarily by the frontal lobes. They support their model with rough comparisons between cognitive deficits associated with frontal lobe damage and general RHD. It is not hard to find executive function explanations for RHD communication deficits. For example, difficulties with organizing and planning can result in problems telling a complete, coherent story; problem-solving deficits can result in difficulties fixing communication breakdowns when they occur. There have been no studies to examine whether benefits of treatment for general executive function deficits might generalize to communication. However, Ylvisaker and colleagues (Ylvisaker, Szekeres, & Feeney, 2008) have reported that most successful cognitive treatments are focused and create benefits for circumscribed skills: Essentially, what you treat in therapy gets better, but there is not much generalization to other skills. Thus, it may not be prudent to expect improvements in communication from treatment of general executive function skills.

One final account of RHD deficits is the cognitive resources hypothesis (Monetta & Joanette, 2003; Monetta et al., 2006). According to this hypothesis, many deficits associated with RHD are due to complexity factors. Thus, problems arise not on simple, straightforward tasks but on those that are complex or require increased processing. The account is based on data indicating that performance by adults with RHD decreases as complexity level increases and that adults without brain damage can exhibit patterns of performance that are similar to adults with RHD when complexity increases. This latter result suggests that deficits associated with RHD are not qualitatively different from normal performance but quantitatively different. The authors emphasize that this hypothesis does not replace any of the others but should be considered in combination with others.

SLPs generally are adept at modifying treatments to alter complexity. These can include manipulations such as the length of a stimulus passage, the number of cues and/or distractors present, the number of relevant versus irrelevant cues that must be considered, or the number of characters mentioned within a text.

Treatments Designed for Other Populations. As mentioned above in reference to treatment for cognitive deficits, when treatments designed specifically for a population of interest are not available, another option is to select treatments initially designed for other patient groups (Myers, 1999b; Tompkins & Scott, 2013). This is a good first step, but careful consideration of the treatments and measurement of outcomes are needed. There are very few direct comparisons between TBI and RHD groups, and so while many of the deficits appear similar, it is not clear whether they may differ in terms of response to treatment. Clinicians must carefully review the literature, examine the strength of the existing treatment studies, and then determine whether or not a specific treatment may be appropriate for any one client with RHD.

The following six questions (Cicerone, 2005; based on Sackett, Straus, Richardson, Rosenberg, & Haynes, 2000) are used as a framework for guiding the selection of treatments for individuals with RHD. Table 4–6 provides a direct comparison between a pragmatic treatment designed for young adults with TBI and a hypothetical client with RHD.

1. Is my client sufficiently similar, in most important ways, to those described in the treatment study? The clinician must determine what factors are important to consider. These may include age, etiology, location, acute versus chronic stage, and degenerative condition.

When using treatments designed for other groups, obviously the etiology will differ. The location and extent of lesion(s) also may differ, given that most clients with RHD have damage due to a focal stroke while TBI generally results in diffuse damage (in addition to focal damage in some cases). Age often will differ between these groups, as young adults are most susceptible to TBIs, and strokes occur most often in older adults. The course of both etiologies is stable or improving (i.e., neither is degenerative). Whether a client is in acute versus chronic stages should be considered. In acute stages, the potential for spontaneous recovery exists. In chronic stages, if clients have had negative experiences due to their disorders (e.g., a loss of friends due to pragmatic deficits), then they may be more motivated to seek out treatment and participate in therapy, as opposed to those in acute stages who do not have a clear understanding of the implications of their deficits.

2. Is the nature of my client's cognitive impairment similar to that targeted in the treatment research? As mentioned above, deficits in attention, memory, executive function, and discourse/pragmatics have been reported to be similar across TBI and RHD groups. Again, one should be careful with these comparisons as they have not been carefully evaluated to determine the extent to which the symptoms actually do overlap.

McDonald (Martin & McDonald, 2003, 2006; McDonald, 2000) has published several reviews of pragmatic disorders following brain injury. The reviews provide descriptions of pragmatic deficits based on the separate RHD and traumatic brain injury literatures but do not directly compare the two groups on the same tasks. One conclusion drawn from the comparisons was that while adults with either RHD or traumatic brain injury had problems interpreting nonliteral language (e.g., sarcasm), only difficulties due to RHD were linked to individuals' abilities to interpret emotional cues.

Prigatano (1996) directly compared adults with RHD to those with TBI in a study of awareness of deficits. Although both groups demonstrated better awareness of physical than social/emotional behaviors, participants with traumatic brain injury were most likely to overestimate their abilities (as compared to relatives' ratings of the same behaviors). The self-ratings from the RHD group, in contrast to the other participants, did not correspond to their performance on a neurologic inventory.

The few studies available suggest that while deficits in pragmatics and awareness may appear similar across TBI and RHD, the deficits are not necessarily equivalent. Future studies are needed to specifically compare deficits caused by diffuse traumatic brain injury and focal RHD, and determine to what extent the behavioral consequences of different types of etiologies can validly be equated.

Table 4–6. Example of Guided Selection of Treatment

To illustrate the selection of treatments based on a different population, a randomized clinical trial of a pragmatic treatment for young adults with TBI will be used as an example. Helffenstein and Wechsler (1982) evaluated an interpersonal process recall (IPR) treatment. The program involved 20 hours of treatment in which clients participated in social interactions and role-playing activities within a treatment group. Clinicians facilitated interactions between the clients and a variety of communication partners in a variety of settings. Interactions were videotaped, and then the clinician and client participated in a structured review of the interaction, with feedback from the clinician. Clinicians worked with clients to develop alternative skills to replace those that were inappropriate or lacking. Modeling and practice were used to reinforce the new skills, and clients were encouraged to self-monitor. Following treatment, in comparison to a control group, the participants exhibited reduced anxiety, improved self-concept, and improved interpersonal communication. The gains generalized to interactions outside of the clinic, and the gains were maintained at a 1-month follow-up. For illustrative purposes, the comparison will be a hypothetical 65-year-old female on a residential rehabilitation unit 2 weeks following a single RHD MCA stroke. She demonstrates anosognosia, mild visuospatial neglect, inappropriate pragmatics, and difficulty with discourse comprehension and production. No general attentional deficits, executive dysfunction, or aprosodia are present.

	Helffenstein & Weschsler (1982)	Hypothetical RHD Client
1. Is my patient/client sufficiently similar, in most important ways, to those described in the treatment study?		
Age	17–35 years	65 years
Etiology/location	Traumatic brain injury: diffuse axonal injury and possibly focal (coup/ contecoup) lesions	Stroke in right MCA; likely affected fronto-temporo-parietal regions
Stage of recovery: acute vs. chronic	Chronic	Acute
Course	Stable/improving	Stable/improving
Symptoms	Not well described; mild-moderate language problems at most; pragmatic deficits	Anosognosia, mild visuospatial neglect, inappropriate pragmatics, and difficulty with discourse comprehension and production. No general attentional deficits, frank executive dysfunction, or aprosodia are present.

Table 4–6. *continued*

	Helffenstein & Weschsler (1982)	Hypothetical RHD Client
2. Is the nature of my client's cognitive impairment similar to that targeted in the treatment research?		
Pragmatics	Deficits present; not well described	Inappropriate pragmatics
Executive function	Not described	None
Awareness	Not described	Anosagnosia
3. Are there coexisting cognitive impairments that are likely to influence the effectiveness of the treatment?		
Anosagnosia	Not described	Present
General attention deficits	Not described	None
Neglect	Not described	Mild neglect present
4. Is it feasible to apply the intervention in this setting?		
Time	Twenty 1-hour sessions	The clinician would need to determine if 1-hour treatment sessions were possible; if there were available, willing, and appropriate partners; and if video equipment was available.
Group treatment	Interaction partners	
Equipment needed	Video equipment	
5. What are the expected benefits and potential costs of applying the intervention?		
Benefits	Improved pragmatics, social interactions, reduced anxiety, improved self-concept	If the benefits were likely to generalize to this client, the treatment could create positive changes.
Costs	Time, resources	Due to unknown generalization of benefits to this client, who differs in age, etiology, deficits, and awareness, the clinician must decide whether the potential benefits might justify the costs.
6. Is the treatment consistent with the patient's own preferences, values, and expectations?		
This question must be considered individually for each specific client.		

3. Are there coexisting cognitive impairments that are likely to influence the effectiveness of the treatment? Likely problems associated with RHD include neglect and anosognosia. Additional deficits in attention, executive function, or memory also may be present. Clinicians must judge the extent to which co-occurring deficits might impact the implementation of treatment or the potential gains. Anosognosia is especially important to consider: If individuals are not aware of their deficits, they may not be willing to participate in treatment or, if they do, may have trouble self-monitoring.

4. Is it feasible to apply the intervention in this setting? Feasibility concerns may include the amount of time available, the location/environment where treatment was conducted (e.g., inpatient, outpatient, academic research setting, intensive day program), and access to materials, including computers and software. Additionally, if treatments were provided in group settings, one must consider whether there is support for group treatments in the facility and, if so, whether there are appropriate group members.

5. What are the expected benefits and potential costs of applying the intervention? Given that it is not clear how well treatments may generalize across populations, the benefits may be unknown. Clinicians must determine whether or not the potential for change is worth the cost of time and money for conducting the treatment. The situation is not too different from what is done in clinical practice currently, in which treatments with no established efficacy or effectiveness are used routinely due to the paucity of treatments for which evidence is available. Clinical expertise and past experience with treatments should be considered in selection of treatments. Additionally, clinicians should consider whether potential treatments are consistent with existing theories of RHD deficits. If so, and if the treatment goals are commensurate with the client's values, then the potential benefits may outweigh the costs.

6. Is the treatment consistent with the patient's own preferences, values, and expectations? This question must be considered individually for each specific client. One consideration for clients with RHD is the presence of anosognosia. As mentioned earlier, individuals who are not aware of their deficits or the consequences of those deficits may prefer not to participate in treatment, and may not expect improvements (because they do not see the need for them). Cherney (2006) outlined four factors that should be considered in this type of situation, and how much the clinician and/or family should work to provide treatment for a person who is not aware of his or her need for it: (1) *Medical indications* must be considered, including the diagnosis and prognosis. If the person had an RH stroke and is likely to remain stable or improve over time, then treatment may be indicated. If, however, the deficits are related to a progressive, degenerating condition, then other options may be considered. (2) The *client's preferences* must always be considered; however, the weight given to them may be dependent on the client's level of understanding and decision-making ability. If the client with RHD is interested in improving social interactions, then discourse/pragmatic treatment may be appropriate. If she is not aware of her deficits and not interested in treatment, it may be encouraged anyway if she is at risk of losing social contacts and interactions due to her inefficient communication and/or inappropriate behaviors. (3) *Quality of life* is a third component to consider. A client with pragmatic deficits may become increasingly more isolated and lonely if family and friends are not comfortable interacting with him anymore. The amount of burden and subsequent quality of life of a caregiver also should be considered. (4) *Contextual features* include economic, legal, and social circumstances. The clinician should consider the client's ability to afford treatment (taking into account insurance, if available); to afford (in terms of time and money) to travel to appointments, particularly if the client lives in a rural area or has no easy method of transportation; and religious, cultural, or personal beliefs that guide his decision making.

The series of questions can be used to select any treatment for any client; they are not restricted to selecting treatments originally designed for a different population. For example, a clinician may want to use the questions to determine if the motoric-imitative treatment for aprosodia is appropriate for a given client with RHD. It is important to remember that the quality of the research behind any treatment must be evaluated first. If a treatment has little or no evidence of effectiveness and little or no theoretical basis, then it is probably inappropriate to use even if your client and situation match well with those in the treatment study.

Conclusions

Damage to the right side of the brain often causes deficits in a variety of areas, including attention, executive function, speech, language, and pragmatics. Communication deficits often affect one's ability to interpret communicative intent. In general, there is little research on treatment for CCDs associated with RHD, with the exceptions of UN. Development and use of theoretically based treatments or careful selection of treatments designed for other populations with similar symptoms are recommended. There is much work that lies ahead. Theories need to be tested, sensitive theoretically based assessment measures need to be developed, treatments need to be developed and carefully tested to measure efficacy and effectiveness, and education is necessary for individuals with RHD, families, and medical professionals so that they can recognize the deficits and provide appropriate referrals.

Case Study

Chart Review

A. A 67-year-old female admitted to the emergency department (ED) following 2 days of seeming "out of it" per her husband. Her husband noticed that she was clumsy with her left hand but the patient denied that anything was wrong except that she was tired. He finally convinced her to go to the hospital when she fell getting out of bed. Neurological assessment revealed reduced strength of left arm and leg but patient continued to assert that she was fine. Clock drawing was incomplete with only numbers 1 to 6 drawn, indicating unilateral neglect. Husband reported that her voice sounded flat and that she was not as expressive as usual. MRI revealed an infarct in the right frontotemporoparietal region extending into the deep white matter.

B. Patient had 12 years of education and had worked a variety of secretarial jobs. For the past 5 years had worked as a classroom assistant in a child care center and volunteered at the local library. She was an avid reader.

C. You receive a consult to evaluate the patient after she is transferred to the inpatient rehab floor.

Assessment Plan

A. Cognitive assessment: A variety of tests are available, including the Cognitive Linguistic Quick Test (Helm-Estabrooks, 2017) and the Repeatable Battery for the Assessment of Neuropsychological Status (Randolph, 1998). The Functional Assessment of Verbal Reasoning and Executive Strategies may be used for more in-depth assessment of reasoning (MacDonald, 2005).

   a. Patient exhibits mild deficits in focused attention and problem solving. Short-term memory within normal limits.

B. Awareness: Awareness Questionnaire (Sherer, Hart, & Nick, 2003)

   a. Questionnaire given to both patient and spouse. Patient's responses indicated some awareness of left hemiparesis but no acknowledgment of any change in vision (used as a proxy for neglect), concen-

tration, planning, or ability to express thoughts or feelings. Spouse's responses indicated the following changes: left hemiparesis, expressing thoughts and feelings, emotional adjustment, concentration.

C. Unilateral Neglect assessment: Behavioural Inattention Test (Wilson et al., 1987), the Apples test cancellation task from the Birmingham Cognitive Screen (Humphreys, Bickerton, Samson, & Riddoch, 2012), is a cancellation task that assesses both stimulus-centered and viewer-centered peripersonal neglect.

   a. Mild unilateral viewer-centered visuospatial neglect noted on cancellation tasks with a lot of stimuli. Simple cancellation and drawing tasks were within normal limits.

D. Communication: the Montreal Evaluation of Communication (Joanette et al., 2015) covers a variety of speech, language, and pragmatic areas.

   a. Moderate-severe deficit in expressive and receptive emotional prosody, mild deficit in linguistic prosody.

   b. Mild deficit in verbal fluency with poor use of strategies.

   c. Discourse comprehension within normal limits for her age and education (NOTE: educational bias apparent in this subtest for older adults).

E. Conversation with husband and daughter

   a. Husband reported changes as listed above for the awareness questionnaire. In reviewing test scores, he was surprised at her performance on the MEC discourse comprehension; his wife was an avid reader and prior to the stroke would have had no difficulty with understanding paragraphs or short stories. Husband and daughter both felt patient was withdrawn, not expressing feelings as she usually did, and seemed unconcerned about other people, which was very different from her prestroke tendency to take care of others before herself.

Treatment Goals and Suggested Approaches

A. Long-term goal is to improve communication to allow return to volunteer and/or work activities and effective social communication with family and friends.
B. Areas of focus:
  a. Expressive prosody—motoric-imitative or cognitive-affective treatment. Recommend to family that they question patient about mood/emotion if there is any doubt (Are you feeling angry about this?)
  b. Receptive prosody—use descriptions of prosodic contours provided in the cognitive-affective treatment to aid in identification of prosody; use techniques for identification and use of contextual cues to determine meaning (facial expression, body language, what was said, any information about the broader conversation, etc.). Recommend to family that they explicitly state emotion to preface a conversation ("I've had a bad day and I'm angry right now . . .").
  c. Awareness—use verbal and video feedback
  d. Discourse comprehension—use techniques described for contextually based treatments. Metacognitive strategies also can be used.
  e. Theory of Mind—further assessment needed to determine if a theory of mind deficit may be present.
C. Education: provide education to patient and family about the kinds of cognitive and communication deficits that are present.
  a. http://www.righthemisphere.org—website with information about RHD for clinicians, patients, and families. Free, downloadable flyer available on the website to give to families.
D. Resources for clinicians:
  a. https://rhd.talkbank.org/—website for students, clinicians, and instructors. The Grand Rounds section has videos, descriptions, and questions to demonstrate communication disorders related to RHD.

References

Aboulafia-Brakha, T., Christe, B., Martory, M.-D., & Annoni, J.-M. (2011). Theory of mind tasks and executive functions: A systematic review of group studies in neurology. *Journal of Neuropsychology*,

5(Pt 1), 39–55. https://doi.org/10.1348/174866410X533660

Adamit, T., Maeir, A., Ben Assayag, E., Bornstein, N. M., Korczyn, A. D., & Katz, N. (2015). Impact of first-ever mild stroke on participation at 3 and 6 month post-event: The TABASCO study. *Disability and Rehabilitation, 37*(8), 667–673. https://doi.org/10.3109/09638288.2014.923523

Anderson, B., Mennemeier, M., & Chatterjee, A. (2000). Variability not ability: Another basis for performance decrements in neglect. *Neuropsychologia, 38*, 785–796. https://doi.org/10.1016/S0028-3932(99)00137-2

Appelros, P. (2007). Prediction of length of stay for stroke patients. *Acta Neurologica Scandinavica, 116*(1), 15–19. https://doi.org/10.1111/j.1600-0404.2006.00756.x

Appelros, P., Nydevik, I., Karlsson, G. M., Thorwalls, A., & Seiger, A. (2004). Recovery from unilateral neglect after right-hemisphere stroke. *Disability and Rehabilitation, 26*(8), 471–477. https://doi.org/10.1080/09638280410001663058

Arene, N. U., & Hillis, A. E. (2007). Rehabilitation of unilateral spatial neglect and neuroimaging. *Eura Medicophysiology, 43*(2), 255–269.

Bailey, M. J., Riddoch, M. J., & Crome, P. (2002). Treatment of visual neglect in elderly patients with stroke: A single-subject series using either a scanning and cueing strategy or a left-limb activation strategy. *Physical Therapy, 82*(8), 782–797.

Balaban, N., Friedmann, N., & Ariel, M. (2016). The effect of theory of mind impairment on language: Referring after right hemisphere damage. *Aphasiology, 7038*(1066), 1–38. https://doi.org/10.1080/02687038.2015.1137274

Balaban, N., Friedmann, N., & Ziv, M. (2016). Theory of mind impairment after right hemisphere damage. *Aphasiology, 7038*, 1–33. https://doi.org/10.1080/02687038.2015.1137275

Baron, C., Goldsmith, T., & Beatty, P. W. (1999). Family and clinician perceptions of pragmatic communication skills following right hemisphere stroke. *Topics in Stroke Rehabilitation, 5*(4), 55–64. https://doi.org/10.1310/78XM-RVMK-NNJ1-3NV9

Barrett, A. M., Buxbaum, L. J., Coslett, H. B., Edwards, E., Heilman, K. M., Hillis, A. E., . . . Robertson, I. H. (2006). Cognitive rehabilitation interventions for neglect and related disorders: Moving from bench to bedside in stroke patients. *Journal of Cognitive Neuroscience, 18*(7), 1223–1236. https://doi.org/10.1162/jocn.2006.18.7.1223

Barrett, A. M., & Muzaffar, T. (2014). Spatial cognitive rehabilitation and motor recovery after stroke. *Current Opinion in Neurology, 27*(6), 653–658. https://doi.org/10.14440/jbm.2015.54.A

Bartolomeo, P., & Chokron, S. (2002). Orienting of attention in left unilateral neglect. *Neuroscience and Biobehavioral Reviews, 26*(2), 217–234. https://doi.org/10.1016/S0149-7634(01)00065-3

Bartolomeo, P., Thiebaut De Schotten, M., & Doricchi, F. (2007). Left unilateral neglect as a disconnection syndrome. *Cerebral Cortex, 17*(11), 2479–2490. https://doi.org/10.1093/cercor/bhl181

Baum, S. R., & Pell, M. D. (1999). The neural bases of prosody: Insights from lesion studies and neuroimaging. *Aphasiology, 13*(8), 581–608.

Beeman, M. J. (1998). Coarse semantic coding and discourse comprehension. In M. Beeman & C. Chiarello (Eds.), *Right hemisphere language comprehension: Perspectives from cognitive neuroscience* (pp. 255–284). Mahwah, NJ: Lawrence Erlbaum.

Beeman, M. J., Bowden, E. M., & Gernbacher, M. A. (2000). Right and left hemisphere cooperation for drawing predictive and coherence inferences during normal story comprehension. *Brain and Language, 71*, 310–336.

Ben-David, B. M., van Lieshout, P. H. H. M., & Leszcz, T. (2011). A resource of validated affective and neutral sentences to assess identification of emotion in spoken language after a brain injury. *Brain Injury, 25*(2), 206–220. https://doi.org/10.3109/02699052.2010.536197

Benowitz, L. I., Moya, K. L., & Levine, D. N. (1990). Impaired verbal reasoning and constructional apraxia in subjects with right hemisphere damage. *Neuropsychologia,* (28), 231–241.

Blake, M. L. (2006). Clinical relevance of discourse characteristics after right hemisphere brain damage. *American Journal of Speech-Language Pathology, 15*(3), 256–267. https://doi.org/10.1044/1058-0360(2006/024)

Blake, M. L. (2007). Perspectives on treatment for communication deficits associated with right hemisphere brain damage. *American Journal of Speech-Language Pathology, 16*(4), 331–342. https://doi.org/10.1044/1058-0360(2007/037)

Blake, M. L. (2018). *The right hemisphere and disorders of cognition and communication: Theory and clinical practice.* San Diego, CA: Plural Publishing.

Blake, M. L., Duffy, J. R., Myers, P. S., & Tompkins, C. A. (2002). Prevalence and patterns of right hemisphere cognitive/communicative deficits: Retrospective data from an inpatient rehabilitation unit. *Aphasiology, 16*(4–6), 537–547. https://doi.org/10.1080/02687030244000194

Blake, M. L., & Lesniewicz, K. (2005). Contextual bias and predictive inferencing in adults with and without right hemisphere brain damage. *Aphasiology, 19*(3–5), 423–434. https://doi.org/10.1080/02687030444000868

Blake, M. L., & Ramsey, A. (2018). *Snapshot of clinical practice with adults with right hemisphere brain damage.* Boston, MA: American Speech-Language-Hearing Association.

Blake, M. L., Tompkins, C. A., Scharp, V. L., Meigh, K. M., & Wambaugh, J. (2015). Contextual Constraint Treatment for coarse coding deficit in adults with right hemisphere brain damage: Generalisation to narrative discourse comprehension. *Neuropsychological Rehabilitation,*

25(1), 15–52. https://doi.org/10.1080/09602011.2014.932290

Blonder, L. X., Heilman, K. M., Ketterson, T., Rosenbek, J. C., Raymer, A., Crosson, B., . . . Gonzalez-Rothi, L. (2005). Affective facial and lexical expression in aprosodic versus aphasic stroke patients. *Journal of the International Neuropsychological Society, 11*(6), 677–685. https://doi.org/10.1017/S1355617705050794

Bloom, R. L., Borod, J. C., Obler, L. K., & Gerstman, L. J. (1992). Impact of emotional content on discourse production in patients with unilateral brain damage. *Brain and Language, 42*(2), 153–164. https://doi.org/10.1016/0093-934X(92)90122-U

Bloom, R. L., Borod, J. C., Obler, L. K., & Koff, E. (1990). A preliminary characterization of lexical emotional expression in right and left brain-damaged patients. *International Journal of Neuroscience, 55*(2–4), 71–80. https://doi.org/10.3109/00207459008985952

Borgaro, S. R., & Prigatano, G. P. (2003). Modification of the Patient Competency Rating Scale for use on an acute neurorehabilitation unit: the PCRS-NR. *Brain Injury, 17*(10), 847–853. https://doi.org/10.1080/0269905031000089350

Borod, J. C., Koff, E., Lorch, M. P., & Nicholas, M. (1985). Channels of emotional expression in patients with unilateral brain damage. *Archives of Neurology, 42,* 345–348. https://doi.org/10.1001/archneur.1985.04060040055011

Borod, J. C., Rorie, K. D., Pick, L. H., Bloom, R. L., Andelman, F., Campbell, A. L., . . . Sliwinski, M. (2000). Verbal pragmatics following unilateral stroke: Emotional content and valence. *Neuropsychology, 14*(1), 112–124. https://doi.org/10.1037/0894-4105.14.1.112

Borod, J. C., Welkowitz, J., & Obler, L. K. (1992). *New York Emotion Battery.* Unpublished manuscript.

Bouaffre, S., & Faita-Ainseba, F. (2007). Hemispheric differences in the timecourse of semantic priming processes:

evidence from event-related potentials (ERPs). *Brain and Cognition*, *63*(2), 123–135. https://doi.org/10.1016/j.bandc.2006.10.006

Bowen, A., Hazelton, C., Pollock, A., & Lincoln, N. B. (2013). Cognitive rehabilitation for spatial neglect following stroke. *Cochrane Database of Systematic Reviews*, (7). https://doi.org/10.1002/14651858.CD003586.pub3

Bowen, A., McKenna, K., & Tallis, R. C. (1999). Reasons for variability in the reported rate of occurrence of unilateral spatial neglect after stroke. *Stroke: A Journal of Cerebral Circulation*, *30*(6), 1196–1202. https://doi.org/10.1161/01.STR.30.6.1196

Bowers, D., Blonder, L., & Heilman, K. M. (1991). *The Florida Affect Battery*. Center for Neuropsychological Studies Cognitive Neuroscience Laboratory. University of Florida. Retrieved from http://neurology.ufl.edu/files/2011/12/Florida-Affect-Battery-Manual.pdf

Braden, C., Hawley, L., Newman, J., Morey, C., Gerber, D., & Harrison-Felix, C. (2010). Social communication skills group treatment: A feasibility study for persons with traumatic brain injury and comorbid conditions. *Brain Injury*, *24*(11), 1298–1310. https://doi.org/10.3109/02699052.2010.506859

Brady, M., Armstrong, L., & Mackenzie, C. (2006). An examination over time of language and discourse production abilities following right hemisphere brain damage. *Journal of Neurolinguistics*, *19*(4), 291–310. https://doi.org/10.1016/j.jneuroling.2005.12.001

Brady, M., Mackenzie, C., & Armstrong, L. (2003). Topic use following right hemisphere brain damage during three semistructured conversational discourse samples. *Aphasiology*, *17*(9), 881–904. https://doi.org/10.1080/02687030344000292

Brooks, J. L., Wong, Y., & Robertson, L. C. (2005). Crossing the midline: Reducing attentional deficits via interhemispheric interactions. *Neuropsychologia*, *43*, 572–582. https://doi.org/10.1016/j.neuropsychologia.2004.07.009

Brookshire, R. H., & Nicholas, M. (1983). *Discourse Comprehension Test*. Minneapolis, MN: BRK Publishers.

Brownell, H. H., Michel, D., Powelson, J., & Gardner, H. (1983). Surprise but not coherence: Sensitivity to verbal humor in right-hemisphere patients. *Brain and Language*, *18*(1), 20–27. https://doi.org/10.1016/0093-934X(83)90002-0

Brownell, H. H., Potter, H. H., & Bihrle, A. M. (1986). Inference deficits in right brain-damaged patients. *Brain and Language*, *27*, 310–321. https://doi.org/http://dx.doi.org/10.1016/0093-934X(86)90022-2

Brownell, H. H., Potter, H. H., Mishelow, D., & Gardner, H. (1984). Sensitivity to lexical decision and connotation in brain damaged patients: A double dissociation? *Brain and Language*, *22*, 253–265.

Brozzoli, C., Demattè, M. L., Pavani, F., Frassinetti, F., & Farnè, A. (2006). Neglect and extinction: Within and between sensory modalities. *Restorative Neurology and Neuroscience*, *24*(4–6), 217–232.

Bryan, K. (1994). *Right Hemisphere Language Battery-2*. Chichester, UK: John Wiley & Sons.

Burns, M. S. (1997). *Burns Brief Inventory of Communication and Cognition*. San Antonio, TX: Pearson Assessment.

Buxbaum, L. J., Ferraro, M. K., Veramonti, T., Farne, A., Whyte, J., Ladavas, E., . . . Coslett, H. B. (2004). Hemispatial neglect: Subtypes, neuroanatomy, and disability. *Neurology*, *62*, 749–756. https://doi.org/10.1212/01.WNL.0000113730.73031.F4

Cappa, S. F., Benke, T., Clarke, S., Rossi, B., Stemmer, B., & Heugten, C. M. (2005). EFNS guidelines on cognitive rehabilitation: report of an EFNS task force. *European Journal of Neurology*, *12*(9), 665–680. https://doi.org/10.1111/j.1468-1331.2005.01330.x

Chantraine, Y., Joanette, Y., & Ska, B. (1998). Conversational abilities in patients with right hemisphere damage. *Journal of Neurolinguistics*, 11(1–2), 21–32.

Chatterjee, A. (1994). Picturing unilateral spatial neglect: Viewer versus object centred reference frames. *Journal of Neurology, Neurosurgery, and Psychiatry*, 57, 1236–1240. https://doi.org/10.1136/jnnp.57.10.1236

Cheang, H. S., & Pell, M. D. (2006). A study of humour and communicative intention following right hemisphere stroke. *Clinical Linguistics & Phonetics*, 20(6), 447–462. https://doi.org/10.1080/0269 9200500135684

Chechlacz, M., Rotshtein, P., Demeyere, N., Bickerton, W. L., & Humphreys, G. W. (2014). The frequency and severity of extinction after stroke affecting different vascular territories. *Neuropsychologia*, 54(1), 11–17. https://doi.org/10.1016/j.neuropsychologia.2013.12.016

Cheng, S. K. W., & Man, D. W. K. (2006). Management of impaired self-awareness in persons with traumatic brain injury. *Brain Injury*, 20(6), 621–628. https://doi.org/10.1080/02699050600677196

Cherney, L. R. (2006). Ethical issues involving the right hemisphere stroke patient: To treat or not to treat? *Topics in Stroke Rehabilitation*, 13(4), 47–53. https://doi.org/10.1310/tsr1304-47

Cherney, L. R., Drimmer, D. P., & Halper, A. S. (1997). Informational content and unilateral neglect: A longitudinal investigation of five subjects with right hemisphere damage. *Aphasiology*, 11(4/5), 351–363. https://doi.org/10.1080/02687039708248476

Cicerone, K. D. (2005). Methodological issues in evaluating the effectiveness of cognitive rehabilitation. In P. W. Halligan & D. T. Wade (Eds.), *Effectiveness of rehabilitation for cognitive deficits*. New York, NY: Oxford University Press.

Cicerone, K. D., Langenbahn, D. M., Braden, C., Malec, J. F., Kalmar, K., Fraas, M., . . . Ashman, T. (2011). Evidence-based cognitive rehabilitation: Updated review of the literature from 2003 through 2008. *Archives of Physical Medicine and Rehabilitation*, 92(4), 519–530. https://doi.org/10.1016/j.apmr.2010.11.015

Cimino, C. R., Verfaellie, M., Bowers, D., & Heilman, K. M. (1991). Autobiographical memory: Influence of right hemisphere damage in emotionality and specificity. *Brain and Cognition*, 15, 106–118. https://doi.org/10.1016/0278-2626(91)90019-5

Cocchini, G., Beschin, N., & Della Sala, S. (2012). Assessing anosognosia: A critical review. *Acta Neuropsychologica*, 10(3), 419–443.

Cocchini, G., Gregg, N., Beschin, N., Dean, M., & Della Sala, S. (2010). Vata-L: Visual-Analogue Test Assessing Anosognosia for language impairment. *The Clinical Neuropsychologist*, 24(8), 1379–1399. https://doi.org/10.1080/13854046.2010.524167

Coelho, C., Ylvisaker, M., & Turkstra, L. S. (2005). Nonstandardized assessment approaches for individuals with traumatic brain injuries. *Seminars in Speech and Language*, 26(4), 223–241. https://doi.org/10.1055/s-2005-922102

Côté, H., Payer, M., Giroux, F., & Joanette, Y. (2007). Towards a description of clinical communication impairment profiles following right-hemisphere damage. *Aphasiology*, 21(6–8), 739–749. https://doi.org/10.1080/02687030701192331

Critchley, E. M. R. (1991). Speech and the right hemisphere. *Behavioural Neurology*, 4(3), 143–151. https://doi.org/10.3233/BEN-1991-4302

Cubelli, R., Guiducci, A., & Consolmagno, P. (2000). Afferent dysgraphia after right cerebral stroke: An autonomous syndrome? *Brain and Cognition*, 44(3), 629–644. https://doi.org/10.1006/brcg.2000.1239

Dahlberg, C. A., Cusick, C. P., Hawley, L. A., Newman, J. K., Morey, C. E., Harrison-Felix, C. L., & Whiteneck, G. G. (2007). Treatment efficacy of social communication skills training after traumatic brain injury: A randomized treatment and deferred treatment controlled trial. *Archives of Physical Medicine and Rehabilitation, 88*(12), 1561–1573. https://doi.org/10.1016/j.apmr.2007.07.033

Dara, C., Bang, J., Gottesman, R. F., & Hillis, A. E. (2014). Right hemisphere dysfunction is better predicted by emotional prosody impairments as compared to neglect. *Journal of Neurology and Translational Neuroscience, 2*(1), 1037–1051.

de Haan, B., Karnath, H.-O., & Driver, J. (2012). Mechanisms and anatomy of unilateral extinction after brain injury. *Neuropsychologia, 50*(6), 1045–1053. https://doi.org/10.1016/j.neuropsychologia.2012.02.015

DeGutis, J. M., & Van Vleet, T. M. (2010). Tonic and phasic alertness training: A novel behavioral therapy to improve spatial and non-spatial attention in patients with hemispatial neglect. *Frontiers in Human Neuroscience, 4*, 1–17. https://doi.org/10.3389/fnhum.2010.00060

Delis, D. C., Wapner, W., Gardner, H., & Moses, J. A. J. (1983). The contribution of the right hemisphere to the organization of paragraphs. *Cortex, 19*(1), 43–50.

Eisenson, J. (1962). Language and intellectual modifications associated with right cerebral damage. *Language and Speech, 5*(2), 49–53. https://doi.org/10.1177/002383096200500201

Ellis, A. W. (1998). Normal writing processes and peripheral acquired dysgraphias. *Language and Cognitive Processes, 3*(2), 99–127. https://doi.org/10.1080/01690968808402084

Ellis, C., Henderson, A., Wright, H. H., & Rogalski, Y. (2016). Global coherence during discourse production in adults: A review of the literature. *International Journal of Language and Communication Disorders, 51*(4), 359–367. https://doi.org/10.1111/1460-6984.12213

Eramudugolla, R., Irvine, D. R. F., & Mattingley, J. B. (2007). Association between auditory and visual symptoms of unilateral spatial neglect. *Neuropsychologia,* 45, 2631–2637. https://doi.org/10.1016/j.neuropsychologia.2007.03.015

Ethofer, T., Anders, S., Wiethoff, S., Erb, M., Herbert, C., Saur, R., . . . Wildgruber, D. (2006). Effects of prosodic emotional intensity on activation of associative auditory cortex. *NeuroReport, 17*(3), 249–253.

Ferré, P., Fonseca, R. P., Ska, B., & Joanette, Y. (2012). Communicative clusters after a right-hemisphere stroke: are there universal clinical profiles? *Folia Phoniatrica et Logopaedica, 64*(4), 199–207. https://doi.org/10.1159/000340017

Fleming, J. M., Strong, J., & Ashton, R. (1996). Self-awareness of deficits in adults with traumatic brain injury: How best to measure? *Brain Injury, 10*(1), 1–15.

Fortis, P., Maravita, A., Gallucci, M., Ronchi, R., Grassi, E., Senna, I., . . . Vallar, G. (2010). Rehabilitating patients with left spatial neglect by prism exposure during a visuomotor activity. *Neuropsychology, 24*(6), 681–697. https://doi.org/10.1037/a0019476

Froming, K., Levy, M., Schaffer, S., & Ekman, P. (2006). *The Comprehensive Affect Testing System.* Sanford, FL: Psychology Software.

Gardner, H., & Denes, G. (1973). Connotative judgements by aphasic patients on a pictorial adaptation of the semantic differential. *Cortex, 9*(2), 183–196. https://doi.org/10.1016/S0010-9452(73)80027-9

Gardner, H., Silverman, J., Wapner, W., & Zurif, E. (1978). The appreciation of antonymic contrasts in aphasia. *Brain and Language, 6*(3), 301–317. https://doi.org/10.1016/0093-934X(78)90064-0

Garrod, S., Brien, E. J. O., Morris, R. K., & Rayner, K. (1990). Elaborative inferencing as an active or passive process. *Journal of Experimental Psychology: Learning, Memory, and Cognition, 16*(2), 250–257.

Gernsbacher, M. A. (1990). *Language comprehension as structure building.* New York, NY: Psychology Press. https://doi.org/10.4324/9780203772157

Giacino, J. T., & Cicerone, K. D. (1998). Varieties of deficit unawareness after brain injury. *Journal of Head Trauma Rehabilitation*, *13*(5), 1–15.

Gillen, R., Tennen, H., & McKee, T. (2005). Unilateral spatial neglect: Relation to rehabilitation outcomes in patients with right hemisphere stroke. *Archives of Physical Medicine and Rehabilitation*, *86*, 763–767.

Goverover, Y., Johnston, M. V, Toglia, J., & Deluca, J. (2007). Treatment to improve self-awareness in persons with acquired brain injury. *Brain Injury*, *21*(9), 913–923. https://doi.org/10.1080/0269 9050701553205

Graesser, A. C., Singer, M., & Trabasso, T. (1994). Constructing inferences during narrative text comprehension. *Psychological Review*, *101*(3), 371–395.

Griffin, R., Friedman, O., Ween, J., Winner, E., Happé, F., & Brownell, H. H. (2006). Theory of mind and the right cerebral hemisphere: Refining the scope of impairment. *Laterality*, *11*(3), 195–225. https://doi.org/10.1080/13576500500450552

Halper, A. S., Cherney, L. R., & Burns, M. S. (2010). *The Rehabilitation Institute of Chicago evaluation of communication problems in right hemisphere dysfunction* (3rd ed.). Chicago, IL: Rehabilitation Institute of Chicago.

Happe, F., Brownell, H. H., & Winner, E. (1999). Acquired 'theory of mind' impairments following stroke. *Cognition*, *70*, 211–240.

Heath, R. L., & Blonder, L. X. (2003). Conversational humor among stroke survivors. *Humor*, *16*(1), 91–106.

Heilman, K. M., Watson, R. T., & Valenstein, E. (1985). Neglect and related disorders. In K. M. Heilman & E. Valenstein (Eds.), *Clinical neuropsychology* (2nd ed., pp. 243–294). New York, NY: Oxford University Press.

Helm-Estabrooks, N. (2017). *Cognitive Linguistic Quick Test Plus (CLQT+)*. San Antonio, TX: Pearson Assessment.

Hewetson, R., Cornwell, P., & Shum, D. (2017). Social participation following right hemisphere stroke: influence of a cognitive-communication disorder. *Aphasiology*, *32*, 164–182. https://doi.org /10.1080/02687038.2017.1315045

Hillis, A. E. (2006). Rehabilitation of unilateral spatial neglect: New insights from magnetic resonance perfusion imaging. *Archives of Physical Medicine and Rehabilitation*, *87*(12, Suppl.), 43–49. https://doi .org/10.1016/j.apmr.2006.08.331

Hillis, A. E. (2014). Inability to empathize: Brain lesions that disrupt sharing and understanding another's emotions. *Brain: A Journal of Neurology*, *137*(Pt 4), 981–997. https://doi.org/10.1093/brain/awt317

Hillis, A. E., Mordkoff, J. T., & Caramazza, A. (1999). Mechanisms of spatial attention revealed by hemispatial neglect. *Cortex: A Journal Devoted to the Study of the Nervous System and Behavior*, *35*(3), 433–442. https://doi.org/10.1016/S0010-9452(08)70811-6

Hillis, A. E., & Tippett, D. C. (2014). Stroke recovery: Surprising influences and residual consequences. *Advances in Medicine*, *2014*. http://dx.doi.org/10.1155/2014/378263

Hough, M. (1990). Narrative comprehension in adults with right and left hemisphere brain damage: Theme organisation. *Brain and Language*, *38*, 253–277.

Huckans, M., Pavawalla, S., Demadura, T., Kolessar, M., Seelye, A., Roost, N., . . . Storzbach, D. (2010). A pilot study examining effects of group-based Cognitive Strategy Training treatment on self-reported cognitive problems, psychiatric symptoms, functioning, and compensatory strategy use in OIF/OEF combat veterans with persistent mild cognitive disorders. *Journal of Rehabilitation Research and Development*, *47*(1), 43–60. https://doi.org/10.1682/JRRD.2009.02.0019

Humphreys, G. W., Bickerton, W.-L., Samson, D., & Riddoch, M. J. (2012). *BCoS Cognition Screen*. Hove, UK: Psychology Press.

Jehkonen, M., Ahonen, J.-P., Dastidar, P., Koivisto, A.-M., Laippala, P., Vilkki, J., & Molnar, G. (2001). Predictors of discharge to home during the first year after right hemisphere stroke. *Acta Neurologica Scandinavica, 104*(3), 136–141. https://doi.org/10.1034/j.1600-0404.2001.00025.x

Joanette, Y., & Ansaldo, A. I. (1999). Clinical note: Acquired pragmatic impairments and aphasia. *Brain and Language, 68,* 529–534.

Joanette, Y., Goulet, P., Ska, B., & Nespoulous, J.-L. (1986). Informative content of narrative discourse in right-brain-damaged right-handers. *Brain and Language, 29,* 81–105. https://doi.org/10.1016/0093-934X(86)90035-0

Joanette, Y., Ska, B., Côté, H., Ferré, P., Lapointe, L., Coppens, P., & Small, S. (2015). *Montreal Protocol for the Evaluation of Communication (MEC).* Sydney, Australia: ASSBI Resources.

Karnath, H.-O., Fruhmann Berger, M., Küker, W., & Rorden, C. (2004). The anatomy of spatial neglect based on voxelwise statistical analysis: A study of 140 patients. *Cerebral Cortex, 14*(10), 1164–1172. https://doi.org/10.1093/cercor/bhh076

Katz, N., Hartman-Maeir, A., Ring, H., & Soroker, N. (2000). Relationships of cognitive performance and daily function of clients following right hemisphere stroke: Predictive and ecological validity of the LOTCA Battery. *Occupational Therapy Journal of Research, 20*(1), 3–17.

Kennedy, M. R. T. (2000). Topic scenes in conversations with adults with right-hemisphere brain damage. *American Journal of Speech-Language Pathology, 9,* 72–86. https://doi.org/10.1044/1058-0360.0901.72

Kerkhoff, G., & Schenk, T. (2012). Rehabilitation of neglect: An update. *Neuropsychologia, 50*(6), 1072–1079. https://doi.org/10.1016/j.neuropsychologia.2012.01.024

Kiefer, R. F. (1993). The role of predictive inferences in situation model construction. *Discourse Processes, 16*(1–2), 99–124. https://doi.org/10.1080/01638539309544831

Kotz, S. A., Kalberlah, C., Bahlmann, J., Friederici, A. D., & Haynes, J.-D. (2013). Predicting vocal emotion expressions from the human brain. *Human Brain Mapping, 34*(8), 1971–1981. https://doi.org/10.1002/hbm.22041

Laplane, D., & Degos, J. D. (1983). Motor neglect. *Journal of Neurology, Neurosurgery & Psychiatry, 46*(2), 152–158. https://doi.org/10.1136/jnnp.46.2.152

Lehman Blake, M. (2018). *The right hemisphere and disorders of cognition and communication: Theory and clinical practice.* San Diego, CA: Plural Publishing.

Lehman-Blake, M. T., & Tompkins, C. A. (2001). Predictive inferencing in adults with right hemisphere brain damage. *Journal of Speech, Language, and Hearing Research, 44,* 639–654. https://doi.org/10.1044/1092-4388(2001/052)

Leon, S. A., Rosenbek, J. C., Crucian, G. P., Hieber, B., Holiway, B., Rodriguez, A. D., . . . Gonzalez-Rothi, L. (2004). Active treatments for aprosodia secondary to right hemisphere stroke. *Journal of Rehabilitation Research and Development, 41*(1), 93. https://doi.org/10.1682/JRRD.2003.12.0182

Leonard, C. L., Waters, G. S., & Caplan, D. (1997). The use of contextual information related to general world knowledge by right brain-damaged individuals in pronoun resolution. *Brain and Language, 57*(57), 343–359. https://doi.org/10.1006/brln.1997.1744

Levine, D. A., Galecki, A. T., Langa, K. M., Unverzagt, F. W., Kabeto, M. U., Giordani, B., & Wadley, V. G. (2015). Trajectory of cognitive decline after incident stroke. *JAMA, 314*(1), 41–51. https://doi.org/10.1001/jama.2015.6968

Lindell, A. B., Jalas, M. J., Tenovuo, O., Brunila, T., Voeten, M. J. M., & Hämäläinen, H. (2007). Clinical assessment of hemispatial neglect: Evaluation of different measures and dimensions. *The Clinical Neuropsychologist, 21*(3), 479–497. https://doi.org/10.1080/13854040600630061

Luauté, J., Halligan, P., Rode, G., Rossetti, Y., & Boisson, D. (2006). Visuo-spatial neglect: A systematic review of current interventions and their effectiveness. *Neuroscience and Biobehavioral Reviews, 30*(7), 961–982. https://doi.org/10.1016/j.neubiorev.2006.03.001

Lundgren, K., Brownell, H. H., Cayer-Meade, C., Milione, J., & Kearns, K. (2011). Treating metaphor interpretation deficits subsequent to right hemisphere brain damage: Preliminary results. *Aphasiology, 25*(4), 456–474. https://doi.org/10.1080/02687038.2010.500809

Luukkainen-Markkula, R., Tarkka, I. M., Pitkänen, K., Sivenius, J., & Hämäläinen, H. (2009). Rehabilitation of hemispatial neglect: A randomized study using either arm activation or visual scanning training. *Restorative Neurology and Neuroscience, 27*(6), 663–672. https://doi.org/10.3233/RNN-2009-0520

MacDonald, S. (2005). *Functional Assessment of Verbal Reasoning and Executive Strategies.* Guelph, Ontario: CCD Publishers.

Mackenzie, C., Begg, T., Brady, M., & Lees, K. R. (1997). The effects on verbal communication skills of right hemisphere stroke in middle age. *Aphasiology, 11*(10), 929–945. https://doi.org/10.1080/02687039708249420

Mackenzie, C., Begg, T., Lees, K. R., & Brady, M. (1999). The communication effects of right brain damage on the very old and the not so old. *Journal of Neurolinguistics, 12*, 79–93. https://doi.org/10.1016/S0911-6044(99)00004-4

Mackisack, E. L., Myers, P. S., & Duffy, J. R. (1987). Verbosity and labeling behavior: The performance of right hemisphere and non-brain-damaged adults on an inferential picture description task. In *Clinical aphasiology conference proceedings* (pp. 143–151). Minneapolis, MN: BRK Publishers.

Marini, A., Carlomagno, S., Caltagirone, C., & Nocentini, U. (2005). The role played by the right hemisphere in the organization of complex textual structures. *Brain and Language, 93*(1), 46–54. https://doi.org/10.1016/j.bandl.2004.08.002

Mark, V. W., Kooistra, C. A., & Heilman, K. M. (1988). Hemispatial neglect affected by non-neglected stimuli. *Neurology, 38*, 1207–1211.

Marshall, J. C., & Halligan, P. W. (1988). Letter: Blindsight and insight in visuo-spatial neglect. *Nature, 336*(22/29), 766–767.

Martin, I., & McDonald, S. (2003). Weak coherence, no theory of mind, or executive dysfunction? Solving the puzzle of pragmatic language disorders. *Brain and Language, 85*(3), 451–466. https://doi.org/10.1016/S0093-934X(03)00070-1

Martin, I., & McDonald, S. (2006). That can't be right! What causes pragmatic language impairment following right hemisphere damage? *Brain Impairment, 7*(3), 202–211. https://doi.org/10.1375/brim.7.3.202

Matsuki, K., Chow, T., Hare, M., Elman, J. L., Scheepers, C., & McRae, K. (2011). Event-based plausibility immediately influences on-line language comprehension. *Journal of Experimental Psychology: Learning, Memory, and Cognition, 37*(4), 913–934. https://doi.org/10.1037/a0022964

McDonald, S. (2000). Exploring the cognitive basis of right-hemisphere pragmatic language disorders. *Brain and Language, 75*(1), 82–107. https://doi.org/10.1006/brln.2000.2342

McDonald, S., Flanagan, S., & Rollins, J. (2002). *The Awareness of Social Inference Test (TASIT).* Randwick, Australia: Australasian Society for the Study of Brain Impairment.

McKoon, G., & Ratcliff, R. (1992). Inference during reading. *Psychological Review, 99*(3), 440–466.

Mesulam, M.-M. (1981). A cortical network for directed attention and unilateral neglect. *Annals of Neurology, 10*, 309–325.

Mesulam, M.-M. (2000). Attentional networks, confusional states and neglect syndromes. In *Principles of behavioral and cognitive neurology* (2nd ed., pp. 174–256). New York, NY: Oxford University Press.

Middleton, L. E., Lam, B., Fahmi, H., Black, S. E., McIlroy, W. E., Stuss, D. T., . . . Turner, G. R. (2014). Frequency of domain-specific cognitive impairment in sub-acute and chronic stroke. *Neuro-Rehabilitation, 34*(2), 305–312. https://doi.org/10.3233/NRE-131030

Milders, M., Fuchs, S., & Crawford, J. R. (2003). Neuropsychological impairments and changes in emotional and social behaviour following severe traumatic brain injury. *Journal of Clinical and Experimental Neuropsychology, 25*(2), 157–172. https://doi.org/10.1076/jcen.25.2.157.13642

Monetta, L., & Joanette, Y. (2003). Specificity of the right hemisphere's contribution to verbal communication: The cognitive resources hypothesis. *Journal of Medical Speech-Language Pathology, 11*(4), 203–211.

Monetta, L., Ouellet-Plamondon, C., & Joanette, Y. (2006). Simulating the pattern of right-hemisphere-damaged patients for the processing of the alternative metaphorical meanings of words: Evidence in favor of a cognitive resources hypothesis. *Brain and Language, 96*(2), 171–177. https://doi.org/10.1016/j.bandl.2004.10.014

Moya, K. L., Benowitz, L. I., Levine, D. N., & Finklestein, S. (1986). Covariant defects in visuospatial abilities and recall of verbal narrative after right hemisphere stroke. *Cortex, 22*(3), 381–397. https://doi.org/http://dx.doi.org.ezproxy.lib.uh.edu/10.1016/S0010-9452(86)80003-X

Myers, P. S. (1979). Profiles of communication deficits in patients with right cerebral hemisphere damage: Implications for diagnosis and treatment. In *Clinical aphasiology conference proceedings* (pp. 38–46). Minneapolis, MN: BRK Publishers.

Myers, P. S. (1990). Inference failure: The underlying impairment in right-hemisphere communication disorders. In T. E. Prescott (Ed.), *Clinical aphasiology con-ference proceedings* (pp. 167–180). Austin, TX: Pro-Ed.

Myers, P. S. (1999a). Process-oriented treatment of right hemisphere communication disorders. *Seminars in Speech and Language, 20*(4), 319–333.

Myers, P. S. (1999b). *Right hemisphere damage: Disorders of communication and cognition.* San Diego, CA: Singular.

Myers, P. S. (2001). Toward a definition of RHD syndrome. *Aphasiology, 15*(10–11), 913–918. https://doi.org/10.1080/02687040143000285

Myers, P. S., & Linebaugh, C. W. (1981). Comprehension of idiomatic expressions by right-hemisphere-damaged adults. In R. Brookshire (Ed.), *Clinical aphasiology conference proceedings* (pp. 254–261). Minneapolis, MN: BRK Publishers.

Newport, R., & Schenk, T. (2012). Prisms and neglect: What have we learned? *Neuropsychologia, 50*(6), 1080–1091. https://doi.org/10.1016/j.neuropsychologia.2012.01.023

Niemeier, J. P., Cifu, D. X., & Kishore, R. (2001). The Lighthouse Strategy: Improving the functional status of patients with unilateral neglect after stroke and brain injury using a visual imagery intervention. *Topics in Stroke Rehabilitation, 8,* 10–18. https://doi.org/10.1310/7UKK-HJ0F-GDWF-HHM8

Orfei, M. D., Robinson, R. G., Prigatano, G. P., Starkstein, S., Rüsch, N., Bria, P., . . . Spalletta, G. (2007). Anosognosia for hemiplegia after stroke is a multifaceted phenomenon: A systematic review of the literature. *Brain: A Journal of Neurology, 130*(Pt 12), 3075–3090. https://doi.org/10.1093/brain/awm106

Osborne-Crowley, K., & McDonald, S. (2016). Hyposmia, not emotion perception, is associated with psychosocial outcome after severe traumatic brain injury. *Neuropsychology, 37*(7), 820–829.

Park, Y. H., Jang, J.-W., Park, S. Y., Wang, M. J., Lim, J.-S., Baek, M. J., . . . Kim, S. (2015). Executive function as a strong predictor of recovery from disability in patients with acute stroke: A preliminary study. *Journal of Stroke and Cerebrovascular Diseases*, 24(3), 554–561. https://doi.org/10.1016/j.jstrokecerebrovasdis.2014.09.033

Pavani, F., Husain, M., Ladavas, E., & Driver, J. (2004). Auditory deficits in visuospatial neglect patients. *Cortex*, 40, 347–365.

Pavani, F., Làdavas, E., & Driver, J. (2002). Selective deficit of auditory localisation in patients with visuospatial neglect. *Neuropsychologia*, 40(3), 291–301. https://doi.org/10.1016/S0028-3932(01)00091-4

Pell, M. D. (2006). Cerebral mechanisms for understanding emotional prosody in speech. *Brain and Language*, 96(2), 221–234. https://doi.org/10.1016/j.bandl.2005.04.007

Pell, M. D. (2007). Reduced sensitivity to prosodic attitudes in adults with focal right hemisphere brain damage. *Brain and Language*, 101(1), 64–79. https://doi.org/10.1016/j.bandl.2006.10.003

Penn, C. (1999). Pragmatic assessment and therapy for persons with brain damage: What have clinicians gleaned in two decades? *Brain and Language*, 68, 535–552. https://doi.org/10.1006/brln.1999.2127

Peppé, S. J. (2009). Why is prosody in speech-language pathology so difficult? *International Journal of Speech-Language Pathology*, 11(4), 258–271. https://doi.org/10.1080/17549500902906339

Perecman, E. (Ed.). (1983). *Cognitive processing in the right hemisphere*. New York, NY: Academic Press.

Pernet, L., Jughters, A., & Kerckhofs, E. (2013). The effectiveness of different treatment modalities for the rehabilitation of unilateral neglect in stroke patients: A systematic review. *NeuroRehabilitation*, 33(4), 611–620. https://doi.org/10.3233/NRE-130986

Pimental, P. A., & Kingsbury, N. A. (2000). *Mini Inventory of Right Brain Injury-2* (2nd ed.). Austin, TX: Pro-Ed.

Pitteri, M., Arcara, G., Passarini, L., Meneghello, F., & Priftis, K. (2013). Is two better than one? Limb activation treatment combined with contralesional arm vibration to ameliorate signs of left neglect. *Frontiers in Human Neuroscience*, 7, 1–10. https://doi.org/10.3389/fnhum.2013.00460

Priftis, K., Passarini, L., Pilosio, C., Meneghello, F., & Pitteri, M. (2013). Visual scanning training, limb activation treatment, and prism adaptation for rehabilitating left neglect: Who is the winner? *Frontiers in Human Neuroscience*, 7, 1–12. https://doi.org/10.3389/fnhum.2013.00360

Prigatano, G. P. (1996). Behavioral limitations TBI patients tend to underestimate: A replication and extension to patients with lateralized cerebral dysfunction. *Clinical Neuropsychologist*, 10(2), 191–201. https://doi.org/10.1080/13854049608406680

Prigatano, G. P. (2014). Anosognosia and patterns of impaired self-awareness observed in clinical practice. *Cortex*, 61, 81–92. https://doi.org/10.1016/j.cortex.2014.07.014

Prigatano, G. P., & Klonoff, P. S. (1998). A clinician's rating scale for evaluating impaired self-awareness and denial of disability after brain injury. *The Clinical Neuropsychologist*, 12(1), 56–67. https://doi.org/10.1076/clin.12.1.56.1721

Randolph, C. (1998). *Repeatable Battery for the Assessment of Neuropsychological Status*. San Antonio: Psychological Corporation.

Rehak, A., Kaplan, J. A., Weylman, S. T., Kelly, B., Brownell, H. H., & Gardner, H. (1992). Story processing in right-hemisphere brain-damaged patients. *Brain and Language*, 42(3), 320–336. https://doi.org/10.1016/0093-934X(92)90104-M

Reinhart, S., Schaadt, A. K., Adams, M., Leonhardt, E., & Kerkhoff, G. (2013). The frequency and significance of the word length effect in neglect dyslexia. *Neuropsychologia*, 51(7), 1273–1278. https://doi.org/10.1016/j.neuropsychologia.2013.03.006

Reinhart, S., Schindler, I., & Kerkhoff, G. (2011). Optokinetic stimulation affects word omissions but not stimulus-centered reading errors in paragraph reading in neglect dyslexia. *Neuropsychologia, 49*(9), 2728–2735. https://doi.org/10.1016/j.neuropsychologia.2011.05.022

Robertson, I. H., McMillan, T. M., MacLeod, E., Edgeworth, J., & Brock, D. (2002). Rehabilitation by limb activation training reduces left-sided motor impairment in unilateral neglect patients: A single-blind randomised control trial. *Neuropsychological Rehabilitation, 12*(5), 439–454. https://doi.org/10.1080/09602010244000228

Robertson, I. H., Tegnér, R., Tham, K., Lo, A., & Nimmo-Smith, I. (1995). Sustained attention training for unilateral neglect: Theoretical and rehabilitation implications. *Journal of Clinical and Experimental Neuropsychology, 17*, 416–430. https://doi.org/10.1080/01688639508405133

Ronchi, R., Algeri, L., Chiapella, L., Gallucci, M., Spada, M. S., & Vallar, G. (2016). Left neglect dyslexia: Perseveration and reading error types. *Neuropsychologia, 89*, 453–464. https://doi.org/10.1016/j.neuropsychologia.2016.07.023

Ronchi, R., Rode, G., Cotton, F., Farnè, A., Rossetti, Y., & Jacquin-Courtois, S. (2013). Remission of anosognosia for right hemiplegia and neglect after caloric vestibular stimulation. *Restorative Neurology and Neuroscience, 31*(1), 19–24. https://doi.org/10.3233/RNN-120236

Rosenbek, J. C., Crucian, G. P., Leon, S. A., Hieber, B., Rodriguez, A. D., Holiway, B., ... Gonzalez-Rothi, L. (2004). Novel treatments for expressive aprosodia: A phase I investigation of cognitive linguistic and imitative interventions. *Journal of the International Neuropsychological Society, 10*, 786–793. https://doi.org/10.1017/S135561770410502X

Ross, E. D. (1981). The aprosodias: Functional-anatomic organization of the affective components of language in the right hemisphere. *Archives of Neurology, 38*(9), 561–569.

Ross, E. D., Thompson, R. D., & Yenkosky, J. (1997). Lateralization of affective prosody in brain and the callosal integration of hemispheric language functions. *Brain and Language, 56*, 27–54.

Rossetti, Y., Rossetti, Y., Rode, G., Rode, G., Pisella, L., Pisella, L., ... Lyon, D. (1998). Prism adaptation to a rightward optical deviation rehabilitates left hemispatial neglect. *Nature, 395*, 8–11.

Rusconi, M. L., & Carelli, L. (2012). Long-term efficacy of prism adaptation on spatial neglect: Preliminary results on different spatial components. *Scientific World Journal, 2012*, 1–8. https://doi.org/10.1100/2012/618528

Sackett, D. L., Straus, E., Richardson, W. S., Rosenberg, W., & Haynes, R. B. (2000). *Evidence-based medicine: How to practice and teach EBM.* New York, NY: Churchill Livingstone.

Saevarsson, S., Halsband, U., & Kristjansson, A. (2011). Designing rehabilitation programs for neglect: could 2 be more than 1+1? *Applied Neuropsychology, 18*(2), 95–106. https://doi.org/10.1080/09084282.2010.547774

Saxton, M. E., Younan, S. S., & Lah, S. (2013). Social behaviour following severe traumatic brain injury: Contribution of emotion perception deficits. *NeuroRehabilitation, 33*(2), 263–271. https://doi.org/10.3233/NRE-130954

Shamay-Tsoory, S. G., Tomer, R., Goldsher, D., Berger, B. D., & Aharon-Peretz, J. (2004). Impairment in cognitive and affective empathy in patients with brain lesions: Anatomical and cognitive correlates. *Journal of Clinical and Experimental Neuropsychology, 26*(8), 1113–1127. https://doi.org/10.1080/13803390490515531

Shammi, P., & Stuss, D. T. (1999). Humour appreciation: A role of the right frontal lobe. *Brain, 122*, 657–666. Retrieved from papers2://publication/uuid/BF7DE5B9-70CF-4A2A-B04F-FA2E301BCA9B

Sherer, M., Hart, T., & Nick, T. G. (2003). Measurement of impaired self-awareness after traumatic brain injury: A comparison of the Patient Competency rating Scale and the Awareness Questionnaire. *Brain Injury, 17*(1), 25–37.

Shinoura, N., Suzuki, Y., Yamada, R., Tabei, Y., Saito, K., & Yagi, K. (2009). Damage to the right superior longitudinal fasciculus in the inferior parietal lobe plays a role in spatial neglect. *Neuropsychologia, 47*(12), 2600–2603. https://doi.org/10.1016/j.neuropsychologia.2009.05.010

Siéroff, E., Decaix, C., Chokron, S., & Bartolomeo, P. (2007). Impaired orienting of attention in left unilateral neglect: A componential analysis. *Neuropsychology, 21*(1), 94–113. https://doi.org/10.1037/0894-4105.21.1.94

Sturm, W., Thimm, M., Kust, J., Karbe, H., & Fink, G. R. (2006). Alertness-training in neglect: Behavioral and imaging results. *Restorative Neurology and Neuroscience, 24*, 371–384.

Sturm, W., & Willmes, K. (1991). Efficacy of a reaction training on various attentional and cognitive functions in stroke patients. *Neuropsychological Rehabilitation, 1*(4), 259–280. https://doi.org/10.1080/09602019108402258

Thimm, M., Fink, G. R., Küst, J., Karbe, H., & Sturm, W. (2006). Impact of alertness training on spatial neglect: A behavioural and fMRI study. *Neuropsychologia, 44*(7), 1230–1246. https://doi.org/10.1016/j.neuropsychologia.2005.09.008

Toglia, J., & Kirk, U. (2000). Understanding awareness deficits following brain injury. *NeuroRehabilitation, 15*(1), 57–70. Retrieved from http://search.ebscohost.com/login.aspx?direct=true&db=cin20&AN=2003055532&site=ehost-live

Tompkins, C. A. (1995). *Right hemisphere communication disorders: Theory and management*. San Diego, CA: Singular.

Tompkins, C. A., Baumgaertner, A., Lehman, M. T., & Fassbinder, W. (2000). Mechanisms of discourse comprehension impairment after right hemisphere brain damage: Suppression in lexical ambiguity resolution. *Journal of Speech, Language, and Hearing Research, 43*, 62–78.

Tompkins, C. A., Bloise, C. G. R., Timko, M. L., & Baumgaertner, A. (1994). Working memory and inference revision in brain-damaged and normally aging adults. *Journal of Speech and Hearing Research, 37*(4), 896–912. https://doi.org/10.1044/jshr.3704.896

Tompkins, C. A., Fassbinder, W., Blake, M. L., Baumgaertner, A., & Jayaram, N. (2004). Inference generation during text comprehension by adults with right hemisphere brain damage: Activation failure versus multiple activation. *Journal of Speech, Language, and Hearing Research, 47*, 1308–1395.

Tompkins, C. A., Klepousniotou, E., & Scott, A. G. (2013). Nature and assessment of right hemisphere disorders. In I. Papthanasiou, P. Coppens, & C. Potagas (Eds.), *Aphasia and related neurogenic communication disorders* (pp. 297–343). Burlington, MA: Jones & Bartlett.

Tompkins, C. A., Lehman-Blake, M. T., Baumgaertner, A., & Fassbinder, W. (2001a). Divided attention impedes suppression by right-brain-damaged and non-brain-damaged adults. *Brain and Language, 79*(1), 57–59.

Tompkins, C. A., Lehman-Blake, M. T., Baumgaertner, A., & Fassbinder, W. (2001b). Mechanisms of discourse comprehension after right hemisphere brain damage: Inferential ambiguity resolution. *Journal of Speech, Language, and Hearing Research, 44*, 400–415.

Tompkins, C. A., Scharp, V. L., Meigh, K., Blake, M. L., & Wambaugh, J. (2012). Generalization of a novel, implicit treatment for coarse coding deficit in right hemisphere brain damage: A single subject experiment. *Aphasiology, 26*(5), 689–708. https://doi.org/10.1080/02687038.2012.676869

Tompkins, C. A., Scharp, V. L., Meigh, K. M., & Fassbinder, W. (2008). Coarse coding and discourse comprehension in adults with right hemisphere brain damage. *Aphasiology, 22*(2), 204–223. https://doi.org/10.1080/02687030601125019

Tompkins, C. A., & Scott, A. G. (2013). Treatment of right hemisphere disorders. In I. Papathanasiou, P. Coppens, & C. Potagas

(Eds.), *Aphasia and related neurogenic communication disorders* (pp. 345–364). Burlington, MA: Jones & Bartlett.

Trupe, E. H., & Hillis, A. E. (1985). Paucity vs. verbosity: Another analysis of right hemisphere communication deficits. In *Clinical aphasiology* (pp. 83–96). Rockville, MD: BRK Publishers.

Turkstra, L., Ylvisaker, M., Coelho, C., Kennedy, M., Sohlberg, M. M., Avery, J., & Yorkston, K. (2005). Practice guidelines for standardized assessment for persons with traumatic brain injury. *Journal of Medical Speech-Language Pathology*, *13*(2), ix–xxxviii. https://doi.org/10.1037/t05 377-000

Vallar, G., Burani, C., & Arduino, L. S. (2010). Neglect dyslexia: A review of the neuropsychological literature. *Experimental Brain Research*, *206*(2), 219–235. https:// doi.org/10.1007/s00221-010-2386-0

Van Lancker, D. R., & Kempler, D. (1987). Comprehension of familiar phrases by left- but not by right-hemisphere damaged patients. *Brain and Language*, *32*, 265–277.

Virk, S., Williams, T., Brunsdon, R., Suh, F., & Morrow, A. (2015). Cognitive remediation of attention deficits following acquired brain injury: A systematic review and meta-analysis. *NeuroRehabilitation*, *36*(3), 367–377. https://doi.org/10 .3233/NRE-151225

Vossel, S., Weiss, P. H., Eschenbeck, P., & Fink, G. R. (2013). Anosognosia, neglect, extinction and lesion site predict impairment of daily living after right-hemispheric stroke. *Cortex*, *49*(7), 1782–1789. https://doi.org/10.1016/j.cortex.2012 .12.011

Vuilleumier, P., Schwartz, S., Clarke, K., Husain, M., & Driver, J. (2002). Testing memory for unseen visual stimuli in patients with extinction and spatial neglect. *Journal of Cognitive Neuroscience*, *14*(6), 875–886.

Vuilleumier, P., Schwartz, S., Husain, M., Clarke, K., & Driver, J. (2001). Implicit processing and learning of visual stimuli in parietal extinction and neglect. *Cortex*, *37*(5), 741–744. https://doi.org/10.1016/ S0010-9452(08)70629-4

Walker, J. P., Daigle, T., & Buzzard, M. (2002). Hemispheric specialisation in processing prosodic structures: Revisited. *Aphasiology*, *16*(12), 1155–1172. https://doi .org/10.1080/02687030244000392

Walker, J. P., Pelletier, R., & Reif, L. (2004). The production of linguistic prosodic structures in subjects with right hemisphere damage. *Clinical Linguistics & Phonetics*, *18*(2), 85–106. https://doi.org/ 10.1080/02699200310001596179

Wapner, W., Hamby, S., & Gardner, H. (1981). The role of the right hemisphere in the apprehension of complex linguistic materials. *Brain and Language*, *14*, 15–33. https://doi.org/10.1016/0093-93 4X(81)90061-4

Wee, J. Y. M., & Hopman, W. M. (2005). Stroke impairment predictors of discharge function, length of stay, and discharge destination in stroke rehabilitation. *American Journal of Physical Medicine and Rehabilitation*, *84*, 604–612. https:// doi.org/10.1097/01.phm.0000171005 .08744.ab

Wildgruber, D., Ethofer, T., Grandjean, D., & Kreifelts, B. (2009). A cerebral network model of speech prosody comprehension. *International Journal of Speech-Language Pathology*, *11*(4), 277–281. https://doi. org/10.1080/17549500902943043

Wilson, B. A., Cockburn, J., & Halligan, P. W. (1987). *Behavioural Inattention Test*. Oxford, UK: Pearson Assessment.

Winner, E., Brownell, H. H., Happe, F., Blum, A., & Pincus, D. (1998). Distinguishing lies from jokes: Theory of Mind deficits and discourse interpretation in right hemisphere brain-damaged patients. *Brain and Language*, *62*(62), 89–106. https://doi.org/10.1006/brln.1997.1889

Witteman, J., van Ijzendoorn, M. H., van de Velde, D., van Heuven, V. J. J. P., & Schiller, N. O. (2011). The nature of hemispheric specialization for linguistic and emotional prosodic perception: A meta-analysis of the lesion literature. *Neuropsychologia*, *49*(13), 3722–3738. https://doi.org/10.1016/j.neuropsychologia.2011.09.028

Wright, H. H. (Ed.). (2016). *Cognition, language and aging*. Philadelphia, PA: John Benjamins BV.

Yang, N. Y. H., Zhou, D., Chung, R. C. K., Li-Tsang, C. W. P., & Fong, K. N. K. (2013). Rehabilitation interventions for unilateral neglect after stroke: A systematic review from 1997–2012. *Frontiers in Human Neuroscience*, *7*, 1–11.

Ylvisaker, M., Szekeres, S. F., & Feeney, T. J. (2008). Communication disorders associated with traumatic brain injury. In R. Chapey (Ed.), *Language intervention strategies in aphasia and related neurogenic communication disorders* (5th ed., pp. 879–962). Philadelphia, PA: Lippincott, Williams & Wilkins.

Youngjohn, J. R., & Altman, I. M. (1989). A performance-based group approach to the treatment of anosognosia and denial. *Rehabilitation Psychology*, *34*(3), 217–222.

Yue, Y., Song, W., Huo, S., & Wang, M. (2012). Study on the occurrence and neural bases of hemispatial neglect with different reference frames. *Archives of Physical Medicine and Rehabilitation*, *93*(1), 156–162. https://doi.org/10.1016/j.apmr.2011.07.192

Zimmer, U., Lewald, J., & Karnath, H. (2003). Disturbed sound lateralization in patients with spatial neglect. *Journal of Cognitive Neuroscience*, *15*(5), 694–703.

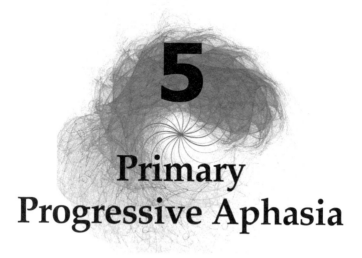

5

Primary Progressive Aphasia

Heather Dial and Maya Henry

Introduction

Primary progressive aphasia, or PPA, is a neurodegenerative disorder wherein speech and language functions gradually deteriorate. This loss of function occurs in the presence of relatively spared general cognition, at least in the initial stages of the disease (Gorno-Tempini et al., 2011; Mesulam, 1982, 2001). Although the existence of this language-specific dementia was first documented in the late 1800s (Kertesz & Kalvach, 1996; Pick, 1977), in-depth research into PPA symptoms, progression, and treatment is a relatively new endeavor. Since speech and language impairments are the primary deficits observed in this relatively rare form of dementia, speech-language pathologists (SLPs) serve an important role in the diagnosis and management of this disorder. In order to provide the best care for individuals with PPA, SLPs require a thorough understanding of the nature of the deficits observed in

PPA, its typical patterns of progression, and potential treatment options.

Brief History

PPA was first described by Arnold Pick in 1892 (Kertesz & Kalvach, 1996; Pick, 1977). Pick, a psychiatrist at a medical university in Prague, had seen several patients who presented with gradually worsening aphasia. Following the patients' deaths, he examined their brains, observing that atrophy was relatively circumscribed to areas of the brain that had recently been identified as related to language. This led him to refer to the disorder as a "focal" dementia. Nearly 100 years after the first documentation of this "focal," language-based dementia, Marsel Mesulam reintroduced the disorder as a "slowly progressive aphasia without generalized dementia" (Mesulam, 1982). In this seminal work, Mesulam presented his clinical impressions regarding several individuals who had experienced gradually worsening language impairments. Most of the individuals presented with anomia, with two individuals also presenting with "nonfluent aphasias similar to the Broca type" (p. 597). He noted that these individuals were fairly young, with four of the cases in their late 40s to early 60s, suggesting an average age of onset that is younger than the more common Alzheimer's dementia. Mesulam noted that, as the disease progressed, many of the individuals developed additional deficits in language comprehension, repetition, and general cognitive processing.

Other researchers and clinicians began to document individuals who had anomia and a progressive loss of semantic knowledge. Some of the first cases of this nature were presented by Elizabeth Warrington in 1975. She described three individuals who had word-finding difficulties and demonstrated evidence of a loss of knowledge of everyday objects and common words but who had relatively preserved visuospatial processing and episodic memory. These individuals were noted to have fluent speech "using an impoverished vocabulary" (Warrington, 1975, p. 638). In 1989, Julie Snowden and colleagues presented three cases that were very similar to those presented by Warrington (1975). They coined the term "semantic dementia" to refer to this disorder, noting that it was likely related to "dementia of the frontal lobe type" and "slowly progressive aphasia" (Snowden, Goulding, & Neary, 1989, p. 179).

A few years later, John Hodges and colleagues presented five cases of semantic dementia (Hodges, Patterson, Oxbury, & Funnell, 1992). Unlike Snowden et al. (1989), they argued that semantic dementia should be considered as distinct from progressive aphasia, since the observed deficits are not isolated to language processes and include a disruption of core semantic knowledge, evidenced by a visual agnosia. They further suggested that progressive aphasia should be limited to nonfluent aphasic presentations but that the likely underlying cause of both semantic dementia and progressive aphasia is frontotemporal lobar degeneration (FTLD). The link between semantic dementia, progressive aphasia, and FTLD was formalized in a paper from David Neary and colleagues that outlined clinical criteria for syndromic diagnosis. This paper presents diagnostic criteria for three syndromes related to FTLD: frontotemporal dementia, semantic dementia, and progressive nonfluent aphasia (Neary et al., 1998). While the discussion of the relation between progressive aphasia and semantic dementia continued, and shortly after the publication of the Neary et al. (1998) criteria, Mesulam introduced clinical criteria for diagnosing PPA (Mesulam, 2001). By the mid-2000s, three behavioral phenotypes had been identified that fit under the PPA umbrella: semantic variant (svPPA), logopenic variant (lvPPA), and nonfluent variant (nfvPPA), and formal diagnostic criteria for each subtype quickly followed (Bonner, Ash, & Grossman, 2010; Gorno-Tempini et al., 2004; Gorno-Tempini et al., 2011; Henry & Gorno-Tempini, 2010).

As can be seen, there is a history of inconsistent and evolving nomenclature associated with PPA. Focal dementia, slowly progressive aphasia, fluent progressive aphasia, nonfluent progressive aphasia, and semantic dementia were all terms being used in the 1970s, 1980s, and 1990s for conditions that are now considered to be part of the PPA classification system. Focal dementia and slowly progressive aphasia have been used to describe PPA generally, fluent progressive aphasia and semantic dementia often refer to svPPA, and nonfluent progressive aphasia has encompassed both lvPPA and nfvPPA. In fact, in the criteria laid out by Neary et al. (1998), progressive nonfluent aphasia includes diagnostic features of nfvPPA (agrammatism) and lvPPA (phonemic paraphasias, anomia). As such, it can be difficult to ascertain whether cases of nonfluent progressive aphasia from the 1980s and 1990s represent lvPPA or nfvPPA. When considering research from this period to aid in the development of appropriate treatment plans for individuals with PPA, care should be taken in interpreting diagnostic labels. Although the relevance of the various nosologic traditions may not be immediately obvious, it is important to be aware of the various naming conventions if one wants to gain a thorough understanding of the PPA literature.

Clinical Criteria for PPA Diagnosis

Formalized diagnostic criteria for PPA were only developed in the last two decades. Whereas Neary et al. presented the first diagnostic criteria for FTLD variants, which included semantic dementia and progressive nonfluent aphasia, Mesulam was the first to present diagnostic criteria for PPA

proper (Mesulam, 2001). According to Mesulam (2001), in order to be conferred a diagnosis of PPA, an individual's language disturbance must have had a gradual onset and should be the initial and primary symptom for at least the first 2 years and must remain the most prominent impairment throughout disease progression. In the early stages of the disease, any disruptions in daily life should be related to language problems. PPA diagnosis is not appropriate if visuospatial processing impairments, episodic memory deficits, or behavioral disruptions are prominent in the initial stages of the disease or if deficits can be clearly linked to stroke, brain tumor, traumatic brain injury, or psychiatric conditions. Once a diagnosis of PPA is made, diagnosis by clinical subtype, if possible, follows.

Gorno-Tempini et al. (2011) reiterated the diagnostic criteria for PPA that were originally enumerated by Mesulam (2001), with the only modification being that the language disturbance must be isolated in the "initial phases of the disease" (p. 1008) rather than the first 2 years. More importantly, they presented clinical criteria for diagnosing three PPA subtypes: the semantic variant (svPPA), the logopenic variant (lvPPA), and the nonfluent variant (nfvPPA; Table 5–1). In broad terms, lexical retrieval difficulties are the most prominent impairment in svPPA and lvPPA, due to a loss of core semantic knowledge in svPPA and phonological processing impairments in lvPPA. For example, an individual with relatively mild svPPA may mistakenly identify an octopus as a jellyfish, which is both semantically and visually similar, whereas an individual with relatively

Table 5–1. Consensus Clinical Criteria for Diagnosis by PPA Subtype

PPA Subtype	Core Clinical Features	Supporting Features
Semantic Variant	Both of the following: 1. Picture naming deficit 2. Single-word comprehension deficit	At least three of the following: 1. Loss of object knowledge 2. Surface dyslexia/dysgraphia 3. Relatively preserved repetition 4. Intact grammar and motor speech
Logopenic Variant	Both of the following: 1. Difficulty with single-word retrieval in spontaneous speech and picture naming 2. Phrase and sentence repetition deficit	At least three of the following: 1. Phonemic paraphasias in spontaneous speech and picture naming 2. Relatively preserved comprehension of single words and intact object knowledge 3. Lack of motor speech impairments 4. Spared syntactic processing
Nonfluent Variant	At least one of the following: 1. Agrammatism 2. Apraxia of speech	At least two of the following: 1. Syntax comprehension deficit, particularly for complex syntax 2. Relatively preserved comprehension of single words 3. Relatively preserved object knowledge

Note. Criteria originally presented by Gorno-Tempini et al. (2011).

mild lvPPA may have difficulty assembling the constituent sounds and produce something like /ɑkpətʊs/. In nfvPPA, agrammatism and/or apraxia of speech are the first symptoms (Gorno-Tempini et al., 2011; see Montembeault, Brambati, Gorno-Tempini, & Migliaccio, 2018, for a review of clinical and anatomical correlates of each PPA subtype). The core linguistic deficits observed in each PPA variant are most distinct in the mild to moderate stages of the disorder. As the symptoms and underlying disease progress, the behavioral profile of each PPA subtype becomes less distinct (Cerami et al., 2017; Rogalski et al., 2011).

PPA Subtypes and Etiology

Semantic Variant

SvPPA is characterized by a loss of semantic knowledge. This manifests as a progressively worsening anomia and single-word comprehension impairment, the two core clinical features for svPPA diagnosis (see Table 5–1; Gorno-Tempini et al., 2011; Henry, Rising, et al., 2013; Hodges & Patterson, 2007). Although the primary cause of anomia is loss of semantic knowledge, anomia may also be related to a weakening of the link between a concept and its verbal label, such that the person knows what he or she is trying to talk about but is unable to retrieve the word for it (Wilson, Dehollain, Ferrieux, Christensen, & Teichmann, 2017). Individuals are likely to make semantic errors in language production when the incorrect verbal label is selected, but, in some mild cases, they may be able to successfully cue themselves or their conversation partners via circumlocution.

In addition to the core linguistic impairments, at least three of the following supporting features must be present: loss of object knowledge, surface dyslexia/dysgraphia, spared repetition, and intact grammatical processing and motor speech. Individuals with svPPA may fail to recognize items and objects, especially those that are relatively uncommon. With progressive loss of object knowledge, they may begin to use objects inappropriately. Another potential consequence

of loss of semantic knowledge is surface dyslexia and dysgraphia, wherein individuals have selective difficulty reading and spelling irregular words (Coltheart, Rastle, Perry, Langdon, & Ziegler, 2001). Individuals with svPPA tend to produce regularization errors when attempting to read or spell irregular words. For example, the word *island* might be read as /ɪzlænd/. By contrast, reading and spelling of regular words and nonwords remains relatively intact. Phonological processing is typically unaffected, such that performance on repetition tasks is generally within normal limits, especially in the early stages of the disease. Grammatical processing impairments or motor speech deficits are not observed in svPPA, as regions in the brain that are devoted to these processes are generally spared.

As the disease progresses, language production becomes progressively empty, while remaining intelligible and grammatical. Additionally, individuals may develop dysexecutive symptoms consistent with frontotemporal dementia such as compulsive behaviors, disinhibition, changes in personality, and altered eating preferences (Cerami et al., 2017; Macoir, Lavoie, Laforce, Brambati, & Wilson, 2017; Seeley et al., 2005). For example, Macoir and colleagues (2017) describe an individual with svPPA who, 6 years after symptom onset and after visiting the clinic for assessment for 3 years, began insisting that all assessment materials be disinfected prior to use.

The deficits observed in svPPA are related to temporal lobe atrophy, with peak atrophy observed in the anterior temporal lobe in the language-dominant hemisphere (Gorno-Tempini et al., 2004; Figure 5–1). This is consistent with

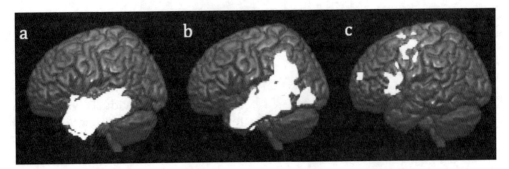

Figure 5–1. Left hemisphere cortical atrophy patterns in svPPA (**a**), lvPPA (**b**), and nfvPPA (**c**). Regions of significant atrophy for 25 individuals with each variant relative to 40 age-matched controls.

a proposed role for the anterior temporal lobes in semantic memory (Patterson, Nestor, & Rogers, 2007; Simmons & Martin, 2009). With progression, atrophy will spread throughout the semantic network (Seeley, Crawford, Zhou, Miller, & Greicius, 2009), and worsening symptoms will emerge. Eventually, the frontal and parietal lobes will also be affected by the disease process (Cerami et al., 2017). The underlying cause of neurodegeneration may vary across individuals, but the most likely pathological finding is FTLD-TDP, with one study observing that 83% of a sample of *n* = 29 svPPA cases had FTLD-TDP pathology at autopsy (Spinelli et al., 2017). Knowledge of the underlying disease process may ultimately inform decisions regarding pharmaceutical intervention. Unfortunately, at this time, there is no way to conclusively test for FTLD-TDP in vivo. Moreover, no pharmacological intervention currently exists for treating the underlying disease, although medications such as selective serotonin reuptake inhibitors (SSRIs) may be prescribed to alleviate behavioral symptoms (Young, Lavakumar, Tampi, Balachandran, & Tampi, 2018).

Logopenic Variant

LvPPA is the most recently identified PPA subtype and is characterized by a phonological processing impairment, which results in anomia and deficits in repeating phrases and sentences, the two core clinical features for lvPPA diagnosis (see Table 5–1). Individuals with lvPPA struggle with confrontation naming, and spontaneous speech may contain frequent pauses due to lexical retrieval difficulties, contributing to a slow rate of production. In addition, these individuals have trouble repeating phrases and sentences and may rely upon semantic memory when performing repetition tasks, causing them to produce semantically similar but not identical utterances (Gorno-Tempini et al., 2008; Henry & Gorno-Tempini, 2010; Leyton & Hodges, 2013).

At least three of the following supporting features must also be present for an lvPPA diagnosis: phonemic paraphasias in spontaneous speech and picture naming, intact single-word comprehension and object knowledge, intact motor speech, and spared syntactic processing. In spontaneous speech and picture naming, individuals with lvPPA may produce phonemic paraphasias via substitution, transposition, deletion, or addition of phonemes. For example, one individual with relatively mild lvPPA, when presented with a picture of a candelabra, remarked that "I've got parts of this rattling around in my head. It's like having two out of three syllables. It's a cal, a candeluh, candelagra." These errors suggest difficulty assembling and producing the phonemes necessary to successfully say "candelabra." However, the proximity to the correct phonological form suggests intact object knowledge for this low-frequency word. Indeed, most individuals with lvPPA, at least in the early stages of the disease process, have intact comprehension of single words and spared object knowledge. In this example, the errors produced were nondistorted sound errors of a phonological nature and not attributable to apraxia of speech. This provides evidence for the supporting clinical feature of intact motor speech. Finally, although individuals with lvPPA may appear to be agrammatic at times, this can be attributed to their lexical retrieval and phonological working memory deficits, and frank agrammatism is not typically noted.

As the disease progresses, individuals may develop jargon-like symptoms, including semantic paraphasias and neologisms (Caffara et al., 2013). At this point, the message the individual is attempting to convey may be indecipherable. Comprehension deficits are also likely to occur in later stages of the disease (Caffara et al., 2013). Individuals may also begin to have difficulty with verbal memory and may begin to develop symptoms consistent with Alzheimer's dementia, such as episodic memory impairment (Brambati et al., 2015; Cerami et al., 2017; Rohrer et al., 2013).

The deficits observed in lvPPA are attributed to temporoparietal atrophy that is greater in the language-dominant hemisphere (Gorno-Tempini et al., 2004; see Figure 5–1), consistent with a role for this region in phonological processing and phonological working memory (Buchsbaum, Hickok, & Humphries, 2001; Henry et al., 2016). The parietal lobe atrophy in lvPPA may also affect an individual's ability to perform simple math, and so these individuals may struggle with math calculations (Henry & Gorno-Tempini, 2010; Rohrer et al., 2010). Although the observed neurodegeneration may be related to different disease processes in different lvPPA cases, an atypical manifestation of Alzheimer's disease is the most likely cause, with recent research reporting that 100% of a sample of $n = 11$ lvPPA cases had Alzheimer's pathology at autopsy (Spinelli et al., 2017). Unlike FTLD, there are pharmaceutical interventions designed to manage Alzheimer's disease, such as cholinesterase inhibitors, although the efficacy of these drugs may vary across individuals (Kobayashi, Ohnishi, Nakagawa, & Yoshizawa, 2016; Trinh, Hoblyn, Mohanty, & Yaffe, 2003).

Nonfluent Variant

In nfvPPA, the core clinical features are agrammatism and apraxia of speech, with some individuals presenting with both features and some presenting with one or the other (Gorno-Tempini et al., 2011; Henry, Meese, et al., 2013). Individuals with agrammatism produce short, simple utterances and may omit function words, resulting in telegraphic output. Speech output of individuals with apraxia of speech is slow, effortful, and aprosodic, often with prominent distortions that affect intelligibility. Although dysarthria is not a diagnostic feature of nfvPPA, it may co-occur with apraxia of speech (Ogar, Dronkers, Brambati, Miller, & Gorno-Tempini, 2007).

To confirm nfvPPA diagnosis, at least two of the following supporting features must be present: comprehension deficit for syntactically complex utterances, intact single-word comprehension, and intact object knowledge. Individuals with nfvPPA may have difficulty understanding noncanonical utterances. For example, an individual with nfvPPA might interpret the passive voice sentence, "The cat was chased by the dog" as if it were active voice, with the resulting interpretation that a cat was chasing a dog. It is unlikely that an individual with nfvPPA will have difficulty understanding single words, as comprehension deficits are related to a syntactic processing impairment. Finally, object knowledge is typically spared in nfvPPA. These individuals will continue to recognize and use objects appropriately, at least as long as additional nonspeech motor impairments are not present.

As the disease progresses, language becomes increasingly agrammatic and speech increasingly unintelligible. In some cases, an individual may become completely mute early in the disease process in the presence of relatively spared general cognitive function (Gorno-Tempini et al., 2006). Unfortunately, depending on the underlying etiology, many individuals with nfvPPA will

develop a generalized movement disorder such as corticobasal syndrome or progressive supranuclear palsy (Cerami et al., 2017). Therefore, regular swallowing evaluations are warranted in order to monitor for signs of dysphagia (Langmore, Olney, Lomen-Hoerth, & Miller, 2007).

The deficits observed in nfvPPA are related to frontoinsular atrophy, with a greater degree of atrophy in the language-dominant hemisphere (Gorno-Tempini et al., 2004; see Figure 5–1). This area is critically involved in grammatical processing (Friederici, 2002; Friederici, Ruschemeyer, Hahne, & Fiebach, 2003) and motor programming for speech (Dronkers, 1996). As with svPPA and lvPPA, the etiology of the neurodegenerative process may vary across individuals, but the most likely cause is FTLD-tau, either in the form of Pick's disease, progressive supranuclear palsy, or corticobasal degeneration. Spinelli and colleagues recently reported that 88% of a sample of $n = 25$ nfvPPA cases had FTLD-tau pathology at autopsy (Spinelli et al., 2017).

Mixed PPA

In a minority of cases, an individual may present with clinical features that do not fit within one of the three PPA subtypes described above. Some researchers and clinicians suggest that these cases be classified as mixed PPA (Mesulam et al., 2009; Mesulam, Wieneke, Thompson, Rogalski, & Weintraub, 2012; Sajjadi, Patterson, & Nestor, 2014). Sajjadi and colleagues argue that mixed PPA is most often observed in PPA with Alzheimer's pathology and that the inclusion criteria for lvPPA may be too narrow to capture the full range of observed deficits in this clinical syndrome (Sajjadi et al., 2014). Alternatively, the underlying pathology may be a disease process known to target frontal and temporal regions, such as Pick's disease. For example, an individual with Pick's disease may present with lexical retrieval difficulties, single-word comprehension impairment, and apraxia of speech, thus meeting core criteria for both svPPA and nfvPPA (Spinelli et al., 2017). Still others have argued that the current clinical consensus criteria simply do not capture all possible PPA phenotypes (Harris et al., 2013). When designing clinical care plans and behavioral interventions for individuals with a mixed PPA presentation, it is important to consider the best way to address and compensate for the observed core linguistic and motoric deficits.

Before moving on to assessment and treatment of PPA, it is important to note that there is ongoing debate regarding PPA subclassification. For example, Mesulam et al. (2009) proposed criteria for subtyping PPA into semantic PPA (PPA-S), logopenic PPA (PPA-L), and agrammatic PPA (PPA-G) types, which largely overlap with svPPA, lvPPA, and nfvPPA, respectively. Others have proposed a distinction between agrammatic PPA and primary progressive apraxia of speech (Duffy & Josephs, 2012; Josephs et al., 2012), which would both be considered nfvPPA in the Gorno-Tempini et al. (2011) framework. That being said, the criteria presented in this section were agreed upon by a group of leading PPA experts and have been widely accepted by clinical and research communities.

Assessment and Diagnosis

Cognitive-linguistic assessment and diagnosis by PPA subtype are important components of clinical care (see Henry & Grasso, 2018, for a thorough discussion of PPA assessment). Knowledge of PPA subtype will help patients and families better understand the nature of the disease and its likely progression, will serve to inform potential treatment options, and may help in determining underlying etiology, which has implications for pharmaceutical interventions and clinical trials. In order to determine an accurate PPA diagnosis, it is important to obtain relevant case history and perform a comprehensive cognitive-linguistic evaluation. Following confirmation of a general PPA diagnosis, clinicians should use assessments that evaluate relevant speech and language domains implicated in svPPA, lvPPA, and nfvPPA, as enumerated in current consensus criteria.

General PPA Diagnosis

As in any speech-language evaluation, a comprehensive case history is obtained in order to determine the pattern of onset and progression of speech-language symptoms and to discern areas of greatest functional communication impairment from the patient and family's perspective. Table 5–2 presents a series of questions that may be helpful in acquiring the most relevant information. For example, clinicians should ask questions regarding individuals' initial symptoms, how long they have been experiencing these symptoms, and

Table 5–2. Screening Questions to Obtain Relevant Case History and to Inform PPA Diagnosis and Treatment

To Acquire Information Regarding:	Example Questions	Responses That Do Not Support PPA Diagnosis
Demographics and medical history	1. What was/is your occupation?	
	2. What is your highest level of education? If you completed college, what field of study?	
	3. Do you have a history of brain injury, stroke, heart disease, seizures, alcohol or drug abuse, depression, diabetes, brain tumor, etc.?	History of brain injury, stroke, heart disease, brain tumor, alcohol or drug abuse, psychiatric condition, etc. that are the likely cause of observed impairments
	4. Do you speak more than one language? If so, what languages do you speak? In what settings do you use each language?	
	5. Have you consulted with a neurologist regarding your communication difficulties? If so, what were the results of the consultation?	If an individual has not yet consulted with a neurologist, a neurological assessment should be recommended to rule out other causes of speech-language decline.
Symptoms and disease progression	1. What were the first symptoms you noticed that made you realize something was wrong? Do you ever have trouble with: a. finding or pronouncing words? b. calling things the wrong name? c. speaking in sentences? d. reading or writing? e. recognizing objects or words? f. remembering the names of people you know? g. recognizing people you know?	First signs and symptoms include episodic memory loss or general cognitive impairment. If the individual indicates they experience memory loss, query further to determine whether this refers specifically to words and names or whether this includes memory for events. Early changes in mobility and loss of motor control beyond the speech domain.

Table 5–2. *continued*

To Acquire Information Regarding:	Example Questions	Responses That Do Not Support PPA Diagnosis
Symptoms and disease progression *continued*	2. When did you first notice these symptoms? 3. Have you noticed that your symptoms are getting worse? 4. What are your greatest communication challenges at present? 5. Do you also experience difficulty with remembering things such as conversations, events, or where you left objects? If so, when did you first notice these symptoms? 6. Have you ever gotten lost in a familiar place? 7. Do you also experience difficulty with gross motor skills such as walking or fine motor skills such as tying shoes? If so, when did you first notice these symptoms?	Symptoms do not show evidence of progression.
Premorbid language abilities	1. Before your current symptoms began, how would you rate your ability to read? 2. Before your current symptoms began, how would you rate your ability to spell? 3. Do you have a history of developmental language impairment? Did you receive special help in school for speech or language?	Premorbid speech-language impairment is not exclusionary but should be noted in order to inform interpretation of language assessments.

whether they have noticed progression or worsening of deficits. Demographic information and medical history will be of value when attempting to rule out alternative causes for speech-language impairment. In some instances, especially in more advanced cases, the individual with PPA may have difficulty understanding and responding to questions. It is thus recommended that, whenever possible, the patient be accompanied by a family member or friend who may assist in answering questions.

Second, it is important to confirm a general PPA diagnosis. Speech and language can be evaluated using batteries developed for use in stroke-induced aphasia, such as the Western Aphasia Battery–Revised (WAB; Kertesz, 2007), the Boston Diagnostic Aphasia Exam (BDAE; Goodglass, Kaplan, & Barresi, 2001), and the Comprehensive Aphasia Test (CAT; Swinburn, Porter, & Howard, 2004). However, aphasia classification systems designed for use in stroke-induced aphasia should not be applied in PPA. In addition to the use of these batteries, engaging in conversation (i.e., getting a spontaneous speech sample) can provide insight into an individual's overall speech and language function while serving to build rapport.

It is critical that clinicians also examine extralinguistic domains, including general cognitive function, visuospatial processing and visual memory, episodic memory, motor skills, and emotional processing, in order to rule out alternative diagnoses. The Mini-Mental State Exam (Folstein, Folstein, & McHugh, 1975) or the Montreal Cognitive Assessment (Nasreddine et al., 2005) can be used to assess general cognitive function, although both are linguistically loaded, and so interpretation of performance should be considered in the con-

text of the language impairment. Visuospatial processing and visual memory should also be evaluated, which can be accomplished using a complex figure copy and recall task. If complex figure copy is performed without error, poor recall of the figure may be related to visual or episodic memory impairment. Episodic memory can be further evaluated via self-report and caregiver report. Poor performance on complex figure copy could be related to impaired motor control and is most likely to be observed in moderate-to-severe nfvPPA. Emotional processing can be evaluated via observation and using tests such as the Emotional Evaluation subtest of the Awareness of Social Inference Test (TASIT; McDonald, Flanagan, Rollins, & Kinch, 2003, discussed in relation to PPA in Binney et al., 2016). Disruptions in emotional processing are often observed in svPPA as the atrophic process begins to encroach upon the amygdala and right ATL, but these disruptions should be less severe than the loss of verbal and object semantics (Binney et al., 2016; Cerami et al., 2017; Miller, Hsieh, Lah, Savage, Hodges, & Piguet, 2012; Rosen et al., 2002). If this is not the case, then a diagnosis of behavioral variant or right temporal lobe variant of frontotemporal dementia should be considered (Neary et al., 1998; Rascovsky et al., 2007). For all of the extralinguistic domains presented above, impairments may be noted, but the speech and language impairments should be the most severe in order to confirm PPA diagnosis.

Diagnosis by PPA Subtype

After confirming a PPA diagnosis, clinicians can diagnose PPA subtype via examination of patterns of performance on tasks designed to assess core and supporting clinical features for each variant. A good first step is to evaluate spontaneous speech (Table 5–3 provides sample responses to the "Cat Rescue" picture, Nicholas & Brookshire, 1993).

Wilson and colleagues presented information on speech rate and error patterns on the WAB-R picnic description for individuals with svPPA, lvPPA, and nfvPPA, which can be helpful in considering diagnosis by PPA subtype (Wilson et al., 2010). In svPPA, connected speech was characterized as fluent with a large proportion of high-frequency nouns, pronouns, and verbs, reflecting lexical retrieval difficulties, and a normal speech rate. In nfvPPA, connected speech was characterized as nonfluent, agrammatic, and slow, with frequent speech sound distortions. Speech rate for lvPPA was intermediate between svPPA and nfvPPA, with fewer syntactic errors than nfvPPA and lexical retrieval difficulties that were

Table 5–3. Sample Transcriptions of the Cat Rescue Picture Description (Nicholas & Brookshire, 1993) for Each PPA Subtype

PPA Subtype	Sample Cat Rescue Description
Semantic Variant	"There's a little girl and she's . . . got her . . . .cat up on the roof or I mean up in the tree . . . and she has a little . . . not a bicycle . . . it has three . . . .um . . . and there's a dog by the tree or just trying to . . . um . . . run, not run, he's just barking by the tree and there's a guy up in the tree and, um, there's a little bird in the tree and there's, um, men who do the fires running over to get the guy off the ladder and they have a . . . fire truck in the back and they also have another ladder that is sitting in the back of the tree."
Logopenic Variant	"Ok we have, um . . . a big tree that is, uh . . . he's in trouble because he's up on top and he needs to get down out of there. So, we have a . . . um . . . depart the fire department is coming up with two of them and their great big, uh, thing that drives it, and the, um . . . away from him well the guy who's up on top he has a young daughter that is on the ground looking up at a cat that is up above where she can't get to it and the bicycle is still there. Then there is, um, something to go up some, um, things to, um, you can, it's not set up to be able to go up it because it's on the ground. A ladder! The dog is at the bot, the bottom of it, for the tree, and it's making noise for the man who is still up there, and there's a bird out on the right side."
Nonfluent Variant	"A girl . . . um . . . girl is . . . um . . . calling . . . um . . . up tree . . . cat . . . tree . . . .dog there . . . it barks . . . .man in tree . . . .sturk . . . uh . . . stuck . . . in . . . tree . . . there bird . . . in . . . on banch . . . barnch . . . branch. Ferman run . . . have ladder . . . .fertruck back there . . . oh . . . um . . . and girl . . . um . . . has . . . tri . . . cyc . . . le."

less severe than svPPA. Phonemic paraphasias were present in some individuals with lvPPA.

It is also of value to examine patterns of performance on batteries such as the WAB, BDAE, or CAT. Individuals with svPPA perform poorly on auditory comprehension subtests, reflecting single-word comprehension deficits. Individuals with lvPPA and nfvPPA typically perform relatively well on auditory comprehension subtests, reflecting intact single-word comprehension. On naming subtests, impairments will be observed in svPPA and lvPPA. Individuals with svPPA typically produce semantic errors and errors of omission and may not be aided by phonemic cues. Individuals with lvPPA may produce phonological errors and are more likely to benefit from phonemic cues than individuals with svPPA. Individuals with nfvPPA often produce sound distortions, although these errors may be difficult to differentiate from phonological errors and should be interpreted in the context of other speech features (e.g., rate and prosody). On repetition subtests, individuals with lvPPA will have pronounced difficulty, whereas individuals with svPPA should perform relatively well. Individuals with nfvPPA may struggle with repetition, although impaired performance is linked to motor speech or grammatical processing impairments.

With regard to assessment of motor speech, evaluations such as those developed by Wertz, LaPointe, and Rosenbek (1984) and Duffy (2013) may be employed, which include such tasks as diadochokinesis, repetition of words and sentences of increasing length and complexity, and passage reading. Individuals with nfvPPA will have the most difficulty with this series of tasks due to apraxia of speech and, often, concomitant dysarthria. However, individuals with lvPPA may struggle with sentence repetition and diadochokinesis because of their phonological working memory and sequencing deficits, and not because of motor speech impairment. Individuals with svPPA demonstrate relative sparing on tasks assessing motor programming and coordination for speech.

Regular, irregular, and nonword reading and spelling can be used to inform PPA subtype diagnosis (Brambati, Ogar, Neuhaus, Miller, & Gorno-Tempini, 2009; Gorno-Tempini et al., 2011). Surface dyslexia/dysgraphia may be observed in svPPA, with patients exhibiting selective impairment of irregular word reading and spelling. Individuals with lvPPA often have impaired nonword reading and spelling due to phonological processing impairment. Reading and spelling in nfvPPA may be affected by motor speech deficits or limb apraxia, respectively, but error patterns (e.g., distortions) should not be influenced by word regularity or word/nonword status.

Semantic processing should be evaluated in the nonverbal domain to identify loss of object knowledge. The picture version of the Pyramids and Palm Trees task (PPT; Howard & Patterson, 1992), an object association task, may be used. Individuals with svPPA will have greatest difficulty with the PPT, whereas those with lvPPA and nfvPPA typically perform this type of task relatively well, reflecting intact object knowledge.

Finally, expressive and receptive grammatical processing should be assessed. The Northwestern Anagram Test (NAT; Weintraub et al., 2009) and the Sentence Comprehension Test/ Make a Sentence Test (SECT/MAST; Billette, Sajjadi, Patterson, & Nestor, 2015) may be useful for this purpose. The NAT, which requires that written words be arranged to describe pictures, is very useful in assessing syntax production without the need for overt speech (which may be affected by motor speech impairment). Of the three variants, individuals with nfvPPA have the most difficulty performing this type of task. Individuals with svPPA and lvPPA typically perform the NAT relatively well, reflecting a lack of frank agrammatism. The SECT requires a single-word response to demonstrate comprehension of auditorily or visually presented sentences with varying degrees of syntactic complexity, and the MAST requires individuals to produce sentences of varying syntactic complexity when provided with four nouns and a verb in a specific order. Impaired comprehension of syntactically complex utterances is a supporting feature in nfvPPA, reflecting a core deficit in grammatical processing. The NAT may be preferable to the MAST for use in individuals with motor speech disorders as it does not rely on overt speech production.

There are now several assessments designed specifically for use in PPA, which may eventually obviate the need to use batteries designed for stroke-induced aphasia (see Battista et al., 2017, for review). One of these is the Sydney Language Battery (SydBat), which consists of a simple series of tasks designed to aid diagnosis by PPA subtype. The SydBat includes confrontation naming, auditory word-picture matching (select target picture from among six semantically or visually

similar distractors), semantic association (select one of four pictures that is most closely associated with a target picture), and single-word repetition subtests (Savage, Foxe, & Piguet, 2013). Another assessment is the Repeat and Point Test, which was created to aid differential diagnosis of semantic dementia (svPPA) and progressive nonfluent aphasia. The Repeat and Point Test involves, not surprisingly, repeating a word or pointing to a picture following auditory presentation of a single word (Hodges, Martinos, Woollams, Patterson, & Adlam, 2008). This test was shown to reliably distinguish between semantic dementia and progressive nonfluent aphasia, although its utility in distinguishing between lvPPA and nfvPPA has not been addressed. Both the SydBat and the Repeat and Point Test are freely available online (see companion website).

Finally, two scales have been designed to aid in tracking disease severity in PPA. Both the Progressive Aphasia Severity Scale (PASS; Sapolsky, Domoto-Reilly, & Dickerson, 2014) and the Progressive Aphasia Language Scale (PALS; Leyton et al., 2011) were developed to assess severity and progression of impairments within specific speech and language domains, such as articulation, grammar, word retrieval, and word comprehension. The PASS and the PALS both rely on a clinician's subjective ratings via a Likert scale (5-point or 3-point scale, respectively). Sapolsky and colleagues (2014) recommend the use of the PASS in evaluating treatment efficacy and determining the appropriateness of speech and language interventions (e.g., when to shift the focus of treatment to the use of alternative and augmentative communication strategies). The PALS was also designed as a means to aid in PPA subtyping via a simple algorithm and was demonstrated to have 94% concordance with diagnosis provided by PPA experts (Leyton et al., 2011). Both of these scales are freely available online (see companion website).

Although not strictly necessary, structural neuroimaging (magnetic resonance imaging [MRI], computed tomography [CT]) may aid in the diagnostic process. In early/mild PPA cases, radiological reports may indicate that an MRI scan is within normal limits, with subtle brain atrophy attributed to the aging process. In conjunction with the medical team, clinicians involved in PPA diagnosis should review MRI scans for patterns of asymmetry or focal brain atrophy, which may have been previously undetected. Notable features include lateralization of neural changes to the language dominant hemisphere—typically the left, although in a minority of individuals, language may be right lateralized. Focal changes are typically observed in the anterior temporal lobe in svPPA, the left temporoparietal junction in lvPPA, and frontoinsular regions in nfvPPA (see Figure 5–1).

Treatment

The evidence base supporting the utility of speech and language intervention in PPA has grown over the last two decades, with more than 75 peer-reviewed research studies to date. The vast majority of these studies utilized single-case, case series, or single-subject experimental designs and were intended to treat lexical retrieval defi-

cits. More than half present treatment in svPPA (e.g., Beales, Cartwright, Whitworth, & Panegyres, 2016; Bier et al., 2009; Bier et al., 2011; Bier et al., 2015; Croot et al., 2015; Dewar, Patterson, Wilson, & Graham, 2009; Dial et al., 2019; Dressel et al., 2010; Evans, Quimby, Dickey, & Dickerson, 2016; Farrajota et al., 2012; Frattali, 2004; Graham, Patterson, Pratt, & Hodges, 1999, 2001; Henry, Beeson, & Rapcsak, 2008; Henry, Rising, et al., 2013; Henry et al., 2019; Heredia, Sage, Lambon Ralph, & Berthier, 2009; Hoffman, Clarke, Jones, & Noonan, 2015; Jokel, Rochon, & Anderson, 2010; Jokel, Rochon, & Leonard, 2002, 2006; Jokel & Anderson, 2012; Jokel et al., 2016; Macoir et al., 2015; Mayberry, Sage, Ehsan, & Lambon Ralph, 2011a, 2011b; McNeil, Small, Masterson, & Fossett, 1995; Meyer, Faria, Tippett, Hillis, & Friedman, 2017; Meyer, Getz, Brennan, Hu, & Friedman, 2016; Meyer, Snider, Eckmann, & Friedman, 2015; Meyer, Tippett, & Friedman, 2016; Newhart et al., 2009; Reilly, 2016; Robinson, Druks, Hodges, & Garrard, 2009; Routhier et al., 2011; Savage, Ballard, Piguet, & Hodges, 2013; Savage, Piguet, & Hodges, 2014, 2015; Senaha, Brucki, & Nitrini, 2010; Snowden & Neary, 2002; Suarez-Gonzalez et al., 2015; Villanelli, Russo, Nemni, & Farina, 2011; Wong, Anand, Chapman, Rackley, & Zientz, 2009), with approximately 15 studies presenting treatment in lvPPA (e.g., Beales et al., 2016; Beeson et al., 2011; Croot et al., 2015; Dial et al., 2019; Farrajota et al., 2012; Henry, Rising, et al., 2013; Henry et al., 2019; Koenig-Bruhin, Studer-Eichenberger, Donati, Zwahlen, & Hohl, 2005; Meyer et al., 2015; Meyer et al., 2016; Meyer et al., 2017; Newhart et al., 2009; Tsapkini, Frangakis, Gomez, Davis, & Hillis, 2014; Tsapkini & Hillis,

2013) and about 20 studies presenting treatment in nfvPPA (e.g., Andrade-Calderón, Salvador-Cruz, & Sosa-Ortiz, 2015; Cotelli et al., 2012; Cotelli et al., 2016; Croot et al., 2015; Dial et al., 2019; Farrajota et al., 2012; Flanagan, Copland, Van Hees, Byrne, & Angwin, 2016; Hameister, Nickels, Abel, & Croot, 2016; Henry, Meese, et al., 2013; Henry et al., 2018; Jokel, Cupit, Rochon, & Leonard, 2009; Louis, Espesser, Rey, Daffaure, Di Cristo, & Habib, 2001; Machado, Campanha, Caramelli, & Carthery-Goulart, 2014; Marcotte & Ansaldo, 2010; Meyer et al., 2017; Murray, 1998; Pattee, Von Berg, & Ghezzi, 2006; Schneider, Thompson, & Luring, 1996; Tsapkini et al., 2014).

In svPPA, researchers have most often implemented treatment protocols in which a picture is paired and rehearsed with the spoken and/or written word form. The goal of this form of treatment is to strengthen the link between the phonological and/or orthographic representations and the semantic representation, which is presumed to be activated via presentation of the picture (e.g., Graham et al., 1999; Graham et al., 2001; Heredia et al., 2009; Jokel et al., 2006; Jokel & Anderson, 2012; Mayberry et al., 2011a, 2011b; Meyer et al., 2017; Savage et al., 2013; Savage et al., 2015; Snowden & Neary, 2002). In these studies, individuals with svPPA had significantly improved naming performance for trained items, but the majority of these gains did not generalize to untrained items or contexts. In terms of maintenance of treatment-induced gains, few studies have examined treatment outcomes past the immediate posttreatment phase, although some studies have reported maintenance up to 6 months posttreat-

ment (Heredia et al., 2009; Jokel et al., 2006; Savage et al., 2015).

The item- and context-specific gains demonstrated in these studies suggest that vocabulary relearning in svPPA may depend on episodic memory and rote memorization to compensate for degraded semantic representations (e.g., Graham et al., 1999; Graham et al., 2001; Snowden & Neary, 2002). In a direct test of this hypothesis, Hoffman and colleagues (2015) manipulated factors related to episodic memory. In an initial experiment, treatment items were presented in either a fixed or random order during the treatment phase, with random presentation hypothesized to prevent context- and order-dependent learning. In a second experiment, items were either presented with a single exemplar or with multiple exemplars, with the use of multiple exemplars designed to prevent rigid relearning of picture-word pairs and to promote generalization to novel exemplars (Hoffman et al., 2015). The researchers found that treatment outcomes were greatest in the random presentation and multiple exemplars conditions, lending support to an episodic basis for relearning in svPPA. However, there is evidence that residual semantic knowledge plays an important role in treatment outcomes, with research suggesting that items lacking residual conceptual knowledge are unlikely to be relearned (Jokel et al., 2006; Jokel et al., 2010; Jokel et al., 2012; Jokel et al., 2016).

Given the hypothesis that episodic memory and residual semantic knowledge may support treatment outcomes in svPPA, a growing number of studies have implemented cueing hierarchies that utilize semantic feature analysis and encourage the retrieval of autobiographical and episodic information in relation to each picture. Participants are also trained to use phonological and orthographic cues to support word retrieval. Pictures are then presented with spoken or written word forms if cueing is unsuccessful (Beales et al., 2016; Bier et al., 2009; Dial et al., 2019; Dressel et al., 2010; Henry et al., 2008; Henry, Rising, et al., 2013; Henry et al., 2019; Jokel & Anderson, 2012; Jokel et al., 2010; Newhart et al., 2009). These studies report improved naming of trained items, generalization to untrained items (Beales et al., 2016; Henry et al., 2008; Henry, Rising, et al., 2013; Jokel & Anderson, 2012; Jokel et al., 2010), and maintenance of gains at 3 months (e.g., Jokel et al., 2010; Jokel et al., 2012), 4 months (e.g., Dressel et al., 2010; Henry et al., 2008; Henry, Rising, et al., 2013), or 12 months posttreatment (e.g., Henry et al., 2019). Overall, the evidence supporting treatment in svPPA suggests that episodic memory and residual semantic knowledge are important factors and that a richer variety of cueing modalities may lead to the largest gains.

As in svPPA, the majority of treatment studies in lvPPA have targeted lexical retrieval deficits (cf. Tsapkini et al., 2013, and Tsapkini et al., 2014, for treatment designed to improve spelling in lvPPA and nfvPPA). In general, treatment targeting lexical retrieval in lvPPA has utilized similar approaches as those implemented with svPPA, namely the pairing of pictures with spoken and/or written word forms (Croot et al., 2015; Meyer et al., 2015; Meyer et al., 2016; Meyer et al., 2017). In these studies, significant treatment effects were observed on trained items, but no maintenance was observed and no generalization to untrained items or connected speech was found. Researchers have also implemented cueing hierarchies utilizing semantic, autobiographical and episodic, phonological, and orthographic cues to treat anomia in lvPPA. In these studies, improved naming of trained items was observed, as was generalization to untrained items. Moreover, maintenance of gains was observed at 6 months (Beales et al., 2016; Newhart et al., 2009; Henry, Rising, et al., 2013) or 12 months posttreatment (Henry et al., 2019). Finally, one study implemented semantic elaboration training and generative naming in a brief but intensive protocol (Beeson et al., 2011). Treatment effects in naming were significant for trained sets, with generalization observed for untrained sets. Gains were maintained for trained items up to 6 months posttreatment. As in svPPA, it seems that a richer variety of cues may lead to greater and longer lasting gains.

Finally, as with svPPA and lvPPA, the majority of intervention research in nfvPPA has focused on lexical retrieval treatment. In several studies, lexical retrieval treatment was implemented such that a picture was paired and rehearsed with the spoken and/or written word form (Cotelli et al., 2014; Cotelli et al., 2016; Croot et al., 2014; Jokel et al., 2009; Meyer et al., 2016; Meyer et al., 2017). In these studies, significant treatment effects were observed on treated items but did not generalize to untreated items, with maintenance at 1 month observed in some participants (Jokel et al., 2009; Meyer et al., 2016; Meyer et al., 2017). Studies using a richer variety of training techniques (semantic feature analysis: Marcotte & Ansaldo, 2010; multimodality treatment: Farrajota et al., 2012) also documented gains on trained items; however, these studies did not measure generalization or maintenance of treatment-induced gains.

Other studies have focused on a range of linguistic deficits associated with the nfvPPA syndrome, such as word retrieval and grammar (Hameister et al., 2016), verb and sentence production (Schneider et al., 1996), and apraxia of speech (Henry, Meese, et al., 2013; Henry et al., 2018). Hameister et al. (2016) used a "go-fish" style card game wherein participants requested cards via description of the action on the card. They observed significant gains for trained items, generalization to untrained items, and maintenance up to 2 months posttreatment. Schneider et al. (1996) utilized a treatment that involved repeating gestures and sentences with verbs in the past, present, or future tense. Following treatment, improvement was noted on the use of trained gestures and verbs, with generalization to untrained noun and verb phrase combinations. The use of gestures and the production of future tense verbs was maintained up to 3 months posttreatment. Finally, Henry and colleagues (2018) utilized a video-implemented script training technique to address speech production and fluency in nfvPPA. In this study, which leveraged home-based practice, participants rehearsed production of personalized scripts by speaking in unison with a video model of a healthy speaker. Video practice at home was complemented by sessions with a clinician targeting memorization and conversational usage of scripts. Significant gains were observed in production of correct, intelligible words for trained scripts, as was generalized improve-

ment in intelligibility and maintenance of gains for trained topics up to 1 year posttreatment.

Across PPA variants and treatment designs, behavioral intervention for speech and language deficits has shown great promise. In most studies, treatment-induced gains have been observed immediately posttreatment, with some studies also documenting generalization to untrained items and tasks and maintenance of gains up to 1 year posttreatment. However, the majority of these studies implemented treatment in individuals with mild-to-moderate PPA, and there is limited work examining treatment for individuals with more advanced PPA. If the speech-language pathologist determines that treatment targeting spoken communication will not be effective or appropriate, multimodality or augmentative and alternative communication (AAC) interventions should be considered. It may be of value to implement AAC training relatively early in the disease course, as increased success using AAC devices may be observed if the individual begins to use AAC before deficits in general cognitive function emerge.

Few studies have examined the use of AAC in PPA. In one study, Laura Murray (1998) presented a phased treatment approach implemented with an individual with nonfluent primary progressive aphasia (consistent with Neary et al., 1998, criteria). In one phase, the individual was trained to use drawing to communicate intended messages, leading to improved performance on the trained drawing task, but generalization to other tasks and contexts was not observed. In another phase of treatment, the individual created communication boards with symbols that were subsequently transferred to an electronic AAC device, which presented written and spoken statements that had been programmed with each symbol. The individual was noted to use the device successfully both within and outside of therapy sessions, including adding new symbols to the device as needed. Several months later, the individual and her spouse reported that she had spontaneously started drawing to communicate messages and continued to use the AAC device. Cress and King (1999) trained two individuals with PPA (unspecified subtype) on the use of low-tech AAC boards. Both individuals were reported to produce more comprehensible and complex messages following development of the AAC boards. One individual's family reported that he was using his communication boards regularly, that their use aided communication, and that he maintained his ability to use the boards after a year, despite a decline in general cognition. Pattee et al. (2006) trained an individual with PPA and apraxia of speech in the use of a text-to-speech device and American Sign Language. Following treatment, the individual produced more content for trained targets, but generalization was not observed and maintenance was not assessed. Of note, the participant stated a preference for the Sign Language approach and decided to discontinue use of the text-to-speech device. Lastly, Mooney and colleagues trained participants with svPPA, lvPPA, and nfvPPA to use a beta version of an AAC application called CoChat (Mooney, Bedrick, Noethe, Spaulding, & Fried-Oken, 2018). With CoChat, participants take photos and share them

with close friends and family, who then comment on the photos. The comments are analyzed using a natural language processor, which creates a list of the 10 most salient words and concepts and places the written words in an array around the photo (visual scene display). In this study, participants used the visual scene display to aid in story retell, leading to increased production of target words relative to a picture-only condition in the majority of participants immediately posttreatment. Maintenance was assessed for only one of the participants, who showed maintenance of treatment-induced gains at 9 months posttreatment. Despite the limited evidence, findings from these studies are promising and warrant further research, including use of AAC in the context of group therapy for PPA, as recent evidence suggests that group therapy sessions targeting AAC may be beneficial (Mooney, Beale, & Fried-Oken, 2018).

Conclusion

PPA is a relatively rare neurodegenerative disorder that predominantly affects speech and language. In PPA, general cognitive and motoric abilities are spared in the initial stages of the disease process, although additional impairments emerge over time. There are three widely recognized PPA subtypes: the semantic variant, characterized by a loss of core semantic knowledge; the logopenic variant, characterized by phonological processing deficits; and the nonfluent variant, characterized by agrammatism and/or apraxia of speech. The underlying disease etiology varies across the three subtypes. In this chapter, we presented information regarding PPA assessment, clinical criteria for general PPA diagnosis and diagnosis by PPA subtype, and evidence-based treatment approaches that have proven beneficial in PPA. It is imperative that researchers continue to investigate the nature and progression of deficits in PPA and focus efforts on the development of novel approaches to intervention as well as optimization of existing treatment approaches for this population. Given their unique set of skills, speech-language pathologists will play a critical role in these endeavors.

Case Study

The following case serves to illustrate the principles of assessment, diagnosis, and intervention in PPA that were described in this chapter.

Ms. Smith is a 55-year-old lawyer who has been having increasing difficulty finding words. She first noticed the problem in high-stress situations, such as when arguing a case in court, but was generally able to compensate by substituting a different word for words she could not find. At first, she thought that she was just tired and stressed, so she tried getting more rest. However, the problem continued to worsen. Recently, her word-finding problems have been affecting her ability to communicate in a significant way and are negatively impacting her work performance. She sometimes uses the wrong word in conversation. She was particularly worried when she was preparing for a big case and did not

recognize an important piece of evidence. She asked her partner what the object was, and after being told that it was a checkbook, she said that she "felt foolish and laughed it off." Her family began to notice that she was having more and more trouble and, at her daughter's suggestion, she visited a neurologist.

At the neurologist, she reports that there is something wrong with her memory. Given her relatively young age, the neurologist thinks this is stress related or that she may be anxious or depressed. In order to be thorough, an MRI scan is acquired and a comprehensive physical and cognitive-linguistic exam are performed. The neurologist notes that she is well groomed and behaves in a socially appropriate manner. Lab tests confirm that she is generally healthy, although a radiologist notes atrophy in the temporal lobes bilaterally. She performs well on measures of visual memory, visuospatial processing, and motor speech, but makes semantic errors on a confrontation naming task. She is mildly impaired on a nonverbal measure of semantic processing (an object association test) and the Mini Mental State Exam. With this formal testing, it becomes clear that she does not have an episodic memory problem but instead is experiencing lexical retrieval difficulties and a mild loss of semantic knowledge. The neurologist diagnoses her with svPPA, and she is referred to an SLP for further evaluation and treatment. The neurologist asks her to schedule follow-up appointments every 6 months.

The SLP meets with Ms. Smith and her daughter. The clinician first engages in casual conversation with Ms. Smith to get a general idea of her current language abilities and to better understand the nature of the communication challenges from her perspective. Given the recent neuropsychological testing, she does not conduct a full language assessment but does conduct a dynamic assessment of naming, evaluating Ms. Smith's potential for generating residual semantic, phonological, and orthographic information in the event of naming difficulty and her potential to self-cue for word retrieval. The SLP also takes the opportunity to offer some counseling regarding the PPA diagnosis and answers questions the two women have regarding the nature and progression of svPPA. She also discusses potential treatment options with Ms. Smith and her daughter and together they identify goals for treatment. In the first phase, they will work on word finding via semantic and phonological self-cueing strategies, as Ms. Smith has demonstrated the ability to retrieve residual semantic and phonological information during word-retrieval difficulty. Subsequently, they begin to work on developing a simple alternative communication system (a picture book with functional items grouped by category and paired with written words). Even though Ms. Smith doesn't feel as though she needs the book at this point, she understands that it will be easier to use in the future if she begins working with it now and learning to use it as a conversational support. The SLP and Ms. Smith and her daughter all agree that Ms. Smith can benefit from practicing word-finding strategies and using her communication book at home with her family's support so that she can get the most out of treatment.

Additionally, the SLP engages in structured communication partner training with Ms. Smith's daughter, emphasizing ways to maximize and support communication for her mother such as using high-frequency vocabulary, giving plenty of time to speak, and using and modeling multimodality communication strategies (e.g., writing, drawing, and gesture). After this round of treatment, Ms. Smith will have follow-up appointments every 6 months with her neurologist and SLP to monitor symptom progression and to discern whether new goals for treatment should be developed and an additional "dose" of treatment undertaken.

References

Andrade-Calderón, P., Salvador-Cruz, J., & Sosa-Ortiz, A. L. (2015). Impacto positivo de la terapia del lenguaje en afasia progresiva no fluente [Positive impact of speech therapy in progressive non-fluent aphasia]. *Acta Colombiana De Psicologia, 18*(2), 101–114.

Battista, P., Miozzo, A., Piccininni, M., Catricalà, E., Capozzo, R., Tortelli, R., . . . Logroscino, G. (2017). Primary progressive aphasia: A review of neuropsychological tests for the assessment of speech and language disorders. *Aphasiology, 31*(12), 1359–1378.

Beales, A., Cartwright, J., Whitworth, A., & Panegyres, P. K. (2016). Exploring generalisation processes following lexical retrieval intervention in primary progressive aphasia. *International Journal of Speech-Language Pathology, 18*(3), 299–314.

Beeson, P. M., King, R. M., Bonakdarpour, B., Henry, M. L., Cho, H., & Rapcsak, S. Z. (2011). Positive effects of language treatment for the logopenic variant of primary progressive aphasia. *Journal of Molecular Neuroscience, 45*(3), 724–736.

Bier, N., Brambati, S., Macoir, J., Paquette, G., Schmitz, X., Belleville, S., . . . Joubert, S. (2015). Relying on procedural memory to enhance independence in daily living activities: Smartphone use in a case of semantic dementia. *Neuropsychological Rehabilitation, 25*(6), 913–935.

Bier, N., Macoir, J., Gagnon, L., Van der Linden, M., Louveaux, S., & Desrosiers, J. (2009). Known, lost, and recovered: Efficacy of formal-semantic therapy and spaced retrieval method in a case of semantic dementia. *Aphasiology, 23*(2), 210–235.

Bier, N., Macoir, J., Joubert, S., Bottari, C., Chayer, C., Pigot, H., . . . Team, S. (2011). Cooking "shrimp a la creole": A pilot study of an ecological rehabilitation in semantic dementia. *Neuropsychological Rehabilitation, 21*(4), 455–483.

Billette, O. V., Sajjadi, S. A., Patterson, K., & Nestor, P. J. (2015). SECT and MAST: New tests to assess grammatical abilities in primary progressive aphasia. *Aphasiology, 29*(10), 1135–1151.

Binney, R. J., Henry, M. L., Babiak, M., Pressman, P. S., Santos-Santos, M. A., Narvid, J., . . . Binney, R. J. (2016). Reading words and other people: A comparison of exception word, familiar face and affect processing in the left and right temporal variants of primary progressive aphasia. *Cortex, 82*, 147–163.

Bonner, M. F., Ash, S., & Grossman, M. (2010). The new classification of primary progressive aphasia into semantic, logopenic, or nonfluent/agrammatic variants. *Current Neurology and Neuroscience Reports, 10*(6), 484–490.

Brambati, S. M., Amici, S., Racine, C. A., Neuhaus, J., Miller, Z., Ogar, J., . . . Gorno-Tempini, M. L. (2015). Longitudinal gray matter contraction in three variants of primary progressive aphasia: A tenser-based morphometry study. *NeuroImage: Clinical, 8*, 345–355.

Brambati, S. M., Ogar, J., Neuhaus, J., Miller, B. L., & Gorno-Tempini, M. L. (2009). Reading disorders in primary progressive aphasia: A behavioral and neuroimaging study. *Neuropsychologia, 47*(8–9), 1893–1900.

Buchsbaum, B. R., Hickok, G., & Humphries, C. (2001). Role of left posterior superior temporal gyrus in phonological processing for speech perception and production. *Cognitive Science, 25*(5), 663–678.

Caffarra, P., Gardini, S., Cappa, S., Dieci, F., Concari, L., Barocco, F., . . . Prati, G. D. R. (2013). Degenerative jargon aphasia: Unusual progression of logopenic/phonological progressive aphasia? *Behavioural Neurology, 26*, 89–93.

Cerami, C., Dodich, A., Greco, L., Iannaccone, S., Magnani, G., Marcone, A., . . . Perani, D. (2017). The role of single-subject brain metabolic patterns in the early differential diagnosis of primary progressive aphasias and in prediction of progression to dementia. *Journal of Alzheimer's Disease, 55*, 183–197.

Coltheart, M., Rastle, K., Perry, C., Langdon, R., & Ziegler, J. (2001). DRC: A dual route cascaded model of visual word recognition and reading aloud. *Psychological Review, 108*(1), 204.

Cotelli, M., Manenti, R., Alberici, A., Brambilla, M., Petesi, M., Cosseddu, M., . . . Borroni, B. (2012). Using transcranial direct current stimulation (tDCS) to treat agrammatic variant of primary progressive aphasia. *Dementia and Geriatric Cognitive Disorders, 34*, 164–165.

Cotelli, M., Manenti, R., Paternicò, D., Cosseddu, M., Brambilla, M., Petesi, M., . . . Borroni, B. (2016). Grey matter density predicts the improvement of naming abilities after tDCS intervention in agrammatic variant of primary progressive aphasia. *Brain Topography, 29*(5), 738–751.

Cress, C. J., & King, J. M. (1999). AAC strategies for people with primary progressive aphasia without dementia: Two case studies. *Augmentative and Alternative Communication, 15*(4), 248–259.

Croot K., Taylor C., Abel S., Jones K., Krein L., Hameister I., . . . Nickels, L. (2015).

Measuring gains in connected speech following treatment for word retrieval: A study with two participants with primary progressive aphasia. *Aphasiology, 29*(11), 1265–1288.

Dewar, B. K., Patterson, K., Wilson, B. A., & Graham, K. S. (2009). Re-acquisition of person knowledge in semantic memory disorders. *Neuropsychological Rehabilitation, 19*(3), 383–421.

Dial, H., Hinshelwood, H., Grasso, S., Hubbard, H., Gorno-Tempini, M. L., & Henry, M. (2019). Investigating the utility of teletherapy in individuals with primary progressive aphasia. *Clinical Interventions in Aging, 14*, 1–19.

Dressel, K., Huber, W., Frings, L., Kümmerer, D., Saur, D., Mader, I., . . . Abel, S. (2010). Model-oriented naming therapy in semantic dementia: A single-case fMRI study. *Aphasiology, 24*(12), 1537–1558.

Dronkers, N. (1996). A new brain region for coordinating speech articulation. *Nature, 384*, 159–161.

Duffy, J. R. (2013). *Motor speech disorders: Substrates, differential diagnosis, and management.* Saint Louis, MO: Elsevier Health Sciences.

Duffy, J. R., & Josephs, K. A. (2012). The diagnosis and understanding of apraxia of speech: Why including neurodegenerative etiologies may be important. *Journal of Speech, Language, and Hearing Research, 55*(5), S1518–S1522.

Evans, W. S., Quimby, M., Dickey, M. W., & Dickerson, B. C. (2016). Relearning and retaining personally-relevant words using computer-based flashcard software in primary progressive aphasia. *Frontiers in Human Neuroscience, 10*, 1–8.

Farrajota, L., Maruta, C., Maroco, J., Martins, I. P., Guerreiro, M., & De Mendonca, A. (2012). Speech therapy in primary progressive aphasia: A pilot study. *Dementia and Geriatric Cognitive Disorders Extra, 2*(1), 321–331.

Flanagan, K. J., Copland, D. A., Van Hees, S., Byrne, G. J., & Angwin, A. J. (2016).

Semantic feature training for the treatment of anomia in Alzheimer disease: A preliminary investigation. *Cognitive and Behavioral Neurology, 29*(1), 32–43.

Folstein, M. F., Folstein, S. E., & McHugh, P. R. (1975). "Mini-mental state": A practical method for grading the cognitive state of patients for the clinician. *Journal of Psychiatric Research, 12*(3), 189–198.

Frattali, C. (2004). An errorless learning approach to treating dysnomia in frontotemporal dementia. *Journal of Medical Speech-Language Pathology, 12*(3), xi–xxiv.

Friederici, A. D. (2002). Towards a neural basis of auditory sentence processing. *TRENDS in Cognitive Sciences, 6*(2), 78–84.

Friederici, A. D., Ruschemeyer, S.-A., Hahne, A., & Fiebach, C. J. (2003). The role of left inferior frontal and superior temporal cortex in sentence comprehension: Localizing syntactic and semantic processes. *Cerebral Cortex, 13*, 170–177.

Goodglass, H., Kaplan, E., & Barresi, B. (2001). *The Boston Diagnostic Aphasia Examination (BDAE-3).* New York, NY: Lippincott Williams & Wilkins.

Gorno-Tempini, M. L., Brambati, S. M., Ginex, V., Ogar, J., Dronkers, N. F., Marcone, A., . . . Miller, B. L. (2008). The logopenic/phonological variant of primary progressive aphasia. *Neurology, 71*(16), 1227–1234.

Gorno-Tempini, M. L., Dronkers, N. F., Rankin, K. P., Ogar, J. M., Phengrasamy, L., Rosen, H. J., . . . Miller, B. L. (2004). Cognition and anatomy in three variants of primary progressive aphasia. *Annals of Neurology, 55*(3), 335–346.

Gorno-Tempini, M. L., Hillis, A. E., Weintraub, S., Kertesz, A., Mendez, M., Cappa, S. F., . . . Grossman, M. (2011). Classification of primary progressive aphasia and its variants. *Neurology, 76*(11), 1006–1014.

Gorno-Tempini, M. L., Ogar, J. M., Brambati, S. M., Wang, P., Jeong, J. H., Rankin, K. P., . . . Miller, B. L. (2006). Anatomical correlates of early mutism in progressive nonfluent aphasia. *Neurology, 67,* 1849–1851.

Graham, K. S., Patterson, K., Pratt, K. H., & Hodges, J. R. (1999). Relearning and subsequent forgetting of semantic category exemplars in a case of semantic dementia. *Neuropsychology, 13*(3), 359.

Graham, K. S., Patterson, K., Pratt, K. H., & Hodges, J. R. (2001). Can repeated exposure to "forgotten" vocabulary help alleviate word-finding difficulties in semantic dementia? An illustrative case study. *Neuropsychological Rehabilitation, 11*(3–4), 429–454.

Hameister, I., Nickels, L., Abel, S., & Croot, K. (2016). "Do you have mowing the lawn?" —Improvements in word retrieval and grammar following constraint-induced language therapy in primary progressive aphasia. *Aphasiology, 31*(13) 1–24.

Harris, J. M., Gall, C., Thompson, J. C., Richardson, A. M. T., Neary, D., du Plessis, D., . . . Jones, M. (2013). Classification and pathology of primary progressive aphasia. *Neurology, 81*(21), 1832–1839.

Henry, M., Beeson, P., & Rapcsak, S. (2008). Treatment for lexical retrieval in progressive aphasia. *Aphasiology, 22*(7–8), 826–838.

Henry, M., & Gorno-Tempini, M. L. (2010). The logopenic variant of primary progressive aphasia. *Current Opinion in Neurology, 23*(6), 633–637.

Henry, M., & Grasso, S. (2018). Assessment of individuals with primary progressive aphasia. *Seminars in Speech and Language, 39*(3), 231–241.

Henry, M. L., Hubbard, H. I., Grasso, S. M., Dial, H. R., Beeson, P. M., Miller, B. L., & Gorno-Tempini, M. L. (2019). Treatment for word retrieval in semantic and logopenic variants of primary progressive aphasia: Immediate and long-term outcomes. *Journal of Speech, Language and Hearing Research.*

Henry, M. L., Hubbard, H. I., Grasso, S. M., Mandelli, M. L., Wilson, S. M., Sathishkumar, M. T., . . . Gorno-Tempini, M. L.

(2018). Retraining speech production and fluency in non-fluent/agrammatic primary progressive aphasia. *Brain, 141*(6), 1799–1814.

Henry, M. L., Meese, M. V, Truong, S., Babiak, M. C., Miller, B. L., & Gorno-Tempini, M. L. (2013). Treatment for apraxia of speech in nonfluent variant primary progressive aphasia. *Behavioural Neurology, 26*(1–2), 77–88.

Henry, M. L., Rising, K., DeMarco, A. T., Miller, B. L., Gorno-Tempini, M. L., & Beeson, P. M. (2013). Examining the value of lexical retrieval treatment in primary progressive aphasia: Two positive cases. *Brain and Language, 127*(2), 145–156.

Henry, M. L., Wilson, S. M., Babiak, M. C., Mandelli, M. L., Beeson, P. M., Miller, Z. A., & Gorno-Tempini, M. L. (2016). Phonological processing in primary progressive aphasia. *Journal of Cognitive Neuroscience, 28*(2), 210–222.

Heredia, C. G., Sage, K., Lambon Ralph, M. A., & Berthier, M. L. (2009). Relearning and retention of verbal labels in a case of semantic dementia. *Aphasiology, 23*(2), 192–209.

Hodges, J. R., Martinos, M., Woollams, A. M., Patterson, K., & Adlam, A. R. (2008). Repeat and point: Differentiating semantic dementia from progressive non-fluent aphasia. *Cortex, 44,* 1265–1270.

Hodges, J. R., & Patterson, K. (2007). Semantic dementia: A unique clinicopathological syndrome. *Lancet Neurology, 6*(11), 1004–1014.

Hodges, J. R., Patterson, K., Oxbury, S., & Funnell, E. (1992). Semantic dementia: Progressive fluent aphasia with temporal lobe atrophy. *Brain, 115*(6), 1783–1806.

Hoffman, P., Clarke, N., Jones, R. W., & Noonan, K. A. (2015). Vocabulary relearning in semantic dementia: Positive and negative consequences of increasing variability in the learning experience. *Neuropsychologia, 76,* 240–253.

Howard, D., & Patterson, K. (1992). *The Pyramids and Palm Trees Test: A test of semantic access from words and pictures*. London, UK: Thames Valley Test Company.

Jokel, R., & Anderson, N. D. (2012). Quest for the best: Effects of errorless and active encoding on word re-learning in semantic dementia. *Neuropsychological Rehabilitation*, 22(2), 187–214.

Jokel, R., Cupit, J., Rochon, E., & Leonard, C. (2009). Relearning lost vocabulary in non-fluent progressive aphasia with MossTalk words. *Aphasiology*, 23(2), 175–191.

Jokel, R., Kielar, A., Anderson, N. D., Black, S. E., Rochon, E., Graham, S., . . . Tang-Wai, D. F. (2016). Behavioural and neuroimaging changes after naming therapy for semantic variant primary progressive aphasia. *Neuropsychologia*, 89, 191–216.

Jokel, R., Rochon, E., & Anderson, N. D. (2010). Errorless learning of computer-generated words in a patient with semantic dementia. *Neuropsychological Rehabilitation*, 20(1), 16–41.

Jokel, R., Rochon, E., & Leonard, C. (2002). Therapy for anomia in semantic dementia. *Brain and Cognition*, 49(2), 241–244.

Jokel, R., Rochon, E., & Leonard, C. (2006). Treating anomia in semantic dementia: Improvement, maintenance, or both? *Neuropsychological Rehabilitation*, 16(3), 241–256.

Josephs, K. A., Duffy, J. R., Strand, E. A., Machulda, M. M., Senjem, M. L., Master, A. V., . . . Whitwell, J. L. (2012). Characterizing a neurodegenerative syndrome: Primary progressive apraxia of speech. *Brain*, 135(5), 1522–1536.

Kertesz, A. (2007). *Western Aphasia Battery–Revised*. San Antonio, TX: The Psychological Corporation.

Kertesz, A., & Kalvach, P. (1996). Arnold Pick and German neuropsychiatry in Prague. *Archives of Neurology*, 53(9), 935–938.

Kobayashi, H., Ohnishi, T., Nakagawa, R., & Yoshizawa, K. (2016). The comparative efficacy and safety of cholinesterase inhibitors in patients with mild-to-moderate Alzheimer's disease: A Bayesian network meta-analysis. *International Journal of Geriatric Psychiatry*, 31(8), 892–904.

Koenig-Bruhin, M., Studer-Eichenberger, F., Donati, F., Zwahlen, J., & Hohl, B. (2005). Language therapy in fluent primary progressive aphasia—A single case study. *Brain and Language*, 95(1), 135–136.

Langmore, S. E., Olney, R. K., Lomen-Hoerth, C., & Miller, B. L. (2007). Dysphagia in patients with frontotemporal lobar dementia. *Archives of Neurology*, 64(1), 58–62.

Leyton, C. E., & Hodges, J. R. (2013). Towards a clearer definition of logopenic progressive aphasia. *Current Neurology and Neuroscience Reports*, 13(11), 396.

Leyton, C. E., Villemagne, V. L., Savage, S., Pike, K. E., Ballard, K. J., Piguet, O., . . . Hodges, J. R. (2011). Subtypes of progressive aphasia: Application of the international consensus criteria and validation using b-amyloid imaging. *Brain*, 134, 3030–3043.

Louis, M., Espesser, R., Rey, V., Daffaure, V., Di Cristo, A., & Habib, M. (2001). Intensive training of phonological skills in progressive aphasia: A model of brain plasticity in neurodegenerative disease. *Brain and Cognition*, 46(1–2), 197–201.

Machado, T. H., Campanha, A. C., Caramelli, P., & Carthery-Goulart, M. T. (2014). Intervençã breve para agramatismo em afasia progressiva primária não fluente: relato de caso [Brief intervention for agrammatism in primary progressive nonfluent aphasia a case report]. *Dementia e Neuropsychologia*, 8(3), 291–296.

Macoir, J., Lavoie, M., Laforce, R., Brambati, S. M., & Wilson, M. A. (2017). Dysexecutive symptoms in primary progressive aphasia: Beyond diagnostic criteria. *Journal of Geriatric Psychiatry and Neurology*, 30(3), 151–161.

Macoir, J., Leroy, M., Routhier, S., Auclair-Ouellet, N., Houde, M., & Laforce, R. (2015). Improving verb anomia in the semantic variant of primary progressive aphasia: The effectiveness of a semantic-phonological cueing treatment. *Neurocase, 21*(4), 448–456.

Marcotte, K., & Ansaldo, A. I. (2010). The neural correlates of semantic feature analysis in chronic aphasia: Discordant patterns according to etiology. *Seminars in Speech and Language, 31*, 52–63.

Mayberry, E., Sage, K., Ehsan, S., & Lambon Ralph, M. (2011a). An emergent effect of phonemic cueing following relearning in semantic dementia. *Aphasiology, 25*(9), 1069–1077.

Mayberry, E., Sage, K., Ehsan, S., & Lambon Ralph, M. (2011b). Relearning in semantic dementia reflects contributions from both medial temporal lobe episodic and degraded neocortical semantic systems: Evidence in support of the complementary learning systems theory. *Neuropsychologia, 49*, 3591–3598.

McDonald, S., Flanagan, S., Rollins, J., & Kinch, J. (2003). TASIT: A new clinical tool for assessing social perception after traumatic brain injury. *Journal of Head Trauma Rehabilitation, 18*(3), 219–238.

McNeil, M. R., Small, S. L., Masterson, R. J., & Fossett, T. (1995). Behavioral and pharmacological treatment of lexical-semantic deficits in a single patient with primary progressive aphasia. *American Journal of Speech-Language Pathology, 4*, 76–87.

Mesulam, M. M. (1982). Slowly progressive aphasia without generalized dementia. *Annals of Neurology, 11*(6), 592–598.

Mesulam, M. M. (2001). Primary progressive aphasia. *Annals of Neurology, 49*(4), 425–432.

Mesulam, M., Wieneke, C., Rogalski, E., Cobia, D., Thompson, C., & Weintraub, S. (2009). Quantitative template for subtyping primary progressive aphasia. *Archives of Neurology, 66*(12), 1545–1551.

Mesulam, M., Wieneke, C., Thompson, C., Rogalski, E., & Weintraub, S. (2012). Quantitative classification of primary progressive aphasia at early and mild impairment stages. *Brain, 135*(5), 1537–1553.

Meyer, A. M., Faria, A. V., Tippett, D. C., Hillis, A. E., & Friedman, R. B. (2017). The relationship between baseline volume in temporal areas and post-treatment naming accuracy in primary progressive aphasia. *Aphasiology, 31*, 1059–1077.

Meyer, A. M., Getz, H. R., Brennan, D. M., Hu, T. M., & Friedman, R. B. (2016). Telerehabilitation of anomia in primary progressive aphasia. *Aphasiology, 30*(4), 483–507.

Meyer, A. M., Snider, S. F., Eckmann, C. B., & Friedman, R. B. (2015). Prophylactic treatments for anomia in the logopenic variant of primary progressive aphasia: Cross-language transfer. *Aphasiology, 29*(9), 1062–1081.

Meyer, A. M., Tippett, D. C., & Friedman, R. B. (2018). Prophylaxis and remediation of anomia in the semantic and logopenic variants of primary progressive aphasia. *Neuropsychological Rehabilitation, 28*(3), 352–368..

Miller, L. A., Hsieh, S., Lah, S., Savage, S., Hodges, J. R., & Piguet, O. (2012). One size does not fit all: Face emotion processing impairments in semantic dementia, behavioural-variant frontotemporal dementia and Alzheimer's disease are mediated by distinct cognitive deficits. *Behavioural Neurology, 25*(1), 53–60.

Montembeault, M., Brambati, S. M., Gorno-Tempini, M. L., & Migliaccio, R. (2018). Clinical, anatomical, and pathological features in the three variants of primary progressive aphasia: A review. *Frontiers in Neurology, 9*, 692. doi:10.3389/fneur.2018.00692

Mooney, A., Beale, N., & Fried-Oken, M. (2018). Group communication treatment for individuals with PPA and their partners. *Seminars in Speech and Language, 39*, 257–269.

Mooney, A., Bedrick, S., Noethe, G., Spaulding, S., & Fried-Oken, M. (2018). Mobile technology to support lexical retrieval during activity retell in primary progressive aphasia, *Aphasiology, 32*(6), 666–692.

Murray, L. L. (1998). Longitudinal treatment of primary progressive aphasia: A case study. *Aphasiology, 12,* 651–672.

Nasreddine, Z. S., Phillips, N. A., Bédirian, V., Charbonneau, S., Whitehead, V., Collin, I., . . . Chertkow, H. (2005). The Montreal Cognitive Assessment, MoCA: A brief screening tool for mild cognitive impairment. *Journal of the American Geriatrics Society, 53*(4), 695–699.

Neary, D., Snowden, J. S., Gustafson, L., Passant, U., Stuss, D., Black, S., . . . Benson, D. F. (1998). Frontotemporal lobar degeneration: A consensus on clinical diagnostic criteria. *Neurology, 51*(6), 1546–1554.

Newhart, M., Davis, C., Kannan, V., HeidlerGary, J., Cloutman, L., & Hillis, A. E. (2009). Therapy for naming deficits in two variants of primary progressive aphasia. *Aphasiology, 23*(7–8), 823–834.

Nicholas, L. E., & Brookshire, R. H. (1993). A system for quantifying the informativeness and efficiency of the connected speech of adults with aphasia. *Journal of Speech, Language, and Hearing Research, 36*(2), 338–350.

Ogar, J. M., Dronkers, N. F., Brambati, S. M., Miller, B. L., & Gorno-Tempini, M. L. (2007). Progressive nonfluent aphasia and its characteristic motor speech deficits. *Alzheimer Disease and Associated Disorders, 21*(4), S23–S30.

Pattee C., Von Berg S., & Ghezzi, P. (2006). Effects of alternative communication on the communicative effectiveness of an individual with a progressive language disorder. *International Journal of Rehabilitation Research, 29*(2), 151–153.

Patterson, K., Nestor, P. J., & Rogers, T. T. (2007). Where do you know what you know? The representation of semantic knowledge in the human brain. *Nature Reviews Neuroscience, 8*(12), 976–987.

Pick, A. (1977). On the relation between aphasia and senile atrophy of the brain. In D. Rottenberg & F. Hochberg (Eds.), *Neurological classics in modern translation* (pp. 35–40). New York, NY: Hafner Press.

Rascovsky, K., Hodges, J. R., Kipps, C. M., Johnson, J. K., Seeley, W. W., Mendez, M. F., . . . Miller, B. M. (2007). Diagnostic criteria for the behavioral variant of frontotemporal dementia (bvFTD): Current limitations and future directions. *Alzheimer Disease & Associated Disorders, 21*(4), S14–S18.

Reilly, J. (2016). How to constrain and maintain a lexicon for the treatment of progressive semantic naming deficits: Principles of item selection for formal semantic therapy. *Neuropsychological Rehabilitation, 26*(1), 126–156.

Robinson, S., Druks, J., Hodges, J., & Garrard, P. (2009). The treatment of object naming, definition, and object use in semantic dementia: The effectiveness of errorless learning. *Aphasiology, 23*(6), 749–775.

Rogalski, E., Cobia, D., Harrison, T. M., Wieneke, C., Weintraub, S., & Mesulam, M.-M. (2011). Progression of language decline and cortical atrophy in subtypes of primary progressive aphasia. *Neurology, 76*(21), 1804–1810.

Rohrer, J. D., Caso, F., Mahoney, C., Henry, M., Rosen, H. J., Rabinovici, G., . . . Gorno-Tempini, M. L. (2013). Patterns of longitudinal brain atrophy in the logopenic variant of primary progressive aphasia. *Brain and Language, 127,* 121–126.

Rohrer, J. D., Ridgway, G. R., Crutch, S. J., Hailstone, J., Goll, J. C., Clarkson, M. J., . . . Warrington, E. K. (2010). Progressive logopenic/phonological aphasia: Erosion of the language network. *NeuroImage, 49*(1), 984–993.

Rosen, H. J., Gorno-Tempini, M. L., Goldman, W. P., Perry, R. J., Schuff, N., Weiner, M., . . . Miller, B. L. (2002). Patterns of brain atrophy in frontotemporal dementia and semantic dementia. *Neurology, 58,* 198–208.

Routhier, S., Macoir, J., Imbeault, H., Jacques, S., Pigot, H., Giroux, S., . . . Bier, N. (2011). From smartphone to external semantic memory device: The use of new technologies to compensate for semantic deficits. *Non-Pharmacological Therapies in Dementia*, 2, 81–99.

Sajjadi, S. A., Patterson, K., & Nestor, P. J. (2014). Logopenic, mixed, or Alzheimer-related aphasia? *Neurology*, *82*(13), 1127–1131.

Sapolsky, D., Domoto-Reilly, K., & Dickerson, B. C. (2014). Use of the Progressive Aphasia Severity Scale (PASS) in monitoring speech and language status in PPA. *Aphasiology*, *28*(8–9), 993–1003.

Savage, S. A., Ballard, K. J., Piguet, O., & Hodges, J. R. (2013). Bringing words back to mind—Improving word production in semantic dementia. *Cortex*, *49*(7), 1823–1832.

Savage, S. A., Foxe, D., & Piguet, O. (2013). Distinguishing subtypes in primary progressive aphasia: Application of the Sydney Language Battery. *Dementia and Geriatric Cognitive Disorders*, *35*, 208–218.

Savage, S. A., Piguet O., & Hodges, J. R. (2014). Giving words new life: Generalization of word retraining outcomes in semantic dementia. *Journal of Alzheimer's Disease*, *40*(2), 309–317.

Savage, S. A., Piguet, O., & Hodges, J. R. (2015). Cognitive intervention in semantic dementia: Maintaining words over time. *Alzheimer Disease and Associated Disorders*, *29*(1), 55–62.

Schneider, S. L., Thompson, C. K., & Luring, B. (1996). Effects of verbal plus gestural matrix training on sentence production in a patient with primary progressive aphasia. *Aphasiology*, *10*(3), 297–317.

Seeley, W. W., Bauer, A. M., Miller, B. L., Gorno-Tempini, M. L., Kramer, J. H., Weiner, M., & Rosen, H. J. (2005). The natural history of temporal variant frontotemporal dementia. *Neurology*, *64*(8), 1384–1390.

Seeley, W. W., Crawford, R. K., Zhou, J., Miller, B. L., & Greicius, M. D. (2009). Neurodegenerative diseases target large-scale human brain networks. *Neuron*, *62*(1), 42–52.

Senaha, M. L. H., Brucki, S. M. D., & Nitrini, R. (2010). Reabilitação na demência semântica: Estudo da eficácia da reaquisição lexical em três pacientes [Rehabilitation in semantic dementia: Study of the effectiveness of lexical reacquisition in three patients]. *Dementia e Neuropsychologia*, *4*(4), 306–312.

Simmons, W. K., & Martin, A. (2009). The anterior temporal lobes and the functional architecture of semantic memory. *Journal of the International Neuropsychological Society*, *15*, 645–649.

Snowden, J. S., Goulding, P. J., & Neary, D. (1989). Semantic dementia: A form of circumscribed cerebral atrophy. *Behavioural Neurology*, *2*, 167–182.

Snowden, J. S., & Neary, D. (2002). Relearning of verbal labels in semantic dementia. *Neuropsychologia*, *40*(10), 1715–1728.

Spinelli, E. G., Mandelli, M. L., Miller, Z. A., Santos-Santos, M. A., Wilson, S. M., Agosta, F., . . . Gorno-Tempini, M. L. (2017). Typical and atypical pathology in primary progressive aphasia variants. *Annals of Neurology*, *81*(3), 430–443.

Suarez-Gonzalez, A., Heredia, C. G., Savage, S. A., Gil-Neciga, E., Garcia-Casares, N., Franco-Macias, E., . . . Caine, D. (2015). Restoration of conceptual knowledge in a case of semantic dementia. *Neurocase: The Neural Basis of Cognition*, *21*(3), 309–321.

Swinburn, K., Porter, G., & Howard, D. (2004). *Comprehensive Aphasia Test*. Hove, UK: Psychology Press.

Trinh, N. H., Hoblyn, J., Mohanty, S., & Yaffe, K. (2003). Efficacy of cholinesterase inhibitors in the treatment of neuropsychiatric symptoms and functional impairment in Alzheimer disease: A meta-analysis. *JAMA*, *289*(2), 210–216.

Tsapkini, K., Frangakis, C., Gomez, Y., Davis, C., & Hillis, A. E. (2014). Augmentation of spelling therapy with transcranial direct current stimulation in primary progressive aphasia: Preliminary results and challenges. *Aphasiology*, *28*(8–9), 1112–1130.

Tsapkini, K., & Hillis, A. E. (2013). Spelling intervention in post-stroke aphasia and primary progressive aphasia. *Behavioural Neurology, 26,* 55–66.

Villanelli, F., Russo, A., Nemni, R., & Farina, E. (2014). Effectiveness (or not?) of cognitive rehabilitation in a person with semantic dementia. *Non-pharmacological Therapies in Dementia, 2,* 111–117.

Warrington, E. K. (1975). The selective impairment of semantic memory. *Quarterly Journal of Experimental Psychology, 27*(4), 635–657.

Weintraub, S., Mesulam, M. M., Wieneke, C., Rademaker, A., Rogalski, E. J., & Thompson, C. K. (2009). The Northwestern Anagram Test: Measuring sentence production in primary progressive aphasia. *American Journal of Alzheimer's Disease & Other Dementias, 24*(5), 408–416.

Wertz, R. T., LaPointe, L. L., & Rosenbek, J. C. (1984). *Apraxia of speech in adults: The disorder and its management.* New York, NY: Grune and Stratton.

Wilson, S. M., Dehollain, C., Ferrieux, S., Christensen, L. E. H., & Teichmann, M. (2017). Lexical access in semantic variant PPA: Evidence for a post-semantic contribution to naming deficits. *Neuropsychologia, 106,* 90–99.

Wilson, S. M., Henry, M. L., Besbris, M., Ogar, J. M., Dronkers, N. F., Jarrold, W., . . . Gorno-Tempini, M. L. (2010). Connected speech production in three variants of primary progressive aphasia. *Brain, 133,* 2069–2088.

Wong, S. B., Anand, R., Chapman, S. B., Rackley, A., & Zientz, J. (2009). When nouns and verbs degrade: Facilitating communication in semantic dementia. *Aphasiology, 23*(2), 286–301.

Young, J. J., Lavakumar, M., Tampi, D., Balachandran, S., & Tampi, R. R. (2018). Frontotemporal dementia: Latest evidence and clinical implications. *Therapeutic Advances in Psychopharmacology, 8*(1), 33–48.

6

Dementia: Concepts and Contemporary Practice

Nidhi Mahendra

Introduction

The world's population has been aging at an unprecedented rate as a result of increasing longevity and declining fertility rates. Indeed, by 2050, people aged over 60 years will more than double and account for over 16% of the world's population (Population Reference Bureau, 2018). In the 2010 census, more Americans were aged 65 years or older than in any previous recorded census, with this segment of the population having increased at a faster rate than the total population between 2000 and 2010 (U.S. Census Bureau, 2011). Further, the number of older Americans aged 65 years or older is expected to increase from 46 million at present to over 98 million by the year 2060 (Population Reference Bureau, 2015).

Rapid global aging has significant implications for all health care practitioners, including speech-language pathologists (SLPs) and audiologists. As providers have increasing numbers of older adults on their caseloads, there is a critical need for better understanding biopsychosocial changes that accompany normal and pathological aging, as well as for renewing efforts to ensure that extensions in human life span go alongside an extended health span. One consequence of these demographic changes is the increasing likelihood of age-related syndromes such as dementia. Indeed, the World Health Organization (WHO) recently declared a public health priority to provide health care and social services for an estimated 50 million persons with dementia, worldwide (WHO, 2017). Dementia deserves the greatest attention because of its rising global incidence and prevalence, its progressive nature, the economic burden of providing care, and its tremendous impact on individuals, families, and society at large.

There has always been a strong focus on basic and applied research to better understand dementia, its cellular-molecular pathology, pattern of neurodegeneration, clinical symptomatology, distinct types, and differential diagnosis. In the last three decades, there has been an explosion of research aimed at enhancing early identification, timely diagnosis, pharmacological and nonpharmacological interventions, and palliative care for persons with dementia. The success of much research aimed at diagnosing dementia early eventually revealed mild cognitive impairment (MCI) as a prodromal state for dementia. This emergence of the construct of MCI has demonstrated that a person might present with very subtle yet measurable changes in brain functioning and cognitive-communicative performance years prior to a clinical diagnosis of dementia (Amieva et al., 2005; Petersen, 2003, 2016). Thus, it is imperative that SLPs have expert knowledge of evidence-based practice and practice-based evidence for optimally serving persons with dementia and MCI, as well as engaging in research and community education about lifelong practices and activities that build cognitive reserve. Speech-language pathologists have unique skills to serve persons with dementia and MCI given their strong foundation in understanding typical and atypical changes in communication, cognition, swallowing, health status, and quality of life across the life span. Further, SLPs work with persons with dementia in varied clinical settings, including acute care, skilled nursing settings, community-based settings (e.g., senior centers), and home-based health care.

The following sections introduce definitions of dementia, MCI, and the latest diagnostic criteria that must be fulfilled for a diagnosis of dementia or MCI.

Dementia, Mild Cognitive Impairment, and the *DSM-5* Criteria

Dementia

Dementia is a syndrome comprising a cluster of symptoms that can have many different causes. Dementia is characterized by acquired, persistent impairment of multiple cognitive domains that significantly alters communication, social interaction, occupational function, and the ability to perform instrumental activities of daily living (Grabowski & Damasio, 2004). Further, these pervasive cognitive impairments must exist in the absence of delirium and any other neurologic or psychiatric disorder. In most dementia types, the most commonly affected neuropsychological domain is memory, with related impairments in attention, executive function, language and communication, visuospatial function, and reduced ability to complete activities of daily living (i.e., daily self-care activities) or ADLs (Figure 6–1).

Mild Cognitive Impairment (MCI)

Mild cognitive impairment or MCI is considered a preclinical condition that may suggest a person is at risk for developing dementia. Mild cognitive impairment has been defined as a transition stage or condition of intermediate symptoms between the cognitive changes associated with healthy aging and the salient cognitive impairments seen in Alzheimer's disease or other dementias (Petersen, 2003, 2016).

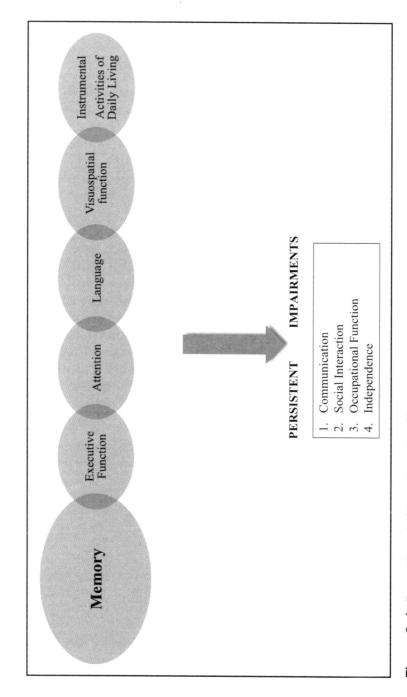

Figure 6–1. Dementia and affected domains of functioning.

Figure 6–2 illustrates the idea that a disease process may begin and progress in its pathogenesis for considerable time before the appearance of observable clinical symptoms. Typically, a clinical diagnosis of dementia indicating the confirmed presence of a neurodegenerative disease process is made much after the first appearance of symptoms. A diagnosis of MCI is made on the basis of mild, measurable changes in a person's cognitive functioning that are noticed by the affected person and usually confirmed by family members. Identifying MCI is important because of its higher likelihood of possible progression to a dementia (Jack et al., 2010; Mitchell & Shiri-Feshki, 2009), particularly when the MCI profile includes memory impairments. Further, timely identification of MCI allows affected persons to initiate a combination of pharmacological and cognitive interventions that may delay or halt the conversion to dementia (Alves et al., 2013).

In 2001, the American Academy of Neurology (AAN; Ganguli, Tangalos, Cummings, & DeKosky, 2001) identified three criteria for a diagnosis of MCI: (a) self-report of memory problems, with corroboration from a family member or caregiver; (b) measurable memory impairment on standardized testing, outside the range expected for age- and education-matched healthy older adults; and (c) no impairments in reasoning, general thinking skills, or ability to perform ADLs. In 2011, the Alzheimer's Association and the National Institute on Aging (McKhann et al., 2011) revised long-standing criteria for the diagnosis of dementia due to Alzheimer's disease. In these new criteria, MCI became elevated in its importance because of the strong suggestion that in some persons, MCI may represent an early stage of AD particularly when biomarkers (e.g., neuronal atrophy, presence of beta-amyloid protein in the brain) are present that indicate a high risk for conversion to AD (Albert

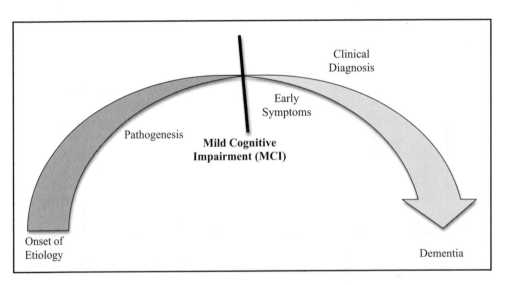

Figure 6–2. Relationship between mild cognitive impairment (MCI) and dementia.

et al., 2011; Jack et al., 2010; Petersen & Negash, 2008). Currently, MCI is classified into two types (Mariani, Monastero & Mecocci., 2007; Petersen, 2003, 2016)—amnestic MCI that initially affects memory only and nonamnestic MCI in which nonmemory cognitive functions are initially affected (e.g., language or executive function). Both amnestic and nonamnestic MCI may be single domain (i.e., affecting one cognitive domain) or multiple domain (affecting two or more cognitive domains). This leads to discussion of the latest criteria for dementia and MCI from the fifth edition of the *Diagnostic and Statistical Manual of Mental Disorders* (*DSM-5;* American Psychiatric Association [APA], 2013).

Diagnostic and Statistical Manual of Mental Disorders (DSM-5) Criteria

The 2013 *DSM-5* criteria (APA, 2013) reframe the dementia syndrome by placing it under two diagnostic categories of Mild Neurocognitive Disorders and Major Neurocognitive Disorders (NCDs). According to Ganguli and colleagues (2011), for a person to meet these *DSM-5* diagnostic criteria for Major NCD, there must be evidence of significant cognitive decline (e.g., in memory or language/communication or executive function) and this observed, quantifiable cognitive decline must be severe enough to disrupt independence in ADLs. To meet the *DSM-5* criteria for Mild NCD, evidence must exist of modest cognitive decline that does not interfere with independent completion of

ADLs. Typically, a person with a Mild NCD would be able to perform tasks requiring money management, taking medications, remembering daily events or appointments but likely will report that these tasks are becoming difficult. One clear advantage of these *DSM-5* criteria for Major NCD is that physicians are required to be specific about the cause of dementia—whether it is Alzheimer's disease (AD), frontotemporal lobar degeneration (FTLD), vascular dementia, dementia with Lewy bodies (DLB), Parkinson's disease, or mixed dementia (i.e., bearing hallmark characteristics of more than one dementia type).

Types of Dementia

Dementia may be caused by over 50 known conditions, and many types of dementia involve progressive and degenerative changes in neurons, neuronal networks, and entire cortical regions responsible for cognitive functions. However, in some cases, dementia-like symptoms may occur in the absence of any degenerative brain disease. Some common causes of such reversible dementia-like symptoms include depression, delirium, side effects from medications, thyroid disorders, specific vitamin deficiencies, excessive use of alcohol, and normal pressure hydrocephalus (Alzheimer's Association, 2018).

Irreversible dementias are characterized by progressive deterioration in cognitive functioning and the capacity for independent living and are most often caused by Alzheimer's disease, vascular dementia, DLB, and FTLD (Alzheimer's Association, 2018; Prince et al., 2013). Each of these types of dementia has specific symptoms, patterns of symptom onset and progression, signature areas of neuropathology, and differential responses to pharmacological and cognitive-communicative interventions. In the next sections, we discuss the leading causes of irreversible dementia.

Alzheimer's Disease

Alzheimer's disease (AD) is the single most common cause of dementia, accounting for 60% to 80% of all dementia diagnoses, currently affecting nearly 5.7 million Americans (Alzheimer's Association, 2018). This number includes 5.5 million adults over the age of 65 years and approximately 200,000 adults below 65 years of age who have young-onset AD. In the United States, AD affects more women than men. Further, African American and Caribbean Hispanic older adults are significantly more likely to have AD or other dementias, as compared to non-Latino white populations (Mehta & Yeo, 2016).

Alzheimer's disease is thought to result from a convergence of factors rather than a single cause. The most significant nonmodifiable risk factors for developing AD are older age, a positive family history of AD (especially in a first-degree relative), and carrier status for the e4 allele of the APOE gene, which governs the production of a protein involved in transporting cholesterol in the blood. Modifiable risk factors are factors that can be managed in order to reduce the risk of cognitive decline and dementia. These include ensuring a heart-healthy diet, social and cognitive engagement, regular physical activity, controlling cardiovascular risk factors, and preventing a traumatic brain injury (Baumgart, Snyder, Carrillo, Fazio, Kim & Johns, 2015).

The earliest-appearing, hallmark symptom of AD involves the human memory systems of episodic memory (Bayles, 1991; Mahendra, Hickey, & Bourgeois, 2018; Mahendra, Scullion, & Hamerschlag, 2011; Salmon & Bondi, 2009) and working memory (Baddeley, Baddeley, Bucks, & Wilcock 2001). The signature neuropathology of AD begins in the medial temporal lobe within the hippocampus and the enthorhinal and perirhinal cortices—regions crucial to episodic memory. Episodic memory is the ability to consciously recall episodes and unique personal experiences (Bayles, McCullough, & Tomoeda, 2018; Baddeley, 2002; Squire & Zola-Morgan, 1991; Tulving, 1983), which allows us to perform everyday tasks like retaining a phone message, remembering the discussion at a meeting, or details of a special event (Dickerson & Eichenbaum, 2010).. Alzheimer's disease also results in significant impairments of attention (Foldi, Lobosco, & Schaefer, 2002) and executive function from the early stages (Collette, Delrue, Van Der Linden, & Salmon, 2001; Martyr & Clare, 2012). These executive function impairments influence planning, goal setting, decision making, self-monitoring, and cognitive flexibility—all components of complex everyday tasks. Thus, executive impairments precede impairments of praxis or the ability to carry out skilled motor procedures like driving (Martyr & Clare, 2012), dressing, and self-feeding (Baudic et al., 2006). Collectively, these impairments of attention, working memory, episodic memory, and executive function adversely affect linguistic communication—this is discussed more in a later section of this chapter.

Vascular Dementia (VaD)

Vascular dementia (VaD) consists of impaired cognitive functions and ADL performance that are most commonly caused by ischemic or hemorrhagic cerebrovascular disease, cardiovascular disease, or circulatory disturbances that damage brain areas vital for memory and cognitive functions (Román, 2005). Conditions that increase the risk of developing VaD include hypertension, hypercholesterolemia, Type II diabetes mellitus, prior history of stroke, and smoking (Elzaguirre, Rementeria, Gonzalez-Torres, & Gaviria, 2017). The concept of VaD has been evolving as evidence accumulates that the brain changes associated with vascular dementia alone are found in 10% of brains of persons with dementia. Yet these brain changes exist in approximately 40% of brains of persons with dementia because the neuropathology associated with VaD and AD commonly coexists (Alzheimer's Association, 2018; Schneider, Arvanitakis, Bang, & Bennett, 2007).

For a diagnosis of VaD, there must be objective evidence of cardiac and/or other systemic vascular conditions and evidence of cerebrovascular disease etiologically tied to the onset of dementia symptoms. Focal neurological signs and symptoms (e.g., slow gait, altered balance) or brain imaging evidence for ischemic, hemorrhagic, or white matter lesions on computed tomog-raphy (CT) or magnetic resonance imaging (MRI) scans (Randolph, 1997) must be present while ensuring that the symptoms of VaD do not occur only during delirium (an acute state of confusion). A unique characteristic of VaD is that its symptoms may be marked either by sudden onset (e.g., from an acute event) or chronic onset from accumulating ischemic changes in the brain over a period of time. Further, a stepwise deterioration of cognitive function may occur in VaD, with affected persons being stable between ischemic events and experiencing significant functional decline with subsequent vascular episodes. Unlike the early appearing memory impairments in AD, the initial symptom in VaD is more likely to be impaired judgment, decision making, planning, or organizing.

In reviewing the literature on differences between AD and VaD across cognitive domains, Mahendra and Engineer (2009) summarized that persons with VaD perform:

a. Better than persons with AD on tasks of verbal episodic memory, semantic memory, and category fluency

b. Worse than persons with AD on tasks of attention, executive function, visuospatial ability, and letter fluency

c. Similar to persons with AD on tasks assessing digit span, constructional ability, processing speed, and on language batteries

For a case study on the longitudinal effects of VaD on cognitive-communicative function, readers are directed to Mahendra and Engineer (2009).

Dementia With Lewy Bodies (DLB)

This dementia type gets its name from Lewy bodies aggregating in the cerebral cortex. Lewy bodies are abnormal clumps of the neuronal protein, alphasynuclein. This same protein is implicated in the neuropathology of Parkinson's disease (PD) along with severe neuronal loss in the substantia nigra. Thus, dementia with Lewy bodies (DLB) is biologically related to PD such that both conditions have a shared pathological hallmark of the presence of Lewy bodies.

Persons presenting with DLB have some overlapping symptoms with those of AD yet are much more likely to present with early symptoms of persistent and complex visual hallucinations or other sensory hallucinations (Ballard, Aarsland, Francis, & Corbett, 2013), visuospatial impairment, sleep disturbance, fluctuating attention and vigilance (Schneider et al., 2012), gait imbalances or Parkinsonian movement features (Hanson & Lippa, 2009), and reduced speech rate and fluency (Ash et al., 2012). Other observed characteristics of DLB include executive dysfunction, cognitive inflexibility, and perseveration during decision making. It is noteworthy that these symptoms occur in the absence of the type of episodic memory impairments seen in AD (McKeith, Taylor, Thomas, Donaghy, & Kane, 2016).

Frontotemporal Lobar Degeneration (FTLD)

Another important dementia type is frontotemporal lobar degeneration (FTLD) that accounts for 10% of dementia cases, most diagnosed before the age of 65 years (Alzheimer's Association, 2018). Nearly 60% of persons diagnosed with FTLD are between 45 and 60 years in age. Frontotemporal lobar degeneration is a heterogeneous group of rare neurodegenerative disorders that result in significant impairments of behavior, personality and distinct types of language impairment (National Institute on Aging, 2012). Frontotemporal dementias are characterized by progressive, focal atrophy of the frontal and anterior temporal brain regions and spongiform changes in the cortex with abnormal tau protein inclusions (Cairns et al., 2007; Sieben et al., 2012). Early symptoms of FTLD generally develop in one of three domains—personality and behavior, language and communication, or movement and motor skills. It is crucial for SLPs to note that isolated speech and language impairments may be the earliest-appearing symptoms of FTLD language variants (Gorno-Tempini et al., 2004; Gorno-Tempini et al., 2011).

The syndromes associated with FTD include a behavioral variant of FTD (bvFTD) and three language variants of FTD, also called primary progressive aphasias or PPA (Gorno-Tempini et al., 2004; Gorno-Tempini et al., 2011; Harciarek & Kertesz, 2011; Henry & Grasso, 2018; Kertesz, 2006a). The behavioral variant of FTLD accounts for about half of all cases with a frontotemporal dementia and is characterized by marked changes in personality, behavior, and social pragmatics. Primary progressive aphasias are of three distinct types (Figure 6–3)—a semantic variant (sv-PPA) characterized by fluent speech and rapid loss of semantic knowledge,

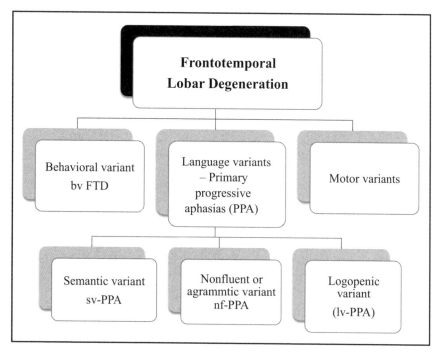

Figure 6–3. Frontotemporal lobar degeneration (FTLD).

a nonfluent or agrammatic variant of PPA (nf-PPA), and a logopenic variant or lv-PPA (Gorno-Tempini et al., 2008; Gorno-Tempini et al., 2011; Mahendra, 2012). Readers are referred to Chapter 5 by Henry in this text for a detailed discussion of PPA. Finally, FTLD also has motor variants that include persons with corticobasal degeneration, motor neuron disease, multiple system atrophy (MSA), and progressive supranuclear palsy. Table 6–1 illustrates select parameters that can be useful in differentially diagnosing AD from VaD, DLB, and FTLD, based on published literature.

This section concludes with brief discussion about the term "mixed dementia," in which a person presents with brain abnormalities associated with more than one type of dementia. Converging evidence from longitudinal studies, autopsy studies, brain imaging, and histopathologic investigations indicates that nearly half of the older adults with dementia have mixed dementia (Schneider et al., 2007) and the likelihood of being diagnosed with mixed dementia is highest past 85 years of age (Alzheimer's Association, 2018).

Impact of Dementia on Cognition and Communication

The syndrome of dementia impacts multiple cognitive domains severely. This impact on multiple cognitive domains adversely influences social interactions, occupational function, everyday activities, and communication. Because AD accounts for the vast majority of dementia cases, we discuss

Table 6–1. Differential Diagnosis of Types of Dementia

	AD	VaD	DLB	FTLD
Age of onset	Mostly past age 65. Early onset AD is rarer.	Mostly past age 65. Age of onset is variable.	Most often past age 65 years.	Most often between 45 and 60 years of age.
Known risk factors	Genetic risk (APOE-e4 allele), higher age, family history of AD in first-degree relative, cardiovascular risk factors, diabetes, hypertension, prior TBI, smoking	Cardiovascular disease, prior stroke/infarct, diabetes, hypertension, high cholesterol, obesity, smoking	Genetic risk, family history of PD, history of depression or anxiety, history of stroke	Genetic risk, family history of dementia, diabetes, prior TBI, autoimmune disease
Neuroimaging findings	Classic medial temporal lobe damage to the hippocampus and surrounding cortex	Multiple ischemic lesions, silent strokes, lacunar infarcts, white matter lesions	Nigrostriatal degeneration, occipital area hypoperfusion affecting primary visual cortex and visual association areas, altered white matter integrity, spared medial temporal lobe	Focal atrophy of frontal and temporal brain regions, spongiform changes to cortex, tau protein inclusions
Earliest symptoms	Episodic memory, working memory, executive function affected earliest	Impaired judgment or impaired planning/decision making	Sleep disturbance, visual or other sensory hallucination, fluctuating confusion	Noticeable changes in behavior (bv-FTD) or speech/language (PPA)
Language	Early impairment in generative naming, discourse. Phonology, syntax, reading mechanics and fluency relatively spared.	Impaired word retrieval and performance on semantic memory tasks, disorganized discourse	Impaired naming and severely impaired conceptual knowledge, reduced speech rate and fluency	Dramatic impairment of language and communication in PPA, worsens rapidly

its broad impact on cognition and communication here. In AD, the earlier mentioned deficits in episodic memory, attention, working memory, and executive function negatively influence language processing and communicative function. Two aspects of linguistic communication affected earliest are naming ability and discourse performance. Confrontation naming and generative naming or the ability to name and generate exemplars of a category is significantly impaired in persons with AD when compared to age-matched healthy older controls (Arkin & Mahendra, 2001; Clark et al., 2009; Martin & Fedio, 1983; Sailor, Antoine, Diaz, Kuslansky, & Kluger, 2004). Similarly, discourse breakdowns are common from the earliest stages of dementia (Bayles, McCullough, & Tomoeda, 2018; Mahendra et al., 2018) with consistent evidence of empty speech (Nicholas, Obler, Albert, & Helm-Estabrooks, 1985), impaired cohesion (i.e., more wordiness and reduced relevant ideas conveyed), increased use of tangential utterances, more sentence fragments and incomplete ideas (Ripich & Terrell, 1988; Tomoeda & Bayles, 1993), and reduced comprehension of sentences (Small, Kemper, & Lyons, 1997).

In the early stages of AD, affected individuals also are frequently disoriented to time and place, getting easily confused and experiencing communication breakdowns (e.g., repetitive question-asking). However, persons with mild dementia present with several spared abilities, including orientation to self and to other persons, ability to produce fluent sentences, engage in conversation, and frequently follow two-step to three-step commands (Hopper, Bayles, & Kim, 2001). Also,

persons with mild AD retain semantic memory (e.g., the ability to describe attributes of an object, define a concept, or sort objects by semantic category), although this deteriorates as dementia severity increases (Bayles, Tomoeda, & Rein, 1996; Bayles, Tomoeda, & Cruz, 1999; Cox, Bayles, & Trosset, 1996). With progression to the middle stages of AD, affected persons may retain the ability to follow one-step and two-step commands, sustain attention for some time, and make relevant on-topic statements or comments about tangible stimuli during conversation (Ashida, 2000; Mahendra, 2001). In the late stages of AD, cognitive-communicative functioning is severely affected (Bayles, Tomoeda, Cruz, & Mahendra, 2000) but persons with AD can still attend to pleasant stimuli (e.g., music, sensory stimulation) for brief periods of time. Table 6–2 provides a list of cognitive domains affected in AD and examples of tasks used to assess these domains.

Role of the Speech-Language Pathologist With Persons With Dementia and MCI

In a position statement and related technical report as well as in the Scope of Practice document in Speech-Language Pathology (ASHA, 2016), the American Speech-Language-Hearing Association has indicated that SLPs play a key role in the screening, assessment, diagnosis, treatment, and research of dementia-based communication disorders (ASHA, 2005a). The range of professional roles and activities performed by SLPs includes the aforementioned

Table 6–2. Cognitive Domains Affected in AD

Cognitive Domain Affected in AD	Sample Assessment Task/Stimulus
Orientation	Answering Questions about Time and Place e.g., *What year is it? What month are we in? What is the name of this building we are in?*
Attention	Letter Scanning e.g., *Please look at this sheet of paper containing letters of the alphabet. Circle every letter A that you can find.*
Executive function	Clock Drawing Test (CDT), Assessment of Activities of Daily Living (ADL) or Instrumental ADLs e.g., *CDT: Please draw a clock with the arms indicating the time is ten after eleven.* *ADL Assessment: Show me how you make a pot of coffee.*
Working memory	Forward or Backward Digit Span Tasks e.g., *Please repeat these numbers after me in the same order: 8, 2, 7*
Episodic memory	Story or Word List Recall e.g., *I am going to tell you a short story. When I'm done, I'd like you tell it back to me.*
Semantic memory	Similarities and Differences Task e.g., *How are an apple and a banana alike? How are they different?*
Language	Confrontation Naming Tasks e.g., *Please name these pictures.* Generative or Category Naming Tasks e.g., *I'd like you to name as many animals as you can, in one minute.* Object Description e.g., *I'd like you to describe this object for me, in as much detail as possible.* Discourse e.g., *Conversation Analysis*
Visuospatial function	Figure Copying e.g., *I'd like you to copy this picture.*

components as well as client and family education, counseling, case management, advocacy and prevention efforts, and interdisciplinary collaboration to ensure the highest quality of care for persons with dementia (ASHA, 2005a, 2005b). Aligning with this view, the next sections address screening, assessment, and interventions for persons with dementia from the perspective of an SLP.

Screening and Assessment of Persons With Dementia and MCI

Screening

The purpose of a brief screening, prior to a comprehensive assessment, aids a clinician in identifying if a subsequent evaluation is necessary, identifying comorbidities (e.g., hearing loss, depression), providing information that informs the nature and type of evaluation conducted, and determining the need for referrals (e.g., for neuropsychological or audiological testing). For persons with suspected dementia or MCI, screenings should include the following components:

Thorough Review of Medical History

Medical records should be reviewed to provide details regarding a client's prior and current health conditions, active diagnoses, list of medications, recent medical history, any report of cognitive-communicative impairments, and psychosocial history. Information

from medical records, direct observations, client self-report, and caregiver input might allow a clinician to derive a Hachinski Ischemia Score (HIS; Hachinski et al., 1975). Using the HIS allows clinicians to screen for the possibility of vascular dementia. The HIS consists of 13 clinical features determined to be present or absent based on a client's medical history. Research studies have validated that a score of 4 or below 4 fits a profile of AD, whereas a score of 7 or greater is more suggestive of VaD (Hachinski et al., 1975; Moroney et al., 1997).

Sensory Impairments Affecting Hearing and Vision

Sensory impairments of hearing and vision are very prevalent in older adults past the age of 65 years (Desai, Pratt, Lentzner, & Robinson, 2001; Yueh, Shapiro, MacLean, & Shekelle, 2003). Indeed, the presence of a hearing or vision impairment can easily confound the reliability and validity of test results. For example, adults with age-related hearing loss may underperform on a cognitive test leading to a spurious dementia diagnosis (Cacciatore et al., 1999; Weinstein, 2019). Further recent research has revealed that hearing loss is a potent, midlife modifiable risk factor that greatly predicts the likelihood of cognitive decline and later-life dementia (Livingston et al., 2017; Weinstein, 2019). ASHA offers clinicians guidance that a hearing screening for older adults with suspected or confirmed dementia should include otoscopy, pure-tone audiometric hearing screening, hearing aid inspection (as needed), and a check of word recognition performance (ASHA, 2005b).

Regarding visual impairments, many screening measures and comprehensive tests that SLPs routinely use for evaluating cognitive-communicative function require clients to identify objects, describe pictures, read words or sentences, and copy figures. Persons with age-related visual impairments such as cataracts, diabetic retinopathy, and macular degeneration may perform poorly on such subtests. Thus, it is necessary to quickly screen for visual impairments by presenting letter/number cancellation tasks, literacy screening tasks, and simple visual agnosia screening tasks. A popular test used by SLPs and developed exclusively for assessing cognitive communication disorders in dementia is the Arizona Battery for Communication Disorders of Dementia (ABCD; Bayles & Tomoeda, 1993) with a forthcoming second edition. This test includes short tasks, appropriate for screening vision and speech discrimination function.

Depression

Depression is common among persons with dementia or MCI. Depressed mood is a significant variable that negatively influences cognitive function. For instance, depression negatively affects clients' motivation and engagement, as well as their desire to participate in assessment and treatment, and is often associated with social withdrawal, loss of interest in daily activities, and poorer well-being. As such, depression can magnify cognitive and ADL impairments associated with dementia or MCI. Whereas the comprehensive treatment of depression falls outside the SLP scope of practice, SLPs are qualified to screen for depression and assist in clients obtaining timely referrals and management. SLPs can use any one of multiple tools to screen for depression—including the Geriatric Depression Scale–Short Form or GDS-15 (Sheikh & Yesavage, 1986), the Beck Depression Inventory (BDI-II; Beck, Steer, & Brown, 1996), and the Patient Health Questionnaire (PHQ-9; Kroenke, Spitzer, & Williams, 2001). Depending on the clinical setting, SLPs may need to consult with psychologists, counselors, neuropsychologists, social workers, and nurse practitioners to manage screening and referrals for depression.

Cognitive Function

Given that clear evidence for modest or significant cognitive decline is required for a *DSM-5* supported diagnosis of mild or major NCD, respectively, screening for cognitive impairment is an essential first step in aiding the diagnosis of MCI or dementia. Some of the most widely used tools for screening cognitive function are the Mini-Mental State Examination (MMSE; Folstein, Folstein, & McHugh, 1975), the Clock Drawing Test (CDT; Agrell & Dehun, 1998; Sunderland et al., 1989), the Montreal Cognitive Assessment (MoCA©; Nasreddine et al., 2005), and the Veterans Affairs Medical Center Saint Louis University Mental Status Exam (SLUMS; Tariq, Tumosa, Chibnall, Perry, & Morley, 2006).

The MMSE is among the most well-known general screening measures of cognitive status. It can be administered quickly within 10 minutes and has 11 items that result in a maximum possible score of 30 points. It has high sensitivity and specificity, particularly when population norms are used to correct scores for age and number of years of education (Crum, Anthony, Bassett, & Folstein, 1993; Harvan & Cotter, 2006). Because the MMSE lacks sensitivity for detecting MCI, clinicians and researchers increasingly prefer the MoCA© or the SLUMS. The SLUMS also features 11 items in a 30-point test and improves on the MMSE by including measures of forward and backward digit span, story recall, and clock-drawing. Further, the SLUMS examination provides education-corrected scores.

The MoCA© is another 30-point test comprising 12 items covering eight domains and has the advantage of being specifically developed to distinguish between healthy aging, MCI, and AD based on obtained scores. This test makes substantial improvements over the MMSE by being much more sensitive to detecting MCI and AD and for differentiating between healthy aging and MCI. Further, the MoCA© features availability in many languages (including a version for blind participants), alternate forms, an electronic version (the eMoCA©), an app, and a 5-minute mini-MOCA© version currently in development. The MoCA© provides reliable assessment of attention, executive function, episodic memory, and semantic memory. Finally, the CDT requires clients to draw a clock showing a specific time or to draw the face of a clock and its hands given a circle already drawn. Performance on the CDT worsens as dementia severity increases and enables distinguishing healthy aging from mild, moderate, or severe dementia. The CDT has low sensitivity for distinguishing very mild dementia from healthy aging, yet has

improved sensitivity and specificity when used in conjunction with age- and education-corrected MMSE scores (Powlishta et al., 2002). Some version of a clock-drawing task appears in multiple assessment measures including the MoCA© and the SLUMS. In summary, these screening tools also may serve as one key component of a comprehensive evaluation of cognitive-communicative function in MCI or dementia. Table 6–3 compares the MMSE, MoCA©, SLUMS, and CDT to assist readers in comparing these screening tools.

Assessment

Evidence-based assessment for persons with dementia and MCI should be informed by federal mandates under the Nursing Home Reform Act (part of the Omnibus Budget Reconciliation Act [OBRA] 1987), the Patient Protection and Affordable Care Act (PPACA, 2010) and its related Elder Justice Act,

Table 6–3. Suggested Areas for Screening for Persons With Dementia or MCI

Thorough Review of Prior and Current Medical History (e.g., risk factors, comorbidities, medications)
Hearing impairment
Vision impairment
Speech/language/communication
Depression
Global cognitive function
Mobility or balance impairments/history of falls

the Speech-Language Pathology Scope of Practice (ASHA, 2016), ASHA position statement on SLPs' role in serving persons with dementia, and the International Classification of Functioning, Disability, and Health (ICF)—a conceptual framework put forward by the World Health Organization (WHO, 2001). This ICF model suggests that a chronic health condition, like dementia, affects an individual's *Body Functions and Structures* (i.e., anatomical/physiological or psychological functioning), *Activities* (i.e., ability to perform specific tasks), and *Participation* (i.e., ability to participate fully in life roles). For instance, a person with dementia is often unable to recall a short story on a standardized test (Body Functions and Structures), consequently being unable to remember what is said (Activity), thus being restricted from participating effectively in social conversations (Participation). Beyond these three levels, per the ICF model, personal and environmental factors are strong determinants of how dementia impacts each affected person (Hopper, 2007). The critical contribution of the ICF model is that it gives clinicians a foundation to conceptualize assessment from multiple perspectives (i.e., at the distinct levels of Body Functions and Structures, Activity, and Participation levels).

The OBRA mandate influences assessment practices in all Medicare-certified long-term care facilities, mandating an initial assessment of resident functional status—the Minimum Data Set (Centers for Medicare and Medicaid Services, 2001), within 14 days for all newly admitted residents and regular quarterly assessments as well as in the event of a change in a resident's functioning (i.e., decline or improvement). The Patient Protection and Affordable Care Act (PPACA or ACA) also has added a Medicare benefit via an Annual Wellness Visit, which now requires an assessment to detect cognitive impairment (Cordell et al., 2013) beyond routine checks of medical history, physical and ADL status, medication review, and consideration of necessary referrals to specialists. These federal mandates suggest strongly that clinicians must be knowledgeable and skilled about screening and assessment methods for persons with suspected MCI or dementia, to contribute to these required evaluations of functional status.

As suggested previously, any measures useful in screening for MCI and dementia may be components of a comprehensive evaluation. There is widespread consensus that the objectives of a comprehensive evaluation of a client with dementia are (Aguirre, Woods, Specter, & Orrell, 2013; Bayles, McCollough, & Tomoeda, 2018; Hickey & Bourgeois, 2018; Mahendra & Apple, 2007; Mahendra & Hopper, 2017):

1. Identifying early the presence of cognitive communication disorder resulting from dementia or MCI
2. Documenting impaired and spared cognitive and communicative abilities
3. Establishing a baseline of cognitive-communicative functioning prior to the onset of any intervention
4. Assessing personal and environmental factors that influence a particular client or family
5. Providing information and resources about dementia or MCI and counseling family members about expected progression
6. Using dynamic assessment approaches or structured therapy

trials to determine a client's candidacy for particular interventions (Mahendra & Hopper, 2017) or need for stimulus presentation in an alternate modality (Mahendra, Bayles, & Harris, 2005)

With these objectives in mind, presented next are selected assessment measures that may be useful for SLPs assessing persons with dementia. This is not an exhaustive review of all assessment measures available but is meant to provide direction to clinicians in selecting assessment measures.

Standardized Tests for Profiling Performance Across Cognitive Domains

Many existing standardized tests allow clinicians to obtain a profile of client functioning across cognitive domains such as attention, memory, language, visuospatial ability, and executive function. These tests allow an immediate understanding of which domains seem to be most affected versus least affected for a particular client. Examples of tests in this category include the Repeatable Battery for the Assessment of Neuropsychological Status (RBANS; Randolph, Tierney, Mohr, & Chase, 1998), the Dementia Rating Scale (DRS-2; Mattis, Jurica, & Leitten, 1991), and the Cognitive Linguistic Quick Test (CLQT [Helm-Estabrooks, 2001]; CLQT+ [Helm-Estabrooks, 2017]).

The RBANS (Randolph et al., 1998) and the RBANS® Update (Randolph, 2012) were specifically developed to provide a stand-alone test for detecting and characterizing dementia in older adults, designed to serve as a screening neuropsychological test when a full-

length battery is inappropriate, and to provide multiple parallel forms to allow reliable retesting while controlling for practice effects (Randolph et al., 1998). This test allows for the assessment of immediate memory, visuospatial/constructional ability, language, attention, and delayed memory using 12 subtests. It provides norms for persons aged 12 through 89 years and provides index scores, percentile ranks, and a total scale score. The RBANS also provides group data for multiple dementia types (e.g., AD, VaD, HIV-related dementia) and other neurogenic (e.g., head injury) and psychiatric causes (e.g., depression, schizophrenia) of cognitive impairments. The RBANS has been validated in multiple studies for use with persons with MCI, AD (Duff et al., 2008), and for assessing community-dwelling healthy older adults. Further, performance on the RBANS reliably predicts functional limitations in persons with MCI and dementia (Freilich & Hyer, 2007; Hobson, Hall, Humphreys-Clark, Schrimsher, & O'Bryant, 2010). Other advantages of the RBANS include availability of two parallel forms in Spanish and options for web-based administration and scoring.

Next, the DRS-2 was designed particularly for persons with dementia and assesses client performance on five subscales—Attention, Initiation/Perseveration, Construction, Conceptualization, and Memory. This test provides age and education corrections for the total DRS-2 score and also has parallel forms to allow retesting without confounding learning effects from repeated test administrations. Finally, the CLQT+ (Helm-Estabrooks, 2017) is a criterion-referenced test that allows clinicians to assess attention, memory, executive function, language, and visuospatial function in persons with dementia, traumatic brain injury, or stroke. This test provides norms for ages 18 through 89 years, with test scores yielding a composite severity rating ranging from performance within functional limits (WFL) through severe impairment. Particular advantages of the CLQT and CLQT+ are the availability of test materials in Spanish, a traditional test version (10 subtests), and an aphasia-friendly version (with an added semantic comprehension task).

Standardized Tests for In-Depth Assessment of Select Cognitive Domains

Tests in this group allow SLPs to assess one or two domains in more depth. For instance, if a clinician wishes to know much more about a client's cognitive-communicative functioning, the Arizona Battery for Communication Disorders of Dementia (ABCD; Bayles & Tomoeda, 1993) or the Western Aphasia Battery–Revised (WAB-R; Kertesz, 2006b) may be appropriate for selection. The ABCD was among the first comprehensive tests of linguistic communication designed for persons with mild AD. This test includes vision, literacy, and hearing screening subtests along with 14 distinct subtests to assess linguistic expression and comprehension, verbal episodic memory, semantic memory, visuospatial construction, and mental status. The ABCD provides performance data on healthy young and older participants, persons with mild and moderate dementia, and persons with PD with and without dementia. This test has a forthcoming second edition featuring expanded norms and data from persons with MCI.

The WAB-R is a well-respected, robust, and validated measure of linguistic communication for domains of auditory comprehension, speech and language production, repetition, and naming for persons with dementia and those with PPA (Henry & Grasso, 2018). It also allows for the assessment of reading comprehension, written language production, motor speech production, and nonverbal cognition (e.g., Raven's Progressive Matrices), and it also offers a shorter, bedside screening version.

Standardized Tests for Functional Assessment of Select Cognitive Domains

Tests in this category are unique in their focus on functional cognition, everyday communication, and for documenting performance on real-life activities. Given the progressive nature of dementia, it is imperative that interventions focus on functional tasks and behaviors that optimize a client's functioning in everyday situations and routines. Thus, tests in this category are extremely useful in honing in on person-centered intervention goals and for informing the selection of specific therapeutic techniques. Two examples of tests useful for the assessment of functional communication are the Communication Activities for Daily Living (CADL-3; Holland, Fromm, & Wozniak, 2018) and the Functional Linguistic Communication Inventory (FLCI; Bayles & Tomoeda, 1994).

The CADL-3 has been recently revised and was developed initially for assessing functional communication in persons with aphasia. Previous versions of the test have been validated for assessing functional communication in persons with mild to moderate dementia (Fromm & Holland, 1989). The CADL-3 is normed on a mixed group of adults with stroke, traumatic brain injury (TBI), dementia, and PPA. This test contains 50 test items that assess communication activities in seven areas: reading-writing-number use, social interaction, divergent communication, contextual communication, nonverbal communication, sequential relationships, and comprehension of humor/metaphor. Unique to the CADL-3 is the use of real-life scenarios and situations for sampling functional communication strategies used by persons with neurogenic communication disorders. For example, one item requires the client to read a sample prescription medication label and then communicate information about the prescribed medication dose and schedule. Another item requires the person to convey how he or she might place a 9-1-1 call in the event of a home fire.

The FLCI was designed to assess functional communication in persons with moderate or greater dementia severity. It contains 10 subtests that assess the ability of a client with dementia to greet someone, name objects, answer questions, write, comprehend signs (e.g., an exit door or restroom sign), match objects to pictures, read and comprehend words, reminisce, follow commands, use gestures, and engage in conversation. A second edition of the FLCI is forthcoming and features expanded norms to further extend its clinical utility.

Similarly, in the vein of functional assessment of memory, the Rivermead Behavioral Memory Test (RBMT-3; Wilson et al., 2008) is an excellent choice for assessing everyday memory performance. The RBMT-3 is an ecologically valid, efficient test that includes 14 subtests that assess visual and verbal memory, immediate and delayed recall and recognition, prospective memory (e.g., setting an alarm to remember to do something), and the ability to learn new information (e.g., a story, a route around a room). This test was developed in the United Kingdom and features four parallel forms, a U.K. and North American version of test stimuli, and norms from typical individuals aged 16 to 96 years and from persons with brain injury.

Nonstandardized Assessment Using Subtests of Comprehensive Tests

Depending on dementia severity, time allocated for client evaluation, and the intended purpose of an evaluation, clinicians can always use subtests of any aforementioned test as a component of a comprehensive evaluation. For example, the Story Recall subtest on the ABCD is very useful clinically to establish whether a client is having episodic memory impairments more in line with those expected with typical aging or those more consistent with AD. Similarly, the RBANS-Update has a forward and backward digit span subtest that offers a precise way to assess working memory performance.

Other Assessment Options—Beyond Routine Standardized Testing

These include the use of naturalistic observation across contexts or during routine activities, interviews with professional or personal caregivers, and rating scales that allow for quantitative or qualitative measurement of behaviors or careful assessment of the environment. For example, clinicians may use rating scales to assess affect and engagement of clients participating in therapeutic or recreational activities. One well-known scale is the Observed Emotion Rating Scale (Lawton, Van Haitsma, & Klapper, 1999. Another important tool is the Environment and Communication Toolkit (ECAT) for Dementia Care (Brush, Calkins, Bruce, & Sanford, 2012). These authors developed the ECAT as an assessment protocol to evaluate client performance using yes/no questions, to assess the environment and barriers in it, and to select and customize interventions for persons with dementia. The ECAT provides clinicians over 300 specific recommendations for interventions and environmental modifications for reducing communication or behavior problems that persons with dementia encounter while completing ADLs. With this backdrop of conceptual understanding of dementia, screening, and assessment methods, we turn to intervention in the final section of this chapter.

Interventions for Persons With Dementia

Two dichotomies deserve mention when categorizing interventions for persons with dementia. The first dichotomy is between pharmacological and nonpharmacological interventions. SLPs do not make decisions about pharmacological interventions for dementia. However, a thorough screening and evidence-based assessment can be invaluable in establishing a dementia diagnosis and related severity of cognitive impairment. This, in turn, can help initiate appropriate pharmacological management. Nonpharmacological interventions are typically directed toward compensating for cognitive-communicative impairments resulting from AD (e.g., using a scheduling app to provide reminders and notifications about appointments) or toward managing behavioral problems resulting from dementia (e.g., reducing disruptive vocalization or repetitive questions). Another subgroup of nonpharmacological interventions is aimed directly at supporting the well-being and quality of life of persons affected by dementia and their immediate family members. Such interventions frequently include psychoeducational approaches, counseling, support groups, and respite services.

A second dichotomy is between direct and indirect interventions (Hopper, 2001; Mahendra, 2001; Mahendra & Hopper, 2017). Direct interventions are those in which persons with dementia themselves participate in compensatory programs or strategy instruction. One example of a direct intervention is applying spaced retrieval training to teach a client to use a memory aid for recalling important information or procedures (e.g., timing of meals or a safe swallowing strategy). Indirect interventions take the form of clinicians providing training to professional and personal caregivers, modifying the physical or social environment to ease demands on cognitive function, and developing stimulating, engaging, and meaningful therapeutic activities in collaboration with others (Hickey & Bourgeois, 2018; Hopper, 2001).

Given the vast literature on direct and indirect interventions, it is not possible to exhaustively review all interventions SLPs can consider for persons with dementia. A sound place to begin thinking about interventions is to consider key evidence-based features of interventions that have proven efficacious for persons with dementia. Based on published research (Aguire et al., 2013; Bayles et al., 2018; Hickey & Bourgeois, 2018; Hill, Kolanowski, & Gill, 2011; Hopper et al., 2013; Mahendra et al., 2011), some of these core features include providing persons with dementia:

1. Repeated and rich presentation of target information
2. Contexts for learning-by-doing and multiple opportunities to practice generating target responses
3. Cognitive stimulation to activate experience-dependent neuroplasticity
4. Task formats that reduce the likelihood of errors during initial learning and increase the chance of early success
5. Ways to capitalize on relatively spared sustained attention
6. Exposure to personally meaningful, tangible sensory stimuli
7. Structured cues or cueing hierarchies that support information retrieval
8. Opportunities for creative and symbolic activity (e.g., using art, music, gardening)
9. Experiences that offer community engagement, intergenerational programming, and sustained physical activity

Table 6–4 lists these core features, with examples of intervention techniques based on these features. This section ends with providing readers pertinent information on three direct intervention approaches that may be of particular significance for SLPs. These approaches were selected based on availability of empirical evidence for their efficacy, particular utility for dementia, and their proven success for facilitating functional cognition, enhancing communication, and social engagement in persons with dementia. The exemplar approaches discussed next include Spaced Retrieval Training, Memory Books/Memory Wallets, and a Montessori-based intervention called Reading Roundtable®.

Spaced Retrieval Training (SRT)

First described by Landauer and Bjork (1978) as a technique to improve episodic learning of information in young adults, spaced retrieval training (SRT) is a shaping paradigm for facilitating recall of information or procedures. Camp (1989) modified and adapted SRT for persons with AD, and since then, the technique has been used with impressive success for persons with mild and moderate dementia. Spaced retrieval training (Hopper et al., 2005; Lee et al., 2009; Mahendra, 2011) involves teaching new facts or a new motor procedure to a person with dementia, who then practices recalling the information or procedure immediately and over gradually increasing lengths of time. Time intervals after a successful recall attempt are doubled while those after a recall failure are maintained or reduced to support successful retrieval. In this way, persons with dementia can learn and recall functional information (e.g.,

Table 6–4. Key Features of Successful Interventions for Dementia, With Examples

Features of Successful Interventions	Sample Intervention
1. Repeated presentation of target information	Spaced retrieval training Computer-assisted cognitive training Memory books/wallets/aids
2. Provide contexts for learning-by-doing and multiple opportunities to generate target responses	Spaced retrieval training Computer-assisted cognitive training, Reading Roundtable®, Montessori-based interventions
3. Task formats that reduce error likelihood during initial learning	Environmental modifications, written cues Technology-assisted interventions (e.g., automated coaching systems)
4. Capitalize on relatively spared sustained attention during intervention	Montessori-based interventions, Reading Roundtable®
5. Exposure to meaningful sensory stimuli	Reading Roundtable®, reminiscence therapy, simulated presence therapy, music-based or art-based therapy activities
6. Opportunities for meaningful social engagement	Community volunteering, intergenerational programming

a room number, meal schedule) or skills (e.g., a safe swallowing strategy, compensatory maneuver) over extended time. Such functional learning optimizes client functioning, independence, and safety and reduces the need for one-on-one assistance.

Spaced retrieval training has been hugely successful for persons with memory disorders (Schacter, Rich, & Stampp, 1985), traumatic brain injury (Bourgeois, Lenius, Turkstra, & Camp, 2007), and dementia (Brush & Camp, 1998; Hopper et al., 2005; Hopper, Drefs, Bayles, Tomoeda & Dinu, 2009; Hopper et al., 2013; Mahendra, 2011). Types of information and skills trained in dementia vary from teaching names of relevant people (Cherry, Walvoord, & Hawley, 2010; Hopper et al., 2009; Mahendra, 2011), prospective memory tasks (Ozgis, Rendell, & Henry, 2009), safe swallow strategies (Brush & Camp, 1998), communicative strategies, and use of memory aids (Bourgeois et al., 2003). For a recent evidence-based systematic review on cognitive interventions for dementia that includes SRT, readers are directed to the work of Hopper and colleagues (2013).

Spaced retrieval training is efficacious because it involves repeated presentation of target information and extensive opportunities to practice retrieving target information while extending the time interval over which recall is successfully maintained. Incidentally, by requiring successful recall prior to lengthening a retention interval, SRT utilizes the principle of errorless learning (Baddeley, 1992). This type of learning is likely superior to trial-and-error learning for persons with dementia because it discourages guessing, constrains response choices, and restricts the number of errors possible during initial learning. Reducing errors during early learning greatly advantages information or skill acquisition for persons with dementia because it renders the learning more stable, without the confound of intervening errors that can derail learning (Clare & Jones, 2008). Hopper, Mahendra, and colleagues (Hopper et al., 2005) have suggested that persons with mild to moderately severe dementia, episodic memory impairments, and the ability to sustain attention to structured learning tasks are suitable candidates for SRT. It is key for clinicians to think about SRT as an effective modality in which to nest intervention for goals ranging from enhancing on-topic communication, retaining a safety strategy, supporting dysphagia therapy, or learning to use a low-tech augmentative alternative communication device or memory aid. Currently, SRT can now be effectively carried out using the Spaced Retrieval Training therapy app from Tactus Therapy Solutions. Next, we talk about the use of memory books and wallets for persons with dementia.

Memory Books/Memory Wallets

Memory aids such as memory books and memory wallets are examples of low-tech supports that can enhance cognitive-communicative function, social engagement, and quality of life for persons with dementia by facilitating orientation, increasing meaningful and on-topic conversations (Bourgeois, 1990), turn-taking, and fruitful exchanges of information with caregivers (Bourgeois, 1992; Hoerster, Hickey, & Bourgeois, 2001). Further, using memory books and wallets can effectively reduce negative behaviors (Bourgeois, 2013; Bourgeois et al., 1997) stemming from episodic memory loss and resulting confusion (e.g., disruptive vocalizations, repeating the same question). A memory book or wallet usually consists of a collection of relevant information, supported by salient and accessible visual cues (e.g., large-font text, pictures, pictographs, or photographs). A memory wallet is designed to be a smaller, portable version of a memory book that can be carried by a client easily and integrated into any communicative situation or activity routine.

Memory books and wallets utilize previously familiar information and clear visual supports to prime personally relevant facts and to promote expression of needs and preferences to communication partners. Such memory aids reduce the burden on a fragile episodic memory, yet simultaneously engage spared language abilities while fostering enhanced engagement and independence during communication. Memory books and wallets are most suitable for persons with mild to moderate dementia, who can read and process visual information and have the desire to learn a functional strategy for supporting communication. For specific ideas and adaptations to design versatile memory aids, Bourgeois (2013) provides an excellent guide on developing memory books and other graphic cuing systems.

Reading Roundtable®

There is a vast literature on Montessori-based dementia programming (Camp, 1999; Mahendra et al., 2006; Mahendra et al., 2011) and Reading Roundtable® is one exemplary technique of this type. Reading Roundtable® is a Montessori-based group activity based on an original idea by Alan Stevens (Malone & Loehr, 2007) at the Myers Research Institute (MRI) of Menorah Park Center for Senior Living (Myers Research Institute, 2008). Reading Roundtable® is a structured reading and discussion activity that uses specifically developed stories, designed and adapted for communicative access for persons with dementia. This intervention utilizes stories characterized by a supportive sensory format (e.g., using large font, high-contrast paper, durable book covers) and layout (e.g., single-sided printing), interesting facts, and accompanying cues and questions designed to engage clients and foster discussion. Clients participate in this intervention in a group with other clients, taking turns to read aloud from their individual books and then answer questions about the read material. Importantly, these myriad features have been designed with the intent to increase positive engagement of clients with this task and materials.

The development of the Reading Roundtable® was preceded by extended testing of a technique called Question Asking Reading (QAR; Judge, Camp, & Orsulic-Jeras, 2000; Orsulic-Jeras, Schneider, & Camp, 2000). This predecessor QAR approach involved a group of clients with dementia, led by a clinician or facilitator, taking turns reading text on a topic while others followed along with their own copies of the same printed text. Another important feature of QAR that extended to Reading Roundtable® was that the same text or storybook was repeated several times over a few weeks to reinforce content and facilitate implicit learning of the intervention procedure while facilitating explicit learning of the material. It is important to analyze why Reading Roundtable® works for persons with dementia. This technique incorporates many core features that make an intervention successful (see Table 6–4) by priming information using structured repetition, supporting retrieval of learned information, positively engaging residents, fostering reminiscence (e.g., in selection of story or text topics), and emphasizing learning-by-doing of taking turns to read and answer questions. Further, this technique utilizes spared reading mechanics and reading comprehension as well as sustained attention ability in persons with dementia while invoking the supportive and engaging milieu of a group intervention technique. Finally, this technique is flexible enough to be merged with reminiscence for added therapeutic and narrative value (Gibson, 1994; Harris, 1997), making it particularly useful when working with culturally and linguistically diverse older adults.

Future Directions

As the population in the United States and the rest of the world ages rapidly, changes are needed in health care legislation (e.g., the National Alzheimer's

Project Act in the United States), service delivery mechanisms (e.g., the Affordable Care Act in the United States), and large-scale investment in a public health approach for focused screening, assessment, and intervention for and prevention of dementia and MCI (e.g., Building Our Largest Dementia [BOLD] Infrastructure for Alzheimer's Act, 2019). Technology is increasingly shaping the approach to research and development of cognitive and behavioral interventions with many exciting emerging developments relative to the design of smart homes, deployment of sensor technology, use of mobile health networks, automated coaching systems, therapy apps, tele-rehabilitation, and use of self-administered computer programs for improving memory and communication. Further, given the implications of the dementia epidemic facing our country and the globe, urgent emphasis is needed on expanding didactic and clinical training in geriatrics and dementia within the speech-language pathology and audiology curriculum. Finally, training the next generation of providers must be infused with rich opportunities for service learning, interprofessional practice, and engaging in community education and outreach to diverse populations.

the San Francisco Bay Area for 3 years. She had a degree in nursing and had worked as a nurse practitioner for 24 years, prior to retiring. Her medical history was significant for hypertension, coronary artery disease, osteoporosis, and a diagnosis of mild cognitive impairment (MCI) made 3 years ago at the time of admission to her current facility. Her diagnosis of MCI was made based on the findings of an interdisciplinary team, using the *DSM-5* criteria for a neuroimaging-supported diagnosis. At the time, her physician prescribed a low-dose (2.5 mg/day) of Aricept for her. Additionally, Mrs. N was taking Fosamax (for osteoporosis) and Tenormin (a beta-blocker). Her older sister (now deceased) also had dementia due to Alzheimer's disease. She has one daughter, who lives close by and is actively involved in Mrs. N's care. Mrs. N was referred to the SLP by the charge nurse requesting a comprehensive assessment after observing disorientation, worsening memory, communication breakdowns, limited participation in recreational activities, frequent expressions of boredom (e.g., "I have nothing to do"), confusion about the daily schedule (e.g., "I don't know what's next"), and frustration with being unable to use her cellphone to call her daughter.

Case Study

Background Information and Chart Review

Mrs. N was a 78-year old, monolingual, third-generation Japanese American who had lived in an assisted living unit (within a continuum-of-care facility) in

Person-Centered Assessment Approach

In implementing a person-centered assessment (Hopper, Douglas, & Khayum, 2015) for Mrs. N, we conducted:

a. Otoscopy and an audiometric hearing screening (to check for hearing loss)

b. An interview to understand her concerns while examining conversational interaction and insight into her cognitive functioning (this interview was also conducted via Skype with her daughter to obtain information about her observations and any concerns). This interview revealed that Mrs. N liked to talk about her family and her career as a nurse. She also expressed the desire to be able to do some of her favorite activities including gardening or "helping patients" as a nurse. She had limited insight about her worsening memory or repetitive discourse.

c. Brief, standardized assessment using the MoCA© (to establish an index of the severity of cognitive impairment)

d. Nonstandardized assessment of language and communicative function using select subtests from the ABCD (i.e., Immediate and Delayed Story Recall, Object Naming, Object Description, Reading Comprehension)

e. Nonstandardized assessment using sections of the ECAT, pertinent for Mrs. N

f. Brief observation of Mrs. N in her room and during an art activity session

Results obtained from these tasks are summarized in the box below.

Short-Term and Long-Term Goals

Based on these results, long-term and short-term goals are selected:

Long-Term Goal: Mrs. N will enhance her social and communicative participation by engaging in stimulating recreational activities, social interaction, and communication with family, independently or with minimal cueing.

Short-Term Goal 1: Mrs. N's room environment will be modified to enhance her orientation to time, place, and her daily schedule using an accessible print calendar and a large-font, activity schedule (in her room and also attached to her walker).

Short-Term Goal 2: Mrs. N will be trained using spaced retrieval training (SRT) to use graphic cue cards (located next to her phone and also adhered to the back of her phone), listing the sequence of steps (with pictographs) so she could call her daughter.

Short-Term Goal 3: Mrs. N will be taught to use a memory wallet (with text and photographic stimuli) to initiate conversation about her life and family.

Short-Term Goal 4: Mrs. N will be verbally encouraged (by staff/family) to attend at least one social activity daily.

Additionally, the SLP may collaborate with recreational therapy or activities staff to create opportunities for Mrs. N to engage in therapeutic gardening or flower arranging given that these were some of her cherished activities. Also, Mrs. N could be encouraged to assist the certified nurse aides with measuring blood pressure for other residents given her observed accuracy and automaticity with performing this task (overly familiar to her because of her prior occupation as a nurse). Mrs.

Test/Measure	Result Obtained
Otoscopy and Audiometric Hearing Screen	Outcome: *Pass*
Interview	– Client primary concerns: Boredom, difficulty navigating schedule; difficulty using cell phone to call daughter – Limited insight into altered cognition – Preferred activities and conversation topics identified
MoCA	Score: 16/30 (consistent with mild dementia)
ABCD	
Immediate Story Recall	Score: 7/17
Delayed Story Recall	Score: 1/17
Following Commands	Score: 9/9
Confrontation Naming	Score: 15/20
Object Description	Score: 4/10
Reading Comprehension	Score: 14/15
ECAT	
Evaluating Orientation Cues in Environment	Intervention needed
Evaluating Appliance Use (phone, iPad, TV)	Intervention needed
Evaluating Social Environment	Intervention needed

Client Observation	– Mrs. N enjoyed social interaction
	– Mrs. N accurately checked her own blood pressure
	– Mrs. N was easily frustrated with art activity
	  – Insufficient dementia-friendly instructions
	  – No graphic cues were used to support task completion

N was seen for twelve 45-minute sessions over 4 weeks to address these goals using a combination of SRT and tangible memory aids. The SRT was implemented to sequentially teach Mrs. N to use her memory wallet to initiate biographical conversations and to use her cell phone to call her daughter.

The first procedure was trained by asking Mrs. N, "What can you use to share information about your family?" Mrs. N was to answer, "I can use my memory wallet," followed by using the wallet to share at least one piece of information. To begin a trial, the target question was presented verbally in the same form, followed by stating the correct response and modeling how to use the memory wallet to share information. One minute later, Mrs. N was asked the target question. If she did not recall the answer, the clinician provided the answer and had Mrs. N repeat it. Then, she was asked the same question again 1 minute later and if she answered accurately this time and used the wallet, this question was repeated after 2 minutes (i.e., the recall interval was doubled after every successful recall). In this way, her intentional recall of using her individualized memory wallet was extended over a full therapy session. When she successfully recalled that she could use her memory wallet in conversation beyond a 32-minute recall interval, maintained over two consecutive sessions, she was encouraged to practice sharing details from the wallet to begin a conversation. She maintained her ability to use her memory wallet, over the remainder of therapy, with a gradual increase in the number of facts she shared using this memory wallet.

Subsequently, SRT was used to teach Mrs. N a second procedure in response to the prompt, "Show me how you would make a call to your daughter." Mrs. N had to show four steps on her iPhone—namely, to press the green phone icon 📞, press the Contacts icon 👥, press the name **Anna** (daughter's name), then press 📞 to make the call. During initial training, she was only asked to point to the final icon (so as not to call her daughter on each trial). Repeated SRT shaping trials were conducted until Mrs. N was able to recall this sequence of four steps over the duration of a therapy session and called her daughter successfully at the end of the session with minimal assistance from the clinician. One of the advantages of SRT is that it can be nested within other therapy goals for a client. For instance, if a client is recalling information over a 16-minute interstimulus interval, the clinician can address other therapy goals (i.e., learning to read and review her activity schedule) or carry out language stimulation activities or games.

Acknowledgments. Preparation of this chapter was supported, in part, by grants awarded to the author by the El Camino Hospital and the Gary and Mary West Foundation.

References

Agrell, B., & Dehun, O. (1998). Review: The Clock Drawing Test. *Age and Ageing, 27,* 399–403.

Aguirre, E., Woods, R. T., Spector, A., & Orrell, M. (2013). Cognitive stimulation for dementia: A systematic review of the evidence of effectiveness from randomized controlled trials. *Ageing Research Reviews, 12*(1), 253–262.

Albert, M. S., DeKosky, S. T., Dickson, D., Dubois, B., Feldman, H. H., Fox, N. C., . . . Phelps, C. H. (2011). The diagnosis of mild cognitive impairment due to Alzheimer's disease: Recommendations from the National Institute on Aging-Alzheimer's Association workgroups on diagnostic guidelines for Alzheimer's disease. *Alzheimer's and Dementia, 7,* 270–279.

Alves, J., Magalhães, R., Machado, A., Gonçalves, O. F., Sampaio, A., & Petrosyan, A. (2013). Nonpharmacological cognitive intervention for aging and dementia: Current perspectives. *World Journal of Clinical Cases, 1*(8), 233–241.

Alzheimer's Association. (2018). 2018 Alzheimer's disease facts and figures. *Alzheimer's and Dementia: The Journal of the Alzheimer's Association, 14*(3), 367–429.

American Psychiatric Association. (2013). *Diagnostic and statistical manual of mental disorders* (5th ed.). Washington, DC: Author.

American Speech-Language-Hearing Association. (2005a). *The roles of speech-language pathologists working with dementia-based communication disorders* [Position statement]. Retrieved from http://www.asha .org/policy

American Speech-Language-Hearing Association. (2005b). *The roles of speech-language pathologists working with individuals with dementia: Technical report.* Rockville, MD: Author. Retrieved from http://www.asha .org/policy

American Speech-Language-Hearing Association. (2016). *Scope of practice in speech-language pathology.* Retrieved from http://www.asha.org/policy

Amieva, H., Jacqmin-Gadda, H., Orgogozo, J. M., Le Carret, N., Helmer, C., . . . Dartigues, J. F. (2005). The 9-year cognitive decline before dementia of the Alzheimer type: A prospective population based study. *Brain, 128*(5), 1093–1101.

Arkin, S., & Mahendra, N. (2001). Discourse analysis of Alzheimer's patients before and after intervention: Methodology and outcomes. *Aphasiology, 15*(6), 533–569.

Ash, S., McMillan, C., Gross, R. G., Cook, P., Gunawardena, D., Morgan, B., . . . Grossman, M. (2012). Impairments of speech fluency in Lewy Body Spectrum Disorder. *Brain and Language, 120*(3), 290–302.

Ashida, S. (2000). The effect of reminiscence music therapy sessions on changes in depressive symptoms in elderly persons with dementia. *Journal of Music Therapy, 37*(3), 170–182.

Baddeley, A. D. (1992). Implicit memory and errorless learning: A link between cognitive theory and neuropsychological rehabilitation? In L. R. Squire & N. Butters (Eds.), *Neuropsychology of memory* (2nd ed., pp. 309–314). New York, NY: Guilford Press.

Baddeley, A. D. (2002). The concept of episodic memory. In A. Baddeley & M. A. Conway (Eds.), *Episodic memory: New directions in research* (pp. 1–10). Oxford, UK: Oxford University Press.

Baddeley, A. D., Baddeley, H. A., Bucks, R. S., & Wilcock, G. K. (2001). Attentional control in Alzheimer's disease. *Brain, 124,* 1492–1508.

Ballard, C., Aarsland, D., Francis, P., & Corbett, A. (2013). Neuropsychiatric symptoms in patients with dementias associated with cortical Lewy bodies: Pathophysiology, clinical features, and pharmacological management. *Drugs & Aging, 30,* 603–611.

Baudic, S., Barba, G. D., Thibaudet, M. C., Smagghe, S., Remy, P., & Traykov, L. (2006). Executive function deficits in early Alzheimer's disease and their relations with episodic memory. *Archives of Clinical Neuropsychology, 21*(1), 15–21.

Baumgart, M., Snyder, H. M., Carrillo, M. C., Fazio, S., Kim, H., & Johns, H. (2015). Summary of the evidence on modifiable risk factors for cognitive decline and dementia: A population-based perspective. *Alzheimers Dementia, 11*(6), 718–726.

Bayles, K. A. (1991). Alzheimer's disease symptoms: Prevalence and order of appearance. *Journal of Applied Gerontology, 10*(4), 419–430.

Bayles, K. A., McCullough, K., & Tomoeda, C. K. (2018). *Cognitive-communication disorders of MCI and dementia* (3rd ed.). San Diego, CA: Plural Publishing.

Bayles, K. A., & Tomoeda, C. K. (1993). *The Arizona Battery for Communication Disorders of Dementia.* Tucson, AZ: Canyonlands Publishing.

Bayles, K. A., & Tomoeda, C. K. (1994). *Functional Linguistic Communication Inventory.* Tucson, AZ: Canyonlands Publishing.

Bayles, K. A., Tomoeda, C. K., & Cruz, R. (1999). Performance of Alzheimer's disease patients in judging word relatedness. *Journal of the International Neuropsychological Society, 5,* 668–675.

Bayles, K. A., Tomoeda, C. K., Cruz, R. F., & Mahendra, N. (2000). Communication abilities of individuals with late-stage Alzheimer disease. *Alzheimer Disease and Associated Disorders, 14*(3), 176–181.

Bayles, K. A., Tomoeda, C. K., & Rein, J. A. (1996). Phrase repetition in Alzheimer's disease: Effect of meaning and length. *Brain & Language, 54*(2), 246–261.

Beck, A. T., Steer, R. A., & Brown, G. K. (1996). *Beck Depression Inventory (BDI®-II).* San Antonio, TX: Psychological Corporation.

Bourgeois, M. S. (1990). Enhancing conversation skills in patients with Alzheimer's disease using a prosthetic memory aid. *Journal of Applied Behavior Analysis, 23*(1), 29–42.

Bourgeois, M. S. (1992). Evaluating memory wallets in conversations with patients with dementia. *Journal of Speech and Hearing Research, 35,* 1344–1357.

Bourgeois, M. S. (2013). *Memory and communication aids for people with dementia.* Baltimore, MD: Health Professions Press.

Bourgeois, M. S., Burgio, L. D., Schultz, R., Beach, S., & Palmer, B. (1997). Modifying repetitive verbalizations of community-dwelling patients with Alzheimer's disease. *Gerontologist, 37*(1), 30–39.

Bourgeois, M. S., Camp, C. J., Rose, M., White, B., Malone, M., Carr, J., & Rovine, M. (2003). A comparison of training strategies to enhance use of external aids by persons with dementia. *Journal of Communication Disorders, 36,* 361–378.

Bourgeois, M. S., Lenius, K., Turkstra, L., & Camp, C. (2007). The effects of cognitive teletherapy on reported everyday memory behaviours of persons with chronic traumatic brain injury. *Brain Injury, 21*(12), 1245–1257.

Brush, J., Calkins, M., Bruce, C., & Sanford, J. (2012). *Environment and Communication Assessment Toolkit (ECAT) for dementia care.* Baltimore, MD: Health Professions Press.

Brush, J., & Camp, C. (1998). *A therapy technique for improving memory: Spaced-retrieval.* Beachwood, OH: Menorah Park Center for the Aging.

Cacciatore, F., Napoli, C., Abete, P., Marciano, E., Triassi, M., & Rengo, F. (1999). Quality of life determinants and hearing function in an elderly population: Observatorio Geriatrico Campano Study Group. *Gerontology, 45,* 323–328.

Cairns, N. J., Bigio, E. H., Mackenzie, I. R., Neumann, M., Lee, V. M., Hatanpaa, K. J., . . . Mann, D. M. (2007). Neuropathologic diagnostic and nosologic criteria for frontotemporal lobar degeneration: Consensus of the Consortium for Frontotemporal Lobar Degeneration. *Acta Neuropathologica, 114* (1), 5–22.

Camp, C. J. (1989). Facilitation in learning of Alzheimer's disease. In G. Gilmore, P. Whitehouse, & M. Wykle (Eds.), *Memory and aging: Theory, research, and practice.* New York, NY: Springer.

Camp, C. J. (1999). *Montessori-based activities for persons with dementia* (Vol. 1). Beachwood, OH: Menorah Park Center for Senior Living.

Centers for Medicare and Medicaid Services. (2001, September 25). Transmittal AB-01-135. Medical review of services for patients with dementia. Retrieved from https://www.cms.gov/Regulations-and-Guidance/Guidance/Transmittals/downloads/AB-01-135.pdf

Cherry, K. E., Walvoord, A. G., & Hawley, K. S. (2010). Spaced retrieval enhances memory for a name-face-occupation association in older adults with probable Alzheimer's disease. *Journal of General Psychology, 171*(2), 168–181.

Clare, L., & Jones, R. S. P. (2008). Errorless learning in the rehabilitation of memory impairment: A critical review. *Neuropsychology Review, 18*, 1–23.

Clark, L. J., Gatz, M., Zheng, L., Chen, Y.-L., McCleary, C., & Mack, W. J. (2009). Longitudinal verbal fluency in normal aging, preclinical and prevalent Alzheimer's disease. *American Journal of Alzheimer's Disease and Other Dementias, 24*(6), 461–468.

Collette, F., Delrue, G., Van Der Linden, M., & Salmon, E. (2001). The relationships between executive dysfunction and frontal hypometabolism in Alzheimer's disease. *Brain and Cognition, 47*, 272–275.

Cordell, C. B., Borson, S., Boustani, M., Chodosh, J., Reuben, D., Verghese, J., . . . Fried, L. B. (2013). Alzheimer's Association recommendations for operationalizing the detection of cognitive impairment during the Medicare Annual Wellness Visit in a primary care setting. *Alzheimer's & Dementia, 9*, 141–150.

Cox, D. M., Bayles, K. A., & Trosset, M. W. (1996). Category and attribute knowledge deterioration in Alzheimer's disease. *Brain and Language, 52*(3), 536–550.

Crum, R. M., Anthony, J. C., Bassett, S. S., & Folstein, M. F. (1993). Population-based norms for the Mini-Mental State Examination by age and education level. *Journal of the American Medical Association, 269*(18), 2386–2391.

Desai, M., Pratt, L. A., Lentzner, H., & Robinson, K. N. (2001). *Trends in vision and hearing among older Americans.* Hyattsville, MD: National Center for Health Statistics.

Dickerson, B. C., & Eichenbaum, H. (2010). The episodic memory system: Neurocircuitry and disorders. *Neuropsychopharmacology, 35*(1), 86-104.

Duff, K., Humphreys-Clark, J., O'Bryant, S., Mold, J., Schiffer, R., & Sutker, P. (2008). Utility of the RBANS in detecting cognitive impairment associated with Alzheimer's disease: Sensitivity, specificity, and positive and negative predictive powers. *Archives of Clinical Neuropsychology, 23*(5), 603–612.

Elzaguirre, N. O., Rementeria, G. P., Gonzalez-Torres, M., & Gaviria, M. (2017). Updates in vascular dementia. *Heart and Mind, 1*, 22–35.

Foldi, N. S., Lobosco, J. J., & Schaefer, L. A. (2002). The effect of attentional dysfunction in Alzheimer's disease: Theoretical and practical implications. *Seminars in Speech and Language, 23*(2), 139–150.

Folstein, M. F., Folstein, S. E. & McHugh, P. R. (1975). Mini-Mental State: A practical method for grading the cognitive state of patients for the clinician. *Journal of Psychiatric Research, 12*, 189–198.

Freilich, B. M., & Hyer, L. A. (2007). Relation of the Repeatable Battery for Assessment of Neuropsychological Status (RBANS) to measures of daily functioning in dementia. *Psychological Reports, 101*(1), 119–129.

Fromm, D., & Holland, A. L. (1989). Functional communication in Alzheimer's disease. *Journal of Speech and Hearing Disorders, 54*, 535–540.

Ganguli, M., Blacker, D., Blazer, D. G., Grant, I., Jeste, D. V., . . . Sachdev, P. S. (2011). Classification of neurocognitive disorders in *DSM-5*: A work in progress. *American Journal of Geriatric Psychiatry, 19*(3), 205–210.

Ganguli, M., Tangalos, E. G., Cummings, J. L., & DeKosky, S. T. (2001). Practice parameter: Early Detection of dementia: Mild cognitive impairment (an evidence-based review). Report of the Quality Standards Subcommittee of the American Academy of Neurology. *Neurology, 56*, 1133–1142.

Gibson, F. (1994). What can reminiscence contribute to people with dementia? In J. Bornat (Ed.), *Reminiscence reviewed: perspectives, evaluations, achievements.* Buckingham, UK: Open University Press.

Gorno-Tempini, M. L., Brambati, S. M., Ginex, V., Ogar, J., Dronker, N. F., Marcone, A., . . . Miller, B. L. (2008). The logopenic/phonological variant of primary progressive aphasia. *Neurology, 71*, 1227–1234.

Gorno-Tempini, M. L., Dronker, N. F., Rankin, K. P., Ogar, J. M., Phengarasamy, L., Rosen, H. J., . . . Miller, B. L. (2004). Cognition and anatomy in three variants of primary progressive aphasia. *Annals of Neurology, 55*, 335–346.

Gorno-Tempini, M. L., Hillis, A. E., Weintraub, S., Kertesz, A., Mendez, M., . . . Grossman, M. (2011). Classification of primary progressive aphasia and its variants. *Neurology, 76*(11), 1006–1014.

Grabowski, T. J., & Damasio, A. R. (2004). Definition, clinical features, and neuroanatomical basis of dementia. In M. Esiri, V. Lee, & J. Trojanowski (Eds.), *Neuropathology of dementia* (2nd ed., pp. 1–10). Cambridge, UK: Cambridge University Press.

Hachinski, V. C., Iliff, L. D., Zilhka, E., DuBoulay, G. H., McAlister, V. L., Marshall, J., . . . Symon, L. (1975). Cerebral blood flow in dementia. *Archives of Neurology, 32*(9), 632–637.

Hanson, J. C., & Lippa, C. F. (2009). Lewy body dementia. *International Review of Neurobiology, 84*, 215–228.

Harciarek, M., & Kertesz, A. (2011). Primary progressive aphasias and their contribution to the contemporary knowledge about the brain-language relationship. *Neuropsychology Review, 21*, 271–287.

Harris, J. (1997). Reminiscence: A culturally and developmentally appropriate language intervention for older adults. *American Journal of Speech Language Pathology, 6*(3), 19–26.

Harvan, J. R., & Cotter, V. (2006). An evaluation of dementia screening in the primary care setting. *Journal of the American Academy of Nurse Practitioners, 18*(8), 351–360.

Helm-Estabrooks, N. (2001). *Cognitive Linguistic Quick Test (CLQT)*. San Antonio, TX: Pearson.

Helm-Estabrooks, N. (2017). *Cognitive Linguistic Quick Test-Plus (CLQT™+)*. San Antonio, TX: Pearson.

Henry, M. L., & Grasso, S. M. (2018). Assessment of individuals with primary progressive aphasia. *Seminars in Speech and Language, 39*, 231–241.

Hickey, E. L., & Bourgeois, M. S. (2018). *Dementia: Person-centered assessment and intervention*. New York, NY: Routledge.

Hill, N. L., Kolanowski, A. M., & Gill, D. J. (2011). Plasticity in early Alzheimer's disease: An opportunity for intervention. *Topics in Geriatric Rehabilitation, 27*(4), 257–267.

Hobson, V. L., Hall, J. R., Humphreys-Clark, J. D., Schrimsher, G. W., & O'Bryant, S. E. (2010). Identifying functional impairment with scores from the Repeatable Battery for the Assessment of Neuropsychological Status (RBANS). *International Journal of Geriatric Psychiatry, 25*(2), 525–530.

Hoerster, L., Hickey, E., & Bourgeois, M. (2001). Effects of memory aids on conversations between nursing home residents with dementia and nursing assistants. *Neuropsychological Rehabilitation, 11*, 399–427.

Holland, A. L., Fromm, D., & Wozniak, L. (2018). *Communication Activities of Daily Living–Third Edition (CADL 3)*. Austin, TX: Pro-Ed.

Hopper, T. (2001). Indirect interventions to facilitate communication in Alzheimer's disease. *Seminars in Speech and Language, 22*(4), 305–315.

Hopper, T. (2007). The ICF and dementia. *Seminars in Speech and Language, 28*, 273–282.

Hopper, T., Bayles, K. A., & Kim, E. (2001). Retained neuropsychological abilities of individuals with Alzheimer's disease. *Seminars in Speech and Language, 22*(4), 261–273.

Hopper, T., Bourgeois, M., Pimentel, J., Qualls, C. D., Hickey, E., Frymark, T., Schooling, T. (2013). An evidence-based systematic review on cognitive interventions for individuals with dementia. *American Journal of Speech-Language Pathology, 22*, 126–145.

Hopper, T., Douglas, N., & Khayum, B. (2015). Direct and indirect interventions for cognitive-communication disorders of dementia. *Perspectives on Neurophysiology and Neurogenic Speech and Language Disorders, 25*(4), 142–157.

Hopper, T., Drefs, S., Bayles, K., Tomoeda, C. K., & Dinu, I. (2009). The effects of modified spaced-retrieval training on learning and retention of face-name associations by individuals with dementia. *Neuropsychological Rehabilitation, 5*, 1–22.

Hopper, T., Mahendra, N., Kim, E., Azuma, T., Bayles, K. A., Cleary, S., & Tomoeda, C. K. (2005). Evidence-based practice recommendations for individuals working with dementia: Spaced retrieval training. *Journal of Medical Speech-Language Pathology, 13*(4), xxvii–xxxiv.

Jack, C. R., Wiste, H. J., Vemuri, P., Weigand, S. D., Senjem, M. L., . . . Knopman, D. S. (2010). Brain beta-amyloid measures and magnetic resonance imaging atrophy both predict time-to-progression from mild cognitive impairment to Alzheimer's disease. *Brain, 133*, 3336–3348.

Judge, K., Camp, C., & Orsulic-Jeras, S. (2000). Use of Montessori-based activities for clients with dementia in adult day care: Effects on engagement. *American Journal of Alzheimer's Disease, 15*(1), 42–46.

Kemper, S., LaBarge, E., Farraro, R., Cheung, H., Cheung, H., & Storandt, M. (1993). On the preservation of syntax in Alzheimer's disease. *Archives of Neurology, 50*, 81–86.

Kertesz, A. (2006a). *The banana lady and other stories of curious behavior and speech.* British Columbia, Canada: Trafford.

Kertesz, A. (2006b). *Western Aphasia Battery–Revised.* San Antonio, TX: Pearson.

Kroenke, K., Spitzer, R. L., & Williams, J. B. (2001). The PHQ-9: Validity of a brief depression severity measure. *Journal of General Internal Medicine, 16*(9), 606–661.

Landauer, T. K., & Bjork, R. A. (1978). Optimum rehearsal patterns and name learning. In M. M. Grunenberg, P. S. Morris, & R. N. Sykes (Eds.), *Practice aspects of memory* (pp. 625–632). New York, NY: Academic Press.

Lawton, M. P., Van Haitsma, K., & Klapper, J. A. (1999). *Observed Emotion Rating Scale.* Retrieved from https://www.abramson center.org/media/1199/observed-emo tion-rating-scale.pdf

Lee, S. B., Park, C. S., Jeong, J. W., Choe, J. Y., Hwang, Y. J., Park, C.-A. . . . Kim, K. W. (2009). Effects of spaced retrieval training on cognitive function in Alzheimer's disease patients. *Archives of Gerontology and Geriatrics, 49*, 289–293.

Livingston, G., Sommerlad, A., Orgeta, V., Costafreda, S. G., Huntley, J., Ames, D., . . . Mukadam, N. (2017). Dementia prevention, intervention and care. *Lancet, 390*, 2673–2734.

Mahendra, N. (2001). Direct interventions for improving the performance of individuals with Alzheimer's disease. *Seminars in Speech & Language, 22*(4), 289–302.

Mahendra, N. (2011). Computer-assisted spaced retrieval training of faces and names for persons with dementia. *Nonpharmacological Therapies in Dementia, 1*(3), 217–238.

Mahendra, N. (2012). The logopenic variant of primary progressive aphasia: Effects on linguistic communication. *Perspectives on Gerontology, 17*(2), 50–59.

Mahendra, N., & Apple, A. (2007). Human memory systems: A framework for understanding dementia. *The ASHA Leader, 12*(16), 8–11.

Mahendra, N., Bayles, K. A., & Harris, F. P. (2005). Effect of presentation modality on immediate and delayed recall in individuals with Alzheimer's disease. *American Journal of Speech-Language Pathology, 14*(2), 144–155.

Mahendra, N., & Engineer, N. (2009). Effects of vascular dementia on cognition and linguistic communication: A case study. *Perspectives on Neurophysiology and Neurogenic Speech and Language Disorders, 19*(4), 107–116.

Mahendra, N., Hickey, E., & Bourgeois, M. S. (2018). Cognitive-communicative characteristics: Profiling types of dementia. In E. Hickey & M. S. Bourgeois (Eds.),

Dementia: Person-centered assessment and intervention (pp. 42–80). New York, NY: Routledge.

Mahendra, N., & Hopper, T. (2017). Dementia and related neurocognitive disorders. In I. Papathanasiou, P. Coppens, & C. Potagas (Eds.), *Aphasia and related neurogenic communication disorders* (2nd ed.). Boston, MA: Jones and Bartlett.

Mahendra, N., Hopper, T., Bayles, K., Azuma, T., Cleary, S., & Kim, E. (2006). Evidence-based practice recommendations for working with individuals with dementia: Montessori-based interventions. *Journal of Medical Speech Language Pathology, 14*(1), xv–xxv.

Mahendra, N., Scullion, A., & Hamerschlag, C. (2011). Cognitive-linguistic interventions for persons with dementia: A practitioner's guide to three evidence-based techniques. *Topics in Geriatric Rehabilitation, 27*(4), 1–12.

Malone, M. L., & Loehr, J. (2007, November). *Using Montessori-based reading stories to improve treatment with older adults.* Paper presented at the American Speech-Language-Hearing Association Convention, Boston, MA.

Mariani, E., Monastero, R., & Meocci, P. (2007). Mild cognitive impairment: A systematic review. *Journal of Alzheimer's Disease, 12,* 22-35.

Martin, A., & Fedio, P. (1983). Word production and comprehension in Alzheimer's disease: The breakdown of semantic knowledge. *Brain and Language, 19,* 124–141.

Martyr, A., & Clare, L. (2012). Executive function and activities of daily living in Alzheimer's disease: A correlational metaanalysis. *Dementia and Geriatric Cognitive Disorders, 33*(2–3), 189–203.

Mattis, S., Jurica, P., & Leitten, C. (1991). *Dementia Rating Scale (DRS-2).* Lutz, FL: Psychological Assessment Resources.

McKeith, I., Taylor, J. P., Thomas, A., Donaghy, P., & Kane, J. (2016). Revisiting DLB diagnosis: A consideration of prodromal DLB and of the diagnostic overlap with Alzheimer disease. *Journal of Geriatric Psychiatry & Neurology, 29*(5), 249–253.

McKhann, G., Knopman, D. S., Chertkow, H., Hyman, B. T., Jack, C. R., Kawas, C. H., . . . Phelps, C. H. (2011). The diagnosis of dementia due to Alzheimer's disease: Recommendations from the National Institute on Aging and the Alzheimer's Association workgroup. *Alzheimer's & Dementia, 7*(3), 263–269.

Mehta, K., & Yeo, G. (2016). Systematic review of dementia prevalence and incidence in US race/ethnic populations. *Alzheimer's and Dementia, 13*(1), 72–83.

Mitchell, A. J., & Shiri-Feshki, M. (2009). Rate of progression of mild cognitive impairment to dementia: Meta-analysis of 41 robust inception cohort studies. *Acta Psychiatrica Scandinavica, 119,* 252–265.

Moroney, J. T., Bagiella, E., Desmond, D. W., Hachinski, V. C., Molsa, P. K., Gustafson, L., . . . Tatemichi, T. K. (1997). Meta-analysis of the Hachinski Ischemia Score in pathologically verified dementias. *Neurology, 49,* 1096–1105.

Myers Research Institute. (2008). *Reading Roundtable®.* Retrieved from http://www.myersresearch.org

Nasreddine, Z. S., Phillips, N. A., Bédirian, V., Charbonneau, S., Whitehead, V., Collin I., . . . Chertkow, H. (2005). The Montreal Cognitive Assessment (MoCA): A brief screening tool for mild cognitive impairment. *Journal of the American Geriatric Society, 53,* 695–699.

National Institute on Aging. (2012). *Frontotemporal disorders: Information for patients, families and caregivers.* Retrieved from www.nia.nih.gov/sites/default/files/frontotemporal_disorders_information_for_patients_families_and_caregivers_0.pdf

Nicholas, M., Obler, L., Albert, M., & Helm-Estabrooks, N. (1985). Empty speech in Alzheimer's disease and fluent aphasia. *Journal of Speech and Hearing Research, 28,* 405–410.

Omnibus Budget Reconciliation Act of 1987. Public Law 100-203 (101 Stat. 1330) (1987).

Orsulic-Jeras, S., Schneider, N., & Camp, C. (2000). Special feature: Montessori-based activities for long-term care residents with dementia. *Topics in Geriatric Rehabilitation, 16*(1), 78–91.

Ozgis, S., Rendell, P. G., & Henry, J. D. (2009). Spaced retrieval significantly improves prospective memory performance of cognitively impaired older adults. *Gerontology, 55,* 229–232.

Patient Protection and Affordable Care Act. (2010). *The Patient Protection and Affordable Care Act: Detailed summary.* Retrieved from https://www.dpc.senate.gov/healthreformbill/healthbill04.pdf

Petersen, R. C. (Ed.). (2003). *Mild cognitive impairment: Aging to Alzheimer's disease.* New York, NY: Oxford University Press.

Petersen, R. C. (2016). Mild cognitive impairment. *Continuum, 22*(2), 404–418.

Petersen, R., & Negash, C. (2008). Mild cognitive impairment: An overview. *CNS Spectrums, 13*(1), 45–53.

Population Reference Bureau. (2015). *Population bulletin—Aging in the United States.* Retrieved from https://www.prb.org/wp-content/uploads/2016/01/aging-us-population-bulletin-1.pdf

Population Reference Bureau. (2018). *2018 world population data sheet.* Retrieved from https://www.prb.org/wp-content/uploads/2018/08/2018_WPDS.pdf

Powlishta, K. K., Von Dras, D. D., Stanford, A., Carr, B. B., Tsering, C., Miller, J. P., & Morris, J. C. (2002). The clock drawing test is a poor screen for very mild dementia. *Neurology, 59,* 898–903.

Prince, M., Bryce, R., Albanese, E., Wimo, A., Ribeiro, W., & Ferri, C. P. (2013). The global prevalence of dementia: A systematic review and metaanalysis. *Alzheimer's and Dementia, 9*(1), 63–75.

Randolph, C. (1997). Differentiating vascular dementia from Alzheimer's disease: The role of neuropsychological testing. *Clinical Geriatrics, 5*(8), 77–84.

Randolph, C. (2012). *Repeatable Battery for the Assessment of Neuropsychological Status update.* San Antonio, TX: Pearson.

Randolph, C., Tierney, M., Mohr, E., & Chase, T. (1998). The Repeatable Battery for the Assessment of Neuropsychological Status (RBANS™): Preliminary clinical validity. *Journal of Clinical and Experimental Neuropsychology, 20,* 310–319.

Ripich, D. N., & Terrell, B. (1988). Patterns of discourse cohesion and coherence in Alzheimer's disease. *Journal of Speech and Hearing Disorders, 53,* 8–15.

Román, G. C. (2005). Clinical forms of vascular dementia. In R. H. Paul, R. Cohen, B. R. Ott, & S. Salloway (Eds.), *Vascular dementia: Cerebrovascular mechanisms and clinical management* (pp. 7–21). Totowa, NJ: Humana Press.

Sailor, K., Antoine, M., Diaz, M., Kuslansky, G., & Kluger, A. (2004). The effects of Alzheimer's disease on item output in verbal fluency tasks. *Neuropsychology, 18*(2), 306–314.

Salmon, D. P., & Bondi, M. W. (2009). Neuropsychological assessment of dementia. *Annual Review of Psychology, 60,* 257–282.

Schacter, D. L., Rich, S. A., & Stampp, M. S. (1985). Remediation of memory disorders: Experimental evaluation of the spaced retrieval technique. *Journal of Clinical and Experimental Neuropsychology, 7*(1), 79–96.

Schneider, J. A., Arvanitakis, Z., Bang, W., & Bennett, D. A. (2007). Mixed brain pathologies account for most dementia cases in community-dwelling older persons. *Neurology, 69,* 2197–2204.

Schneider, J. A., Arvanitakis, Z., Yu, L., Boyle, P. A., Leurgans, S. E., & Bennett, D. A. (2012). Cognitive impairment, decline and fluctuations in older community-dwelling subjects with Lewy bodies. *Brain, 135*(10), 3005–3014.

Sheikh, J. I., & Yesavage, J. A. (1986). Geriatric Depression Scale (GDS): Recent evidence and development of a shorter version. *Clinical Gerontologist, 5*(1–2), 165–173.

Sieben, A., Van Langenhove, T., Engelborghs, S., Martin, J. J., Boon, P., Cras, P., . . . Cruts, M. (2012). The genetics and neuropathology of frontotemporal lobar degeneration. *Acta Neuropathologica, 124*(3), 353–372.

Small, J., Kemper, S., & Lyons, K. (1997). Sentence comprehension in Alzheimer's disease: Effects of grammatical complexity, speech rate and repetition. *Psychology & Aging, 12,* 3–11.

Squire, L. R., & Zola-Morgan, S. (1991). The medial temporal lobe memory system. *Science, 253,* 1380–1386.

Sunderland, T., Hill, J. L., Mellow, A. M., Lawlor, B. A., Gundersheimer, J., Newhouse, P.A., Grafman, J.H. (1989). Clock drawing in Alzheimer's disease: A novel measure of dementia severity. *Journal of the American Geriatrics Society, 37*(8), 725–729.

Tariq, S. H., Tumosa, N., Chibnall, J. T., Perry, M. H., & Morley, J. E. (2006). Comparison of the Saint Louis University Mental Status Examination and the Mini-Mental State Examination for detecting dementia and mild neurocognitive disorder: A pilot study. *American Journal of Geriatric Psychiatry, 14,* 900–910.

Threats, T. T. (2008). Use of the ICF for clinical practice in speech-language pathology. *International Journal of Speech-Language Pathology, 10*(1–2), 50–60.

Tomoeda, C. K., & Bayles, K. A. (1993). Longitudinal effects of AD on discourse production. *Alzheimer Disease and Associated Disorders, 7*(4), 223–236.

Tulving, E. (1983). *Elements of episodic memory.* New York, NY: Oxford University Press.

U.S. Census Bureau. (2011). *The older population: 2010 Census briefs.* Retrieved from http://www.census.gov/prod/cen2010/briefs/c2010br-09.pdf

Weinstein, B. E. (2019). The cost of age-related hearing loss: To treat or not to treat? *Speech, Language and Hearing, 22*(1), 9–15. https://doi.org/10.1080/2050571X.2018.1533622

Wilson, B. A., Greenfield, E., Clare, L., Baddeley, A., Cockburn, J., . . . Nannery, R. (2008). *The Rivermead Behavioural Memory Test–3rd Edition (RBMT-3).* London, UK: Pearson Assessment.

World Health Organization. (2001). *International classification of functioning, disability and health.* Geneva, Switzerland: Author.

World Health Organization. (2017). *Global action plan on the public health response to dementia 2017–2025.* Geneva, Switzerland: Author.

Yueh, B., Shapiro, N., MacLean, C. H., & Shekelle, P. G. (2003). Screening and management of adult hearing loss in primary care: Scientific review. *Journal of the American Medical Association, 289,* 1976–1985.

7

Cognitive Communication Disorders of Mild Traumatic Brain Injury

Carole Roth and Kathryn Hardin

Introduction to Mild TBI

Mild traumatic brain injury (mTBI), also referred to as concussion, is a significant concern for civilian, active-duty military, and veteran populations (Soble et al., 2018). It is estimated that every year, 42 to 62 million individuals sustain mTBI or concussions worldwide and perhaps as many as 6 to 8 million individuals in the United States (Dewan et al., 2018; Haarbauer-Krupa et al., 2018; Hunt et al., 2016). Individuals experience a constellation of symptoms, including changes in cognitive, physical, and psychological functioning, likely representing the effects of neural injury. While many recover relatively quickly, for a significant subset, postinjury symptomology lasts for months or even years (Makdissi, Cantu, Johnston, McCrory, & Meeuwisse, 2013). This common condition affects young children, healthy youth, and the elderly. It impacts sports legends, military service members, veterans, and civilians. Individuals describe marked changes in sense of self post-mTBI as well as decreased job and/or academic performance, social engagement, financial stability, and overall quality of life (Iadevaia, Roiger, & Zwart, 2015; Snell, Martin, Surgenor, Siegert, & Hay-Smith, 2017; Stergiou-Kita et al., 2016; Wäljas et al., 2015). The estimated financial burden for medical care and lost time wages is $26 billion per year for new injuries in the United States (Jagnoor & Cameron, 2015).

TBI is recognized as the silent epidemic due to the large incidence, both nationally and worldwide, yet there was limited public awareness, until recently, of the lifelong cognitive, physical, emotional, and social consequences. Despite the rapid expansion of information, and ongoing research related to TBI, mTBI, the most common severity subset of TBI, continues to be little understood in terms of its diagnosis, interventions, and long-term consequences. Not long ago, concussions were considered a virtual "rite of passage," particularly in certain sports. Despite the rapid increase in recognition of its significance, there remain countless mTBIs that go undiagnosed every year as a result of a confluence of underawareness, underreporting, underdiagnosis, and misdiagnosis (Helgeson, 2010). For these reasons, completing a careful assessment of symptoms as soon as possible following injury is important for making an accurate initial diagnosis, especially when the patient may experience alteration of consciousness and be unable to recall what happened at the time of the injury.

Mild TBI/concussion remains the "condition-de-jour" within the current media, leading to an increased awareness, paired with a high likelihood of misinformation for clinicians and the greater public (McCrory et al., 2017). The significant increase in mTBI and potential long-term effects has led to a need for well-trained rehabilitation specialists in both educational and medical settings. This chapter will provide a review of the most current research and evidence-based clinical practice guidelines for evaluating and treating cognitive communication deficits following mTBI. A case study is used to illustrate clinical practices, and supporting resources are made available for additional learning. Due to the high incidence of mTBI associated with military service, the Veteran Affairs/Department of Defense (VA/DoD) has created many clinical recommendations that can be applied to both military and civilian care, and information regarding mTBI in service members and veterans

is incorporated throughout the chapter. Within this chapter, the reader will find a special section devoted to service members and veterans, with extended information specifically regarding military injury.

mTBI Terminology and Presentation Timelines

There are many operationalized definitions of mTBI/concussion found in the literature, each of which has slight variations in terminology or historical philosophy. Key groups working to define mTBI include the American Congress of Rehabilitation Medicine, the American Academy of Neurology, the World Health Organization, Consensus in Sport Group, and the VA/DoD. The breadth of these organizations reflects the far-reaching populations impacted by mTBI and consequently may have some unique characteristics outside the scope of this chapter. That being said, for most speech-language pathologists, it is the unifying features that remain most important to our clinical practice.

Nearly all groups agree that mTBI diagnoses are based on the initial signs and symptoms at the time of the event and that these symptoms are based on physiological disruption within the brain. Diagnosis of mTBI is based on the presence of one or more of the following criteria: (1) change in neurologic function such as possible loss of consciousness, altered mental status, amnesia, or confusion; (2) loss of consciousness (LOC) < 30 minutes; (3) Glasgow Coma Scale score of 13 to 15; and (4) posttraumatic amnesia (PTA) <24 hours. For *uncomplicated* mTBI/concussion, there is an absence of structural changes on standard imaging techniques. For injuries where the above criteria are met and there are positive structural neuroimaging findings, *complicated* mTBI is a commonly used diagnostic label.

Despite centralized diagnostic definitions, there is little consensus over terminology. "Concussion" is the preferred term of the robust sport-related injuries community, though a 2015 article in *BMJ Practical Neurology* recommended that the term "concussion" be avoided and preferred "traumatic brain injury" (Sharp & Jenkins, 2015). The terms "concussion" and "mTBI" have been used interchangeably by many, including the VA/DoD. The VA/DoD further advocates the use of the reference for "patients with a history of mTBI" over the phrase "patients with mTBI" (VA/DoD Guideline, 2016). Newer guidelines in the pediatric literature specifically recommend the use of "mTBI" regardless of neuroimaging findings (Lumba-Brown et al., 2018). Practicing clinicians continue to struggle with what terminology to use with clients, and the lack of consistency in labeling can make interpretation of research studies difficult. In this chapter, which covers both traumatic and sports-related injuries, the terms "concussion" and "mTBI" will be used interchangeably to describe uncomplicated mild injuries.

Additional confusion reigns for individuals with slower-than-average recovery times. Historically, individuals have used the terms "postconcussive symptoms," "postconcussion syndrome" (PCS), and "persistent postconcussion syndrome." These are terms that have marked variability in clinical use, defining the disorder anywhere from 1 day to 6 months postinjury.

The field is trying to unify the concept of protracted recovery as "persistent symptoms" after mTBI, which can be defined by symptoms lasting over 14 days for adults or 30 days for children depending on the age of the individual. While psychology has removed the term "postconcussion syndrome" from the *DSM-5*, this change in terminology is actively in process, and clinicians may continue to receive referrals with these labels for several years to come.

Functional Recovery From mTBI

The idea of recovery after mTBI typically refers to returning to baseline levels of performance in daily activity. This is an important distinction as research indicates that there may continue to be changes in cellular performance even after an individual feels well. However, in terms of recovery, our profession will consider our client's care and recovery in terms of daily functionality.

Mild TBI is typically a transient event with the normal recovery trajectory for a single mTBI considered to be back to full function occurring quickly (Soble et al., 2018). Early data from collegiate and professional athletics indicated that most adults recovered from acute concussion within 7 to 10 days and children took only slightly longer (Eisenberg, Andrea, Meehan, & Mannix, 2013; McCrea et al., 2013). The timeline has shifted slightly with improved research. Today a typical recovery for adults occurs within 14 days of injury and within 1 month for children; however, there is a significant subset of individuals who will have a more protracted recovery (Guerriero, Hawash,

Pepin, Wolff, & Meehan, 2015). The physical and cognitive development inherent in childhood may be slowing the neural resilience experienced by older populations.

Functional recovery statistics continue to vary widely with some findings across population groups showing that up to 40% or greater will have persistent symptoms several months to years following mTBI (Makdissi et al., 2013; Zemek et al., 2016). Studies of veterans with histories of mTBI have found that 7.5% to 40% have at least three postinjury symptoms more than 3 months postinjury (Morissette et al., 2011; Schneiderman et al., 2008; Terrio et al., 2009). It is important to note that these recovery statistics vary widely and may have been impacted by unsuccessful clinical care models. Over time, the symptoms are likely increasingly influenced by co-occurring psychological, social, and environmental factors (Soble et al., 2018). Psychoeducation and gradual return to activity are key to successful return to functional status (VA/DoD, 2016) and improved clinical intervention will likely speed up recovery for many individuals. At this point, best estimates remain that at any time, 10% to 30% of individuals are living with persistent symptoms of mTBI. Moreover, individuals seen in speech-language pathology (SLP) outpatient settings are likely those who are experiencing a more protracted recovery profile. It is also important to consider that chronic symptoms of mTBI reported by patients include changes in their cognition, behavior, and physical functioning (Dikmen, Corrigan, Levin, Machamer, Stiers, & Weisskopf, 2009; McAllister et al., 2012; Yamamoto, DeWitt, & Prough, 2018). The role of the SLP will almost certainly shift depending on the time since injury for the client.

Neurobiopsychosocial Modeling

A neurobiopsychosocial model of acute and persistent symptoms in concussion accounts for the unique variables that impact one's overall success postinjury (McCrea & Manley, 2018), meaning that it is critical to consider the neurologic, biologic, psychological, and social factors when treating mTBI. Wäljas et al. (2015) concluded, "The manifestation of post-concussion symptoms likely represents the cumulative effect of multiple variables, such as genetics, mental health history, current life stress, general medical problems, chronic pain, depression, and substance abuse" (p. 544). For example, the high comorbidity of mental health conditions among service members/veterans is an important consideration. It has been estimated that as many as 89% of veterans with a history of TBI receiving VA services were also diagnosed with a comorbid mental health condition (Taylor et al., 2012). Clinicians need to consider an individual's perceptions of illness and wellness, external variables such as media attention, workplace environments, school support systems, and early parent education as each of these has been shown to impact clinical outcomes (Mah, Hickling, & Reed, 2018; Snell, Macleod, & Anderson, 2016).

Neurobiopsychosocial modeling is directly relevant to protracted recovery in mTBI. Risk factors for ongoing symptoms include preinjury factors, including lower education, female sex, lower military rank, previous TBI or other neurologic events, history of learning disability, attention deficit disorder, and personal or family histories of migraine/behavioral health (Covassin, Elbin, Harris, Parker, & Kontos, 2012; Dick, 2009; McCrory et al., 2017; Mollayeva, El-Khechen-Richandi, & Colantonio, 2018; Sandel, Schatz, Goldberg, & Lazar, 2017; Scheenen et al., 2017; Zemek et al., 2016). There are also peri-injury factors to consider, such as context and mechanism of injury, and postinjury factors, including emerging psychiatric diagnoses and possible secondary gain (Carroll et al., 2004; Cooper et al., 2011; Lange, Edmed, Sullivan, French, & Cooper, 2013). As an example, there are higher estimates of persistent symptoms among service members and veterans with a history of multiple TBI events, and those with concomitant mental health conditions such as depression and posttraumatic stress disorder (PTSD) (O'Neil et al., 2013). While these are indeed many factors to consider in a client's health history, a strong clinical interview will help guide clinicians to incorporate these relevant variables.

Epidemiology and Causality

An estimated 69 million individuals sustain TBI every year worldwide, with approximately 90% of TBIs being mild in nature (Dewan et al., 2018). In the United States, the incidence of mTBI remains surprisingly hard to capture. The primary problem associated with estimating the incidence of mTBI is that the "mild" nature of the injury directly impacts when and if an individual pursues medical care.

Individuals seen in emergency rooms typically have experienced falls (44%) with mixed mechanisms of falls, assault, and motor vehicle accidents combined for nearly 70%. These same individuals tracked by the Nationwide Emergency Department Sample from the Healthcare Cost and Utilization Project have found that the majority of these mTBIs occur in young children (<4 years), males aged 16 to 24, and women over 65 years (Cancelliere, Cornonado, Taylor, & Xu, 2017). A known problem with this data set from the Centers for Disease Control and Prevention (CDC) is that millions of mTBIs every year are either treated outside of emergency settings or receive no medical care at all (Taylor, Bell, Breiding, & Xu, 2017). In fact, it has been estimated that 50% of individuals with a history of mTBI never receive medical care, whether that is related to geographic access problems, financial constraints with medical care, or rapid recovery of symptoms (Voss, Connolly, Schwab, & Scher, 2015). When looking beyond emergency departments only, Haarbauer-Krupa and colleagues (2018) found that sports injuries accounted for the majority of pediatric concussion (70%), with very few patients under the age of 5 (4.5%). This discrepancy is at least in part related to the fact that the Haarbauer-Krupa study included numerous sites of TBI care and that families rely on front-line practitioners such as pediatricians (53.4%) or specialty clinics (27%), rather than emergency department (ED)/urgent care only (16.6%). When combining the data from the CDC estimating annual incidence at 2.5 million (807.9 per 100,000 Americans) with that of Haarbauer-Krupa et al. (2018), overall U.S. mTBI incidence rates may be more accurately estimated at an additional 2- to 3-fold, perhaps 6 to 8 million concussions per year. It is clear that additional research on the incidence of mTBI is needed.

In addition to challenges with incidence, prevalence estimates are also difficult to discern. Although mTBI has been considered a relatively benign injury with rapid and complete recovery occurring within days to weeks following injury, some civilians, service members, and veterans report persistent symptoms several months to years following mTBI (Bolzenius et al., 2015; Helmick & Members of the Consensus Conference, 2010; Mooney & Speed, 2001). Therefore, determining prevalence of mTBI remains unclear in the literature (Carlson et al., 2011; Carroll et al., 2004; Kristman et al., 2008; Rabinowitz et al., 2015).

Inherent in the epidemiology of mTBI are considerations of causality and prognosis. There are three main categories of mTBI: sport-related, mixed-mechanism, and military-related mTBI. Sport-related or sport-related concussion (SRC) typically refers to mTBI sustained in athletic training or competition and, depending on the level of sport, may imply individuals with a generally healthy physical condition. Mixed-mechanism (MM) is a catchall category that describes traumatic mTBI cases identified from hospital emergency departments and includes falls, motor vehicle accidents, assaults, and other related causalities. Mechanism of injury seems to be a factor with longer recoveries occurring following MM mTBI compared with SRC (Seiger, Goldwater, & Deibert, 2015). Military-related mTBI can have numerous cau-

salities, including intracranial pressure changes from blast waves and blunt-force trauma. These injuries can occur in combat but also in the daily operations of a military professional. As with MM injuries, military-related injuries may co-occur with psychological stressors, contributing to greater levels of disability than civilians with a history of mTBI (MacDonald et al., 2014; Soble et al., 2018). Learn more about the blast injuries in the special military-care section. Clinicians should always find out about etiology of the injury and consider it as a possible factor related to the prognosis for a patient.

Neurophysiology of Concussion

Giza and Hovda (2001) published a pivotal paper reporting neurophysiological changes of concussion in animal models, essentially creating impact injuries that are similar to sport-related concussion. Understanding the cellular function after injury can be a valuable teaching tool to help explain symptoms and dysfunction with patients. Early on, there is a significant disruption in the ionic balance of the neurons with potassium rushing out of the cells, while sodium and calcium flood into the cells. At the same time, excess amounts of the neurotransmitter glutamate are released. Dysfunction in the sodium-potassium pump and too much glutamate ultimately results in toxic synapses and slowed communication between neurons. Shortly after injury, the brain temporarily goes into a "hyperactive" state, requiring lots of energy and resources quickly, followed by an extended 7- to 10-day decrease in cerebral blood flow and hypometabolism. This period of hypoactivity has been found to be even longer in adolescence (Grady, Master, & Gioia, 2012). These immediate physiologic changes result in many of the acute symptoms associated with mTBI, such as slow processing and motor changes.

In addition to impairments in cellular communication, microstructural changes occur. Diffuse axonal injury remains a hallmark of mTBI, with axons being stretched or broken as a result of the linear and rotational forces on the cells. Axonal injury will not necessarily result in neuronal death; however, the impaired synaptic communication can result in increased dysfunction in the frontal lobe, cerebellum, and corpus callosum (Choe & Giza, 2015). Unmyelinated cells are particularly susceptible to damage as they lack the structural support provided by the myelin. It has been hypothesized that one reason for greater deficits in children postinjury is related to their incomplete myelination (Dennis, Babikian, Giza, Thompson, & Asarnow, 2017). Some researchers have argued that in addition to the diffuse axonal injury model of mTBI, changes in thalamic structure and function may also occur (Grossman & Inglese, 2016). The thalamus acts as a central relay station for sensory gating and processing and also has cortical projections tied to many cognitive functions, including language and working memory (Chien, Cheng, & Lenz, 2017). Edema, or inflammation, postinjury can also occur. Early work documented rapid edema following repeated mTBI (Kelly et al., 1991). This is an important con-

sideration as ongoing research indicates that neurophysiologic functioning at the cellular level may remain impaired after behavioral functioning has returned to baseline (Kamins et al., 2017; McCrory et al., 2017).

The extent to which the neurological system remains vulnerable to repeated injury during the acute phase of recovery from mTBI, or if an increased vulnerability exists, remains unknown. The acute stage is defined as time of injury to 7 days postinjury (Management of Concussion/mTBI Working Group, 2009), with additional timelines for subacute and chronic or persistent symptoms. Most of what is known about cumulative effects of TBI comes from civilian athletes (Soble et al., 2018), though this research remains in its infancy. Much remains to be learned about the long-term effects of multiple blast exposures, blast-plus-blunt injuries, and non-combat-related concussions preceding military service and during military service on the brain. The military continues to fund extensive research to further the understanding of the effects of blasts on the brain and how best to diagnose the neurotrauma of mTBI.

Clinical Neuroimaging for mTBI

In the acute stage of traumatic brain injury, computed tomography (CT) and conventional magnetic resonance imaging (MRI) are used to rule out severe complications such as skull fracture, intracranial hemorrhage, and brain edema. In mTBI, conventional CT and MRI are frequently insensitive to more subtle changes in the brain such as diffuse axonal injury (Shenton et al., 2012), and conventional imaging modalities do not provide accurate information relevant to long-term prognosis (Iverson, 2005; Le & Gean, 2009; Mittl et al., 1994). Consequently, it is very common that most individuals seen in an emergency department will not have experienced structural imaging. A review of the research using more advance neuroimaging techniques to diagnose objective physiological correlates of persistent symptoms, regardless of the technology, demonstrates abnormalities associated with mTBI in some participants. These neuroimaging techniques include diffusion tensor imaging (DTI), magnetization transfer imaging (MTI), magnetic resonance spectroscopy (MRS), magnetic source imaging (MSI), functional magnetic resonance imaging (fMRI), positron emission tomography (PET), and single-photon emission computed tomography (SPECT). Belanger et al. (2007) suggest that there is "particular promise evident with fMRI, PET, and SPECT scanning, as demonstrated by associations between brain activation and clinical outcomes" (p. 5). There are no current or definitive biomarkers, neuroimaging procedures, or neuropsychological tests that can determine a remote event resulted in a mTBI (Vanderploeg et al., 2012).

In light of the limited diagnostic and prognostic benefit of neural imaging studies, the Defense Centers of Excellence, in their July 2013 Clinical Recommendations report, state, "Neuroimaging is not recommended as part of a routine evaluation for all service members following mTBI. A physical exam, individual history and provider judgment should be combined to develop the best evaluation and treatment plan for each individual" (Defense Centers of Excellence, 2013, p. 1). The report goes on to say that the clinical diagnosis of mTBI is based on a history of a traumatic injury in the context of a change in alteration in consciousness. With current imaging standards and practices, most individuals with a diagnosis of mTBI will have normal imaging findings, and this should not deter the need for specialty referral when clinically indicated. These findings are echoed in civilian medicine. Neuroimaging is not recommended as part of a routine evaluation for individuals following mTBI, even in emergency medicine; however, neuroimaging may be recommended medically for the evaluation of any individuals with clinical red flags: progressive declining level of consciousness, focal neurological deficits, failure to recognize people, disorientation, seizures, worsening headache, and repeated vomiting.

Physical and Emotional Changes Associated With mTBI

Both acute and persistent symptoms of mTBI can be classified broadly into three categories: physical, emotional, and cognitive. Physical symptoms include headaches, sleep disturbance, dizziness, balance problems, fatigue, vision changes/light sensitivity, and tinnitus. Emotional changes involve irritability, anxiety, depression, posttraumatic stress, and mood swings. Cognitive symptoms include trouble concentrating, attention problems, poor memory, slowed thinking, and word-finding difficulty when speaking.

Headache

Headache pain remains the most reported symptom post-mTBI and one that often persists the longest (Stillman, Madigan, & Alexander, 2016). One study of 95 soldiers with histories of mTBI identified 166 distinct types of postconcussive headaches and posttraumatic headache symptoms, and not surprisingly, presence of headaches has been tied to poor performance on neurocognitive testing (Finkel et al., 2017; Kontos, Sufrinko, Womble, & Kegel, 2016). Pain is a common comorbidity among service members/veterans with a history of combat-related mTBI and headache is the most frequent pain complaint reported (Evans, 1994). The prevalence of headache pain is 90% (Lew et al., 2006) with the most common types categorized as tension, migraine, and a combination of migraine and tension type.

Dizziness and Balance Problems

"Dizziness," a term often used to describe multiple symptoms, including vertigo, disequilibrium (unsteadiness or imbalance), and lightheadedness, is a common symptom following mTBI. Postconcussive dizziness has multiple causes; therefore, it can be clinically challenging to diagnose and treat (Akin et al., 2017; Lau et al., 2011). It frequently occurs following mTBI across causal mechanisms. The etiology for dizziness or imbalance following mTBI has been linked to white matter abnormalities, diffuse axonal injury in the brain, and central and peripheral vestibular damage, such as inner ear damage from blast exposure. Estimates are that between 30% and 65% of people with TBI suffer from dizziness and disequilibrium (Akin et al., 2017). Management for persistent vestibular dysfunction requires an examination of hearing, balance, coordination, and vision that may be performed by a variety of specialists, including neurology, otolaryngology, audiology, ophthalmology or optometry, and vestibular therapy. Once the etiology of the vestibular dysfunction is defined, then an appropriate treatment plan is implemented. For example, the most common cause of posttraumatic peripheral vestibular dysfunction is benign paroxysmal positional vertigo, with canalith repositioning therapy and vestibular rehabilitation as effective treatments, (Akin et al., 2017). Vestibular intervention is becoming a mainstay of mTBI rehabilitation, frequently within the first week postinjury. While historically, individuals post-mTBI who had symptoms of dizziness and imbalance required a longer recovery period (Chamelian & Feinstein, 2004), this may shift with improved intervention practices.

Visual Changes

In mTBI, impairments in the visual system are well documented. Hypersensitivity to light (photophobia) and feelings of increased visual noise remain hallmark symptoms that can persist for months (Yuhas, Shorter, McDaniel, Earley, & Hartwick, 2017). This common experience led in part to the early, and erroneous, treatment recommendations that individuals should spend extended time in the darkness and persistently wear sunglasses to decrease overall symptom presence. Newer research indicated that these strategies for accommodations long term may have had iatrogenically harmful effects (Silverberg & Iverson, 2013). Impairments in oculomotor functioning are also extremely common post-mTBI, and it is estimated that as many as 90% of patients present with some form of dysfunction (Thiagarajan, Ciuffreda, & Ludlam, 2011). Common impairments occur in convergence and tracking, and somewhat rarer occurrences such as a fourth cranial nerve palsy and diplopia. This disruption directly impacts daily skills like including reading and related academic/work activities requiring near-point convergence. It is reportedly a primary limiting factor in successful return to work (Capó-Aponte et al., 2017; Swanson et al., 2017). Interestingly, a consistent presentation of visual dysfunction has been found for individuals exposed to blast and those with civilian impact-related injuries, and it has been hypothesized that these deficits can remain even at 1 year postinjury (Heitger et al., 2006). Oculomotor dysfunction post-mTBI has responded well to interventions, and this therapeutic change has been found to be both effective and enduring (Thiagarajan & Ciuffreda, 2015).

Auditory Changes

Changes within the auditory system also occur postconcussion even in the absence of injury to the ear or temporal lobe. Hypersensitivity to noise (hyperacusis) is a common occurrence in all types of mTBI (Callahan et al., 2018; Chorney, Suryadervara, & Nicholas, 2017), though also a common symptom in healthy adults (Callahan et al., 2018). Dischinger and colleagues (2009) found that 27% of patients seen in an emergency department reported hyperacusis early on and that noise sensitivity was a significant predictor of ongoing symptoms 3 months postinjury. Similar studies have found hyperacusis to be predictive of severity of symptoms and speed of return to sport and that hypersensitivity can develop over time (Chorney et al., 2017; Landon, Shepherd, Stuart, Theadom, & Freundlich, 2012). Both hypersensitivity to noise and tinnitus impact the overall functioning and quality of life for individuals post-mTBI as their presence likely increase levels of discomfort, fatigue, and cognitive overwhelm as well as any impact on audiologic function.

Tinnitus and auditory sensitivity can be experienced in isolation, but individuals also report decreased auditory functioning in social situations. Vander Werff (2016) in an excellent review article that reported audiological consequences of mTBI in the WHO International Classification of Functioning, Disability and Health (ICF), including impairments in communication such as understanding speech in noise, conversation, and complex interpersonal interactions. A significant amount of daily interaction can occur in noisy environments such as restaurants, stores, workplaces, athletic facilities, and schools. Decreased functioning in noisy environments (speech-in-noise) has been found post-mTBI in adults exposed to blast (Gallun, Papesh, &

Lewis, 2017) and in 84% of adults with uncomplicated, community-acquired mTBI (Hoover et al., 2017). Auditory processing disorder (APD), a condition where the integration and interpretation of sound becomes disordered, is estimated to be as high as 85% to 89% in certain populations post-mTBI (Oleksiak et al., 2012). Although there has been less investigation in APD outside military medicine, deficits have been documented in SRC and MM as well (Atcherson & Steele, 2016; Turgeon, Champoux, Lapore, Leclerc, & Ellemberg, 2011). Explore additional information related to hearing changes in service members in the special section.

Sleep

Changes in sleep patterns are a common occurrence after mTBI. Fatigue, insomnia, hypersomnia, and daytime sleepiness changes are consistently listed as some of the most prominent characteristics after concussion (Eisenberg, Meehan, & Mannix, 2014). While the exact prevalence is unknown, sleep changes after mTBI have been estimated to be between 30% and 70% (Viola-Saltzman & Watson, 2012; Wiseman-Hakes, Colantonio, & Gargaro, 2009). Insomnias and hypersomnias are both reported in the literature, with dysfunction tied to increased deficits in energy, pain, cognitive, and psychological functioning (Mah et al., 2018; Ouellet, Beaulieu-Bonneau, & Morin, 2015). Raikes and Schaefer (2016) found an increase in sleep shortly after injury but a decrease in total sleep time by 1 month after. Individuals without concussion have been found to test with neurocognitive impairments when

lacking sufficient sleep (Sufrinko et al., 2015). Poor sleep is also a known modifier of neurocognitive assessment, and consideration of sleep remains critical in the broader characterization of mTBI symptomatology.

Posttraumatic Stress Disorder, Depression, and Other Psychological Health Concerns

Changes in behavioral health and emotional regulation are both acute and persistent factors in mTBI. As noted above, individuals with histories of needs related to psychological health may be more likely to experience mTBI as well as have a slower recovery. Preexisting issues related to behavioral health are a key area of assessment for all individuals regardless of age or mechanism of injury. Changes in psychological health are more common in military injuries but occur in SRC as well. Of critical clinical importance, the influence of depression, anxiety, and trauma response on cognitive function may facilitate referrals to speech-language pathology when behavioral health needs may be of equal or potentially primary importance.

It is unquestionable that the most robust literature on psychological health and mTBI comes from military medicine, particularly related to posttraumatic stress disorder (PTSD). Briefly, PTSD requires that an individual experience directly or be personally impacted by a stressful event. In response to this event, an individual may reexperience this event or be emotionally triggered by situations in daily life. Subsequently, an individual often avoids those triggers and becomes increasingly isolated.

These are all behaviors that are caused by the physiological response to the traumatic event, but behaviors such as sleep disorders, aggression, and cognitive dysfunction can become worse over time. PTSD, depression, and other psychological diagnoses are commonly reported following military deployments to combat regions, and there is clear overlap with many symptoms of mTBI that are also symptoms of changes in psychological health. Slowed processing speed, decreased memory and attention, and changes in initiation and follow-through can all occur in each of these disorders, and this overlap remains challenging, if not impossible, for clinicians to parse out. The importance of behavioral health in veterans and service members can be critical in clinical care and, therefore, there is extended discussion on this topic at the end of the chapter.

The civilian literature describes early psychological changes following mTBI, including frustration, irritability, dysthymia, increased anxiety/restlessness, apathy, and emotional lability (Eisenberg et al., 2013 McCrory et al., 2017). Significantly higher levels of depression have been found in male and female young adult athletes, with significant increases in symptom scores by day 2 (Kontos, Covassin, Elbin, & Parker, 2012), though not consistently with diagnosable depressive disorders. Elevated levels of anxiety have also been found in collegiate athletes within the first week post-SRC and for adults with MM injuries (Wood, O'Hagan, Williams, McCabe, & Chadwick, 2014; Yang, Peek-Asa, Covassin, & Torner, 2015), which parallels animal model literature that mTBI may induce physiologic changes in behavioral health

systems. Persistent symptomatology nearly always has components of deficits related to behavioral health, even if an individual has not had preexisting needs related to psychological well-being. When someone continues to try to function in the face of persistent physical and cognitive deficits, emotional deficits may manifest themselves as an after-effect to the TBI.

Cognitive Communication Changes Associated With mTBI

Cognitive communication deficits encompass difficulty with any aspect of communication and language that is affected by a disruption of cognition (ASHA, 2005a, 2005b). Deficits in cognitive processes, including attention, perception, memory, organization, and executive function, may impact an individual's behavioral self-regulation, social interaction, academic and vocational performance. Semistructured interviews and symptom checklists can be used to identify cognitive communication complaints frequently reported following mTBI. The most frequently described concerns described include changes in concentration and attention; processing speed; working memory; executive function; social communication; language, including auditory comprehension, word-finding, and reading skills; and stuttering.

Attention

Deficits in concentration and attention post-mTBI are commonly reported

(Cicerone, 1996; Ozen, Itier, Preston, & Fernandes, 2013). Impairments in arousal are a highly visible but relatively rare sign of acute concussion, with loss of consciousness occurring in less than 10% of individuals. For most, impairments in attention seem more functionally impaired such as difficulties maintaining concentration, losing train of thought, and problems focusing on workplace and academic tasks. In terms of persistent symptoms, impairments in both visual and verbal attention have been found (Halterman et al., 2005 Howell, Osternig, Van Donkelaar, Mayr, & Chou, 2013). Impairments in sustained attention are also described as being problematic, though the literature base for these changes postconcussion is less robust. Inconsistent patterns of hyper/hypoactivation had been found in fMRI data for other attention tasks, implying that while there are clear changes in resources allocation post-mTBI (Mayer et al., 2012), additional research is needed to clarify patterns of attentional deficits.

Processing Speed

Objective assessments of processing speed indicated slowing beginning immediately after injury and that slowing may continue for an extended period of time. Impaired reaction time may be the clearest sign of slowed processing speed, with examples of decreased speed of finger tapping or speed of stick drop (Del Rossi, 2017; Eckner, Kutcher, Broglio, & Richardson, 2014). In the field of speech-language pathology, interpretation of motor reaction time is outside of the standard scope of practice, and additional specialized training would be required. Rather, as a

clinical standard, SLPs look to processing speed tasks that load more heavily on cognitive resources like computerized response time, cancellation tasks, speeded verbal-response tasks, or complex multistep tasks such as are found in the *Functional Assessement of Verbal Reasoning and Executive Strategies* (Isaki & Turkstra, 2000; MacDonald, 1998). In one of the most creative studies of functional, long-term changes in processing speed, Wasserman and colleagues (2015) compared the batting statistics of Major League Baseball players who were placed on the injured list after mTBI with players who were not playing due to a nonmedical condition, like bereavement. Four weeks after returning to play, the injured athletes had lower batting averages, slugging percentages, and on-base percentages than the uninjured players. The deconditioning of the athletes was comparable, but the injured players had an additional factor that their processing speed of the pitches or swings remained impaired. Moreover, the athletes from 2011 and later years had "returned to baseline" on standardized computerized testing, including measures of reaction time.

Memory and Learning

Immediate impairments in working memory (WM) are nearly universally agreed upon when considering acute concussion in people and animal models (Creed et al., 2011; Milman et al., 2005). Young adolescents and college students have shown deficits in verbal and visual working memory 3 to 5 days after injury, with verbal dysfunction being worse (Covassin, Stearne, & Elbin, 2008; Green, Keightley, Lobaugh,

Dawson, & Mihailidis, 2018). While both verbal and visual WM are compromised long term for at least a subset of individuals post-mTBI, the impact of dysfunction in the verbal domain is likely more impactful. Verbal WM directly impacts comprehension of language as well as verbal production (Acheson & Mac-Donald, 2009), with communication needs shifting rapidly based on conversational interactions. As most individuals live in a highly verbal world, even mild dysfunction in verbal WM will directly impact academic, vocational, and social success.

In acute concussion, amnesia and duration of posttraumatic amnesia remains a diagnostic factor differentiating mTBI from other conditions (McCrory et al., 2017), and reports have noted up to 79% of individuals experiencing changes in memory (Hall, Hall, & Chapman, 2005). Traditional memory deficits have been linked to acute concussion, with impairments in verbal memory encoding and learning efficiency (Lezak, Howieson, Loring, & Fischer, 2004; Nolin, 2006). Individuals with a history of mTBI improved less from practice effects of repeat trials, implying that the learning curve for individuals postconcussion may be diminished (O'Jile et al., 2006). This is recognizable on tasks outside of traditional memory assessments, including academic learning struggles after mTBI. Delayed recall, comprising storage and retrieval domains, is frequently impaired after mTBI though for various reasons. At times, individuals have decreased recall as initial encoding is limited and the total information recalled is also diminished, but it remains an encoding deficit, rather than a decay of information over time. Some individuals also seem to experience deficits in delayed recall of new information (Keightley et al., 2014). Episodic memory, such as memory for events, is frequently reported as decreased after injury and can negatively impact people's quality of life (Brunger et al., 2014; Daggett, Bakas, Buelow, Habermann, & Murray, 2013; Mansfield et al., 2015).

Executive Function

Early on, it was known that executive functions can be impaired after mTBI and impairments in executive function are routinely cited in qualitative literature (Brooks, Fos, Greve, & Hammond, 1999; Brunger et al., 2014; Daggett et al., 2013; Stergiou-Kita, et al., 2016). Specific deficits noted included planning, organization, emotional regulation, and decision making, though self-awareness is often considered to be a strength of the individuals post-mTBI. Changes in executive functioning have been reported in children, adolescents, and adults in acute mTBI and in persistent presentations as well (Howell et al., 2013). Seichepine and colleagues (2013) evaluated current and retired elite football players with a mixed history of concussion and subconcussive blows using a self-report measure called the Behavioral Rating Inventory of Executive Function–Adult. Significant changes at all levels of executive function were found when compared with unexposed controls, and the degree of impairment increased with age. Deficits included changes in inhibition, shifting, emotional control, planning/organization, initiation, and task monitoring.

Social Cognition/Social Communication

There is broad overlap between the concepts of social cognition and social communication as both deal directly with "the capacity to attend to, recognize, and interpret interpersonal cues that guide social behavior" (McDonald, 2013, p. 231). All social interactions are interdependent on communication messages between partners, whether intended or not, and hence the unextractable overlap between social cognition and social communication. Social communication skills require rapid evaluation of the context and listener, prior to initiating an appropriate topic, providing sufficient but not excessive relevant details, controlling utterance length to enable others to comment, and use of both verbal and nonverbal methods to convey stated and implied meaning (Burgess & Turkstra, 2010). In mTBI, there is emerging evidence from young pediatrics that social communication is impacted after injury in several ways. Parents and young children with histories of mTBI were found to have less mutual engagement, less success in reading interpersonal cues, poorer communication shifting and flow, and overall less successful engagement than interactions with uninjured children (Lalonde, Bernier, Beaudoin, Gravel, & Beauchamp, 2018). These interactions were also found to be more negative in tone than those with uninjured children. Young children with mTBI were found to have reduced emotional recognition of conversational partners and, at 2 years postinjury, decreased theory of mind (Bellerose, Bernier, Beaudoin, Gravel, & Beauchamp, 2017; D'Hondt

et al., 2017). There are no published works that specifically evaluate social cognition in adolescents or adults postconcussion, though there are numerous articles that cite changes in social participation, social success, and increased isolation (Childers & Hux, 2016; Finebilt et al., 2016; Snell et al., 2017; Sveen et al., 2013). Speech-language pathologists have reported success treating social communication deficits after mTBI in peer-focused groups (Hardin & Kelly, 2019; Schneider & Van Auken, 2018). Refer to Table 7–1.

Language Presentation in mTBI

Changes in communication have been largely overlooked in mTBI, though there is an evolving evidence base. Impairments in word finding have the strongest literature, and many other areas have qualitative and emerging quantitative research. Despite a limited evidence base for communication changes in mTBI, changes in functional auditory comprehension, verbal expression, reading, and writing have been documented.

Deficits in auditory comprehension are well documented in moderatesevere TBI (Kewman, Yanus, & Kirsch, 1988; Nicholas & Brookshire, 1995), but the presence/absence of auditory comprehension changes in mTBI remains minimally explored. Changes in auditory functioning such as impairments in speech-in-noise or changes in timing and perception of pitch likely impact auditory comprehension, the ability to interpret receptive auditory communication. Two articles have targeted the assessment of auditory comprehension

Table 7–1. Cognitive Communication Domains

Domain	Functional Examples
Attention	Difficulties paying attention, easily distracted, struggling to follow conversations, poor concentration when reading or watching a movie, limited multitasking, difficulties shifting between tasks, problems with sustained attention
Processing speed	Feeling slowed down or foggy, problems following a conversation and actively contributing thoughts, taking phone messages
Working memory	Walking into a room to get something and forgetting what it was; losing track mid-conversation
Memory and learning	Forgetting personal items at home (e.g., cell phone, wallet); forgetting shopping items, losing personal items; forgetting appointments and social events, remembering people's names
Executive function	Difficulties planning, skipping appointments, drinking alcohol while taking medications, poor choices, time management deficits, excessive spending
Social cognition/ communication	Problems in group conversation, poor turn taking, excessive talking, speaking one's mind without filtering; decreased understanding of sarcasm, social isolation
Receptive language	Functional auditory comprehension, decreased reading speed, rereading materials, decreased reading comprehension
Expressive language	Word finding, difficulties organizing and expressing ideas either verbally or in writing
Speech	Diagnosable speech deficits seem to be rare unless in acute injury. Psychogenic stuttering should be considered for fluency changes.

in adults using a traditional linguistic measure, *the Computerized Revised Token Test*, with motor responses (Bialuńska & Salvatore, 2017; Salvatore et al., 2017). While overall results varied slightly, adolescents and adults with SRC were consistently slower than healthy controls, were less efficient overall, and made more errors. While there is limited information on auditory compre- hension post-mTBI, a study by Kutas and Federmeier (2000) offers an interesting explanation beyond that of simple slower processing speed. By using electroencephalography (EEG), the authors showed a relationship between semantic memory and sentence comprehension, where the semantic memory system is in essence "priming" the language system based on previous experiences. A functional example of this occurs when an individual can predict the end of sentence, even with unfamiliar conversational partners. Semantic memory is one of several subtypes of declarative memory known to be dysfunctional after TBI, and as such, a decline in semantic memory would likely impact successful priming post-mTBI.

The ability to produce a targeted single word is an inherently complex task, and slowed word finding is a commonly cited communication disorder after mTBI (Barrow et al., 2006; Crewe-Brown, Stipinovich, & Zsilavecz, 2011; Keightley et al., 2014). In general, speeded conditions for naming tasks are considered to have an increase in overall processing load and are frequently preferred in mTBI assessments of naming and cognition. Slowed naming has been found in confrontational naming tasks for adults with acute and subacute mTBI (Barrow et al., 2003; King, Hough, Vos, Walker, & Givens, 2006; King, Hough, Walker, Rastatter, & Holbert, 2006), and this slowing has been identified longitudinally at 60 days. A pattern has been described in children and young adults aged 10 to 22 years with both acute and subacute injuries (Stockbridge, Doran, King, & Newman, 2018). Decreased categorical fluency has been found in young adults with traumatic blows to the head and/ or injuries resulting from exposure to blast, with a range of acuity of injury (Keightley et al., 2014; Parrish, Roth, Roberts, & Davie, 2009). It is important to note that correct diagnostic label for patients is likely cognitive communication impairment, despite that Norman and colleagues (2013) found that "aphasia" was the most common

diagnosis in young veterans with histories of mTBI, likely reflecting the word-finding errors present post-mTBI and the limitations of the VA diagnostic system. These errors are not limited to VA practitioners as the ASHA Special Interest Group 2 Neurogenic Communication Disorders frequently receives queries on diagnostic labels for anomia in mTBI.

Modalities for expressive discourse of conversation and writing have parallel presentations in mTBI. As discourse relies on extended production, numerous components of the individual's output can be evaluated. Discourse analysis often targets both microlinguistic factors, which impact quality of information within a single phrase, and macrolinguistic factors, which address clarity and cohesion across sentences and throughout the narrative as a whole. Microlinguistic verbal production does indicate some deficits, including slower production and decreased word variety; however, macrolinguistic areas can be markedly impaired with deficits, including decreased content units, mazing, abandoned utterances, vague language, and irrelevant and tangential content (Berisha, Wang, LaCross, Liss, & Garcia-Fillion, 2017; Marini, Galetto, Zampieri, Vorano, Zettin, & Carlomagno, 2011; Stout, Yorkston, & Pimentel, 2000; Tucker & Hanlon, 1998). Barry and Tomes (2015) examined remote autobiographical narratives in asymptomatic college students and found that their personal narratives were more challenging for individuals to remember, as well as lacking in vividness and linguistic complexity. There have been similar, but limited, findings in writing, including micro- and macrolinguistic errors, including run-on sentences, fragments, grammatical errors, semantic errors, and agreement errors for both verbs and pronouns (Dinnes & Hux, 2017). The only published cohort research targeting writing intervention post-mTBI indicates improvements in macrolinguistic functioning (Ledbetter, Sohlberg, Fickas, Horney, & McIntosh, 2017).

Decreased reading comprehension is a frequent characteristic post-mTBI. Karlin (2011) described numerous academic impacts of concussion, including decreased reading comprehension of speeded sentences. This is a significant concern when working with school-age/collegiate clients. Oral reading fluency as well as challenges with paraphrasing have also been found (Sohlberg, Griffiths, & Fickas, 2014). In a well-designed qualitative study from Norway that evaluated the ICF framework in relationship to mTBI, reading was a self-identified problem (Sveen et al., 2013). Decreased processing speed, visual dysfunction, and changes in memory will likely impact reading comprehension skills, and it is critical for a client's visual functioning to be assessed in order to drive appropriate therapeutic interventions. While additional research is needed on reading and reading comprehension in mTBI, interventions have been found to be effective (Laatsch & Guay, 2005; Sohlberg et al., 2014).

Speech Presentation in mTBI

Given the common changes in gross motor function after mTBI, it is not surprising that researchers are looking into speech functioning as well. "Slurred speech," one aspect of dysarthria, is a frequently cited symptom of acute concussion. It was included as a sign of SRC in the first International Conference on Concussion in Sport, and slow, labored motor movements remain present into the current fifth version (Aubry et al., 2002; McCrory et al., 2017). Subsequent to sideline-type assessments, there are minimal objective longitudinal data describing the ongoing dysarthric symptomatology. The presence of dysarthric speech patterns is clearly a sign of a more severe neurological picture, one that implicates focal, multifocal, or diffuse involvement of the central and/or peripheral nervous system (Duffy, 2012). For example, hypokinetic dysarthria or a mixed hypokinetic/ataxic dysarthria diagnosed in a boxer implicates lesions at the subcortical level of the central nervous system, similar to dysarthria seen in patients with Parkinson's disease or Parkinsonism, while a mixed dysarthria with an ataxic component implicates cerebellar involvement, which may also occur with repeated head strikes or motor vehicle accidents, for example, that cause the brain to experience acceleration and deceleration forces that ripple down the brainstem. These types of speech findings are diagnostic of a more severe brain injury and warrant neuroimaging to diagnose neuropathology (Bailes, Darshaw, Petraglia, & Turner, 2014; Corsellis, Bruton, & Freeman-Browne, 1973; Rabadi & Jordan, 2001; Tarazi et al., 2018). Recent work has explored speech articulation and changes in vocal acoustics post-mTBI. Daudet and colleagues (2017) evaluated vocal production of alternate motion rates (AMRs), sequential motion rates (SMRs), and polysyllabic words for average pitch, pitch variations, and phonemic amplitudes in very acute SRC. Statistical analyses indicated group differences for numerous aspects of temporal performance, including diadochokinetic (DDK) rates and variance, and acoustic performance of pitch, pitch variability, as well as amplitude and amplitude variability. This remains an area to be further explored in research.

Finally, stuttering has been reported in mTBI. There are four main categories of stuttering: developmental, neurogenic (e.g., palilalia), psychogenic, and medication induced, known as tardive dyskinesia. A fifth diagnosis described by Baumgartner and Duffy (1997) is psychogenic stuttering in adults with neurologic disease. Overall, adult-onset stuttering remains relatively rare, yet the majority of documented cases are determined to have a psychogenic etiology (Duffy, Manning, & Roth, 2012; Roth, Aronson, & Davis, 1989; Roth, Cornis-Pop, & Beach, 2015). The differential diagnosis can be most challenging when occurring with a history of mTBI, complicated by comorbidities of disordered sleep, PTSD, depression, and medications. Acquired stuttering in mTBI, in the absence of PTSD, is extremely rare (Norman et al., 2013; Norman et al., 2018). For individuals with histories of mTBI and PTSD, ruling out medication-induced stuttering is the first step in differential diagnosis. A review of medications and, if possible, withdrawing a symptom-inducing medication by substituting an alternative without speech effects can quickly determine whether tardive dyskinesia is responsible for the symptoms by observing improvement in the speech symptoms within a day to weeks. Symptoms of neurogenic stuttering (the most commonly occurring is palilalia, as observed in Parkinson's disease) are consistent and predictable. Unlike developmental and psychogenic stuttering symptoms, the symptoms do not wax and wane. Other motor speech stuttering-like symptoms usually are categorized as apraxia of speech or ataxic dysarthria, both of which are relatively easy to differentially diagnose. Therefore, during the initial speech evaluation or within two to three diagnostic treatment sessions, neurogenic-type stuttering can be confirmed when present. The presence of developmental stuttering is easily ruled out in the absence of a history of stuttering. Psychogenic stuttering, the fourth category, is probably the most challenging form of stuttering to diagnose, for no two patients present the same pattern of speech behaviors. Although the speech behaviors in psychogenic stuttering can sometimes resemble developmental stuttering characteristics, there are many more speech behaviors that differentiate acquired stuttering from developmental stuttering (Duffy et al., 2012; Roth et al., 2015). Diagnosis is usually made based on exclusion of the other types. Finally, the confirmation of diagnosis is based on symptom resolution through systematic symptomatic treatment.

Military medicine cites multiple examples of psychogenic stuttering post-mTBI in conjunction with post-traumatic stress (Mattingly, 2015; Norman et al., 2018; Roth et al., 2015), though authors are cautious to infer that neurogenic stuttering should not be ruled out as a viable option post-mTBI, in part due to complexities associated with diagnosis (Norman et al., 2013). While neurogenic stuttering does occur post-TBI, there have not been validated reports of this in the mTBI literature and while the literature base remains small, it does seem that true neurogenic stuttering post-mTBI would be a rare occurrence. SLPs need to keep in mind, when evaluating a patient with a history of a neurologic event, that it is less likely that sudden onset of stuttering is neurogenic in etiology and more likely that it is psychogenic in the presence of neurologic disease or etiology—the fifth diagnostic category of stuttering.

Long-Term Effects of mTBI and Chronic Traumatic Encephalopathy

The chronic effects of mTBI and possible changes in daily function have received considerable media attention, and for SLPs, there is no more rapidly evolving evidence base for these potential cognitive communication disorders. At this point, the unknowns related to serial mTBI remain greater than facts. As clinicians, it is critical that we have the most current information to guide our assessment and treatment decision making. It is also important that SLPs consider information distinguishing possible impacts of serial mTBI from that of chronic traumatic encephalopathy (CTE) (Randolph, 2014).

For nearly a century, clinicians have been concerned about repetitive head trauma accompanying long-term effects on functioning. The notion of being "punch drunk" was first reported in boxers in the 1920s, referring to broad changes in cognition after serial head injury (Martland, 1928). Subsequent references to dementia pugilistica and CTE expanded on these cases (Critch-

ley, 1949; Millspaugh, 1937). More recently, neuropsychological assessments and postmortem neuropathological findings of retired professional football players reignited interests in these potentially chronic conditions (Guskiewicz et al., 2003; Omalu et al., 2011). Researchers today are considering the potential impacts to long-term functioning from diagnosable mTBI as well as repeated subconcussive blows, hits to the head that do not cross the threshold into a concussive event (McAllister et al., 2014; Talavage et al., 2014).

It is well documented that repeated hits to the head may have significant after-effects and that those after-effects can be exponentially impactful (Jordan, 2000). Patients commonly cite how life becomes increasing difficult after a third or fourth TBI. In the consensus article resulting from the 2016 Berlin conference, Manley et al. (2017) reported that some athletes with repeated head trauma "suffer from depression and cognitive deficits later in life" (p. 7) and that these can be associated with a history of multiple concussive events. The increase in public awareness evolving from media coverage, stimulated by reports of CTE, marked by neuropsychiatric features including dementia, parkinsonism, depression, agitation, psychosis, and aggression, has become recognized as a potential late outcome of repetitive TBI (DeKosky, Blennow, Ikonomovic, & Gandy, 2013). The research into chronic effects of serial mTBI remains in its infancy, with minimal longitudinal research available. At this point, it remains unknown what neuro-bio-psychosocial factors may be associated with these longer-term changes, and it remains incumbent on medical professionals to reiterate these unknowns. The incidence, prevalence, and the role of genetic factors remain uncertain, and the contribution of age, gender, stress, and alcohol and substance abuse to the development of CTE is undetermined (Stein, Alvarez, & McKee, 2014). It is also critical to remember that these changes in function may or may not be related to CTE, which is a rare condition despite significant media attention (Willer et al., 2018). It is also possible that clinicians are witness to multiple types of outcomes from repeated mild neurotrauma, with blast-related injuries unique characteristics from those in sport (Shively et al., 2016). Moderate-severe TBI has been associated with progressive neurologic conditions such as Alzheimer's disease, Parkinson's disease, and amyotrophic lateral sclerosis, and research is emerging at this point as to if/how this research may apply in mTBI (Baker et al., 2018; DeKosky, Jaffee, & Bauer, 2018). Despite widespread media coverage, serial mTBI has not been correlated with increased risk of suicide (McAllister & McCrea, 2017).

Proceeding with caution regarding possible long-term effects from serial mTBI, it is important that SLPs be aware of the current (2019) literature base on CTE. CTE is presumed to be a condition where hyperphosphorylated tau protein accumulates in the brain and causes progressive deterioration of neurologic function, resulting in dementia. This form of tau protein is a distinct form of tau from the one associated with plaques and tangles in Alzheimer's disease. In CTE, tau accumulates throughout the brain, including within the hippocampus, amygdala, and various cortical areas. It has been reported in retired athletes, veterans, and civilians

(Mez et al., 2017). Diagnostic criteria of CTE remain somewhat unsettled and largely based on postmortem evaluation of these areas (McKee et al., 2016). Four grades of severity of CTE have been proposed with symptomatology of decreased memory and executive function, aggression, depressed mood, erratic behaviors, and changes in motor function and balance. Behavioral symptoms have been reported to be some of the earlier signs of CTE.

Diagnosis of CTE based on the neuropathological presence of tau remains problematic. In one highly publicized study of deceased football players, brains were analyzed postmortem for the presence of CTE-related tau (Mez et al., 2017). Within the convenience sample, 101 of 102 retired NFL players had CTE pathology and 71% of them were diagnosed as severe. While not designed as a prevalence study, one might incorrectly infer that 99% of retired NFL players will develop CTE. In contrast, a neuropathology group in Winnipeg, Canada, analyzed the brains of 111 "everyday folks" aged 18 to 60 years who were autopsied due to a standard medical process (Noy, Krawitz, & Del Bigio, 2016). Fully 35% of these individuals died with detectable CTE pathology, which may imply that CTE-related tau is a common and unremarkable event for many individuals. These two studies are highlighted to reinforce the infancy of research into CTE and that clinicians should proceed with caution when discussing CTE pathology with patients. Future research and advances in imaging techniques will likely help identify behavioral phenotypes and offer additional guidance regarding assessment and intervention (Iverson, Keene, Perry, & Castellani, 2018).

Special Population: Service Members/ Veterans and mTBI

Incidence of mTBI in the U.S. Military

According to the Department of Defense (DoD), 383,947 of more than 2 million troops, who served worldwide between 2000 and 2018 (first quarter), sustained a traumatic brain injury (TBI), with 82.3% classified as mild (Defense and Veterans Brain Injury Center, 2018). Many service members sustained multiple mTBIs during their two or more deployments in both Iraq and Afghanistan. A visual comparison of the total number of diagnosed TBIs by severity occurring in the military worldwide since 2000 is presented in Figure 7–1.

Military service members are at greater risk for mTBI than civilians, due to their demographics. Most are young healthy males, representing a high-risk group, and they are engaged in risk-related training, operational engagements, and deployments to combat zones (Soble et al., 2018). Deployments to combat theaters of operation put individuals at risk for concussive blast exposures from improvised explosive devices (IEDs), suicide bombers, land mines, mortar rounds, and rocket-propelled grenades. TBI is recognized as the "signature injury" of modern warfare.

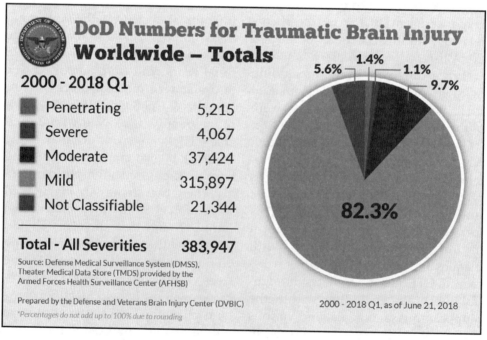

DoD Numbers for Traumatic Brain Injury Worldwide – Totals

2000 - 2018 Q1

Penetrating	5,215	
Severe	4,067	
Moderate	37,424	
Mild	315,897	
Not Classifiable	21,344	

Total - All Severities 383,947

5.6% — 1.4% — 1.1% — 9.7% — 82.3%

Source: Defense Medical Surveillance System (DMSS), Theater Medical Data Store (TMDS) provided by the Armed Forces Health Surveillance Center (AFHSB)

Prepared by the Defense and Veterans Brain Injury Center (DVBIC)

2000 - 2018 Q1, as of June 21, 2018

Percentages do not add up to 100% due to rounding

Figure 7–1. Worldwide numbers for TBI in the military, 2000–2018 Q1.

Military-related mTBI seems more likely to be accompanied by persistent symptoms than SRC, with 47% of individuals remaining symptomatic 3 months postinjury or longer (Schwab & Cernich, 2011). Although deployment/combat-related mTBI receives much attention in the media, the majority of recorded TBIs among service members occur in nondeployed contexts (Defense and Veterans Brain Injury Center [DVBIC], 2018). Military-related activities, including boxing and combat training, put service members at risk for concussion and repeated subconcussive blows. Former service members with a history of mTBI often receive subsequent health care in the Veterans Health Administration, where the risk for TBI (primarily from falls) increases with aging (70+ years) (Soble et al., 2018). This estimate may be higher among service members with a history of one or more combat deployments, given the frequency of multiple TBI events, concomitant mental health conditions such as depression and PTSD, and other factors unique to combat deployments. As such, deployment-related mTBI is a significant issue for the VA (O'Neil et al., 2013).

The incidence of military members sustaining TBI ranges from 11% to 23%, with a recent independent study citing 17.3% of post-9/11 service members and veterans met criteria for TBI, with 87% sustaining mTBI. Half of the respondents with TBI reported multiple TBIs and 46% reported a loss of consciousness, which is far higher than is commonly reported (Lindquist, Love, & Elbogen, 2017). In the absence of a biomarker for diagnosing TBI, this number is based largely on self-reports. However, even when there is opportunity to self-report, military values of self-sacrifice and "warrior ethos" can lead to underreporting potential occurrences. In 2005, the DoD saw a sharp rise in the identification of combat-related mTBI due to troop surges and increased recognition and acknowledgment of the diagnosis, followed by mandatory concussion screening in 2007 requiring troops to administer the Military Acute Concussion Evaluation to screen all service members who were at risk for a concussion (Belanger et al., 2011; Helmick et al., 2015). Years later, McCrea and colleagues (2014) demonstrated the validity of this screening tool to assess for cognitive dysfunction in military service members during the acute phase after mTBI.

Following years of limited information about the incidence of TBI impacting the troops in Iraq, the military established policies for screening troops in combat. Every deployed service member was trained to screen any service member who was at risk of a concussion by administering the Military Acute Concussion Evaluation (MACE) (DVBIC, 2012; French, McCrea, & Baggett, 2008) at the time of the event and making mandatory and detailed evaluation for soldiers who have sustained three concussions before being released back to combat (Belanger et al., 2007; Helmick et al., 2015). To be most effective, all service members experiencing a concussive injury should have the MACE administered within the first 24 hours of the event in order to make certain that they receive proper care in a timely fashion. The MACE, in combination with a medical exam, can be used to help determine if it is safe for a service member to return to duty or if further medical monitoring and supervision is required. McCrea and colleagues (2014) conducted a retrospective analysis of MACE data of Operation Enduring Freedom (OEF)/Operation Iraqi Freedom (OIF) deployed service members with a history of mTBI. Their findings support the validity of the MACE as a screening tool to assess for cognitive dysfunction in military service members during the acute phase after mTBI.

Mechanism of Blast Injuries

Blast injuries result from the impact of a blast overpressurization wave, or a complex pressure wave generated by an explosion, that causes an instantaneous rise in atmospheric pressure that is much higher than normal for humans to withstand (CDC, 2003). There are four basic mechanisms of blast injuries. They are classified as primary, secondary, tertiary, and quaternary.

Primary blast injuries result directly from the explosion. Blast explosives generate a sudden rise in atmospheric pressure that strikes the individual and pushes on all of the organs of the body. Air-filled organs such as the ears, lungs, gastrointestinal tract, and organs surrounded by fluid-filled cavities including the brain and spinal cord are especially susceptible to primary blast injury (Elsayed, 1997; Mayorga, 1997). The overpressurization causes the greatest risk of injury to bodies closest to the explosion. An increasing number of animal studies suggest that primary blast waves can cause structural injuries to the brain (Belanger et al., 2009).

Secondary blast injuries result from the blast fragments flying through the air, or any objects that are set in motion by the blast. IED explosions create debris of glass, wood, or metal that can lodge in limbs or any exposed surface of the body or cause penetrating brain injury or contusion damage from the impact (Phillips, 1986). Tertiary blast injuries occur when an individual is thrown against other moving or stationary objects by the force of the blast (Finkel, 2006).

Quaternary blast-related injuries include all other injuries or medical complications caused by explosions, including burns, toxic inhalation of gases, exposure to radiation, asphyxiation, and inhalation of dust containing coal or asbestos (DePalma et al., 2005; Lavonas & Pennardt, 2006). An individual may have experienced injury from any of these types of blasts.

Because there are differences between the mechanism of injury in primary blast trauma and blunt trauma, studies have examined the sequelae of these mechanisms of injury to determine whether different pathways of care are warranted (Soble et al., 2018). Blast and nonblast TBI groups had similar rates of vision loss, vestibular dysfunction, functional status, depression, sleep disorders, and alcohol misuse. Comparative outcomes were inconsistent with respect to headache, neurocognitive outcomes, hearing loss, and presence of PTSD (Greer, Sayer, Koeller, Velasquez, & Wilt, 2018). There is evidence that the neurological, psychological, and behavioral consequences of blast and nonblast TBIs are similar (Belanger et al., 2011; Dretsch, Kelly, Coldren, Parish, & Russell, 2015; Lange et al., 2012; MacDonald et al., 2014); however, there is also evidence that there may be unique neurophysiological changes associated with blast injuries (Shively et al., 2016). Similarly, differences in the frequency of long-term complications in mTBIs between blast and nonblast TBIs have been described (Luethcke, Bryan, Morrow, & Isler, 2010).

Blast-Plus-Impact TBI

While falls, athletic activities, and motor vehicle accidents are the major causes of civilian-related mTBI, blasts from explosive devices, causing repeated blast-induced neurotrauma over the course of multiple and prolonged deployments (Terrio et al., 2009; Warden, 2006), are responsible for most mTBIs among military service members and veterans. Advances in medical care and technology, including protective equipment, medical evacuation systems, and life-saving procedures, contribute to greater survival rates following combat-related as well as noncombat, training-related injuries sustained by service members previously (Bagalman, 2014; Martin et al., 2008; Owens et al., 2008). The surviving individuals, who in earlier conflicts might have died, are facing a complex combination of impairments in physical, cognitive, and psycho-social functioning (Zeitzer & Brooks, 2008) that requires a comprehensive, coordinated, evidence-based standard of care.

Combat-related primary blast injury is almost always accompanied by psychological and/or blunt trauma. MacDonald, Johnson, Nelson, and colleagues (2014) utilized the term "blast-plus-impact" (or "blast-plus") to describe the frequently reported history of being exposed to multiple blasts as well as impact-related blows during military service; for example, when the power of a blast explosion throws the individual off his or her feet and against a hard surface, this is known as a blast-plus-impact injury. Blast injuries often are accompanied by the psychological trauma of war in the context fear, anxiety, and emotional shock. Clinical outcomes of combat-injured U.S. military troops who were evacuated to Landstuhl Regional Medical Center in Germany following "blast-plus-impact" concussive TBIs were studied over time. Glasgow Outcome Scale–Extended assessments and neuropsychological test batteries were completed 6 to 12 months after injury (MacDonald, Johnson, Wierzechowski, et al., 2014), and findings showed high rates of PTSD and depression, but not cognitive impairments or focal neurological deficits. Much remains to be learned about the effects of blast injuries and of the short- and long-term effects of multiple blast exposures and blast-plus concussions on the brain. The military continues to fund extensive research to further the understanding of the effects of blasts on the brain and how best to diagnose the neurotrauma of mTBI.

Unique Clinical Considerations

When considering clinical care, there are additional unique considerations for veterans and service members for clinicians to consider.

Miller and colleagues (2013) evaluated symptom endorsement in soldiers during peacetime and found increased symptom reporting among those with a history of mTBI within 3 months compared to those with no prior TBI. Because active-duty and reserve service members are at greater risk of TBI than their civilian counterparts (DVBIC, 2018), and many military service members have sustained mTBI prior to military service (Ivins, Kane, & Schwab, 2009), it is important for clinicians to screen for a history of TBI prior to military service, as well as non-combat-related TBI. The traumatic nature of combat and the co-occurrence of posttraumatic stress increase the complexity of these injuries, and injury characteristics (e.g., distance from blast) are often based on self-report that may have questionable accuracy because of the intense psychological stress during the time of injury (Soble et al., 2018). Having a history of a TBI greater than 3 months prior to the current TBI did not influence symptom reporting (Miller et al., 2013). However, given the current interest and growing literature on the long-term consequences of repeated head trauma, documentation of any history of TBI would seem beneficial for clients/patients.

Hearing loss and tinnitus occur in up to 60% of individuals with blast-related TBI, a rate higher than in non-blast-related TBI (Fausti et al., 2009). When exposed to the primary blast wave of an explosion, the human auditory system is at risk for both peripheral and central damage from the pressure wave. Permanent pure sensorineural hearing loss is the most prevalent type of auditory impairment in blast exposure with a 35% to 100% incidence rate in blast-injured patients (Lew et al., 2007). Rupture of the tympanic membrane from the blast pressure, causing a con-

ductive hearing loss, is also common, with clinical reports of incidence ranging from 4% to 79% (de Ceballos et al., 2004; Gondusky & Reiter, 2005; Lucic, 1995). A significant association between tympanic membrane perforations and loss of consciousness has been noted (Xydakis et al., 2007); therefore, a finding of a tympanic membrane perforation following blast exposure has been recommended as a diagnostic tool for concussive injury (Chandler, 2006).

PTSD, Depression, and Other Psychological Health Considerations in mTBI

U.S. military veterans who deployed during Operation Enduring Freedom, Operation Iraqi Freedom, and Operation New Dawn (OEF/OIF/OND) were found to have an increased risk of developing posttraumatic stress disorder compared to the general population as demonstrated by a recent meta-analysis showing a 23% overall prevalence rate (Fulton et al., 2015). Psychiatric comorbidity, including major depressive disorder and/or generalized anxiety disorder postdeployment, was reported in 18% of OEF veterans following combat-related mTBI relative to other OEF veterans who did not sustain a mTBI (Stein et al., 2015). Alcohol and substance abuse were also identified in 19% (Carlson et al., 2010). PTSD is described as the most commonly diagnosed comorbid psychiatric diagnosis in OEF/OIF veterans with deployment-related mTBIs (Carlson et al., 2010). In comparison to OEF/OIF veterans who sustained a single TBI during deployment (28%), OEF/OIF veterans with a history of multiple TBIs during deployment had a 68% prevalence of PTSD (Lindquist et al., 2017). In another recent study, over 80% of OEF/OIF/OND combat veterans who sustained a TBI met criteria for PTSD, and over 35% met criteria for depressive disorder (McGlinchey et al., 2017).

Research findings suggest that PTSD and major depressive disorder contribute to cognitive dysfunction. Cooper et al. (2011) reported that OIF/OEF service members with PTSD symptoms and major depressive disorder had a high risk for self-reported cognitive dysfunction, even in the absence of a history of mTBI. The highest risk for self-reported cognitive dysfunction occurred in the context of comorbid PTSD and major depressive disorder, while mTBI alone accounted for only a small increased risk (Seal et al., 2016). In a comparison of OEF/OIF veterans with PTSD to those with PTSD and mTBI, Soble et al. (2013) found no neuropsychological functioning differences between groups. These findings suggest that PTSD symptoms are likely associated with cognitive complaints. In a similar study, Nelson et al. (2012) found that OIF/OEF veterans with only psychiatric disorders and veterans with comorbid psychiatric disorders and mTBI did not differ on neuropsychological functioning compared to veteran controls, suggesting that neuropsychological deficits are likely driven by psychiatric symptoms.

Similar findings were reported by Verfaellie et al. (2014), who found no differences in neuropsychological functioning among three groups of service members exposed to blasts during deployment (no TBI, mTBI with no loss of consciousness (LOC), and mTBI with LOC); however, symptoms of PTSD and depression were consistently associated with neuropsychological performance. On the other hand, Combs and colleagues (2015) reported possible mild effects of mTBI on processing speed and visual attention in OEF/OIF veterans; although similar to other studies, the most significant effects on neuropsychological functioning in their sample were attributed to comorbidities of mTBI and PTSD. A comparison study of measures of psychiatric functioning, postconcussive symptoms, deployment-related PTSD, pain coping, and a brief neuropsychological evaluation completed by 90 post-9/11 veterans, including 15 females and 75 males, demonstrated veterans with comorbid mTBI and PTSD reported significantly higher postinjury symptoms across domains, as well as greater pain intensity and maladaptive coping, and also performed more poorly on measures of recall but not on measures of attention, encoding, or executive functioning (Aase et al., 2018). In summary, research findings across numerous studies suggest neuropsychological deficits and persistent symptoms are driven by PTSD in the context of mTBI, and in the absence of mTBI, neuropsychological deficits can be caused by PTSD and depression.

Cognitive Communication Assessment

Assessment models in mTBI are variable depending on how recently an individual was injured. In acute injury, fatigue is particularly pronounced and clinicians must consider fatigue and cognitive overwhelm in their assessment planning. Similarly, visual impairments may directly impact test performance of visually heavy assessments. Evaluations after acute injury are often brief and primarily focused on an interview for gathering information and symptom description or checklist. For persistent symptoms, a more comprehensive assessment battery is common practice.

Since most acute cognitive symptoms resolve within 90 days following mTBI (Helmick & Members of the Consensus Conference, 2010; Levin, Goldstein, & MacKenzie, 1997), comprehensive evaluation is typically deferred until after the acute phase (14–28 days post-injury). Cognitive assessment, for those with persisting symptoms, is typically used to guide treatment and recommend referrals for other services. The cognitive communication assessment serves to identify and describe underlying strengths and weaknesses of cognitive, language, and social skills; the effects of cognitive communication impairments on the individual's capabilities and performance in everyday contexts; and participation. Outcomes of assessment provide diagnosis and clinical description of the cognitive communication disorder, prognosis, recommendations for intervention and support, and referral for other assessments or services (ASHA, 2004).

A combination of standardized and nonstandardized assessments to document real-world functioning is recommended (Coelho et al., 2005; Sohlberg & Mateer, 1989; Turkstra et al., 2005). According to Turkstra and McCarty (2006), communication competence,

which is the use of language within social contexts, is best assessed in real-world situations and is more sensitive to communication breakdowns than in structured monologue in the clinic. The majority of formal, standardized cognitive assessments have not been shown to be sensitive to postconcussive impairments (Helmick & Members of the Consensus Conference, 2010).

Purpose of Assessment

When conducting an assessment of cognitive communication impairments, the clinicians need to have a clear purpose for their assessment. Assessment of persisting cognitive communication impairments resulting from mTBI provides the following information:

- the nature and severity of the impairments, as well as co-occurring factors contributing to cognitive communication impairments;
- whether the onset and history of the cognitive communication symptoms are consistent with the diagnosis of mTBI;
- the underlying strengths and weaknesses related to attention, information processing, memory, executive function, and social communication skills;
- the effects of cognitive communication impairments on the individual's performance in everyday communication contexts and participation; and
- contextual factors that serve as barriers to or facilitators of successful communication and participation for individuals with

cognitive communication impairment (WHO, 2001).

These functions assist the clinician in identifying a need for behavioral intervention, for developing an appropriate treatment plan, and for making referrals to other health care providers. Initial assessment measures are used to define baseline functioning and later provide the outcome measures to demonstrate treatment effectiveness and to assist the patient in returning to work or school.

Interview

Assessment of cognitive communication begins with a patient interview. Krug and Turkstra (2015) describe a problem-focused interview they developed for use in a college concussion clinic. Their interview includes four components: a detailed history to evaluate risk factors for persistent symptoms, assessment of cognitive communicative complaints, assessment of academic needs and environmental demands, and assessment of client-generated compensations and strategies that the student attempted to use and/or used on an ongoing basis. The traditional structured interview often includes a combination of open- and closed-ended questions that gather information about the injury, symptoms, education and work history, medications, and so on.

In a patient-centered interview, described by the Working Group to Develop a Clinician's Guide to Cognitive Rehabilitation in mTBI (2016), the patient is asked to tell his or her story and the interview is guided by what the patient describes; therefore, it is less structured. If the individuals have previously told their story to other providers, they may not want to retell it. In this case, a patient-centered, semi-structured interview can be used to gather the patients' background information. The clinician asks open-ended questions organized from general to more specific to gather the following information:

■ Reason for referral
■ Chief concern(s)
■ History of onset
■ Pattern of onset and progression or recovery
■ Nature and severity of symptoms
■ Frequency, consistency, and contextual influences on symptoms
■ Functional consequences to work and home life
■ How the symptoms have been addressed to date (e.g., has the patient learned ways to lessen or eliminate symptoms)
■ How the patient has coped with or altered daily routines because of symptoms
■ Other concerns regarding potential comorbidities (i.e., "What else is going on?")

While listening to the story, the clinician periodically asks to summarize his or her understanding of what has been said by the patient, notably about:

■ Initial trigger or trauma that led to change in the patient's function
■ Other symptoms and events that may be contributing to or maintaining symptoms
■ Services received and benefits gained

- How symptoms have impacted the patient's work and personal life

Symptom Checklist

Postconcussion symptom checklists are a means of efficiently documenting and tracking a client's symptoms (Krug & Turkstra, 2015), although some research cautions against administering symptom checklists prior to interviewing patients due to the risk of gathering an exaggerated number and/or severity rating of symptoms. Iverson et al. (2010) found that when individuals with a history of mTBI were asked about their symptoms in an open-ended question-style interview about their symptoms and then completed a symptom checklist, they reported more symptoms on the checklist and often listed them as moderate or severe, although they had not endorsed them at all on the free-response symptom review. Checklists frequently are used as treatment outcome measures and therefore administered as part of the initial patient intake process. Cicerone and Kalmar (1995) created a symptom checklist, the Neurobehavioral Symptom Inventory (NSI), based on Levin and colleagues' (1987) outcomes from interviewing 57 patients with mTBI at 1 month postinjury. In contrast to the Levin et al. study, Cicerone and Kalmar administered their symptom checklist to adults with a history of persisting symptoms following a mTBI, ranging from 3 to 52 months postinjury. Additional checklists include the Acute Concussion Evaluation (ACE) (Gioia & Collins, 2006), Post-Concussion Scale (PCS, Lovell et al., 2006), and the Symptom Evaluation portion of Sports Concussion Assessment Tool 5 (SCAT5) (Echemendia et al., 2017) and the Self-

Awareness of Deficits Interview, a standardized self-report measure (Fleming, Strong, & Ashton, 1996).

Formal Standardized Evaluation

For the majority of patients with a history of mTBI, an interview and symptom checklist may provide enough information to identify treatment goals and strategies to help the patient return to work or school. Formal standardized cognitive or neuropsychological testing may not be necessary in certain cases for the clinician to design and implement an appropriate cognitive rehabilitation plan; however, formal assessment may be required for administrative reasons, such as insurance coverage and to clarify clinical presentation. If the patient has had a formal neuropsychological assessment, the speech-language pathologist can refer to it in developing treatment goals. The goal of cognitive therapy is to treat functional concerns described by the patient. The clinician should never dispute the patient's complaints of cognitive problems; they should be accepted as a valid reflection of his or her day-to-day life. The clinician can use cognitive test scores to educate the patient that his or her brain is intact and can focus and attend, learn, and remember; together, the patient and clinician need to figure out what is causing the patient to have memory problems in his or her everyday life and then help deal with them.

The Clinician's Guide to Cognitive Rehabilitation in mTBI (2016) lists the following reasons for administering formal standardized testing:

- Education and feedback. When patients are convinced that they have significant cognitive impairments that reflect underlying brain damage, good performance on standardized testing can provide valuable therapeutic feedback that the patient's brain is fully capable of performing in areas the individual believes are damaged. This feedback can provide a starting point in educating patients and exploring why they tested so well yet are experiencing functional problems in their daily activities. Appropriate positive, supportive feedback can be effective in avoiding or minimizing disability beliefs.

■ Identify cognitive strengths. Formal testing may be useful in identifying specific cognitive strengths that can be applied in a cognitive rehabilitation program. For example, good attention and concentration can help facilitate learning and memory, or strong visual skills may compensate for verbal challenges.

■ Identify and quantify preexisting deficits such as attention deficit disorder or learning disabilities.

■ Track cognitive rehabilitation goals or treatment targets. If a patient has a particular area of weakness, the test can be used to identify this weakness; treatment goals can be developed to improve the weaker function, and repeat testing can be used to demonstrate treatment progress.

■ Plan vocational or educational programs. Formal standardized testing may be important in vocational planning or return-to-school decisions. In some cases, it may be necessary to document a need for accommodations, while in other cases, it may be important in identifying cognitive strengths for vocational or academic planning.

■ Assess clinical program needs. Some clinical settings and programs may require formal testing for administrative purposes. In those cases, the results can still be clinically beneficial for providing positive feedback and education to the patient, avoiding or minimizing disability self-beliefs, identifying strengths for facilitating performance success, establishing goals, and tracking progress.

Once the clinician has completed the patient interview, the patient-recorded symptom checklist is completed, and if indicated, the patient has completed standardized testing, the clinician reviews and integrates the assessment information, sorts through the issues, and begins to formulate the "big picture" of initial etiology, maintaining factors, and comorbidities and defines:

■ functional deficits, symptom triggers, and factors contributing to maintaining symptoms;

■ situational variables, supports, barriers, and comorbidities affecting symptoms.

Once the "big picture" is defined, the clinician is ready to develop a treatment plan in collaboration with the patient.

Assessment Instruments

The following is a list of assessment instruments generated by experts from the DoD/VA and academia with expertise and experience working with mTBI (Cornis-Pop et al., 2012; Hardin & Kelly, 2019). This list is not meant to be comprehensive or exclusive. Few of the tests used by speech-language pathologists in the evaluation of postconcussive cognitive communication deficits have been standardized on people with mTBI.

Broad Assessment of Cognitive-Linguistic Abilities

Woodcock-Johnson III Tests of Cognitive Abilities (WJ III COG) (Woodcock, Mather, & McGrew, 2001)

Woodcock-Johnson IV Tests of Cognitive Abilities (Schrank, McGrew, & Mather, 2014)

Cognitive Screening Measures

Repeatable Battery for the Assessment of Neuropsychological Status (RBANS) (Randolph, 2012)

Domain-Specific Tests

Attention

Test of Everyday Attention (TEA) (Robertson, Ward, Ridgeway, & Nimmo-Smith, 1994)

WAIS III subtest Digit Symbol Coding (Woodcock et al., 2001)

Trail Making Tests A and B (Reitan & Wolfson, 1985)

Information Processing Speed

Speed and Capacity of Language Processing (SCOLP) (Baddeley, Emslie, & Nimmo-Smith, 1992)

Woodcock-Johnson III COG Subtest 6: Visual Matching, Subtest 16: Decision Speed, Subtest 18: Rapid Picture Naming, Subtest 20: Pair Cancellation (Woodcock et al., 2001)

WJ-IV-COG Subtest 4: Letter-Pattern Matching, Subtest 11: Number-Pattern Matching, Subtest 17: Pair Cancellation; WJ-IV-OL Subtest 8: Rapid Picture Naming (Shrank et al., 2014)

Executive Functions

Functional Assessment of Verbal Reasoning and Executive Strategies (FAVRES, SFAVRES- Student) (MacDonald, 1998, 2013)

Behavior Rating Inventory of Executive Function (Adult and pediatric versions) (BRIEF; BRIEF-A) (Gioia, Isquith, Guy & Kenworthy, 2000; Roth, Isquith, & Gioia, 2005)

Behavioral Assessment of the Dysexecutive Syndrome (BADS) (Wilson et al., 2005)

Memory

Rivermead Behavioral Memory Test–Third Edition (RBMT- 3) (Wilson et al., 2008)

Contextual Memory Test (Toglia, 1993)

California Verbal Learning Test (CVLT) (Delis et al., 2000)

Everyday Memory Questionnaire (Sunderland, Harris, & Baddeley, 1987)

Wechsler Memory Scale IV (Wechsler, 2009)

Social Communication

The Awareness of Social Inference Test (TASIT) (McDonald, Flanagen, & Rollins, 2002)

LaTrobe Communication Questionnaire & Informant Report (LCQ) (Douglas, O'Flaherty, & Snow, 2000)

Language

Controlled Oral Word Association (COWA) (FAS) (Benton, Hamsher, & Sivan, 1994)

Woodcock-Johnson IV Tests of Achievement: Oral Language (Shrank et al., 2014)

WJ III COG Subtest 12: Retrieval Fluency; WJ III COG Subtest 1: Verbal Comprehension; WJ-III ACH Subtest 3 Story Recall; Subtest 4: Understanding Directions (Woodcock et al., 2001)

WJIV-OL Subtest 4: Rapid Picture Naming, Subtest 8: Retrieval Fluency, Subtest 2: Oral Comprehension (Shrank et al., 2014)

Administering formal standardized tests can assist clinicians in developing hypotheses about the underlying cognitive impairments and deficits that impact a person's functional behavior, which leads to treatment planning. Formal standardized testing is less informative about the functional difficulties the patient is experiencing with friends and strangers. Formal, nonstandardized assessments can be useful for providing a baseline measure of functioning for a particular skill area, establishing a starting point for therapy based on baseline performance, and then measuring the effectiveness of therapy targeting the particular skill area. Examples are the Attention Process Training (APT) II Questionnaire, which is completed by the patient, and the APT Test, which is administered prior to initiating the APT therapy program (Sohlberg et al., 2001).

Measurement of functional outcomes is important for demonstrating the effectiveness and efficacy of cognitive rehabilitation therapy with mTBI.

Interdisciplinary Rehabilitation

The goal of cognitive rehabilitation is to return the patient to their previous level of functioning. The diagnosis of a "history" of mTBI corresponds to a positive prognosis for recovery. Given the complex needs of patients with a history of mTBI and persisting cognitive and emotional sequelae, cognitive rehabilitation therapy is best delivered in the context of an interdisciplinary holistic rehabilitation model comprising a specialized team of medical-surgical physicians, mental health and social work providers, and rehabilitation specialists (Cornis-Pop et al., 2012; Malia et al., 2004). A patient-centered approach to rehabilitation is designed by incorporating results of the team members' evaluations into a comprehensive treatment plan with long- and short-term goals that are targeted and monitored regularly. Intervention strategies for cognitive communication impairments of mTBI include education, counseling, direct therapy, modifications, and group therapy.

The past decade has seen marked changes in mTBI/concussion research and care. The resulting changes in the research base have prompted changes in best practice of clinical care. At a conceptual level, care for mTBI has shifted significantly with a move away from cocooned, quiet rest after injury to a model of active rehabilitation (Schneider et al., 2017), although anecdotal evidence supports that ongoing "rest" models continue to be applied despite clear changes in guidelines. Multidisciplinary care is now recommended to address the breadth of symptoms post-mTBI (Collins et al., 2016), with a team including medicine, physical therapy, behavioral health, and cognitive therapy, most commonly provided by speech-language pathology. These mTBI guidelines are in concert with the NIH Consensus Panel on TBI (1999), but implementation of revised practice guidelines can be slow to be adopted in mTBI and other areas of clinical care (Cranney, Warren, Barton, Gardner, & Wally, 2001; Lebrun et al., 2013).

There are several examples of high-profile multiprovider care models for persistent symptoms of mTBI. One such model is the Marcus Institute from Brain Health (MIBH) at the University of Colorado Anschutz medical campus, where care moves from multiprovider to true interdisciplinary care (Hardin & Kelly, 2019). Interdisciplinary care requires that providers interact regularly and that care planning incorporates all discipline perspectives in client-centered care. At the MIBH, clinicians practice in a co-located group of spaces, allowing for easy communication throughout the day on specific patient performance and concerns. The MIBH intensive outpatient care team is led by neurology with accompanying providers from speech-language pathology, physical therapy, sleep, behavioral health, clinical pharmacy, mind-body medicine, art therapy, and case management. During 3-day evaluations, SLPs participate in a patient-centered group clinical interview, screen auditory processing skills, and assess cognitive and communication

factors. Interventionally, speech-language pathology has three roles on the team, providing both individual and group-based care. Individual sessions occur approximately 3 days per week and often target communication strategies, metacognitive strategy instruction, and memory strategies. Patient group sessions are transdisciplinary in nature, where SLPs go with patients outside of the traditional clinic environments to practice strategies from physical therapy, speech, and behavior in a more real-world setting (Hardin & Kelly, 2019). Working with family members, the speech team also co-treats with behavioral health on how mTBI symptoms can impact communication at home and offering strategies to increase success. While the MIBH offers civilian-centered care, similar models for care exist within military medicine, including the National Intrepid Center for Excellence (NICoE) in Bethesda, Maryland, and Intrepid Spirit Centers across the country. SLPs can look to these interdisciplinary programs as examples of rehabilitation for mTBI in practice.

Acute mTBI Intervention

In the presence of an acute mTBI, the purpose of an initial visit is to acknowledge symptoms, provide education, and track and facilitate the resolution of symptoms to assist the individual in returning to his or her preinjury state and initiate intervention. Reduction in both the severity and duration of persisting postconcussion symptoms has been demonstrated following a brief psychoeducational intervention during the acute postinjury period (Comper, Bisschop, Carnide, & Tricco, 2005;

Mittenberg, Tremont, Zielinski, Fichera, & Rayls, 1996). Therefore, as early as the first visit, intervention is initiated through education and symptomatic treatment. While using psychoeducational interventions in the acute phase of recovery is considered a standard of care (VA/DoD Clinical Practice Guideline for the Management of Concussion-Mild Traumatic Brain Injury, 2016), it has not been shown to be effective among individuals with chronic persisting symptoms (Soble et al., 2018).

Education consists of providing information regarding the nature of the injury (e.g., the temporary neurologic events of concussion) relative to the presenting symptoms, the recovery process, the anticipated recovery time, and strategies that may assist with compensating and facilitating improved performance to maximize successes and minimize frustration and stress until symptoms resolve. Support takes the form of active listening and conveying empathy, optimism, and encouragement. Providing reassurance and instilling the expectation of recovery (within weeks to months) is key to the recovery process and, therefore, should be communicated on a regular basis. Recovery is facilitated by conveying a positive prognosis that rapid and full recovery is very likely and that patients can help themselves by returning to modulated physical and cognitive activity within 1 to 2 days following injury.

Intervention is provided in the form of a multidisciplinary team approach to symptomatic treatment of the comorbidities to minimize the risk of persisting cognitive communication deficits and to increase the likelihood of full recovery. Specialists on the team are called upon to address sleep hygiene, diet, social communication, recreation and exercise as tolerated, psychological intervention, and cognitive stimulation. Outpatient follow-up consultation is recommended to monitor patient status and to provide reassurance as improvement occurs (Miller & Mittenberg, 1998).

Speech-language pathologists can be called upon to provide education, facilitation, and compensation for symptoms while emphasizing the expectation of recovery and return to work/school. One option for acute intervention is the SMART trial that, through psychoeducation, focuses on symptom management, return to activity, positivity, and metacognitive strategy instruction (Kurowski et al., 2016). In addition to reinforcing the information being communicated by the other team members, treatment goals may include:

- Providing strategies for controlling environmental distractors
- Training strategies for behavioral management of symptoms
- Reviewing memory strategies
- Encouraging routine use of cognitive tools and strategies (e.g., calendar, notepad, smartphone, tablet, and smart watch)

Rehabilitation for Persisting Postconcussive Cognitive Communication Deficits

Persons who complain of persisting cognitive communication difficulties following a concussion should be assessed and treated symptomatically regardless of the time elapsed since injury. Multiple factors, including demographic, psychiatric, and psychosocial-emotional variables, and mTBI comorbidities and their interactions all contribute to ongoing persistent symptoms in persons with mTBI (Vanderploeg, Belanger, & Curtiss, 2009). Regardless of the etiology of the symptoms, whether they are the result of the initial brain trauma or to current comorbidities, interventions should be designed to reduce the level of functional disability caused by cognitive communication symptoms (Cornis-Pop, 2008). There is increasing evidence that functional cognitive improvements may continue years postinjury and be supported through active treatment (Draper & Ponsford, 2008).

Motivational Interview

Motivational interviewing (MI) is a method of communication designed to facilitate moving individuals in the direction of change. MI can be used for engaging the patient to explore areas of concern and ways his or her difficulties are impacting performance at work, at school, or in the home. This process leads to defining functional goals that provide the focus for rehabilitation.

In MI, the clinician adopts a "following" style to allow the patient to freely share concerns (Working Group to Develop a Clinician's Guide to Cognitive Rehabilitation in mTBI, 2016). For example:

Clinician: "I understand you would like to work on remembering your schedule."

Patient: "I keep losing my appointment slips."

Clinician: "Paper schedules are not working for you."

Patient: "No, I need to use my smartphone but I'm not consistent entering my appointments."

Clinician: "You would like to be more consistent entering your appointments in your smartphone?"

Patient: "I would remember my schedule better."

The clinician can use the following mnemonic to remember strategies used in MI, "OARS"—open-ended questions (e.g., "How do memory challenges affect you at work?"), affirmations (e.g., "You may have forgotten your appointment earlier this morning, but it sounds like you remembered all your appointments yesterday. You must feel good about that."), reflections (e.g., "Paper schedules get lost easily."), and summaries (e.g., "You are having difficulty remembering your schedule because the paper schedules keep getting lost. You would like to have your appointments in your smartphone so you will remember and attend them more consistently."). Affirmations and reflections are statements that reassure the patient that he or she is being heard and understood and can yield specific information that may help in formulating treatment goals. Summaries of the patient's comments can be used to tie together information within an interview and to highlight and focus information for identifying goals and strategies. MI is used to elicit patients' motivation to change, not telling why or how they are to change, and in this way the clinician conveys respect for patients' autonomy to decide to change.

Therapeutic Alliance

Cognitive intervention involves a collaborative effort between a motivated patient and a dedicated clinician who together form a therapeutic alliance or partnership that is based on trust and credibility among the clinician, the patient, and his or her family (Cornis-Pop et al., 2012). The clinician actively listens to the patient to understand the concerns and impact of the patient's impairments on quality of life. Once a shared trust and clinician credibility are established with the patient, the clinician can facilitate and support the patient to gradually regain functional cognitive communication skills. A strong therapeutic working alliance can positively influence outcomes in postacute TBI rehabilitation (Schonberger, Humle, & Teasdale, 2007; Sherer et al., 2009).

Education

The first step in a treatment program for a person with a history of mTBI is to provide education and validation of symptoms (Kay et al., 1992; Rosenthal, 1993; Sohlberg, 2000). TBI education begins with an interview, such as the motivational interview, and continues with the individual's participation in functional goal setting. Education should focus on assisting the individual in understanding the relationship between the acute event that caused his or her mTBI and its consequences, the history of mTBI including the typical recovery process, the interplay of comorbid symptoms and persisting cognitive communication deficits, and

the positive prognosis and expectation of recovery.

The Demands and Capacities (DC) model (Adams, 1990), frequently referred to in the treatment of stuttering, can be applied in working with SMs/veterans with persisting postconcussive cognitive communication deficits. Based on the premise that each person has a finite resource (capacity) of cognitive abilities, the presence of comorbidities of pain, disordered sleep, medication effects, sensory deficits, and psychosocial-emotional issues represents demands or conditions that deplete the individual's finite capacity. Thus, reducing comorbidities through interventions may enhance the individual's cognitive communication functioning. The DC model may assist the patient in acknowledging the benefit of focusing interventions on the comorbidities either before initiating or in conjunction with his or her cognitive communication rehabilitation.

Counseling

Counseling is inherently a component of cognitive communication rehabilitation and includes a patient-centered approach that engages the patient's participation in goal setting and integrates goal-directed counseling for eliciting behavior change. The implementation of goal attainment scaling (GAS) in establishing treatment goals is an effective way to ensure the patient sets the direction for his or her therapy. Goal attainment scaling has a long history of use for program evaluation in mental health settings and more recently in neurorehabilitation. It is a method that allows the patient to establish personal individualized functional goals and as a vehicle to measure clinical outcomes. GAS has been found to be a valuable procedure for ensuring that treatment is goal directed and for guiding social reinforcement in behavioral treatment in both mental health and rehabilitation settings (Malec, Smigielski, & DePompolo, 1991).

Modifications

Maintaining communications with the patient's family members, employers, teachers, and peers is an essential component of cognitive communication intervention. The inclusion of the patient's support team in his or her rehabilitation process facilitates a greater understanding of the challenges and needs of the individual as he or she reenters the community. Working with family members or caregivers may include recommending strategies for modifying the environment to remove communication barriers and for enhancing community participation. When providing cognitive communication rehabilitation in the military, the unique needs of the military need to be understood, including returning to duty or work, balancing military and family relationships, readjusting to civilian life, and considering risk for posttraumatic stress (Trudel, Nidiffer, & Barth, 2007).

Modifications may take the form of making adaptations to the patient's home or work environment such as adjusting the lighting or reducing noise. The patient may find it best to work in a space with fewer distractions rather than working in a large open space with many people and few barriers. Restructuring the environment

to compensate for memory deficits may include adding visual or auditory (alarm) reminders and establishing a special location for placing important personal items that go back and forth between home and work (e.g., keys, phone, wallet, hat).

Direct Therapy

Cognitive communication treatment is a systematic, functionally oriented program of therapeutic activities that is based on assessment and understanding of a patient's brain-behavioral deficits (Cicerone et al., 2000). Interventions include strengthening previously learned patterns of behavior, establishing new patterns through use of internal and external compensatory cognitive strategies, and enabling the individual to adapt to the changes in his or her revised approaches to cognitive communicative functioning. Increased performance success is reinforced through repetition, errorless learning, and gradually increasing task stimuli and complexity in a structured systematic approach.

Systematic instruction (Ehlhardt et al., 2008), founded on the theory that persons with learning challenges benefit most from structured training, is an effective intervention model for cognitive communication impairments of mTBI (Sohlberg & Turkstra, 2011). Structured training includes presentation of explicit models and reinforcement of errorless learning when first acquiring new information, use of facilitation and compensatory strategies, structured and guided practice to enhance mastery, and maintenance and generalization across contexts (Sohlberg & Turkstra, 2011). Errorless learning is an effective approach for training complex, multistep processes, by breaking the process down into discrete steps that are trained one step at a time, building each step on the next, until the process is sequentially performed error free. This approach is typically used when training new tasks or new facts. Effective treatments incorporate principles of learning theory that enhance neuroplasticity, including intensive, repetitive practice of functional targets with careful consideration of salience, potential for generalization, and personal factors (Sohlberg & Turkstra, 2011).

Several recent studies have examined compensatory cognitive rehabilitation approaches in SMs/veterans (Huckans et al., 2010; Storzback et al., 2017; Twamley, Jak, Delis, Bondi, & Lohr, 2014). Compensatory strategy training involves teaching individuals to cope with cognitive difficulties through use of functional adaptive skills, techniques, and use of external aids such as smart devices such as smartphone applications. Twamley and colleagues (2014) developed one of the most widely implemented cognitive rehabilitation interventions that includes both didactics and compensatory strategy training. The program is presented in cognitive modules that can be adapted for both individual and group interventions. In a randomized controlled trial, the authors reported improved postconcussive symptoms and prospective memory (Twamley et al., 2014) at completion of the study, and at 1-year follow-up, there was evidence of continued reduction in symptomatology (Caplan et al., 2015).

Clinical experience with patients with persistent symptoms suggests that a comprehensive holistic approach to rehabilitation, which provides individual- and group-based treatment of cognitive, emotional, and interpersonal skills, within an integrated therapeutic environment addresses the functional impairment and promotes meaningful and satisfactory quality of life, even in the presence of persisting limitations (Cicerone et al., 2008; Cornis-Pop et al., 2012; Helmick & Members of the Consensus Conference, 2010). The most recent and largest cognitive rehabilitation trial to date, the SCORE clinical trial (Cooper et al., 2017), compared four 6-week treatment arms: (1) psychoeducation, (2) independent self-administered computer-based cognitive rehabilitation, (3) therapist-directed manualized cognitive rehabilitation, and (4) therapist-directed cognitive rehabilitation integrated with cognitive behavioral therapy (CBT) psychotherapy. In total, 126 service members participated in the study. Results showed that treatment arms involving therapist-directed cognitive rehabilitation had superior outcomes compared to treatments without therapist involvement as demonstrated by a self-report measure of day-to-day cognitive functioning (Soble et al., 2018). Cognitive rehabilitation delivered by the clinicians in this study included psychoeducation, external aids, cognitive strategies, drills, and generalization tasks. As reported in these studies, cognitive rehabilitation addresses one or more of the following domains, specific to individual patient complaints: attention, speed of information processing, memory, executive function, and social pragmatics.

Attention

Treatment for attention may focus on direct attention training, use of compensatory strategies, and education. Many studies have demonstrated efficacy and utility for direct attention training (Ben-Yishay, Silver, Piasetsky, & Rattock, 1987; Fasotti, Kovacs, Eling, & Brouwer, 2000; Sinotte & Coelho, 2003; Sohlberg, McLaughlin, Pavese, Heidrich, & Posner, 2000; Tiersky et al., 2005), including studies of populations with mTBI (Cicerone, 2002; Palmese & Raskin, 2000). Treatments that focus on strategies to allocate attention resources (e.g., rehearsal, self-pacing) and reduce anxiety and frustration related to high-level working memory demands are effective for addressing attention impairments in people with mTBI (Cicerone, 2002).

Sohlberg and Mateer (2001) described one of the earliest approaches to attention process training (APT) that served as the foundation for many well-designed research studies and is commonly used in clinics nationally. Currently, there are three published versions of the APT program: APT-I (Sohlberg & Mateer, 1987, 2005); APT II, an attention training program for persons with mild traumatic brain injury (Sohlberg et al., 2001); and APT-3 (Sohlberg & Mateer, 2010). Sohlberg et al. (2000) demonstrated improved performance on a wide range of tasks that involved executive functions and attentional control with a combination of brain injury education and APT training. A review of the evidence for cognitive interventions for attention supports direct attention training and metacognitive training for developing compensatory strategies that "foster generalization to real world tasks" (Cicerone et al., 2011, p. 521). Independent practice using computer-based programs in the absence of therapeutic interventions with a clinician is not recommended (Cicerone et al., 2011).

Processing Speed

Individuals with mTBI often describe slowed thinking and concentration problems. Slowing of information processing has been attributed to attention deficits (Gentilinia, Nichell, & Schoenhube, 1989), memory functioning (Cicerone, 1996), and cognitive communication processes, including encoding information, verbal comprehension, and responding to novel situations (Cornis-Pop et al., 2012). Demonstrated improvements in processing speed have targeted increasing awareness and management of the temporal demands of tasks (Fasotti et al., 2000; Gray et al., 1992). Use of compensatory strategies (e.g., verbal meditation, self-pacing, self-monitoring of mental effort, and management of secondary emotional reactions during a task) to allocate attention resources and manage the flow rate of information represents an effective strategy training model of remediation (Cicerone, 2002; Fasotti et al., 2000; Gray et al., 1992). Minimizing distractions, allocating sufficient time to complete tasks, planning for rest breaks, and reducing demands of competing tasks are additional strategies for assisting an individual with slowed information processing. There are a variety of cognitive assistive technologies that may also be of benefit (e.g., smart pen or computer application that audio-records lectures as one takes notes or using reminder alarms for staying on task or for remembering to take a break). Comorbidities and factors, including sleep deprivation, PTSD, and other mental health conditions, must be considered in addition to underlying cognitive processes that may impact processing speed (Belanger et al., 2009).

Memory

Helmick and Members of the Consensus Conference (2010) state, "Memory training is the most frequently prescribed form of cognitive rehabilitation" (p. 245). Levin and Goldstein (1986) suggested that the memory problems experienced after a TBI represent difficulty retrieving information because of deficits in the encoding stage of memory as a result of decreased ability to generate semantic associations and visual imagery. Consequently, a variety of mnemonic training and visual imaging strategies have been developed to create associations and images (Crovitz, 1979; Crovitz, Harvey, & Horn, 1979; Gianutsos & Gianutsos, 1979; Wilson, 1987). Unfortunately, people may not use these strategies outside of therapy in functional situations. It is important that SLPs educate clients about the application of these strategies outside the clinic environment to ensure generalization.

Several studies (Lawson & Rice, 1989; Ownsworth & McFarland, 1999; Sohlberg & Mateer, 1989) demonstrated generalization of memory strategy training approaches using a memory book or diary. The effectiveness of these programs is the addition of a training element for transferring and using these external memory strategies in everyday situations. In a similar study, Wilson et al. (2001) demonstrated the effectiveness of training in the uses of a portable pager to improve independence in people with memory and planning problems. These studies support the current practice of clinicians around the world, who are training SMs/veterans to use compensatory memory devices with the support of the Computer/Electronic Accommodations Program (CAP), a federally funded program for government employees with disabilities. Based on guidance from the DCoE/DVBIC consensus, "efficacy has been demonstrated for memory training" (Helmick & Members of the Consensus Conference, 2010, p. 245), particularly for patients with mTBI and mild memory impairment. The benefits of training in the use of external memory strategies and devices in functional real-life contexts cannot be underestimated.

Executive Functions

Executive functions comprise those mental capacities necessary for formulating goals, planning steps to achieve them, and carrying out the plans effectively (Lezak, 1982). In working with patients with a history of mTBI and persistent symptoms, executive function disorders are often difficult to tease out from their baseline level of functioning and the individual's unique personal factors, including, age, social background, education, and past and current experiences. Deficits in executive functions should be addressed in cognitive communication therapy since they are likely to affect functional activities and participation in everyday life events (Cornis-Pop et al., 2012). A robust literature supports the use of metacognitive strategy training as an intervention for executive function impairments due to TBI (Helmick & Members of the Consensus Conference, 2010). Metacognitive strategy training uses direct instruction to facilitate behavioral self-control and to deliberately monitor performance of a task, then to modify the behavior if the performance is not optimal (Sohlberg, Ehlhardt, & Kennedy, 2005). The steps frequently applied in metacognitive skills training for problem-solving deficits are (Sohlberg & Turkstra, 2011):

1. Identify an appropriate goal
2. Anticipate what needs to be done to reach the goal
3. Identify possible solutions to challenges
4. Self-monitor and evaluate progress
5. Modify behavior or strategy use if adequate progress is not being made
6. Self-monitor and evaluate progress through to the outcome
7. Review what was successful and unsuccessful

Although remediation of executive functions initially focuses on external strategies and explicit instructions and feedback, it should gradually shift to the internalization of self-regulation strategies through internalized self-instruction and self-monitoring (Cicerone et al., 2005; Kennedy & Coelho, 2005). These same metacognitive strategies are beneficial in addressing attentional deficits as well.

Assistive Technology for Cognition. The training in the use of assistive technology for cognition (ATC) to compensate for deficits can be beneficial to the transition of the patients back into the community. Assistive technology includes smart mobile devices (e.g., smartphones, smart pads/tablets, recording devices, etc.) and applications for the devices that assist with planning, organization, time management, information storage and retrieval, note taking (manually or voice to text), reminder alarms, accessing new information, navigation, and virtual assistance with placing calls, getting directions, and taking messages. One of the most promising features of these devices is they normalize the patient when integrated into cognitive rehabilitation.

There is a growing literature documenting the benefits of ATC among individuals with cognitive disabilities (de Joode, van Heugten, Verhey, & van Boxtel, 2010; Gillespie, Best, & O'Neill, 2012). The strength of research evidence for the inclusion of external memory aids and ATC into cognitive rehabilitation is sufficient that it is considered a practice standard for individuals with mild memory impairments according to the American Congress of Rehabilitation Medicine (Cicerone et al., 2011; Haskins, Keith, & Trexler, 2012). When new device and strategy use are being implemented to substitute or compensate for cognitive impairments, training is essential for the successful generalization to real-life functioning. In the case of the more complex assistive technology devices, use of errorless learning in functional applications may be optimal for training acquiring skills in using the devices and their respective applications.

Social Communication

While there is extensive literature documenting social pragmatic impairment in people with moderate to severe TBI, there is little research specifically describing such difficulties in people with mTBI. In a randomized controlled study, Dahlberg and colleagues (2007) demonstrated improved social communication skills, maintained through a 9-month follow-up, using a curriculum that emphasized self-awareness and self-assessment; individual goal setting; use of the group process to foster interaction, feedback, problem solving, and social support; and generalization of skills through the involvement of family, friends, and weekly assignments completed in the home or community.

Impairments of social communication may result from both cognitive and behavioral changes associated with concussion and/or mTBI and comorbid conditions (Cornis-Pop et al., 2012). Persisting irritability and anger may manifest as negative self-talk, verbal abusiveness to others, or physical aggression that can negatively affect social interactions (Raskin & Mateer, 2000). Breakdowns in social communication, originating from chronic emotional and self-esteem problems, can contribute to loss of meaningful relationships and result in social isolation and loneliness (Brooks et al. 1987; Ylvisaker & Feeney, 2001). Cornis-Pop et al. (2012) suggest that social communication treatment focus on affective-behavioral impairments (e.g., anger and anxiety) and working with family and friends within the individual's circle of support on techniques that facilitate improved communication skills. These strategies would best be imple-

mented through collaboration with a mental health provider. Ylviskaker and colleagues (2005) suggest the following components of social skills intervention for persons with TBI:

- Educate and train communication partners to interact supportively
- Select personally important social interactive competencies
- Provide extensive practice of socially appropriate behaviors
- Provide situational coaching and training specifically designed to improve social perception and interpretation of others' behaviors and to improve self-monitoring of stress levels, so that individuals can remove themselves from the situation as needed
- Situational training
- Coach the individual to evaluate and reward personal "social successes"
- Counsel to develop the individual's sense of self that includes positive social interaction strategies

Clinical experience with the military population with mTBI and PTSD supports the need to address impairments in social communication and optimally in a group setting with interdisciplinary facilitators (Helmick & Members of the Consensus Conference, 2010).

Group Intervention

The culture of the military, as well as many civilian work environments, is one of teamwork, trust, and working toward shared goals. Therefore, group therapy is ideal for working with individuals on cognitive-social communication skills. Group treatment within community settings provides a more natural communicative context and should be considered as a strategy to facilitate generalization of improved cognitive communication abilities beyond the clinic and into real-life situations. Recent studies demonstrate that group-based interventions with combat veterans are effective in training social (Dahlberg et al., 2007) and cognitive skills (Huckans et al., 2010). Twamley et al. (2014) developed the Cognitive Symptom Management and Rehabilitation Therapy (CogSMART) program that is effective in training cognitive skills and symptom management and can be delivered in a group or individual setting. These are many other examples of the benefits of group-based programs for cognitive communication rehabilitation. A service member/veteran peer group can be very powerful by supporting the individual, influencing positive change among the participants, and providing a work team that is consistent with the military ethos. Similar models are continuing to evolve in civilian care as well (Hardin & Kelly, 2019; Schneider & Van Auken, 2018).

Discharge From Cognitive Communication Treatment

Discharge from cognitive communication treatment begins at the start of therapy with the development of the treatment plan or including the long- and short-term goals, frequency, and duration of treatment. Goal setting is a collaborative effort between the clinician and the patient. GAS is a flexible system of measuring objective, measurable, and time-based outcome goals,

based on a 5-point scale. During the process of establishing the treatment goals, the patient and clinician agree on the anticipated frequency and duration of therapy. The process of collaboration in the treatment planning and goal setting engages the patient in the therapy process, facilitates realistic goal setting, and establishes a shared responsibility in the therapeutic outcome. The transition plan should also be discussed as it can define the time frame for therapy.

Optimally, discharge is defined by the patient's achievement of his or her individualized treatment plan. There are no established thresholds on standardized testing that can substitute for clinician judgment and patient goals, perceptions, and preferences (Cornis-Pop et al., 2012). When a patient completes therapy by achieving his or her goals, recommendations are provided to facilitate a smooth transition back to work or school by including (1) gradual work reentry, (2) flexibility in setting a work schedule that allows for a shortened work schedule or breaks during the day, (3) environmental modifications, and (4) reduced work responsibilities. At the completion of the therapy program, the successful return to the community, whether it be returning to active-duty status or to a civilian position, to school or to employment, is measured by the patient's successful maintenance at the level of functioning achieved at discharge (Management of Concussion/mTBI Working Group, 2009).

For some patients, treatment goals may need to be adjusted to realistically fit a time schedule that is dictated by a discharge plan based on other factors than achievement of the long-term goals, and when working with service members, this is especially true. Discharges from therapy may occur when the patient either retires or is medically discharged from the military or is transferred back to his or her command. Sometimes admission to an intensive treatment program for substance abuse or PTSD leads to discontinuation of cognitive communication therapy that may be reinstated at a later date. When a service member is discharging from the military and relocating, a transition to the VA health care system in the new location can be facilitated by the patient's case manager. Whenever possible, the clinician will facilitate a smooth transition to another SLP provider for continuation of cognitive communication therapy.

Outcome Measures

Although adequate literature and expert consensus exist to support use of cognitive rehabilitation for persisting symptoms of mTBI, there is a paucity of well-designed clinical trials. It is important for individual providers and rehabilitation programs to collect and publish their outcome data and clinical experiences. In the current era of evidence-based clinical practice, measuring treatment outcomes is a practice standard (Helmick & Members of the Consensus Conference, 2010). Given a standard set of outcome measures, clinicians can compare their outcomes and pull their data to demonstrate the effectiveness and efficacy of intervention for persons with mTBI. Carefully describing the patients receiving cognitive communication therapy will be a particular challenge as the population of persons with mTBI is complex due to

the influence of comorbidities and other personal factors on cognitive communication impairment. Therefore, it is essential that programs include data elements to capture the nature and severity of comorbidities potentially affecting cognitive status (Helmick & Members of the Consensus Conference, 2010).

The recommended functional outcome measures are:

a. goal attainment scaling;
b. job performance, need for job redesignation/duty restrictions or limitations;
c. ongoing comparisons between preinjury fitness evaluations and current functional abilities as they improve;
d. performance on simulators (planes, computers, machinery, etc.);
e. quality of life assessment;
f. community participation assessment; and
g. social skills pragmatics assessment.

Outcome measures used in rehabilitation include team assessments of rehabilitation team goals, strengths and limitations of functional performance, discipline-specific outcomes (e.g., neuropsychological, speech pathology, and occupational therapy assessments), patient assessments of their functional outcome, and patient and family ratings of satisfaction and quality of life. Outcome measurement is necessary for advancing our understanding of who will benefit the most and which cognitive communication interventions are most effective with patients with a history of mTBI and persisting symptoms (Cornis-Pop et al., 2012; Helmick & Members of the Consensus Conference, 2010).

A Case Study of mTBI

JC, a 37-year-old U.S. Marine Corps Gunnery Sergeant (GySGT), sustained a TBI during his second deployment to Afghanistan in April 2010 when the Humvee he was riding in drove over a buried improvised explosive device. The blast pressure forces turned the vehicle into a mangled, barely recognizable pile of metal. He estimated that his loss of consciousness could not have been more than a minute. Although still confused and disoriented when he regained consciousness, he was able to organize his men for the ambush that ensued, secure the area, and move to a safe location. He was unable to provide an estimate of how long it took for these events to transpire or how long his confusion lasted.

Following the blast and ambush, JC was medically evacuated to a forward operating base (FOB) rehabilitation center for over a month before being able to join his troops in theater to complete their mission several months later. He continued to suffer from headaches, dizziness, balance problems, vision and hearing problems, disordered sleep, and cognitive communication deficits, including memory, word finding, and slow information processing.

JC's acute symptoms met the diagnostic criteria for mTBI.

■ A few minutes of LOC and less than 6 hours of PTSD
■ Gaps in his recall of the first 6 hours after the event
■ Alteration in mental state at the time of the accident (e.g., feeling dazed, disoriented, confused)
■ Focal neurological deficit(s) including vision, hearing, headache, dizziness, imbalance, and cognitive communication symptoms: memory, processing speed, and word finding
■ Negative neuroimaging
■ Negative screening for symptoms of PTSD or other mental health concerns

On returning home, JC resumed his duties supervising the motor pool. Over time, he became increasingly aware that he was having difficulties at work but internalized his thoughts. At home he avoided talking about work and became increasingly irritable and short-tempered. His wife and children noted his unusual behavior and knew something was wrong.

About 18 months after his second deployment, JC completed a third deployment in Afghanistan. However, he was restricted to his base, required to continue with outpatient therapy, and was not allowed to join his troops in combat. On returning stateside, he was transferred to a new command to continue supervising the motor pool. The stress of relocating across country with his family and transitioning to a new work group escalated his physical, cognitive, and emotional deficits and his command physician strongly recommended he go to the major military medical enter nearest to his base to be seen at the TBI clinic there. His family convinced him he needed to follow through with the advice of his command.

Thirty months after his injury, JC followed up with the recommendation to be seen for an evaluation at the TBI Clinic. He underwent a comprehensive TBI evaluation including assessments of his hearing, vision, headaches, dizziness and balance, sleep, mental health, and cognitive abilities. He underwent medical and surgical interventions for his hearing and vision impairments. Headaches, dizziness, balance, and sleep concerns were assessed and determined to be resolved. He was evaluated for PTSD and other mental health issues and cleared for these concerns. Results of neuropsychological assessment revealed borderline to mild deficits in attention and processing speed, verbal learning and memory, executive functions, and verbal skills. A test of his emotional functioning could not be interpreted due to his strong tendency to minimize symptoms and present himself in a positive light.

Initial screening of cognitive communication revealed intact naming, repeating simple sentences, and following simple commands, and moderately severe deficits in following complex commands and sentence repetition. He recalled only 50% of detail from a short story and had difficulty reading and answering simple yes/no questions. He became confused and frustrated when attempting both oral and silent reading comprehension tasks. Word definitions and proverb explanations were incomplete and concrete. He had difficulty verbally elaborating. His conversational speech was dysfluent and characterized by difficulties with word-finding sentence formulation and expression.

Many of JC's communication deficits were thought to be due to attention and processing impairments. On two occasions 6 months apart, the APT test was initiated. He consistently scored 30/30 on Level I, Sustained Attention. He became anxious and frustrated with the testing. In treatment, he eventually was able to complete the complex sus-

tained attention task, when the stimuli were presented at about a 50% slower rate. He was not able to complete the selective attention task due to its verbal distraction component, nor was he able to complete the divided or alternating attention task.

Task 2 of the FAVRES was administered. JC was able to complete this task accurately given a substantial amount of time. He demonstrated logical reasoning and problem solving, as well as use of strategies, and provided sound rationale for his responses. He required an hour to complete the independent portion of the task and his verbal responses reflected slow information processing and verbal formulation and expression.

JC was enrolled in the TBI program where he received physical therapy for vestibular and balance problems, speech-language pathology for cognitive communication interventions, and occupational therapy for functional cognitive skills training. He also attended medical appointments to address his hearing and vision impairments. In speech therapy, he participated in cognitive communication goal setting.

The motivational interview was conducted with JC prior to goal setting. Motivational interviewing is used to engage the patient in the goal-planning process, first by exploring areas of concern and then defining functional goals that provide the focus of intervention. The interview was semistructured with an emphasis on asking open-ended questions to indirectly guide JC through a process of providing information but also reflecting on what he was saying. Periodically, his messages would be reflected back in the form of offering a short summary of what the provider heard to demonstrate she was actively listening to JC as well as to give him a chance to reflect on what he was saying.

JC shared that he was frustrated at work because he was having such a tough time processing information and remembering what was said. He knew people had noticed he was not able to do his job, which really worried him because at his new command, he had no history with the people, and he was not a member of "their family" like he was at his previous command where he had deployed multiple times with his team. He stated he was unable to cover up his errors at work because he constantly was forgetting what he was doing and what someone told him, forgetting meetings and appointments, and having difficulty tracking projects. He described his frustration with his speech difficulties, including word-finding difficulties and forgetting what he just said as he tried to engage in a conversation, and he had difficulties maintaining the topic of conversation as demonstrated by his sudden shift from the topic of the conversation to another topic without awareness.

From the information shared during the motivational interview, JC was able to identify the following functional goals he wished to target in his cognitive communication therapy. The goals were written in the format of GAS with a baseline level of functioning defined as one level below the target level, with an additional two levels above the target to reflect levels of advanced achievement and one level below baseline to reflect regression.

The initial goal he selected focused on increasing his self-monitoring and management for visual and auditory distractors in his environment to im-

prove his attention and concentration (e.g., lower lights and blinds, reduce extraneous noise and visual distractors). This was a challenging goal for him to accomplish, as he was uncomfortable accepting his limitations and requesting assistance. After 6 months, he met the goal with 90% consistency.

The second goal he defined was to increase verbal fluency by focusing on word retrieval in conversations. His baseline was 40%, and by the completion of the goal, 4 months later, his word retrieval was 90%, consistent with mild delays 20% of the time.

Another treatment goal developed by JC was to depend less on his wife to manage his schedule. Early in his cognitive communication therapy, JC was provided a smart tablet for organizing and managing his schedule. With family support, he established a habit of checking his schedule and "to do" list twice daily before leaving the house in the morning and before going to bed at night. At the conclusion of his therapy, he stated that he was no longer dependent on his wife for his scheduling, and he was attending his appointments regularly.

His therapy progress was relatively slow until his fourth month of therapy, when during a follow-up visit with the team psychologist, he began to admit that he was experiencing flashbacks, random anxiety attacks, and sudden bursts of uncontrolled temper with his wife and children, among other symptoms of PTSD. JC finally admitted to his neurologist, a uniformed officer, that as much as he wanted to remain in the Marines, he realized he was unable to lead his troops safely through another mission. Through counseling, he was able to let go of the heavy burden of denying the physical, emotional, and cognitive communication deficits he was experiencing. His progress in therapies seemed to accelerate with his acceptance. Over the course of the next few weeks, he talked openly about his decision to get out of the military and began to discuss his future plans to return to Florida and to go back to school.

With JC's decision to return to school, the focus of cognitive communication therapy was redirected to addressing functional compensatory strategies for preparing him, including listening, reading, note taking, asking and responding to questions, engaging in conversations, and organizing and retrieving information. He was provided a smart pen that records lectures as you take notes and a smart pad and applications to address his goals.

He established GAS goals to:

a. Listen to lectures and record key points; read an article and highlight key points
b. Organize key points into a visual graphic maps or outlines
c. Write summaries or prepare verbal briefs of the material outlined
d. Plan and complete projects with specified due dates for each step through completion of the project
e. Manage a complex time-ordered agenda with contact and location information
f. Create to do lists and tasks and track progress in completing them
g. Efficiently store and retrieve passwords, resource information, documents, and so on

Through instructional training and practice, he accomplished these goals. At the conclusion of therapy, on the occasion of his retirement from the U.S. Marine Corps, GySGT JC completed a self-assessment of functional skills related to his use of assistive technology for cognition. He reported that he was effective to very effective at:

- remembering his schedule, appointments, and belongings;
- learning, storing, and retrieving new information (passwords, procedures, instructions);
- taking messages when talking on the telephone;
- having a conversation with an instructor or supervisor;
- taking notes during a meeting or lecture;
- completing tasks without distractions;
- completing tasks after being interrupted or distracted;
- organizing, scheduling, and completing tasks, appointments, and activities;
- preparing outlines, briefs, or written assignments;
- maintaining organized records, work/school, or personal files and papers;
- planning and completing projects;
- using daily routines; and
- feeling confident, independent, and capable using ATC.

GySGT JC was discharged from therapy and transitioned to the VA for follow-up in his home state.

The views expressed in this chapter are those of the authors and do not reflect the official policy or position of the Department of the Navy, Department of Defense, or the United States Government.

Additional Resources Available for Working With Individuals Following mTBI

- Defense Centers of Excellence for Psychological Health and Traumatic Brain Injury (DCoE) https://health.mil/News/Authors/ Defense-Centers-of-Excellence-for -Psychological-Health-and -Traumatic-Brain-Injury
- Defense and Veterans Brain Injury Center (DVBIC) http://dvbic.dcoe.mil
- Clinician's Guide to Cognitive Rehabilitation in Mild Traumatic Brain Injury: Application for Military Service Members and Veterans https://www.asha.org/uploaded Files/ASHA/Practice_Portal/ Clinical_Topics/Traumatic_Brain_ Injury_in_Adults/Clinicians-Guide-to-Cognitive-Rehabilitation-in-Mild-Traumatic-Brain-Injury.pdf
- Mild Traumatic Brain Injury Rehabilitation Toolkit http://www.cs.amedd.army.mil/ FileDownloadpublic.aspx?docid= e454f2ce-00ae-4a2d-887d-26d547 4c8d1a

References

Aase, D. M., Babione, J. M., Proescher, E., Greenstein, J. E., DiGangi, J. A., Schroth, C., . . . Phan, L. (2018). Impact of PTSD on post-concussive symptoms, neuropsychological functioning, and pain in post-9/11 veterans with mild traumatic brain injury. *Psychiatry Research, 268,* 460–466.

Acheson, D. J., & MacDonald, M. C. (2009). Verbal working memory and language production: Common approaches to the serial ordering of verbal information. *Psychological Bulletin, 135*(1), 50–58.

Adams, M. R. (1990) The demands and capacities model I: Theoretical elaborations. *Journal of Fluency Disorders, 15*(3), 135–141.

Akin, F. W., Murnane, O. D., Hall, C. D., & Riska, K. M. (2017). Vestibular consequences of mild traumatic brain injury and blast exposure: A review. *Brain Injury, 31*(9), 1188–1194.

American Speech-Language-Hearing Association. (2004). *Preferred practice patterns for the profession of speech-language pathology* [Preferred practice patterns]. Retrieved from http://www.asha.org/policy

American Speech-Language-Hearing Association. (2005a). *Knowledge and skills needed by speech-language pathologists providing services to individuals with cognitive-communication disorders* [Knowledge and skills]. Retrieved from http://www.asha.org/policy

American Speech-Language-Hearing Association. (2005b). *Roles of speech-language pathologists in the identification, diagnosis, and treatment of individuals with cognitive-communication disorders* [Position statement]. Retrieved from http://www.asha.org/policy

Atcherson, S. R., & Steele, M. (2016). Auditory processing deficits following sport-related or motor vehicle accident injuries. *Brain Disorders & Therapy, 5*(204), 1–5.

Aubry, M., Cantu, R., Dvorak, J., Graf-Baumann, T., Johnston, K., Kelly, J. P., . . . Schamasch, P. (2002). Summary and agreement statement of the first International Conference on Concussion in Sport, Vienna 2001. *British Journal of Sports Medicine, 36*(1), 6–7.

Baddeley, A., Emslie, H., & Nimmo-Smith, I. (1992). *Speed and Capacity of Language Processing (SCOLP).* Bloomington, MN: Pearson Education.

Bagalman, E. (2014, January 4). *Traumatic brain injury among veterans* (Congressional Report No. R40941). Washington,

DC: Library of Congress Congressional Research Service. Retrieved from http://www.ncsl.org/documents/statefed/health/TBI_Vets2013.pdf

Bailes, J. E., Dashnaw, M. L., Petraglia, A. L., & Turner, R. C. (2014). Cumulative effects of repetitive mild traumatic brain injury. *Concussion*, *28*, 50–62.

Baker, J. G., Leddy, J. J., Hinds, A. L., Haider, M. N., Shucard, J., Sharma, T., . . . Willer, B. S. (2018). An exploratory study of mild cognitive impairment of retired professional contact sport athletes. *Journal of Head Trauma Rehabilitation*, *33*(5), E16–E23.

Barrow, I. M., Collins, J. N., & Britt, L. D. (2006). The influence of an auditory distraction on rapid naming after a mild traumatic brain injury: A longitudinal study. *Journal of Trauma and Acute Care Surgery*, *61*(5), 1142–1149.

Barrow, I. M., Hough, M., Rastatter, M. P., Walker, M., Holbert, D., & Rotondo, M. F. (2003). Can within-category naming identify subtle cognitive deficits in the mild traumatic brain-injured patient? *Journal of Trauma and Acute Care Surgery*, *54*(5), 888–897.

Barry, N. C., & Tomes, J. L. (2015). Remembering your past: The effects of concussion on autobiographical memory recall. *Journal of Clinical and Experimental Neuropsychology*, *37*(9), 994–1003.

Baumgartner, J., & Duffy, J. R. (1997). Psychogenic stuttering in adults with and without neurologic disease. *Journal of Medical Speech Language Pathology*, *5*(2), 75–95.

Belanger, H. G., Kretzmer, G., Yoash-Gantz, R., Pickett, T., & Tupler, L. A. (2009). Cognitive sequelae of blast-related versus other mechanisms of brain trauma. *Journal of the International Neuropsychological Society*, *15*(1), 1–8.

Belanger, H. G., Proctor-Weber, Z., Kretzmer, T., Kim, M., French, L. M., & Vanderploeg, R. D. (2011). Symptom complaints following reports of blast versus non-blast mild TBI: Does mechanism of injury matter? *Clinical Neuropsychology*, *25*(5), 702–715.

Belanger, H. G., Vanderploeg, R., Curtiss, G., & Warden., D. (2007). Recent neuroimaging techniques in mild traumatic brain injury. *Journal of Neuropsychiatry and Clinical Neurosciences*, *19*(1), 5–20.

Bellerose, J., Bernier, A., Beaudoin, C., Gravel, J., & Beauchamp, M. H. (2017). Long-term brain-injury-specific effects following preschool mild TBI: A study of theory of mind. *Neuropsychology*, *31*(3), 229.

Benton, A. L., Hamsher, K., & Sivan, A. B. (1994). *Multilingual Aphasia Examination* (3rd ed.). Iowa City, IA: AJA Associates.

Ben-Yishay, Y., Silver, S. L., Piasetsky, E., & Rattock, J. (1987). Vocational outcome after holistic cognitive rehabilitation: Results of a seven-year study. *Journal of Head Trauma Rehabilitation*, *1*, 90.

Berisha, V., Wang, S., LaCross, A., Liss, J., & Garcia-Filion, P. (2017). Longitudinal changes in linguistic complexity among professional football players. *Brain and Language*, *169*, 57–63.

Białuńska, A., & Salvatore, A. P. (2017). The auditory comprehension changes over time after sport-related concussion can indicate multisensory processing dysfunctions. *Brain and Behavior*, *7*(12), e00874. https://doi.org/10.1002/brb3.874

Bolzenius, J. D., Roskos, P. T., Salminen, L. E., Paul, R. H., & Bucholz, R. D. (2015). Cognitive and self-reported psychological outcomes of blast-induced mild traumatic brain injury in veterans: A preliminary study. *Applied Neuropsychology Adult*, *22*(2), 79–87.

Brooks, J., Fos, L. A., Greve, K. W., & Hammond, J. S. (1999). Assessment of executive function in patients with mild traumatic brain injury. *Journal of Trauma and Acute Care Surgery*, *46*(1), 159–163.

Brooks, N., McKinlay, W., Symington, C., Beattie, A., & Campsie, L. (1987). Return to work within the first seven years of severe head injury. *Brain Injury*, *1*, 5–19.

Brunger, H., Ogden, J., Malia, K., Eldred, C., Terblanche, R., & Mistlin, A. (2014). Adjusting to persistent post-concussive symptoms following mild traumatic brain injury and subsequent psycho-educational intervention: A qualitative analysis in military personnel. *Brain Injury, 28*(1), 71–80.

Burgess, S., & Turkstra, L. S. (2010). Quality of communication life in adolescents with high-functioning autism and Asperger syndrome: A feasibility study. *Language, Speech, and Hearing Services in Schools, 41*, 474–487.

Callahan, M. L., Binder, L. M., O'Neil, M. E., Zaccari, B., Roost, M. S., Golshan, S., . . . Storzbach, D. (2018). Sensory sensitivity in Operation Enduring Freedom/Operation Iraqi Freedom veterans with and without blast exposure and mild traumatic brain injury. *Applied Neuropsychology: Adult, 25*(2), 126–136.

Cancelliere, C., Coronado, V. G., Taylor, C. A., & Xu, L. (2017). Epidemiology of isolated versus nonisolated mild traumatic brain injury treated in emergency departments in the United States, 2006–2012: Sociodemographic characteristics. *Journal of Head Trauma Rehabilitation, 32*(4), E37–E46.

Caplan, B., Bogner, J., Brenner, L., Twamley, E. W., Thomas, K. R., Gregory, A. M., . . . Lohr, J. B. (2015). CogSMART compensatory cognitive training for traumatic brain injury: effects over 1 year. *Journal of Head Trauma Rehabilitation, 30*(6), 391-401.

Capó-Aponte, J. E., Jorgensen-Wagers, K. L., Sosa, J. A., Walsh, D. V., Goodrich, G. L., Temme, L. A., & Riggs, D. W. (2017). Visual dysfunctions at different stages after blast and non-blast mild traumatic brain injury. *Optometry and Vision Science, 94*(1), 7–15.

Carlson, K. F., Kehle, S. M., Meis, L. A., Greer, N., MacDonald, R., Rutks, I., . . . Wilt, T. J. (2011). Prevalence, assessment, and treatment of mild traumatic brain injury and posttraumatic stress disorder: A systematic review of the evidence. *Journal of Head Trauma Rehabilitation, 26*(2), 103–115.

Carlson, K. F., Nelson, D., Orazem, R. J., Nugent, S., Cifu, D. X., & Sayer, N. A. (2010). Psychiatric diagnoses among Iraq and Afghanistan war veterans screened for deployment-related traumatic brain injury. *Journal of Traumatic Stress, 23*(1), 17–24.

Carroll, L., Cassidy, J. D., Peloso, P., Borg, J., Von Holst, H., Holm, L., . . . Pépin, M. (2004). Prognosis for mild traumatic brain injury: Results of the WHO Collaborating Centre Task Force on Mild Traumatic Brain Injury. *Journal of Rehabilitation Medicine, 36*, 84–105.

Centers for Disease Control and Prevention (CDC), National Center for Injury Prevention and Control. (2003). *Report to Congress on mild traumatic brain injury in the United States: Steps to prevent a serious public health problem.* Atlanta, GA: Author.

Chamelian, L., & Feinstein, A. (2004). Outcome after mild to moderate traumatic brain injury: The role of dizziness. *Archives of Physical Medicine and Rehabilitation, 85*(10), 1662–1666.

Chandler, D. (2006). Blast-related ear injury in current US military operations. *The ASHA Leader, 11*(9), 8–9.

Chien, J. H., Cheng, J. J., & Lenz, F. A. (2016). The thalamus. In P. M. Conn (Ed.), *Conn's translational neuroscience* (pp. 289–297). London, UK: Academic Press.

Childers, C., & Hux, K. (2016). Invisible injuries: The experiences of college students with histories of mild traumatic brain injury. *Journal of Postsecondary Education and Disability, 29*(4), 389–405.

Choe, M. C., & Giza, C. C. (2015). Diagnosis and management of acute concussion. *Seminars in Neurology, 35*(1), 29–41.

Chorney, S. R., Suryadevara, A. C., & Nicholas, B. D. (2017). Audiovestibular symptoms as predictors of prolonged sports-related concussion among NCAA athletes. *Laryngoscope, 127*(12), 2850–2853.

Cicerone K. D. (1996). Attention deficits and dual task demands after mild traumatic brain injury. *Brain Injury, 10,* 79–89.

Cicerone, K. D. (2002). Remediation of 'working attention' in mild traumatic brain injury. *Brain Injury, 16*(3), 185–195.

Cicerone, K. D., Dahlberg, C., Kalmar, K., Langenbahn, D. M., Malec, J. F., Bergquist, T. F., . . . Morse, P. A. (2000). Evidence-based cognitive rehabilitation: recommendations for clinical practice. *Archives of Physical Medicine and Rehabilitation, 81*(12), 1596–1615.

Cicerone, K. D., Dahlberg, C., Malec, J. F., Langenbahn, D. M., Felicetti, T., Kneipp, S., . . . Catanese, J. (2005). Evidence-based cognitive rehabilitation: Updated review of the literature from 1998 through 2002. *Archives of Physical Medicine and Rehabilitation, 86*(8), 1681–1692.

Cicerone, K. D., & Kalmar, K. (1995). Persistent postconcussion syndrome: The structure of subjective complaints after mild traumatic brain injury. *Journal of Head Trauma Rehabilitation, 10*(3), 1–17.

Cicerone, K. D., Langenbahn, D. M., Braden, C., Malec, J. F., Kalmar, K., Fraas, M., . . . Ashman, T. (2011). Evidence-based cognitive rehabilitation: Updated review of the literature from 2003 through 2008. *Archives of Physical Medicine and Rehabilitation, 92*(4), 519–530.

Cicerone, K. D., Mott, T., Azulay, J., Sharlow-Galella, M. A., Ellmo, W. J., Paradise, S., & Friel, J. C. (2008). A randomized controlled trial of holistic neuropsychologic rehabilitation after traumatic brain injury. *Archives of Physical Medicine and Rehabilitation, 89*(12), 2239–2249.

Coelho, C., Ylvisaker, M., & Turkstra, L. S. (2005). Nonstandardized assessment approaches for individuals with traumatic brain injuries. *Seminars in Speech and Language, 26*(4), 223.

Collins, M. W., Kontos, A. P., Okonkwo, D. O., Almquist, J., Bailes, J., Barisa, M., . . . Cardenas, J. (2016). Statements of agreement from the targeted evaluation and active management (TEAM) approaches to treating concussion meeting held in Pittsburgh, October 15–16, 2015. *Neurosurgery, 79*(6), 912–929.

Combs, H. L., Berry, D. T., Pape, T., Babcock-Parziale, J., Smith, B., Schleenbaker, R., . . . High, W. M., Jr. (2015). The effects of mild traumatic brain injury, post-traumatic stress disorder, and combined mild traumatic brain injury/post-traumatic stress disorder on returning veterans. *Journal of Neurotrauma, 32*(13), 956–966.

Comper, P., Bisschop, S. M., Carnide, N., & Tricco, A. (2005). A systematic review of treatments for mild traumatic brain injury. *Brain Injury, 19,* 863–880.

Cooper, D. B., Bowles, A. O., Kennedy, J. E., Curtiss, G., French, L. M., Tate, D. F., & Vanderploeg, R. D. (2017). Cognitive rehabilitation for military service members with mild traumatic brain injury: A randomized clinical trial. *Journal of Head Trauma Rehabilitation, 32*(3), E1–E15.

Cooper, D. B., Kennedy, J. E., Cullen, M. A., Critchfield, E., Amador, R. R., & Bowles, A. O. (2011). Association between combat stress and post-concussive symptom reporting in OEF/OIF service members with mild traumatic brain injuries. *Brain Injury, 25*(1), 1–7.

Cornis-Pop, M. (2008). The role of speech-language pathologists in the cognitive-communication rehabilitation of traumatic brain injury. *California Speech-Language Hearing Association Magazine, 38*(1),14–18.

Cornis-Pop, M., Mashima, P., Roth, C., MacLennan, D., Picon, L., Hammond, C., . . . Frank, E. M. (2012). Cognitive-communication rehabilitation for combat-related mild traumatic brain injury. *Journal of Rehabilitation and Research Development, 49*(7), xi–xxxii.

Corsellis, J. A. N., Bruton, C. J., & Freeman-Browne, D. (1973). The aftermath of boxing. *Psychological Medicine, 3*(3), 270–303.

Covassin, T., Elbin, R. J., Harris, W., Parker, T., & Kontos, A. (2012). The role of age and sex in symptoms, neurocognitive performance, and postural stability in athletes after concussion. *The American Journal of Sports Medicine, 40*(6), 1303–1312.

Covassin, T., Stearne, D., & Elbin, R., III. (2008). Concussion history and postconcussion neurocognitive performance and symptoms in collegiate athletes. *Journal of Athletic Training, 43*(2), 119–124.

Cranney, M., Warren, E., Barton, S., Gardner, K., & Walley, T. (2001). Why do GPs not implement evidence-based guidelines? A descriptive study. *Family Practice, 18*(4), 359–363.

Creed, J. A., DiLeonardi, A. M., Fox, D. P., Tessler, A. R., & Raghupathi, R. (2011). Concussive brain trauma in the mouse results in acute cognitive deficits and sustained impairment of axonal function. *Journal of Neurotrauma, 28*(4), 547–563.

Crewe-Brown, S. J., Stipinovich, A. M., & Zsilavecz, U. (2011). Communication after mild traumatic brain injury: A spouse's perspective. *South African Journal of Communication Disorders, 58*(1), 1–21.

Critchley, M. (1949). *Punch-drunk syndromes: The chronic traumatic encephalopathy of boxers.* Hommage a Clovis Vincent. Paris: Maloine.

Crovitz, H. F. (1979). Memory retraining in brain-damaged patients: The airplane list. *Cortex, 15*(1), 131–134.

Crovitz, H. F., Harvey, M. T., & Horn, R. W. (1979). Problems in the acquisition of imagery mnemonics: Three brain damaged cases. *Cortex, 15*, 225–234.

Daggett, V. S., Bakas, T., Buelow, J., Habermann, B., & Murray, L. M. (2013). Needs and concerns of male combat veterans with mild traumatic brain injury. *Journal of Rehabilitation Research and Development, 50*(3), 327–340.

Dahlberg, C. A., Cusick, C. P., Hawley, L. A., Newman, J. K., Morey, C. E., Harrison-Felix, C. L., & Whiteneck, G. G. (2007). Treatment efficacy of social communication skills training after traumatic brain injury: A randomized treatment and deferred treatment controlled trial. *Archives of Physical Medicine and Rehabilitation, 88*, 1561–1573.

Daudet, L., Yadav, N., Perez, M., Poellabauer, C., Schneider, S., & Huebner, A. (2017). Portable mTBI assessment using temporal and frequency analysis of speech. *IEEE Journal of Biomedical and Health Informatics, 21*(2), 496–506.

Davis, G. A., et al. (2017). Sport Concussion Assessment Tool 5th edition (SCAT 5). *British Journal of Sports Medicine, 1–8.*

de Ceballos, J. P. G., Turégano-Fuentes, F., Pérez-Diaz, D., Sanz-Sanchez, M., Martin-Llorente, C., & Guerrero-Sanz, J. E. (2004). 11 March 2004: The terrorist bomb explosions in Madrid, Spain—an analysis of the logistics, injuries sustained and clinical management of casualties treated at the closest hospital. *Critical Care, 9*(1), 104.

de Joode, E., van Heugten, C., Verhey, F., & van Boxtel, M. (2010). Efficacy and usability of assistive technology for patients with cognitive deficits: A systematic review. *Clinical Rehabilitation, 24*(8), 701–714.

Defense and Veterans Brain Injury Center (DVBIC). (2012). Retrieved from https://www.jsomonline.org/TBI/MACE_Revised_2012.pdf

Defense and Veterans Brain Injury Center (DVBIC). (2018). *TBI & the military.* Retrieved from http://dvbic.dcoe.mil/tbi-military

Defense Centers of Excellence. (2013). *Neuroimaging following mild traumatic brain injury in the non-deployed setting.* DCoE Clinical Recommendations.

DeKosky, S. T., Blennow, K., Ikonomovic, M. D., & Gandy, S. (2013). Acute and chronic traumatic encephalopathies: Pathogenesis and biomarkers. *Nature Reviews Neurology, 9*(4), 192.

DeKosky, S. T., Jaffee, M., & Bauer, R. (2018). Long-term mortality in NFL professional football players: No significant increase, but questions remain. *JAMA, 319*(8), 773–775.

Delis, D. C., Kramer, J. H., Kaplan, E., & Ober, B. A. (2000). *California Verbal Learning Test–Second Edition (CVLT-II)*. Bloomington, MN: Pearson Education.

Del Rossi, G. (2017). Evaluating the recovery curve for clinically assessed reaction time after concussion. *Journal of Athletic Training, 52*(8), 766–770.

Dennis, E. L., Babikian, T., Giza, C. C., Thompson, P. M., & Asarnow, R. F. (2017). Diffusion MRI in pediatric brain injury. *Child's Nervous System, 33*(10), 1683–1692.

DePalma, R. G., Burris, D. G., Champion, H. R., & Hodgson, M. J. (2005). Blast injuries. *New England Journal of Medicine, 352*(13), 1335–1342.

Dewan, M. C., Rattani, A., Gupta, S., Baticulon, R. E., Hung, Y. C., Punchak, M., . . . Rosenfeld, J. V. (2018). Estimating the global incidence of traumatic brain injury. *Journal of Neurosurgery*, 1–18.

D'Hondt, F., Lassonde, M., Thebault-Dagher, F., Bernier, A., Gravel, J., Vannasing, P., & Beauchamp, M. H. (2017). Electrophysiological correlates of emotional face processing after mild traumatic brain injury in preschool children. *Cognitive, Affective, & Behavioral Neuroscience, 17*(1), 124–142.

Dick, R. W. (2009). Is there a gender difference in concussion incidence and outcomes? *British Journal of Sports Medicine, 43*(Suppl. 1), i46–i50.

Dikmen, S. S., Corrigan, J. D., Levin, H. S., Machamer, J., Stiers, W., & Weisskopf, M. G. (2009). Cognitive outcome following traumatic brain injury. *Journal of Head Trauma Rehabilitation, 24*(6), 430–438.

Dinnes, C., & Hux, K. (2017). A multicomponent writing intervention for a college student with mild brain injury. *Communication Disorders Quarterly, 4*, 1–11.

Dischinger, P. C., Ryb, G. E., Kufera, J. A., & Auman, K. M. (2009). Early predictors of postconcussive syndrome in a population of trauma patients with mild traumatic brain injury. *Journal of Trauma and Acute Care Surgery, 66*(2), 289–297.

Douglas, J., O'Flaherty, C. A., & Snow, P. (2000). Measuring perception of communicative ability: The development and evaluation of the La Trobe Communication Questionnaire. *Aphasiology, 14*, 251–268.

Draper, K., & Ponsford, J. (2008) Cognitive functioning ten years following traumatic brain injury and rehabilitation. *Neuropsychology, 22*, 618–625.

Dretsch, M. N., Kelly, M. P, Coldren, R. L., Parish, R. V., & Russell, M. L. (2015). Significant acute and subacute differences between blast and blunt concussions across multiple neurocognitive measures and symptoms in deployed soldiers. *Journal of Neurotrauma, 32*, 1217–1222.

Duffy, J. R. (2012). *Motor speech disorders: Substrates, differential diagnosis, and management* (3rd ed.). St. Louis, MO: Mosby.

Duffy, J. R., Manning, R. K., & Roth, C. R. (2012, November). *Acquired stuttering in post-deployed service members*. ASHA convention podium presentation, Atlanta, GA.

Echemendia, R. J., Meeuwisse, W., McCrory, P., Davis, G. A., Putukian, M., Leddy, J., . . . Schneider, K. (2017). The Sport Concussion Assessment Tool 5th edition (SCAT5): Background and rationale. *British Journal of Sports Medicine, 51*(11), 848–850.

Eckner, J. T., Kutcher, J. S., Broglio, S. P., & Richardson, J. K. (2014). Effect of sport-related concussion on clinically measured simple reaction time. *British Journal of Sports Medicine, 48*, 112–118.

Ehlhardt, L. A., Sohlberg, M. M., Kennedy, M., Coelho, C., Ylvisaker, M., Turkstra, L. S., & Yorkston, K. (2008). Evidence based practice guidelines for instructing individuals with neurogenic memory impairments: What have we learned in the past 20 years? *Neuropsychological Rehabilitation, 18*(3), 300–342.

Eisenberg, M. A., Andrea, J., Meehan, W., & Mannix, R. (2013). Time interval between concussions and symptom duration. *Pediatrics, 132*(1), 8–17.

Eisenberg, M. A., Meehan, W. P., & Mannix, R. (2014). Duration and course of post-concussive symptoms. *Pediatrics, 133*(6), 999–1006.

Elsayed, N. M. (1997). Toxicology of blast overpressure. *Toxicology, 121*(1), 1–15.

Evans, R. (1994). The postconcussion syndrome: 130 years of controversy. *Seminars in Neurology, 14,* 31–39.

Fasotti, L., Kovacs, F., Eling, P. A., & Brouwer, W. H. (2000). Time pressure management as a compensatory strategy training after closed head injury. *Neuropsychological Rehabilitation, 10*(1), 47–65.

Fausti, S. A., Wilmington, D. J., Gallun, F. J., Myers, P. J., & Henry, J. A. (2009). Auditory and vestibular dysfunction associated with blast-related traumatic brain injury. *Journal of Rehabilitation Research and Development, 46*(6), 797–810.

Fineblit, S., Selci, E., Loewen, H., Ellis, M., & Russell, K. (2016). Health-related quality of life after pediatric mild traumatic brain injury/concussion: A systematic review. *Journal of Neurotrauma, 33*(17), 1561–1568.

Finkel, A. G., Ivins, B. J., Yerry, J. A., Klaric, J. S., Scher, A., & Sammy Choi, Y. (2017). Which matters more? A retrospective cohort study of headache characteristics and diagnosis type in soldiers with mTBI/concussion. *Headache: The Journal of Head and Face Pain, 57*(5), 719–728.

Finkel, M. F. (2006). The neurological consequences of explosives. *Journal of the Neurological Sciences, 249*(1), 63–67.

Fleming, J. M., Strong, J., & Ashton, R. (1996). Self-awareness of deficits in adults with traumatic brain injury: How best to measure? *Brain Injury, 10*(1), 1–15.

French, L., McCrea, M., & Baggett, M. (2008). The Military Acute Concussion Evaluation (MACE). *Journal of Special Operations Medicine, 8*(1), 68–77.

Fulton, J. J., Calhoun, P. S., Wagner, H. R., Schry, A. R., Hair, L. P., Feeling, N., Elbogen, E., & Beckham, J. D. (2015). The prevalence of posttraumatic stress disorder in Operation Enduring Freedom/Operation Iraqi Freedom (OEF/OIF) veterans: A meta-analysis. *Journal of Anxiety Disorders, 31,* 98–107.

Gallun, F. J., Papesh, M. A., & Lewis, M. S. (2017). Hearing complaints among veterans following traumatic brain injury. *Brain Injury, 31*(9), 1183–1187.

Gentilinia, M., Nichell, P., & Schoenhube, R. (1989). Assessment of attention in mild head injury. In H. S. Levin, H. M. Eisenberg, & A. L. Benton (Eds.), *Mild head injury* (pp. 162–175). New York, NY: Oxford University Press.

Gianutsos, R., & Gianutsos, J. (1979). Rehabilitating the verbal recall of brain-injured patients by mnemonic training: An experimental demonstration using single-case methodology. *Journal of Clinical and Experimental Neuropsychology, 1*(2), 117–135.

Gillespie, A., Best, C., & O'Neill, B. (2012). Cognitive function and assistive technology for cognition: A systematic review. *Journal of the International Neuropsychological Society, 18*(1), 1–19.

Gioia, G., & Collins, M. (2006). Acute Concussion Evaluation (ACE): Physician/clinician office version. Retrieved from http://www.cdc.gov/concussion/headsup/pdf/ace-a.pdf

Gioia, G. A., Isquith, P. K. Guy, S. C. & Kenworthy, L. (2002) *Behavior Rating Inventory of Executive Function*® (BRIEF®). Lutz, FL: PAR.

Giza, C. C., & Hovda, D. A. (2001). The neurometabolic cascade of concussion. *Journal of Athletic Training, 36*(3), 228–235.

Gondusky, J. S., & Reiter, M. P. (2005). Protecting military convoys in Iraq: An examination of battle injuries sustained by a mechanized battalion during Operation Iraqi Freedom II. *Military Medicine, 170*(6), 546–549.

Grady, M. F., Master, C. L., & Gioia, G. A. (2012). Concussion pathophysiology: Rationale for physical and cognitive rest. *Pediatric Annals*, *41*(9), 377–382.

Gray, J. M., Robertson, I., Pentland, B., & Anderson, S. (1992). Microcomputer-based attentional retraining after brain damage: A randomized group controlled trial. *Neuropsychological Rehabilitation*, *2*, 97–115.

Green, S. L., Keightley, M. L., Lobaugh, N. J., Dawson, D. R., & Mihailidis, A. (2018). Changes in working memory performance in youth following concussion. *Brain Injury*, *32*(2), 182–190.

Greer, N., Sayer, N., Koeller, E., Velasquez, T., & Wilt, T. J. (2018). Outcomes associated with blast versus nonblast-related traumatic brain injury in US military service members and veterans: A systematic review. *Journal of Head Trauma Rehabilitation*, *33*(2), E16–E29.

Grossman, E. J., & Inglese, M. (2016). The role of thalamic damage in mild traumatic brain injury. *Journal of Neurotrauma*, *33*(2), 163–167.

Guerriero, R., Hawash, K., Pepin, M., Wolff, R., & Meehan III, W. (2015). Younger children recover faster and have less premorbid conditions than adolescents with concussion (I5–5E). *Neurology*, *84*(14, Suppl.), I5–5E.

Guskiewicz, K. M., McCrea, M., Marshall, S. W., Cantu, R. C., Randolph, C., Barr, W., . . . Kelly, J. P. (2003). Cumulative effects associated with recurrent concussion in collegiate football players: The NCAA Concussion Study. *JAMA*, *290*(19), 2549–2555.

Haarbauer-Krupa, J., Arbogast, K. B., Metzger, K. B., Greenspan, A. I., Kessler, R., Curry, A. E., . . . Master, C. L. (2018). Variations in mechanisms of injury for children with concussion. *Journal of Pediatrics*. Advance online publication.

Hall, R. C., Hall, R. C., & Chapman, M. J. (2005). Definition, diagnosis, and forensic implications of postconcussional syndrome. *Psychosomatics*, *46*(3), 195–202.

Halterman, C. I., Langan, J., Drew, A., Rodriguez, E., Osternig, L. R., Chou, L. S., & Donkelaar, P. V. (2005). Tracking the recovery of visuospatial attention deficits in mild traumatic brain injury. *Brain*, *129*(3), 747–753.

Hardin, K. Y., & Kelly, J. P. (2019). The role of speech-language pathology in an interdisciplinary care model for persistent symptomatology of mild traumatic brain injury. *Seminars in Speech and Language*, *40*(1), 65–78.

Haskins, E. C., Keith, C., & Trexler, L. E. (2012). *Cognitive rehabilitation manual: Translating evidence-based recommendations into practice*. Reston, VA: American Congress of Rehabilitation Medicine.

Heitger, M. H., Jones, R. D., Dalrymple-Alford, J. C., Frampton, C. M., Ardagh, M. W., & Anderson, T. J. (2006). Motor deficits and recovery during the first year following mild closed head injury. *Brain Injury*, *20*(8), 807–824.

Helgeson, S. R. (2010). Identifying brain injury in state juvenile justice correlations, and homeless populations: Challenges and promising practices. *Brain Injury Professional*, *7*(4), 18–20.

Helmick, K., & Members of the Consensus Conference. (2010). Cognitive rehabilitation for military personnel with mild traumatic brain injury and chronic postconcussional disorder: Results of April 2009 consensus conference. *NeuroRehabilitation*, *26*(3), 239–255.

Helmick, K. M., Spells, C. A., Malik, S. Z., Davies, C. A., Marion, D. W., & Hinds, S. R. (2015). Traumatic brain injury in the US military: Epidemiology and key clinical and research programs. *Brain Imaging Behavior*, *9*(3), 358–366.

Hoover, E. C., Souza, P. E., & Gallun, F. J. (2017). Auditory and cognitive factors associated with speech-in-noise complaints following mild traumatic brain injury. *Journal of the American Academy of Audiology, 28*(4), 325–339.

Howell, D., Osternig, L., Van Donkelaar, P., Mayr, U., & Chou, L. S. (2013). Effects of concussion on attention and executive function in adolescents. *Medical and Science in Sports and Exercise, 45*(6), 1030–1037.

Huckans, M., Pavawalla, S., Demadura, T., Kolessar, M., Seelye, A., Roost, N., . . . Storzbach, D. (2010). A pilot study examining effects of group-based cognitive strategy training treatment on self-reported cognitive problems, psychiatric symptoms, functioning, and compensatory strategy use in OIF/OEF combat veterans with persistent mild cognitive disorder and history of traumatic brain injury. *Journal of Rehabilitation Research and Development, 47,* 43–60.

Hunt, C., Zanetti, K., Kirkham, B., Michalak, A., Masanic, C., Vaidyanath, C., . . . Ouchterlony, D. (2016). Identification of hidden health utilization services and costs in adults awaiting tertiary care following mild traumatic brain injury in Toronto, Ontario, Canada. *Concussion, 1*(4), CNC21.

Iadevaia, C., Roiger, T., & Zwart, M. B. (2015). Qualitative examination of adolescent health-related quality of life at 1 year postconcussion. *Journal of Athletic Training, 50*(11), 1182–1189.

Isaki, E., & Turkstra L. (2000). Communication abilities and work re-entry following traumatic brain injury. *Brain Injury, 14,* 441–453.

Iverson, G. L. (2005). Outcome from mild traumatic brain injury. *Current Opinions in Psychiatry, 18,* 301–317.

Iverson, G. L., Brooks, B. L., Ashton, V. L., & Lange, R. T. (2010). Interview versus questionnaire symptom reporting in people with the postconcussion syndrome. *Journal of Head Trauma Rehabilitation, 25*(1), 23–30.

Iverson, G. L., Keene, C. D., Perry, G., & Castellani, R. J. (2018). The need to separate chronic traumatic encephalopathy neuropathology from clinical features. *Journal of Alzheimer's Disease, 61*(1), 17–28.

Ivins, B. J., Kane, R., & Schwab, K. A. (2009). Performance on the automated neuropsychological assessment metrics in a nonclinical sample of soldiers screened for mild TBI after returning from Iraq and Afghanistan: A descriptive analysis. *Journal of Head Trauma Rehabilitation, 24*(1), 24–31.

Jagnoor, J., & Cameron, I. (2015). Mild traumatic brain injury and motor vehicle crashes: Limitations to our understanding. *Injury, 46*(10), 1871–1874.

Jordan, B. D. (2000). Chronic traumatic brain injury associated with boxing. *Seminars in Neurology, 20*(2), 179–186.

Kamins, J., Bigler, E., Covassin, T., Henry, L., Kemp, S., Leddy, J. J., . . . McLeod, T. C. V. (2017). What is the physiological time to recovery after concussion? A systematic review. *British Journal of Sports Medicine, 51*(12), 935–940.

Karlin, A. M. (2011). Concussion in the pediatric and adolescent population: Different population, different concerns. *Physical Medicine and Rehabilitation, 3*(10), S369–S379.

Kay, T., Newman, B., Cavallo, M., Ezrachi, O., & Resnick, M. (1992). Toward a neuropsychological model of functional disability after mild traumatic brain injury. *Neuropsychology, 6*(4), 371.

Keightley, M. L., Singh Saluja, R., Chen, J. K., Gagnon, I., Leonard, G., Petrides, M., & Ptito, A. (2014). A functional magnetic resonance imaging study of working memory in youth after sports-related concussion: Is it still working? *Journal of Neurotrauma, 31*(5), 437–451.

Kelly, J. P., Nichols, J. S., Filley, C. M., Lillehei, K. O., Rubinstein, D., & Kleinschmidt-DeMasters, B. K. (1991). Concussion in sports. *JAMA, 266*(20), 2867–2869.

Kennedy, M. R., & Coelho, C. (2005). Self-regulation after traumatic brain injury: A framework for intervention of memory and problem solving. *Strategies, 12,* 13.

Kewman, D. G., Yanus, B., & Kirsch, N. (1988). Assessment of distractibility in auditory comprehension after traumatic brain injury. *Brain Injury*, 2(2), 131–137.

King, K. A., Hough, M. S., Vos, P., Walker, M. M., & Givens, G. (2006). Word retrieval following mild TBI: Implications for categorical deficits. *Aphasiology*, 20, 233–245.

King, K. A., Hough, M. S., Walker, M. M., Rastatter, M., & Holbert, D. (2006). Mild traumatic brain injury: Effects on naming in word retrieval and discourse. *Brain Injury*, 20(7), 725–732.

Kontos, A. P., Covassin, T., Elbin, R. J., & Parker, T. (2012). Depression and neurocognitive performance after concussion among male and female high school and collegiate athletes. *Archives of Physical Medicine and Rehabilitation*, 93(10), 1751–1756.

Kontos, A. P., Sufrinko, A., Womble, M., & Kegel, N. (2016). Neuropsychological assessment following concussion: An evidence-based review of the role of neuropsychological assessment pre- and post-concussion. *Current Pain and Headache Reports*, 20(6), 1–7.

Kristman, V. L., Côté, P., Van Eerd, D., Vidmar, M., Rezai, M., Hogg-Johnson, S., . . . Cassidy, J. D. (2008). Prevalence of lost-time claims for mild traumatic brain injury in the working population: Improving estimates using workers compensation databases. *Brain Injury*, 22(1), 51–59.

Krug, H., & Turkstra, L. S. (2015). Assessment of cognitive-communication disorders in adults with mild traumatic brain injury. *Perspectives on Neurophysiology and Neurogenic Speech and Language Disorders*, 25, 17–35.

Kurowski, B. G., Wade, S., Dexheimer, J. W., Dyas, J., Zhang, N., & Babcock, L. (2016). Feasibility and potential benefits of a Web-based intervention delivered acutely after mild traumatic brain injury in adolescents: A pilot study. *The Journal of Head Trauma Rehabilitation*, 31(6), 369.

Kutas, M., & Federmeier, K. D. (2000). Electrophysiology reveals semantic memory use in language comprehension. *Trends in Cognitive Sciences*, 4(12), 463–470.

Laatsch, L., & Guay, J. (2005). Rehabilitation of reading comprehension fluency in adults with acquired brain injury. *Journal of Cognitive Rehabilitation*, 23, 5–12.

Lalonde, G., Bernier, A., Beaudoin, C., Gravel, J., & Beauchamp, M. H. (2018). Investigating social functioning after early mild TBI: The quality of parent–child interactions. *Journal of Neuropsychology*, 12(1), 1–22.

Landon, J., Shepherd, D., Stuart, S., Theadom, A., & Freundlich, S. (2012). Hearing every footstep: Noise sensitivity in individuals following traumatic brain injury. *Neuropsychological Rehabilitation*, 22(3), 391–407.

Lange, R. T., Edmed, S. L., Sullivan, K. A., French, L. M., & Cooper, D. B. (2013). Utility of the Mild Brain Injury Atypical Symptoms Scale to detect symptom exaggeration: An analogue simulation study. *Journal of Clinical and Experimental Neuropsychology*, 35(2), 192–209.

Lange, R. T., Pancholi S., Brickell, T. A., Sakura, S., Bhagwat, A., Merritt, V., & French, L. M. (2012). Neuropsychological outcome from blast versus non-blast: Mild traumatic brain injury in U.S. military service members. *Journal of the International Neuropsychological Society*, 18, 595–605.

Lau, B. C., Kontos, A. P., Collins, M. W., Mucha, A., & Lovell, M. R. (2011). Which on-field signs/symptoms predict protracted recovery from sport-related concussion among high school football players? *American Journal of Sports Medicine*, 39(11), 2311–2318.

Lavonas, E., & Pennardt, A. (2006). *Blast injuries*. Retrieved from http://www.emedicine.com/emerg/topic63.htm

Lawson, M. J., & Rice, D. N. (1989). Effects of training in use of executive strategies on a verbal memory problem resulting from closed head injury. *Journal of Clini-*

cal and Experimental Neuropsychology, *11*(6), 842–854.

Le, T. H., & Gean, A. D. (2009). Neuroimaging of traumatic brain injury. *Mount Sinai Journal of Medicine, 76*(2), 145–162.

Lebrun, C. M., Mrazik, M., Prasad, A. S., Tjarks, B. J., Dorman, J. C., Bergeron, M. F., . . . Valentine, V. D. (2013). Sport concussion knowledge base, clinical practices and needs for continuing medical education: A survey of family physicians and cross-border comparison. *British Journal of Sports Medicine, 47*(1), 54–59.

Ledbetter, A. K., Sohlberg, M. M., Fickas, S. F., Horney, M. A., & McIntosh, K. (2017). Evaluation of a computer-based prompting intervention to improve essay writing in undergraduates with cognitive impairment after acquired brain injury. *Neuropsychological Rehabilitation, 27,* 1–30.

Levin, H. S., & Goldstein, F. C. (1986). Organization of verbal memory after severe closed-head injury. *Journal of Clinical and Experimental Neuropsychology, 8*(6), 643–656.

Levin, H. S., Goldstein, F. C., & MacKenzie, E. J. (1997). Depression as a secondary condition following mild and moderate traumatic brain injury. *Seminars in Clinical Neuropsychiatry, 2*(3), 207–215.

Levin, H. S., Mattis, S., Ruff, R. M., Eisenberg, H. M., Marshall, L. F., Tabaddor, K., & Frankowski, R. F. (1987). Neurobehavioral outcome following minor head injury: A three center study. *Journal of Neurosurgery, 66,* 234–243.

Lew, H. L., Lin, P. H., Fuh, J. L., Wang, S. J., Clark, D. J., & Walker, W. C. (2006). Characteristics and treatment of headache after traumatic brain injury: A focused review. *American Journal of Physical Medicine & Rehabilitation, 85*(7), 619–627.

Lezak, M. D. (1982). The problem of assessing executive functions. *International Journal of Psychology, 17,* 281–297.

Lezak, M. D., Howieson, D. B., Loring, D. W., & Fischer, J. S. (2004). *Neuropsychological assessment.* New York, NY: Oxford University Press.

Lindquist, L. K., Love, H. C., & Elbogen, E. B. (2017). Traumatic brain injury in Iraq and Afghanistan veterans: New results from a National Random Sample Study. *Journal of Neuropsychiatry and Clinical Neurosciences, 29*(3), 254–259.

Lovell, M. R., Iverson, G. L., Collins, M. W., Podell, K., Johnston, K. M., Pardini, D., . . . Maroon J. C. (2006). Measurement of symptoms following sports-related concussion: Reliability and normative data for the Post-Concussion Scale. *Applied Neuropsychology, 13*(3), 166–174.

Lucic, M. (1995). Therapy of middle ear injuries caused by explosive devices. *Vojnosanit Pregl, 52*(3), 221–224.

Luethcke, C. A., Bryan, C. J., Morrow, C. E., & Isler, W. C. (2010). Comparison of concussive symptoms, cognitive performance, and psychological symptoms between acute blast-versus nonblast-induced mild traumatic brain injury. *Journal of the International Neuropsychological Society, 17,* 36–45.

Lumba-Brown, A., Yeates, K. O., Sarmiento, K., Breiding, M. J., Haegerich, T. M., Gioia, G. A., . . . Joseph, M. (2018). Centers for Disease Control and Prevention guideline on the diagnosis and management of mild traumatic brain injury among children. *JAMA Pediatrics, 172*(11), e182853.

MacDonald, C. L., Johnson, A. M., Nelson, E. C., Werner, N. J., Fang, R., Flaherty, S. F., & Brody, D. L. (2014). Functional status after blast-plus-impact complex concussive traumatic brain injury in evacuated United States military personnel. *Journal of Neurotrauma, 31*(10), 889–898.

MacDonald, C. L., Johnson, A. M., Wierzechowski, L., Kassner, E., Stewart, T., Nelson, E. C., . . . Brody, D. L. (2014). Prospectively assessed clinical outcomes in concussive blast vs nonblast traumatic brain injury among evacuated US military personnel. *JAMA Neurology, 71,* 994–1002.

MacDonald, S. (1998). *Functional assessment of verbal reasoning and executive strategies.* Guelph, Canada: Clinical Publishing.

MacDonald, S. (2013). *Student Version Functional assessment of verbal reasoning and executive strategies*. Guelph, Canada: Clinical Publishing.

Mah, K., Hickling, A., & Reed, N. (2018). Perceptions of mild traumatic brain injury in adults: A scoping review. *Disability and Rehabilitation*, *40*(8), 960–973.

Makdissi, M., Cantu, R. C., Johnston, K. M., McCrory, P., & Meeuwisse, W. H. (2013). The difficult concussion patient: What is the best approach to investigation and management of persistent (>10 days) postconcussive symptoms?. *British Journal of Sports Medicine*, *47*(5), 308–313.

Malec, J. F., Smigielski, J. S., & DePompolo, R. W. (1991). Goal attainment scaling and outcome measurement in postacute brain injury rehabilitation. *Archives of Physical Medicine and Rehabilitation*, *72*(2), 138–143.

Malia, K., Law, P., Sidebottom, L., Bewick, K., Danzinger, S., Schold-David, E., . . . Vaidya, A. (2004). *Recommendations for best practice in cognitive rehabilitation therapy: Acquired brain injury*. Exton, PA: The Society for Cognitive Rehabilitation.

Management of Concussion/mTBI Working Group. (2009). VA/DoD clinical practice guideline for management of concussion/mild traumatic brain injury. *Journal of Rehabilitation Research and Development*, *46*(6), CP1–68.

Manley, G. T., Gardner, A. J., Schneider, K. J., Guskiewicz, K. M., Bailes, J., Cantu, R. C., . . . Dvořák, J. (2017). A systematic review of potential long-term effects of sport-related concussion. *British Journal of Sports Medicine*, *51*(12), 969–977.

Mansfield, E., Stergiou-Kita, M., Cassidy, J. D., Bayley, M., Mantis, S., Kristman, V., . . . Moody, J. (2015). Return-to-work challenges following a work-related mild TBI: The injured worker perspective. *Brain Injury*, *29*(11), 1362–1369.

Marini, A., Galetto, V., Zampieri, E., Vorano, L., Zettin, M., & Carlomagno, S. (2011). Narrative language in traumatic brain injury. *Neuropsychologia*, *49*(10), 2904–2910.

Martin, E., Lu, W., Helmick, K., French, L., & Warden, D. (2008). Traumatic brain injuries sustained in the Afghanistan and Iraq wars. *Journal of Trauma Nursing*, *15*(3), 94–101.

Martland, H. S. (1928). Punch drunk. *Journal of the American Medical Association*, *91*(15), 1103–1107.

Mattingly, E. O. (2015). Dysfluency in a service member with comorbid diagnoses: A case study. *Military Medicine*, *180*(1), e157–e159.

Mayer, A. R., Yang, Z., Yeo, R. A., Pena, A., Ling, J. M., Mannell, M. V., . . . Mojtahed, K. (2012). A functional MRI study of multimodal selective attention following mild traumatic brain injury. *Brain Imaging and Behavior*, *6*(2), 343–354.

Mayorga, M. A. (1997). The pathology of primary blast overpressure injury. *Toxicology*, *121*(1), 17–28.

McAllister, T. W., Flashman, L. A., Maerlender, A., Greenwald, R. M., Beckwith, J. G., Tosteson, T. D., . . . Grove, M. R. (2012). Cognitive effects of one season of head impacts in a cohort of collegiate contact sport athletes. *Neurology*, *78*(22), 1777–1784.

McAllister, T. W., Ford, J. C., Flashman, L. A., Maerlender, A., Greenwald, R. M., Beckwith, J. G., . . . Jain, S. (2014). Effect of head impacts on diffusivity measures in a cohort of collegiate contact sport athletes. *Neurology*, *82*(1), 63–69.

McAllister, T., & McCrea, M. (2017). Long-term cognitive and neuropsychiatric consequences of repetitive concussion and head-impact exposure. *Journal of Athletic Training*, *52*(3), 309–317.

McCrea, M., Guskiewicz, K., Doncevic, S., Helmick, K., Kennedy, J., Boyd, C., . . . Jaffee, M. (2014). Day of injury cognitive performance on the Military Acute Concussion Evaluation (MACE) by U.S. military service members in OEF/OIF. *Military Medicine*, *179*(9), 990–997.

McCrea, M., Guskiewicz, K., Randolph, C., Barr, W. B., Hammeke, T. A., Marshall, S. W., . . . Kelly, J. P. (2013). Incidence, clinical course, and predictors of prolonged recovery time following sport-related concussion in high school and college athletes. *Journal of the International Neuropsychological Society, 19*(1), 22–33.

McCrea, M., & Manley, G. (2018). State of the science on pediatric mild traumatic brain injury: Progress toward clinical translation. *JAMA Pediatrics, 172*(11), e182846.

McCrory, P., Meeuwisse, W., Dvorak, J., Aubry, M., Bailes, J., Broglio, S., . . . Davis, G. A. (2017). Consensus statement on concussion in sport—the 5th international conference on concussion in sport held in Berlin, October 2016. *British Journal of Sports Medicine, 51*(11), 1–10.

McDonald, S. (2013). Impairments in social cognition following severe traumatic brain injury. *Journal of the International Neuropsychological Society, 19*(3), 231–246.

McDonald, S., Flanagen, S., & Rollins, J. (2002). *The Awareness of Social Interference Test.* Austin TX: Harcourt Assessment.

McGlinchey, R. E., Milberg, W. P., Fonda, J. R., & Fortier, C. B. (2017). A methodology for assessing deployment trauma and its consequences in OEF/OIF/OND veterans: The TRACTS longitudinal prospective cohort study. *International Journal of Methods in Psychiatric Research, 26*(3), e1556.

McKee, A. C., Cairns, N. J., Dickson, D. W., Folkerth, R. D., Keene, C. D., Litvan, I., . . . Tripodis, Y. (2016). The first NINDS/NIBIB consensus meeting to define euro-pathological criteria for the diagnosis of chronic traumatic encephalopathy. *Acta Neuropathologica, 131*(1), 75–86.

Mez, J., Daneshvar, D. H., Kiernan, P. T., Abdolmohammadi, B., Alvarez, V. E., Huber, B. R., . . . Cormier, K. A. (2017). Clinicopathological evaluation of chronic traumatic encephalopathy in players of American football. *JAMA, 318*(4), 360–370.

Miller, K. J., Ivins, B. J., & Schwab, K. A. (2013). Self-reported mild TBI and post-concussive symptoms in a peacetime activity duty military population: Effect of multiple TBI history versus single mild TBI. *Journal of Head Trauma Rehabilitation, 28*(1), 31–38.

Miller, L. J., & Mittenberg, W. (1998). Brief cognitive behavioral interventions in mild traumatic brain injury. *Applied Neuropsychology, 5*(4), 172–183.

Millspaugh, J. A. (1937). Dementia pugilistica. *US Naval Medical Bulletin, 35*(297), 303.

Milman, A., Rosenberg, A., Weizman, R., & Pick, C. G. (2005). Mild traumatic brain injury induces persistent cognitive deficits and behavioral disturbances in mice. *Journal of Neurotrauma, 22*(9), 1003–1010.

Mittenberg, W., & Burton, D. B. (1994). A survey of treatment for post-concussion syndrome. *Brain Injury, 8*, 429–437.

Mittenberg, W., Tremont, G., Zielinski, R. E., Fichera, S., & Rayls, K. R. (1996). Cognitive-behavioral prevention of post-concussion syndrome. *Archives of Clinical Neuropsychology, 11*, 139–145.

Mittl, R. L., Grossman, R. I., Hiehle, J. F., Hurst, R. W., Kauder, D. R., Gennarelli, T. A., & Alburger, G. W. (1994). Prevalence of MR evidence of diffuse axonal injury in patients with mild head injury and normal head CT findings. *American Journal of Neuroradiology, 15*(8), 1583–1589.

Mollayeva, T., El-Khechen-Richandi, G., & Colantonio, A. (2018). Sex & gender considerations in concussion research. *Concussion, 3*(1), CNC51.

Mooney, G., & Speed, J. (2001). The association between mild traumatic brain injury and psychiatric conditions. *Brain Injury, 15*(10), 865–877.

Morissette, S. B., Woodward, M., Kimbrel, N. A., Meyer, E. C., Kruse, M. I., Dolan, S., & Gulliver, S. B. (2011). Deployment-related TBI, persistent post-concussive symptoms, PTSD, and depression in OEF/OIF veterans. *Rehabilitation Psychology, 56*(4), 340–350.

Nelson, N. W., Hoelzle, J. B., Doane, B. M., McGuire, K. A., Ferrier-Auerbach, A. G., Charlesworth, M. J., . . . Sponheim, S. R.

(2012). Neuropsychological outcomes of US veterans with report of remote blast-related concussion and current psychopathology. *Journal of the International Neuropsychological Society, 18*(5), 845–855.

Nicholas, L. E., & Brookshire, R. H. (1995). Comprehension of spoken narrative discourse by adults with aphasia, right-hemisphere brain damage, or traumatic brain injury. *American Journal of Speech-Language Pathology, 4*(3), 69–81.

NIH Consensus Development Panel on Rehabilitation of Persons With Traumatic Brain Injury. (1999). Rehabilitation of persons with traumatic brain injury. *JAMA, 282*(10), 974–983.

Nolin, P. (2006). Executive memory dysfunctions following mild traumatic brain injury. *Journal of Head Trauma Rehabilitation, 21*(1), 68–75.

Norman, R. S., Jaramillo, C. A., Amuan, M., Wells, M. A., Eapen, B. C., & Pugh, M. J. (2013). Traumatic brain injury in veterans of the wars in Iraq and Afghanistan: Communication disorders stratified by severity of brain injury. *Brain Injury, 27*(13–14), 1623–1630.

Norman, R. S., Jaramillo, C. A., Eapen, B. C., Amuan, M. E., & Pugh, M. J. (2018). Acquired stuttering in veterans of the wars in Iraq and Afghanistan: The role of traumatic brain injury, post-traumatic stress disorder, and medications. *Military Medicine, 183*(11-12), e512-e534.

Noy, S., Krawitz, S., & Del Bigio, M. R. (2016). Chronic traumatic encephalopathy-like abnormalities in a routine neuropathology service. *Journal of Neuropathology & Experimental Neurology, 75*(12), 1145–1154.

O'Jile, J. R., Ryan, L. M., Betz, B., Parks-Levy, J., Hilsabeck, R. C., Rhudy, J. L., & Gouvier, W. D. (2006). Information processing following mild head injury. *Archives of Clinical Neuropsychology, 21*(4), 293–296.

Oleksiak, M., Smith, B. M., St. Andre, J. R., Caughlan, C. M., & Steiner, M. (2012).

Audiological issues and hearing loss among veterans with mild traumatic brain injury. *Journal of Rehabilitation Research and Development, 49*, 995–1004.

Omalu, B., Bailes, J., Hamilton, R. L., Kamboh, M. I., Hammers, J., Case, M., & Fitzsimmons, R. (2011). Emerging histomorphologic phenotypes of chronic traumatic encephalopathy in American athletes. *Neurosurgery, 69*(1), 173–183.

O'Neil, M. E., Carlson, K. F., Storzbach, D., Brenner, L.A., Freeman, M., Quinones, A., . . . Kansagara, D. (2013). *Complications of mild traumatic brain injury in veterans and military personnel: A systematic review.* Washington, DC: Department of Veterans Affairs. Retrieved from https://www.ncbi.nlm.nih.gov/books/NBK189785/

Ouellet, M. C., Beaulieu-Bonneau, S., & Morin, C. M. (2015). Sleep-wake disturbances after traumatic brain injury. *The Lancet Neurology, 14*(7), 746–757.

Owens, B. D., Kragh, J. F., Jr., Wenke, J. C., Macaitis, J., Wade, C. E., & Holcomb, J. B. (2008). Combat wounds in operation Iraqi Freedom and operation Enduring Freedom. *Journal of Trauma and Acute Care Surgery, 64*(2), 295–299.

Ownsworth, T. L., & McFarland, K. (1999). Memory remediation in long-term acquired brain injury: Two approaches in diary training. *Brain Injury, 13*(8), 605–626.

Ozen, L. J., Itier, R. J., Preston, F. F., & Fernandes, M. A. (2013). Long-term working memory deficits after concussion: Electrophysiological evidence. *Brain Injury, 27*(11), 1244–1255.

Palmese, C. A., & Raskin, S. A. (2000). The rehabilitation of attention in individuals with mild traumatic brain injury, using the APT-II programme. *Brain Injury, 14*(6), 535–548.

Parrish, C., Roth, C., Roberts, B., & Davie, G. (2009). Assessment of cognitive-communicative disorders of mild traumatic brain injury sustained in combat. *Perspectives on Neurophysiology and Neurogenic Speech and Language Disorders, 19*(2), 47–57.

Phillips, Y. Y. (1986). Primary blast injuries. *Annals of Emergency Medicine, 15*(12), 1446–1450.

Rabadi, M. H., & Jordan, B. D. (2001). The cumulative effect of repetitive concussion in sports. *Clinical Journal of Sport Medicine, 11*(3), 194–198.

Rabinowitz, A. R., Li, X., McCauley, S. R., Wilde, E. A., Barnes, A., Hanten, G., . . . Levin, H. S. (2015). Prevalence and predictors of poor recovery from mild traumatic brain injury. *Journal of Neurotrauma, 32*(19), 1488–1496.

Raikes, A. C., & Schaefer, S. Y. (2016). Sleep quantity and quality during acute concussion: A pilot study. *Sleep, 39*(12), 2141–2147.

Randolph, C. (2012). *RBANS update: Repeatable Battery for the Assessment of Neuropsychological Status.* Bloomington, MN: Pearson Education & PsychCorp.

Randolph, C. (2014). Is chronic traumatic encephalopathy a real disease? *Current Sports Medicine Reports, 13*(1), 33–37.

Raskin, S. A., & Mateer, C. A. (2000). *Neuropsychological management of mild traumatic brain injury.* New York, NY: Oxford University Press.

Reitan, R. M., & Wolfson, D. (1985). *The Halstead–Reitan Neuropsychological Test Battery: Therapy and clinical interpretation.* Tucson, AZ: Neuropsychological Press.

Robertson, I. H., Ward, T., Ridgeway, V., & Nimmo-Smith, I. (1994). *Test of Everyday Attention (TEA).* New York, NY: Pearson Education.

Rosenthal, M. (1993). Mild traumatic brain injury syndrome. *Annals of Emergency Medicine, 22*(6), 1048–1051.

Roth, C. R., Aronson, A. E., & Davis, L. J. (1989). Clinical studies in psychogenic stuttering of adult onset. *Journal of Speech and Hearing Disorders, 54*(4), 634–646.

Roth, C. R., Cornis-Pop, M., & Beach, W. A. (2015). Examination of validity in spoken language evaluations: Adult onset stuttering following mild traumatic brain injury *NeuroRehabilitation, 36*(4), 415–426.

Roth, R. M., Isquith, P. K., & Gioia, G. A. (2005). *Behavior Rating Inventory of Executive Function®–Adult Version (BRIEF®-A).* Lutz, FL: PAR.

Salvatore, A. P., Cannito, M., Brassil, H. E., Bene, E. R., & Sirmon-Taylor, B. (2017). Auditory comprehension performance of college students with and without sport concussion on Computerized–Revised Token Test Subtest VIII. *Concussion, 2*(2), 1–12.

Sandel, N. K., Schatz, P., Goldberg, K. B., & Lazar, M. (2017). Sex-based differences in cognitive deficits and symptom reporting among acutely concussed adolescent lacrosse and soccer players. *American Journal of Sports Medicine, 45*(4), 937–944.

Scheenen, M. E., Spikman, J. M., de Koning, M. E., van der Horn, H. J., Roks, G., Hageman, G., & van der Naalt, J. (2017). Patients "at risk" of suffering from persistent complaints after mild traumatic brain injury: The role of coping, mood disorders, and post-traumatic stress. *Journal of Neurotrauma, 34*(1), 31–37.

Schneider, E., & Van Auken, S. (2018). Bridging the gap: Pragmatic language group approach for cognitive-communication deficits postconcussion. *Perspectives of the ASHA Special Interest Groups, 3*(2), 31–43.

Schneider, K. J., Leddy, J. J., Guskiewicz, K. M., Seifert, T., McCrea, M., Silverberg, N. D., . . . Makdissi, M. (2017). Rest and treatment/rehabilitation following sport-related concussion: A systematic review. *British Journal of Sports Medicine, 51*(12), 930–934.

Schneiderman, A. I., Braver, E. R., & Kang, H. K. (2008). Understanding sequelae of injury mechanisms and mild traumatic brain injury incurred during the conflicts in Iraq and Afghanistan: Persistent postconcussive symptoms and posttraumatic stress disorder. *American Journal of Epidemiology, 167*(12), 1446–1452.

Schonberger, M., Humle, F., & Teasdale, T. W. (2007). The relationship between clients' cognitive functioning and the therapeutic working alliance in post-acute brain injury rehabilitation. *Brain Injury, 21*(8), 825–836.

Schrank, F. A., McGrew, K. S., & Mather, N. (2014). *Woodcock-Johnson IV*. Rolling Meadows, IL: Riverside.

Schwab, K., & Cernich, A. (2011). Comments on "Longitudinal effects of mild traumatic brain injury and posttraumatic stress disorder comorbidity on postdeployment outcomes in National Guard soldiers deployed to Iraq." *Archives of General Psychiatry, 68*, 79–89.

Seal, K. H., Bertenthal, D., & Kumar, S. (2016). Association between mild traumatic brain injury and mental health problems and self-reported cognitive dysfunction in Iraq and Afghanistan veterans. *Journal of Rehabilitation Research and Development, 53*(2), 185–189.

Seichepine, D. R., Stamm, J. M., Daneshvar, D. H., Riley, D. O., Baugh, C. M., Gavett, B. E., . . . Cantu, R. C. (2013). Profile of self-reported problems with executive functioning in college and professional football players. *Journal of Neurotrauma, 30*(14), 1299–1304.

Seiger, A., Goldwater, E., & Deibert, E. (2015). Does mechanism of injury play a role in recovery from concussion? *Journal of Head Trauma Rehabilitation, 30*(3), E52–E56.

Sharp, D. J., & Jenkins, P. O. (2015). Concussion is confusing for us all. *BMJ Practical Neurology, 15*(3), 172–186.

Shenton, M. E., Hamoda, H. M., Schneiderman, J. S., Bouix, S., Pasternak, O., Rathi, Y., . . . Zafonte, R. (2012). A review of magnetic resonance imaging and diffusion tensor imaging findings in mild traumatic brain injury. *Brain Imaging and Behavior, 6*(2), 137–192.

Sherer, M., Evans, C. C., Leverenz, J., Irby, J. W., Lee, J. E., & Yablon, S. A. (2009). Therapeutic alliance in post-acute brain injury rehabilitation: Predictors of strength of alliance and impact of alliance on outcome. *Brain Injury, 21*(7), 663–672.

Shively, S. B., Horkayne-Szakaly, I., Jones, R. V., Kelly, J. P., Armstrong, R. C., & Perl, D. P. (2016). Characterisation of interface astroglial scarring in the human brain after blast exposure: A post-mortem case series. *The Lancet Neurology, 15*(9), 944–953.

Silverberg, N. D., & Iverson, G. L. (2013). Is rest after concussion "the best medicine?": Recommendations for activity resumption following concussion in athletes, civilians, and military service members. *Journal of Head Trauma Rehabilitation, 28*(4), 250–259.

Sinotte, M., & Coelho, C. A. (2003). Attention training for reading impairment in mild aphasia: A follow-up study. *Journal of Medical Speech Pathology, 21*, 11–19.

Snell, D. L., Macleod, A. S., & Anderson, T. (2016). Post-concussion syndrome after a mild traumatic brain injury: A minefield for clinical practice. *Journal of Behavioral and Brain Science, 6*(6), 227–232.

Snell, D. L., Martin, R., Surgenor, L. J., Siegert, R. J., & Hay-Smith, E. J. C. (2017). What's wrong with me? Seeking a coherent understanding of recovery after mild traumatic brain injury. *Disability and Rehabilitation, 39*(19), 1968-1975.

Soble, J. R., Cooper, D. B., Lu, L. H., Eapen, B. C., & Kennedy, J. E. (2018). Symptom reporting and management of chronic post-concussive symptoms in military service members and veterans. *Current Physical Medicine Rehabilitation Reports, 6*, 62–73.

Soble, J. R., Spanierman, L. B., & Fitzgerald Smith, J. (2013). Neuropsychological functioning of combat veterans with posttraumatic stress disorder and mild traumatic brain injury. *Journal of Experimental Clinical Neuropsychology, 35*(5), 551–561.

Sohlberg, M. M. (2000). Psychotherapy approaches. In S. A. Raskin & C. A. Mateer, (Eds.), *Neuropsychological management of mild traumatic brain injury* (pp. 137–156). New York, NY: Oxford University Press.

Sohlberg, M. M., Ehlhardt, L., & Kennedy, M. (2005). Instructional techniques in cognitive rehabilitation: A preliminary report. *Seminars in Speech and Language, 26*(4), 268.

Sohlberg, M. M., Griffiths, G. G., & Fickas, S. (2014). An evaluation of reading comprehension of expository text in adults with traumatic brain injury. *American Journal of Speech-Language Pathology, 23*(2), 160–175.

Sohlberg, M. M., Johnson, L., Paule, L., Raskin, S., & Mateer, C. (2001). *Attention Process Training APT-2 for persons with mild cognitive dysfunction* (2nd ed.). Wolfeboro, NJ: Lash & Associates.

Sohlberg, M. M., & Mateer, C. A. (1987). Effectiveness of an attention-training program. *Journal of Clinical and Experimental Neuropsychology, 9*(2), 117–130.

Sohlberg, M. M., & Mateer, C. A. (1989). *Introduction to cognitive rehabilitation: Theory and practice.* New York: Guilford Press.

Sohlberg, M. M., & Mateer, C. A. (2001). Improving attention and managing attentional problems. *Annals of the New York Academy of Sciences, 931*(1), 359–375.

Sohlberg, M. M., & Mateer, C. A. (2005). *Attention Process Training: A program for cognitive rehabilitation to address persons with attentional deficits ranging from mild to severe* (3rd ed.). Wake Forest, NC: Lash & Associates.

Sohlberg, M. M., & Mateer, C. A. (2010). *APT-III: Attention Process Training: A direct attention training program for persons with acquired brain injury.* Youngville, NC: Lash & Associates.

Sohlberg, M. M., McLaughlin, K. A., Pavese, A., Heidrich, A., & Posner, M. I. (2000). Evaluation of attention process training and brain injury education in persons with acquired brain injury. *Journal of Clinical and Experimental Neuropsychology, 22*(5), 656–676.

Sohlberg, M. M., & Turkstra, L. S. (2011). *Optimizing cognitive rehabilitation: Effec-tive instructional methods.* New York, NY: Guilford Press.

Stein, M. B., Kessler, R. C., Heeringa, S. G., Jain, S., Campbell-Sills, L., Colpe, L. J. & Fullerton, R. J. (2015). Prospective longitudinal evaluation of the effect of deployment-acquired traumatic brain injury on posttraumatic stress and related disorders: Results from the Army Study to Assess Risk and Resilience in Service Members (Army STARRS). *American Journal of Psychiatry, 172*(11), 1101–1111.

Stein, T. D., Alvarez, V. E., & McKee, A. C. (2014). Chronic traumatic encephalopathy: A spectrum of neuropathological changes following repetitive brain trauma in athletes and military personnel. *Alzheimer's Research & Therapy, 6*(4), 1–11.

Stergiou-Kita, M., Mansfield, E., Sokoloff, S., & Colantonio, A. (2016). Gender influences on return to work after mild traumatic brain injury. *Archives of Physical Medicine and Rehabilitation, 97*(2), S40–S45.

Stillman, A., Madigan, N., & Alexander, M. (2016). Factors associated with prolonged, subjective post-concussive symptoms (P3. 325). *Neurology, 86*(16, Suppl.), P3–325.

Stockbridge, M. D., Doran, A., King, K., & Newman, R. S. (2018). The effects of concussion on rapid picture naming in children. *Brain Injury, 32*(4), 506–514.

Storzback, D., Twamley, E. W., Roost, M. S., Golshan, S., Williams, R. M., O'Neil, M., . . . Huckans, M. (2017). Compensatory cognitive training for Operation Enduring Freedom/Operation Iraqi Freedom/Operation New Dawn veterans with mild traumatic brain injury. *Journal of Head Trauma Rehabilitation, 32,* 16–24.

Stout, C. E., Yorkston, K. M., & Pimentel, J. I. (2000). Discourse production following mild, moderate, and severe traumatic brain injury. *Journal of Medical Speech-Language Pathology, 8*(1), 15–25.

Sufrinko, A., Pearce, K., Elbin, R. J., Covassin, T., Johnson, E., Collins, M., & Kontos,

A. P. (2015). The effect of preinjury sleep difficulties on neurocognitive impairment and symptoms after sport-related concussion. *American Journal of Sports Medicine, 43*(4), 830–838.

Sullivan, K. A., & Wade, C. (2017). Does the cause of the mild traumatic brain injury affect the expectation of persistent postconcussion symptoms and psychological trauma? *Journal of Clinical and Experimental Neuropsychology, 39*(4), 408–418.

Sunderland, A., Harris, J. E., & Baddeley, A. D. (1987). Do laboratory tests predict everyday memory? A neuropsychological study. *Journal of Verbal Learning & Verbal Behavior, 22*, 341–357.

Sveen, U., Østensjø, S., Laxe, S., & Soberg, H. L. (2013). Problems in functioning after a mild traumatic brain injury within the ICF framework: The patient perspective using focus groups. *Disability and Rehabilitation, 35*(9), 749–757.

Swanson, M. W., Weise, K. K., Dreer, L. E., Johnston, J., Davis, R. D., Ferguson, D., . . . Lee, S. D. (2017). Academic difficulty and vision symptoms in children with concussion. *Optometry and Vision Science, 94*(1), 60–67.

Talavage, T. M., Nauman, E. A., Breedlove, E. L., Yoruk, U., Dye, A. E., Morigaki, K. E., . . . Leverenz, L. J. (2014). Functionally-detected cognitive impairment in high school football players without clinically-diagnosed concussion. *Journal of Neurotrauma, 31*(4), 327–338.

Tarazi, A., Tator, C. H., Wennberg, R., Ebraheem, A., Green, R. E., Collela, B., . . . Tartaglia, M. C. (2018). Motor function in former professional football players with history of multiple concussions. *Journal of Neurotrauma, 35*(8), 1003–1007.

Taylor, B. C., Hagel, E. M., Carlson, K. F., Cifu, D. X., Cutting, A., Bidelspach, D. E., & Sayer, N. A. (2012). Prevalence and costs of co-occurring traumatic brain injury with and without psychiatric disturbance and pain among Afghanistan

and Iraq war veteran VA users. *Medical Care, 50*(4) 342–346.

Taylor, C. A., Bell, J. M., Breiding, M. J., & Xu, L. (2017). Traumatic brain injury–related emergency department visits, hospitalizations, and deaths—United States, 2007 and 2013. *Morbidity and Mortality Weekly Report. Surveillance Summaries, 66*(9), 1–16.

Terrio, H., Brenner, L. A., Ivins, B., Cho, J. M., Helmick, K., & Schwab, K. (2009). Traumatic brain injury screening: Preliminary findings in a U.S. army brigade combat team. *Journal of Head Trauma Rehabilitation, 24*, 14–23.

Thiagarajan, P., & Ciuffreda, K. J. (2015). Short-term persistence of oculomotor rehabilitative changes in mild traumatic brain injury (mTBI): A pilot study of clinical effects. *Brain Injury, 29*(12), 1475–1479.

Thiagarajan, P., Ciuffreda, K. J., & Ludlam, D. P. (2011). Vergence dysfunction in mild traumatic brain injury (mTBI): A review. *Ophthalmic and Physiological Optics, 31*(5), 456–468.

Tiersky, L. A., Anselmi, V., Johnston, M. V., Kutyka, J., Roosen, E., Schwartz, T., & DeLuca, J. (2005). A trial of neuropsychologic rehabilitation in mild-spectrum traumatic brain injury. *Archives of Physical Medicine and Rehabilitation, 86*(8), 1565–1574.

Toglia, J. P. (1993). *Contextual Memory Test.* New York, NY: Pearson Education.

Trudel, T. M., Nidiffer, F. D., & Barth, J. T. (2007). Community-integrated brain injury rehabilitation: Treatment models and challenges for civilian, military, and veteran populations. *Journal of Rehabilitation Research and Development, 44*(7), 1007.

Tucker, F. M., & Hanlon, R. E. (1998). Effects of mild traumatic brain injury on narrative discourse production. *Brain Injury, 12*(9), 783–792.

Turgeon, C., Champoux, F., Lepore, F., Leclerc, S., & Ellemberg, D. (2011). Auditory processing after sport-related concussions. *Ear and Hearing, 32*(5), 667–670.

Turkstra, L., & McCarty, J. (2006, November 1). *Evidence based practice in traumatic brain injury: Assessment and intervention for cognitive communication disorders.* ASHA Webinar. Rockville, MD: American Speech, Language, and Hearing Association.

Turkstra, L. S., Coelho, C., & Ylvisaker, M. (2005, November). The use of standardized tests for individuals with cognitive-communication disorders. *Seminars in Speech and Language, 26*(4), 215.

Twamley, E. W., Jak, A. J., Delis, D. C., Bondi, M. W., & Lohr, J. B. (2014). Cognitive symptom management and rehabilitation therapy (CogSMART) for veterans with traumatic brain injury: Pilot randomized controlled trial. *Journal of Rehabilitation Research and Development, 51,* 59–70.

Twamley, E. W., Thomas, K. R., Gregory, A. M., Jak, A. J., Bondi, M. W., Delis, D. C., & Lohr, J. B. (2015). CogSMART compensatory cognitive training for traumatic brain injury: Effects over 1 year. *Journal of Head Trauma Rehabilitation, 30,* 391–401.

VA/DoD Clinical Practice Guideline for the Management of Concussion-Mild Traumatic Brain Injury. Version 2.0. (2016). Retrieved from https://www.healthquality.va.gov/guidelines/Rehab/mtbi/mTBICPGFullCPG50821816.pdf

Vanderploeg, R. D., Belanger, H. G., & Curtiss, G. (2009). Mild traumatic brain injury and posttraumatic stress disorder and their associations with health symptoms. *Archives of Physical Medicine and Rehabilitation, 90*(7), 1084–1093.

Vanderploeg, R. D., Groer, S., & Belanger, H. G. (2012). Initial development process of a VA semistructured clinical interview for TBI identification. *Journal of Rehabilitation Research & Development, 49*(4), 545-556.

Vander Werff, K. R. (2016). The application of the International Classification of Functioning, Disability and Health to functional auditory consequences of mild traumatic brain injury. *Seminars in Hearing, 37*(3), 216–232.

Verfaellie, M., & Lafleche, G., & Spiro, A., III, & Bousquet, K. (2014). Neuropsychological outcomes in OEF/OIF veterans with self-report of blast exposure associations with mental health, but not MTBI. *Neuropsychology, 28*(3), 337–346.

Viola-Saltzman, M., & Watson, N. F. (2012). Traumatic brain injury and sleep disorders. *Neurologic Clinics, 30*(4), 1299–1312.

Voss, J. D., Connolly, J., Schwab, K. A., & Scher, A. I. (2015). Update on the epidemiology of concussion/mild traumatic brain injury. *Current Pain and Headache Reports, 19*(7), 1–8.

Wäljas, M., Iverson, G. L., Lange, R. T., Hakulinen, U., Dastidar, P., Huhtala, H., . . . Öhman, J. (2015). A prospective biopsychosocial study of the persistent post-concussion symptoms following mild traumatic brain injury. *Journal of Neurotrauma, 32*(8), 534–547.

Warden, D. (2006). Military TBI during the Iraq and Afghanistan wars. *Journal of Head Trauma Rehabilitation, 21*(5), 398–402.

Wasserman, E. B., Abar, B., Shah, M. N., Wasserman, D., & Bazarian, J. J. (2015). Concussions are associated with decreased batting performance among Major League Baseball players. *American Journal of Sports Medicine, 43*(5), 1127–1133.

Wechsler, D. (2009). *Wechsler Memory Scale–Fourth Edition.* San Antonio, TX: Pearson.

Willer, B. S., Zivadinov, R., Haider, M. N., Miecznikowski, J. C., & Leddy, J. J. (2018). A preliminary study of early-onset dementia of former professional football and hockey players. *Journal of Head Trauma Rehabilitation, 33*(5), E1–E8.

Wilson, B. A. (1987). *Rehabilitation of memory.* New York, NY: Guilford.

Wilson, B. A., Alderman, N., Burgess, P. W., Emslie, H., & Evans, J. J. (2005). *Behavioural assessment of the dysexecutive syndrome.* New York, NY: Pearson Education.

Wilson, B. A., Emslie, H. C., Quirk, K., & Evans, J. J. (2001). Reducing everyday memory and planning problems by means of a paging system: A randomised control crossover study. *Journal of Neurology, Neurosurgery & Psychiatry, 70*(4), 477–482.

Wilson, B. A., Greenfield, E., Clare, L., Baddeley, A., Cockburn, J., Watson, P., . . . Nannery, R. (2008). *Rivermead Behavioral Memory Test–Third Edition (RBMT-3).* London, UK: Pearson Assessment.

Wiseman-Hakes, C., Colantonio, A., & Gargaro, J. (2009). Sleep and wake disorders following traumatic brain injury: A systematic review of the literature. *Critical Reviews™ in Physical and Rehabilitation Medicine, 21*(3–4), 317–374.

Wood, R. L., O'Hagan, G., Williams, C., McCabe, M., & Chadwick, N. (2014). Anxiety sensitivity and alexithymia as mediators of postconcussion syndrome following mild traumatic brain injury. *Journal of Head Trauma Rehabilitation, 29*(1), E9–E17.

Woodcock, R. W., Mather, N., & McGrew, K. S. (2001). *Woodcock-Johnson III Tests of Cognitive Abilities.* Itasca, IL: Riverside.

Working Group to Develop a Clinician's Guide to Cognitive Rehabilitation in mTBI: Application for Military Service Members and Veterans. (2016). *Clinician's guide to cognitive rehabilitation in mild traumatic brain injury: Application for military service members and veterans.* Rockville, MD: American Speech-Language-Hearing Association. Retrieved from http://www.asha.org/uploadedFiles/ASHA/Practice_Portal/Clinical_Topics/Traumatic_Brain_Injury_in_Adults/Clinicians-Guide-to-Cognitive-Rehabilitation-in-Mild-Traumatic-Brain-Injury.pdf

World Health Organization. (2001). *ICIDH-2: International classification of functioning, disability and health: Final draft, full version.* Geneva, Switzerland: Author.

Xydakis, M. S., Bebarta, V. S., Harrison, C. D., Conner, J. C., Grant, G. A., & Robbins, A. S. (2007). Tympanic-membrane perforation as a marker of concussive brain injury in Iraq. *New England Journal of Medicine, 357*(8), 830–831.

Yamamoto, S., DeWitt, D. S., & Prough, D. S. (2018). Impact & blast traumatic brain injury: Implications for therapy. *Molecules, 23,* 245–255.

Yang, J., Peek-Asa, C., Covassin, T., & Torner, J. C. (2015). Post-concussion symptoms of depression and anxiety in division I collegiate athletes. *Developmental Neuropsychology, 40*(1), 18–23.

Ylvisaker, M., & Feeney, T. (2001). Supported behavior and supported cognition: An integrated, positive approach to serving students with disabilities. *Educational Psychology in Scotland, 6*(1), 17–30.

Ylvisaker, M., Turkstra, L. S., & Coelho, C. (2005). Behavioral and social interventions for individuals with traumatic brain injury: A summary of the research with clinical implications. *Seminars in Speech and Language, 26*(4), 256–267.

Yuhas, P. T., Shorter, P. D., McDaniel, C. E., Earley, M. J., & Hartwick, A. T. (2017). Blue and red light-evoked pupil responses in photophobic subjects with TBI. *Optometry and Vision Science, 94*(1), 108–117.

Zeitzer, M. B., & Brooks, J. M. (2008). In the line of fire: Traumatic brain injury among Iraq War veterans. *American Association of Occupational Health Nurses, 56*(8), 347–353.

Zemek, R., Barrowman, N., Freedman, S. B., Gravel, J., Gagnon, I., McGahern, C., . . . Craig, W. (2016). Clinical risk score for persistent postconcussion symptoms among children with acute concussion in the ED. *JAMA, 315*(10), 1014–1025.

8

Traumatic Brain Injury

Jessica A. Brown, Sarah E. Wallace, and Michael L. Kimbarow

Introduction[1]

Traumatic brain injury (TBI) is an acquired injury to the brain due to an applied force that results in widespread damage to cortical and subcortical structures. TBIs often cause a range of symptoms, including cognitive, language, speech, motor, and sensory impairments. No matter the cause, whether from falls, blunt force injury, motor vehicle accidents, blast injuries, or other mechanisms, the devastating social, emotional, physical, and cognitive effects of the injury often lead to substantial and permanent changes to a person's life. The deficits associated with TBI are devastating to the people who survive the TBI as well as their loved ones and community. In this chapter, we will focus on the cognitive and communication deficits commonly experienced by individuals with TBI and will provide guidelines for assessment and treatment practices.

Incidence and Risk Factors

Estimates suggest that in 2013, 2.8 million people sustained a TBI in the United States resulting in emergency department visits, hospitalization, and death; with even greater numbers of injuries likely occurring without documentation (Taylor, Bell, Breiding, & Xu, 2017). This epidemic results in approximately 153 people dying from TBI-related injuries each day in the United States (Taylor et al., 2017). Information about the prevalence of the effects of TBI is limited; however, estimates suggest that in the United States between

---

[1]Although the focus of this chapter is primarily adults with TBI, unfortunately, children are also significantly affected by TBI. Much of the strategies and information presented within this chapter may still apply to children with TBI, but readers should seek additional information about TBI rehabilitation within an educational system and developmental issues that affect children with TBI.

3.2 million and 5.3 million survivors of TBI are living with varying degrees of permanent disability resulting from their injury (Selassie et al., 2008; Thurman, Alverson, Dunn, Guerrero, & Sniezek, 1999; Zaloshnja, Miller, Langlois, & Selassie, 2008). Long-term deficits impair an individual's ability to live independently such that 76% of adults with moderate-severe brain injury reside in assisted living facilities or require total support from a caregiver for completion of daily living activities (Colantonio et al., 2004). Due to these deficits, costs of TBI rehabilitation and therapy total over $76 billion annually (Coronado, McGuire, Faul, Sugarman, & Pearson, 2012; Thurman, 2001).

These data are perhaps an underestimate because TBIs are often underreported due to poor recognition of the symptoms or reluctance to report the injury (Lovell et al., 2002; McCrea, Hammeke, Olsen, Leo, & Guskiewicz, 2004; Sosin, Sniezek, & Thurman, 1996; Summers, Ivins, & Schwab, 2009). Additionally, these statistics do not include data from TBIs treated in federal, military, or Veterans Affairs hospitals. Estimates suggest that between 2000 and June 2018, 383,947 service members were diagnosed with a TBI. Approximately 82% of these were considered mild.

A disproportionate number of people with TBIs have preexisting conditions including substance abuse, a previous TBI, and medical conditions. Alcohol or other controlled substances are often a factor in motor vehicle accidents, pedestrian accidents, assaults, and falls that can result in TBI. Additionally, their continued use and abuse often affect rehabilitation success. Previous TBIs are a risk factor for a second or subsequent TBI due to changes in problem solving, judgment, motor control, and impulsivity. Pre-existing medical conditions such as heart disease and high blood pressure, as well as psychiatric illnesses appear to put people at greater risk for a TBI. In addition to these pre-existing conditions, as many as 25% to 87% of prisoners report having experienced a head injury or TBI compared to about 8.5% of the general population (CDC, n.d.) with frequency of TBI associated with more convictions, greater violent offenses, decreased mental health, and increased drug use in this population (Williams, Cordan, Mewse, Tonks, & Burgess, 2010). Additionally, a South Carolina study provided data suggesting that 60% of men and 72% of women who are incarcerated experienced a TBI (Ferguson, Pickelsimer, Corrigan, Bogner, & Wald, 2012). Individuals who experience homelessness or have a low socioeconomic status also are at greater risk for TBI and for underreporting TBIs (Kraus, Fife, Ramstein, Conroy, & Cox, 1986; Topolovec-Vranic et al., 2012). The increased incidence and risk in certain segments of the population highlight the need for screenings and targeted education efforts.

Pathophysiology

To fully appreciate cognitive communication deficits associated with TBI, it is useful to understand the nature of the neurologic damage sustained during and after traumatic events. TBIs are often categorized based on two types of brain damage: penetrating TBI (i.e., open-head injury) and nonpenetrating blunt force TBI (i.e., closed head injury).

Penetrating TBI

A penetrating TBI occurs when a foreign object, such as a high-velocity bullet, shrapnel from an explosive device, or a sharp weapon, passes through the skull. This type of open-head injury results in brain tissue destruction from the foreign objects as well as from the generation of a pressure wave within the skull. Additionally, people with TBI may experience secondary complications (e.g., infections) from the presence of foreign material, such as bone fragments embedded in the brain. Penetrating TBIs are more likely than non-penetrating injuries to result in focal damage to the brain and therefore, often result in cognitive deficits specific to the area of brain damage.

Non-Penetrating TBI

Non-penetrating TBIs may occur when a head accelerates and strikes an external object, when an external object hits a stationary head, or when the head experiences significant movement without impact. For example, an injury may occur during a motor vehicle crash when the driver's head accelerates forward and hits the windshield or is propelled through the windshield and hits the pavement. Similarly, a motor vehicle crash can result in extreme forward and backward movement of the head with no significant impact with an external object (i.e., whiplash injuries). Finally, non-penetrating injuries can result from an external object such as a baseball hitting a stationary head.

People who survive blunt force injuries are often left with widespread neurological damage resulting in part due to acceleration/deceleration and rotational forces. The mechanical forces associated with violent movement of the brain may lead to coup (damage at the point of impact) and countrecoup (damage opposite the original point of impact or acceleration) damage, lacerations of brain tissue, and widespread shearing and tearing of neurons known as diffuse axonal injury resulting from rotational forces (Baron & Jallo, 2007) (Figure 8–1).

Blast-related TBIs, such as those associated with Iraq and Afghanistan wars, have a unique signature. The injuries can be described as being primary (i.e., resulting from a pressure wave impacting air-filled cavities), secondary (i.e., similar to the injuries found in penetrating TBIs and blunt trauma), tertiary (i.e., resulting from the body being thrown with force at another object), and quaternary (i.e., burns and chemical exposure; DePalma, Burris, Champion, & Hodgson, 2005). Additionally, these TBIs may be compounded by multiple injuries to the limbs as well as loss of vision and hearing. The damaged peripheral sensory and motor systems may have a significant effect on the person's ability to participate in and benefit from rehabilitation.

Injury Severity

In addition to the variety of characteristics clinicians might encounter when working with people with TBI, the severity of the injury contributes to the heterogenic nature of this population. Injury severity has significant implications for prognosis, participation in rehabilitation, and selection of formal assessment tools. Injuries are generally labeled as mild, moderate, and severe (CDC, 2017).

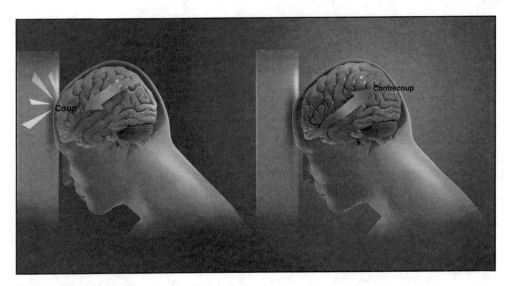

Figure 8–1. Coup and contrecoup damage occurring during brain injury. By Manu5 (http://www.scientificanimations.com/wiki-images/), CC BY-SA 4.0 (https://commons.wikimedia.org/w/index.php?curid=71496323).

The Glasgow Coma Scale (GCS) is often used to determine severity classification of initial TBI. The GCS guides measurements of eye opening, verbal response, and motor response. Additional information about the GCS is available in the assessment section within this chapter. Because of the limitations inherent to the GCS, additional items are typically considered when classifying TBI severity. Those include results of structural imaging testing, length of time for which the individual has lost consciousness, the length of time the person has experienced post-traumatic amnesia, and Abbreviated Injury Scale score for the head and neck region (Baker et al., 1974; Brasure et al., 2012; CDC, 2015).

Another measurement of severity is post-traumatic amnesia (PTA) which is defined as the time between injury and recovery of continuous memory; the individual must demonstrate ability to remember events for a 24-hour period before being considered out of PTA. There is a relationship between the length of PTA and the severity of the TBI as displayed in Table 8–1 (Armed, Bigsley, Sheikh, & Date, 2000; Levin, Peters, & Hulonen, 1983; Ponsford, Spitz, & McKenzie, 2016). Although using a comprehensive approach and considering all of these factors is critically important to classification, limitations still exist in using any severity criteria as a predictor of outcome without considering other personal and environmental factors.

Mild TBI

About 75% of TBIs are categorized as mild TBIs (or concussions) each year based on initial symptoms (CDC, 2003). They are generally described as having normal results on structural imaging, and involve the person experiencing less than 30 minutes or 0 to 1 day of post traumatic amnesia. Addi-

Table 8–1. Length of PTA and Initial Injury Severity

Length of PTA	Initial Injury Severity
Less than 5 minutes	Very mild deficits
5–59 minutes	Mild deficits
1–24 hours	Moderate long-term deficits
1–7 days	Severe long-term deficits
Greater than 7 days	Very severe long-term consequences

tionally, mild TBI is classified when the person receives a score between 13 and 15 as their best score on the GCS within 24 hours or a score between 1 and 2 on the Abbreviated Injury Scale score.

Despite the term "mild," the long-term consequences of these injuries can be substantial. Because of the mildness of the injury many people neglect seeking medical attention and if they do seek medical attention, they may not receive complete information about the potential long term deficits. Signs and symptoms of a concussion such as difficulty thinking clearly, a headache or balance problems, sleeping disturbances, and difficulty concentrating, may go unnoticed for a few days or months after injury (CDC, National Center for Injury Prevention and Control, Division of Unintentional Injury Prevention, 2014a). Some disagreement about the definition of mild TBI exists.

Moderate and Severe TBI

Moderate TBIs result in normal or abnormal structural imaging results and involve the person experiencing between 30 minutes and 24 hours of loss of consciousness and greater than 1 and fewer than 7 days of post traumatic amnesia. Additionally, moderate TBIs are those that result in characteristics consistent with a GCS scale between 9 and 12 and an Abbreviated Injury Scale score: Head of 3. Severe injuries are those during which the structural imaging may be normal or abnormal and the person experiences a loss of consciousness greater than 24 hours and a period of post traumatic amnesia greater than 7 days. People with severe TBI typically score between 3 and 8 on the GCS and between 4 and 6 on the Abbreviated Injury Scale score: Head (Brasure et al., 2012; CDC, 2017).

Impaired Consciousness

When an injury to the brain is severe enough, a person may become unconscious. In a coma, the eyes remain closed and the person cannot be aroused even by noxious stimuli. There is no purposeful motor activity and no indication of receptive or expressive language skills (American Congress of Rehabilitation Medicine, 1995; Jennet & Teasdale, 1977, The Multi-Society Task Force on PVS, 1994). Coma is indicative of widespread cortical and subcortical damage; consequently, the length of coma has previously been used as a useful predictor of long-term disability (Wilson, Vizor, & Bryant, 1991; Zafonte et al., 1996). Coma lasting less than a day is generally associated with a good recovery, whereas coma durations of 1 to 2 weeks leads to moderate disability, and coma durations of 3 or more weeks typically will result in severe long-term disability.

Controversy exists about the exact terminology to use to describe people with prolonged disorders of consciousness (DoC). The term *coma* denotes a complete state of unconsciousness (i.e., no environmental interaction) with no eye opening and an absence of sleep/wake cycles. The person does not communicate and does not respond to sound, touch, or pain. A *vegetative state* is defined as the complete lack of environmental interaction with some eye opening and periods of wakefulness and sleep; however, the person will exhibit a lack of visual tracking, objective recognition, and other environmental interaction. Responses such as smiling or crying as a reaction to visual or auditory stimuli, is a reflex that is beyond the person's control. A person may be determined to be in a *minimally conscious state* with eye opening and sleep/wake cycles, and some visual tracking despite having limited environmental international. During this state of limited awareness, the person may inconsistently follow some simple instructions or may communicate with yes/no spoken responses or gestures. These types of responses are referred to as purposeful behaviors. Some people may never improve beyond a minimally conscious state, but others may improve to a state of confusion and demonstrate disorientation and severe cognitive impairments. Emergence from a minimally conscious state is characterized as consistent ability to communicate and purposeful use of at least two objectives. The person may follow simple commands.

TBI Characteristics

Cognitive Impairments

Cognitive deficits following TBI vary significantly depending on the location and extent of the brain areas damaged. Additionally, although most people with TBI may have deficits in one or many areas of cognition, the extent of impairment in each area may vary. Generally, many people with TBI experience deficits in orientation, attention, memory, executive functions, and awareness. Although many of these aspects of cognition were discussed in Chapters 1, 2, and 3, a review of these deficits as they manifest in people with TBI is provided here.

Orientation

Orientation to the environment is a significant problem for many people with TBI. Orientation is typically measured in terms of person, place, time, and purpose or situation. Orientation may be evaluated on a daily basis or multiple times a day. Typically, orientation to person returns before orientation to place (e.g., city, state, hospital). Orientation to place is usually followed by improved orientation to time (e.g., season, year, month, week, day, date). Orientation to purpose or situation (e.g., injury, rehabilitation goals) may return last and may continue to be significantly impaired as the result of impaired self-awareness typical after TBI.

Attention

Attention deficits are common in people with TBI regardless of the severity of their injury. People with TBI may have deficits in all areas of attention including focused, sustained, selective, alternating, and divided. Specific information about impairments in different types of attention is provided in Chapter 1. Additionally, sometimes people with TBI can be hypervigilant, become overstimulated, and are unable to be redirected (Stierwalt & Murray, 2002). In particular, most people with TBI have difficulty selecting and prioritizing the most important information to which they should attend. These attention deficits are critical to cognitive rehabilitation because attention is believed to be foundational for all other cognitive abilities. Thus, attention deficits in people with TBI are likely to interfere with successful rehabilitation outcomes (Brooks, McKinlay, Symington, Beattie, & Campsie, 1987). After consciousness is regained and during states of minimal awareness, attention impairments may be severe and occur across multiple attention types creating difficulty even orienting to simple stimuli (Stierwalt & Murray, 2002). After some confusion has resolved, higher-level attention skills such as divided attention are impaired, particularly during complex, demanding tasks.

Memory

As many as 75% of people with TBI report persistent memory problems that may be very mild or may be characterized as permanent amnesia (Thomsen, 1984). Additionally, different types of memory may be impaired in people with TBI (e.g., short-term memory, long-term memory) for various types of information (e.g., declarative memory, non-declarative memory, visual, verbal). These types of memory are described in more detail in Chapter 2. Despite the multiple potential profiles of memory impairments, most people with TBI have more difficulty storing and retrieving declarative information than procedural information (Sohlberg, et al., 2007). Even people with mild or moderate TBI demonstrate deficits in episodic memory (i.e., immediate and delayed verbal memory recall, verbal recognition, immediate and delayed visual memory recall; Miotto et al., 2010).

Executive Functions

As described in Chapter 3, executive functions are a group of cognitive processes that facilitate goal-directed behavior. Much like impairments in attention and memory following TBI, executive functions resulting from TBI deficits vary significantly in severity and type. Two general categories of executive function impairments include initiation-related and inhibition related. Some examples of characteristics of executive function impairments exhibited by people with TBI include difficulty setting reasonable goals, planning and organizing their behavior to reach goals, and initiating behaviors that help achieve goals. People with TBI may also experience challenges related to inhibiting behaviors that are incompatible with reaching goals, as well as to monitoring their performance and revising plans as needed. They may also exhibit poor judgment and struggle to anticipate the difficulty of daily tasks.

Awareness and Theory of Mind

Researchers have reported up to 97% of individuals with TBI demonstrate self-awareness impairments (Sherer et al., 1998). Failure to recognize one's deficits can take a significant emotional toll on the person with TBI and act as a barrier to successful rehabilitation outcomes (Giacino & Cicerone, 1998; Schmidt, Lannin, Fleming, & Ownsworth, 2011; Sherer, Boake, Levin, Silver, Righolz, & High, 1998; Wallace & Bogner, 2000). Crosson and his colleagues (1989) described an awareness pyramid built on a foundation of intellectual awareness, defined as the cognitive capacity to understand that a particular cognitive function is diminished from pre-injury levels. They defined the middle level of the pyramid as emergent awareness. Emergent awareness is evident when the person with TBI recognizes a problem or deficits in real time. People with TBI must reach this level to activate situational specific strategies to compensate for their deficits. Crosson and colleagues (1989) suggested that, when a person with TBI reaches the top of the pyramid, he or she demonstrates anticipatory awareness. Anticipatory awareness is the ability to recognize that, because a deficit is present, the person can predict when a problem may happen and take appropriate steps to mitigate the effect or avoid a situation completely through anticipatory compensations.

Awareness deficits may be a precursor to deficits in theory of mind. Impaired theory of mind suggests that a person has difficulty in taking another person's perspective. People who experience theory of mind deficits have difficulty determining the intentions of others, lack understanding about how their behaviors affects others, and struggle with social reciprocity (Happé, Brownell, & Winner, 1999). These impairments may significantly affect a person's ability to make friends, succeed in school, and return to work.

Communication Impairments

People with TBI experience a variety of types and severities of speech and language impairments (Sarno, Buonaguro, & Levita, 1986). Mutism is common during early stages of recovery, usually due to severe cognitive (e.g., impaired consciousness) or physical impairments (e.g., locked-in-syndrome; Levin et al., 1983). People with TBI can also have aphasia, most often characterized as anomic aphasia. Sometimes their aphasia may present as transient word finding problems during the early stages of recovery. However, in about one-third of severe TBIs, the resulting communication impairment is aphasia (Sarno, 1980; Sarno et al.,1986). Usually aphasia following TBI is the result of focal damage to the areas responsible for language functions. About one-third of people with severe TBI have characteristics of dysarthria. Finally, in addition to dysarthria and aphasia, almost all people with severe TBI experience cognitive communication impairments.

Cognitive-communication impairments result in ineffective or inefficient communication due to deficits in areas of cognition which support communication (e.g., attention, memory, executive functions). Cognitive-communication deficits may be subtle, and therefore may only be detected through analysis of discourse tasks. Discourse produced by people with TBI may include poor topic maintenance, cohesion, and coherence (Coelho, Ylvisaker, & Turkstra, 2005). They may also have difficulty understanding the gist and abstract language. Although deficits in discourse production and comprehension are subtle, these may also significantly affect a person's participation in daily activities as well as return to school or work.

For people with severe communication impairments after TBI, recovery of natural speech may occur over an extended period of time. As a result, clinicians should continue to reassess people with TBI over time, particularly as cognitive abilities change (Light, Beesley & Collier, 1988). Of the people with severe TBI who initially cannot use natural speech to meet communication needs, 55 to 59% recover functional natural speech during the middle stages of recovery (Dongilli, Hakel, & Beukelman, 1992). By *Ranchos Los Amigos Scale Levels of Cognitive Functioning-Revised* (Hagen, 1982; 2000) Level V, if the person is unable to rely on natural speech, it is often due to severe, motor speech or language disorders (Dongilli et al., 1992).

Other Relevant Areas of Impairment

In addition to cognitive and communication impairments, many people with TBI experience auditory or vestibular symptoms such as dizziness and vertigo, tinnitus and hyperacusis, hearing loss, and loudness sensitivity (Dennis, 2009). Injuries specifically resulting from a blast may include tympanic membrane rupture, dislocations of the ossicles, or cochlea damage. This dam-

age may be a sign of blast exposure despite the lack of other signs or symptoms. Immediately following blast injury, people may experience temporary hearing loss and tinnitus that should be closely monitored.

In addition to communication impairments, people with TBI often also have dysphagia. The severity of swallowing impairment and prognosis can vary greatly in this population. The primary concern for individuals with swallowing impairments is aspiration which occurs when food or liquids are present below the vocal folds. Some people may cough or have a wet "gurgly" voice as a result of aspiration, while others may not exhibit signs or symptoms of aspiration. Assessment and treatment for dysphagia can be complicated by other physical, sensory, and cognitive impairments experienced by many people with TBI.

As the purpose of this chapter is to provide information about cognitive and communication impairments following TBI, readers are referred to resources in Table 8–2 for additional information about hearing loss and swallowing after TBI.

Assessment

General Assessment Considerations

As part of a comprehensive TBI evaluation, speech-language pathologists should consider a number of factors. Injury severity is an important factor that is described in detail in the next section. In addition to determining severity, it is important that clinicians consider that poor performance on for-

Table 8–2. Resources About Dysphagia and Hearing Loss in People With TBI

Audiology
Dennis, K. C. (2009). Current perspectives on traumatic brain injury. *ASHA Access Audiology*, http://www.asha.org/aud/articles/currentTBI.htm (Retrieved May 11, 2014).
Dodd-Murphy, J. (2014). Auditory effects of blast exposure: Community outreach following an industrial explosion. Retrieved from http://www.asha.org/aud/Articles/Auditory-Effects-of-Blast-Exposure/?utm_source=asha&utm_medium=enewsletter&utm_campaign=accessaud051214#sthash.zOdcZBFb.dpuf
Myers, P., Henry, J., Zaugg, T., & Kendall, C. (2009). Tinnitus evaluation and management considerations for persons with mild traumatic brain injury. First published in *ASHA Access Audiology, 8.* Retrieved from http://www.asha.org/aud/articles/TinnitusTBI/

Dysphagia
American Speech-Language-Hearing Association Evidence maps. Retrieved from http://ncepmaps.org/ptbi/tx/
Mackay, L. E., Morgan, A. S., & Bernstein, B. A. (1999). Swallowing disorders in severe brain injury: Risk factors affecting return to oral intake. *Archives of Physical Medicine and Rehabilitation, 80,* 365–371.
Mandaville, A., Ray, A., Robertson, H., Foster, C., & Jesser, C. (2014). A retrospective review of swallow dysfunction in patients with severe traumatic brain injury. *Dysphagia, 29,* 1–9.
Morgan, A. S., & Mackay, L. E. (1999). Causes and complications associated with swallowing disorders in traumatic brain injury. *The Journal of Head Trauma Rehabilitation, 14,* 454–461.

mal and informal assessment measures may reflect motor or sensory-perceptual problems, pre-existing academic difficulties, or emotional-behavioral deficits. Additionally, during the acute stages of TBI, people often make dramatic performance changes so it is helpful to use scales to describe their overall function and to continue to assess their abilities throughout treatment. Finally, people with TBI tend to perform better within structured tasks in a clinical setting than they do in the real world, thus emphasizing the need for assessment measures that reflect functional performance in the real-world.

Interprofessional collaborations may be particularly vital for successfully evaluating and documenting deficits following TBI. The unique challenges faced by TBI survivors across a variety of domains (e.g., physical, sensory, cognitive, and emotional) require a team-approach to ensure best practice and implementation of evidence-based techniques to serve the individual as a whole rather than as someone experiencing distinct deficits and challenges. In rehabilitative settings, interdisciplinary assessment practices may include, but are not limited to, audiologists, occupational therapists, physical therapists, respiratory therapists, recreation therapists, nurses, physicians, and neuropsychologists. Navigating the team dynamic and determining the various roles and responsibilities of each professional involved is necessary for thorough evaluation and treatment post-injury (Sander, Raymer, Wertheimer, & Paul, 2009).

In addition to these factors for consideration, rehabilitation professionals must consider potential constraints that may serve as barriers to the assessment process. Some such barriers may include time constraints, availability of testing measures, and reimbursement practices. Specifically, depending on the setting in which an evaluation is conducted, time and procedural constraints may inhibit the type and length of assessments chosen by an SLP. Little evidence is available to inform the average length of evaluation in acute, post-acute, outpatient, and skilled nursing settings; however, it is likely that many therapists are encouraged or required to complete a full evaluation of cognitive, communicative, and swallowing competencies in a single, often short session. Co-occurring deficits post-TBI such as decreased processing speed, motor challenges, sensory challenges, and neurobehavioral deficits (e.g., agitation) may further contribute to these difficulties. In such instances, clinicians should consider selecting assessment subtests or tasks that are reflective of a variety of domains simultaneously, which may require access from more than one assessment tool. A model suggested by the World Health Organization may assist clinicians in developing holistic testing protocols when time and procedural constraints confound testing practices.

Models of Assessment

The World Health Organization's Classification of Functioning, Disability, and Health (WHO-ICF) provides a logical, globally recognized model for assessing deficits at the impairment, activity, and functioning levels within the recovery continuum of TBI (McDougall, Wright, & Rosenbaum, 2010; Wade, 2005); however, a great deal of focus has recently emerged regarding evaluation of patient deficits in real-world, functional settings. According to the WHO-ICF model, a person's functioning ability, including participation in everyday activities, comprises the interaction among the experienced health condition, contextual real-world factors, and personal characteristics. Thus, a variety of factors must be considered when evaluating the outcomes of a disorder or disease given this biopsychosocial health perspective—encompassing both the individual (i.e., personal factors) and societal perspective (i.e., environmental factors). The WHO-ICF model offers a unifying conceptual and terminological framework for rehabilitation professionals (Figure 8–2, used with permission).

Adequately assessing functioning at the individual levels requires an assessment protocol which meets the following five primary objectives (Constantinidou, Wertheimer, Tsanadis, Evans, & Paul, 2012):

- Evaluate strengths and weaknesses and their effect on pre-morbid abilities
- Guide the development and implementation of short- and long-term treatment goals
- Guide the development of remedial and compensatory strategies

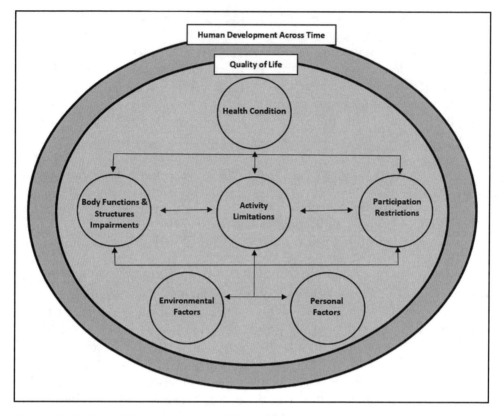

Figure 8–2. World Health Organization's Classification of Functioning, Disability, and Health. Used with permission from the World Health Organization (WHO).

- Steer discussion with patients and family members regarding challenges within the recovery process
- Serve as an anchor for future changes resulting from recovery and treatment

In the sections that follow we will discuss various methods available to rehabilitation professionals attempting to reach these aims during the assessment process. Globally, this will include consideration of injury severity and patient demographics; self-report and quality of life measures; standardized, objective testing methods; and functional, ecologically-valid tasks.

Early Assessment Techniques

The most widely used tool for quantifying coma is *Glasgow Coma Scale* (Teasdale & Jennett, 1974). This 15-point scale measures behaviors associated with eye opening, as well as best motor and best verbal responses within 24 hours of injury (Table 8–3). A total score of 3 to 8 represents a severe TBI, a score of 9 to 12 represents a moderate TBI, and a score of 13 to 15 represents a mild TBI (CDC, 2017; Teasdale & Jennett, 1974). These results should be interpreted carefully because factors, such as time post-injury, pharmaceutical treatments to control brain swelling or to relax muscles, high blood alcohol levels,

Table 8–3. Glasgow Coma Scale Responses

	Eye-Opening Response	Best Motor Response	Best Verbal Response
1	No response	No response	No response
2	Eye opening to pain	Extension of limbs	Incomprehensible
3	Eye opening to speech	Flexion of limbs	Inappropriate
4	Spontaneous eye opening	Withdraws from stimulus	Confused
5		Localizes sensory stimulus	Oriented ×3
6		Obeys commands	

paralysis or hemiparesis, and communication disorders such as aphasia and dysarthria may affect performance within each area assessed.

The use of coma length as a measure of TBI severity is complicated primarily by the use of pharmaceutical treatments to induce coma for medical stabilization and the potential presence of alcohol or drugs at the time of the injury. An additional complication is the use of motor and speech/language-dependent responses to measure coma in a population who is likely to have associated damage in one or both of these areas separate from their cognitive impairments as described previously. For these reasons, coma length alone should not be used as an index of TBI severity.

Posttraumatic Amnesia

As stated previously, PTA is another indicator of TBI severity, which also has prognostic utility. PTA can be formally assessed using one of the two following tools.

The Galveston Orientation and Amnesia Test (Levin, O'Donnell, & Grossman, 1979) was the first test of PTA. The test has 10 questions that are heavily weighted toward orientation but also tap into the person's recall of information. For example, the first few questions require the person to provide his or her name, place of birth, and place of residence. The examiner also asks the person to describe details about the first event he or she recalls after the injury and the last event they can recall before the injury. This helps the clinician determine what the person remembers about their experience. A person can obtain a maximum score of 100 on the test. Scores between 80 to 100 points indicated normal performance. Scores between 66 and 79 points suggest borderline disability, and scores ranging from 0 to 65 points are representative of clear difficulty with PTA (Levin et al., 1979). An individual who receives a consistent score of 75 or greater three tries in a row is considered to have recovered from PTA. The *Children's Orientation and Amnesia Test* (Ewing-Cobbs, Levin, Flectcher, Miner, & Eisenberg, 1990) was normed on 146 school-age children 3 and 15 years old. The 16-item scale assesses general orientation, temporal orientation, and memory (i.e., immediate, short-term, and remote) and takes about 5 to 10 minutes to administer. The test can be administered daily. A score of 78 or greater on three consecutive occasions indicates that the child is no longer in a state of PTA.

Scales and Observational Checklists

Severity of injury is also measured through medical chart reviews, case history interviews, and completion of general observational scales. Particularly relevant case history questions for this population include questions about demographics such as age and date of injury (i.e., measures orientation and memory), goals (i.e., measure self-awareness), and level of education (i.e., education may correlate with performance on standardized tests). The provided case form (Appendices 8–A and 8–B) serves as a starting point for clinicians when performing medical chart reviews and establishing basic patient case history. As a supplement, both patient and caregiver interviews should be initiated.

With information from the case history, as well as from observational scales or checklists, clinicians may plan an appropriate, comprehensive evaluation for the person with TBI. In particular, formal or structured assessment of some areas of cognition (e.g., attention) is inappropriate during early stages of cognitive recovery because test results obtained during this phase are typically unreliable and invalid due to the person's state of generalized confusion and agitation. Moreover, testing procedures and stimuli may cause overstimulation and increased agitation. These scales and checklists will help speech-language pathologists determine a general sense of severity, thereby conveying the attention and behavioral abilities of the person with TBI.

Ranchos Los Amigos Levels of Cognitive Functioning-Revised (RLA-R) (Hagen Malkmus, & Durham, 1972; Hagen, 2000) is perhaps the most widely used measure of cognitive status of people with TBI. The original scale described eight categories that effectively evaluated a person's level of cognitive ability at a given point in time. Individuals are assigned to a level according to a number of behavioral variables. The written descriptors capture in detail the behavior of a person with TBI as he or she moves from coma to minimally responsive behavioral states to purposeful and independent behavior. This scale was revised from an 8-point to a 10-point scale (Hagen, 2000; "Ranchos Los Amigos Cognitive Scale Revised," 2014). Levels IX and X were added to provide greater definition of purposeful and appropriate behaviors, which are more sensitive to individuals at the higher end of the recovery spectrum. The revision also provided clearer descriptions of the behaviors at each level, so that it is easier to differentiate from people who are high functioning. This scale is a valid and sensitive measure of the behaviors that are associated with long-term functional improvement and can guide development of a comprehensive assessment and treatment plan. It is important for clinicians to remember that people progress through the levels at different rates and that at times one person might demonstrate characteristics that are associated with more than one level.

Another commonly administered scale that provides a description of a person's general level of function is the *Functional Independence Measure* (*FIM*™; Guide for the Uniform Data Set for Medical Rehabilitation, 1996; Wright, 2000; Table 8–4). The purpose of this assessment tool is to measure the person's level of disability and the amount of assistance required for him or her to complete everyday tasks. Five of the 18 items assessed relate to cognitive abilities. The clinician uses a seven-point scale to rate the person as either being dependent or independent in that particular activity such that a score of one refers to complete dependence and a score of seven refers to complete independence. The five cognitive items include: cognitive comprehension, expression, social interaction, problem solving and memory. Several benefits exist regarding implementation of *FIM* scores in practice. First, this scale pro-

vides for a common language across rehabilitative disciplines such that professionals in a variety of domains (e.g., occupational therapy and physical therapy) subjectively rate client independence and supportive needs on a well-established, standardized scale. Furthermore, this assessment measure provides quantifiable data for initial evaluation and progress monitoring for primarily subjective clinical observations.

Finally, the *Disability Rating Scale* (Rappaport, Hall, Hopkins, Belleza, & Cope, 1982) was designed to measure functional changes in people with moderate and severe TBI as they progress through various stages of recovery. The clinician rates the person's behavior in four categories: consciousness (i.e., eye opening, verbal response, motor response), cognitive abilities (i.e., feeding, toileting, grooming), level of dependence on others, and employability.

Table 8–4. Functional Independence Measure Rating Scale and Interpretations

Score	Description
7	100% Functional—independent (I)
6	Functional with assistance of a device or extra time
5	Occasional difficulty, 90% functional—requires assistance less than 10% of the time (supervision)
4	Minimally impaired; 75%–90% functional—requires assistance 10%–25% of the time
3	Moderately impaired; 50%–74% functional—assistance 25%–50% of the time
2	Maximally impaired; 25%–49% functional—assistance 50%–75% of the time
1	Profoundly impaired; 0%–24% functional—assistance 75%–100% of the time

Because it covers a wide range of recovery, it may not be as sensitive to subtle changes, particularly at the mild end of the scale. Malec and his colleagues' (2012) modified telephone interview protocol, the Disability Rating Scale-Postacute Interview, was found to be an efficient approach to standardized follow-up assessment for people with TBI. Additionally, this modified version was found to be more sensitive and provide more detail for people with mild impairments than the original *Disability Rating Scale.*

Self-Report and Quality of Life Measures

Many professionals rely on client self-report to diagnose and determine symptomatology for individuals with TBI. This is due to the fact that performance on standardized, objective measures can be skewed based on a variety of environmental and personal factors and provide inconsistent identification of deficits (Wood & Liossi, 2006). Current suggested models from the WHO encourage rehabilitation professionals and researchers to collect information from the perspective of individuals themselves, as well as from other sources. Additionally, self-report elicited through structured screening tools or client interviews are increasingly recognized as the best, or perhaps only, way to estimate TBI incidence and chronic TBI prevalence (Dams-O'Connor et al., 2014). In fact, a 2010 panel of rehabilitation specialists documented the importance of self-report measures, indicating that a multidimensional approach to patient-reported outcomes was a promising

evaluative tool across the brain injury severity spectrum (Wilde et al., 2010).

Initiation of person-centered care relies on involvement of the client during both the assessment and treatment process. Thus, inclusion of measures which solicit perspectives of patients, family members, and caregivers are vital to selecting functional, real world treatment goals. Many self-report measures are available to professionals working with individuals with TBI. The following sections briefly highlight some of the available tools.

Behavior Rating Inventory of Executive Function– Adult (BRIEF-A)

This self-rating scale captures the participants' executive functions and self-regulation in everyday environments (Roth, Isquith, & Gioia, 2005). This 75-item measure includes nine non-overlapping scales that measure various aspects of executive functioning (i.e., inhibition, self-monitoring, planning/organization, shifting, initiation, task monitoring, emotional control, working memory, and organization). Three scores are comprised from this measure: Behavioral Regulation, Metacognition, and the Global Executive Composite. This self-report scale is normed on U.S. men and women from a variety of ethnic, geographical, and educational backgrounds. Higher raw scores, T scores, and percentile ranks indicate a greater degree of executive dysfunction (Roth et al., 2005).

Quality of Life After Brain Injury (QOLIBRI)

The QOLIBRI is the first instrument specifically developed to assess health-related quality of life (HRQoL) of individuals after traumatic brain injury (http://www.qolibrinet.com/index/htm). This questionnaire is designed to measure physical, psychological, daily life, and psychosocial changes typical of brain injury. Questions are coded as "satisfaction" or "feeling bothered" items and are queried using a 5-point Likert-type scale. The comprehensive measure includes 37 items covering six health related dimensions of quality of life following TBI—cognition, self, daily life & autonomy, social relations, emotions, and physical problems. The questionnaire provides a profile of quality of life through a total score value and domain scores ranging from zero to 100; scores of zero indicate very poor quality of life and scores of 100 equal very high quality of life.

National Institute of Health Toolbox

The National Institutes of Health created a validated, standardized toolbox for evaluation of deficits across a variety of cognitive domains (i.e., the NIH Toolbox). Within this collection of instruments are several client self-report measures that may be useful in documenting symptomatology post-injury and effect on daily functioning. Two such examples are the Neuro-QOL Cognitive Function measure (National Institute of Neurological Disorders and Stroke, 2015) and the PROMIS Cognitive Function measure (Health Measures, 2018). The Neuro-QOL queries individuals regarding current difficulties with cognitive functions as well as difficulties experienced over the previous seven-day period. Questions are formed in a manner to provide example activities relative to distinct cognitive functions. Participants are tasked with responding on a 5-point Likert-type scale indicating frequency with which a symptom occurs such from very often (1) to never (5). Similarly, the PROMIS item bank queries individuals regarding cognitive function across the previous seven-day period using a 5-point Likert-type scale; however, the PROMIS differs from the Neuro-QOL in that it does not provide contextual examples of cognitive deficits but rather explicitly queries respondents regarding particular cognitive domains.

Brain Injury Screening Questionnaire (BISQ)

The three-part tool is an evidence-based, self-report instrument designed to screen for and document history related to TBI (Dams-O'Connor et al., 2014). The BISQ was developed based on the mTBI diagnosis criteria set by the American Congress of Rehabilitation Medicine with the goal of creating a screening tool that could document lifetime history of self-reported TBI and symptoms. The BISQ, which is divided into three distinct parts: TBI History, Symptoms, and Other Health Conditions, rules out alternative explanations for symptoms (e.g., neurological or developmental conditions). The inventory includes 100 possible cognitive, physical, emotional, and behavioral symptoms for endorsement. When the BISQ is used in evaluations, inferences can be made regarding the extent to which symptoms are specifically attributable to TBI. Furthermore, the BISQ reportedly has increased sensitivity compared to other commonly used self-assessment measures for the mTBI population.

Mayo-Portland Adaptability Inventory

The Mayo-Portland Adaptability Inventory–Fourth Edition (MPAI-4; Malec et al., 2003; Malec & Lezak, 2008) is a subjective rating form which can be completed by a single professional, professional consensus, the person with brain injury, or a caregiver. Each part of the scale queries the respondent on various domains associated with daily living and specifically targets an individual with brain injury's abilities, adjustment, and participation using a 5-point Likert-type scale. Additionally, the scale takes into consideration pre-existing and associated conditions that may be substantially contributing to results. Obtained raw scores are converted to standard scores and can be used clinically to judge the level of impairment such that a higher score indicates a more advanced level of impairment and increased reliance on others for daily task completion.

Motivational Interview Techniques

Motivational interview techniques combine a supportive and empathic counseling style with a conscious, directive method for client self-analysis (Hettema, Steele, & Miller, 2005; Medley & Powell, 2010). Motivational interviewing emphasizes and honors client autonomy through clinician and client co-construction of challenges and needs. Motivational interview techniques involve the clinician beginning with an open-ended question (e.g., "What can I help you with?"). The clinician then follows client responses with open-ended, directive prompts (e.g., "Tell me more about why that bothers you."), reflects on client responses (e.g., "It's hard to stay focused for long periods of time."), and summarizes/synthesizes client remarks (e.g., "So what I hear you saying is . . . "). Such techniques assist in developing client-centered care plans and enhancing client buy-in for therapy goals and targets.

Standardized Assessment Measures

In addition to self-report tools and observational scales, clinicians use standardized, objective assessment tools to measure the cognitive and communicative abilities of people with TBI. These may take the form of screening tools, subtests, or holistic testing batteries. Due to the extensive number of tests available and the challenges faced by clinicians in determining the most appropriate formal assessment tools for people with TBI, the Academy of Neurological Communication Disorders and Sciences created a committee to review the evidence for commonly used assessment tools (Turkstra et al., 2005). As described in Chapter 3, only seven tests met the committee's criteria. Additionally, the committee emphasized that standardized assessments, although valuable for identifying cognitive and communication deficits, should only be one component of a comprehensive evaluation.

Benefits include procurement of a standardized score, potential comparison of patient performance to age and gender norms, commonalities among test-taking procedures and questions, and provision of a quantitative diagnosis of a problem. However, the adequacy of these measures when utilized in isolation is substantially lacking. A recent survey of speech-language pathologists (Brown, 2018) revealed that on average, approximately 80% of respondents reported less than complete satisfaction and/or dissatisfaction with available assessment tools across cognitive domains. Furthermore, when asked to provide cons to assessments, respondents commonly reported issues such as (a) lack of norm-referenced data, poor psychometrics, and poor standardization, (b) problems with test length or administration ease, and (c) challenges related to the functional, realistic, or patient-specific nature of assessments. In fact, of the 467 reported cons, a staggering 32% related to challenges with the functional, realistic nature of assessments. Thus, at this time, an ideal approach to assessing cognition and communication in individuals with neurogenic disorders likely includes administering a variety of tools and developing personally-relevant, function tasks.

Screening Tools

As an initial step in the assessment process, clinicians may wish to administer screening tools. Such tests are meant to detect the presence of a disorder and serve to alert clinicians as to whether in-depth exploration and assessment in a given area is a necessary next step. Screening tools do not provide information regarding deficit severity nor do they elucidate the specific characteristics of challenges faced by individuals with TBI. For example, completion of a screening tool for left neglect may reveal a potential deficit in visual

attention and processing and provide guidance for the clinician to initiate in-depth assessment in these areas. A variety of screening tools are available to rehabilitation professionals working with individuals with TBI that highlight a variety of cognitive, linguistic, and visuospatial domains. Such tools include, but are not limited to, the *Mini Mental State Exam* (MMSE; Folstein, Folstein, & McHugh, 1975), *Montreal Cognitive Assessment* (MOCA; Nasreddine at al., 2005), and *St. Louis University Mental Status Examination* (SLUMS; Morley & Tumosa, 2002). Such tools are intended to be administered in a short time frame (e.g., 30 minutes or less) and provide initial evaluation of deficits in areas such as: orientation, visuospatial skills, attention, memory (immediate and delayed), language comprehension and expression, and executive functioning skills. Additional brief assessments for consideration include the *Repeatable Battery for the Assessment of Neuropsychological Status* (*RBANS*, Randolph, 2012) and the *Cognitive Linguistic Quick Test–Plus* (*CLQT+*; Helm-Estabrooks, 2017). Although useful in settings where initial deficit detection is vital (e.g., acute care), brief assessments and screening tools should only be used as a component to a comprehensive evaluation and should not replace in-depth, holistic deficit testing post-injury.

Cognitive Subtests and Batteries

Often speech-language pathologists may evaluate people with TBI using subtests from various batteries or by selecting measures related to specific areas of deficits. For example, the clinicians might combine subtests from the

Functional Assessment of Verbal Reasoning and Executive Strategies (MacDonald, 2005) for assessment of executive functioning, the *Test of Everyday Attention* (Robertson, Ward, Ridgeway, & Nimmo-Smith, 1994) for attention, and the *Rivermead Behavioural Memory Test-Third Edition* (Wilson, et al., 2008) for memory. Please refer to previous chapters for descriptions of assessment tools that are appropriate for these areas. Two batteries specifically designed for people with TBI are the *Brief Test of Head Injury* (Helm-Estabrooks & Hotz, 1991) and the *Scales of Cognitive Ability for Traumatic Brain Injury* (Adamovich & Henderson, 1992). The *Brief Test of Head Injury* may be most appropriate for people at *RLA-R* levels IV to VI particularly because its administration lasts about 20 to 30 minutes so attention deficits will be less impactful and because it scores gestural and verbal responses. In contrast, the *Scales of Cognitive Ability for Traumatic Brain Injury* (Adamivich & Henderson, 1992) may be most appropriate for people at *RLA-R* levels VI and above. This battery takes 30 to 120 minutes and progresses to levels of difficulty that will likely be challenging for some adults without brain injury.

Communication Subtests and Batteries

Speech-language pathologists may also wish to administer standardized tests aimed at evaluating various components of communication. Although we will not discuss physical deficits associated with TBI in detail in this book, it is important to note that clinicians should complete thorough motor speech and swallowing evaluations on all people with history of TBI. As a focus of this chapter, we provide suggestions for assessment practices relative to various aspects of communication (e.g., aphasia, reading, writing, social communication). Evaluating communication at an appropriate stage in recovery is crucial for accurate representation of linguistic ability such that a patient's current cognitive status may interfere with assessment results. For example, evaluating communicative functioning may be inappropriate for patients at *RLA-R* V or below given their continued agitation, confusion, and severe attention and memory deficits. Thus, consideration of language and communication evaluation for individuals at *RLA-R* VI or above may be most appropriate. Table 8–5 provides potential standardized measures for clinicians to evaluate communication in individuals following TBI. Because the evidence related to some areas of assessment following TBI is limited (ASHA, 2019), clinicians may consider tools that are validated with other populations; however, further research examining their use is needed. These areas may also be evaluated using informal measures until validated tools are available.

Functional Assessment Measures

Given some of the challenges described in the above sections, ecologically-valid assessments are critically important to a thorough TBI assessment. These evaluations may include, among other things, observational reports; discourse analysis; and completion of functional, personally-relevant tasks that may or may not reflect a set of standardized, objective procedures. Understanding

Table 8–5. Standardized Assessments for Evaluation of Communication Deficits Following TBI

Communicative Domain	Measure
Aphasia diagnosis	Western Aphasia Battery–Revised (WAB-R)
	Boston Naming Test (BNT)
	Comprehensive Aphasia Test (CAT)
	Test of Adolescent/Adult Word Finding (TAWF)
Holistic language evaluation	American Speech Language Hearing Association Functional Assessment of Communication Skills for Adults (ASHA FACS)
	Communication Activities of Daily Living–Third Edition (CADL-3)
	Scales of Cognitive and Communicative Ability for Neurorehabilitation (SCCAN)
Reading	Wechsler Test of Adult Reading (WTAR)
Writing	Western Aphasia Battery–Revised Part II
Social skills	Mini Inventory of Right Brain Injury–Second Edition (MIRBI-2)
	Scales of Cognitive Ability for Traumatic Brain Injury (SCATBI)
Apraxia and motor speech disorders	Frenchay Dysarthria Assessment–Second edition
	Assessment of Intelligibility of Dysarthric Speech (AIDS)

the contribution of real-world constraints to the performance of individuals with TBI is vital. In fact, a wealth of research exists documenting that individuals with TBI perform relatively well given structured and routine tasks (e.g., standardized tests), but may perform poorly during novel functional tasks. Specifically, ample evidence exists to suggest that cognitive and executive difficulties are often more pronounced when a reminder cue must be self-generated, when the cognitive load of the ongoing task is high, or when distractors are present (Carlesimo, Casadio, & Caltagirone, 2004; Knight, Titov, & Crawford, 2006; Maujean, Shum, & McQueen, 2003). These factors are indicative of naturalistic, real-world settings and, thus, important to note. Inclusion of tasks during the assessment process which attempt to mimic personally-relevant, real-world situations are necessary in order to select and implement effective treatment plans for return to functional status post-injury.

The literature investigating the ecological validity of common neuropsychological tests of cognition in particular is inconsistent (Chaytor, Schmitter-Edgecombe, & Burr, 2006). However, many researchers and clinicians have acknowledged the usefulness of ecologically-valid assessments to: (a) determine competency when standardized assessments do not exist for a particular skill, (b) identify unique demands of a client's personal contexts, (c) describe performance within natural contexts, and (d) evaluate the effectiveness of potential supports to enhance competency (Coelho, Ylvisaker, & Turkstra, 2005). Past researchers have assessed ecological validity using a variety of measurement tools including self-questionnaires, clinician rating scales, and observation of simulated everyday tasks (Chaytor et al., 2006). The following sections highlight functional assessment tools available to rehabilitation professionals across a variety of cognitive and communicative domains.

Observational Reports

Observational reports may assess general behaviors (e.g., alertness, restlessness) during standardized assessments, simulated situations (e.g., role-play, phone calls, ordering food), or real-world situations (e.g., grocery store, bank). Behaviors to evaluate include those related to social appropriateness (e.g., proxemics, turn taking, eye contact) as well as, fatigue (i.e., how long it takes performance to decline), and emotional lability (e.g., uncontrollable emotional displays). Role-play tasks can be simple (e.g., look up number and call for a pet store's hours) or complex (e.g., budget and plan a trip to Italy for two couples). The opportunity to select personally relevant tasks may enable the speech-language pathologist to get a complete picture of how the person's constellation of strengths and deficits affect his or her daily functioning. This

type of assessment may also help the clinician detect subtle deficits that may not be identified using standardized assessments.

Discourse Analysis

People with TBI may have communicative deficits not readily captured by standardized testing methods. Discourse analysis in particular is another approach that may identify these subtle deficits. Discourse analysis can be particularly powerful because it can measure various areas of deficits ranging from those less likely to be affected in TBI (e.g., topic maintenance) to those likely be affected (topic maintenance, organization). Coelho, Ylvisaker, and Turkstra (2005) reviewed several types of discourse analysis used with people with TBI including both non-interactive (e.g., description, procedural) and conversational. Non-interactive discourse is elicited through story retelling, story generation, personal event retelling, and procedural descriptions. Coelho and his colleagues (2005) recommend the analysis of the following elements because they produced the most consistent findings: verbal output, content accuracy and organization, story grammar, and coherence. Measures of syntax, grammatical complexity, and cohesion resulted in inconsistent findings across studies. Conversational analyses often made use of rating scales such as Daminco's Clinical Discourse Analysis (1992), but training is required and the four basic psychometric properties should be considered (Coelho et al., 2005). Two categories of measurements (i.e., measures of initiation and manipulation of content) are appropriate for analysis of conversational discourse, with content and topic management probably being the most useful. Conversational discourse analyses appear to better distinguish people with TBI from people without brain injury than non-interactive analyses.

Additional analyses may focus on coherence and cohesion of expressive language output produced by individuals with TBI. Cohesion refers to the linking of meaning across sentences that occur through the use of cohesive markers. Such markers are words that lead the listener to information elsewhere in the conversation. Coherence, on the other hand, refers to the relation of an expressed utterance to the overall content or topic and is defined in two ways—that is, local and global. Local coherence is established by relating the content of one utterance to the content of the previous utterance; global coherence occurs by relating the content of one utterance to the general theme or topic of conversation (Glosser & Deser, 1990). In both instances of cohesion and coherence deficits, underlying cognitive issues associated with skills such as attention, memory, organization, and theory of mind may play a role. Objectively analyzing expressive language for these characteristics may shed light on communication difficulties attributable, in part, to common cognitive deficits following brain injury (Van Leer & Turkstra, 1999).

Functional, Personally-Relevant Tasks

The development of ecologically-valid tools in addition to standardized measurements is necessary to successfully evaluate clients at the participation level and within their natural contexts (Constantinidou et al., 2012; Eslinger, Zappala, Chakara, & Barrett, 2011; Wood & Liossi, 2006). Several methods exist to aid clinicians in administering functionally, personally-relevant assessments that do not require development for each individual. For example, the Multiple Errands Test, available in many forms both paper-based and electronically (e.g., Dawson et al., 2009; Knight, Alderman, & Burgess, 2002; Raspelli et al., 2012), requires the individual with TBI to perform tasks similar to those experienced in daily life while outside of the therapy room setting (e.g., in a mall, within a rehabilitation facility campus). Similarly, the Party Planning Task (Shanahan, McAllister, & Curtin, 2011) facilitates planning of a party while following various restrictions and guidelines; again, a task that may be relevant to functional, real-world need. Furthermore, other researchers have developed and evaluated functional tasks that include both planning and execution and encompass constraints for both immediate and prospective memory (Brown & Hux, 2016; 2017) and have been specifically created for use with individuals with TBI. However, many researchers and clinicians have acknowledged the usefulness of functional assessments to: (a) determine competency when standardized assessments do not exist for a particular skill, (b) identify unique demands of a client's personal contexts, (c) describe performance within natural contexts, and (d) evaluate the effectiveness of potential supports to enhance competency (Coelho et al., 2005). Thus, in times when functionally, relevant tools are not readily available to clinicians, creation of client-specific tasks may be of value to the assessment process.

Treatment

Treatment of TBI ideally involves a team of rehabilitation professionals; thus, it is critical that services are carefully coordinated. Additionally, although interventions emphasized through this section focus on cognitive and communication impairments, consideration of potential impairments in swallowing, hearing, and visual processing are important to the development of a successful, comprehensive intervention program. Finally, for people with TBI, evidence suggests comprehensive neuropsychological programs are beneficial. These programs are often interdisciplinary in nature and may offer group and individual interventions during post-acute rehabilitation (Cicerone et al., 2011).

Multiple systematic reviews examining the evidence for cognitive rehabilitation have been conducted (e.g., Cicerone et al., 2011; Kennedy et al., 2008; Sohlberg et al., 2007; Sohlberg et al., 2003). Many of these reviews have examined interventions within the areas of attention, memory, executive functions, and communication. Although it is difficult to isolate cognitive impairments during interventions due to multiple areas of overlap, each is discussed in separate sections below. Typically, in clinical practice, a group of intervention strategies may be implemented with consideration of the specific needs of the client.

A variety of methods are available to treat cognitive and communicative deficits in individuals with TBI such that no one, standard approach should be utilized. Selection of a specific approach may depend on a number of factors (e.g., timeline for treatment, patient preference, research evidence) and, thus, understanding underlying principles of treatment is a vital clinical skill. Following completion of in-depth assessments, clinicians and their clients should initiate co-construction of goals, when possible, to enhance the treatment process and maintain personal relevance during therapy. Other chapters in this textbook describe various methods available to clinicians when selecting cognitive-communication goals post-TBI (e.g., Goal Attainment Scaling). Subsequently, clinicians may wish to decide whether a selected goal and subsequent treatment is aimed at restoring functioning and remediating deficits (e.g., drill and practice), compensating for present deficits (e.g., strategy training), or environmental management. The sections below highlight some potential treatment approaches for various cognitive and communicative deficits typically experienced by individuals with TBI.

Sensory Stimulation

The following principles are important considerations for providing sensory stimulation to individuals with altered consciousness (e.g., Ranchos Levels I, II, or III). First, the person must always be treated with dignity and respect. Second, it is important to remember that the person may understand what is said near him or her, so be careful to only say things that you would want him or her to hear. Finally, the person may be able to perceive pain without a way to respond or communicate about it, so it is important that he or she is monitored for possible discomfort or pain. For example, watch that the person's limbs are free from any moving parts of a wheelchair before moving him or her.

Although further research is needed regarding the use of sensory stimulation programs (Lombardi, Taricco, De Tanti, Telaro, & Liberati, 2002), they are appropriate for people in states of altered consciousness because they prevent sensory deprivation, facilitate increased arousal and responsiveness, and prevent sensory overload by controlling the amount and type of stimulation (Ansell, 1991). Specifically, sensory stimulation treatment is aimed at increasing a person's frequency, variety, and specificity of response by manipulating the rate, amount, duration, and complexity of stimulation but should ideally be administered for periods no greater than 15 minutes in length. Typically, sensory stimulation may be provided in a structured manner via six types of stimulation: visual, auditory, tactile, olfactory, gustatory, and kinesthetic and should only target one sensory modality at a time. It is important that speech-language pathologists collaborate with other health care professionals, as sensory stimulation in many of these areas overlaps with other disciplines' scope of practice. Examples of strategies that might be implemented in each area are included in Table 8–6.

Attention

Direct attention training (as described in Chapter 1), includes improvement of the neurocognitive system through repetition of exercises that stimulate attention. Attention Process Training is one well-known example of direct attention training that targets multiple areas of

Table 8–6. Examples of Sensory Stimulation Strategies

Stimulation Type	Strategies
Visual	Visual tracking of the following: photos of family and friends, balloons, printed signs, get well cards, mirror
Auditory	Preferred music or television shows, voices of family and friends, spoken commands
Tactile	Rub face or limbs with lotion, brush hair, massage hands, feet, arms, or legs
Olfactory	Bring the person in the kitchen while food is being cooked, flowers, spices, coffee, mints, soap, perfume or cologne
Gustatory	(Be sure to evaluate swallowing and oral reflexes first) lemon glycerin swabs, brushing teeth
Kinesthetic	Elevate bed (if medically approved), sit person in rocking chair, perform range-of-motion exercise

attention (Sohlberg & Mateer, 2001a). During post-acute care and for individuals with mild impairments, Sohlberg and colleagues (2007) recommend combining direct attention training with metacognitive strategy instruction (e.g., goal setting, feedback, self-monitoring) (as described in Chapters 1 and 3). In this way, direct attention training can be combined with compensatory strategy instruction, perhaps increasing the overall affect. There is limited evidence that these strategies automatically generalize to improvements in functional attention; thus, the guidelines provided within Chapter 1 for direct attention training and self-management strategies warrant careful consideration (Sohlberg & Mateer, 2001b). Additionally, little evidence is available to explain the effect of these interventions during acute rehabilitation (Cicerone et al., 2011). Computer-based interventions may be added as a supplement to other clinician-guided treatments, but should not be implemented as the sole intervention (Cicerone et al., 2011).

Memory

Memory interventions for TBI can be categorized as external memory aids and internalized strategies. In 2003, written communication notebooks or daily planners were reported to be the most commonly used external memory aid while electronic memory aids were reported to be infrequently used, perhaps due to their complexity (Evans et al., 2003). Given the many advances in computerized memory aids and the increased presence of technology in society, electronic aids may be increasing in use. Evidence suggests that external memory aids (described in Chapter 2) are appropriate intervention strategies for people with mild and severe memory impairments (Cicerone et al., 2011). People with severe memory impairments may most easily use external aids to complete a specific task. Instruction in the use of external aids is critical to successful use. Sohlberg and Mateer (1989) described a three-stage approach that includes acquisition (e.g., listing contents and use of different sections), application (e.g., completing role-play activities using the aid), and adaptation (e.g., using aid in a community setting). Many studies have modified this approach for use with external memory aids with incorporation of massed practice and an errorless learning approach (e.g., Donaghy & Williams, 1998; Schmitter-Edgecomb et al., 1995).

For people with mild memory impairments, long-standing evidence supports the use of internalized strategies such as visual imagery (Cicerone et al., 2011), verbal rehearsal (Harris, 1996), storytelling, or mnemonics (Gianutsos & Gianutsos, 1979; Richardson, 1995). However, current evidence regarding the use of internal memory strategies does not delineate for whom and under what conditions such strategies are most beneficial (O'Neil-Pirozzi, Kennedy, & Sohlberg, 2015). Regardless, a systematic review of such techniques with the TBI population supports interventions which encompass internal memory strategies as one component to the therapeutic plan. For people with severe memory impairments, use of errorless learning for specific skills or information (e.g., taking medication at a meal) may also be effective; however, it is important to note that carryover to other memory tasks may be limited. One such method is to initiate spaced retrieval techniques in therapy (Schacter, Rich, & Stampp, 1985). Spaced retrieval involves the selection of distinct pieces of information for later recall. In this method, the clinician systematically increases the amount of time between which a client successfully recalls the target information. This is completed using an errorless learning approach such that if a client incorrectly recalls the target information, the correct answer is provided and the time interval is reduced.

Group memory interventions might be also appropriate for individuals with TBI at all severity levels and should focus primarily on teaching compensatory strategies (Cicerone et al., 2011). Group participants can discuss memory problems and generate multiple solutions with real-time feedback from other group members (Thickpenny-Davis & Barker-Collo, 2007). Often this discussion focuses on prospective memory tasks, however, discussion of memory for information at shorter intervals may also be useful. Time spent in group therapy can also be used to practice implementing memory strategies learned through errorless learning strategies (Thickpenny-Davis & Barker-Collo, 2007). Clinicians may use multiple methods for presenting information in groups to support retention of learned strategies.

Executive Functions

In a review of the literature examining executive function interventions for TBI, Kennedy and her colleagues (2008) found that although the interventions focused on different aspects of executive functions, three general intervention approaches were used: metacognitive strategy instruction, training strategic thinking, and multitasking instruction. Metacognitive strategies can increase participation and improve problem solving skills for personally-relevant activities (Kennedy et al., 2008). Although specific instructional programs for metacognition may differ, they typically involve solving a problem or achieving a goal through the deliberate use of multistep instructions such as "go-plan-do" (Kennedy et al., 2008). Generally, the steps of a metacognitive program include: creating goals, self-monitoring and documenting performance, and adjusting plans based on feedback. Goal management training (Levine et al., 2000) and goal attainment scaling (Webb & Glueckauf, 1994) are examples of metacognitive interventions that use variations of these steps and are described in detail in Chapter 2. These strategies emphasize the inclusion of the client in developing treatment goals. Additionally, evidence for goal management training suggests that it should be integrated within a comprehensive treatment plan to maximize effectiveness (Krasny-Pacini, Chevignard, Evans, 2014).

Few studies have examined the use of strategic thinking and multitasking instruction. Strategic thinking interventions typically have the clinician prompt the person with TBI to engage in verbal reasoning and then provide feedback. This strategy is described in the Interactive Strategy Modeling Training Section in Chapter 3 (Marshall, Karow, Morelli, Iden, Dixon, & Cranfill, 2004). Another such example is to initiate the IDEAL approach. This method prompts the client to evaluate different components of the problem in order to generate a variety of solutions while recalling the acronym IDEAL. This acronym refers to: identifying a problem, defining the problem, exploring alternative approaches, acting on a plan, and looking at the effects. Despite the potential usefulness of these tools, it is important to note that people with TBI and particularly those with significant communication impairments may struggle to use these language-mediated problem solving strategies.

Multitasking interventions are designed to improve the person's ability to do two things at once or dual-task. These studies provide instruction in multitasking during simulated real-life activities or through the use of a computerized program that requires a response to different and changing features of stimuli.

Communication

Communication interventions for people with TBI may aim to address aphasia, dysarthria, or pragmatic language impairments. There is limited evidence concerning specific treatments for the people with TBI who have aphasia (e.g., Massaro & Tompkins, 1994). Many people with TBI are included in studies that have examined interventions for stroke-induced aphasia (e.g., Ballard & Thompson, 1999; Hinckley & Craig, 1992); however, rarely do the results indicate what worked best for the people with TBI separate from the people with aphasia from a stroke.

Motor Speech and Voice

Similarly, studies examining motor speech interventions for people with

TBI are limited. Typically, treatments for dysarthria following TBI would be selected based on the specific speech characteristics (e.g., vocal weakness or fatigue, slurred speech, impaired intonation and rate). Thus, these treatments have been included in systematic reviews for dysarthria that included other etiologies such as Parkinson's disease (e.g., Yorkston, Hakel, Beukelman, & Fager, 2007). For example, Solomon, McKee, and Garcia-Barry (2001) found that *Lee Silverman Voice Treatment* when combined with respiratory exercises was effective for a person with moderate to severe hypokinetic-spastic dysarthria resulting from a TBI. Additionally, one systematic review found that external pacing strategies such as a metronome or pacing board increase intelligibility by reducing rate of speech (Teasell et al., 2012).

Discourse and Pragmatics

Individuals with brain injury typically display two variations of discourse deficits: (1) problems in narrative and conversational discourse, and (2) social disconnection and reduced awareness. For individuals with deficits in narrative and conversational discourse, challenges with inferences, quantity and quality of expressed language, and recognition of alternative meanings may be apparent. Targeting these domains directly or through compensatory approaches (e.g., strategy implementation) may result in improved outcomes (Gabbatore et al., 2015). Individuals with TBI may also experience difficulties connecting in social situations and may benefit from treatment aimed at various pragmatic goals (e.g., increasing awareness of listener needs, improving use of social conventions, reducing Theory of Mind deficits). Available evidence related to communication skills for people with TBI suggests benefits of specific interventions aimed at improving pragmatic conversational skills (e.g., turn taking, initiating a conversation, prosodic comprehension and expression). Additionally, group-based interventions, sometimes called social communication skills training, have been found to increase effective communication skills after TBI (e.g., Dahlberg et al., 2007; McDonald et al., 2008). Such treatments appear to achieve gains that are maintained over time and enhance overall life satisfactions for patients (Dahlberg et al., 2007). Included in this type of therapy should be counseling with the person and family members to assist with increasing deficit awareness and focusing on potential strategy implementation during social interactions. Potential effective methods for increasing awareness of social deficits could include, but are not limited to, video recording patient conversations (Bornhofen & McDonald, 2008) and asking family members to record or document socially inappropriate situations (McDonald et al., 2008). An example compensatory strategy may include encouraging the individual to explicitly state or label his or her emotions to reduce confusion (e.g., "I feel angry.").

Augmentative and Alternative Communication

People who cannot meet their communication needs through natural speech often rely on augmentative and alternative communication (AAC) strategies (Beukelman & Mirenda, 2013). People with TBI may use AAC to supplement or replace insufficient or ineffective expressive or receptive communication (Burke, Beukelman, & Hux, 2004; Doyle Kennedy, Jausalaitis, & Phillips, 2000). When considering AAC methods to support or replace oral communication, clinicians should include occupational and physical therapists to assist with access and positioning of such systems.

Strategies used by people with TBI range significantly based on characteristics of the individuals as well as the severity of their deficits (Wallace, 2010). Speech-language pathologists should consider the evolution of AAC strategy use during recovery in the development of an AAC treatment plan for people with TBI (Doyle & Fager, 2011; Fager & Karantounis, 2011; Light et al., 1988). The framework of AAC strategies for people with TBI based on cognitive stage appears in Table 8–7. This framework highlights AAC strategies for each of three stages: Early Stage (*RLA-R I-III*), Middle Stage (*RLA-R IV-VI*), and Late Stage (*RLA-R VII-X*) and can provide a starting point for clinicians to determine appropriate strategies.

Cognitive considerations are important aspects of an AAC assessment for people with TBI. Cognitive abilities affect how people with TBI learn to use an AAC device or strategy, as well as selection of appropriate organizational approaches. For many people with TBI, clinicians should develop strategies that avoid new learning and tap residual knowledge. For example, people with TBI who do not have aphasia may prefer to use text-to-speech devices that make use of overlearned spelling and typing skills (Fager, Hux, Beukelman, & Karatounis, 2006). Investigation of organizational approaches for high-technology AAC devices used by people with TBI suggests that accuracy

Table 8–7. Staging of AAC Strategies Using the Ranchos Los Amigos Scale Levels of Cognitive Functioning–Revised as Described by Fager and Karantounis (2011)

Early Stage	Middle Stage	Late Stage
RLA-R I-III	*RLA-R IV-VI*	*RLA-R VII-X*
• Simple choice-based systems Yes/no systems • Eye gaze or direct selection	• Complex choice making with picture, letter, or word board • Written Choice Communication Strategy • Simple voice output for basic information	*Familiar listeners:* • Alphabet board for supplemented speech • Gestures combined with natural speech *Unfamiliar listener and specific contexts:* • Text-to-speech • Stored message complex voice output systems

and efficiency increase with the use of an alphabetically organized device, but that people with TBI tend to prefer a topical (i.e., semantic) organization strategy (Burke et al., 2004). Similarly, other studies have identified idiosyncratic organizational strategies and significant heterogeneity in the use and preference of organizational strategies (Brown, Hux, Kenny, & Funk, 2014; Snyder & Hux, 2000). Additionally, cognitive flexibility affects the accuracy and efficiency with which people with TBI navigate dynamic display AAC devices with semantic organizations (Wallace, Hux, & Beukelman, 2010). These results highlight the need for individualized assessments of AAC organization with multiple trials with various organizations, as well as instruction in the use of strategies and devices.

The instruction clinicians provide to teach people with TBI and their facilitators to use AAC is critical to eventual successful communication participation. Recommendations include pro-viding a structured environment for practice (e.g., therapy room) before expecting functional use in a natural setting, using errorless learning (described in previous chapters) to support strategy initiation as well as navigation of high technology devices (Baddeley & Wilson, 1994), and encouraging repetitive practice to facilitate overlearning (e.g., at least four times the amount of practice required by individuals without brain injury; Wilson, Baddeley, Evans, & Shiel, 1994). Finally, facilitator instruction and buy-in are critically important to the eventual success of AAC strategies with people with TBI. Lack of facilitator support is the primary reason for device abandonment (Fager et al., 2006).

Group Treatment

As described in previous sections, group therapy for people with TBI and/or their caregivers can support various areas of cognition and communication (Cicerone et al., 2011) and may focus on intervention of skills, counseling and education, or psychosocial support. Clinicians can implement group therapy with people with TBI across different severity levels and lengths of time post-onset; however, clinicians should carefully assess cognitive and communication abilities prior to placing people with TBI in a particular group. Additional considerations include fatigue, behavioral challenges, age, and interest in group theme which may impact an individual's engagement with and performance in a particular group.

Clinicians may wish to structure group treatment for individuals with TBI based on the overall group goal. For example, a group which focuses on direct treatment of skills would likely be highly structured, clinician directed, and target specific language processes (e.g., a group aimed at improving naming and word retrieval abilities). Conversely, a group whose goal is indirect treatment of skills might be low in structure, provide a rich cognitive communicative environment, and focus on facilitating general involvement of group members (e.g., conversation, role-playing activities). Additional foci of group treatment include sociolinguistic groups (i.e., emphasize interaction among group participants), transition groups (i.e., intended to ease transition from treatment to discharge and emphasize a person's independence), or maintenance groups (i.e., opportunities to practice skills to prevent deterioration). Additionally, groups may be structured based on a common theme or therapeutic goal with some group themes being more appropriate for outpatient or community-based settings and some being better implemented

during inpatient rehabilitation (Gillis, 1999a, 1999b). For instance, group interventions that emphasize executive function skills and problem solving may be appropriate after TBI (Cicerone et al., 2011). Other ideas for group themes appear in Table 8–8.

Summary

Cognitive-communication deficits result in permanent and profound social emotional, educational, and vocational challenges for people with TBI and their family members. The unique nature of generalized brain damage and the resultant deficits in attention, memory, and executive function paired with deficits in awareness and theory of mind lead to reduced participation in daily activities. Speech-language pathologists are faced with the challenge of identifying deficits primarily through informal non-standardized tests and treating deficits with an array of creative approaches. More research is needed to identify the relationships between communication skills and various cognitive functions (e.g., attention, memory, and executive functions). Increased understanding

Table 8–8. Group Therapy Themes

- Problem-Solving Group
- Psychosocial Adjustment Group
- Job Skills Group
- Parenting Group
- Money Management Group
- Orientation Group
- Meal Planning Group
- Communication Skills Group
- External Memory Aid Group

of these relationships will facilitate development of interventions that can best address the complex constellation of symptoms in people with TBI. The encouraging findings associated with the evidence-based guidelines developed through the Academy of Neurologic Communication Disorders and Sciences suggest the science of rehabilitation is moving forward and that we will continue to improve and refine our treatment approaches with this unique clinical population.

References

Adamovich, B. B., & Henderson, J. (1992). *Scales of cognitive ability for traumatic brain injury.* Austin, TX: Pro-Ed.

American Congress of Rehabilitation Medicine. (1995). Recommendations for use of uniform nomenclature pertinent to patients with severe alterations in consciousness. *Archives of Physical Medicine and Rehabilitation, 76*(2), 205–209.

American Speech-Language Hearing Association. (2019). The practice portal. Retrieved from https://www.asha.org/practice-portal/

American Speech-Language-Hearing Association Evidence maps. (n.d.) Retrieved from http://ncepmaps.org/ptbi/tx/

Ansell, B. J. (1991). Slow-to-recover brain-injured patients: Rationale for treatment. *Journal of Speech, Language, and Hearing Research, 34*, 1017–1022.

Baddeley, A., & Wilson, B. A. (1994). When implicit learning fails: Amnesia and the problem of error elimination. *Neuropsychologia, 32*, 53–68.

Ballard, K. J., & Thompson, C. K. (1999). Treatment and generalization of complex sentence production in agrammatism. *Journal of Speech, Language, and Hearing Research, 42*, 690–707.

Baron, E., & Jallo, J.I. (2007). TBI: Pathology, pathophysiology, acute care and surgical management, critical care principles, and outcomes. In N. D. Zasler, D. Katz, & R. D. Zafonte (Eds.), *Brain injury medicine: Principles and practice* (pp. 265–282). New York, NY: Demos.

Beukelman, D., & Mirenda, P. (2013). *Augmentative and alternative communication: Supporting children and adults with complex communication needs.* Baltimore, MD: Brookes.

Bornhofen, C., & McDonald, S. (2008). Treating deficits in emotion perception following traumatic brain injury. *Neuropsychological Rehabilitation, 18*, 22–44.

Brasure, M.,Lamberty, G. J., Sayer, N. A., Nelson, MacDonald, R., Ouellette, J., . . . Wilt, T. J. (2012). *Multidisciplinary post-acute rehabilitation for moderate to severe traumatic brain injury in adults.* Retrieved from https://www.ncbi.nlm.nih.gov/books/NBK98993/pdf/Bookshelf_NBK98993.pdf

Brooks, N., McKinlay, W., Symington, C., Beattie, A., & Campsie, L. (1987). Return to work within the first seven years of severe head injury. *Brain Injury, 1*, 5–19.

Brown, J. (2018, November). *Cognitive assessment for adults with acquired neurological disorders: Speech-language pathologist practices.* Poster presentation at the American Speech Language Hearing Association Annual Convention, Boston, MA.

Brown, J., & Hux, K. (2016). Functional assessment of immediate task planning and execution by adults with acquired brain injury. *NeuroRehabilitation, 39*, 191–203.

Brown, J., & Hux, K. (2017). Ecologically-valid assessment of prospective memory task planning and execution by adults with acquired brain injury. *American Journal of Speech Language Pathology, 26*, 819–831.

Brown, J. A., Hux, K., Kenny, C., & Funk, T. (2015). Consistency and idiosyncrasy of semantic categorization by individuals with traumatic brain injuries. *Disability and Rehabilitation: Assistive Technology, 10*(5), 378–384.

Burke, R., Beukelman, D. R., & Hux, K. (2004). Accuracy, efficiency and preferences of survivors of traumatic brain injury when using three organization strategies to retrieve words. *Brain Injury, 18*, 497–507.

Carlesimo, G. A., Casadio, P., & Caltagirone, C. (2004). Prospective and retrospective components in the memory for actions to be performed in patients with severe closed-head injury. *Journal of the International Neuropsychological Society, 10*, 679–688.

Centers for Disease Control and Prevention (CDC). (n.d.). *Traumatic brain injury in prisons and jails: An unrecognized problem.* Retrieved from http://www.cdc.gov/traumaticbraininjury/pdf/Prisoner_TBI_Prof-a.pdf

Centers for Disease Control and Prevention (CDC). (2015). *Heads Up: Concussion signs and symptoms.* Retrieved from https://www.cdc.gov/headsup/basics/concussion_symptoms.html

Centers for Disease Control and Prevention (CDC). (2017). *Severe traumatic brain injury.* Retrieved from https://www.cdc.gov/traumaticbraininjury/severe.html

Centers for Disease Control and Prevention (CDC), National Center for Injury Prevention and Control. (2003). *Report to Congress on mild traumatic brain injury in the United States: Steps to prevent a serious public health problem.* Atlanta, GA.

Chaytor, N., Schmitter-Edgecombe, M., & Burr, R. (2006). Improving the ecological validity of executive functioning assessment. *Archives of Clinical Neuropsychology, 21*, 217–227.

Cicerone, K. D., Langenbahn, D. M., Braden, C., Malec, J. F., Kalmar, K., Fraas, M., . . . Ashman, T. (2011). Evidence-based cognitive rehabilitation: Updated review of the literature from 2003 through 2008. *Archives of Physical Medicine and Rehabilitation, 92*, 519–530.

Coelho, C., Ylvisaker, M., & Turkstra, L. (2005). Nonstandardized assessment approaches for individuals with traumatic brain injuries. *Seminars in Speech and Language, 26*, 223–241.

Colantonio, A., Ratcliff, G., Chase, S., Kelsey, S., Escobar, M., & Vernich, L. (2004). Long-term outcomes after moderate to severe traumatic brain injury. *Disability and Rehabilitation, 26*(5), 253–261.

Constantinidou, F., Wertheimer, J. C., Tsanadis, J., Evans, C., & Paul, D. R. (2012). Assessment of executive functioning in brain injury: Collaboration between speech-language pathology and neuropsychology for an integrative neuropsychological perspective. *Brain Injury, 26*, 1549–1563.

Coronado, V. G., McGuire, L. C., Faul, M., Sugerman, D. E., & Pearson, W. S. (2012). In N. D. Zasler, D. L. Katz, & R. Zafonte (Eds.), *Brain injury medicine, second edition: Principles and practice* (pp. 84–100). New York, NY: Demos Medical Publishing.

Crosson, B., Barco, P. P., Velozo, C. A., Bolesta. M. M., Cooper, P. V., Werts, D., & Brobeck, T. (1989). Awareness of compensation in postacute head injury rehabilitation. *Journal of Head Trauma Rehabilitation, 4*(3), 46–54.

Dahlberg, C. A., Cusick, C. P., Hawley, L. A., Newman, J. K., Morey, C. E., Harrison-Felix, C. L., & Whiteneck, G. G. (2007). Treatment efficacy of social communication skills training after traumatic brain injury: A randomized treatment and deferred treatment controlled trial. *Archives of Physical Medicine and Rehabilitation, 88*, 1561–1573.

Damico, J. S. (1992). Systematic observation of communicative interaction: A valid and practical descriptive assessment technique. *Best Practice in School Speech-Language Pathology, 2*, 133–144.

Dams-O'Connor, K., Cantor, J. B., Brown, M., Dijkers, M. P., Spielman, L. A., & Gordon, W. A. (2014). Screening for traumatic brain injury: Findings and public health implications. *Journal of Head Trauma Rehabilitation, 29*, 479–489.

Dawson, D. R., Anderson, N. D., Burgess, P., Cooper, E., Krpan, K. M., & Stuss, D. T. (2009). Further development of the Multiple Errands Test: Standardized scoring, reliability, and ecological validity for the Baycrest version. *Archives of Physical Medicine and Rehabilitation, 90*, S41–S51.

Dennis, K. C. (2009). Current perspectives on traumatic brain injury. *ASHA Access Audiology.* Retrieved from http://www.asha.org/aud/articles/currentTBI.htm

DePalma, R. G., Burris, D. G., Champion, H. R., & Hodgson, M. J. (2005). Blast injuries. *New England Journal of Medicine, 352*, 1335–1342.

Dodd-Murphy, J. (2014). *Auditory effects of blast exposure: Community outreach following an industrial explosion.* Retrieved from http://www.asha.org/aud/Articles/Auditory-Effects-of-Blast-Exposure/?utm_source=asha&utm_medium=enewsletter&utm_campaign=accessaud 051214#sthash.zOdcZBFb.dpuf

Donaghy, S., & Williams, W. (1998). A new protocol for training severely impaired patients in the usage of memory journals. *Brain Injury, 12(12)*, 1061–1076.

Dongilli, P. A., Hakel, M. E., & Beukelman, D. R. (1992). Recovery of functional speech following traumatic brain injury. *Journal of Head Trauma Rehabilitation, 7(2)*, 91–101.

Doyle, M., & Fager, S. (2011, February 15). Traumatic brain injury and AAC: Supporting communication through recovery. *The ASHA Leader.* https://doi.org/10.1044/leader.FTR8.16022011.np

Doyle, M., Kennedy, M., Jausalaitis, G., & Phillips, B. (2000). AAC and traumatic brain injury. In D. R. Beukelman, K. M. Yorkston, & J. Reichle (Eds.), *Augmentative and alternative communication for adults with acquired neurological disorders* (pp. 271–304). Baltimore, MD: Brookes.

Eslinger, P., Zappala, G., Chakara, F., & Barrett, A. (2011). Cognitive impairments after TBI. In N. D. Zasler, D. I., Katz, & R. D. Zafonte (Eds.), *Brain injury medicine* (2nd ed., pp. 779–790). New York, NY: Demos.

Evans, J. J., Wilson, B. A., Needham, P., & Brentnall, S. (2003). Who makes good use of memory aids? Results of a survey of people with acquired brain injury. *Journal of the International Neuropsychological Society, 9(6)*, 925–935.

Ewing-Cobbs, L., Levin, H. S., Fletcher, J. M., Miner, M. E., & Eisenberg, H. M. (1990). The Children's Orientation and Amnesia Test: Relationship to severity of acute head injury and to recovery of memory. *Neurosurgery, 27*, 683–691.

Fager, S., Hux, K., Beukelman, D. R., & Karantounis, R. (2006). Augmentative and alternative communication use and acceptance by adults with traumatic brain injury. *Augmentative and Alternative Communication, 22(1)*, 37–47.

Fager, S., & Karantounis, R. (2011). AAC assessment and interventions in TBI. In K. Hux (Ed.), *Assisting survivors of traumatic brain injury* (2nd ed., pp. 227–254). Austin, TX: Pro-Ed.

Ferguson, P. L., Pickelsimer, E. E., Corrigan, J. D., Bogner, J. A., & Wald, M. (2012). Prevalence of traumatic brain injury among prisoners in South Carolina. *Journal of Head Trauma Rehabilitation, 27(3)*, E11–E20.

Folstein, M. F., Folstein, S. E., & McHugh, P. R. (1975). "Mini-mental state": A practical method for grading the cognitive state of patients for the clinician. *Journal of Psychiatric Research, 12(3)*, 189–198.

Gabbatore, I., Sacco, K., Angeleri, R., Zettin, M., Bara, B. G., & Bosco, F. M. (2015). Cognitive pragmatic treatment: A rehabilitative program for traumatic brain injury individuals. *Journal of Head Trauma Rehabilitation, 30(5)*, E14–E28.

Giacino, J. T., & Cicerone, K. D. (1998). Varieties of deficit unawareness after brain injury. *Journal of Head Trauma Rehabilitation, 13*, 1–15.

Gianutsos, R., & Gianutsos, J. (1979). Rehabilitating the verbal recall of brain-injured patients by mnemonic training: An experimental demonstration using single-case methodology. *Journal of Clinical and Experimental Neuropsychology, 1*, 117–135.

Gillis, R. J. (1999a). Traumatic brain injury: Cognitive-communicative needs and early intervention. In R. J. Elman (Ed.),

Group treatment of neurogenic communication disorders: The expert clinician's approach (pp. 141–151). Boston, MA: Butterworth-Heinemann.

Gillis, R. J. (1999b). Cotreatment and community-oriented group treatment for traumatic brain injury. In R. J. Elman (Ed.), *Group treatment of neurogenic communication disorders: The expert clinician's approach* (pp. 153–163). Boston, MA: Butterworth-Heinemann.

Glosser, G., & Deser, T. (1990). Patterns of discourse production among neurological patients with fluent language disorders. *Brain and Language, 40*, 67–88.

Hagen, C. (1982). Language-cognitive disorganization following closed head injury: A conceptualization. In L. E. Trexler (Ed.), *Cognitive rehabilitation* (pp. 131–151). New York, NY: Plenum.

Hagen, C. (2000, February). *Rancho Levels of Cognitive Functioning–Revised.* Presentation at TBI rehabilitation in a managed care environment: An interdisciplinary approach to rehabilitation, Continuing Education Programs of America, San Antonio, TX.

Hagen, C., Malkmus, D., & Durham, P. (1972). *Rancho Los Amigos Levels of Cognitive Functioning Scale.* Downey, CA: Professional Staff Association.

Happé, F., Brownell, H., & Winner, E. (1999). Acquired theory of mind impairments following stroke. *Cognition, 70*, 211–240.

Harris, J. R. (1996). Verbal rehearsal and memory in children with closed head injury: A quantitative and qualitative analysis. *Journal of Communication Disorders, 29*, 79–93.

Health Measures. (2018). *Patient-Reported Outcomes Measurement Information System–Cognitive Function.* Retrieved from http://www.healthmeasures.net/images/PROMIS/manuals/PROMIS_Cognitive_Function_Scoring_Manual.pdf

Helm-Estabrooks, N. (2017). *Cognitive Linguistic Quick Test–Plus (CLQT+).* San Antonio, TX: Pearson.

Helm-Estabrooks, N., & Hotz, G. (1991). *Brief Test of Head Injury.* Austin, TX: Pro-Ed.

Hettema, J., Steele, J., & Miller, W. R. (2005). Motivational interviewing. *Annual Review of Clinical Psychology, 1*, 91–111.

Hinckley, J. J., & Craig, H. K. (1992). A comparison of picture-stimulus and conversational elicitation contexts: Responses to comments by adults with aphasia. *Aphasiology, 6*, 257–272.

Jennett, B., & Teasdale, G. (1977). Aspects of coma after severe head injury. *Lancet, 309*(8017), 878–881.

Kennedy, M. R., Coelho, C., Turkstra, L., Ylvisaker, M., Moore Sohlberg, M., Yorkston, K., . . . Kan, P. F. (2008). Intervention for executive functions after traumatic brain injury: A systematic review, meta-analysis and clinical recommendations. *Neuropsychological Rehabilitation, 18*, 257–299.

Knight, C., Alderman, N., & Burgess, P. W. (2002). Development of a simplified version of the Multiple Errands Test for use in hospital settings. *Neuropsychological Rehabilitation, 12*, 231–255.

Knight, R. G., Titov, N., & Crawford, M. (2006). The effects of distraction on prospective remembering following traumatic brain injury assessed in a simulated naturalistic environment. *Journal of the International Neuropsychological Society, 12*, 8–16.

Krasny-Pacini, A., Chevignard, M., & Evans, J. (2014). Goal Management Training for rehabilitation of executive functions: A systematic review of effectiveness in patients with acquired brain injury. *Disability and Rehabilitation, 36*(2), 105–116.

Kraus, J. F., Fife, D., Ramstein, K., Conroy, C., & Cox, P. (1986). The relationship of family income to the incidence, external causes, and outcomes of serious brain injury, San Diego County, California. *American Journal of Public Health, 76*(11), 1345–1347.

Levin, H. S., Madison, C. F., Bailey, C. B., Meyers, C. A., Eisenberg, H. M., & Guinto, F. C. (1983). Mutism after closed head injury. *Archives of Neurology, 40*(10), 601–606.

Levin, H. S., O'Donnell, V. M., & Grossman, R. G. (1979). The Galveston Orientation and Amnesia Test: A practical scale to assess cognition after head injury. *Journal of Nervous and Mental Disease, 167,* 675–684.

Levine, B., Robertson, I. H., Clare, L., Carter, G., Hong, J., Wilson, B. A., . . . Stuss, D. T. (2000). Rehabilitation of executive functioning: An experimental-clinical validation of goal management training. *Journal of the International Neuropsychological Society, 6*(3), 299–312.

Light, J., Beesley, M., & Collier, B. (1988). Transition through multiple augmentative and alternative communication systems: A three-year case study of a head injured adolescent. *Augmentative and Alternative Communication, 4,* 2–14.

Lombardi, F., Taricco, M., De Tanti, A., Telaro, E., & Liberati, A. (2002). Sensory stimulation of brain-injured individuals in coma or vegetative state: Results of a Cochrane systematic review. *Clinical Rehabilitation, 16,* 464–472.

Lovell, M. R., Collins, M. W., Maroon, J. C., Cantu, R., Hawn, M. A., Burke, C. J., & Fu, F. (2002). Inaccuracy of symptom reporting following concussion in athletes. *Medicine & Science in Sports & Exercise, 34*(5), S298.

MacDonald, S. (2005). *Functional Assessment of Verbal Reasoning and Executive Strategies.* Ontario, Canada: CCD.

Mackay, L. E., Morgan, A. S., & Bernstein, B. A. (1999). Swallowing disorders in severe brain injury: Risk factors affecting return to oral intake. *Archives of Physical Medicine and Rehabilitation, 80,* 365–371.

Malec, J. F., Hammond, F. M., Giacino, J. T., Whyte, J., & Wright, J. (2012). Structured interview to improve the reliability and psychometric integrity of the Disability Rating Scale. *Archives of Physical Medicine and Rehabilitation, 93*(9), 1603–1608.

Malec, J. F., Kragness, M., Evans, R. W., Finlay, K. L., Kent, A., & Lezak, M. D. (2003). Further psychometric evaluation and revision of the Mayo-Portland Adapt-ability Inventory in a national sample. *The Journal of Head Trauma Rehabilitation, 18*(6), 479–492.

Malec, J. F., & Lezak, M. D. (2008). *Manual for the Mayo-Portland Adaptability Inventory (MPAI-4) for adults, children and adolescents.* Retrieved from: http://www.tbims.org/mpai/manual.pdf

Mandaville, A., Ray, A., Robertson, H., Foster, C., & Jesser, C. (2014). A retrospective review of swallow dysfunction in patients with severe traumatic brain injury. *Dysphagia, 29,* 1–9.

Marshall, R., Karow, C., Morelli, C., Iden, K., Dixon, J., & Cranfill, T. (2004). Effects of interactive strategy modelling training on problem-solving by persons with traumatic brain injury. *Aphasiology, 18,* 659–673.

Massaro, M., & Tompkins, C. A. (1994). Feature analysis for treatment of communication disorders in traumatically brain-injured patients: An efficacy study. *Clinical Aphasiology, 22,* 245–256.

Maujean, A., Shum, D., & McQueen, R. (2003). Effect of cognitive demand on prospective memory in individuals with traumatic brain injury. *Brain Impairment, 4,* 135–145.

McCrea, M., Hammeke, T., Olsen, G., Leo, P., & Guskiewicz, K. (2004). Unreported concussion in high school football players: Implications for prevention. *Clinical Journal of Sport Medicine, 14*(1), 13–17.

McDonald, S., Tate, R., Togher, L., Bornhofen, C., Long, E., Gertler, P., & Bowen, R. (2008). Social skills treatment for people with severe, chronic acquired brain injuries: A multicenter trial. *Archives of Physical Medicine and Rehabilitation, 89,* 1648–1659.

McDougall, J., Wright, V., & Rosenbaum, P. (2010). The ICF model of functioning and disability: Incorporating quality of life and human development. *Developmental Neurorehabilitation, 13*(3), 204–211.

Medley, A. R., & Powell T. (2010). Motivational interviewing to promote self-awareness and engagement in rehabilitation following acquired brain injury: A conceptual review. *Neuropsychological Rehabilitation, 20*(4), 481–508.

Miotto, E. C., Cinalli, F. Z., Serrao, V. T., Benute, G. G., Lucia, M. C. S., & Scaff, M. (2010). Cognitive deficits in patients with mild to moderate traumatic brain injury. *Arquivos de Neuro-psiquiatria, 68*, 862–868.

Morgan, A. S., & Mackay, L. E. (1999). Causes and complications associated with swallowing disorders in traumatic brain injury. *Journal of Head Trauma Rehabilitation, 14*, 454–461.

Morley, J. E., & Tumosa, N. (2002). Saint Louis University Mental Status Examination (SLUMS). *Aging Successfully, 12*(1), 4.

Multi-Society Task Force on PVS. (1994). Medical aspects of the persistent vegetative state. *New England Journal of Medicine, 330*, 1499–1508.

Myers, P., Henry, J., Zaugg, T., & Kendall, C. (2009). Tinnitus evaluation and management considerations for persons with mild traumatic brain injury. First published in *ASHA Access Audiology, 8*. Retrieved from http://www.asha.org/aud/articles/TinnitusTBI/

Nasreddine, Z. S., Phillips, N. A., Bédirian, V., Charbonneau, S., Whitehead, V., Collin, I., . . . Chertkow, H. (2005). The Montreal Cognitive Assessment, MoCA: A brief screening tool for mild cognitive impairment. *Journal of the American Geriatrics Society, 53*, 695–699.

National Institute of Neurological Disorders and Stroke (NINDS). (2015). *User Manual for the Quality of Life in Neurological Disorders (Neuro-QOL) Measures, Version 2.0.* Retrieved from http://www.healthmeasures.net/images/neuro_qol/Neuro-QOL_User_Manual_v2_24Mar2015.pdf

O'Neil-Pirozzi, T. M., Kennedy, M. R. T., & Sohlberg, M. M. (2015). Evidence-based practice for the use of internal strategies as a memory compensation technique after brain injury: A systematic review. *Journal of Head Trauma Rehabilitation, 15*, 32–42.

Ponsford, J. L., Spitz, G., & McKenzie, D. (2016). Using post-traumatic amnesia to predict outcome after traumatic brain injury. *Journal of Neurotrauma, 33*(11), 997–1004.

Rancho Los Amigos Cognitive Scale Revised. (2014). Retrieved from http://www.northeastcenter.com/rancho_los_amigos_revised.htm

Randolph, C. (2012). *Repeatable Battery for the Assessment of Neuropsychological Status: Manual.* London, UK: Pearson.

Rappaport, M., Hall, K. M., Hopkins, K., Belleza, T., & Cope, D. N. (1982). Disability rating scale for severe head trauma: Coma to community. *Archives of Physical Medicine and Rehabilitation, 63*, 118–123.

Raspelli, S., Pallavicini, F., Carelli, L., Morganti, F., Pedroli, E., Cipresso, P., . . . Riva, G. (2012). Validating the Neuro VR-based virtual version of the Multiple Errands Test: Preliminary results. *Presence: Teleoperators and Virtual Environments, 21*, 31–42.

Richardson, J. T. (1995). The efficacy of imagery mnemonics in memory remediation. *Neuropsychologia, 33*, 1345–1357.

Robertson, I. H., Ward, T., Ridgeway, V., & Nimmo-Smith, I. (1994). *Test of Everyday Attention.* Suffolk, UK: Thames Valley Test Company.

Roth, R. M., Isquith, P. K., & Gioia, G. A. (2005). *Behavior Rating Inventory of Executive Function–Adult Version (BRIEF-A).* Lutz, FL: PAR.

Sander, A. M., Raymer, A., Wertheimer, J., & Paul, D. (2009). Perceived roles and collaboration between neuropsychologists and speech-language pathologists in rehabilitation. *The Clinical Neuropsychologist, 23*, 1196–1212.

Sarno, M. T. (1980). The nature of verbal impairment after closed head injury. *Journal of Nervous and Mental Disease, 168*(11), 685–692.

Sarno, M. T., Buonaguro, A., & Levita, E. (1986). Characteristics of verbal impairment in closed-head injured patients.

Archives of Physical Medicine and Rehabilitation, 67(6), 400–405.

Schacter, D. L., Rich, S. A., & Stampp, M. S. (1985). Remediation of memory disorders: Experimental evaluation of the spaced-retrieval technique. *Journal of Clinical and Experimental Neuropsychology, 7,* 79–96.

Schmidt, J., Lannin, N., Fleming, J., & Ownsworth T. (2011). Feedback interventions for impaired self-awareness following brain injury: A systematic review. *Journal of Rehabilitation Medicine, 43,* 673–680.

Schmitter-Edgecombe, M., Fahy, J. F., Whelan, J. P., & Long, C. J. (1995). Memory remediation after severe closed-head injury: Notebook training versus supportive therapy. *Journal of Consulting and Clinical Psychology, 63(3),* 484.

Selassie, A. W., Zaloshnja, E., Langlois, J. A., Miller, T., Jones, P., & Steiner, C. (2008). Incidence of long-term disability following traumatic brain injury hospitalization, United States, 2003. *Journal of Head Trauma and Rehabilitation, 23*(2), 123–131.

Shanahan, L., McAllister, L., & Curtin, M. (2011). The Party Planning Task: A useful tool in the functional assessment of planning skills in adolescents with TBI. *Brain Injury, 25,* 1080–1090.

Sherer, M., Boake, C., Levin, E., Silver, B. V., Ringholz, G., & High, W. M. (1998). Characteristics of impaired awareness after traumatic brain injury. *Journal of the International Neuropsychological Society, 4*(4), 380–387.

Snyder, C., & Hux, K. (2000). Traumatic brain injury survivors' ability to reduce idiosyncrasy in semantic organization. *Journal of Medical Speech-Language Pathology, 8,* 187–197.

Sohlberg, M., Avery, J., Kennedy, M. R. T., Coelho, C., Ylvisaker, M., Turkstra, L., & Yorkston, K. (2003). Practice guidelines for direct attention training. *Journal of Medical Speech-Language Pathology, 11,* xix–xxxix

Sohlberg, M. M., Kennedy, M., Avery, J., Coelho, C., Turkstra, L., Ylvisaker, M., & Yorkston, K. (2007). Evidence-based practice for the use of external aids as a memory compensation technique. *Journal of Medical Speech Language Pathology, 15,* xv–li.

Sohlberg, M. M., & Mateer, C. A. (1989). *Introduction to cognitive rehabilitation: Theory and practice.* New York, NY: Guilford Press.

Sohlberg, M. M., & Mateer, C. A. (2001a). Improving attention and managing attentional problems. *Annals of the New York Academy of Sciences, 931,* 359–375.

Sohlberg, M. M., & Mateer, C. A. (Eds.). (2001b). *Cognitive rehabilitation: An integrative neuropsychological approach.* New York, NY: Guilford Press.

Solomon, N. P., McKee, A. S., & Garcia-Barry, S. (2001). Intensive voice treatment and respiration treatment for hypokinetic-spastic dysarthria after traumatic brain injury. *American Journal of Speech-Language Pathology, 10,* 51–64.

Sosin, D. M., Sniezek, J. E., & Thurman, D. J. (1996). Incidence of mild and moderate brain injury in the United States, 1991. *Brain Injury, 10,* 47–54.

Stierwalt, J. A., & Murray, L. L. (2002). Attention impairment following traumatic brain injury. *Seminars in Speech and Language, 23,* 129–138.

Summers, C. R., Ivins, B., & Schwab, K. A. (2009). Traumatic brain injury in the United States: An epidemiologic overview. *Mount Sinai Journal of Medicine, 76,* 105–110.

Taylor, C. A., Bell, J. M., Breiding, M. J., & Xu, L. (2017). Traumatic brain injury-related emergency department visits, hospitalizations, and deaths—United States, 2001 and 2013. *Morbidity and Mortality Weekly Report—Surveillance Summaries, 66*(9), 1–16.

Teasdale, G., & Jennett, B. (1974). Assessment of coma and impaired consciousness: A practical scale. *Lancet, 304*(7872), 81–84.

Teasell, R., Marshall, S., Cullen, N., Bayley, R., Rees, L., Weiser, M., . . . Aubut, J.

(2012). *Evidence-based review of moderate to severe acquired brain injury*. Retrieved from http://www.abiebr.com/pdf/exec utiveSummary.pdf

Thickpenny-Davis, K. L., & Barker-Collo, S. L. (2007). Evaluation of a structured group format memory rehabilitation program for adults following brain injury. *Journal of Head Trauma Rehabilitation, 22,* 303–313.

Thomsen, I. V. (1984). Late outcome of very severe blunt head trauma: A 10–15 year second follow-up. *Journal of Neurology, Neurosurgery & Psychiatry, 47,* 260–268.

Thurman, D. (2001). The epidemiology and economics of head trauma. In L. Miller & R. Hayes (Eds), *Head trauma: Basic, preclinical, and clinical directions.* (pp. 327–347). New York, NY: Wiley and Sons.

Thurman, D. J., Alverson, C., Dunn, K. A., Guerrero, J., & Sniezek, J. E. (1999). Traumatic brain injury in the United States: A public health perspective. *Journal of Head Trauma and Rehabilitation, 14*(6), 602–615.

Topolovec-Vranic, J., Ennis, N., Colantonio, A., Cusimano, M. D., Hwang, S. W., Kontos, P., . . . Stergiopoulos, V. (2012). Traumatic brain injury among people who are homeless: A systematic review. *BMC Public Health, 12*(1), 1059.

Turkstra, L., Ylvisaker, M., Coelho, C., Kennedy, M., Sohlberg, M. M., & Avery, J. (2005). Practice guidelines for standardized assessment for persons with traumatic brain injury. *Journal of Medical Speech-Language Pathology, 13,* ix–xxvii.

Uniform Data Set for Medical Rehabilitation. (1996). *Guide for the use of the uniform data set for medical rehabilitation, Version 5.0.* Buffalo: State University of New York at Buffalo Research Foundation.

Van Leer, E., & Turkstra, L. (1999). The effect of elicitation task on discourse coherence and cohesion in adolescents with brain injury. *Journal of Communication Disorders, 32,* 327–349.

Wade, D. T. (2005). Applying the WHO ICF framework to the rehabilitation of patients with cognitive deficits. In P. W. Halligan & D. T. Wade (Eds.), *Effectiveness of rehabilitation for cognitive deficits.* Oxford, UK: Oxford University Press.

Wallace, C. A., & Bogner, J. (2000). Awareness of deficits: Emotional implications for persons with brain injury and their significant others. *Brain Injury, 14*(6), 549–562.

Wallace, S. E. (2010). AAC use by people with TBI: Effects of cognitive impairments. *Perspectives on Augmentative and Alternative Communication, 19,* 79–86.

Wallace, S. E., Hux, K., & Beukelman, D. R. (2010). Navigation of a dynamic screen AAC interface by survivors of severe traumatic brain injury. *Augmentative and Alternative Communication, 26,* 242–254.

Webb, P. M., & Glueckauf, R. L. (1994). The effects of direct involvement in goal setting on rehabilitation outcome for persons with traumatic brain injuries. *Rehabilitation Psychology, 39,* 179.

Wilde, E. A., Whiteneck, G. G., Bogner, J., Bushnik, T., Cifu, D. X., Dikmen, S., . . . Millis, S. R. (2010). Recommendations for the use of common outcome measures in traumatic brain injury research. *Archives of Physical Medicine and Rehabilitation, 91,* 1650–1660.

Williams, W. H., Cordan, G., Mewse, A. J., Tonks, J., & Burgess, C. N. (2010). Self-reported traumatic brain injury in male young offenders: A risk factor for reoffending, poor mental health and violence. *Neuropsychological Rehabilitation, 20*(6), 801–812.

Wilson, B., Vizor, A., & Bryant, T. (1991). Predicting severity of cognitive impairment after severe head injury. *Brain Injury, 5*(2), 189–197.

Wilson, B. A., Baddeley, A., Evans, J., & Shiel, A. (1994). Errorless learning in the rehabilitation of memory impaired people. *Neuropsychological Rehabilitation, 4,* 307–326.

Wilson, B. A., Greenfield, E., Clare, L., Baddeley, A., Cockburn, J., Watson, P., . . . Nannery, R. (2008). *The Rivermead Behavioural Memory Test–Third Edition.* Bury

St Edmunds, UK: Thames Valley Test Company.

Wood, R. L., & Liossi, C. (2006). The ecological validity of executive tests in a severely brain injured sample. *Archives of Clinical Neuropsychology, 21,* 429–437.

Wright, J. (2000). *The FIM™. The Center for Outcome Measurement in Brain Injury.* Retrieved from http://www.tbims.org/combi/FIM

Yorkston, K. M., Hakel, M., Beukelman, D. R., & Fager, S. (2007). Evidence for effectiveness of treatment of loudness, rate or prosody in dysarthria: A systematic review. *Journal of Medical Speech-Language Pathology, 15,* xi–xxxvi.

Zafonte, R. D., Hammond, F. M., Mann, N. R., Wood, D. L., Black, K. L., & Millis, S. R. (1996). Relationship between Glasgow Coma Scale and functional outcome. *American Journal of Physical Medicine & Rehabilitation, 75(5),* 364–369.

Zaloshnja, E., Miller, T., Langlois, J.A., & Selassie, A.W. (2008). Prevalence of long-term disability from traumatic brain injury in the civilian population of the United States. *Journal of Head Trauma Rehabilitation 23,* 394–400.

Appendix 8–A

Case History Example

SPEECH-LANGUAGE THERAPY CASE HISTORY

NAME: Thomas Casler	ONSET DATE: 1/16/2019 (6 months ago)	
ADDRESS: 593 E. Spencer Boulevard, Columbus, OH	PHONE: 555-2678	
EMERGENCY CONTACT: Joshua (dad) 248-555-1212 Power of Attorney: Joshua (dad) 248-555-1212	AGE: 21 years	DATE OF BIRTH: 5/11/1988

SOCIAL HISTORY			MEDICAL HISTORY		
PARTNER: N/A (single)			DIAGNOSES: History of ADHD managed with medication. Diffuse axonal injury; subdural hematoma on 1/16/19. No other remarkable medical history.		
FAMILY: Younger sister who also lives at home with their parents					
LIVING SITUATION: Lived with parents (mom = Catherine age 49 years; dad = Joshua age 51 years) prior to accident.			PAST MEDICAL HISTORY: Survived a motor vehicle accident 6 months ago. Upon intake to the intensive care unit, he had a GCS of 5: eyes = 1; motor = 2, verbal = 2. He was in a medically induced coma for 13 days. Upon waking up from his coma he was oriented ×2, but still was in a state of PTA as determined by the GOAT for 25 days postinjury. Ranchos Level upon waking was 4. Remained in ICU for 15 days before being transferred to acute care to participate in rehabilitation.		
EMPLOYMENT: Worked part-time at a grocery store approximately 20 hours per week.					
EDUCATION: Enrolled as a full-time student in community college studying art history.					
HOBBIES/INTERESTS: Pottery, running, video games, volunteers for YMCA			GLASSES?	YES	NO
HANDEDNESS?	Left	Right		READING ONLY	
PREVIOUSLY DRIVING?	YES	NO	HEARING AIDS?	YES	NO
LITERATE – READING?	YES	NO		Left	Right
LITERATE – WRITING?	YES	NO	DENTURES?	YES	NO
RESPONSIBLE FOR FINANCES?	YES	NO			

continues

Appendix 8–A. *continued*

ACUTE CARE INFORMATION	
DIET LEVEL: No modifications	HOSPITAL: Southwestern Medical
PREVIOUS MODIFIED BARIUM SWALLOW STUDY: 2/10/19 showed silent aspiration on thin liquids, impulsivity was noted; recommended diet modification and initiation of dysphagia management. 3/10/19 no s/s of aspiration; recommend return to regular diet.	RANCHOS LEVEL: 6
	PREVIOUS IMAGING RESULTS: A noncontrast computed tomography (CT) scan was conducted at the time of injury. A skull fracture and subdural hematoma were identified in the scan.

THERAPY HISTORY

ASSESSMENTS:

Scales of Cognitive and Communicative Ability for Neurorehabilitation: Speech Comprehension and Reading Comprehension were relative strengths (raw scores of 90 and 92, respectively). Concerns with mild memory impairments with greater deficits in the area of delayed versus immediate member (total raw score of 73). Greatest deficits were documented in attention with moderate deficits (raw score of 48). We conducted a follow-up attention evaluation to discern the nature of the attention impairments.

Test of Everyday Attention: Greatest deficits were noted in selective attention and sustained attention. Sample subtest scores include: Map Search subtest Raw scores = 25 for 1 minute and 46 for 2 minutes; Elevator Counting subset score = 5; Elevator Counting with Distraction = 3; Telephone Search = 4.8.

Assessment of Intelligibility of Dysarthric Speech: Determined to be 55% intelligible to unfamiliar listeners when topic is known.

Informal Discourse Sample: Three samples were collected: personal narrative, picture description, and procedural task. Using criteria, characteristics, and procedures from Van Leer and Turkstra (1999) and Hux et al. (2008), no areas of concerns were noted (e.g., intact local and global coherence, adequate number of content units, appropriate use of cohesive markers, and no abnormal presence of redundancies).

THERAPIES RECEIVED: In acute care, he received speech-language therapy related to dysphagia as well as cognitive communication impairments (e.g., external strategies to improve orientation).	AUGMENTATIVE AND ALTERNATIVE COMMUNICATION/SUPPLEMENTAL SUPPORTS: None at this time.

CURRENT PLAN OF CARE	
SAMPLE SHORT-TERM THERAPY GOALS: 1. With physical prompt, Thomas will use a letter board to resolve 65% of communication breakdowns with unfamiliar communication partners. 2. On the Listening for Attention Processing Training III: 1 Number task, Thomas will score 75% current will minimal verbal cues from the clinician. 3. With minimal verbal cues, Thomas will use an external strategy to manage internal distractions at least two times during a 5-minute conversation. 4. With moderate verbal cues, Thomas will use an electronic calendar to schedule daily tasks (e.g., work, school) with 80% accuracy.	CURRENT FUNCTIONAL STATUS: RLA = 7; Transitional rehab with a patient goal of discharging to home environment and live with his parents. Completes ADLs with standby assistance (verbal cues). Patient and family state goal related to him returning to audit some community college courses.

Appendix 8–B

Treatment Protocol Description

Short-Term Goal

With minimal verbal cues, Thomas will use an external strategy to manage internal distractions at least two times during a 5-minute conversation.

Long-Term Goal

Thomas will independently use an external strategy to manage internal distractions at least two times during a 10-minute conversation.

Protocol

This activity will involve teaching Thomas to use compensatory strategies to manage his attention deficits. The clinician will provide instruction on three strategies, including spoken and written description of the strategies. One strategy will be a Key Ideas Log.

Key Ideas Log

At the beginning of each session, the clinician will ask Thomas to write down any ideas or persistent thoughts that were present in his head or things he wanted to comment on. Items that could be dealt with quickly (i.e., a person with blue hair that he saw) were addressed at that time. Other items that might lead to broader discussion were kept until later. The clinician indicates that they will save 5 to 10 minutes at the end of each session to discuss what was written on the log. The key ideas log is kept on the table or another visible location during the therapy session, and if other thoughts or ideas (unrelated to therapy) come to his mind, he can write them in the log. The client will then be able to focus on the therapy tasks because he knows that (a) he will not forget to mention the ideas that are important to him, and (b) he will be given time to talk about them. The introduction of a key ideas log can substantially reduce negative effects of distractibility in therapy. This strategy can generalize to other tasks and can assist with participation in school and work activities.

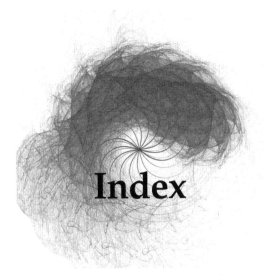

Index

Note: Page numbers in **bold** reference non-text material.